BUSINESS GROUPS
IN THE WEST

BUSINESS GROUPS IN THE WEST

Origins, Evolution, and Resilience

Edited by

ASLI M. COLPAN

and

TAKASHI HIKINO

OXFORD

UNIVERSITY PRESS

UNIVERSITY PRESS

Great Clarendon Street, Oxford, OX2 6DP,
United Kingdom

Oxford University Press is a department of the University of Oxford.
It furthers the University's objective of excellence in research, scholarship,
and education by publishing worldwide. Oxford is a registered trade mark of
Oxford University Press in the UK and in certain other countries

© Oxford University Press 2018

The moral rights of the authors have been asserted

First Edition published in 2018

Impression: 1

Published in the United States of America by Oxford University Press
198 Madison Avenue, New York, NY 10016, United States of America

British Library Cataloguing in Publication Data
Data available

Library of Congress Control Number: 2017954186

ISBN 978-0-19-871797-3

Printed and bound by
CPI Group (UK) Ltd, Croydon, CR0 4YY

PREFACE

How have the organizational models of large business enterprises evolved in different market and institutional settings? This volume on business groups in developed economies over the last century aims to examine the origins, evolution, and resilience of business groups to comprehend the role of the different varieties of large business enterprises in advanced economies. It builds on our earlier work, *The Oxford Handbook of Business Groups*, which focused on business groups in today's developing economies, to understand the evolutionary dynamics of business groups in varied and changing economic settings. While business groups are a dominant and critical business organization in contemporary emerging markets and have lately attracted much attention in academic circles and business presses, interestingly their counterparts in developed economies have not been systematically examined.

We aim to fill this gap in the literature by exploring the evolutionary paths and contemporary roles of business groups in developed economies from an internationally comparative perspective. The present volume thus stands as the first systematic attempt to examine this important yet little-known subject. In doing so, contrary to the widespread assumptions in much of the literature that has associated business groups with low-income economies since the middle of the twentieth century, our research amply shows that the reality is different. Business groups rose to function as a critical factor of industrial dynamics in the context of the Second Industrial Revolution in the late nineteenth century. They have adapted their characteristic roles and transformed to fit the changing market and institutional settings. As they flexibly co-evolve with the environment, the volume shows that business groups can remain as a viable organization model in the world's most advanced economies today.

We hope that readers will find the contents and findings of the volume a stimulating and useful contribution to the understanding not only of business groups but also of large business enterprises in general. This research, however, by no means represents an end to the study of developed economy business groups, but only a beginning. We thus hope that our research will open up new paths for future research, as business groups continue to be an intriguing topic with critical academic, managerial, and policy implications for advanced economies as well as emerging markets.

This volume was long in the making. It is the fruit of a five-year international research project, which included intensive work together with the contributors of this volume. The authors of individual chapters have interacted with each other many times, with each chapter going through repeated revisions, to form a coherent and organized volume. The authors submitted the draft of their chapters for the first time to a workshop on this volume that we hosted at Kyoto University in 2014. Many of the authors revised their chapters for the panel sessions at the World Business History Conference that was held at Goethe University in Frankfurt am Main in 2014 and then the World Economic History Congress in Kyoto in 2015. The authors subsequently rewrote their chapters for the current volume following many rounds of reviews by the editors and outside reviewers. Finally, several of the chapters were presented at the conference titled the "Varieties of Big Business: Business Groups in the West" at the Harvard Business School in 2016. With more comments at that conference, the editors and authors completed the volume to bring it to its present shape.

We are therefore, first and foremost, deeply grateful to the contributors to this volume, who all kindly and enthusiastically committed to take part in this challenging but equally rewarding research project. Without their patient and collaborative work through the many stages of the making of the volume, this project could not possibly have been completed.

We would also like to thank the many individuals and organizations that have made significant contributions to the making of this volume. First, several colleagues have provided invaluable feedback to the volume. We are especially indebted for their comments and suggestions to, in alphabetical order, Franco Amatori, Joseph Bower, David Collis, Louis Galambos, Geoffrey Jones, Tarun Khanna, Randall Morck, Tetsuji Okazaki, and Ben Ross Schneider, as well as to the participants at the seminar at the Institute for Applied Economics, Global Health and the Study of Business Enterprise, Johns Hopkins University, and those at the conference at the Harvard Business School.

We are grateful for the contributions provided by the team of editorial professionals at Oxford University Press, and by three individuals in particular. We very much thank David Musson, the previous Commissioning Editor, who originally supported this project and whose commitment was critical for the volume to become a reality. We are grateful to Adam Swallow, the present Commissioning Editor, for taking the project over and maintaining his supportive and thoughtful encouragement throughout. We are also indebted to Clare Kennedy, Assistant Commissioning Editor, for her friendly professionalism and diligent coordination of many aspects of the volume throughout its compilation, editing, and production.

We gratefully acknowledge the financial backing provided by Mizuho Securities Co. Ltd., whose endowment at the Graduate School of Management at Kyoto University kept this research project progressing through various stages. We single out the continuous support and encouragement provided by Hiroto Koda, Deputy President of the company, who was instrumental in originally establishing and subsequently maintaining the endowment. Without such commitment, this volume would not have been possible.

Asli M. Colpan and Takashi Hikino

Kyoto, 2017

CONTENTS

List of Figures

List of Tables

Notes on Contributors

Bharat Anand is the Henry R. Byers Professor of Business Administration in the Strategy Unit at Harvard Business School, and the faculty chair of the HBX digital initiative. His primary research interests are in digital strategy, corporate strategy, and empirical industrial organization, with an emphasis on competition in information goods markets.

Marco Becht is a Professor of Finance and the Goldschmidt Professor of Corporate Governance at the Solvay Brussels School for Economics and Management at Université libre de Bruxelles, Belgium. Becht is also a founder member, a fellow, and the executive director of the European Corporate Governance Institute, an international non-profit scientific association. He has been a visiting professor at Columbia Law School, the Saïd Business School, University of Oxford, Stanford Law School, and the University of St. Gallen, and is a research fellow at the Centre for Economic Policy Research (CEPR).

Marcelo Bucheli is an Associate Professor at the College of Business, University of Illinois at Urbana-Champaign, USA. He is the author of *Bananas and Business* (New York University Press, 2005), co-editor of *Organizations in Time* (Oxford University Press, 2014), and author of articles studying the political strategies of multinational corporations in historical perspective and the integration of historical research in management studies. He earned his Ph.D. at Stanford and was the Harvard-Newcomen fellow.

Youssef Cassis holds the joint chair in economic history with the RSCAS and the Department of History and Civilization at the European University Institute in Florence, Italy. He also held a long-standing research fellowship at the LSE and has been a visiting professor at the Graduate Institute for International and Development Studies in Geneva, the Cass Business School in London, and the University of St. Gallen. His work focuses on banking and financial history, as well as business history more generally. His most recent book (with Philip Cottrell) is *Private Banking in Europe: Rise, Retreat, and Resurgence* (Oxford University Press, 2015).

J. Yo-Jud Cheng is a doctoral candidate in the Strategy Unit at Harvard Business School, USA. Her research focuses on CEO succession practices, top management teams, corporate governance, and other topics related to strategic human resource management.

Andrea Colli is Professor of Economic History at the Department of Policy Analysis and Public Management at Bocconi University, Milan, Italy. His research interests range from the history of family firms to small and medium-sized enterprises, to the role played by international entrepreneurs and firms in the global economy, and to corporate governance in historical perspective. He has also devoted research activity to the study of the history of entrepreneurship in different contexts.

David Collis is a professor at the Harvard Business School, USA, where he is the Thomas Henry Carroll Ford Foundation Adjunct Professor of Business Administration within the Strategy Unit. His work has been frequently published in the *Harvard Business Review, Academy of Management Journal, Strategic Management Journal,* and in many books including *Managing the Multibusiness Company, International Competitiveness,* and *Beyond Free Trade.* He is currently a consultant to several major US corporations, and on the board of directors of several firms.

Asli M. Colpan is Associate Professor of Corporate Strategy at the Graduate School of Management and Graduate School of Economics, Kyoto University, Japan; and Visiting Associate Professor at Koç University, Turkey. Previously she was the Alfred Chandler visiting scholar at Harvard Business School and visiting scholar at the Department of Political Science at MIT. Her research interests include corporate strategy, corporate governance, and especially the evolution of large enterprises in developed and emerging economies. She co-edited (with Takashi Hikino and James Lincoln) *The Oxford Handbook of Business Groups* (Oxford University Press, 2010).

Alvaro Cuervo-Cazurra is Professor of International Business and Strategy at Northeastern University, USA. He is an expert on the internationalization of firms, with a special interest in emerging market multinationals; capability upgrading, particularly technological capabilities; and governance issues, focusing on corruption in international business. He was elected a Fellow of the Academy of International Business and is co-editor of *Global Strategy Journal.*

Ferry de Goey is Assistant Professor in Economic History and International Relations at the Erasmus School of History, Culture and Communication, Erasmus University, Netherlands. His research interests include business and entrepreneurial history, global history, and international relations.

Takashi Hikino is Mizuho Securities Endowed Chair Professor at the Graduate School of Management at Kyoto University, Japan; and Visiting Professor at Koç University, Turkey. His recent publications include *Big Business and Wealth of Nations* (co-edited with Alfred D. Chandler and Franco Amatori, Cambridge University Press, 1997), *The Global Chemical Industry in the Age of the Petrochemical Revolution* (co-edited with Louis Galambos and Vera Zamagni, Cambridge University Press, 2006), and *The Oxford Handbook of Business Groups* (co-edited with Asli Colpan and James Lincoln, Oxford University Press, 2010).

Geoffrey Jones is Isidor Straus Professor of Business History at Harvard Business School, USA. He researches the evolution, impact, and responsibility of global business.

Abe de Jong is Professor of Corporate Finance at Rotterdam School of Management, Erasmus University, and Professor of Financial Accounting at University of Groningen, both in the Netherlands. His research interests are in corporate finance, corporate governance, business history, and financial history.

Mats Larsson is Professor in Economic History at the Uppsala University and Head of the Uppsala Centre for Business History (UCBH), Sweden. He has mainly worked within the fields of business and financial history. His current research interests concern the development of large-scale enterprises in banking and insurance.

James R. Lincoln is Mitsubishi Bank Professor Emeritus at the Haas School of Business of the University of California, Berkeley, USA. He is the author (with Michael Gerlach) of *Japan's Network Economy: Structure, Persistence, and Change* (Cambridge University Press, 2004); (with Arne Kalleberg) of *Culture, Control, and Commitment: A Study of Work Organizations and Work Attitudes in the US and Japan* (Cambridge University Press, 1990); and of numerous articles and chapters on Japanese business, network theory, and related topics in organization studies. He co-edited (with Asli Colpan and Takashi Hikino) *The Oxford Handbook of Business Groups* (Oxford University Press, 2010).

Randall Morck is Jarislowsky Distinguished Chair in Finance at the Alberta School of Business, Canada, and Research Associate with the National Bureau of Economic Research. He has taught at Harvard University and Yale University. Google Scholar records almost 32,500 citations to his more than 100 research articles and the Social Sciences Research Network ranks him the 53rd most highly cited of 12,000 business authors worldwide. He has advised the governments of Canada, Chile, Israel, and the United States, as well as the IMF and World Bank.

Pedro Neves is Assistant Professor at the Lisbon School of Economics and Management, Universidade de Lisboa, Portugal. His research interests include capital markets, business groups, and corporate networks.

Tom Petersson is Associate Professor in Economic History at Uppsala University, Sweden. His research is mainly concerned with the development and organization of the Swedish financial system since the mid-nineteenth century.

Matthew Sargent is an associate management scientist at RAND Corporation, USA. Previously, he was a lecturer and Mellon Postdoctoral Fellow at the University of Southern California and a research associate at the California Institute of Technology (Caltech). His research explores the structure of Asian business networks and, in historical contexts, the development of long-distance trading networks and the emergence of the corporation as an organizational form.

Ben Ross Schneider is Ford International Professor of Political Science at MIT, USA. He is also the director of the MIT-Brazil program. Prior to moving to MIT, Schneider taught at Princeton University and Northwestern University. His recent books include *Hierarchical Capitalism in Latin America* (2013) and *Designing Industrial Policy in Latin America: Business-Government Relations and the New Developmentalism* (2015).

Harm G. Schröter is Professor of Economic History at the Department of Archaeology, History, Cultural Studies, and Religion, University of Bergen, Norway. He served as president of the European Business History Association and on several advisory and editorial boards. He researches the relation between state and the economy, economic cooperation, European multinational enterprise, technological innovation, European small developed states, institutions and innovation, and the "European enterprise," among other subjects.

Álvaro Ferreira da Silva is Associate Professor and Associate Dean at Nova School of Business and Economics, Portugal, as well as president of the Portuguese Association for Economic and Social History. His research interests currently include business groups and elites in a long-term perspective, technology and business activities in infrastructure projects, foreign investment and political risk.

Gloria Y. Tian is Associate Professor of Finance at University of Lethbridge, Canada. Previously, she was a tenured senior lecturer at the Australian Graduate School of Management (AGSM), University of New South Wales, Australia. Her research interests include corporate governance and business history. She earned her Ph.D. from the University of Alberta, and her thesis examines the evolution of large business groups in Canada.

Michelangelo Vasta is Professor of Economic history at the Department of Economics and Statistics of the University of Siena, Italy. Most of his research work has dealt with Italian economic development from unification to the present. His fields of research range over macro- and micro-perspective and focus on technical change, institutions, international trade, corporate networks, and entrepreneurship. He has published extensively in major economic and business history journals such as *Economic History Review, European Review of Economic History, Explorations in Economic History, Journal of Economic History, Business History,* and *Enterprise & Society.*

Simon Ville is Senior Professor of Economic and Business History at the University of Wollongong, Australia. He is also a fellow of the Academy of Social Sciences in Australia, and a member of the College of Experts at the Australian Research Council. He has previously worked at ANU, University of Auckland, and University of Manchester, and held a visiting fellowship at Harvard Business School. He has written widely on big business, industry associations, social capital, transport history, the

Vietnam War, and the rural and resource industries. His jointly edited *The Cambridge Economic History of Australia* (Cambridge University Press, 2014).

Weihuang Wong is a doctoral candidate in political science at the Massachusetts Institute of Technology (MIT), USA. Previously he worked in the credit markets group at GIC, the Singaporean sovereign wealth fund, focusing on US and European corporates. His current research examines how housing markets shape and are shaped by mass political attitudes.

PART I

CONCEPTS AND ARGUMENTS

CHAPTER 1

···

INTRODUCTION

business groups re-examined

···

ASLI M. COLPAN AND TAKASHI HIKINO

1.1 OBJECTIVES OF THE VOLUME

···

THE major aim of this volume is to explore the long-term evolution of different varieties of large business enterprises in today's *developed* economies. More specifically, the volume focuses on the economic institution of the *business group* and attempts to understand the factors behind its rise, growth, struggle, and resilience; its behavioral and organizational characteristics; and its roles in national economic development. While business groups are a dominant and critical organization model in contemporary *emerging and developing* economies and have lately attracted much attention in academic circles and business presses, interestingly their counterparts in developed economies have *not* been systematically examined. This disregard for business groups in mature market settings stands in sharp contrast to the intensive research that has been conducted on other major models of large modern enterprises in those economies, such as functionally organized firms with a clear product focus and multidivisional enterprises that have diversified into related product lines. The present book aims to fill this gap in the literature by adopting a coherent approach to this elusive subject. In doing so, contrary to the widespread assumptions in much of the literature that associates business groups with low-income economies since the middle of the twentieth century, this volume amply shows that the reality is different. Business groups actually rose to function as a critical factor of industrial dynamics in the context of the Second Industrial Revolution in the late nineteenth century. They have adapted their characteristic roles and transformed to fit the changing market and institutional settings. As business groups flexibly co-evolve with the environment, this volume shows that they can remain as a viable organization model in the world's most advanced economies today.

To date, scholars have generally concentrated on pinning down the reasons for the emergence and development of business groups, particularly those with unrelated product portfolios that are often owned and controlled by families, in developing economies since World War II. Given that it was in the 1970s that scholarly research on business groups as an economic institution commenced, this particular focus on the business groups in *developing* economies is understandable, as they represented the predominant model of large enterprises in such markets. In comparison, it has been argued, multidivisional enterprises with related diversified product portfolios have often come to dominate the large-enterprise economy in many *developed* nations. The contrasting settings in which business groups and multidivisional enterprises have played their developmental functions within the contemporary economy, however, do not necessarily mean that the distinctive roles performed by those two institutions were predetermined throughout the different phases of modern economic growth. Alongside numerous small and medium-sized enterprises with focused product portfolio, business groups *in their prototype* with the characteristics of diversified product portfolios and often pyramidal ownership arrangements have been present and active since the beginning of the nineteenth century. As early as the Renaissance period in Western Europe, premodern large enterprises with international scope, whose industrial domains often ranged from commerce, service, and finance to mining and manufacturing, were owned by such prominent families as the Medicis and Fuggers and adopted the apparent organization of business groups. In the United States, the Boston Associates—a group of investors and entrepreneurs with family and kin networks—were similarly active in a wide scope of economic spheres in the nation's early phase of industrialization in the first half of the nineteenth century. Business groups often controlled by families and their networks have remained the dominant model of large enterprises in some countries (such as Sweden), while in other nations (such as the United States) the conventional varieties of business groups have mostly faded away. Given the significance of the US experience in modern management research, management scholars understandably did not comprehend how different varieties of business groups have played a significant role in the modernizing economy.

In the meanwhile, in the United States it was mostly historians who kept the heritage of business group research alive, although they did not deal with contemporary issues and rarely used the analytical concept of business groups even when they examined that particular business organization. This absence of intellectual exchange between management scholars and historians, as well as economists, did not bring about the synthesis of theoretical and empirical studies on business groups across academic disciplines. We have therefore lacked systematic knowledge regarding the conditions under which business groups emerged, developed, struggled yet remained in today's high-income nations of Western Europe, North America, and Oceania.

This volume stands as the first scholarly attempt to systematically examine the evolutional paths and contemporary roles of business groups in today's developed economies from an international-comparative perspective. It focuses, first, on the long-term evolution of large business groups in Western Europe, North America, and

Oceania.[1] Second, it examines the multiplicity of the ownership, strategies, and structures of those enterprises. Last but not least, it examines the roles that this particular design of large enterprises has played in the economic development of their relevant nations. The volume thus seeks to strengthen scholarly and policy-oriented understanding of business groups in developed economies by bringing together state-of-the-art research on the large enterprises in individual nations from an evolutionary perspective.

1.2 THE BUSINESS GROUP AS A VARIETY OF MODERN BIG BUSINESS

The conventional understanding of the long-term development of business organizations has broadly followed the historical analysis conducted by Alfred Chandler (1962, 1990). Mainly based on the developmental pattern he observed in the United States, Chandler came up with the "convergence model" for the evolution of modern large enterprises based on the ascendancy of product "strategy" of related diversification and administrative "structure" of multidivisional design. The combination and integration of that particular strategy with a specific structure involving strategic planning and control exercised by salaried senior management in corporate headquarters were argued to maximize the efficiency and effectiveness of large modern enterprises. Those enterprises therefore adopted that particular assimilation of strategy and structure in order to survive and grow in competitive market environments.[2]

In the present volume we re-examine the theoretical and empirical validity of this "convergence model" for the development of modern large enterprises that Chandler proposed by taking one of the most influential alternatives to the Chandlerian multidivisional enterprise—*business group*s as an analytical focus. Holding the "strategy and structure" model of multidivisional enterprises as the ultimate goal of efficiency and effectiveness, Chandler and modern-day management theorists—as well as economists—have remained more or less skeptical about the economic role that business groups have played in various national and economic settings in different time

---

[1] A major developed economy omitted in this volume is Japan, as that nation remained as the economy with the strong character of late industrialization until after World War II, and thus was covered in our earlier volume (see Colpan, Hikino, and Lincoln, 2010). Japan also experienced a unique historical development in terms of its business groups, which were dissolved due to external political forces after World War II (Lincoln and Shimotani, 2010).

[2] It is important to note that, while the M-form argument has faced criticism, especially from some sociologists (Fligstein, 1985; Freeland, 1996), that criticism has been targeted more towards the strict theoretical model and formulation of the M-form proposed by Oliver Williamson. This is partially because Chandler's "sensitive use of historical materials shows a broader and more nuanced understanding of the factors driving historical change" (Shanley, 1996). Ultimately, the multidivisional firm and Chandler's interpretations of it remain influential in the management and business history literatures.

periods. Given the prominence of business groups in many dynamic emerging economies such as South Korea and Singapore, and also the notable successful cases of their counterparts in developed economies such as Sweden and Italy, we have now reached the point at which we should be able to systematically examine the role that business groups have played in different phases of nations' industrialization. While acknowledging the effectiveness of multidivisional enterprises with related product portfolios in certain market and institutional environments, we would like to propose in this book a "divergence model" of modern large enterprises, in which firms can, and should, actively nurture the organizational design of business groups as well as other corporate models. Ultimately, we aim to explore in the volume the contingencies in terms of both exogenous environmental factors and endogenous organizational ones, which determine the evolutionary patterns and strategic effectiveness of the business-group model.

The volume categorically separates business groups into several different types (as discussed in detail below), as business groups can take different varieties in any economy and, over time, even in one particular economy. Further, in many cases those varieties overlap and intersect with each other, which makes systematized analyses necessary yet challenging. In addition, the relative significance of different varieties of business groups may differ across national economies. We thus examine business groups from the comprehensive and comparative perspective of the evolutionary dynamics of business organizations (especially large enterprises). Ultimately, however, we aim to provide a logical coherence and analytical robustness to our examination of business groups across national economies and give most attention to diversified business groups.

This volume, therefore, sets its analytical focus on *diversified business groups*. Diversified business groups can broadly be defined as the collections of legally independent enterprises, linked through equity ties and other economic means, which have a central unit at the helm that controls the affiliated enterprises in (technology- or market-wise) *unrelated* industries. They *theoretically* come close to a corporate organizational model of "the firm," rather than networks, in the economics sense.[3] Diversified business groups actually bear some resemblance to multidivisional enterprises owing to their characteristics of diversified portfolio, hierarchical structure, and administrative design (Colpan and Hikino, 2010). Rather than being narrowly concerned with the diversified business group model per se as a variety of modern large enterprises, all contributors to this volume share a common interest in the evolutionary dynamics of corporate organization models and their interaction with the modern growth of national economies. Our close examination of this organization model derives from our understanding that, in the analytical context of competitive market settings, four major models of large enterprises with multi-unit organizational scope can be singled out based on the Chandlerian "strategy and structure" perspective. These models are: first, firms with a focused product portfolio that take the functional

---

[3] We note that the extent of this closeness to a firm (in the economics sense) depends on how constituent companies are integrated and controlled in a business group.

structure; second, and as a variety of the first model, state-owned enterprises (SOEs) with mostly focused product portfolios in such capital-intensive sectors as steelmaking and petroleum refining;[4] third, enterprises operating in multiple yet related product categories that adopt the multidivisional structure; and fourth, firms with an industry portfolio that remains unrelated and take the diversified business group structure.

Those four major models have all faced serious competitive challenges in the liberal market setting at the second half of the twentieth century, particularly since the 1980s. Single-product firms with a functional organizational structure began to steadily reduce their significance in the big business sector, as the diversification strategy that the largest enterprises widely adopted after World War II mostly forced those enterprises to convert their organizational form to the multidivisional structure (Rumelt, 1974). In the meanwhile, however, some new single-product firms with a functional organizational structure (for instance, IT firms in Silicon Valley) have emerged since the 1970s. State-owned enterprises began to be challenged once the liberal market ideology became globally fashionable in the 1980s, when many of them were privatized, especially in developed economies (Tonitelli, 2008). Some state-owned enterprises have, however, survived the privatization process, especially in industries that are regarded by their governments as strategic to the national economy (Musacchio and Lazzarini, 2012).[5] From the remaining two major categories of multi-unit enterprises, multidivisional firms, especially those with a vertically integrated scope, have suffered as transportation and communication costs have fallen in the IT era, and as vertical disintegration, outsourcing, and network of long-term supplier relationships became common (Lamoreaux et al., 2002; Langlois, 2010). Also struggling in competitive and liberalized market environments were diversified business groups, both their conventional varieties with the characteristics of family ownership in emerging and developed economies and the contemporary types, especially the acquisitive conglomerates that flourished in the US and the UK after the 1960s. Ultimately, these four models of large enterprises compete with each other for efficiency, effectiveness, and legitimacy.[6]

It is against this general background that we examine the diversified business group as one major model of large enterprises with multi-unit organizational form. While all the other above-mentioned organization models have attracted much academic

---

[4] We acknowledge that the category of state-owned enterprises differs from others, as it remains a variety of the first model that adopts the focused product strategy but differs in terms of ownership. However, we still classify them separately because they follow a different logic from privately owned firms in pursuing political as well as economic objectives (La Porta et al., 1999; Musacchio and Lazzarini, 2012). Further, it should be noted that some notable state-owned enterprises, such as IRI in Italy and INI in Spain, take the strategy of unrelated diversification and the structure of diversified business groups.

[5] Further, in the privatization movement since the 1980s governments started modifying their majority-owned, state-owned enterprise model and began to hold minority stakes in relevant companies (Musacchio and Lazzarini, 2012).

[6] Lamoreaux et al. (2002), for instance, argue that the top-ten list of the most respected business leaders in a survey conducted by the *Financial Times* in 2001 was occupied by CEOs of diversified business groups like the Virgin group and Berkshire Hathaway, and highly focused companies like Intel, as well as traditional Chandlerian firms such as IBM.

attention and scholarly scrutiny to date (see, for instance, Fligstein, 1985; Freeland, 1996; Lamoreaux et al., 2002; Langlois, 2010; Musacchio and Lazzarini, 2012), the diversified business group model has not yet been systematically examined, except for that in developing economies (Colpan, Hikino, and Lincoln, 2010). The analytical focus on *diversified* business groups can be justified as a critical yet underexplored variety of the organization model, and as the central topical scope of this volume. Nevertheless, other types of business groups will be discussed throughout the volume whenever they are relevant and significant in the economic context of individual nations.[7]

We examine the categorical classifications of various types of business groups in Section 1.3, as conceptual clarification is necessary to distinguish different varieties of this organization model at the outset of the volume.

1.3 Business Groups: Their Nature and Typology

Business groups are broadly defined as the collections of *legally* independent companies bound together by formal and/or informal ties (Granovetter, 1995, 2005; Khanna and Yafeh, 2007). In a comprehensive sense, they characterize "an economic coordination mechanism in which legally independent companies utilize the collaborative arrangements to enhance their collective economic welfare" (Colpan and Hikino, 2010: 17). These encompassing definitions and characterizations are by themselves too broad to be categorically transparent and analytically robust, however, and thus create much confusion in examining business groups in a systematic manner. Even cartel arrangements, which are illegal in most economies for their harmful effects on economic welfare, for instance, can well be included in the broad business group classification.

Further, and relatedly, the categorical boundary of business groups based on *legal* grounds (i.e., legal separation and independence) crucially compromises the logical clarity and analytical robustness for managerial and economic examination. The outcome of this definitional ambiguity has been that individual scholars have referred to different types and varieties of corporate models, organizational forms, and administrative arrangements under the single rubric of *business groups* (Leff, 1978; Goto, 1982; Granovetter, 1995; Guillén, 2000; Morck, Wolfenzon, and Yeung, 2005; Khanna and Yafeh, 2007). Since business groups can come in different and distinct varieties, we differentiate them throughout the volume. The clarification and reclassification of various subcategories of business groups should make the analytical and theoretical examination of the conditions under which each of the organizational variety of business groups emerge, develop, and survive more robust and coherent.

---

[7] For a systematic examination of pyramidal business groups, see Morck (2010).

1.3.1 Categorical Confusion Surrounding Business Groups

While scholars pay primary attention to the *legal nature and organizational form* of various multi-unit firm organizations, they have not quite examined their characteristic resources, strategy models, structural designs, and administrative processes in a systematic manner. The business-group literature took the legal independence of units as the original and core component of its definition, making this legal arrangement a main feature of the analysis. While that arrangement has often been the case thanks to product-unrelatedness between operating units, too much consideration of the legal status has confused the understanding of the business-group organization. Some scholars categorized any enterprise organized under a holding company with more than two legally independent subsidiaries as a business group (Fracchia et al., 2010; Wailerdsak and Suehiro, 2010; Yiu et al., 2013). Other studies argued that changes in tax laws which caused US enterprises to turn their internal divisions into legally independent subsidiaries led to a switch from the multidivisional form with internal divisions to a new form with a holding company at the helm combined with subsidiaries underneath, which they named "multilayer-subsidiaries" (Prechel, 1997; Prechel et al., 2008). A recent study argued that in the US there were as many as 14,146 business groups in 2002 (Belenzon et al., 2012).

This analytical inclination toward the legal nature of organizations may, ironically, have come from Chandler's own work on the multidivisional enterprise which, he observed, mostly took the form of internal divisions for the operating units. Chandler, however, acknowledged that the multidivisional enterprises he examined in the US context took the internal division form *basically for tax and legal reasons* (Chandler, 1982a: 4). As his concern remained the administrative control and coordination of individual operating units exercised by the headquarters, he did not necessarily distinguish legally independent subsidiaries from internal divisions, especially when they were 100-percent-owned by the apex organization, such as a holding company. His analytical concern remained the administrative control and coordination of operating units that were most often organized in an operational, not legal, sense as internal divisions (Chandler, 1962).

Some enterprises that Chandler investigated actually organized their operating units as legally independent subsidiaries, not as internal divisions from a legal perspective. One of the classic cases of multidivisional enterprises that he examined in *Strategy and Structure*—Standard Oil Co. of New Jersey, which established a systematic internal administrative mechanism and clear division of tasks between the holding company and operating units—fit into this example of multisubsidiary organization until as late as the 1950s (Colpan and Hikino, 2010). No wonder Chandler, in one of his works, named the multidivisional enterprise the *American style industrial group*: "groups that were administered from a large corporate office that coordinated and monitored the current activities of their operating divisions and allocated resources for future production and distribution" (Chandler, 1982a: 10). Scholars, however, have long misinterpreted this issue and have narrowly taken Chandler's multidivisional enterprise as the structure that organizes their operating units as *internal divisions only* without legal independence. As has been argued above in the historical context, large US enterprises often arranged their operating units as either internal divisions or legally independent subsidiaries for tax and legal reasons. Either way, the administrative control and coordination of operating units exercised by the headquarters, which is supposed to be the critical issue for corporate management, remained the same.

In sum, to date scholars in general have examined the business-group organization by relying too much on the *legal* nature of operating units. As long as they are legally independent firms, they tend to be classified as business groups. Once scholars ignore the critical features of the strategic aspects of product relatedness and the administrative design of operational processes—both of which Chandler focused on—many business organizations with different basic characteristics of ownership, strategy, and structure, including some Chandlerian multidivisional enterprises, are eventually incorrectly classified as business groups. As long as we aim to pin down the basic nature and characteristics of various business organizations, this logical confusion should be avoided for the sake of categorical clarity and analytical robustness. While broad perspectives that examine the legal nature of operating units may function as a starting point for the identification of business groups, strategic, organizational, and administrative factors should be the key to characterize and classify such groups.

1.3.2 Hierarchy-Type Versus Network-Type Business Groups

With the understanding of business groups as a collaboratively coordinated set of legally independent companies, we first identify two basic yet different types of business groups: network- and hierarchy-types. A network-type business group is one in which the constituent companies adopt the behavioral principle of *alliance*, wherein individual enterprises maintain autonomy in terms of basic strategic and budgetary decisions. These groups typically have no single controlling entity at the helm. They can be alliances of product-diversified or product-focused companies. Examples of the product-diversified variety could be post-World War II Japanese horizontal keiretsu (kigyo-shudan) groups such as Mitsubishi, Mitsui, and Sumitomo that have no controlling unit at the apex, although they have been equipped with a coordinating organ in the form of the monthly Presidents Meeting of constituent operating companies. By contrast, the international alliances of airline companies such as Star Alliance, Sky Team, and One-world are contemporary cases of the network-type business groups that remain focused in terms of product portfolio. Network-type business groups stand somewhere between the polar modes of the market and the hierarchy, and thus differ from a classic firm that internally coordinates its economic activities through administrative instruments.[8] Because the crucial focus of our research is not networks per se, while allocating a chapter to the issue of the characteristics and current trends of network-type business groups (see Chapter 4), we touch on these groups only when they are significant in connection with the hierarchy type of business groups for historical and structural reasons.

In hierarchy-type business groups, in contrast to network-type groups, constituent companies are organized by the *authority* principle. This principle likens the business group "as a coherent organization model in which customarily a holding company at the helm of hierarchy controls legally-independent operating units, usually organized as subsidiaries and affiliates through equity ties and other economic means such as interlocking directorates, budget allocation and intra-group transactions" (Colpan and Hikino, 2010: 20). The authority principle concentrates on the hierarchical design of business groups, with the group headquarters unit or central office typically exercising financial and/or strategic control over operating companies in terms of their market behavior. The apex holding company is often controlled by a family or an entrepreneur, but sometimes the family or entrepreneur directly owns those operating companies underneath without incorporating or formalizing the apex control unit. The hierarchy-type business group, therefore, theoretically comes close to, or even may become identical to, the *firm* itself in the economics sense, depending on the exact design in which constituent companies are integrated and controlled.

Within hierarchy-type business groups, we observe two major varieties: first, diversified business groups and the "holding company" in the Chandler–Williamson denomination from strategic and product-portfolio perspectives; and second, pyramidal business groups from ownership and governance perspectives. As defined above, we refer to those groups that have a (formal or informal) controlling unit at the helm with operating subsidiaries and/or affiliates in *unrelated* industries as diversified business groups.[9] We explore this category in more detail in Section 1.4.

The "holding company" type of business group, following Chandler–Williamson's characteristic definition, denotes a pure holding company with controlling equity ties yet limited and often *unsystematic* administrative mechanism and ultimately *loose* control of operating subsidiaries that are concentrated on focused or narrowly related

---

[8] As diverse as network-type business groups can be, scholars who have studied those economic institutions usually consider them to be *business networks* (Fruin, 2008; Lincoln and Shimotani, 2010). In order to keep the focus and robustness of analytical concepts, we concentrate on the second category, that of hierarchy-type business groups, in this volume. Unless otherwise noted, we mean this sort of hierarchy-type business groups when we refer to business groups hereafter.

[9] We employ the term "unrelated" here following the conventional definitions of "relatedness," or for that matter "unrelatedness," that have focused on similarities in technologies and markets (Rumelt, 1974; Markides and Williamson, 1994; Anand and Jayanti, 2005). However, scholars of a resource-based view of the firm emphasized the need to look beyond such relatedness to include the distinctive resources of the parent company (Collis and Montgomery, 1998).

Table 1.1. Stylized characteristics of comparable corporate organization models.

	Multidivisional enterprises		Business groups			
			"Authority" Principle — Hierarchy-type business groups		Governance and finance perspectives	"Alliance" Principle — Network-type business groups
	(Chandler)	(Williamson, M-form Type D1)	Product portfolio and strategy perspectives — Diversified business groups	"Holding company" (Chandler, Williamson)	Pyramidal business groups	Network-type business groups
Ownership	mostly public	mostly public	Please refer to Table 1.3 for the categorization and characteristics of diversified business groups	mostly public	mainly family	no single controlling owner
Control unit	corporate office or holding company	general office or holding company		holding company	mostly holding company	none
Top management	salaried managers	salaried managers		salaried managers	family and salaried managers	not applicable
Administrative control	strategic planning or strategic control	extensive internal control		internal control (limited and often unsystematic)	internal control (ultimate control)[1]	inter-firm coordination
Operating units	internal divisions and/or subsidiaries (wholly-owned)	internal divisions and/or subsidiaries (wholly-owned)		autonomous subsidiaries (wholly-owned)	tiers of listed group companies (partially-owned)	stand-alone enterprises (partial or no ownership)
Growth pattern	organic growth and acquisitions	organic growth and acquisitions		acquisitions and sell-offs	formation of listed affiliates	proliferation of clustering enterprises
Product portfolios	diversified, related	diversified, related		focused or diversified (related)	focused, diversified (related or unrelated)	focused, diversified (related or unrelated)
Examples	Du Pont in the US since the 1920s			Calico Printers' Association in the UK from the late nineteenth century to the 1960s	Hees Edper (Bronfman) group in Canada from the 1950s to the 1990s[2]	Mitsubishi (horizontal) keiretsu since the early 1950s

Note: Reorganized and extended based on Colpan and Hikino (2010).

[1] Ultimate control here means "in a position to control, or materially to influence, the management of one or more other companies by virtue, in part at least, of its ownership of securities in the other company or companies" (Bonbright and Means, 1932): 10.

[2] The Hees Edper group was pyramidal by the mid-1960's, when detailed intercorporate equity holdings data in Canada became available, but the formation of the group's pyramidal structure predates that. We write 1950s to denote the time period when the holding company of the group, Edper Investments, was established.

product categories.[10] Examples of this category are the British "holding company" entities such as Calico Printers' Association, Associated Portland Cement, and United Alkali in the early decades of the twentieth century, as covered in Chandler's *Scale and Scope* (1990).

Pyramidal business groups, by contrast, are defined by an ownership arrangement which contains a multilayered chain organization of (at least two) *publicly listed* companies (Morck, 2010). Diversified business groups are often structured in this way in terms of their ownership arrangements in many emerging markets and developed economies. Examples in this volume include the Edper Bronfman group in Canada and the Exor group in Italy (see Morck and Tian, and Colli and Vasta, respectively, in this volume). Table 1.1 illustrates the stylized characteristics of the different varieties of business groups in a systematic manner.

Below we delve into the diversified business groups that form the core analytical target of this volume.

1.4 DIVERSIFIED BUSINESS GROUPS AS A "MULTI-UNIT ENTERPRISE" MODEL

1.4.1 The Nature and Characteristics of Diversified Business Groups

Diversified business groups and their comparable organizational models can be examined under the category of "multi-unit enterprises" originally coined by Chandler (1977). In contrast to single unit enterprises that confine their activities to a particular operational function such as production, marketing, or sales, multi-unit enterprises contain several such operating units that concentrate on different functions, with the headquarters unit at the helm of the entire organization. The headquarters and operating units typically exhibit a division of labor between the tasks of *administrative control and coordination* and the actual production of goods and services. Within the broad category of multi-unit enterprises, multidivisional enterprises ultimately became the core model of corporate development as American industrial enterprises began to diversify into technologically related product markets after the 1920s.

Multidivisional enterprises are described in the classic Chandlerian, and also Williamsonian, classification of the M-form category as "the divisionalized enterprise in which a separation of operating from strategic decision-making is provided and for which the requisite internal control apparatus has been assembled and is systematically

---

[10] "Holding company" in this context denotes a specific variety of business groups based on Chandler's and Williamson's "special use of the term" (Williamson, 1975: 143), rather than the general legal arrangement that can be taken by different types of enterprises including the multidivisional enterprise.

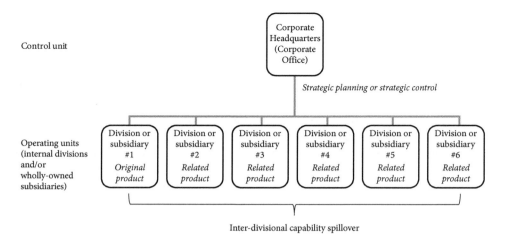

FIGURE 1.1. Archetypal structure of a Chandlerian multidivisional enterprise.

Source: Based on Chandler (1962).

employed" (Williamson, 1975: 152). Administrative control includes the "monitoring of the divisions and the long-term planning for the group as a whole and the allocation of resources" by the headquarters (Chandler, 1982a). Following this characterization, Chandler focused on the product-specific knowledge accumulated within large industrial enterprises functioning as the competitive resource that spilled over to related product categories (Colpan and Hikino, 2010).[11] Accordingly, the multidivisional "structure follows strategy" (Chandler, 1962), which denotes the structure adopted by an enterprise that diversifies into related product lines (see Figure 1.1 for the archetypal structure of a Chandlerian multidivisional enterprise).

In terms of their basic organizational configuration or "structure," diversified business groups bear some apparent similarities to the above descriptions of the multidivisional enterprise: a headquarters unit of the business group is typically responsible for long-term planning, allocation of resources, and monitoring the execution and performance of the operating units (see Figure 1.2 for the archetypal structure of a diversified business group). Nevertheless, the similarities end here, as diversified business groups critically differ from Chandlerian multidivisional enterprises on three fronts related to their product portfolio, administrative control, and ownership composition.

First, and foremost in terms of the product portfolio or "strategy," diversified business groups spread into unrelated business categories. The business-group literature that has developed with the experience of developing economies in mind has argued that such unrelated product portfolio resulted from the environmental conditions of immature markets and institutions where business groups play a filling

---

[11]   Williamson acknowledged the product-related externalities, but his focus remained on capital market imperfections that theoretically yield transaction costs. In this chapter we use Williamson's (1975) category representing "common" product categories that suggests related lines (his D1 classification) as the "multidivisional form," which is comparable to Chandler's classic multidivisional enterprise.

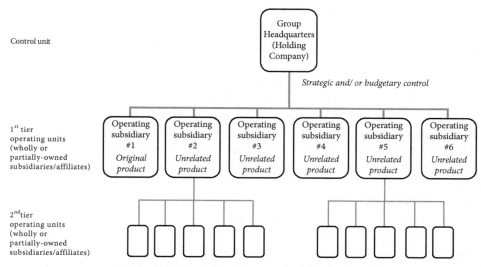

FIGURE 1.2. Archetypal structure of a diversified business group.
Source: Adopted from Colpan and Hikino (2010): 21 with some additions.

role (Khanna and Palepu, 1997). Put it in a different way, these business groups should collapse and disappear, or modify their product portfolio, as the market environment shifts to become mature and competitive. In reality, however, some of these organizations have stayed resilient even in the context of maturing and mature economies (as several national chapters in this volume illustrate), which questions the assumptions of earlier literature. Regardless of the market context, the unrelated-product feature categorically separates diversified business groups from the Chandlerian multidivisional enterprises that possess related product portfolios.

Second, the administrative control "styles" (the terminology Goold and Campbell, 1987, employed) that the headquarters unit exercises over individual operating units differ between Chandlerian multidivisional enterprises and diversified business groups. Given the potential spillover of product-related knowledge between operating units, it is ultimately the systematic administrative apparatus based on strategic planning or control exercised by the headquarters unit that realizes inter-unit sharing of product-related proprietary knowledge and thus constitutes the basic underlying efficiency mechanism in the multidivisional enterprise. Without such organized strategic administration of interdependencies within the firm, any potential spillover cannot be realized to yield a competitive advantage.[12]

---

[12] It is important to note that, within this division of labor, in the original Chandlerian multidivisional enterprises the separation of major roles was solely between the headquarters and operating units. As firms grew, the divisional headquarters themselves took the roles of an administration center within the boundaries of their divisions. Within this evolutional transformation, corporate headquarters remained the final administrative control unit for the entire enterprise, whose role altered from strategic planning to strategic control.

In the conventional business group literature (which is based on the experiences of business groups in developing economies), on the other hand, diversified business groups are often assumed *not* to be equipped with competitive resources that are product-related and, for that matter, not to require an apparatus for systematic internal control. This is primarily because those groups are seen as an opportunistic institutional response to immaturity in capital, labor as well as product markets (especially in emerging economies), and typically operate in less than competitive market environments. Thus, it has been argued, they may not need the same full-fledged level of administrative control as the multidivisional enterprise in competitive markets. With their operating environment being "soft," their administrative design can remain unsystematically developed and can still be loose in terms of execution. As the market environment matures, however, increasingly systematic control is observed even in diversified business groups. Yet, the means of that control, strategic and/or budgetary, may remain different from the multidivisional enterprise (see Chapter 2, this volume; Kock and Guillén, 2001; Colpan and Hikino, 2010).

Last but not least, a basic difference between multidivisional enterprises and diversified business groups lies in their ownership composition and governance features, which in turn critically influence their strategic behavior and administrative design. The multidivisional enterprises that Chandler championed as the most efficient and effective organizational model for large industrial firms in the modern competitive economy are generally characterized by scattered share ownership, which results in the separation of ownership from control that lies with salaried professional management. This characteristic derives from two forces in the product and capital markets.

First, as the Second Industrial Revolution transformed the technological and economic foundation of the modern industrial economy after the late nineteenth century, the amount of financial resources that individuals, families, and kin networks could rally became marginal relative to the amount of investment capital required to exploit economies of scale in those capital-intensive industries which became the driving core of the modern economy. Only with the mobilization and pooling of financial resources available society-wide could the modern large industrial enterprise secure the necessary amount of capital to achieve its potential in the production of goods and services.

Second, while the individual shareholders were no longer capable of, or interested in, managing the enterprises they invested in, salaried professionals at corporate headquarters became competent enough to effectively administer the managerial hierarchy of large modern industrial enterprises. The functional separation of salaried management from scattered ownership thus became common among Chandlerian multidivisional enterprises, as those professionals eventually embodied the managerial capabilities that integrated technological forces and organizational dynamics with competitive market environments. According to the "managerial capitalism" thesis proposed by Chandler, the administrative apparatus within managerial enterprises surpassed external market forces as the efficient and effective coordination mechanism of economic activities. Within those firms, salaried professionals effectively replaced owning investors as the key controlling force and managerial body for basic strategic and financial decisions. This completes the operational model of managerial enterprises in which the principle of the separation and independence of top management functions from shareholders and their control is firmly established.

Diversified business groups, by contrast, are differentiated from multidivisional enterprises in terms of the basic characteristics of ownership and control. Most often, and especially in emerging markets, individual entrepreneurs and their families keep the majority or controlling stake of equity holdings so that the principle of the separation of ownership and control does not hold for diversified business groups. Rather, owners usually maintain a tight grip on the basic strategic and financial decision-making of operating subsidiaries as well as headquarters, even after they hire salaried professionals in senior managerial positions both at headquarters and at operating levels. Even with diversified business groups of bank-centered and state-owned varieties, the controlling owners exercise substantial influence on the basic decision-making of operating affiliates, although, relatively speaking, those affiliates enjoy strategic autonomy, especially compared with the tight control that family-owned groups customarily exhibit (see, for instance, Colli and Vasta, this volume).

1.4.2 Varieties of Diversified Business Groups

Diversified business groups— the collections of legally independent enterprises linked through equity ties and other economic means that have a central unit at the helm controlling the affiliated enterprises in (technology- or market-wise) *unrelated* industries—can be examined as two distinct types. The first is the conventional type controlled by business families, government bureaucracy, or banking institutions, and the second is the contemporary variety made up of conglomerate enterprises and private equity firms. Table 1.2 shows the varieties of diversified business groups and their main features.

Depending on the controlling entity, the conventional varieties of diversified business groups can be further separated into three distinct categories: family-owned, state-owned, and bank-centered business groups.[13] The apex unit of these groups—families, the state, or banks—exerts a sufficient level of control over the operating companies either through full or partial ownership stakes (often organized in pyramidal structures) or through more subtle mechanisms like super voting shares and board interlocks (Morck, 2010).[14] The apex unit is typically organized as a pure holding company and is actively involved in the critical decisions of operating units (some of which may be publicly listed).

---

[13] For a complementary discussion, see Cuervo-Cazurra (2006).

[14] Although we use the term "owned," we mean full or partial ownership adequate enough to exert control. We therefore use "owned" and "controlled" interchangeably in this context, unless otherwise specified.

Table 1.2. Stylized characteristics of diversified business groups.

	Diversified business groups					
	Conventional varieties			Contemporary varieties		
	Family-owned business groups	State-owned business groups	Bank-centered business groups	Conglomerates		Private equity firms
				(Chandler, Berg)	(Williamson, M-form Type D2)[1]	
Ownership	family	state	bank	mostly public	mostly public	partners
Control unit	mostly holding company	state bureaucracy	operating holding company	holding company	general office or holding company	professional partnership
Top management	family and/or salaried managers	state bureaucrats	salaried managers	entrepreneurs and/or salaried managers	entrepreneurs and/or salaried managers	professional partners
Administrative control[3]	strategic and/or budgetary control	strategic and/or budgetary control	mostly financial control	budgetary control	"not extensive internal control"[2]	mostly financial control
Operating units	subsidiaries and affiliates (wholly- or partially- owned)	subsidiaries and affiliates (wholly-or partially-owned)	listed and unlisted companies (partially-owned)	subsidiaries (wholly-owned)	internal divisions and/or subsidiaries (wholly-owned)	subsidiaries (wholly-owned)
Growth pattern	organic growth and acquisitions	strategic investment, acquisitions	strategic investment	acquisitions and sell-offs	organic growth, acquisitions and sell-offs	acquisitions and sell-offs
Product portfolios	diversified, unrelated	diversified, unrelated	diversified, unrelated	diversified, unrelated	diversified, related or unrelated	diversified, unrelated
Examples	Wallenberg group in Sweden since the 1910s	IRI in Italy from the 1930s to early 2000s	Deutsche Bank group in Germany from the late nineteenth century to the late 2000s	Berkshire Hathaway in the US since the 1960s		KKR in the US since the mid 1970s

[1] While in the original Williamson classification (1975, 1985), conglomerate enterprises are classified under the general category of multidivisional enterprises, the two subcategories of his classifications, types D1 and D2, are separated here in order to clarify the characteristics of those two organizational structures.

[2] Less extensive internal control apparatus relative to the original case of multidivisional form of type D1 (Williamson, 1975): 153.

[3] For most conventional varieties of business groups, initially limited and loose administrative control.

[4] Wallenberg family foundations have gradually become the controlling owner of the group, especially from the 1950s and 1960s.

Family-owned (and/or -controlled) business groups are diversified groups that have the entrepreneur and his or her family members at the helm of the group. The two well-known and still-extant examples of this variety of business groups covered in this volume are the groups organized around the Wallenberg and Agnelli families. The Wallenberg group emerged in Sweden towards the end of the 1910s as Stockholms Enskilda Bank, which began controlling Swedish enterprises in numerous industries with partial equity stakes and commercial credits (see Larsson and Petersson, this volume). On the other hand, the Exor group controlled by the Agnelli family in Italy had its origins in the holding company, IFI, founded in 1927 to control and manage Fiat and its related auto businesses. The whole organization, however, turned into an unrelated diversified group, especially after the 1960s, as the company increasingly invested in various businesses (see Colli and Vasta, this volume). A majority of emerging market business groups, such as Samsung and LG in South Korea and Tata and Reliance Industries in India, have basically been organized in similar fashion in terms of their family ownership and control.

State-owned business groups are diversified groups that have a state bureaucracy as the controlling owner. These groups have mostly developed to facilitate a rapid industrialization process in their respective nations, or to rescue and restructure failing banks and their industrial investments. An example to the former type in a Western economy is Instituto Nacional de Industria (INI) of Spain. While INI disappeared in 1995, it left its place to another state-owned business group, State Society of Industrial Participations (SEPI). An example of the latter type is Istituto per la Ricostruzione Industriale (IRI) in Italy, which was originally founded in 1933 but dissolved in 2002 following the privatization of its businesses in the 1980s and 1990s (see Colli and Vasta, this volume; Cuervo-Cazurra, this volume).

Bank-centered business groups have a commercial, investment, or universal bank at the helm of the whole organization. The banks control operating companies by establishing various ties including equity and often also debt. A prominent example of this variety of business group is the Deutsche Bank group in Germany, which divested its industrial activities after the first decade of the twenty-first century. The Deutsche Bank group, whose origins go back to the late nineteenth century, developed into the largest universal banking group in Germany by owning a considerable part of equity in, as well as providing credits to, a number of industrial enterprises. Deutsche Bank owned or had significant influence on such major industrial enterprises as Mannesmann, BMW, and particularly Daimler-Benz (see Schröter, this volume).

The second category of diversified business groups includes more contemporary varieties of business groups that have flourished since the 1960s, starting in the US and UK, which consist of conglomerates and then private equity firms.[15] We categorically

---

[15] See Chapter 2 for why the unrelated diversification wave after the 1960s has occurred as the corporate structure of conglomerates in the US and UK, and as conventional types of diversified business groups in many other nations.

include these as the new varieties of diversified business groups for two reasons. First, they are principally organized in legally independent operating units that exhibit diversified yet unrelated business portfolios.[16] Second, their apex organization exercises administrative (often financial) control over those units. These two new varieties of diversified business groups, however, basically show different ownership characteristics and administrative designs to control their operating units against each other.

Conglomerate firms differ from conventional diversified business groups in that conglomerates typically wholly own their operating units (usually organized as subsidiaries) and thus have no outside shareholders for those units.[17] Conventional business groups, by contrast, often possess a combination of wholly and partially owned operating units, some of which have outside shareholders and are even publicly listed. As such, conglomerates can theoretically have a much stronger administrative control of their operating units—for instance, by having full rights to transfer assets across constituent subsidiaries. By contrast, the presence of outside, yet non-controlling, shareholders in business groups implies that the right over the discretionary use of assets of group firms may be limited and thus intra-group capital allocation may possibly become suboptimal as far as the controlling shareholders are concerned (due to a potential conflict of interest between inside and outside shareholders) (Samphantharak, 2002).

Yet, in reality, the boundaries between the conventional types of diversified business groups and conglomerate firms sometimes get blurred, as diversified business groups increasingly aim to control their invested companies by taking majority, or even full, ownership of equity stakes, and by employing control-enhancing mechanisms over operating subsidiaries such as different classes of stocks (Colpan and Hikino, 2010; Moody's Investors Service, 2015). The Wallenberg group (of Sweden), through its apex organization Investor, for instance, has established a portfolio of wholly owned subsidiaries, and increased its ownership stakes in its listed companies since the 2000s.[18] Haniel Group (of Germany), on the other hand, has either wholly owned subsidiaries or controlling equity stakes in all its group companies (Investor, Annual Report, 2014; Haniel, Annual Report, 2015).

By contrast, private equity firms represent alternative investment funds which exhibit diversified portfolios that are unrelated product-wise. Those alternative funds differ from traditional investments in such established asset classes as stocks, bonds,

---

[16] Some conglomerates like Berkshire Hathaway and Danaher Corporation organize their operating units as legally independent companies only, while others are organized as an amalgamation of internal divisions and legally independent subsidiaries.

[17] This classification of conglomerates is based on the Chandler (1982a) and Berg (1969) classic definition of conglomerates that are unrelated in terms of their product portfolios and acquisitive in terms of their growth orientation.

[18] As discussed in Chapter 2, an important rationale for this change in investment behavior is the increasing active institutional investors and activist shareholders challenging diversified business groups in those economies.

and cash by committing to financial portfolios such as private equity (including venture capital), hedge funds, distressed securities, and financial derivatives. Private equity firms (and even some hedge funds, especially activist ones) eventually come close to the broad category of these diversified business groups for their sizeable equity stake in invested firms, which often leads to direct involvement in the significant decisions of those firms.

Private equity firms, however, differ from all other varieties of diversified business groups by their basic yet different investment and operating principles. Those principles dictate that private equity firms acquire a controlling stake in their operating companies but then exit from those enterprises within a relatively short period of three to seven years through an initial public offer, strategic sell-off, or secondary sale. Further, private equity firms are in principle obliged to separately maximize the financial return to individual investments without transferring resources to or from other investments. Private equity organization does not function as a collaborative arrangement group-wise for invested operating units in this regard. Given such critical differences in investment horizon and principles, and for the sake of conceptual focus of the present volume, we will therefore concentrate on the conglomerate types of business groups among the contemporary varieties of business groups hereafter, without delving into the categories of private equity firms, activist hedge funds, and other varieties of alternative investment funds. Contemporary examples of conglomerates are Berkshire Hathaway and Danaher Corporation, while private equity firms can be represented by firms like KKR and the Carlyle Group, and activist hedge funds include Pershing Square and Third Point—all in the United States.[19]

In order to highlight the basic similarities and differences between the new varieties of diversified business groups and the conventional ones, Figure 1.3 gives a comparative illustration of business organizations with diversified product portfolios in terms of the equity stake in operating units owned by the headquarters unit and the intra-group resource sharing and transfer within the entire organization. Operating units in all these business organizations naturally benefit from the professional talents and management capabilities nurtured and accumulated within the headquarters. Diversified business groups show a wide range of varieties in terms of their nature and level of resource sharing and transfers among operating units. Within that variety, it is interesting to notice that generally their contemporary counterparts, conglomerates, and private equity firms tend to stay away from intensive resource sharing and transfer among operating units, and thus their sources of competitive advantage are becoming more and more concentrated on the skills and capacities in financial resource allocation and monitoring that the headquarters unit possesses and exercises.

---

[19] For more information on conglomerates and private equity firms, see Collis, Anand, and Cheng (this volume) and Baker and Montgomery (1994).

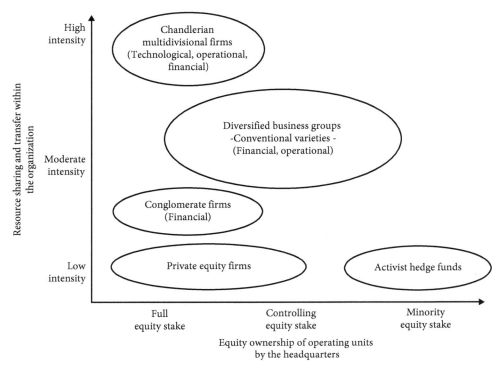

FIGURE 1.3. Comparable business organizations with diversified product portfolios.

Note: The above figure shows the stylized features of each business organization. Characteristic resources shared or transferred within the organization are shown in parentheses. For private equity firms, their equity ownership combined with their investors are represented.

1.5 OUTLINE OF THE VOLUME

The chapters that follow are organized in two distinct parts. Part I, made up of four chapters including this introduction, deals with significant economic, institutional, and organizational subjects related to business groups from a cross-national perspective. These chapters provide comparative analyses that highlight the similarities and differences in the development and functioning of business groups in the diverse national settings of today's developed economies of the West. Chapters 2 and 3 concentrate on diversified business groups, following the overall orientation of the volume as outlined above. Chapter 2 examines the nature, roles, and evolutionary paths of diversified business groups in the West and seeks to explain the origins, growth, and resilience of those groups in different market and institutional settings. Chapter 3 concentrates on the effects of national-level politics and institutions on the evolution of diversified business groups. It examines the experiences of diversified business groups in the developed economies of Western Europe and North America which have exhibited different regimes, political forces, and policy instruments. Chapter 4 then turns toward network-type business groups and the "network form" to provide a complementary view. It explores analytic characteristics, including density, connectivity, centrality, and clustering, that are critical in understanding the internal structuring of business groups.

Part II includes thirteen nation-specific chapters (organized in three groups). The national chapters broadly follow the basic typology laid out in this introduction, with a focus on diversified business groups, although there are differences between chapters in terms of their focal coverage, depending on the existence of different varieties of business groups and also the conventional use of the term "business group" in different countries.[20] These chapters present individual national cases that aim at portraying an organized synthesis of the broad issues pertaining to the analysis of the development and resilience of business groups in developed economies. The approaches that individual contributions take in the volume are developmental and evolutionary, and the chapters cover the period up to the present. More specifically, the chapters address the following six issues (with differences of emphasis between chapters) pertaining to the business group as a variety of the large modern enterprise organization summarized above:

1. The significance of the business group organization in the large-enterprise sector of the individual nations with a long-term evolutionary perspective. How important have these groups been for the national economy over periods of time?
2. The long-term development pattern of business groups in national economic contexts. What forces have facilitated and constrained the emergence and growth of business groups? What have been the roles of political and regulatory factors, in contrast to economic ones, in the formation and evolution of business groups?
3. The reasons for the longevity of business groups in the competitive economy. How have the competitiveness and viability of the business groups been affected by changes in such environmental factors as product, capital, labor markets, and institutional frameworks, as well as organizational factors such as intra-group resources and capabilities?
4. Corporate governance topics such as ownership composition and intra-group control and coordination devices, including the roles of equity ties (especially pyramids), director interlocks, and other mechanisms.
5. What varieties of business groups nurture competitive resources and capabilities? What has been the division of labor between the headquarters unit and operating subsidiaries? How has that division shifted as business groups have evolved?
6. Strategic factors such as primary industry composition, product portfolio, and overseas expansion. Structural considerations such as organizational design and control and administrative mechanisms. How have the relationships between strategy and structure changed in the long term?

---

[20] Each national chapter gives a categorization of the types of business groups that it covers in an opening footnote.

Table 1.3. Levels of per capita GDP in earlier and late industrializing economies, 1820–2010 (1990 international Geary–Khamis dollars).

	1820	1870	*1913*	1950	1960	1970	1980	1990	2000	2010
Historical Front Runners in Europe										
UK	1,706	3,190	*4,921*	6,939	8,645	10,767	12,931	16,430	20,353	23,777
Belgium	1,319	2,692	*4,220*	5,462	6,952	10,611	14,467	17,197	20,656	23,557
Netherlands	1,838	2,757	*4,049*	5,996	8,287	11,967	14,705	17,262	22,161	24,303
Germany	1,077	1,839	*3,648*	3,881	7,705	10,839	14,114	15,929	18,944	20,661
France	1,135	1,876	*3,485*	5,186	7,398	11,410	14,766	17,647	20,422	21,477
Catch-up Nations in Europe										
Sweden	1,198	1,662	*3,096*	6,739	8,688	12,716	14,937	17,609	20,710	25,306
Italy	1,117	1,499	*2,564*	3,502	5,916	9,719	13,149	16,313	18,774	18,520
Spain	1,008	1,207	*2,056*	2,189	3,072	6,319	9,203	12,055	15,622	16,797
Portugal	923	975	*1,250*	2,086	2,956	5,473	8,044	10,826	13,813	14,279
Western Offshoots										
USA	1,257	2,445	*5,301*	9,561	11,328	15,030	18,577	23,201	28,467	30,491
Australia	518	3,273	*5,157*	7,412	8,791	12,024	14,412	17,173	21,732	25,584
Canada	904	1,695	*4,447*	7,291	8,753	12,050	16,176	18,872	22,488	24,941
Late Industrializing Nations in Asia										
Japan	669	737	*1,387*	1,921	3,986	9,714	13,428	18,789	20,738	21,935
Singapore	683	682	*1,279*	2,219	2,310	4,439	9,058	14,220	22,518	29,038
S. Korea	600	604	*869*	854	1,226	2,167	4,114	8,704	14,375	21,701
Thailand	570	608	*841*	817	1,078	1,694	2,554	4,633	6,398	9,372
Taiwan	550	550	*747*	924	1,492	2,980	5,869	9,886	16,835	23,292
India	533	533	*673*	619	753	868	938	1,309	1,892	3,372
China	600	530	*552*	448	662	778	1,061	1,871	3,421	8,032
Late Industrializing Nations in Latin America										
Argentina	n.a.	1,311	*3,797*	4,987	5,559	7,302	8,206	6,433	8,581	10,256
Chile	694	1,290	*2,988*	3,670	4,270	5,231	5,680	6,401	10,309	13,883
Mexico	759	674	*1,732*	2,365	3,155	4,320	6,320	6,085	7,275	7,716
Brazil	646	713	*811*	1,672	2,335	3,057	5,195	4,920	5,532	6,879
Late Industrializing Nations in the Middle East, Eastern Europe, and Africa										
South Africa	415	858	*1,602*	2,535	3,041	4,045	4,390	3,834	3,890	5,080
Russia	688	943	*1,488*	2,841	3,945	5,575	6,427	7,779	5,277	8,660
Turkey	643	825	*1,213*	1,623	2,247	3,078	4,022	5,399	6,446	8,225
Israel	n.a.	n.a.	*n.a.*	2,817	4,663	8,101	10,984	13,067	16,172	19,171

Note: Within individual national groupings, countries are ranked based on the GDP per capita figures for the year 1913.

Source: Compiled from Maddison (2009) and The Maddison-Project, http://www.ggdc.net/maddison/maddison-project/home.htm, 2013 version.

The volume covers the following national cases: Britain, Belgium, the Netherlands, Germany, France, Sweden, Italy, Spain, Portugal, the United States, Australia, and Canada. Table 1.3 shows the GDP per capita (representing the comparative level of economic development) of these nations and selected other countries. It divides them into groups depending on their geographical areas as well as phases of economic maturity. The chapters in Part II are organized in the following groups: historical front runners in Western Europe, catch-up nations in Western Europe, and the economies of Western offshoots. Together these chapters present a comprehensive picture of the similarities and differences between national economies in terms of the historical development paths that business groups have taken and the shifting economic roles they have played. Altogether, then, combined with the previous volume on business groups in contemporary developing economies (Colpan, Hikino, and Lincoln, 2010), this book aims to portray and understand the evolutionary dynamics of business groups in changing global market settings.

Acknowledgments

We thank the contributors to this volume, and in particular David Collis, Alvaro Cuervo-Cazurra, Geoffrey Jones and Álvaro Ferreira da Silva, for their valuable comments on this chapter.

CHAPTER 2

....

THE EVOLUTIONARY DYNAMICS OF DIVERSIFIED BUSINESS GROUPS IN THE WEST

history and theory

....

ASLI M. COLPAN AND TAKASHI HIKINO

2.1 INTRODUCTION

....

THIS chapter aims to amplify the analytical scope of management research on the evolutionary dynamics of large business enterprises in different market and institutional settings. It does so by incorporating historical perspectives on the varied developmental patterns that the corporate organization model of *diversified business groups* has exhibited in the economies of Western Europe, North America, and Oceania from the late nineteenth century to the present. In examining the evolutionary dynamics of diversified business groups in those economies, we aim to propose a new interpretation of the long-term development of large business enterprises in different economic settings. In this context, diversified business groups are defined as the collections of legally independent enterprises, linked through equity ties and other economic means, which have a central unit at the helm that controls the affiliated enterprises in *unrelated* industries.[1]

---

[1] For a detailed description of diversified business groups, see Chapter 1. We employ the term "unrelated" here following the conventional definitions of "relatedness," or for that matter "unrelatedness," that have focused on similarities in technologies and markets (Rumelt, 1974; Markides and Williamson, 1994; Anand and Jayanti, 2005).

At the outset we review and re-examine the influential thesis on the historical primacy of the multidivisional enterprise as the most efficient and effective variety of modern large enterprises associated with the work of Alfred Chandler (1962, 1977, 1990). In doing so we attempt to lay the groundwork for reassessing the role of the diversified business group as an alternative model of modern large enterprises and ultimately for coming up with a more balanced and comprehensive interpretation of the role that different models of business organizations have played in the process of modern economic growth. In the Chandlerian interpretation, it is ultimately large industrial firms that are coined "multi-divisional enterprises" with related product portfolio, representing "scale and scope," and which are strategically managed by salaried senior executives that play the central role in a nation's dynamic economy. By contrast, diversified business groups can be understood as positioning themselves at the opposite end of ownership, strategy, and structure. Often they are owned and controlled by concentrated shareholders in the form of business families, but also financial institutions and the state. As such, many groups have been controlled at the headquarters level by majority shareholders, rather than by salaried, non-owning executives, as Chandler observed in multidivisional enterprises. Strategically, diversified business groups exhibit unrelated product portfolios, not related ones with technological or product-market links to each other. Further, they have their operating units in the form of legally independent subsidiaries and affiliates, some of which can even be publicly listed. In the case of multidivisional firms, operating units are most often organized as internal divisions.

At a more focused level on diversified business groups per se, then, we in effect re-examine the influential "institutional voids" hypothesis proposed by Tarun Khanna and colleagues (1997, 2007) in their research on diversified business groups in emerging markets. Those works emphasize the critical significance of the immaturity of external markets and market institutions, which gives advantages to established firms that are equipped with abundant and often underutilized intra-group resources to exploit market opportunities. As markets develop and their institutions mature as a consequence of economic development, diversified business groups are expected to complete their positive roles and start functioning as negative forces to become an obstacle and thus harm the viability of national economies. As a result, this line of argument suggests that diversified business groups should complete their historical role by exiting from the marketplace altogether or by switching their basic strategic orientation in terms of product portfolio to be more focused and to resemble the Chandlerian multidivisional firm.

The historical development of diversified business groups in today's developed economies will present an appropriate testing ground for these two theories, one on the primacy of multidivisional firms with related product portfolio in developed economies and the other on the rise of diversified business groups with unrelated product portfolio in emerging markets. While the Chandlerian enterprise model may reflect a significant aspect of the corporate development pattern in the US economy, the resilience and even resurgence of the new as well as conventional varieties of business groups in some developed economies force scholars to re-examine and reinterpret the evolution of large multibusiness enterprises from fresh and broader perspectives. This continuing viability of the group model suggests that diversified business groups do not simply fade away as the market and institutional environments become more developed. These empirical realities signify the need to look beyond the theoretical arguments of institutional void-filling as the major function played by the business groups that have occupied the most prominent place of the business-group literature to date. They suggest the significance of looking at the concrete examples of Western nations to explore the rise, growth, struggle, and resilience of diversified business groups in contrasting market and institutional settings. This examination will make it possible to reassess both the interpretations of corporate evolution proposed by Alfred Chandler, which were built on the experiences of the US economy and the economic development theories of diversified business groups that were predominantly based on the experiences of contemporary developing economies.

With a historiographical examination as a starting point, this chapter examines the historical origins, evolutionary paths, and long-term resilience of diversified business groups in contemporary developed economies of the West. Ultimately, the central goal of this chapter is to come up with a new theoretical understanding of diversified business groups and other comparable models of corporate organizations by broadening the analytical perspectives of the earlier approaches in terms of longitudinal and geographical scope. To reach such an end, in Section 2.2 we begin our analysis by reviewing the historical context of the development of diversified business groups in the US economy to reveal their standing within the Chandlerian analyses. In Sections 2.3 to 2.5 we then examine the empirical regularities in the historical evolution of diversified business groups in different Western nations from the late nineteenth century to the present day. Section 2.6 puts forward a theoretical analysis of the critical factors that have led to the divergent developmental patterns of corporate organizations across different economies. Section 2.7 concludes the chapter with the synthesis and implications of our findings.

2.2 DIVERSIFIED BUSINESS GROUPS WITHIN THE CHANDLERIAN FRAMEWORK

Ever since the publication of *Strategy and Structure* in 1962, historical research on the evolution of large enterprises in the modern market economy has been dominated by a single paradigm: the Chandlerian perspective that emphasizes the primacy of the industrial enterprise of the US variety, in which salaried professional management adopts the growth strategy of *related diversification* and the administrative structure of *multidivisional organization*. Despite the theoretical and empirical criticisms that Chandler's interpretation of firm evolution across different economies over time has faced (Fligstein, 1985; Freeland, 1996; Lamoreaux et al., 2002), the supremacy of the Chandlerian large enterprises has remained influential in academic disciplines of management as well as business history.

In order to reassess Chandler's thesis on the primacy of multidivisional firms adopting the strategy of related diversification among the varieties of modern business enterprises, it is critical to recall the historical background of the time when Chandler originally formulated his ideas of corporate growth in the 1950s and 1960s: the supremacy of the United States was firmly established in the global political and economic scene, and large US firms stood at the center of that dominance. After all, in the early 1960s more than 300 of the 500 largest industrial enterprises in the global economy had US headquarters (Chandler and Hikino, 1997). Chandler's championing of the product diversification strategy committed by large US industrial enterprises, complemented by Raymond Vernon's (1966) "product cycle" model of their multinationalization conduct, eventually represented the core mechanism of the US hegemony of the post-World War II global economy. Within this context, below we examine the standing of diversified business groups within the Chandlerian thesis.

2.2.1 Diversified Business Groups in the Chandlerian Historical Interpretation

Long before large modern industrial enterprises with an organized managerial hierarchy became firmly established as the representative and most effective model of big business in the US by the 1920s—and before this became the most emulated model around the world, especially after World War II—the US economy actually had its own varieties of diversified business groups. These can broadly be classified into two basic types. The first is made up of general merchants as the historical predecessors of region-oriented business groups who dealt with varied products and industries, especially in international markets, and who played an influential role in the initial phase of industrialization of the US economy up to the 1840s. After the 1880s they would categorically transform into business groups centered around overseas trading and operating companies. The second type is made up of bank-centered business groups organized typically around investment banks. These bank-centered groups, or "money trusts" (the largest of which was the Morgan group), appeared around the turn of the nineteenth century to invest in and control firms in various industries. The US also saw business groups that were often organized within a single industry sector: the industrial "holding company"-type groups, mostly arranged in pyramidal structures. These groups mostly had their origins in trusts and turned into holding companies after trust arrangements were outlawed by the Sherman Antitrust Act of 1890 (Kandel et al, 2015; Hikino and Bucheli, this volume).

Chandler, in his *Visible Hand* (1977), was categorically dismissive of all of these business groups. For diversified business groups formed around general merchants, Chandler argued: "The general merchant ... dominated the economy and ... was an exporter, wholesaler, importer, retailer, ship owner, banker, and insurer. ... [They] still relied entirely on commercial practices and procedures invented and perfected centuries earlier by British, Dutch, and Italian merchants" (Chandler, 1977). Hence, according to Chandler, because of their "traditional" administrative styles these diversified entities could not nurture competitive resources and capabilities to take advantage of expanding domestic markets. Bank-centered groups organized around investment banks, he claimed, did not have adequate product-related resources and capabilities to control the strategic decision-making of constituent industrial enterprises. The holding company groups, he argued, were "loose" organizations bound together for legal reasons without administrative unity or coordination. Those groups began to be challenged as early as the 1910s, but more decisively within the policy framework of the New Deal in the 1930s, on political, legal, and economic grounds (Chandler, 1977, 1982a; Kandel et al., 2015). At around the same time, another challenge came from the specialized and vertically integrated firm, reducing the role of diversified business groups in the US economy.

In fact, however, bank-centered groups in particular played a critical and complementary role in the original manufacturing and industrial function of Chandlerian firms by meeting their capital needs for investing in large-scale production facilities to achieve economies of scale. The banks customarily attempted to monitor the efficient and effective conduct of industrial enterprises in order to assure their productive operation, and they ultimately functioned as rescuers and reorganizers when those enterprises faced unsolvable financial difficulties (Hikino and Bucheli, this volume). However, these contributions by banking institutions and bank-centered groups to the viability of US economic institutions remained marginalized according to the Chandlerian interpretation. When the early experiences of the United States with the corporate model of diversified business groups ended abruptly in the 1930s, the Chandlerian enterprises that became related-diversified in strategy and multidivisional in structure had come to be hailed as the most effective and efficient combination of strategy and structure regardless of the varieties of market settings and differences in economic maturity. Broadly accepting the theoretical assumption of an eventual convergence on such a single model of large enterprises, then, American consulting companies pressed the rest of the world to emulate this variety of the US model (Whittington et.al, 1999).

2.2.2 Multiplicity of Large Enterprises in Competitive Mature Markets

A turning point for the dominance of the Chandlerian paradigm came from the global competitive dynamics of big business that eventually pushed diversified business groups into becoming the center of attention. The shift in international dynamics in the large enterprise landscape started to urge a reinterpretation of the primacy of Chandlerian multidivisional enterprises, as they struggled against upcoming firms originating in late-industrializing economies such as Japan, South Korea, Taiwan, and then China, which started their modern economic growth in the twentieth century, and especially in the decades following World War II (Hikino and Amsden, 1994). Business groups, which were at the core of competitive dynamics in the late-industrializing nations, differed critically from the Chandlerian enterprises in all the three aspects that Chandler emphasized as the primary reasons for competitive capabilities. First, ownership usually remained with the entrepreneurial family that controlled and often managed their business empire. Second, the firms employed the strategy of unrelated diversification for their long-term growth. Third, in response to that diversification conduct they adopted a group structure with legally independent subsidiaries and affiliates. For each of these three characteristics, business groups remained different from the Chandlerian multidivisional enterprises.

Interestingly, within the Chandlerian framework none of the three characteristics of diversified business groups has a positive connotation. First, family ownership and control eventually deter the development of salaried and professional management that stands as the core of competitive dynamics in modern industrial enterprises. Second, product domains should be related, as in strategy literature, so that an enterprise exploits the benefits of accumulated intra-organizational knowledge that can be transferred to related product categories, ensuring a lower-than-market level of production cost. It has been suggested that unrelated diversification, by contrast, should suffer the "conglomerate discount" problem, i.e., that the market value of the entire group as a whole is lower than that of the sum of the individual operating companies. Third, the group structure hinder the inter-business transfer of accumulated knowledge that remains at the core of the Chandlerian view of competitive advantages of large industrial enterprises. The allegedly limited and often *unsystematic* administrative arrangements deter the coordination mechanism which should function as an instrument for such transfer of knowledge assets across operating units. Relying on these negative connotations of business groups in general, while acknowledging the rise of diversified business groups as global players, advocates of the Chandlerian argument suggested that it was the environment of immature markets and institutions that supported the growth of such groups in developing economies. Ultimately the time will come for their demise, the supporters continued to insist, as markets become mature.

While dynamic diversified business groups have successfully remained as the core business organization in many late-industrializing nations, comparable entities with wide and unrelated product portfolio were destined to lead a checkered life in contemporary developed economies. While in parts of Europe business groups survived the many market and institutional changes their economies experienced and remained intact forms of business enterprise (e.g., in Sweden and Italy), in others they were marginalized—yet individually stayed resilient—as a business organization (e.g., in Spain).[2] Furthermore, the United States itself saw the rise, fall, and resurgence of the noble varieties of diversified business groups such as conglomerates.

---

[2] The organizational design of multidivisional firms spread to Europe in the post-World War II era and especially during the 1960s, whose advance was promoted by American consulting firms, business schools, and global successes of the American enterprise (Mayer and Whittington, 1996).

Chandler remained dismissive of these enterprises as well. He was especially critical of acquisitive conglomerates, such as Harold Geneen's ITT and Charles Bluhdorn's Gulf & Western, which started burgeoning in the US economy in the 1960s. Those conglomerates exhibited the characteristic conduct of *unrelated* diversification, in contrast to the historical development of *diversified* industrial enterprises such as DuPont and General Electric, which adopted the strategy model of *related* diversification. Overall, Chandler claimed that the style of administrative coordination based on financial and budgetary means only is not well suited to modern industrial enterprises that are the major sources of economic growth in competitive market settings (Chandler, 1982a; 1991). He also remained critical of European business groups, especially of their historical prototype of holding companies such as Calico Printers' Association and Associated Portland Cement in Britain. Further he was skeptical of old family-controlled large enterprises in general such as Cadburys (Chandler, 1990), although he did not specifically investigate the concrete cases of European firms at the group level, as his interest remained mainly in individual industrial enterprises strategically administered by salaried senior executives.

Chandler's interpretation could possibly be justified for the central role of multi-divisional enterprises which prospered in the market and institutional contexts of the US economy in the early to mid-twentieth century. Yet he was much too assertive in his managerial theses on ownership (scattered shareholding), strategy (related diversification), and structure (multidivisional structure) to discount the role of diversified business groups altogether and to ignore the influential forces outside the internal managerial dynamics of the *industrial* enterprise. As we now turn to our own examination of the evolutionary dynamics of diversified business groups in different Western nations that have altogether been marginalized within the Chandlerian interpretation, we argue that diversified business groups worked well not only in early economic growth, but also remain an effective and dynamic form of large business enterprise in several developed economies, despite the hostile attitudes that institutional investors have adopted against their diversified product portfolio since the 1980s. We examine in particular the factors behind the development of diversified business groups in different nations to complement the Chandlerian story and come up with a more balanced and comprehensive picture of the dynamic evolution of the modern corporate economy.

Before we delve into their long-term evolution across nations, Table 2.1 shows the state (in 2014) of the largest diversified business groups (including conglomerates)[3] by revenue in the Western nations covered in this volume. The table illustrates the interesting pattern of distribution of diversified business groups in the major developed economies in which they exist side by side with Chandlerian multidivisional

---

[3] Our classification of conglomerates, especially in the US context, is based on the Berg (1969) and Chandler (1982a) classic definition of conglomerates that are unrelated in terms of their product portfolios and acquisitive in terms of their growth orientation. See Chapter 1 for details.

Table 2.1. The largest diversified business groups (including conglomerates) in the West, 2014.

Rank	Group name	Country	Revenues (US$ m)	Year	Controlling ownership	Public listing[a] Apex	Operating units
1	Berkshire Hathaway	USA	194,673	2014	Warren Buffett	O	×
2	Wallenberg Group	Sweden	182,000[b]	2013	Wallenberg family	O	O
3	Exor Group	Italy[c]	148,043	2014	Agnelli family	O	O
4	Handelsbanken Group	Sweden	140,000[b]	2014	None[k]	O	O
5	Koch Industries	USA	115,000	2014	Koch family	×	×
6	Jardine Matheson	UK/Bermuda/ Hong Kong[c]	62,782	2014	Keswick family	O	O
7	Wesfarmers	Australia	49,235	2014	None	O	×
8	Groupe Bouygues	France	40,131	2014	Bouygues family	O	O
9	Groupe Arnault	France	39,020[d]	2014	Arnault family	×	O
10	Weston Group	Canada	37,890	2014	Weston family	O	O
11	Power Corporation of Canada	Canada	36,778	2014	Desmarais family	O	O
12	J.D. Irving Limited	Canada/Bermuda[c]	30,000[b]	2011	Irving family	×	△
13	Swire Group	UK	28,974	2014	Swire family	×	O
14	Américo Amorim Group	Portugal	25,063	2010	Amorim family	×	O
15	Virgin Group[e]	UK	24,000	2012	Richard Branson	×	O
16	Danaher[f]	USA	19,914	2014	None	O	×
17	Icahn Enterprises	USA	18,758	2014	Carl Icahn	O	×
18	SHV Group	Netherlands	18,051	2014	Fentener van Vlissingen family	×	×
19	Rethmann Group	Germany	14,774	2014	Rethmann family	×	×
20	Loews Corporation	USA	14,572	2014	Tisch family	O	O
21	Mondragon Corporation	Spain	14,381	2014	Employees' cooperatives	×	×
22	Espírito Santo Group[g]	Portugal	13,252	2010	Espírito Santo family	×	O
23	Oetker Group	Germany	13,241	2014	Oetker family	×	×
24	Edizione Group	Italy	13,200	2014	Benetton family	×	O
25	Leucadia National Corporation	USA	12,407	2014	None	O	△
26	Groupe Artémis	France	12,110[h]	2014	Pinault family	×	O
27	Groupe Frère- Bourgeois	Belgium	12,106	2014	Frère family	×	O
28	Maxingvest	Germany	11,702	2014	Herz family	×	O
29	Cofra Group	Switzerland/ Netherlands[c]	10,000[b]	2008	Brenninkmeijer family	×	×
30	Axel Johnson	Sweden	8,524	2014	Johnson family	×	O

(continued)

Table 2.1. Continued

Rank	Group name	Country	Revenues (US$ m)	Year	Controlling ownership	Public listing[a] Apex	Public listing[a] Operating units
31	HAL Trust	Curaçao/ Netherlands[c]	8,484	2014	Van der Vorm family	O	O
32	Jim Pattison Group	Canada	8,400	2015	Jim Pattison	×	△
33	Jarden Corporation[i]	USA	8,287	2014	None	O	×
34	Grupo Villar Mir	Spain	7,826	2014	Villar Mir family	×	△
35	Freudenberg Group	Germany	7,244	2014	Freudenberg family	×	×
36	Groupe Wendel	France	7,162	2014	Wendel family	O	O
37	Kinnevik Group	Sweden	6,386	2014	Stenbeck family	O	O
38	Italmobiliare Group	Italy	6,169	2013	Pesenti family	O	O
39	Sonae Group	Portugal	6,024	2014	Belmiro de Azevedo family	×	O
40	Newell Rubbermaid[i]	USA	5,727	2014	None	O	×
41	Fininvest Group	Italy	5,300	2015	Berlusconi family	×	O
42	Fintecna Group	Italy	5,163	2013	Ministry of Economy and Finance, Italy	×	O
43	Renco Group	USA	5000[b]	2014	Ira Rennert	×	×
44	Haniel Group	Germany	4,776	2014	Haniel family	×	O
45	SEPI	Spain	4,433	2014	Treasury and Public Administration Ministry, Spain	×	O
46	Werhahn Group	Germany	4,419	2013	Werhahn family	×	×
47	James Richardson & Sons	Canada	4,200	2010	Richardson family	×	×
48	Bestway Group[j]	UK	3,970	2014	Pervez family	×	O
49	Mota-Engil Group	Portugal	3,195	2013	Mota family	×	O
50	COFIDE Gruppo De Benedetti	Italy	2,952	2014	De Benedetti family	O	O

Note: This table covers only the diversified business groups in the nations covered in this volume. US conglomerates that are technologically and market wise unrelated in their product portfolio and acquisitive in their growth orientation are included. Private equity firms are excluded.

[a] In public listing column for the operating units, O means some operating units are publicly listed, while x means they are not. △ means most companies are privately held. Apex unit represents the central controlling organization of the group, although there may be family offices or other organizations on top of that visible unit.

[b] Approximate figure.

[c] Exor relocated its headquarters to Netherlands in 2016, but remained listed on the Milan Exchange in Italy. Jardine Matheson has standard listing in the UK, is incorporated in Bermuda, and operates from Hong Kong. J.D. Irving is registered in Bermuda. Cofra group belongs to the Brenninkmeijer family in the Netherlands but is headquartered in Switzerland. HAL Trust is based in Curaçao but listed in the Netherlands.

[d] This figure is the revenue of Financière Agache, which is a holding company controlled by Groupe Arnault.

[e] Some companies are connected to the Virgin group only through a licensing agreement.

[f] In 2015 Danaher announced it would split into two companies.

[g] Espírito Santo Group was dismantled in August 2014.

[h] This figure shows the revenue for only one subsidiary named Kering, as the revenue for the whole group is not available.

[i] Newell Rubbermaid and Jarden merged in 2016.

[j] Bestway group has operations in the grocery wholesale, pharmacy, and real-estate industries the UK and cement and banking industries in Pakistan.

[k] The Lundberg family increased its ownership in the holding company, Industrivärden, to more than 20% in 2106.

Source: Orbis/Osiris Database, Bureau van Dijk Electronic Publishing KK; Fortune 500 companies, Fortune; Forbes America's Largest Private Companies, Forbes; Group webpages and annual reports; chapters in this volume.

enterprises. The nations that have the most number of business groups in the list are Italy (6 enterprises), Germany (6), Canada (5), France (4), Sweden (4), the UK (4), Portugal (4), Spain (3), the Netherlands (3), Australia (1), and Belgium (1), as well as the US (9)—which, however, typically has conglomerate-type groups with non-publicly listed operating companies except for the case of Loews Corporation. The largest five business groups consist of the US (2 enterprises), Swedish (2), and Italian (1) groups, which make up almost 50 percent of the whole of the largest 50 business groups in terms of revenue. The table also illustrates the dominance of family control in the largest diversified business groups.

2.3 THE HISTORICAL RISE OF DIVERSIFIED BUSINESS GROUPS, FROM THE LATE NINETEENTH CENTURY TO THE 1910S

Diversified business groups rose to play critical roles in early-industrializing economies in the Second Industrial Revolution. By early-industrializing economies we in this context mean those nations that experienced an initial phase of industrialization by the late nineteenth to early twentieth century, when the economic impact of the Second Industrial Revolution engulfed the whole industrial economy across nations. We argue that the key factors to an understanding of the historical *rise* of diversified business

groups in such economies are twofold. First, the prime factor is related to the characteristic nature of available internal resources and the capabilities of business organizations in individual economies: the industrial enterprises in "early mover" economies
that industrialized by the late nineteenth to early twentieth century typically embodied
proprietary know-how that was technology-intensive and product-centered. These
industrial enterprises often became the first in their respective nations to systematically
nurture technological capabilities by establishing research and development facilities,
and they commercialized new products and processes through exploiting their accumulated capabilities later in the twentieth century (Chandler and Hikino, 1997).
Second, banking institutions often became gradually yet systematically involved in
the debt and/or equity financing of those industrial enterprises in the process of
the Second Industrial Revolution. This technological advancement and ultimately
whole corporate development continuously required industrial enterprises to commit
huge amounts of financial resources to invest in order to keep up with the ever
increasing minimum optimal scale. Only with that investment could the relevant
firms sustainably retain the status of stable oligopolistic players. As the amount of
capital requirement became too massive for individual firms to internally finance or to
rely on the network of owning entrepreneurs and families, banking institutions became
an indispensable part of the modern business dynamics for large industrial enterprises.
Those relationships between industrial enterprises and banking institutions ultimately
became the basis of the formation of diversified business groups. The case of Sweden
illustrates this point in a telling manner.

Experiencing its rapid industrialization between 1870 and 1913, Sweden saw its first
wave of innovation during this period, which led to the establishment of enterprises
specialized in manufacturing and engineering, including Atlas Copco founded in 1873,
L. M. Ericsson in 1876, ASEA in 1883, and others. These family-controlled firms were
originally financed principally by retained earnings, trade credits, and short-term credit
notes (Högfeldt, 2005). Later, and especially after 1900, bank loans and bank connections became important as the demand for capital increased, and in 1911 the bank ties
were boosted when commercial banks were allowed to own shares in industrial
companies (Högfeldt, 2005; Larsson and Petersson, this volume). Diversified business
groups in Sweden therefore had their origins predominantly after that year, when
banks started to invest in industrial companies, and especially in the 1920s, when a
deflation crisis in the country caused the transfer of corporate shares to the banks
(which were the original creditors of the industrial companies) (Larsson and Petersson,
this volume).[4] The prominent business groups of the Wallenbergs (organized around

---

[4] There were also a number of family-owned business groups that to some extent diversified into
unrelated businesses before the 1930s, such as the Johnson group into trading, shipping, and steel
production, and Söderberg into iron and steel trading, and investment. Relative to these groups,
however, the bank-centered groups were much more diversified and larger in size—especially after the
1920s deflation crisis. The banking groups had therefore played a more central role in the Swedish
economy (Larsson and Petersson, this volume).

Stockholms Enskilda Bank controlled by the Wallenberg family) and the Handelsbanken thus came into full existence in the 1920s as they became the controlling owners of many industrial companies. The business groups (and the banks as their apex) therefore mainly served a reorganizing and revitalizing function for established but financially troubled industrial companies.

The experiences of most other early industrializing nations of the West illustrate a strikingly similar pattern: it was product-specialized industrial firms that had historically played a central role in the industrialization processes at earlier stages, and in the later phases banks entered as rescuers and reorganizers of those firms when they experienced financial troubles, to eventually form bank-centered diversified groups. In this context the banks that would stand at the center of the diversified business groups mostly started organizing those industrial firms passively to protect their financial interest, rather than forming the groups actively as a part of their grand growth scheme. This argument fits nicely with recent work that has shown universal banking being developed into significance only after the first push of industrialization in the continental European economies (Fohlin, 2007). Several illustrative examples can be cited.

In Germany it was the self-standing and self-financed product-specialized industrial enterprise that originally carried the industrialization process up to the 1880s, while banking institutions and bank-centered groups came to play a major role in the later stages of German industrialization. The latter were formed as banks aimed at achieving control and security by investing in their customers (Fohlin, 2007; Schröter, this volume).[5] In Belgium bank-centered groups began to be formed when banks reluctantly had to accept the shares of product-specialized companies in exchange for their debts following economic crises in the economy in the mid-nineteenth century that depressed the performance of the borrower industrial enterprises (Daems, 1977). Even Italy, the country known mostly for its contemporary family-owned business groups, had its own share of diversified business groups in the 1910s—as bank-centered groups, which had been formed when banks progressively increased their shareholdings in their most important clients. This was especially so, as the banks had to take over distressed firms and eventually became the controlling shareholders of industrial companies (Colli and Vasta, this volume). The US economy, interestingly, had its own share of bank-centered groups when the major investment banks such as Morgan started owning a substantial proportion of the shares of large corporations in diverse industries. It is important to note, however, that the instrumental means by which these bank-centered groups operated in controlling various industrial enterprises, extending

---

[5] Despite the fact that industrial companies tried to ward off the intervention of banks, the latter achieved success in their policy of controlling their invested companies to a substantial amount especially until World War I (see Schröter, this volume).

from financial control to involvement in more strategic issues, were not uniform in different economies or even within one nation.

In contrast to the above-mentioned cases, Britain and two of its former colonies, Australia and Canada, chose to adopt a different development model due to the relative absence of banking institutions engaged in long-term industrial financing in those nations. In Britain, the "first industrial nation," product-specialized companies drove the country's early industrialization processes, while bank-centered business groups were not formed to play any major economic role. British banks differed from those already mentioned in that they did not take any large shares in industrial firms, while providing mostly short-term financing and, to a lesser extent, eventual long-term loans through rolled-over credits (Jones, this volume; Fohlin, 2007). Even when the capital demand increased with the coming of the Second Industrial Revolution, in Britain it was mainly the "re-invested profits, stock market issues, private placements with stockbrokers and insurance companies, and family" (rather than banks) that provided the necessary financing (Jones, this volume). On the other hand, British enterprises formed business groups in developing economies, especially colonial territories or post-colonial countries, exploiting the underdeveloped markets in those economies with the support of capital markets in London.

The Australian and Canadian cases show a similar pattern to Britain with regard to the absence of bank-centered groups during the late nineteenth to early twentieth century. This was mostly due to the British heritage in those two former colonies, which led to banks remaining minor players in industrial finance (Naylor, 1975; Ville, this volume).[6] However, the two economies depart from each other in the type of large enterprises that became prominent in this period. With the Australian economy lacking breadth, product-specialized companies exploited growth opportunities in the dominant resource industries, while belated manufacturing expansion from the interwar years fell largely under the control of American multinationals. Local companies, in a relatively small and remote market with a developing but regionalized stock exchange, struggled to compete or build business groups. Canada, experiencing its rapid industrial growth from the mid-1890s to World War I, saw the emergence of its business groups (organized around entrepreneurs) as British capital flooded in to finance such expansion. For instance, the largest of the business groups—Aitken group—was formed in the early twentieth century when Max Aitken borrowed money in London and used his investment bank to organize the takeover of several small independent firms in Canada to end up in a widely diversified business group (Morck and Tian, this volume; Ville, this volume).

---

[6] Ville (this volume) argues that Australian banks remained as minor players in industrial finance before the Second World War, as they were tarnished by the financial collapse of the 1890s, and that the British influence might have provided a blueprint for how the relationships between banking institutions and industrial enterprises should be arranged. Naylor (1975) suggests that the banking system in Canada developed as an imitation of, and through regulation from, London.

2.4 THE TRANSFORMATION OF BUSINESS GROUPS IN THE INTERWAR PERIOD

The interwar period, especially from the mid-1920s to the mid-1930s, serves as a significant turning point in the long-term evolution of diversified business groups in the Western economies. Thanks to the inflationary setting in parts of Europe in the 1920s, followed by recessionary economic conditions during the Great Depression, many banks became burdened with non-performing assets in terms of credits given to and shares invested in failing industrial enterprises. While this economic background has been similar across many nations, different political and regulatory responses became the key factor for the transformation, or in some cases demise, of diversified business groups that were especially centered around banks. We see three patterns in particular. First, a few nations, as observed in the experiences of the US economy, came up with newly formulated policies that signaled the eventual end of the business groups that were specifically targeted as one of the main causes of the structural troubles in the economy. Second, some nations preferred to limit the banks' control over industrial enterprises (as evidenced in Sweden and Belgium, for instance), rather than categorically banning those groups altogether. They came up with policies that would eventually transform the structure of business groups from being bank-centered to other forms. Third, in several nations (like in Italy) the government itself directly entered into business domains as the "reorganizer" of failing large enterprises and banks. We discuss each of the three characteristic cases below.

The US economy marks the representative case in our sample that responded to its business groups in the most severe way. While the Great Depression brought the so-called New Deal reforms in general, two specific outcomes were noteworthy in the contextual environment for business groups. First, the Glass-Steagall Act of 1933 separated commercial banking from investment banking, which had a critical impact on bank-centered business groups. Second, the collapse in 1931 of the United Corporation, the apex holding company of the vast Insull group, prompted federal regulators to target inter-corporate dividend tax by enacting the Public Utility Holding Company Act of 1935. Taxing capital transfers between subsidiaries and the holding company at the apex was designed to deter a group structure in which the apex organization often exercised eventual control of hierarchical chains of subsidiaries. President Franklin Roosevelt and his close economic advisors were specifically critical of business groups, suggesting they deterred competition: "Close financial control . . . through the use of financial devices like holding companies and strategic minority interests, creates close control of the business policies of enterprises which masquerade as independent units" (Roosevelt, 1942, in Morck, 2003: 13). Other concerns about business groups included their extensive acquisitions, over-capitalization, and accounting frauds, as well as monopolistic practices and political corruption (Kandel et al., 2013). As a result, regulatory developments in the 1930s in particular led to the demise of the bank-centered as well as industrial business groups in the US.

Sweden also tried to restrain long-term control of banks over large industrial enterprises. The rights of the banks to own and trade shares were curtailed in 1933 and had to be realized over the following five years. However, the Swedish government did not introduce an outright ban on the formation of groups, which led to the opportunistic behavior of bank-centered groups in transforming themselves into other forms. Holding companies that were linked to the banks were established, and those companies were technically owned by the bank-controlled foundations, pension funds, and influential bank shareholders to make sure that the control of the holding companies remained with the banks and their owners. Dual-class shares with differentiated voting rights were used as a critical mechanism to retain control over these companies. In what would become Sweden's largest business group, for instance, the Wallenberg family had significant ownership stakes in both the main Stockholms Enskilda Bank and holding companies, and the family eventually controlled the operating enterprises in diverse industries through its holding companies. Two holding companies, Investor and Providentia, were originally designated to be the center of such a mechanism of control, but the family later placed Investor as the ultimate control apex (Larsson and Petersson, this volume). A similar structural change was seen in some other nations—for instance, in Belgium—in which the government forced the dissolution of bank-centered groups in 1934–5. Those groups, however, transformed themselves into diversified business groups formed around holding companies, rather than dissolving in a straightforward fashion (Daems, 1977; Becht, this volume).

A third variety was the economies in which the government directly intervened in business activities during the Great Depression. In the case of Italy, for example, the government saw a solution in the bailout of the nation's three largest banks, which had been burdened with heavy non-performing credits and depressed stockholdings in industrial firms operating in diverse economic sectors. The state holding company, Istituto per la Ricostruzione Industriale (IRI), was founded in 1933 to rescue the failing banks and protect their industrial interests. When the banks were prohibited from acting as shareholders in industrial companies in 1936, the equity stakes, majority or minority, that the banks had owned in industrial companies became part of IRI's assets. Although IRI was originally set up as a temporary measure, it turned out to be a permanent state-owned business group with equity stakes in large enterprises in diverse industries (Aganin and Volpin, 2005; Colli and Vasta, this volume). Germany also saw the rise of state-owned business groups in the interwar period. In the case of Germany, however, state-owned enterprises that had originally been established along industry lines were grouped together and reorganized under different holding companies. Groups such as Preussag, Veba, and Viag were established in the 1920s and became active in diverse business activities (Schröter, this volume).

2.5 The Rise, Fall, and Resurgence of Diversified Business Groups, from the 1950s to the Present

2.5.1 The Rise of Diversified Business Groups, from the 1950s to 1970s

A new tidal wave in the formation of diversified business groups in Western economies had its beginnings primarily in the conglomeration drive that started in the United States in the early 1950s and accelerated in the 1960s and 1970s (Didrichsen, 1972).[7] This was in particular due to the economic and institutional conditions at the time (including the antitrust legislation against horizontal expansion), as well as the inadequate external sources of growth capital for small firms, low interest rates for corporate loans, and abundant free cash flows of established firms (Anand and Jayanti, 2005; Collis et al., this volume). As a result US firms, particularly those that faced declining markets in their original businesses, began moving into unrelated businesses in a massive manner (Didrichsen, 1972). Many acquisitive conglomerates like Charles Bluhdorn's Gulf & Western and Harold Geneen's ITT developed in the US economy. The British economy also saw a rise in conglomerate firms from the 1960s. Conglomerates that were established specifically for acquisitions and sell-offs, such as Hanson Trust, appeared in that decade. Capital and financial markets were more than supportive of such unrelated diversified growth. In fact, the liberalization of capital and financial markets was a critical turning point that enabled the new and larger sources of capital increase and corporate borrowing for acquisitions and thus the more robust activities of corporate takeovers, ultimately establishing the "market for corporate control" (Jensen and Ruback, 1983; Ville, this volume).

With strong regulations to deter the formation of pyramidal groups (i.e., the multilayered hierarchy of publicly listed firms controlled through partial equity stakes) in place in the United States and later in Britain, investment or operating holding companies at the apex of the conglomerate organizations in those two nations typically held a 100-percent ownership stake in their operating companies. In other Western countries, however, such regulations were usually not the case, and the conventional type of business group structure, especially with pyramidal ownership of their operating subsidiaries that were publicly listed, began to emerge from the 1970s. Italy and Australia are two appropriate examples to illustrate this case.

Italy, after having experienced with state-owned business groups from the 1930s, witnessed another major undertaking of diversified business groups in the 1970s. This time it was family-owned companies that enlarged their industry boundaries

---

[7] Didrichsen (1972) argues that the conglomerate diversification began in about 1953 in the US.

with active acquisitions and via pyramidal ownership structures. Agnellis (through the financial holding companies of IFI and IFIL), for instance, started aggressively shifting their product domain out of their core business of automobiles (Fiat) and into such unrelated fields as insurance, synthetic fibers, and food in that decade. Colli and Vasta (this volume) call this process of diversification the "Italian" version of the conglomeration wave occurring at the international level. In the Italian case, the abolishment of double-taxation laws—a critical obstacle for the formation of pyramidal groups—from the late 1970s and a rapid vibrancy in the stock market, easing access to financial resources through listing subsidiaries, assisted unrelated growth into diversified business groups with pyramidal ownership arrangements (Colli and Vasta, this volume).

The development path of large enterprises in Australia was also disturbed by the discontinuity of the 1970s and 1980s, when the nation saw the initial building of diversified business groups on a large scale (Ville, this volume). The major groups representing this new development included Adelaide Steamship Company (Adsteam), Elders IXL, and Bond Corporation. American thinking on business strategies and structures that was infused into the country through US multinationals was one reason why Australia experienced such a wave of unrelated diversification, mostly through acquisitions, in this period. Other reasons for the rapid formation of diversified business groups were the competition policy in the 1960s that was designed to counter collusive arrangements within an industry, the deregulation of Australian capital and financial markets, and a more active corporate takeover market from the early 1980s (Ville, this volume). Interestingly, the unrelated diversification took the form of partially owned enterprises through pyramidal arrangements, as was the case in Italy and other nations, rather than wholly owned subsidiaries, as in the United States and Great Britain. According to Ville (this volume), this feature of the partial ownership of operating companies in Australia was because acquiring controlling positions through partially owned stakes (tied together via pyramidal and cross-shareholding structures) brought rapid growth and were preferable to slower growth resulting from financing full ownership.

2.5.2 The Fall of Diversified Business Groups, the 1980s and Afterwards

The struggle of diversified business groups, including conglomerate firms, occurred in two waves from the 1980s. Initially, weaknesses in competitive capabilities became the primary cause for the overall decline of business groups. Then, pressures from capital markets under the so-called "conglomerate discount" drive began to further break down several of the diversified groups. The narrative across the nations shows many similar patterns along these lines.

In the case of the United States, many of the original conglomerates first came under pressure due to their financial underperformance from the early 1980s (Collis et al., this volume). One critical factor for their poor performance was the lack of necessary competitive capabilities possessed by the corporate headquarters to manage the many diverse operations that were carried out by subsidiaries in unrelated product markets. Small numbers of executives at head office became overloaded in decision-making related to a huge number of acquisitions and subsequent sell-offs. The role of the headquarters unit was typically to allocate capital at market interest rates to subsidiaries asking for investments and in that sense acting as a "poorly functioning bank lending capital without adequate due diligence or adequate oversight" and also cross-subsidizing those subsidiaries suffering from declining profitability with cash flows of the well-performing ones (Anand and Jayanti, 2005: 6). Tax hikes and interest rates in the economy also overburdened the enterprises that had originally grown by borrowing massive debts at low interest rates (Sobel, 1984).

Business groups in other nations that have grown suddenly and aggressively through acquisitions tell a similar story. In Australia, for instance, groups that developed in the 1970s shared a similar destiny to that of US groups. In diversifying into many varied businesses within a decade, several Australian groups underestimated the administrative tasks and overrated their own capabilities to effectively manage a large number of unrelated businesses organized in intricate pyramidal structures. Increasing indebtedness to fund their rapid growth added up to insoluble problems for these groups (Ville, this volume). Ville also argues that the entrepreneurs at the helm of the groups "proved to be impatient and extreme risk takers, whose moral compasses were misdirected and whose business judgments were often far from sound . . . and [they] destroyed more wealth than they created." As a result, many of the groups were dissolved or simply collapsed altogether within a short period of two decades.

In the case of other nations, even where groups grew in less rushed ways the competitive capabilities of many of the diversified groups became challenged. In Spain, for instance, increased product market competition resulting from pro-market reforms from the 1980s (and the establishment of the European single market in the early 1990s) exposed the groups that had been operating in a relatively protected market setting to a further challenging environment. Faced with foreign competitors that were larger in size and more sophisticated in technology, many Spanish family-owned groups reacted by selling off their operating companies to foreign multinationals that offered attractive prices. Even the groups organized around banks began unloading their industrial holdings in the 1980s to concentrate on achieving global size in their banking operations (Cuervo-Cazurra, this volume). State-owned groups took their own turn to decline as they began to be privatized due to their unpopularity in the global fever of pro-market reforms that preached liberalization, deregulation, and privatization as the three major pillars (see, for instance, Schröter, this volume, and Cuervo-Cazurra, this volume). It is somewhat ironic that some of the operating firms within these state-owned groups were purchased by established private enterprises to form new diversified groups.[8]

---

[8] See, for instance, the case of Benetton/Edizione group, which expanded from textiles into retail distribution and expressways through the acquisition of former state-owned enterprises (Colli and Vasta, this volume).

Once the fate of many earlier diversified business groups was set, capital markets took their turn to unravel the business groups. The capital market liberalization that took place globally from the 1980s ensured that not only domestic but also international, especially institutional, shareholders pressured diversified business groups to narrow their product categories where each group enjoyed the highest competitive position in the product market. In this environment, "conglomerate discount" became a buzzword for the undoing of many diversified business enterprises.

Faced with increased pressure, even established business groups like the Swedish Wallenberg group had to scale down their operations or even exit from some of their investments. Purchasing large blocks of shares in the publicly listed, group-affiliated companies, institutional investors put pressure on the Wallenberg group for higher yields to challenge the group's long-term investment and development strategies. In some cases, hostile takeover bids in operating companies controlled by minority holdings by the Wallenbergs resulted in the sell-off of such companies. The Wallenberg group ultimately strengthened their ownership stakes in their listed companies, exited those companies in which they were not the largest shareholders, and built up a new portfolio of wholly owned subsidiaries (Investor, Annual Report, 2014; Larsson and Petersson, this volume).

In other cases, such hostile takeover bids brought the total demise of business groups. A striking case is that of Société Générale de Belgique (Belgium's largest business group, and one of the largest enterprises in that country, since its establishment in 1822), which became the target of the Italian de Benedetti group in 1988. Société Générale, whose stocks were publicly traded and widely held (having only about 10 percent of its shares in the hands of stable owners by the 1980s), and which directly or indirectly controlled about 1,300 companies around the world at the time, was caught unprepared by the Italian bid. The case ended as the French Suez Lyonnaise des Eaux group was brought in as a white knight to counter the bid. The French firm however later sold off Société Générale's all diverse businesses to focus on its own energy-related business (Lambrecht, 2002; Becht, this volume;). Other Belgian groups (with the sole major exception of Groupe Frère-Bourgeois) followed the destiny of Société Générale and ended in dissolution, with operating subsidiaries and affiliates sold to overseas enterprises.

In some of these cases business groups were inefficient, ineffective, and thus seriously underperforming, while in others such an argument is not entirely justified. Jones (this volume), for instance, argues that several British conglomerates, such as Hanson Trust, BTR, and Grand Metropolitan, actually had respectable performances, and their demise owed more to the unfashionableness of unrelated diversified enterprises and management fads regarding that particular strategy. Unrelated diversified product portfolio came to be loathed, particularly by institutional investors, which caused those enterprises' share prices to decline and the cost of capital to increase. All of these shifts challenged the diversified groups that had particularly relied on the growth strategy of acquisitions based on loans with low interest rates.

2.5.3 The Resurgence of Diversified Business Groups, the 1980s and Thereafter

Section 2.5.2 suggested that several diversified business groups have ended in failure or outright restructuring (for instance, by focusing on a smaller number of competitive business lines) since the 1980s. However, this does not mean that all business groups categorically declined. Indeed, several of the older and more established groups stayed essentially resilient despite all the economic and institutional challenges they faced. We will turn to the key factors behind the robustness and continuity of those groups in Section 2.6. What is more, even when the environment was generally hostile to the model of diversified business groups, we observe the emergence of new varieties of diversified business groups. Below we examine some major cases of these new formations.

First, following the breakdown of many of the diversified business groups, novel forms with critical differences in investment principles and organizational design were born. The leveraged buyout association (LBO, later renamed as private equity), popularized in the United States in the 1980s, was the most important among these new varieties of diversified business groups. Such firms customarily bought a non-core business from diversified enterprises, leveraged it up with debt, and aimed to improve profitability by cost-cutting and other means to ultimately target an IPO or sell-off to strategic or financial buyers. These firms had originally built in their core capabilities in the way they organized financial transactions, but over time they also attempted to build an industry or operational expertise, or specialized in particular forms of investing (Collis et al., this volume). This form became vitalized with the intellectual support of Michael Jensen, who proposed in *The Wall Street Journal* article that "companies should return free cash flow to shareholders rather than retain it inside the firm where it would be dissipated in uneconomic diversification or managerial perks and self-aggrandizement . . . [and] investors themselves rather than corporations should make diversification decisions" (Collis et al., this volume). In 2015 private equity comprised approximately 10 percent of non-financial corporate assets in the US economy (Collis et al., this volume). Other economies have broadly followed this trend initiated by the US, but the US market remained the dominating center and its firms by far the largest in terms of total deal volume and fundraising (Bernstein et al., 2015; Private Equity International; 2016).

Second, taking the opportunities in newly emerging business segments especially related to information technology, in which older business groups, or established enterprises in general, possessed no capabilities or little interest for entry, new business groups still developed from the 1980s onwards. Sweden's Stenbeck (Kinnevik) group is a case in point. Founded in 1936 by the Stenbeck, Klingspor, and von Horn families as an investment company with its industrial base in forestry, pulp, and paper, the enterprise entered into diverse businesses including telecommunications, media, e-commerce, and microfinance from the 1980s. Although much smaller in size than the two largest groups—Wallenberg and Handelsbanken—in Sweden, the group expanded into diverse businesses (Larsson and Petersson, this volume). In a similar context, the new group of companies—for instance those around Google/Alphabet, Facebook, and Amazon in the United States—can also be regarded as a new variety of diversified business groups that have been rapidly extending their product reach in various newly emerging industries (Schneider et al., this volume).

Third, the change of investment ideology, particularly following the relative decline in the influence of the US model, encouraged the formation of diversified business groups in some nations. For instance, Schröter (this volume) argues that in Germany a new trend to diversify into unrelated businesses and to create diversified business groups emerged following the "collapse of [the US] model's influence after the 2008 [financial crisis]." This renewed expansion path has been taken especially by family firms, mostly privately held, although some public as well. Overall, however, those newly established diversified groups stayed small in size compared with the largest German enterprises.

2.6 What Explains the Varied Evolutionary Dynamics of Diversified Business Groups over Time?

We have explored the dynamics of diversified business groups in a longitudinal and comparative context to comprehend the differences as well as similarities of business groups in distinct phases of modern economic growth. Figure 2.1 gives a concise presentation of the changing patterns of the role and significance that the different varieties of diversified business groups exhibited in the various nations examined above. Overall, it illustrates the prominence of bank-centered business groups from the late nineteenth century to the 1930s and state-owned groups from the 1920s to the late 1980s in many nations. Family-owned groups became significant especially from the 1950s, yet we detect significant inter-country variations, especially for this type of business groups. Conglomerate firms remained important from the 1960s to the 1980s in the US and UK economies. Although not illustrated in Figure 2.1, due to their critically distinct characteristics from other types of groups,[9] private equity firms quickly became one of the most active players in the capital markets (especially of the US and the UK) from the 1980s (Bernstein et al., 2015). Diversified business groups as a whole thus occupied significant positions in the economies of the Western nations from the early twentieth century to the 1990s (see the Appendix to this chapter for a detailed summary of the rationales for the rise and fall of diversified business groups in different time periods).

---

[9] See Chapter 1, this volume, and Collis et al., this volume.

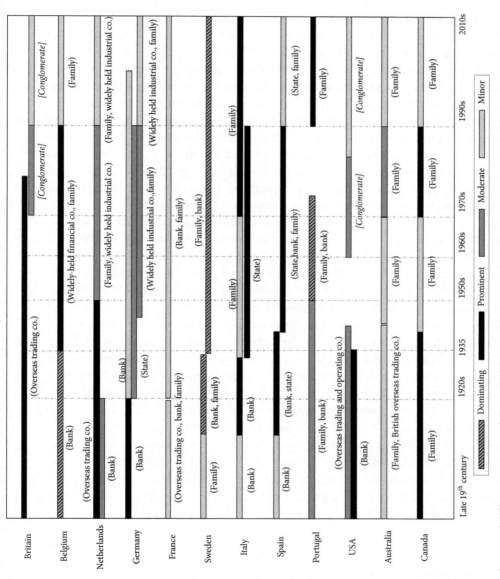

FIGURE 2.1. Significance of different varieties of diversified business groups in the Western economies.

Note: The bars in the above figure illustrate the significance that specific type of business groups played in individual economies over time. The type of the group is shown in parentheses beside the term describing its significance. Diversified business groups have been distinguished according to their distinctive types following the typology of diversified business groups identified in Chapter 1 of this volume. Private equity firms are excluded.

Source: Based predominantly on the national chapters in this volume. For detailed information on the coverage of this figure, see Appendix.

In this section, we attempt to pin down the basic factors that drive the development of different diversified business groups and then explore the reasons why they evolved dissimilarly in varied national economic settings. While the exogenous factors that impact the evolution of corporate models can theoretically be either economic forces or non-economic influences, research on diversified business groups has been strongly influenced by the economics-based perspective adopted by Khanna and colleagues (1997, 2007), who singled out the level of economic development and the maturity of market institutions as the most significant explanatory variable. Especially, they argued, with product markets often working poorly in emerging economies, which potentially provide profit-making opportunities to entrants, established firms take up those opportunities by utilizing internal capital markets to become diversified business groups. As external capital market institutions customarily remain underdeveloped in those economies, the entrepreneurs of start-up firms, by contrast, cannot secure adequate capital to materialize the production and supply of goods and services for those product markets. The "institutional voids," in capital, product, and also labor markets, play a critical role, while exogenous factors beyond immature and imperfect markets and institutions remain marginal in the whole story.

Once the perspective is broadened to comprehend the characteristics of business organizations in general, on the other hand, the current orientation of international scholarship tends to emphasize categorical dissimilarities in broader non-economic as well as economic institutional factors in the different groups of national economies over time. As is typically observed in the "Varieties of Capitalism" literature, institutional approaches focus on the rigidity and continuity of such exogenous forces as legal framework, regulatory orientations, labor organizations, family goals, and societal norms, which ahistorically condition the behavior of business organizations (Hall and Soskice, 2001; Schneider et al., this volume). We argue that, first, those institutional settings are sometimes unstable and actually transform themselves; as such, they do not necessarily function as a binding precondition for the economic behavior of diversified business groups. Second, those business groups have not universally taken those institutions as the controlling might that would force the groups to passively take an adopting response. Rather, business groups have often successfully reacted to the changing institutional settings to survive and grow by flexibly shifting their behavior in ownership arrangements, strategic orientations, and structural accommodations. They have even attempted to change the institutional environment to make it more instrumental and friendly to their business conduct in the marketplace.

2.6.1 Business Groups as a Reorganizing versus Generating Device in Developmental Perspectives

In the above-mentioned process, we observe close interactions between environmental settings in terms of micro- and macro-market forces, economic and non-economic institutions, and the reactive and proactive behavior taken by individual business groups. This relates to *how* different types of business groups have been formed and impacted the national economy in which they were involved. Based on the individual cases compiled in the national chapters in this volume and in our earlier work (see Colpan and Hikino, 2010), we propose that individual diversified business groups have devised distinctive growth models depending on the time-specific historical context of relevant national settings.

Specifically, many of the diversified business groups predominantly rose to serve as a *reorganizing device* of large industrial enterprises in those national economies that experienced their initial industrialization processes before the end of the Second Industrial Revolution by the 1920s. "Reorganizing" in this context means that the prime actor of productive viability remained with already-established independent operating enterprises in respective industries, which would later be *reorganized* and collectively formed into diversified business groups by the reactive involvement of mostly banks, but also the state, and families. The effectiveness of industrial enterprises should be a necessary condition for the economic viability of nations, as Chandler repeatedly claimed. Yet the contributions made by banking and other institutions at the center of group formation as a complementary instrument should be adequately acknowledged in this context. Examples of this type of group formation are typically observed in the cases of Sweden, Germany, Italy, and the United States.

By contrast, in those economies that industrialized relatively late, after the 1920s and especially after World War II—that is, national economies that started their industrialization under the precondition of acute backwardness in the Gerschenkronian sense—diversified business groups became primarily a *generating device* of large enterprises that became the oligopolistic core of respective industries. "Generating" in this context means that it was a central agent, mostly an entrepreneur or a family, which *generated* and developed operating enterprises in many unrelated industries (Colpan and Hikino, 2010). The cases of contemporary emerging market business groups fit in here, as well as the cases of Portugal and Spain that are covered in this volume (see Chapters 12 and 13).[10] The cases of Spain and Portugal are different from other nations discussed in this volume in that they correspond more with the area of acute backwardness, starting their industrial growth after the 1950s. While the state-owned business group INI created (or participated in) industrial enterprises and was the primary actor in facilitating the industrialization process in Spain; the family-controlled groups (some of which were centered around banks) that created industrial companies were the central actors in Portugal.

These historical regularities suggest that the evolutionary experiences of diversified business groups fundamentally differ between those in earlier-industrializing economies and the later-developing economies. This also suggests that the uncritical application of conventional theories of business groups to more advanced economies may cause a misleading assessment of the central role played by business groups in

[10] The case of Japanese pre-war zaibatsu groups also exhibit similar characteristics of serving predominantly as a generating device.

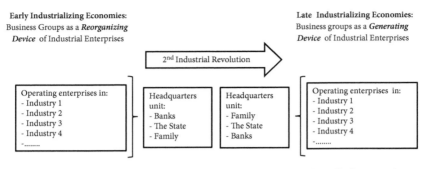

FIGURE 2.2. Two distinctive models of diversified business groups.

Note: By early-industrializing economies, we in this context mean those nations that experienced the initial phase of industrialization drive by the late nineteenth to early twentieth centuries when the economic impact of the Second Industrial Revolution engulfed the whole industrial economy across nations. Late-industrializing economies are those that started their modern economic growth in the mid-twentieth century, especially in the decades since World War II.

different nations with dissimilar levels of economic advance. Figure 2.2 shows these different dynamics in the formation of diversified business groups in early and later industrialization.

2.6.2 Factors that Shape the Evolution of Diversified Business Groups

Below we examine the common threads in understanding the dissimilar evolutionary patterns of diversified business groups in Western economies to understand why different corporate organizations developed in individual nations at a given time. In this sense, our theoretical arguments are based on an inductive approach driving upon the historical analyses in previous sections.

Our following arguments highlight the underlying universal factors that have long shaped the evolution of diversified business groups. They, however, resonate with the primary factors that have tipped to become critical causal inferences that affected the group organization model in each of the historical periods examined above: the early rise of the diversified business group had to do more with relative economic backwardness and the timing of industrialization. Politics, political institutions, and regulatory frameworks, while surely important in different time periods, had their most direct and critical impact on business groups in the interwar period. The rising wave of diversified business groups since the 1960s, in the characteristic form of "conglomeration," first in the United States and then in other nations, and the fall from the 1980s, then, resonates closely with the changing attitudes adopted by the investors, as their characteristic shifts for and then against the strategic conduct of unrelated diversification were elevated to the level of management fads and were transplanted to several nations. The resilience and in part resurgence of various varieties of diversified business groups after the 1980s, on the other hand, had most to do with endogenous factors within the group itself. While these environmental and organizational forces have certainly been constantly interacting with each other, we separate them according to their primarily exogenous or endogenous characters to the firm in general. We then examine them individually to understand their functioning to shape the dissimilar fortunes of business groups in different nations over time.

2.6.2.1 *Exogenous Factors*

The literature on diversified business groups that has extensively been developed based on the experiences of such business organizations in late-industrializing economies predominantly deals with missing markets and economic institutional voids. Those arguments suggest that diversified business groups appear because of a variety of market and institutional immaturities for which those groups can play the role of substitute. This theoretically implies that business groups should disappear as the markets and institutions develop to become more mature and well-functioning in relevant nations. The historical developments of early-industrializing economies, and especially their experiences with business groups (which are summarized above), show that this hypothetical argument is not quite supported in the case of earlier developments of industrialization, which suggests that we need to look beyond the theoretical underpinnings of market immaturity and institutional void-filling. This is not to say that the development of markets and market institutions does not matter. Naturally their developments remain critically important. In reality, however, the process of national markets to mature and their institutions to progress is not a simple and straightforward shift but a complicated and dynamic process. What we propose here is that we need to incorporate larger forces in terms of the historical context and the functioning of non-economic as well as economic institutions within that context. Those forces, directly or sometimes indirectly through their effects on market efficiency and effectiveness, at times functioned as negative and even destructive forces, while at other times they ironically created a positive and favorable environment in which diversified business groups could further expand or rejuvenate.

2.6.2.1.1 HISTORICAL CONTEXT AS A PRECONDITION

Given the basic shift in production scale and thus capital requirements, international intra-industry competition changed fundamentally after the Second Industrial Revolution. Above all, for individual national economies the initial timing of industrialization drive and the genesis of various institutions that emerged in connection with that economic shift played a crucial role in designating particular assignments for specific agents to fulfill. In the classic Gerschenkron thesis, as the first country to start industrialization Great Britain did not need to develop banks that committed to long-term industrial financing for domestic enterprises, as internal funds (without external financing from banks or other institutions) within industrial firms that were customarily owned and managed by business families were adequate for those enterprises to finance additional investment for growth. After all, the demand for capital infusion from outside investors or lenders remained marginal in the early stages of British industrialization, as the national economy embarked on the original drive toward industrial economy in the historical context of the First Industrial Revolution of the late eighteenth to the early nineteenth centuries. Banks thus did not commit to long-term industrial financing within the domestic economy, which later created an institutional rigidity that would be called the Macmillan gap (Collins, 1991), even as the capital requirements increased to finance the massive fixed investments especially in several industries that experienced the technological and structural changes of the Second Industrial Revolution. Rather, the equity and bond markets were mostly perceived as the source of long-term finance for enterprises that engaged in overseas, especially colonial, ventures (Jones, this volume). For the countries that started industrialization later—at the time of, or even after, the Second Industrial Revolution—since capital requirements substantially increased for the optimal size of production facilities to realize economies of scale, while the internal funds in reserve within industrial firms remained insufficient, banks had to fulfill the capital demand on the part of industrial firms. This is the mechanism of capital provision by banks that Gerschenkron identified as the consequence of the "relative backwardness" of relevant national economies (especially Germany in his classification), although he did not quite comprehend the critical significance of the universal setting of the Second Industrial Revolution that substantially raised the minimum optimal size of production facilities and thus, regardless of their level of economic development, increased the capital requirements to achieve that size across the national economies.

The historical context of the Second Industrial Revolution in the late nineteenth to the early twentieth centuries, whose influence changed the basic nature of industrial competition on a global scale, and the progress (or struggle) of industrialization drive at the different historical timing and pace for individual national economies, made a critical difference in terms of the relationship between industrial enterprises and banking and financial institutions. It is precisely at this conjuncture that the structural legacy of industrial financing mattered most for the different evolutionary paths of diversified business groups. Strong and developed capital providers (such as large universal banks)—in the absence of government regulations to prohibit them from committing to long-term industrial investments—took over weak and distressed industrial firms to reorganize them into oligopolistic players, and to eventually form bank-centered business groups. The upshot was that the dominant variety of diversified business groups with adequate size that was observed in several of the early industrializing economies after the Second Industrial Revolution was the bank-centered groups. Banks could be seen here as functioning akin to venture capitalists fulfilling the institutional voids in industrial financing and then, whenever necessary, playing the role of investors in distressed debt for those companies.

Nonetheless, the formation of such groups was not automatic or straightforward in most cases, whereas banks in a few countries like Germany and the United States formed their groups more actively and willingly. Indeed, the emergence of business groups often came reluctantly because of exogenous economic shocks and the resulting financial troubles on the part of industrial enterprises when banks were obliged to take over those distressed firms, as in Sweden, Belgium, and Italy, that would eventually end up in the formation of bank-centered groups.

What is more, the timing of industrialization possibly also mattered for the initial obscurity of diversified business groups formed around industrial companies operating in unrelated businesses. Since those industrial enterprises in the late nineteenth to early twentieth centuries typically embodied proprietary know-how, they focused for competitive reasons on nurturing the know-how and product-specific capabilities they possessed, rather than reinvesting the income earned into unrelated product categories. Such product-specific capabilities plausibly functioned to deter them from entering unknown business terrains and thus prevented them to form diversified business groups around themselves. That was because expected marginal return would remain higher with those investments in product and industry domains in which they could utilize proprietary resources and capabilities and thus possess competitive advantages.

2.6.2.1.2 POLITICS, POLITICAL INSTITUTIONS, AND REGULATORY FRAMEWORKS

While economic backwardness is likely not independent of politics and political institutions, different governmental policies and regulatory regimes played further roles to influence, or at times determine, the fate of business groups in different nations. An immense and early impact came in the way in which different governments and their regulators chose dissimilar policies in different countries in the 1930s, to stand face to face with the strong banks with large industrial interests. Some nations, such as the United States, chose eventually to ban the formation of those groups organized around banks. Some others, such as Sweden and Belgium, tended to be less strict by accepting the opportunistic behavior of bank-centered groups in transforming themselves into other forms. A few like Italy, on the other hand, were more intrusive or active in having the government take over distressed industrial firms from the banks and form state-owned business groups.

Beyond those regulations that directly targeted and were in some ways detrimental to the prevailing business-group organization, government policies also often indirectly affected the formation and operation of business groups. One example is the Celler-Kefauver Act of 1950 that led to the development of new types of business groups in the United States. That act, which amended the loophole of the Clayton Act of 1914 by giving legal foundations to the government to intervene in anti-competitive vertical mergers, eventually became instrumental in supporting the "conglomerate" wave of US firms of the 1960s and 1970s (Hitt et al., 2007). Another example is the trade protection that governments provided in early twentieth-century Italy, (followed by state procurement during the interwar period), which was accompanied by lax corporate governance regulations that assisted the growth of business groups in that country (Colli and Vasta, this volume; Schneider et al., this volume).

Government attitudes toward policy intervention into market processes in fact function in dynamic and intricate ways to influence diversified business groups. An important instance is the pro-market reforms initiated by the US government and followed by the UK and other major nations to lift restrictive regulations and privatize many state-owned enterprises after the 1980s. Given the more liberalized market settings that consequentially emerged, diversified business groups had to face two major challenges. First, with regulatory distortion and protective umbrellas lifted, the competitive forces of open markets confronted each one of the product domains in which subsidiaries within diversified business groups operated. Second, as will be discussed in more detail in the following section, they started coming under strong pressure from the active institutional shareholders to readjust their product portfolio to concentrate on the categories where they possessed competitive advantages and enjoyed higher-than-average rates of return. These shifts, and especially the latter one that specifically targeted the business group organization as a whole, had a critical impact on the way in which diversified business groups conducted their businesses.

These broad policy and regulatory involvements, however, were not unilateral, and these government interventions have not necessarily been abolished altogether in practice despite pro-market reforms since the 1980s (Vietor, 1994). In many ways the government policies and regulations were actually shaped by the political advantages of influential business groups in reinforcing those institutions that favor the groups. Such political advantages, on the other hand, likely depended on the relative power of governments and their dependence on business groups. Government power has been relatively high and dependence on business groups low in the United States, for instance, as opposed to Sweden where cooperation between business groups and the government has long been frequent and dense (Schneider et al., this volume). Evident most from the case of Sweden, the major business groups have long interacted with the political sphere in protecting their own interests. For instance, they worked closely with the political organs to affect the institutional setup including tax regulations and the system of differentiated voting rights of shareholders in facing the challenges stemming from the European Union. Having been considered as long-term, trustable, and responsible owners within Swedish society, large business groups utilized the resources of their social acceptance that contributed to their long-term prevalence in that economy (Larsson and Petersson, this volume).

2.6.2.1.3 THE IDIOSYNCRASY OF CAPITAL MARKETS AND MANAGEMENT FADS

We observe changing investor attitudes and management fads and fever playing decisive roles in shaping business-group behavior, particularly after the 1950s. In this regard a common thread across several nations examined in this volume is the rise of diversified business groups following the conglomeration fever in the United States starting in the early 1950s and accelerating in the 1960s and 1970s. The following conglomerate drive on the international scale in the 1970s and 1980s seems to owe as much to temporal management fads and their transplantation across nations as it does to the liberalized capital and financial markets (and at the same time the lack of venture-capital providers to finance start-ups in product markets with profit-making opportunities, and the abundance of established large firms with access to those resources within their own companies or in capital and financial markets outside). Those fads that appeared and new ideas that developed in a national economy, and the transplantation of such fads and ideas across nations, functioned as crucial factors in shaping group structure.[11] The formation of diversified business groups, both widely held and family-owned, seems to have occurred simultaneously in several countries following a swift change in support of diversification drive in this period. In the case of Italy and Australia in particular, we see many large diversified business groups abruptly coming out from earlier specialized enterprises. Given the eventual absence of active institutional investors (and especially activist ones) at the time, firms were relatively insulated from strong investor preferences and thus jumped on the bandwagon of conglomeration in forming diversified business group structures, often in pyramidal arrangements, from the 1960s to the 1980s (Zorn et al., 2004).

Likewise, once the fate of many original conglomerates ended in financial misery due to their lack of competitive capabilities, capital market players, especially institutional investors that had risen by that time, started to be preoccupied with the idea of "conglomerate discount" from the 1980s. Those institutional investors that had begun investing not only domestically but internationally as well came to frame a new investor-oriented understanding of the firm that should focus on lines of business where individual firms held core competence and thus enjoyed competitive advantages that yielded high profitability. They have thus forced many diversified business groups to disband and concentrate by shunning investment in diversified business groups and thus lowering firm value, and eventually forcing those groups to change their portfolios (Zorn et al., 2004). The more "impatient" and especially "activist" investors and takeover firms in the competitive capital markets of Anglo-Saxon economies have been directly hostile to the diversified business groups and have pushed for the eventual dissolution of many of the diversified groups in those nations.

2.6.2.2 *Endogenous Factors*

What we have argued above should not be taken as implying that environmental differences automatically determine a "one-fits-all" corporate model to be effective in one particular economy at a specific time. We suggest that one also needs to look systematically at the endogenous factors inside the group organization, from its ownership structure and owner ideology to underpinnings in resources, capabilities, and administrative mechanisms, to understand the prevalence and effectiveness of the group organization within individual nations. As discussed above, outside investors in this context can also have an endogenous aspect once the potential investors actually become the shareholders of a firm and affect its behavior and structure, for instance by demanding that management in diversified business groups focus their product portfolio, and thus force those groups to change their strategic nature. In sum we argue

---

[11] See for instance, Zorn et al. (2004) for the impact of management fads on the US firm. Several chapters in this volume, in particular those by Jones and Cuervo-Cazurra, refer to the impact of such fads in owner ideology.

below that those factors that are beyond purely exogenous in character have over time come to play relatively more significant roles in the long-term resilience of various business-group organizations.

2.6.2.2.1 OWNERSHIP STRUCTURE AND SHAREHOLDER IDEOLOGY

Setting aside the political economy arguments on the existence of concentrated ownership in some nations but not in others (see Schneider et al., this volume), ownership structure and the investment ideology of those owners have played critical roles in the diverse evolution of business groups. Foremost, the concentrated owners, often in the form of families or the state, are generally argued to have a long-term horizon as their strategic decisions and investment principle. This difference in time horizon results from the inclination that such owners are willing to forego short-term profits in order to obtain larger financial gains in the long term (Schneider et al., this volume). It can however also be because those owners prefer to pursue other goals such as firm stability, political power, and social prestige, which usually come with large corporate size, rather than immediate profits that often fluctuate for exogenous macroeconomic reasons. For those concentrated owners, in particular, product and industry diversification can function as an effective means to achieve their preferred goals. For instance, in the case of Spain state-owned business groups including SEPI (State Society of Industrial Participations), which was founded in 1995 after its predecessors INI and INH were abolished, long kept its highly diversified business portfolio with the goal of securing employment and providing public services besides maximizing profitability (Cuervo-Cazurra, this volume).

Having concentrated ownership in families or the state, particularly in continental European countries, has therefore possibly been an important factor in keeping several business groups in place for extended periods. Supporting this argument, Table 2.1 shows that many diversified business groups in Western economies have in fact concentrated ownership especially in families. The table shows that dominance of family ownership among the largest diversified business groups is observed even in mature economies, while family ownership of diversified business groups has long been a norm in emerging markets (Colpan and Hikino, 2010). As has been argued earlier, some groups (e.g. the Wallenberg group) have even increased their ownership stakes in their operating companies and also established fully owned subsidiaries to shield them from institutional investor pressures or hostile takeover bids (see Section 2.5.2).

Despite the fact that concentrated ownership has mostly become a necessary condition, it is, however, unlikely that it is a sufficient condition for the resilience of business groups in competitive market settings. As has been argued above, with escalated competitive pressure from increasingly globalized product and capital markets particularly since the 1980s, many groups regardless of their concentrated ownership structure, have begun to be challenged for their viability. Several such instances are examined in this volume, such as family-owned groups being forced to narrow down their product portfolios or even being sold to foreign enterprises (see, for instance, Cuervo-Cazurra, this volume, and Larsson Petersson, this volume). At this juncture, we argue in the following section that intra-group resources, capabilities, and administrative processes inside a business organization become a vital factor.

2.6.2.2.2 RESOURCES, CAPABILITIES, AND ADMINISTRATIVE MECHANISMS

The dynamic resources, capabilities, and administrative mechanisms that groups developed to act and react to the market and institutional developments became decisive factors in shaping the diverse fortunes of business groups in the context of maturing and competitive market environments. In such settings, it is fair to suggest that the conventional characteristics of generic capabilities, and loose, limited, and unsystematic administrative control mechanisms that have usually been associated with business groups would be seriously challenged (Hikino and Amsden, 1994; Kock and Guillén, 2001). In this environment, the systematic integration of industry-transcending resources and capabilities at headquarters level and product-related know-how at the operating company level became a necessary and sufficient condition for the survival and growth of diversified business groups.

At the level of operating companies, needless to say, the affiliated firms had to establish the product-related capability to survive and grow in their own product and industry domain in an increasingly competitive market environment. The corporate office of these affiliated firms controlled the functional operation through the administrative means of strategic planning or strategic control. In this context, the operating companies often came close to a small Chandlerian multidivisional enterprise with related product portfolio. At the level of headquarters unit (often organized as a holding company), however, the business group enterprise showed more characteristic differences that separated it from the traditional Chandlerian multidivisional firm.

The group headquarters usually needed to establish "trans-product" or industry-transcending capabilities to nurture and exploit in a variety of businesses it controlled. These resources and capabilities were often made up of financial instruments (such as budgeting processes as well as financial management systems) but also could be functional ones such as human resources (including incentive mechanisms and per-formance control at the group level) and organizational systems (to enforce mechan-isms for coordination and integration across constituent firms). At the same time, as the headquarters established its distinctive capabilities, it also turned to achieving more administrative efficiency by enforcing systematized control mechanisms. Further, the headquarters' long-term investment horizons also often added value to affiliated companies to commit themselves into nurturing knowledge resources and thus strengthening their competitive positions in the long-run.

A noteworthy example for the changing roles and flexible adaptation of the head-quarters to evolving environments is the case of the Agnelli group (organized under the holding company IFI in 1927, and Exor from 2009) in Italy. Originally the group headquarters—organized under IFI—exerted tight, strategic control over its affiliated companies, which until the mid 1960s were mostly concentrated in automotive manu-facturing. With the core capabilities of the headquarters unit concentrated on know-how in automotive production, the other group companies outside this core business line (where the holding company at the helm usually held fewer equity stakes) were not systematically integrated into the group administrative mechanism and hence remained loosely controlled. The group started to diversify aggressively outside auto-mobile businesses after the 1970s to grasp new opportunities in growing and profitable industries and jumped on the conglomeration bandwagon occurring in Italy in that decade. This was facilitated especially with the establishment of another holding company, IFIL (whose controlling shares remained with IFI), in 1963 to manage the group's non-auto businesses. IFI, which remained as the central headquarters of the group, continued to strategically control its core business of automobile manufacturing, while the non-core businesses in unrelated industries received unequal attention. At this stage the group attempted to systematically combine strategic control of its main business with financial control of its non-core businesses. The whole mechanism of group control, however, was not well designed in that the rules and responsibilities between the two holding companies (IFI and IFIL) and individual operating units remained unclear and unorganized. With the escalated competition in globalized product market (especially in their auto business) and capital market pressures from institutional shareholders after the 2000s, then, the group headquarters became organized under the holding company Exor after IFIL was merged into IFI, which changed its name to Exor S.p.A. in 2009. The newly established headquarters changed its role over time in two dimensions. First, the involvement of the newly formed main holding company, Exor, shifted towards more financial, rather than strategic, control of all the group companies, including the automotive company organized under its subsidiary Fiat (this was partially because Fiat's weight in the group decreased with diversification into selected new industries, particularly insurance). Second, the group headquarters established a much more well-defined control of its several operating companies. As such, the administrative mechanism for the entire group organization became more structured and systematic, and consequently less confused. At this juncture, the core resources and capabilities of the headquarters

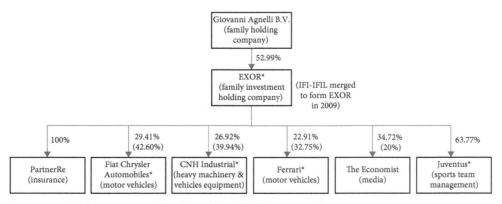

FIGURE 2.3. Basic structure of the Exor (Agnelli) Group, 2016.

Note: * denotes publicly-listed companies. The numbers are the equity stakes held in each company, while voting rights are shown in parentheses. Group companies are indicated in the order of the gross asset value of investments.

Source: Drawn based on Exor, Annual Report (2016); Orbis/Osiris Database, Bureau van Dijk Publishing K.K.

became the disciplined financial and organizational management of constituent group companies (Bianchi, Bianco, and Enriques, 2001; Clark, 2012; Davis, Bertoldi, and Quaglia, 2012; Colli, 2016; Gordon and Sanderson, 2017).[12] Figure 2.3 shows the structure of the Exor group in 2016.

Supporting these arguments on the changing resources, capabilities, and administrative mechanisms of diversified business groups to fit into maturing environments, Collis et al. (this volume) have maintained that those unrelated diversified firms in the United States that crafted their own set of resources and capabilities and built administrative mechanisms continued to add value to their businesses after the 2000s. Anand and Jayanti (2005) further argued that "the use of authority, superior information on the individual businesses, the ability to create a common culture and informational norms, repeated exchange and trust" may imply that such diversified entities could have advantages over market forces, even in developed economy settings. Recent work supporting these claims has shown that several diversified groups have outperformed their rival firms even in well-functioning markets, and the oft-cited "diversification discount" contains measurement problems so that such "discount" cannot be generalizable to all unrelated-diversified enterprises (Anand and Jayanti, 2005; Maksimovic and Philips, 2013). These findings strongly suggest that the effectiveness of the diversified business model is not emphatically predetermined. Rather, depending on the specific arrangements to manage widely diversified product and industry portfolio, strategic implementation and operational execution of such business models should be the ultimate components for the success and failure of those business groups.

2.7 CONCLUSION

This chapter has aimed to explore the evolutionary dynamics of diversified business groups across contemporary developed economies over time and to identify common threads to understand why diversified business groups have evolved dissimilarly in different nations. The empirical examination provided in this chapter questions the theoretical and empirical validity of the progressive interpretation of the development of large-scale modern enterprises that Chandler proposed. Diversified business groups that have been dismissed in the Chandlerian framework have long lived and are still active as an effective form of large business organization in several mature developed economies. Chandler was possibly right in emphasizing the historical significance of the emergence and effectiveness of multidivisional enterprises that eventually dominated the US economy. However, he oversimplified the whole story by eventually demoting historical context and institutional forces outside the internal managerial dynamics of *industrial* enterprises and thus marginalizing the contributions made by

---

[12] We thank Andrea Colli for his input on the Exor group.

such economic players as banking institutions that had functioned as the core of diversified business groups.

Our analysis also suggests the necessity of reconsidering and reformulating the conventional theoretical arguments on diversified business groups that were mostly based on the experiences of contemporary developing economies. The historical experiences of modern developed economies imply that the straightforward association of the general environmental settings of market immaturities and institutional voids with the rise and burgeoning of diversified business groups, which research derived from the basic theoretical assumption in development economics has been preaching to date, is rather incomplete in reality. That understanding may be applied to the experiences of economies that started their industrialization processes at the stage of acute backwardness in the Gershenkronian sense, but it is not universally generalizable to other economies where industrialization was initiated at relatively advanced stages. This contingency suggests that the external environment of immature markets in capital, labor, and product alone does not necessarily function as the sole determining factor in the formation of diversified business groups as an effective model of business organization.

Our findings draw attention to the importance of examining national *differences* and historical *shifts* in larger contexts in understanding the evolution of different varieties of diversified business groups, or comparable models of business organizations as a whole for that matter. Historical context had immense effects in the early emergence of bank-centered business groups, when banks, willingly or reluctantly, formed their own groups in several economies. Those bank-centered groups served as "reorganizing devices" of large industrial enterprises and functioned as critical complements to those enterprises. This critically differentiates their roles from their counterparts in today's developing economies, in which business groups mainly serve as the "generating devices" of industrial enterprises.

This historical beginning did not, however, imprint the evolvement of the business group organization in the long run. Politics and political institutions distorted the development paths, often destroying those business groups altogether, transforming them into other varieties of corporate models, or sometimes even nationalizing them into state-owned groups. The idiosyncrasy of capital markets, changing investor attitudes, and management fads functioned in an interconnected fashion to become decisive as those factors first created and later destroyed business groups. The conglomeration drive that started in the United States in the early 1950s and was supported by waves of liberalization in financial and capital markets was taken up by entrepreneurs in other Western nations to end up in diversified business groups that were often organized in pyramidal structures. The changing investor ideology from the 1980s, especially that of institutional investors following the earlier collapse of many of the groups, worked in the opposite direction to break up the very groups that they pressed for. Those groups that had concentrated ownership were in a favorable position to resist or even reject outright the pressure for deconglomeration.

These dynamics suggest that such broad and diverse exogenous factors beyond the environmental settings of immature and imperfect markets and institutions play critical roles in shaping the basic course of the long-term development of business groups. Those exogenous endowments have at times positively functioned to keep business groups intact. Yet the same environmental factors—and especially political institutions and capital markets—have ultimately turned into powerful agents to dismantle those diversified business groups.

In order to understand the resilience, as well as the effectiveness, of the corporate model of diversified business groups, then, a decisive factor to examine remains inside the group itself: especially the competitive resources, capabilities, and administrative mechanisms within the group and their alignment with ownership structures. What is most important is to acknowledge the fact that groups are not static enterprises with fixed resources, capabilities, and administrative arrangements that suit one market and institutional environment but expire when that environment shifts. Business groups are, in fact, living entities that can co-evolve with the market and institutional settings to ensure they persist. A common thread through the national chapters in this volume is the evolution from unsystematic and looser arrangements of intra-group administration that defied any competitive assets to more systematic and often financial control mechanisms that valued and utilized proprietary resources at both operating and group levels, which have often been organized under concentrated ownership. This is not necessarily to imply that some business groups cannot attempt to sustain themselves via inefficient means, while relying for instance on their closed ownership and cross-subsidization across business units to ensure their longevity. But surely with globalizing capital as well as competitive product markets such behavior alone is unlikely to warrant long-term viability for business groups with broad and unrelated product portfolio.

In sum, we argue that diversified business groups are not simply transitionary organizations that worked well only at the early phase of modern economic growth and will not necessarily become an obstacle for dynamic development as the economies mature. Instead, as the business groups flexibly evolve with changing market and institutional environments, they can stay on as a viable organization model even in mature markets. To understand such flexibility in terms of the internal configurations of diversified business groups, more research inside the black box of the intra-organizational dynamics of business groups is indispensable.

ACKNOWLEDGMENTS

We are grateful for their valuable and helpful comments on earlier versions of this chapter to David Collis, Alvaro Cuervo-Cazurra, Lou Galambos, Geoffrey Jones, Tarun Khanna, Paul Miranti, David Mitch, Randall Morck, Ben Ross Schneider, Harm Schröter, David Sicilia, Álvaro Ferreira da Silva, Simon Ville, participants at the seminar at the Institute for Applied Economics, Global Health and the Study of Business Enterprise, Johns Hopkins University, and participants at the Varieties of Big Business: Business Groups in the West conference at Harvard Business School.

THE ROLE AND SIGNIFICANCE OF DIVERSIFIED BUSINESS GROUPS IN THE WESTERN ECONOMIES

		Britain	Belgium	The Netherlands
1st wave	Time period	From 1870s to 1980s	From 1880s to 1935	From 1870s to 1950s
	Significance in the economy	Prominent in overseas developing economies	Dominating	Prominent in overseas developing economies
	Core actor	Overseas trading company-centered groups	Bank-centered groups	Overseas trading company-centered groups
	Reasons for emergence	Functioning capital markets in the UK to substitute for dysfunctional markets and institutions in developing economies	Industrial revolution funded by universal banks that held a portfolio of industrial stakes and close relationships with management; some independent family groups that created their own banks	Opening of colonies for private investments (after 1860s); development of modern banks
	Reasons for decline (if any)	Changes in political environment in host countries; changes in perception of British capital markets that got hostile to diversified groups	Structural change forced separation of banks and industrial holdings in 1934/35; financial holding companies remained important	Economic crisis of the 1930s; mergers; decolonization after WWII brought an end to many groups
2nd wave	Significance in the economy	Moderate	Prominent	From the late 19th century to 1920s Moderate
	Core actor	Conglomerates	Widely-held financial holding company-centered and family-owned business groups	Bank-centered business groups
	Reasons for emergence	Fluid market for corporate control that functioned instrumentally for acquisitions and sell-offs of enterprises	Earlier groups transformed through the establishment of financial holding companies. Business opportunities after WWII assisted expansion into new business areas	Long-term investment by banks in industrial enterprises

Reasons for decline (if any)	Unfashionability of diversified product portfolio; capital market pressures to refocus on a narrow range of products (a few survived as diversified business groups)	Management mistakes at financial holdings; contestable control structure; opening of Belgian market as part of the European Single Market programme	Dutch financial crisis of the 1920s brought an end to equity investments in industrial firms and led to more conservative attitude towards financing enterprises
3rd wave			
Significance in the economy		From the 1990s to present Minor**	From 1950s to 1990s Moderate
Core actor		Family-owned groups (Groupe Frère-Bourgeois remained as the "surviving" Belgian diversified group)	Family-owned and widely-held industrial company centered business groups (including some earlier trading company centered groups)
Reasons for emergence		Decline of the Belgian groups and the eventual sale of group companies to overseas enterprises (in particular from France but also from the Netherlands)	Diversification for growth in the post-colonial market setting since the 1950s; response to decline in original industry; management of risk through diversification
Reasons for decline (if any)		n.a.	Growing international competition and economic crisis of the 1970s; development of competitive European market; management troubles. Some stay resilient

(continued)

		Germany	France	Sweden*
1st wave	Time period	From 1880s to 1920s	From 1870s to 1920s	From 1910s to 1930s
	Significance in the economy	Prominent	Minor	Dominating
	Core actor	Bank-centered business groups	Overseas trading company centered groups, bank-centered business groups, few family owned groups	Bank-centered groups and few family-owned groups
	Reasons for emergence	Long-term investment by banks in industrial enterprises	Market opportunities in overseas markets; long-term investment by banks in industrial enterprises	For the finance of industrial companies by commercial banks that extended their ownership of industrial enterprises after the financial crises of the 1920s and 1930s
	Reasons for decline (if any)	World War I and hyperinflation (Deutsche Bank group and few others remained resilient as an exception. After 2000s, however, they divested their industrial activities)	Changes in political and economic environment in host countries brought an end to trading groups. Some bank and family groups stayed resilient	Regulations of 1933/34 prohibited banks from directly holding equity; but the groups stayed resilient by transforming their structures
2nd wave	Time period	From 1920s to 1990s	From the 1920s	From 1930s to present
	Significance in the economy	Moderate	Minor	Dominating
	Core actor	State-owned business groups	Family-owned business groups	Family-owned and bank-centered groups

Reasons for emergence	Reorganization of state owned enterprises into holding companies in the interwar period	Business groups formed to seize opportunities in new markets and privatizations, as well as to escape from declines in original industries	Earlier groups transformed through the establishment of holding companies and special investment funds. Business opportunities after WWII assisted expansion into new business areas
Reasons for decline (if any)	Privatization process and focusing on core businesses that ended these groups	not applicable	Not applicable (Groups however face challenges due to deregulation of financial markets and capital market pressures since the 1980s)
3rd wave Time period	From 1945 to 1990s		From the 1980s to present
Significance in the economy	Moderate		Moderate
Core actor	Widely-held industrial company centered and family-owned business groups		Family-owned business groups
Reasons for emergence	Management of risk through diversification; ban of cartelization in 1947 that led to diversification activities		Rise of new sectors such as IT and media, which was taken up by the newly formed business groups
Reasons for decline (if any)	Perception of Anglo-Saxon business model that discouraged unrelated diversification and widely-diversified business groups. After the financial crisis in 2008, a renewed trend towards formation of groups started		Not applicable

(continued)

		Italy*	Spain*	Portugal
1st wave	Time period	From 1910s to 1930s	From 1910s to late 1930s	From the late 19th century to 1975
	Significance in the economy	Prominent	Prominent	Moderate before 1950s; dominating afterwards
	Core actor	Bank-centered groups	Bank-centered groups and some state-owned groups	Family-owned business groups, bank-centered business groups
	Reasons for emergence	Long-term investment by banks in industrial enterprises that often became controlling shareholders as they took over distressed companies	Government encouragement of banks to invest in industrial firms to grow and achieve rapid industrialization; government intervention to speed up industrialization	Subsitute for dysfunctional markets and institutions in the domestic economy
	Reasons for decline (if any)	Bail out of banks and their affiliated companies by the State agency following the economic depression of early 1930s	Civil war (1936-1939), economic collapse and autarchic period at beginning of military dictatorship	Nationalization of business groups in 1975 that led to a sudden end to the business groups
2nd wave	Time period	From 1933 to 1990s	From 1940s to 1990s	From the 1990s to present
	Significance in the economy	Prominent	Prominent	Prominent
	Core actor	State-owned group (IRI and since the 1950s ENI) and few family-owned groups	State-owned group (INI), bank-centered industrial groups, some family owned groups	Family-owned business groups
	Reasons for emergence	IRI emerged in order to rescue the failing banks (and their industrial investments); ENI was created to manage the country's needs in energy	State owned groups facilitated the rapid industrialization; banks invested in industrial firms to increase income; families diversified in search of growth opportunities	Acquisition of assets in privatization programme; capital market liberalization. (Groups maintained unrelated diversification but focused more on fewer core industries and became multinational)

Reasons for decline (if any)	Dissolution of IRI in 2002 following the privatization of its businesses in the 1980s and 1990s; ENI stays intact	End of import substitution; liberalization, privatization and deregulation after the 1970s. Some groups remained resilient by focusing on core activities to gain size to compete on a global scale	Not applicable
3rd wave			
Time period	From the 1970s to present	From 1990s to present	
Significance in the economy	Prominent	Minor	
Core actor	Family-owned groups	Family-owned business groups	
Reasons for emergence	Acquisition of assets in privatization programme and capital market liberalization, both of which assisted established firms to diversify into new business fields	Acquisition and restructuring of firms in difficulties led to the formation of new groups	
Reasons for decline (if any)	Not applicable (There is some decline however in the overall significance of the largest groups in the Italian economy)	Not applicable	

(continued)

		USA	Australia	Canada
1st wave	Time period	From the 1880s to 1940s	From 1850s to 1940s	From the late 19th century to 1940s
	Significance in the economy	Moderate in overseas developing economies	Minor	Prominent
	Core actor	Overseas trading and operating company-centered groups	Family-owned business groups, British overseas trading companies	Family-owned business groups
	Reasons for emergence	Functioning US capital markets to substitute for dysfunctional markets and institutions in developing economies	Close-knit colonial communities, entrepreneurial innovation; conducive environment for emerging British overseas trading groups	Business groups emerged to substitute for dysfunctional markets and institutions in the domestic economy
	Reasons for decline (if any)	Maturing of specialized multinational companies and development of local economies	Maturing domestic capital markets and commercial practices fostered large corporations; waning influence of British trading groups	Role ended by the economic development of the country
2nd wave	Time period	From the 1880s to mid 1930s	From 1970s to 1990s	From 1970s to 1990s
	Significance in the economy	Prominent	Moderate	Prominent
	Core actor	Bank-centered groups	Family-owned business groups	Family-owned business groups
	Reasons for emergence	Well-developed financial and capital markets, and investment opportunities in technological and product markets	Change of competition policy, financial deregulation and active takeover market that led to the rise of diversified business groups	Nationalistic policies and political connections that favored Canadian-controlled firms to enter into specific industries

Reasons for decline (if any)	Development of managerial enterprises, and government regulations that challenged banking groups	Ineffective management, over-leveraged debt structure and the 1987 stock market crash brought the demise of business groups	Major change of policies toward liberal ones that led to the diminishing of business groups
3rd wave			
Time period	From 1960s to 1980s		
Significance in the economy	Moderate		
Core actor	Conglomerates		
Reasons for emergence	Low interest rate and emerging market for corporate control that functioned instrumentally for acquisitions and sell-off of enterprises		
Reasons for decline (if any)	Low profitability and capital market pressures (Wall Street hostility). Some groups, particularly of the value-creating type, remained resilient		

Note: This chart does not include private equity firms due to their critically distinct characteristics from other types of groups. Yet they have become important players, especially in the US and the UK economies, from the 1980s (see Chapter 1, this volume; Collis et al., this volume).

* We observe the moderate role of family-owned groups for Sweden, and the minor role of bank-centered groups for Italy and Spain from the late nineteenth century until the 1910s. However, we do not show them in this chart due to space limitations. For a companion chart, see Figure 2.1 that illustrates the roles of these groups.

** Suez took control of Société Générale de Belgique and its diversified assets in 1988 (as such, it looks like a diversified business group for a transitional period), which however from late 1990s divested the non-core assets to focus on utilities and waste management.

Source: Based mainly on the national chapters in this volume.

CHAPTER 3

....

POLITICS, INSTITUTIONS, AND DIVERSIFIED BUSINESS GROUPS

comparisons across developed countries

....

BEN ROSS SCHNEIDER, ASLI M. COLPAN, AND WEIHUANG WONG

3.1 INTRODUCTION

....

THIS chapter focuses largely on the effects of national-level politics and institutions on the long-term evolution of diversified business groups.[1] In many business groups (especially in emerging economies), product diversification, pyramidal ownership structures, as well as family control and management come together and often reinforce one another (Schneider, 2008). However, these dimensions are analytically distinct and can have different causes. Further, the notion of what constitutes a diversified business group can be context-specific. Empirical cases that fall within our definition of diversified business groups range from Sweden's family-controlled Wallenberg and Italy's Exor Group, to Anglo-Saxon-style conglomerates and private equity.[2] These business groups differ along several dimensions, including the ownership structure, the degree of strategic and operational control, and the turnover rate among subsidiaries of the group.

Accordingly, students of origins, continuity, and change in corporate organizational structures should be attentive to differences among varieties of diversified business groups (Schneider, 2009). The existence of different types of business groups across

---

[1] Diversified business groups are those that are diversified into unrelated sectors, especially into technologically or product market-wise unrelated sectors. For a detailed definition, see Chapter 1.

[2] For conglomerates, as a variety of diversified business groups, we in particular refer to those with legally independent and wholly owned subsidiaries.

Table 3.1. Theoretical perspectives, mechanisms, and effects on business groups.

Theoretical perspective	Mechanism	Effects on business groups
Varieties of capitalism (Hall and Soskice)	Patient capital and high skills in CMEs	Complementarities with diversification and family control
Power resource theory (Roe)	Strong left government; social democracy	Concentrated ownership
Cross-class coalitions (Gourevitch & Shinn)	Proportional representation	Blockholding
Manager preferences (Culpepper)	Strong labor within firm	Resistance to takeovers
Legal system (LLSV)	Weak MSP; dual class shares	Encourages diversification & pyramids
Political regime (Pagano and Volpin)	Proportional representation	Weak minority shareholder protections (MSP)
Entrenchment (Morck et al.)	Lobbying for favorable regulation	Longevity of largest incumbents
Small countries	State protection of domestic firms	Encourages domestic diversification

developed countries raises the likelihood of causal heterogeneity—that various types of business groups have different institutional origins and supports. For example, import substitution policies supported family groups in Spain in the mid-twentieth century, while large, liquid stock markets in the United States facilitated conglomerates then private equity groups in the late twentieth century. Oversimplifying, states (through regulations) and firms (via their corporate practices, especially concentrated ownership and cross-ownership) across much of continental Europe and also Japan protected business groups by forestalling takeovers, while capital markets in liberal economies encouraged the formation of new varieties of business groups (especially after the 1960s) by facilitating takeovers.[3]

A central goal of this chapter is to connect the analysis of business groups to broader debates on the political economy of advanced capitalism. Even though not intended to explain business groups, a large number of these political economy arguments have relevance for analyzing the prevalence of business groups across countries and over time, though the mechanisms affecting business groups vary dramatically. Table 3.1 provides a summary of some of the main arguments and mechanisms that will be fleshed out in later sections. These theories move well beyond a narrow focus on aspects of corporate governance (that might affect conditions for creating business groups) to look at the overall economic structure and political distribution of class and corporate power, including everything from labor power to legal traditions, to country size, and much else in between. As such, the specific impact of these broad factors and

[3] There are examples in other countries of business groups buying up subsidiaries through stock markets (see the chapters on Sweden and Italy, for example). What is distinctive about liberal market economies (LMEs) with large markets for corporate control, especially the United States, is the rapid shifts possible, as in the rise and fall of conglomerates within a few decades.

structures on business groups is usually indirect, facilitating, and probabilistic rather than direct and determining.

This chapter steps back and attempts broad comparisons across all the countries included in this volume, as well as Japan, over the past half-century. Given this breadth, our analysis depends heavily on reviewing the chapters in this volume and other secondary literature, and draws from this review rough classifications of the significance of business groups among the largest firms in a country. This significance ranges from dominating (Sweden), to prominent (Italy), to moderate (the United States during the conglomeration wave), to minor (France), as outlined in Chapter 2 (see Table 2.1). In addition, for the late 1990s we constructed an original estimate for the twelve countries in the volume (as well as Japan) for the percentage of large firms that are diversified business groups themselves or affiliated to one. This estimate ranges from a low of 0 percent in Australia to a high of 75 percent in Sweden (see Appendix, this chapter).

Sections 3.2–3.4 draw on a range of political economic theories of developed countries to elaborate hypotheses on when, how, and where business groups should thrive. Section 3.2 analyzes broad theories of power resource theory (PRT) and varieties of capitalism. Section 3.3 considers theories with a narrower focus on state promotion, institutional gaps, and country size. Lastly, Section 3.4 considers debates on legal families and the regulation of corporate governance. Although these theories do not themselves make predictions about diversified business groups, it is possible to extrapolate from them to show that all these theories would predict business groups in a range of developed countries, though for different reasons. Section 3.5 turns to the analysis of change over time in the fortunes of business groups, focusing especially on the waves of conglomerates and later private equity in liberal economies and the more recent struggle of business groups across most developed countries. Section 3.6 offers several brief case studies in Sweden and the United States to illustrate more concretely the evolution of business groups over time and in very different contexts.

Overall, these theories—and the empirical chapters in this volume—make clear that the formation of diversified business groups is not a one-shot reaction to, or combination of, political, economic, and other institutional factors, but rather an ongoing process with adaptations, exogenous shocks, and endogenous feedback loops. The effects of politics and institutions are thus only fully visible in a longer-term, interactive framework.

3.2 BROAD POLITICAL ECONOMY FRAMEWORKS: VARIETIES OF CAPITALISM AND POWER RESOURCE THEORY

Two approaches have dominated scholarship on the overall political economy of rich countries: varieties of capitalism (VoC) and power resource theory (PRT). Hall and Soskice (2001) developed the VoC framework to explain systematic and persistent

Table 3.2. Diversified business groups and varieties of capitalism.

	Share of diversified business groups among large firms	
	1970s	1995 (percent)
Liberal Market Economies (LMEs)		*11*
Australia	Moderate	0
Britain	Moderate	20
Canada	Prominent	20
USA	Moderate	5
Coordinated Market Economies (CMEs)		*45*
Belgium	Prominent	55
Germany	Moderate	50
Japan	Prominent	30
Netherlands	Moderate	15
Sweden	Dominating	75
Mixed Market Economies (MMEs)		*49*
France	Minor	25
Italy	Prominent	60
Portugal	None (in 1975)	50
Spain	Prominent	60

Source: First column from Chapter 2 (Japan from Lincoln and Shimotani, 2010), second column from our estimates. See appendix for details.

institutional differences in corporate governance, labor relations, and worker skills across more coordinated market economies (CMEs) in northern Europe and Japan compared with more liberal varieties (LMEs) in Anglophone countries. Firms in CMEs tend to organize production through strategic interactions and negotiations with multiple stakeholders, whereas firms in LMEs rely on competitive market arrangements and intra-firm hierarchies. Hall and Soskice suggested (and Hancké, Rhodes, and Thatcher, 2007, later elaborated) a possible third category of mixed market economies (MMEs) of southern European countries where states intervened more in their economies. Table 3.2 categorizes our thirteen countries across these three categories. Power resource theory (PRT) explains most policy outcomes, especially distributional outcomes, by the varying power of labor and business.[4] PRT is generally invoked to explain variations in the generosity of welfare states across developed countries. This section instead focuses more narrowly on the subset of theories which argue that labor power affects variations in corporate governance (Roe, 2003; Gourevitch, and Shinn, 2005; and Culpepper, 2011). Countries with stronger labor tend to be CMEs, but the factors affecting corporate governance operate through

---

[4] See, among others, Rueschemeyer, Stephens, and Stephens (1992), Huber and Stephens (2001), and Korpi (2006).

different mechanisms and channels in the two theoretical approaches, as highlighted in Table 3.1.

Table 3.2 confirms a strong correspondence in the 1990s between the presence of diversified business groups and varieties of capitalism, with many in CMEs and MMEs and few in LMEs.[5] Varieties of capitalism approaches analyze the complementarities among economic institutions and the ways these institutional complementarities support distinctive firm strategies, and from there derive possible cross-class coalitions that support various distributional and institutional outcomes (Hall and Soskice, 2001). Although rarely explicitly applied to explaining diversified business groups, the hypothesis within the VoC framework would be that business groups have some complementarities with other institutions that explain their longevity. In Japan, for example, lifetime employment increased returns to group diversification and size, since larger business groups could shift workers from declining subsidiaries to expanding ones (Milgrom and Roberts, 1992; 1994).

One of the key complementarities in coordinated economies is between highly skilled labor and patient capital. In the VoC framework, providing incentives for workers and their employers to make significant investments in skills requires strong expectations that the workers will have long tenure so they and their employers can fully amortize their investments in skills. Over time, managers need to be able to avoid layoffs in short-run cyclical downturns, which in turn means owners have to be willing to forego short-term profits in order to reap larger gains down the road—i.e., patient capital. Liberal economies with dispersed corporate ownership, of course, have much more impatient capital, and layoffs are the common response to recession. Most of the VoC literature focuses on the role of banks and cross-shareholding in making capital patient in coordinated capitalism (Schneider, 2013).

However, business groups in all three main dimensions—diversification, pyramids, and family—allow owners to be more patient and to delay laying workers off in an economic downturn. Diversification means controlling owners can absorb losses in any subsidiary and cover it with profits from other subsidiaries.[6] Pyramidal structure provides further (tunneling) opportunities to extract resources from one subsidiary to transfer to another. Finally, families reportedly take a longer view of profitability and of employment relations. In cyclical downturns, family-owned firms (business groups or not) are less quick to lay off workers than non-family firms (Stavrou et al., 2007). In

---

[5] Granovetter (2005: 435) provided an early assessment of VoC and business groups and concluded, "This argument implies that business groups will be less prevalent in LMEs than in CMEs, which the empirical data support." As Colpan and Hikino (this volume) illustrate, the significance of diversified business groups in these nations change over time (sometimes from being very prominent to minor); as such the VoC cannot explain these long-term evolutionary dynamics. In a strong critique, Sluyterman (2015) wrote that the "generalizations of Hall and Soskice [VoC framework] captured a moment in time and described the developments [only] in the 1990s."

[6] Some authors argue that the inefficient cross-subsidizing within the business groups contributes to their generally discounted value when listed on stock exchanges (for example, Ferris, Kim, and Kitsabunnarat, 2003).

sum, although not necessary for patient capital, business groups are well prepared to provide it, and are therefore complementary to labor relations and long worker tenure in coordinated capitalism, where we should expect to find more of them.

Other authors use PRT-related models based on the power of labor and the left to explain variations in corporate governance. Mark Roe (2003) argues that ownership was more concentrated in Europe compared with the United States due to the greater strength of social democracy (by which Roe meant a composite left-wing government, strong unions, and more protective labor laws).[7] Where unions were strong both organizationally and institutionally (as in German works councils), the hired managers had incentives to accommodate their demands at the expense of shareholders. Owners therefore had incentives to concentrate ownership in order to counter the power of labor and retain control over managers. Conversely, where, as in the United States, labor was weaker and social democracy non-existent, ownership could be widely dispersed.

Gourevitch and Shinn (2005) make related but broader and more direct arguments. For one, business and labor struggle directly in the political arena over regulations in corporate governance. In addition, the overall political system affects actor preferences and regulation of corporate governance. For example, majoritarian political systems as in the United States generate wider policy swings and therefore favor dispersed ownership, while consensus, parliamentary systems in Europe generate greater policy continuity and more concentrated, blockholder dominance (Gourevitch and Shinn, 2005: 10). And business groups, especially when organized in pyramids, are a corporate form that promotes concentrated ownership.

For Pepper Culpepper (2011), a crucial dimension of variation in corporate governance across developed countries is the ease and frequency of hostile takeovers. In the United States and United Kingdom hostile takeovers have long been common, but most other rich countries had regulations or corporate practices (concentrated ownership and cross-shareholding) that precluded hostile takeovers. Regulations facilitating or restricting takeovers (and thereby overall markets for control) depend, for Culpepper, primarily on manager preferences, which in turn depend on the power of labor within the firm. Following this argument, where labor in firms was weak—e.g., in France and Japan—managers were open to easing restraints on takeovers. In contrast, where codetermination provided workers with strong powers over work organization and layoffs, as in Germany and the Netherlands, managers resisted reforms to ease constraints on takeovers.

Although Roe, Gourevitch and Shinn, and Culpepper all focus on labor, the locus of labor strength shifts across the three arguments, as does the type of the corporate governance outcomes of primary interest. Roe's goal is to explain diffuse versus concentrated ownership, and his independent variable of social democracy is a composite of left power in government, union strength, and labor regulation. Gourevitch

---

[7] See Culpepper (2011: 14–15) for a critique. In a recent update, Belenzon and Tsolmon (2016) find that, in countries with rigid labor markets, group firms outperform stand-alone firms.

and Shinn are also focused on explaining blockholding versus dispersed ownership, but their explanatory variables shift to electoral politics and the coalitions workers are likely to join. In Culpepper's longer causal chain, labor's firm-level representation is the crucial variable affecting managers' preferences, which in turn determine constraints on markets for corporate control. In many instances, labor strength across these loci of contention is correlated; however, the causal mechanisms linking labor power to outcomes in corporate governance differ across these arenas.

Although primarily concerned with ownership concentration rather than business groups, the labor-based arguments can be extended to them. In Roe's (2003) argument, social democracy leads owners to prefer concentrated ownership in order to shift power within the firm from managers to owners who are better able to withstand pressure from labor and the left. Beyond ownership concentration, diversified business groups offer several additional means for shifting power from labor and managers to owners. First, stand-alone firms are more vulnerable to labor holdup and strikes than subsidiaries of diversified groups where owners can back up a firm facing labor conflict with resources from other firms in the group. Second, through pyramids, cross-shareholdings, and other types of controlling schemes, owners of business groups can gain more centralized control over more productive assets, thus affording owners a size advantage in dealing with social-democratic governments as well as more opportunities to shift resources among firms to counter threats from labor (Leff, 1986). Moreover, strong labor governments may prefer to negotiate with fewer but more diversified business groups, just as they prefer to bargain with strong encompassing business associations (as in Sweden, discussed in Section 3.5).

With Culpepper's arguments on labor power and takeover regulation, an intriguing bifurcation emerges when thinking about extending the argument to business groups. On the one hand, where labor is strong, managers prefer restrictions on takeovers which can protect diversified business groups from being acquired and broken up as happened in the deconglomeration wave in the United States. On the other hand, where labor is weak and managers do not oppose regulations facilitating hostile takeovers, conglomerate empire builders and private equity firms—that may have different economic motivations to build diversified portfolios of businesses—can take advantage of active markets for corporate control to pursue diversification strategies. This distinction gets at the need to identify more specific kinds of business groups that are related to particular politics and institutions (see Chapters 1 and 2 on types of business groups).

Looking more broadly at patterns of representation in national political systems, Pagano and Volpin (2005a, 2005b, 2006) develop a theory that revolves around the political institutions that benefit minority shareholders over managers and workers, or vice versa, and allow the winning coalition to entrench their preferred institutions. In simplified form, proportional representation (PR) in electoral systems—as in most of Europe—gives more power to workers and managers, which thus facilitates the adoption of regulations that weaken minority shareholder protections (MSP) and strengthen employment protection.[8] These regulations in turn stunt the development of equity markets, which in turn protect corporate incumbents. These arguments can be extended to business groups in three ways. First, costly unemployment protections increase returns to patient capital and to diversified firms (as noted earlier) that can both shift protected employees among subsidiaries or provide cross-subsidies to weather short-term downturns. Second, weak minority shareholder rights increase returns to, and opportunities for, pyramids and tunneling. Lastly, if business groups are the first incumbents, then they would have incentives to join with workers and managers to entrench weak shareholder protections and strong employment protections.

In sum, a range of arguments from varieties of capitalism and labor power perspectives can be extended to explain variation in the prominence of business groups. Thus, patient capital in CMEs, concentrated ownership in social-democratic countries, restrictions on hostile takeovers where labor has power within the firm, and weak MSP in PR electoral systems all favor business groups. And they may be necessary factors to explain the greater prevalence of long-standing, family-controlled business groups in CMEs, though not for explaining the shorter lived conglomerates in LMEs during the 1960s and 1970s, where factors we return to in section 3.4 had greater influence.

3.3 State Promotion, Institutional Gaps, and Country Size

Several theories devised in the study of business groups in developing countries may also be useful for understanding their evolution in now-developed countries. States in developing countries have often been key movers in pushing economic growth as well as structuring large firms (Schneider, 2009; Khanna and Yafeh, 2010). This statist framework revolves around industrial policy and other forms of direct state promotion and protection of diversified business groups. This perspective seems best suited to understanding the evolution of business groups in MMEs in southern Europe. In her book on business groups in Italy and Spain, Veronica Binda emphasized, "The role of the state was also key in creating and making many very diversified business groups profitable" (2013: 204). While PRT and VoC perspectives look at broad political systems and institutions, the state promotion view focuses more narrowly on direct government interventions to promote diversification in specific business groups.

---

[8] Iversen and Soskice (2009) extend VoC arguments to political institutions. They argue that CMEs tend to adopt PR electoral systems. These systems encourage coalitions between business and skilled workers, and these coalitions in turn support the institutional foundations of CMEs (such as vocational training, patient capital, employment protection, and more generous welfare systems).

Developmental states in Asia were most visible in forcing firms into new sectors deemed essential for development. For example, the South Korean government "chose Hyundai and Daewoo to develop power plant facilities and Hyundai, Samsung, and Daewoo to build ships" (Chang, 2003: 54). In other cases, states may be more narrowly concerned with particular sectors, as with defense industries in Israel, for example, where the state encouraged business-group diversification into and across areas of the defense industry (Maman, 2002).

In general, states can foster business groups directly by subsidizing particular activities or indirectly by generating rents through favorable regulation (e.g., public utilities) that groups can invest in other sectors, or by generally protecting firms from international competition or takeover. In the latter case, protected firms are not internationally competitive, so they expand domestically by diversifying into other sectors rather than internationally in their core activities (see Guillén, 2001).[9] Moreover, fiscal laws and regional development policies promote diversification, as does sporadic pressures from government for business groups to rescue failing firms and add them to their portfolios.[10]

Over more than a century, the Italian government provided a wide and evolving range of supports to business groups, both to the same group over time (as with Agnelli) and to new groups as they emerged (e.g., Edizione) (Collis and Vasta, this volume).[11] Initially, the government provided trade protection in the early twentieth century, followed by procurement during two world wars, and accompanied throughout the century by generally lax corporate governance and weak protection for minority shareholders, which facilitated pyramid building.[12] In postwar decades, Italian groups followed the global conglomeration wave of the 1960s and 1970s, and at the end of the century policies to promote regional development and privatization offered further state aid for diversification. In Portugal, state intervention was even more decisive in the turbulent history of business groups in the twentieth century, first providing trade and other protections during the authoritarian *Estado Novo* through 1974 and then nationalizing the major groups in 1975. Later privatizations allowed business groups, new and old, to reconstitute themselves after the 1980s (Silva and Neves, this volume).

Another framework drawn from the study of diversified business groups in developing countries views politics as secondary, at least initially, and business groups more

---

[9] The entrenchment argument for business groups in developing countries would fit within a statist argument, but with less variation over time and more of a lock-in logic whereby, once powerful, business groups use their influence to create policies and institutions to sustain their advantages and cannot thereafter be dislodged by other firms (Morck, Wolfenzon, and Yeung, 2005).

[10] State action in reverse can also be effective in reducing business groups, as in the United States in the 1930s or in the government nationalization of large groups in Portugal in the 1970s, or in shifts in financial regulation that force banks to unload holdings in non-financial firms (Schneider, 2009).

[11] "If American capitalism can be defined as managerial, British as personal, and German as co-operative, then the Italian model can be termed political" (Amatori, 1997: 116).

[12] It is, however, interesting to note that at the same time there was double taxation on the dividends of the companies belonging to a group until the end of the 1970s, which was a disincentive for pyramid formation (Colli and Vasta, this volume).

as natural responses to environments with immature and imperfect markets and institutions. For example, some theorists take the institutional environment as given, especially at early stages of development, and business groups arise then naturally as an internal, second-best economic organization designed to overcome problems in the institutional environment (Leff, 1978; Khanna and Yafeh, 2010). In this view, economies that lack deep credit and equity markets, pools of capable managers, or informational intermediaries such as consulting firms make business groups a rational corporate response. Business groups are effective substitutes for capital markets (as they can pool resources among firms within the group), can make the most of scarce managerial talent, and can substitute for consulting firms and other informational intermediaries because they have the size and scope to develop these capacities internally.

This institutional gaps hypothesis partially works for the late nineteenth- and early twentieth-century wave of bank-based group formation in Continental Europe and the United States (Colpan and Hikino, Chapter 2 this volume). Following Gerschenkron (1962), banks became core institutions for financing catch-up development, first in financing firms and later in acquiring large ownership stakes. Later regulations often prohibited bank business groups, and financial markets developed alternative means for financing large investments, thereby filling the institutional gap. However, where capital markets did not fully develop (in part because business groups had solved their financing needs), as in parts of southern Europe, business groups continued to fill in for the missing financial development.[13]

A last, overlapping, and related factor to consider, especially in continental Europe, is country size.[14] Excepting the Netherlands, the other three smallest countries in Table 3.2—Belgium, Portugal, and Sweden—all had prominent business groups in the 1990s and throughout much of the twentieth century despite different varieties of capitalism, proclivities for social democracy, labor power, and other macro variables discussed in Section 3.2. Smaller economies may alter incentives in government and business in ways that encourage the formation of large business groups. On the government side, the vulnerability of small economies to international shocks gives political leaders incentives to bargain with organized business and labor (Katzenstein, 1985), and therefore, by a similar logic, gives leaders preferences for longer-term relations with stable large business groups. Policymakers may also prefer to negotiate adjustments with local firms rather than footloose multinationals.

On the business side, specialized firms are likely to be smaller than firms in the same sectors in larger countries and face more difficulties expanding abroad (via either trade or acquisitions), and therefore may prefer to diversify at home.[15] International

---

[13] In recent research, Belenzon et al. (2013) find that business groups continue to be more common in less developed financial markets.

[14] Business groups were also quite prominent in a set of even smaller countries in Central America (Bull et al., 2014).

[15] In Turkey, Vehbi Koç cited the small size and volatility of the country as motives for diversifying the Koç group: "Turkey is a small country relative to the world's developed countries. Here, it was difficult to grow doing business in one field as it is done in big countries. Our economic and political

expansion was especially difficult for business in the late-developing countries of southern Europe, thus making domestic diversification even more attractive (Binda, 2013: 203). Higher returns to local brand recognition, as well as supportive government policies and protections, can reinforce these preferences. Successful capital owners in small economies, particularly in non-tradable sectors like hospitality and retail, may also be compelled by the limited size of the domestic market to reinvest profits in unrelated sectors.

In sum, beyond the broad systemic influences of VoC and PRT considered in Section 3.3, a number of other contextual factors promoted business groups in Europe, especially southern Europe. States were generally more interventionist in latecomer economies, and this intervention often supported group diversification; and over time political pressures by huge business groups reinforced favorable policy. In more passive ways, institutional gaps and lagging market development in areas like finance and managerial talent favored business groups, as did small domestic markets.

3.4 LEGAL TRADITION AND REGULATION

This section turns to research that focuses more narrowly on legal systems and specific regulations on corporate governance that benefit, facilitate, or sustain business groups. Much of this line of research starts with a concern over minority shareholder protections (MSP) and probes the wide variation in the protections countries offer. In the 1990s La Porta et al. (1997, 1999, 2000)—Rafael La Porta, Florencio López-de-Silanes, Andrei Shleifer, and Robert Vishny, also known as LLSV—started a major debate with their arguments that centuries-long legal traditions created distinct clusters of countries, namely common-law and civil-law countries. These clusters overlap significantly with LMEs that are common law and CMEs and MMEs that have various types of civil law. Overall, MSP were stronger in common-law LMEs than in civil-law CMEs and MMEs in long-term, path-dependent ways.

Table 3.3 takes some of the core measures in LLSV and shows their association with varieties of capitalism and prominence of business groups in the 1990s. Anti-director rights (a composite index constructed as a proxy for MSP) were stronger in LMEs than in CMEs and MMEs. Pyramids were also much less common in LMEs than in the other two varieties. Family control was lower in LMEs though more variable across CME and MME countries. Lastly, state ownership in the 1990s was lower everywhere save three of the four MMEs. In sum, civil-law traditions are associated with the classic hierarchical business group that thrives on family control, pyramidal structure, and weak MSP.

status has continuously shown ups and downs. If one business made a deficit, the other would make a profit, and as such I acted in thinking that I would make balance. I believe I did the right thing" (Colpan and Jones, 2011).

Table 3.3. Types of ownership, MSP, and varieties of capitalism in the 1990s.

	Diversified business groups (percent)	Pyramids	Family	State	Anti-director rights
Liberal market economies (LMEs)					
LME average	11	0.09	0.13	0.01	3.8
Australia	0	0.14	0.05	0.05	4
Britain	20	.	0.00	0.00	4
Canada	20	0.13	0.25	0.00	4
USA	5	0.00	0.20	0.00	3
Coordinated market economies (CMEs)					
CME average	45	0.37	0.26	0.10	1.6
Belgium	55	0.79	0.50	0.05	0
Germany	50	0.40	0.10	0.25	1
Japan	30	0.00	0.05	0.05	3
Netherlands	15	0.14	0.20	0.05	2
Sweden	75	0.53	0.45	0.10	2
Mixed market economies (MMEs)					
MME average	49	0.36	0.24	0.28	1.5
France	25	0.38	0.20	0.15	2
Italy	60	0.25	0.15	0.40	0
Portugal	50	0.44	0.45	0.25	2
Spain	60	0.38	0.15	0.30	2

Source: First column from our research (repeated from Table 3.2). Pyramids, family, and state data for largest twenty publicly traded firms in a country are proportions, calculated in La Porta, López-de-Silanes, and Shleifer (1999: 492, 499). Figures for pyramids show the frequency of pyramids in firms with controlling owners. Anti-director rights for largest ten publicly traded firms in a country range from high of 4 to low of 0, calculated in LLSV (1997: 1138).

Other research has identified a long list of more specific regulations that benefit business groups (see Table 3.4). Among those that favor pyramids, for example, are tax cumulation (losses in one subsidiary can be charged against profits in another subsidiary) and lack of restrictions on issuing non-voting shares or multiple classes of shares. By contrast, taxing dividends at both subsidiary and holding-company level encourages business groups to dismantle pyramids, buy full control of subsidiaries, and delist subsidiaries (Morck, 2005; Kandel et al., 2015). Lower taxation of carried interest for the incentive fees paid to private equity managers that are regarded as capital gains (compared to higher income taxes) increases returns to private equity and may encourage those types of groups. Increases in inheritance taxes, on the other hand, may facilitate the downsizing of business groups. This may be because as governments make it expensive for families to pass profits and transfer outright ownership upon death of the existing generation, families may prefer to decrease the scale and scope of their businesses (Morck, Wolfenzon, and Yeung, 2005; Morck and Tian, this volume).

Table 3.4. Effects of selected regulations on business groups.[16]

Regulation	Effect on business groups
Taxes	
Cumulative taxation	Encourages ownership of multiple firms to use profits in one subsidiary to offset losses in others
Dividend taxation at both subsidiary and holding company levels	Discourages pyramids and multisubsidiary structures
Lower taxation of carried interest	Increases returns to private equity
Inheritance tax	Can encourage downsizing of business groups
Sectoral, anti-trust, and other	
Public utilities	Reduction of tiers of pyramids and decline in the scope of activities of public utilities groups (as in the United States in the 1930s)
Prohibition of bank ownership of non-financial firms	Dissolution of bank-centered business groups
Dual class shares	Can facilitate pyramids
Anti-trust regulation against horizontal and vertical acquisitions	Promotes unrelated diversification (e.g., Celler-Kefauver Act of 1950)
Insertion into global economy	
Trade protection	Encourages uncompetitive firms to diversify at home
Restrictions on MNCs	Protects domestic business groups

Regulations that favor diversification move beyond taxes and corporate governance to include more general and sectoral regulation. For example, incentives for banks to form business groups with operating subsidiaries in diverse fields seem especially sensitive to financial regulation, and regulatory reform often prohibits banks from controlling non-financial subsidiaries. Banks have remained the hubs of business groups in Sweden through the establishment of holding companies connected to the banks, despite regulatory efforts to deter them in the 1930s (Larsson and Petersson, this volume). By contrast, the Glass-Steagall Act of 1933 in the United States prohibited banks from owning non-financial firms.[17]

A variety of domestic restrictions on competition, regulation of utilities, or other special concessions can also work as incentives for diversification. Favorable regulation that generates rents in utility sectors, for example, encourages diversification by attracting business groups into utilities, by giving utility firms extra funds they can invest in other sectors, and by limiting growth opportunities in the sectors regulated (see Schneider,

---

[16] Table 3.4 provides a sampling of major regulations that other research and chapters in this volume have identified as affecting business groups. For more detailed lists, see Kandel et al. (2015) and Cuervo-Cazurra (this volume).

[17] Bank-centered groups were prominent in Mexico and Chile until regulations in the 1980s forbade banks from owning non-financial firms (Schneider, 2009).

2013, and Cuervo-Cazurra, this volume).[18] In addition, general competition or anti-trust regulation may affect incentives for diversification (as discussed in Section 3.5).

Other regulations affecting integration into the global economy also affect incentives for the formation of diversified business groups. Widespread tariff protection both reduces the ability of firms to compete abroad and encourages them to expand at home into new sectors once they have reached the limits of expansion in their sectors of origin. This was the common pattern in Spain under Franco (Cuervo-Cazurra, this volume) and in Latin America through much of the twentieth century (Guillén, 2001). Moreover, many governments in Europe and Japan imposed restrictions on the entry of multinational corporations (MNCs) by prohibiting takeovers of national champions or reserving "strategic" sectors of the economy for domestic firms. Such restrictions reduced competition for corporate control and facilitated expansion and diversification by domestic business groups. This protection from foreign firms was part of the social-democratic package in mid twentieth-century Sweden that shielded business groups (see, e.g., Reiter, 2003, and Högfeldt, 2005).

In sum, a wide range of laws and regulations can encourage (or impede) those who create and own business groups. The legal families research focused on the benefits of common-law trajectories for strengthening MSP which in turn lead to greater financial development and dispersed corporate ownership. Although not directly focused on business groups, the non-common-law systems fostered pyramids and concentrated ownership (particularly in the hands of the families), which helped business groups. The overlap between legal families and varieties of capitalism is large, and both make long-term, path-dependent arguments that lead to expectations of continuity (though the causal mechanisms are different). The longer list of other laws and regulations that encourage the formation of business groups are in principle subject to shorter-term shifts, as in, for example, sectoral regulation or deregulation or changes to stock markets on types of shares allowed. To the extent that these regulations persist over time, a prime suspect would be the power of business-group incumbents to block change, especially in arcane rules where business has the upper hand in "quiet politics" (Culpepper, 2011). Yet tendencies toward entrenchment and path dependence notwithstanding, change sometimes does happen.

3.5 Change Over Time: LME Waves and CME Convergence

While most of the factors discussed in previous sections that encouraged business groups—like labor strength, complementarities with skilled workers, and weak protection

---

[18] Early twentieth-century utility pyramids in the United States were not diversified (Kandel et al., 2015).

for minority shareholders—were fairly constant, other regulatory factors, globalization, and management trends were more variable. Taking longer-term perspectives,
the chapters in this volume reveal many fluctuations in the fortunes of business
groups. This section focuses on two major types of changes. In LMEs, change came
in waves, precisely because large, liquid financial markets allowed for more experi-
mentation in corporate governance and more rapid reconfigurations of corporate
assets. Change in CMEs (and MMEs as well) came mostly in the direction of
reduction of protections for business groups and their resulting decline in prominence with overall trends in convergence towards LMEs.

LMEs experienced major changes over the past century with distinct waves of
business-group formation and dissolution from the beginning of the twentieth century
to the start of the twenty-first. Table 3.5 highlights a wave of conglomeration in LMEs
from the 1950s to the 1970s. None of the core institutional dimensions of LMEs (or
common-law tradition) shifted dramatically in this period (though labor strength
waned and capital markets deepened). Researchers have generally sought explanations
for conglomeration elsewhere. For one, in the United States anti-trust regulators were
stricter in the 1950s and 1960s in prohibiting horizontal mergers, and firms then
acquired unrelated firms that promoted giant conglomerates (Fligstein, 1991; Davis,
Diekman, and Tinsley, 1994). Due to their financial underperformance and partly in
response to later anti-trust approval in the 1980s of horizontal mergers, firms decon-
glomerated or shifted from acquiring unrelated subsidiaries to merging with competitors in the same sector (Zorn et al., 2004; Collis et al., this volume). Around the same
time, ideas about best management practice shifted towards a greater focus on core
competence.[19]

Although conglomeration was ephemeral—rising rapidly in the 1960s and declining
precipitously after the 1970s—the underlying constant factors enabling both the rise
and decline were large, liquid markets for corporate control characteristic of LMEs.
Because it was comparatively easy to buy and sell firms in large stock and financial
markets where corporate ownership was dispersed, empire builders could quickly
buy up firms to create large conglomerates. Likewise, when takeover firms emerged
in the 1970s, they found a ready market to allow them to take on debt to buy up
conglomerates, then break them up and find buyers for the pieces. Such rapid shifts in
corporate ownership are rarer in CMEs and MMEs where financial markets are
smaller, ownership is more concentrated, and takeover-blocking cross-shareholding
is more common. Table 3.4 shows little change in business group prominence in CMEs
and MMEs over the course of the mid-twentieth century (with the exception of
Portugal, discussed later).

---

[19] Ideas about best practice in the United States may be one of the causes for the rise and decline of
conglomerates in other LMEs. In addition, institutional investors came to dominate the US stock
market, and preferred to invest in specialized firms in order to build their own diversified portfolios
(Zorn et al., 2004).

Table 3.5. Change over time in prominence of business groups.

	1950s	1970s	Trend 1950s–1970s	2000s and after	Trend 1970s–2000s and after
Liberal market economies (LMEs)					
Australia	Minor	Moderate	More	Minor	Less
Britain	Minor	Moderate	More	Minor	Less
Canada	Minor	Prominent	More	Minor	Less
USA	Minor	Moderate	More	Minor	Less
Coordinated market economies (CMEs)					
Belgium	Prominent	Prominent	Same	Minor	Less
Germany	Moderate	Moderate	Same	Minor	Less
Japan	Prominent	Prominent	Same	Moderate	Less
Netherlands	Moderate	Moderate	Same	Minor	Less
Sweden	Dominating	Dominating	Same	Dominating	Same
Mixed market economies (MMEs)					
France	Minor	Minor	Same	Minor	Same
Italy	Prominent	Prominent	Same	Prominent	Same
Portugal	Dominating	None	Less	Prominent	More
Spain	Prominent	Prominent	Same	Minor	Less

Sources: Chapter 2 (Appendix, and Figure 2.1). Japan from Lincoln and Shimotani (2010).

In LMEs, the trend after the 1980s was towards less diversification among major corporations, save exceptions like Berkshire Hathaway and General Electric. However, this overall trend misses the emergence of new types of business groups, especially in the United States, namely, private equity firms which at their peak in 2007 came to control 12 percent of corporate assets in the United States (Collis et al., this volume). Compared with archetypal zaibatsu or chaebol, private equity firms are speed-dating versions of business groups that buy up firms with the express goal of selling them off in a matter of years rather than using them to build a lasting conglomerate. This rapid-turnover type of business group is a novel corporate invention that—like the conglomerates of the twentieth century—thrives especially in large, liquid LME financial markets where credit is abundant and firms easy to buy.

In CMEs, the trend in recent decades has mostly been toward fewer business groups and more specialization among large firms. This trend results in part from increasing global financial integration and the consequent arrival of LME institutional investors in CME stock markets, as well as general reductions in ownership concentration and cross-shareholding in CMEs (Jackson, 2003).[20] For smaller countries, financial globalization means that domestic groups or parts of them are likely to be acquired by larger foreign rivals in the absence of continuing government and other protections (as in

---

[20] Change has been uneven, however, and Germany and Italy have retained significant cross-shareholding that blocks takeovers (Culpepper, 2005).

Belgium). Yet the exceptional case of Sweden's business groups thriving well into the twenty-first century gives the lie to arguments that convergence is universal and ineluctable. Groups like the Wallenbergs do have special features, such as the family foundation, that make it more difficult to dismantle the group. But thriving exceptional business groups in both CMEs and LMEs make clear that forces of convergence and natural selection have not driven all business groups from the field.

The uneven impact of financial globalization and convergence is also evident in the disparate trends in recent decades in MMEs. Spain best exemplifies the convergence perspective. Business groups declined as Spain opened its economy after the 1970s and later joined the EU. By contrast, Italy (already in the EU) maintained its distinctive family-controlled groups. In Portugal—the only country in Table 3.4 where business groups increased their prominence—the trend was somewhat a reversion to type after the dominant business groups had been nationalized in the 1970s. As noted earlier, in both Italy and Portugal government policies and favorable regulation were key to the continued longevity of business groups.

These changes go against rigid notions of path dependency, continuity, and equilibrium. Hall and Soskice (2001: 60–2) already noted in 2001 that change was underway in corporate governance. On this dimension, LMEs have shifted less than other varieties, and private equity in LMEs is just another corporate innovation that fits with, and depends on, active markets for corporate control.[21] Arguments based on legal families have a harder time explaining convergence tendencies of non-common-law countries, though a plausible hypothesis is that financial globalization brings foreign investors from common-law countries who then press for better MSP. Arguments on labor power and social democracy might also plausibly hypothesize that the decline of unions and weakening or more moderate social democracy would reduce incentives for blockholding and open up opportunities for more dispersed shareholding. The Swedish exception again merits mention, as unions and social democracy retain more power in Sweden than in much of the rest of Europe.

3.6 ILLUSTRATIVE COUNTRY STUDIES: SWEDEN AND THE UNITED STATES

This section looks briefly at two country experiences to examine the evolving political and institutional factors that promoted the emergence and, sometimes, decline of diversified business groups. The preceding Colpan and Hikino chapter (Chapter 2, this volume) helps to identify the specific kinds of business groups that emerged in each country, while the theories in Sections 3.2, 3.3, and 3.4 help specify why these kinds of

---

[21] Although, see the *Economist* briefing (October 22, 2016) on how widespread and potentially transformative private equity has become.

groups emerged and not others. Sweden stands out as the country where business groups have been most stable and most dominant, as well as an emblematic case of labor strength, social democracy, CME, and small-economy vulnerabilities. The United States—the archetype of a weak labor LME—went through successive waves of different sorts of business groups, from financial and industrial groups in the early twentieth century, to conglomerates and private equity later on.

3.6.1 The Case of Sweden

As Larsson and Petersson (this volume) note, the Swedish corporate sector today remains dominated by diversified business groups. Two groups stand out for their historical and contemporary involvement in a broad range of industries: the Wallenberg and Handelsbanken groups. The scope of their businesses extends from primary industries like pulp and paper to manufacturing sectors such as automotive, communications, consumer goods, and engineering, with banking located at the core of the groups. The provenance of these groups can be traced back to the beginnings of Swedish industrialization, which took root in the 1850s and gained pace in the 1870s.

By the mid-1930s Handelsbanken (the successor to Stockholms Handelsbank) and the Wallenbergs' Stockholms Enskilda Bank (SEB) had become owners of diversified portfolios of large industrial companies in Sweden. Although the 1911 Banking Act permitted banks to purchase and own shares of industrials, it was in the wake of the financial crises in the 1920s and early 1930s that the banks amassed large portfolios of shares in major listed firms, having taken over these shares when borrowers went into financial distress. One consequence of the financial crisis of 1932, linked to the collapse of the Kreuger business group, was an effort by policymakers to limit the linkages between banks and industrial companies. The Swedish government established a Banking Commission after the crisis, which in its final report noted that "the right to acquire shares means quite simply that the banks become industrialists, not only sources of credit . . . the risks associated with loan operations are so substantial that the banks should not assume the additional risks of entrepreneurship" (quoted in Lindgren, 1987). The Commission's recommendations were passed into law in 1933, and beginning the following year banks were given five years to divest their holdings of industrial companies.

Regulations against bank ownership of industrial companies did not prevent SEB and Handelsbanken from growing their respective diversified business groups, well into the twenty-first century. By transferring their industrial assets into affiliated investment vehicles, and retaining control of these vehicles through dual-class share structures, the Wallenberg family and Handelsbanken expanded their influence over corporate Sweden, while keeping to the letter of banking regulations. Why did policymakers not move to enforce the spirit of the rules, and why were these diversified business groups so resilient? Part of the answer, we propose, can be found by examining the dynamics of Sweden's political economy.

The dominance of the Swedish Social Democratic Party (SAP), which formed the government from 1932 to 1976, coincided with a period of expansion and diversification for Swedish business groups. Explaining this outcome is a matter of some scholarly debate. One interpretation sees this outcome as a result of a bargain among the SAP, trade unions, and business elites, or what some scholars call the "iron triangle" of Swedish politics: "the mutual purpose has been stable, long-term ownership in exchange for looking after certain interests that are of importance to the economy and the trade unions when making decisions" (Söderström et al., 2003). Like some other small open-market economies, Sweden had a sizeable export sector, and all stakeholders had an interest in maintaining the international competitiveness of Swedish firms. The SAP's objectives of economic stability and orderly social reforms resulted in an antipathy toward the short-termism of public equity markets, and led policymakers to prefer relationship-based bank financing and pyramidal ownership structures (Högfeldt, 2005). Policymaking elites' perception of "concentration of industrial ownership as a favorable feature, since it was thought to enable dialogue and common understandings between the state, employers, and employees in the area of economic policy making" persisted well into the 1980s (Reiter, 2003). Diversified business groups complemented employers' associations in enforcing top-down discipline among constituent firms in the domain of wage-setting and industrial relations.

As discussed in Section 3.2, Mark Roe (2003) has suggested that labor power and social democratic pressures in Sweden gave workers more bargaining power over corporate managers about how to distribute a firm's surplus, and strong owners were necessary to counterbalance this social pressure. This argument explains concentrated corporate ownership, but is perhaps less valuable in helping us to understand why business groups continued to be diversified in the postwar era. In addition, since the 1980s large Swedish industrial companies—particularly those in the Wallenberg group—have steadily shifted production and other business activities offshore, in response to changes in demand dynamics.[22] So, while labor strength may have facilitated the persistence of the diversified business group form in the postwar decades, it appears to have less traction in recent years as an explanation for why large diversified business groups continue to dominate the Swedish economy. Nonetheless, it provides an alternative explanatory framework for pyramidal ownership structures and other mechanisms that owners employ to maintain tight control over their assets. Through these multiple mechanisms, the political power of the SAP and the trade unions played a central role in the resilience of business groups in Sweden, especially through the 1970s.

The enduring nature of Swedish business groups can also be understood with reference to institutional complementarities, a key idea in the VoC literature. Håkan Lindgren and Hans Sjögren make the claim that "the fundamental cause of the implementation of 'German' universal practices into the Swedish 'Scottish-influenced'

---

[22] For instance, Sheldon and Thornwhaite (1999) note that by 1996 Electrolux and Atlas Copco—core Wallenberg holdings—employed just 12 percent of their total workforce in Sweden.

banking system is to be found on the demand side, in the rapid industrial transformation of the Swedish economy during the prolonged 1895–1913 boom" (Lindgren and Sjögren, 2003: 141). Because producers of export-oriented capital goods required long-term, patient capital to fund their expansion, the financial system co-evolved with the real economy, and commercial banks—particularly the *Enskilda*, or private, note-issuing joint stock banks—developed expertise in industrial bond issuance and credit underwriting, as well as financial organization and restructuring. Financiers formed tight-knit relationships with industrialists. The hands-on involvement of bankers in the operations of industrial companies as well as sectoral-level coordination have led scholars to observe that "as regards active participation on the board of large firms, key features of German universal banking were more pronounced and decisive in Sweden than in Germany itself" (Lindgren and Sjögren, 2003: 142). The VoC framework proposes that the resilience of diversified business groups in Sweden has less to do with the hegemony of the SAP or the influence of labor unions, but is conditioned by the structural demands of industrial production. As Glete (1993: 106) notes in his study of the Wallenberg companies, the division of competencies and specialization among ASEA, Ericsson, and Electrolux was achieved through the coordination of the owner in consultation with managers: "It is not difficult to imagine that independent managerial hierarchies within these three great companies would have followed different, possibly competing, strategies."

In the Swedish case, patient capital with interests across multiple sectors played a decisive role in financing and organizing high-skill, high-quality, and internationally competitive production organized by highly concentrated business groups. Many of the other factors listed in previous sections (and Table 3.1), such as labor power, social democracy, civil law, and proportional representation, do not come up in analyses of the Wallenberg and Handelsbanken groups, yet these factors in principle would have pushed in the same direction of concentrated business groups. These factors may then have worked more as background or contextual influences that encouraged the corporate strategies adopted in business groups or that impeded the emergence of other corporate firms that could have challenged the groups.

3.6.2 The Case of the United States

On most dimensions—from labor strength to economic size and corporate turnover—the United States lies at the opposite end of the spectrum from Sweden.[23] The rise and fall of various types of business groups in the United States is largely a story of shifting

---

[23] There were a few Wallenberg-style multigenerational, family-owned, diversified business groups in the United States, like Pritzker, but, significantly, they were mostly unlisted and hence not subject to influences of outside investors in LME-style equity markets.

regulation and evolving corporate strategies, but the indispensable, necessary condition for all types of business groups (save the earliest) were the relatively deep and dynamic financial markets, one of the defining features of LMEs.

At the beginning of the twentieth century business groups active in unrelated businesses (and that also were in pyramidal structure) emerged primarily in two forms.[24] First were the financial groups organized around investment banks, or "money trusts," the largest of which was the Morgan group. These financial groups were the most significant case of diversified groups in the United States at the time, and were formed after banks acquired equity stakes in various industrial companies. Some argued that achieving size and influence, rather than economic efficiency and market power, was the driving force behind the formation of these groups (Kandel et al., 2013).[25] The second type was the pyramidal, industrial group. These business groups mostly had their origins in trusts and turned into industrial holding companies at the turn of the twentieth century after trust arrangements were outlawed by the Sherman Act of 1890. The majority of these groups were holding companies active in single sectors (mainly in utilities and transportation) with pyramidal structures (a smaller minority were widely diversified groups) (Kandel et al., 2013; Hikino and Bucheli, this volume).

Both types of business group began to be challenged as early as the 1910s but mostly after the 1930s on political, legal, and economic grounds (due to concerns including their extensive acquisitions, possible over-capitalization, reduced competition, possible accounting frauds, and political corruption).[26] In the aftermath of the great depression and collapse of the Insull group in 1931, New Dealers' reforms on the inter-corporate dividend tax of 1935 in particular (and the Public Utility Holding Company Act initiated in 1935 that specifically attacked public utility companies) deterred holding companies by taxing capital transfers between subsidiaries and the holding company.[27] These reforms slowly led to the demise of the financial as well as industrial business groups—specifically of the pyramidal type that controlled

---

[24] There were also earlier groups organized around general merchants that played an influential role in the initial phase of industrialization of the US economy up to the 1840s (Hikino and Bucheli, this volume).

[25] "Whole strings of companies with no particular relation to, and often essentially unconnected with, units in the existing system have been absorbed from time to time. Among the subsidiaries in the holding company systems were companies engaged in one or more of a variety of enterprise—coal mining production, refining, and transportation of oil; wood, coal, and oil retailing; foundries; textiles; farming, irrigation, orchards; taxicabs; ice and cold storage; towing and lighterage; real estate, finance and credit, water, street railways, railroads, bus transportation and telephone companies" (SEC Annual Report, 1944, in Kandel et al., 2013: 14).

[26] Early challenges include the Pujo Committee report in 1913 on the concentration of control of money and credit by members of the empire headed by J. P. Morgan, and the 1914 Clayton Antitrust Act that "prohibited one company from holding controlling stocks of a rival company if the result was the substantial lessening of competition between these two firms" (Kandel et al., 2013: 11).

[27] The Glass-Steagall Act that separated commercial banking from investment banking, passed in 1933, was also critical as it brought an end to bank dominance.

businesses with partial stakes in publicly quoted entities—in the US (Prechel, 1997; Kandel et al., 2013).

In the mid-twentieth century another form of diversified business group emerged: large conglomerates with wholly owned subsidiaries and divisions in a range of unrelated industries. This wave of acquisitive conglomeration during the 1960s and 1970s was partly fueled by shifting antitrust regulations (Celler-Kefauver Antimerger Act of 1950) that made horizontal and related mergers and acquisitions more difficult (Fligstein, 1990). Conglomeration was also preferred by CEOs whose compensation was tied to corporate size and who, by virtue of dispersed shareholding, were relatively unconstrained by shareholders.[28] Some of the titans of the conglomerate age included ITT, Gulf & Western, and Textron.

A convergence of factors reversed conglomeration in the 1980s thanks to the financial underperformance of the highly diversified conglomerates (Collis et al., this volume). Institutional investors who came to control more of the stock market and increasingly emphasized short-term returns preferred more specialized firms (Zorn et al., 2004). Leveraged buyout (LBO) firms like KKR thrived in this environment and broke up conglomerates by buying them or their subsidiaries up, leveraging them with debt, and selling them off after improving performance with cost-cutting. The fear of leveraged, hostile buyouts also encouraged other CEOs to sell off subsidiaries and streamline. Lastly, during the 1980s the Reagan administration loosened antitrust regulations and opened up more opportunities for horizontal and related mergers.

Ironically, the last wave of business-group formation evolved from LBO firms into private equity (Collis et al., this volume). The crucial regulation favoring private equity was tax treatment of carried interest where the taxation of gains from buying and selling subsidiaries is considered capital gains and taxed at less than half the rate of personal income. That successive governments (in both US and UK) have been unable to change the taxation of carried interest is due in some, likely large, measure to the growing political influence of private equity firms (showing early signs of entrenchment).

These three waves of business groups, especially the most recent, seem to confound expectations from Section 3.2, especially VoC and PRT, that business groups would thrive mostly in smaller, coordinated economies with stronger labor. However, what emerged in the United States, in particular after the 1980s, were more LME-compatible sorts of business groups—short-lived agglomerations of firms that can be easily assembled and disassembled in deep, active equity markets according to changing investor preferences and regulatory shifts. These fluid business groups were quite different from the long-standing, family-owned groups of Europe, like the Wallenbergs in Sweden or the Agnelli/Exor group in Italy.

---

[28] In Australia, another LME, a brief and smaller wave of conglomeration emerged following the conglomeration wave in the United States (Ville, this volume).

Previous sections outlined the broad institutional contexts which encouraged or discouraged business groups. The vignettes in this section show how specific battles over corporate governance unfolded within the broader institutional landscapes. Even in the US case of large LME financial markets, weak labor, strong common-law MSP, and battles over specific regulations (especially corporate tax and antitrust) led to, or reversed, successive waves of different types of business groups. Similarly, in the Swedish case of a small economy with strong labor in a well-organized CME, firms and policymakers battled over specific forms of corporate governance, though in this case anti-group reformers of the 1930s were unable to dismantle the groups that would go on to dominate the economy (with later government support) through the remainder of the twentieth century.

3.7 CONCLUSIONS

This desperately brief comparative overview reinforces the intuition in the introduction to this volume that it is crucial to distinguish between different types of business groups. Simple measures of the number of Standard Industrial Classification (SIC) codes of major subsidiaries could give the impression of significant similarities across most OECD countries. However, one needs to be careful about the significant differences among these enterprises: Gulf & Western, General Electric, the Wallenberg Group, with emerging private equity groups. Even within one country over time, as seen in the US case, business groups varied greatly from financial groups organized around investment banks and industrial holding companies in the early twentieth century, to conglomerates in the 1960s and 1970s, to private equity (and their leveraged buyout predecessors), since the 1980s. More fine-grained distinctions are useful (Schneider, 2009), but for now it seems important to distinguish broadly the contemporary LME-style groups that are more likely to be looser portfolio groups in contrast to CME-type groups with long-standing patterns of unrelated diversification.

The enduring existence of diversified business groups in developed countries raises serious issues for the extensive literature on corporate governance and strategy in developing countries. As noted in the introduction, most prior theorizing on business groups in poor countries started with the assumption that mature economies mostly lacked business groups (with the corollary implication that business groups would disappear as economies matured). The explanatory challenge then was to uncover the institutions (or missing institutions) and politics that existed in poor countries but not in rich ones. The resulting list of differences was long and subject to a lot of fruitful debate: shallow capital markets (Leff, 1978), authoritarian politics, economies of scope (Amsden, 1992), industrial policy (Schneider, 2009), missing informational intermediaries (Khanna and Palepu, 1997), and the list goes on (Khanna and Yafeh, 2010; Colpan and Hikino, 2010, for reviews). Many of these factors have some relevance for the analysis of business in rich countries, especially earlier in the twentieth century when these countries were themselves industrializing. Although beyond the scope of this chapter, the comparison of factors that have the most analytic purchase in both rich and poor economies is a priority for future scholarship.

Another challenge in the comparative analysis of business groups is to take some of the factors deemed important in understanding business groups in rich countries to see what relevance they could have for the analysis of their counterparts in relatively poor countries. Theories related to PRT and labor power would seem to have the least relevance, as labor unions and statutory representation through mechanisms like codetermination have been weak or nonexistent in most developing countries. Issues in VoC related to patient capital and worker skills might have some relevance to business-group strategies in developing countries, though few business groups there rely on highly skilled workers with long tenure. Industrial policy could have similar effects across rich and poor economies, especially considering earlier periods in European history when states intervened more. Industrial policy also continues under various guises, especially related to defense (United States) and energy (Europe).

To close on a speculative note, the early twenty-first-century evolution of giant technology firms like Apple, Google/Alphabet, Facebook, and Amazon may be the beginning of a new wave of business groups. These firms established dominance in different software platforms, which in turn generated large cash reserves that these firms used to buy up related competitors and unrelated tech firms. From one perspective, any acquired firm that relies heavily on software could be seen as a related firm. However, from another view, cloud-computing for Amazon or driverless cars for Google take them into unknown markets, new products, and distinct technological challenges, and could thus be considered unrelated to their core business. Future expansions and acquisitions by these tech giants should tell us more about whether and how they are evolving into diversified business groups.

ACKNOWLEDGMENTS

We are grateful to Laura Chirot for research assistance, and to Michael Witt and workshop participants at Kyoto University and Harvard Business School for feedback on earlier versions of this chapter.

APPENDIX

	Number of firms in top 20		Percentage of firms in top 20
Country	Diversified business group	Subsidiaries within or affiliates of diversified business groups	Diversified business groups or subsidiaries or affiliates
Australia	0	0	0%
Britain	3	1	20%
Belgium	3	8	55%
Canada	2	2	20%
France	2	7	25%
Germany	5	5	50%
Italy	3	11	60%
Japan	0	6	30%
Netherlands	1	3	15%
Portugal	2	8	50%
Spain	2	10	60%
Sweden	1	16	75%
United States	1	0	5%

Data: The list of top-20 firms in each country in 1995, ranked by market capitalization of common equity, is based on the database collated by and described in La Porta et al., 1999. We coded the firms that were (1) themselves diversified business groups (e.g., Sweden's Investor and Germany's Viag), or (2) subsidiaries within or affiliates of diversified business groups (e.g., Sweden's Atlas Copco, controlled by the Wallenberg family, or Italy's Benetton, which is not itself diversified but is held by Edizione, a financial holding company with interests across various industries). For Japan, we only included horizontal keiretsu groups that have members in unrelated business fields. The rightmost column shows the percentage of firms in the top 20 that are diversified or associated with diversified business groups.

CHAPTER 4

....

BUSINESS GROUPS AS
NETWORKS

....

JAMES R. LINCOLN AND MATTHEW SARGENT

4.1 INTRODUCTION

....

In a definition most scholarship on the topic has come to accept, Granovetter (2005:
95) defined business groups as a set of legally independent firms linked to one another
in "formal and/or informal" ways. This is a broad definition of a business group as an
interfirm network. A casual perusal of the scholarly literature on business groups
reveals much attention to network properties and processes. In our view, however,
most business-group scholars have yet to engage in a rigorous way with the concept of
network and to exploit in their research the considerable power of network models and
methods. This chapter explores how business groups can be viewed as networks;
whether and how some groups are more "network-like" than others; and how formal
network concepts and analytic methods may facilitate the study of a number of salient
problems in business-group research.[1]

There is general consensus among business-group researchers that the literature
suffers from a lack of close attention to problems of group internal structure. This was

---

[1] This chapter deals with network-type business groups as described in Chapter 1, and further
suggests the network characteristics of a hierarchical variety of business groups including diversified
business groups. We acknowledge that our use of the term "network" in multiple senses may at points
confuse readers. First, we contend that all (or nearly all) business groups are "networks" (in the broadest
structuralist sense of interlinked nodes). Then we suggest that some groups are "pyramidal" and others
"horizontal" (network-like) in the narrower morphological sense of whether chains of ties flow vertically
or laterally. Finally, we refer to an even smaller subset of business groups that display to some degree the
idealized "network form" defined not just in morphological terms but also in functional and
performance terms. We regret the potential for confusion here, but the application of the term
"network" to a variety of overlapping yet distinct organizational phenomena did not originate with us
(on this point, see also Podolny and Page, 1998).

the shared view of the participants at a panel session on business groups organized by the editors and senior author at the 2009 Strategic Management Society in Washington, DC. The typical quantitative empirical study in this literature treats a firm's affiliation with a group as an "all or nothing" dichotomy. The unstated and perhaps unintended assumption is that affiliates are all alike in the degree to which they participate in, identify with, and are controlled by the group. Some research on business groups, the pyramidal sort in particular, does give close attention to the relative positioning of firms within chains of ownership and control relations (see Bertrand et al., 2002; Belenzon and Berkovitz, 2010). Yet often the end result of such nuanced measurement is a simple binary coding of whether the firm is in a pyramid or not (Chittoor, Kale, and Puranam, 2015).

Much of the value of the network lens when applied to the study of business groups is that it forces the analyst to unpack the coarse dichotomy of "group" and "stand-alone" into its constituent relations, equivalences, and complementarities. Network analysis enables the identification and measurement of structural properties of networks shown by research in a variety of settings to shape those networks' operation and performance. Several of these are germane to the study of business groups and appear in various guises in the research literature but rarely with the analytic rigor and theoretic clarity provided by the network lens.

The broad multidisciplinary literature on business groups commonly alludes to and analyzes the network characteristics of groups of a wide variety of kinds. Yet it also often draws a distinction between "hierarchical" groups—centrally coordinated, pyramidally shaped, and sharply bounded—and "network" groups—decentralized, horizontally linked, and porously bounded. This is a meaningful and useful dichotomy both in how it factually divides the world of business groups and in its implications for theory and research regarding them. We devote a major section of this chapter early on to exploring it. But we will also attempt to demonstrate that network groups differ from pyramidal groups more in degree than in kind. *All* business groups and many stand-alone firms as well are in fact structured as networks and can fruitfully be analyzed as such (Podolny and Page, 1998). Some—the Korean chaebol, say—are indeed more centralized and vertically coordinated than others, such as the Japanese keiretsu or Taiwanese *qiye jituan* (Hamilton and Biggart, 1988; Chang, 2003). But these differences are best understood as variations along a set of continuous structural dimensions, not apples-and-oranges differences that thwart thoughtful comparison. We will also suggest that the outward appearance of hierarchy and centralization frequently conceals a more flexible underlying reality.

The chapter is laid out as follows. We first review a variety of corporate phenomena from integrated, divisionalized corporations to clusters of strategic alliances that might or might not be viewed as groups. We then consider how attention to such formal network analytic properties as density, connectivity, centrality, and clustering may facilitate business-group research. We finally examine the concept of a "network form," an ideal type that considerable popular and scholarly writing views as a leading-edge mode of business organizing in the global economy.

4.2 IMAGES OF BUSINESS GROUPS: VERTICAL AND HORIZONTAL NETWORKS

Definitions of business groups often explicitly refer to them as "clusters" of interconnected firms (Granovetter, 2005; Khanna and Yafeh, 2005; Morck, 2010; Jones, this volume). The implication is that interfirm ties within the group do not differ in kind from the ties that surround it. Both inside and outside groups of resource exchange, ownership, governance, kinship, information flow, etc., exist. "Groups" are simply patterns in which firms are linked to one another through ties that are denser, closer, stronger, more multiplex, more direct, and more similar than is true of the network as a whole. Thus, the boundaries of groups are not hard and clear but are rather vague, permeable, and transitory. Khanna and Rivkin (2006) describe groups metaphorically as "icebergs" in a sea of economic relations. Lincoln and Gerlach (2004: ch. 3) similarly characterize the generally amorphous Japanese keiretsu as "gravitational fields" in which some firms are situated at the core of the field (e.g., Mitsubishi Corporation) while others hover around the periphery (Honda in relation to the Mitsubishi Group).

Thus, there are zones within a business group's gravitational field such that it is difficult to say with certainty whether any given firm is "in" the group or "out." Colli and Vasta in this volume creatively measure the boundaries of Italian business groups in such a zonal fashion. Unlike most studies that use ownership as the lead criterion of group affiliation, they "take interlocking directorates as proxy of the existence of a formal link between two companies" (18). They apply a kind of confidence interval to gauging the assignment of firms to groups. The upper bound of the interval—unambiguous assignment—is the placement of a high-level executive of firm A on the board of firm B. The lower bound—weak assignment—is satisfied by the less stringent criterion of any kind of interlock between the two firms' boards (e.g., a direct but lower-level interlock; an indirect interlock wherein a third party sits on both boards).

4.2.1 Vertical (Pyramidal) and Horizontal ("Network-Type") Groups

The principal distinction in taxonomies of business groups turns on the structure of their underlying networks. On the one hand, there are centralized, vertically structured groups, often referred to as "pyramids." On the other, there are decentralized, horizontally linked groups, often referred to as "network-type" or sometimes "alliance" groups. We discuss each in turn.

4.2.1.1 *Pyramidal Groups*

Pyramidal groups are defined by the asymmetric chains of equity ties that convey control indirectly but expansively from an apex holding company or founding family to firms at the base or periphery of the pyramid. The constituent companies are independent legal entities in that they have their own charters, issue their own stock, and maintain their own boards, but are nonetheless largely if not wholly controlled by one or more entities higher in the pyramid. Such centralized control is assumed more than demonstrated. Alternatively, such control may be manifested in the decisions on which shareholders are entitled to vote, but it may not pass through to the day-to-day business decisions made by operating managers of the affiliate firms.

Much of the research on pyramidal groups in the finance literature views them negatively, as devices for entrenching family owners and consolidating their control over the numerous enterprises in which their equity stakes—"cash-flow rights"—are small. The evidence from econometric studies appears substantial that pyramidal groups expropriate minority shareholders, clandestinely channeling wealth away from firms low in the pyramid to the apex firm or family. Some recent research, however, challenges the finding that tunneling is what pyramidal groups are all about. Siegel and Choudhury (2013) replicate the much-cited Bertrand et al. (2002) study of tunneling in Indian business groups with improved data and a more rigorous statistical methodology and fail to find evidence of tunneling. Siegel and Choudhury in fact find that Indian-ownership pyramidal groups outperform stand-alone firms, succeeding because, they believe, of the groups' "recombinant capabilities": the capacity to mix, match, and synergize a set of industrially diverse firms linked to one another through the groups' internal networks.

Other studies suggest that the literature on pyramids and tunneling has the causality backward. Almeida et al. (2010) and Bunkanwanicha et al. (2014) find in studies of the Korean chaebol and Thai banks that financial stress and low market valuation may be the cause, not the consequence, of such firms' positioning within the network of equity ties. Groups place such firms in peripheral positions in the pyramid in order to minimize spillover risks to other affiliates.

4.2.1.2 *Horizontal Groups*

The other principal kind of group, horizontal or network-type, has no one firm or holding company or founding family in a clear apex or controlling position in a network of ownership and control relations. As opposed to the vertical, inverted "tree" structure of downward branching equity ties distinctive of pyramidal groups, dispersed, horizontal, and reciprocal cross-shareholdings and interlocking directorates distinguish the horizontal groups.

As the editors of this volume suggest, the Japanese keiretsu is perhaps the best known and most studied example of a horizontal network group. The keiretsu are also the kind of group on which we have done the most research and about which we are most knowledgeable (Lincoln and Gerlach, 2004). Many of our examples in the following pages thus draw on our familiarity with the keiretsu.

Horizontal groups are sometimes termed "alliance" groups (Gerlach, 1992). The implication is that the affiliated firms enjoy more managerial autonomy than in a vertical group, and the coordination and strategic orientation of the group are collectively determined through a network process of aggregating members' strategic choices and operational decisions. Yet horizontal groups are not, strictly speaking, strategic alliances, which are voluntary partnerships of two or more firms aimed at the pursuit of mutual strategic aims. First, most business groups—as highly diversified conglomerate-type entities—do not have the focused and publicly stated goals that distinguish a strategic alliance.

Secondly, unlike a strategic alliance, which we later discuss in greater depth, firms in horizontal groups mostly do not freely elect to affiliate with or participate in the group. Their entry often results from historically and situationally based events of an unanticipated and adventitious sort. Toyota Group members Denso and Toyota Motor Sales, for example, began life as divisions of Toyota Motor Corporation. They were spun off at the behest of TMC's banks in the late 1940s following the automaker's brush with bankruptcy. Fellow affiliate Daihatsu, by contrast, transitioned from stand-alone firm to Toyota keiretsu member when the smaller automaker fell upon financial distress in the 1960s and was bailed out by TMC with an equity stake and other resource transfers. Daihatsu's integration in and subsequent domination by the Toyota Group was not on the whole welcomed by the smaller firm (Ahmadjian and Lincoln, 2001).

Members of a horizontal group need not enjoy complete or even substantial autonomy. The cross-shareholdings typical of such groups are sufficiently small that no one firm is likely to have a controlling stake in any other. But the group as a whole may readily accumulate such control through its aggregate ownership of every individual member firm. Reported instances of the horizontal keiretsu forcing changes on troubled or errant affiliates are not uncommon (see the discussion of the "Mitsukoshi" incident in Gerlach, 1992).

4.2.1.3 *Non-family Groups: Bank- and Trading-Company-Centered*

What determines whether some business groups are configured as decentralized, horizontally linked networks while others take the pyramidal form? Idiosyncratic factors such as culture, institutional setting, and historical circumstance play enormous roles. The rebuilding of the Japanese political economy under US occupation oversight had much to do with the elimination of pyramidal groups from that country and their replacement by the flexible webs of intercorporate relations known as keiretsu (Lincoln and Shimotani, 2010). Another likely factor in the network structuring of the keiretsu was the relative unimportance in comparison to other Asian countries of kinship ties in Japanese business networks (Mehrotra et al., 2013).

Indeed, perhaps the single most important explanatory factor in whether a group takes on the pyramidal or network morphology is the level of founding family ownership and control. In network terms, the question is whether two specific corporate ties—kinship and ownership—suffice to configure the network, or whether the network is more "multiplex" such that relations of diverse content get equal weight. Multiplex networks exhibit intersecting and overlapping channels of communication and control and thus reduced verticality and centralized control. Multiplexity also implies that the ties that configure the network shift with the industry, location, period, and other contextual circumstances. Thus, which actors occupy the center and how long they remain there are apt to be more variable and contingent than in a group built around fewer ties.

Groups at whose peak or core resides, not a family of owners, entrepreneurial firms, or holding company, but a professionally managed legal entity are more likely to cohere as webs of varied and distinct interfirm relations and thus be flexibly coordinated as networks. As several chapters in this volume testify, business groups centered on trading companies and banks often display such network characteristics. Geoffrey Jones's historical treatment of the British case in this volume observes that groups formed around trading companies such as Swire had two rings of affiliated firms. The inner ring comprised the wholly owned divisions and subsidiaries of the trading company. The outer ring subsumed "a cluster of partly owned firms linked not only by equity, but also debt, management, cross directorships, and trading relationships." Such a two-tier network form is evidenced as well in the post-millennium vertical keiretsu clusters that persist in Japan today. With one exception—Denso—the Toyota Group's inner circle (Aisin Seiki, Kanto, Toyota Motor Sales, Daihatsu, Hino, etc.) is composed of majority-owned subsidiaries of Toyota Motor Corporation. But the affiliates below this elite tier connect to one another loosely through the types of ties identified by Jones (Ahmadjian and Lincoln, 2001). Similar centripetal-centrifugal tendencies have in recent years transformed other Japanese vertical groups as well, notably Panasonic (Guillot and Lincoln, 2005).

Powerful banks have combined lending, shareholding, and director interlocks to position themselves at the nexus of constellations of industrial firms. Like other bank-centered groups, such clusters exhibit network-like attributes. Regarding the German economy, Schröter in this volume writes: "Not even Marxist historians claimed that banks formed an (unitary) *entity* with their client firms. [They] spoke of 'families' but not of enterprise." He acknowledges, however, that some banks did exert top-down control over their client enterprises. He further observes that in the last twenty years the rationale behind German bank shareholdings shifted away from network control and coordination to pure financial investment. Thus, as presently constituted, the German bank-centered networks bear little resemblance to the usual understanding of a business group.

Larsson and Petersson's chapter describes the Swedish Handelsbanken group in similar multiplex network terms as "held together by an intrinsic system of cross-wise ownership in combination with strong personal networks and pensions funds, primarily consisting of professional top managers." Their account of the family-centered Wallenberg group, by contrast, fits the portrait of a centrally controlled pyramidal group.

4.2.2 Groups as "Social Constructions"

Whether hierarchical or horizontal in structuring, the business groups discussed so far conform to the usual "network" definition of a cluster of firms bound by formal and informal ties. However, groups may be defined and identified by other criteria as well. Khanna and Rivkin (2006) suggest that many groups are "social constructions," such that their interfirm ties matter less for cohesion and coordination than their shared history, values, legitimacy, and reputation in the eyes of external audiences. Khanna and Rivkin also suggest that the naming of groups and the listing of their members in archival databases reflect those socially constructed identities:

> As products of social construction, groups probably cannot be reduced to specific types of ties between firms, such as equity holdings, family bonds, or director interlocks. Nonetheless, interfirm ties play a role in the process of social construction, and... field observers of groups have consistently identified groups with particular types of ties.

Thus, business groups may both be "taken for granted" socially and culturally constructed categories as well as clusters of interfirm ties. Depending on the period and the circumstances, however, the two principles of organizational identity may diverge or converge.

Clearly, business groups are defined and supported by the shared identities and cultures that their affiliates take on. Cultures are apt to be particularly strong and established in large, old, and highly institutionalized groups such as Mitsubishi, Samsung, Tata, and Wallenberg. Much of the cohesion of the Tata Group, for example, derives from the values of social responsibility and philanthropy that are institutionalized in the charter of Tata Trust, the holding company in which affiliate shareholding is concentrated (Chittoor, Narain, Vyas, and Tolia, 2013). As Khanna and Rivkin (2006) suggest, such group cultures may transcend and outlive the concrete ties among member firms. Japan's horizontal keiretsu have in large measure unraveled as network clusters since the asset bubble burst in 1992 (Lincoln and Gerlach, 2004), but their identities persist as cultural categories maintained by brands, logos, and reputation. This is especially true of the Mitsubishi group and, to a lesser degree, the Sumitomo group, historically the most cohesive of the "big six" horizontal keiretsu (Gerlach, 1992).

Conversely, cross-shareholdings, main bank relations, co-location, employee and resource transfers, etc., may persist even when identifiable "groups" as nominal or cultural categories are not in evidence. As *The Economist* (2015) wrote of Prime Minister Abe's recent efforts to reform the still deeply ingrained network rigidities of the Japanese economy:

> Japan's corporate-governance revolution has had many false dawns... Only 274 of some 40,000 directorships are held by foreigners. A mesh of shareholdings still binds big firms together. Japan's business lobby group, Keidanren, fought to dilute the new reforms. The banks still keep weak companies afloat: the fact that not one of Japan's listed firms went bankrupt last year, for the first time since 1991, reflects not just a zippier economy, but also lenders' clubby ties to borrowers.... Hobbesian, Japan is not.

Thus, cross-cutting keiretsu-type horizontal ties remain institutional fixtures of the Japanese economy, despite reforms in disclosure and governance and the general disintegration of the bounded groups themselves.

Whether groups are viewed as network clusters or social constructions has implications for how they can be studied. In the first view, the usual methodology is an inquiry that gathers data on interfirm ties and infers groups from a network analysis of those ties; how indirect versus direct they are; how symmetric and reciprocated versus asymmetric; how dense, connected, and clustered are the surrounding network environments.

In the second view, the researcher needs a measure of group affiliation that has cultural and institutional meaning distinct from the tie data (trade, debt, etc.) that trace interfirm relations. Archival, often officially designated, designations of groups are widely relied upon in business-group studies. It is not clear, however, that they have independent criterion validity. The designations of group names and affiliate lists provided by an official or other formally prepared directory may be merely impressionistic filterings of information on equity and director ties, name, trade and lending patterns, family connections, and the like. Still, some such nominal classifications may satisfy the criterion of independent cultural validity. Khanna and Rivkin claim this to be true of the official Chilean group affiliate lists they utilize in a 2006 study. They suggest that the records of that country's business groups since its financial crisis in the 1980s have been carefully compiled and accurately represent the groups' standing as Chilean socioeconomic/cultural categories.

4.3 THE STRUCTURAL (NETWORK) ANALYSIS OF GROUPS

We now consider in a somewhat more formalistic fashion the relevance of network analysis for the study of business groups. Specifically, we discuss a number of network properties at varying levels of aggregation—node or actor positioning, dyadic and triadic ties, subnetwork clusters, and whole networks. We then examine various measures and models of these properties that are part of the standard repertoire of network analysis along with examples of business-group research that have productively utilized them.

Merely because a network property appears and is measurable at a given level of aggregation does not mean that its causes and effects can be assumed fixed at that network level. Macrostructures such as "groups" may emerge from processes operating at lower levels, such as nodes and dyads. Those structures, that is, are derivative of the network positioning and bilateral relations of the individual firms (Asanuma, 1985; Khanna and Rivkin, 2006). The multilevel configuring of networks demands that their study be guided by a rule of parsimony. If micro-level relational processes suffice to explain the aggregate patterns, there may in fact be little need, as Khanna and Rivkin (2006) suggest, for the concept of "group."

4.3.1 Node-Level Properties

We reduce to the concept of "centrality" several nodal properties pertaining to the positioning of individual actors within networks. Much network research examines the causes and consequences of a single actor's positioning in the network. A variety of concepts and measures describe that positioning, but all deal with the extent to which the actor can access through chains of relations other nodes and network segments.

An application in the business-group literature is an important recent paper by Almeida et al. (2010), who used a centrality measure to index the total direct and indirect control (voting rights) through equity ties accruing to an affiliate firm. Their measure was designed for the Korean chaebol and other groups wherein horizontal cross-shareholding supplements vertical chains (La Porta et al., 1999). They find central firms to be less profitable and valuable than firms higher in the pyramid but less central in the network overall. Chang (cited in Granovetter, 2005) finds a similar tendency for affiliates on the periphery of the chaebol to enjoy higher profitability. Such a pattern accords with network research outside the business group context that reveals central actors generally having less autonomy and power than actors with fewer but more diverse and expansive ties (Cook, Emerson, and Gillmore, 1983; Burt, 1992).

In keeping with this reasoning, some conceptualizations and measures of centrality focus less on the number of ties into and out of an actor—too many such ties being seen as constraining—and rather on the extent to which actors are positioned so as to mediate or broker relations among others (Bonacich, 1987; Burt, 1992). This was the approach of Vedres and Stark's (2010) study of business groups in Hungary, which focused on "structural folds" in the network: the overlaps of clusters. "Actors at the structural fold," they write, "are multiple insiders, facilitating familiar access to diverse resources." Vedres and Stark found stronger financial performance among Hungarian firms occupying such overlap positions.

4.3.2 Dyad-Level Properties

The irreducible, elementary particle of any network is the "tie," a relation represented graphically by a line connecting a *dyad*— a pair of actors (or nodes). The larger network is then analyzable as aggregations and clusterings of dyadic ties.

4.3.2.1 *Direct/Indirect*

A direct tie means that an observable formal or informal link exists between a pair of actors. One firm is a major shareholder in the other, for example, or has placed a director on the other's board. A direct kinship tie exists if the CEO's or other executives of the two firms are from the same family (Luo and Chung, 2005). Direct transactional ties exist if one firm sells to or lends to another.

A distinctive feature of networks, however, is the many *indirect* paths or channels through which actors connect to one another. Resources, information, and control flow from firm A to firm B, say, through chains of dyadically linked intermediaries. The length of the shortest such chain measures the network "distance" or, conversely, the proximity between the pair (Knoke and Kuklinski, 1982).

A common and useful network analytic strategy is to represent proximities spatially so that directly linked actors are adjacent in network space, and actors indirectly linked through longer chains are proportionally more distant.

The question of direct versus indirect linkage of the affiliate firms has received close attention in the business-group literature. Clusters of firms may derive their cohesion and coherence from indirect linkage. Lincoln, Gerlach, and Takahashi (1992) analyzed indirect and direct equity and board interlock ties among large Japanese groups in the 1990s. The empirical evidence for groups in their data varied with whether the connection analyzed was purely direct (A owns 10 percent of B) or indirect as well (A owns B, which in turn owns C). The boundaries of groups were not discernible in the analysis of direct trade relations but they emerged clearly when indirect links were allowed.

Colli and Vasta perform a network analysis of a similar sort for their chapter in this volume. They provide two pictorial mappings of the "network neighborhood" of the Italian automaker Fiat. One utilizes direct board interlock links; a second considers interlock paths of length two (one intermediary). As expected, the Fiat network is revealed as much more crowded in the latter case.

4.3.2.2 *Multiplexity*

A second dyad-level property with implications for business group research is *multiplexity*, the number of distinct contents bundled into a relationship. As discussed above, the formal and informal ties that join firms in groups are highly varied. How ties of diverse content combine or unravel across economic and institutional environments has been a core theme of business-group research. Luo and Chung (2005), for example, find for Taiwan that, during the turbulent transition from a highly regulated and centrally controlled economy to a market-based and open one, the linkage of executives by kinship and other similar "particularistic" ties played a heightened role in the performance of the firms.

Multiplexity is an aspect of tie "strength" (Granovetter, 1973), and groups built on networks of multiplex ties can be presumed more cohesive and durable than groups grounded in single-content ties. Thus, multiplexity may offset deficits in network cohesion of other sorts. A sparsely linked network is more cohesive, for example, to the extent that its constituent ties are multiplex. An illustration from the keiretsu case is apropos: as compared to the chaebol and other closely linked hierarchical groups, the network densities of the Japanese groups were low. (This was in part due to legal rules.

Banks were forbidden until 1997 to hold shares larger than 5 percent in industrial clients.) But the ties among the affiliate firms were multiplex: overlaying cross-shareholdings were director and other personnel transfers, presidents' council and supplier association affiliations, co-location (e.g., Mitsubishi firms headquartered in the Marunouchi district of Tokyo), and shared corporate culture and identity. Lincoln and Gerlach's (2004: ch. 3) blockmodeling of the Japanese large-firm network from 1980 to 1998 exploits this multiplexity in extracting clusters based on eight distinct ties: the i -> j and j -> i sides of trade, lending, equity, and board connections. Groups inferred from data on multiplex ties, they reasoned, have a firmer basis in reality than clusters derived from single-stranded ties.

4.3.2.3 Symmetry and Reciprocity

Related to whether ties are direct or indirect is whether they are symmetric or reciprocated. This, too, is an important relational property that features importantly in network-analytic business-group research. "Pyramids" are defined by the unidirectional chains of equity ties that convey control indirectly but exhaustively from an apex holding company or founding family to firms positioned at the base or periphery of the network. By contrast, network-type groups such as the horizontal keiretsu are distinguished by high rates of direct reciprocal cross-shareholding.

Japan's vertical manufacturing keiretsu have pyramidal structures of this sort. An apex firm (e.g., Toyota, Hitachi) takes equity stakes in and dispatches directors and technicians to second-tier firms, which link similarly to third-tier firms, and so on down the vertically ordered chain. In the horizontal keiretsu, by contrast, lateral cross-shareholding was the prevailing pattern. The South Korean chaebol exemplify a third pattern. Direct reciprocity of equity ties is illegal, but indirect reciprocity, built into circular ownership chains, is conspicuously present (Chang and Hong, 2000; Almeida et al., 2010).

Among the reasons for the asymmetric sequencing of ties observed in many business groups is that the affiliate firms are arrayed along a supply chain sequenced by value-added stage in a production process. In such a chain, the entire network of asymmetric ownership and control ties functions as a governance structure superimposed upon an economic division of labor. Asanuma (1985: 2) offered such a transaction cost explanation for the keiretsu as a counterpoint to the then-common view that the Japanese groups were legacy institutions devoid of contemporary economic functionality:

> Whereas the conventional view has tended to regard keiretsu...as remnants of feudalist relations or derivatives of the cultural peculiarities of the Japanese, the most important explanatory variable should be the kind and nature of the transaction of goods or services conducted beneath each of these relations.

Khanna and Rivkin (2006: 8) argue similarly that groups arise endogenously from attempts by firms to monitor and regulate exchange relations through governance structures. They write: "The bonds put in place to forestall opportunistic behavior may lead to confederations of firms that outsiders then perceive as groups." Their reasoning supports our point that network structures at the macro-level ("groups") are often rooted in micro-level (e.g., dyadic) network processes.

That the ownership and control ties key to the structuring of business groups might be efficient solutions to the failures of markets clearly represents a very different portrait of the business group phenomenon from the negative one of groups as devices for "tunneling," entrenchment, and expropriation (Siegel and Choudhury, 2013).

4.3.3 Properties of Whole Networks and Subnetworks

4.3.3.1 *Density*

Network density is the ratio of direct ties in the network to potential ties (the number of dyads). It is the most commonly used measure of network cohesion. A maximally dense network is one in which direct ties interconnect all nodes. Business groups vary widely in the densities of their interfirm networks: the horizontal keiretsu have been low on this structural dimension, for example, while the chaebol and Indian family-based groups are high.

Mahmood and his colleagues have made some important attempts to measure with precision the network properties of Asian business groups. In one paper on Taiwanese business groups they model the association of affiliate firm innovativeness with the densities of several interfirm ties: shareholdings, director interlocks, and buyer-supplier trade (Mahmood, Chung, and Mitchell, 2013). They find no significant effects of the equity and director densities, but that of within-group buyer-supplier links proved a significant predictor at a decelerating rate of the patenting productivity of affiliate firms. They interpret the density of buyer–supplier links as a proxy for "combinatorial opportunity." Their results in general align with other work that finds positive but ultimately diminishing returns to network embeddedness: at some threshold level the returns to cohesion are exhausted as constraint and rigidity set in (Uzzi, 1996; Luo and Chung, 2005).

4.3.3.2 *Connectivity*

Connectivity is the ratio of direct and *indirect* ties to the number of dyads, the number of potential ties. A maximally dense network (= 1.0) is a maximally connected one, but full connectivity is also compatible with low levels of density.

The concept of a pyramidal group rests on an assumption of vertically ordered connectivity. The group is fully connected vertically through chains of ownership and control ties emanating from an apex firm, family, or holding company. Pyramidal groups differ from horizontally networked groups in that lateral and reciprocal ties are minimized (Belenzon and Berkovitz, 2010). The usual approach to the measurement of pyramidal structures combines three distinct network properties: (1) the ratio of connectivity to density in the equity network; (2) the asymmetry or verticality of equity ties; and (3) the magnitude of the ties—specifically, the extent to which they exceed the

10-percent threshold commonly assumed to confer voting rights control. A potentially more informative analytical approach, we suggest, is to unpack the pyramid dummy by entering these three component structural variables and their interactions in regressions predicting performance outcomes such as sales growth, profitability, and Tobin's Q. The analyst could then ascertain what precisely it is about the pyramid—its verticality, connectivity, asymmetry, or magnitude of pairwise linkage—that conditions such performance outcomes.

4.3.3.3 *Centralization*

The counterpart to centrality at the node or actor level is centralization at the level of the network as a whole: the extent to which ties issue from one or few central actors and how direct and indirect they are. A long stream of research on groups and organizations finds centralized networks to be more efficient but also more rigid and decentralized ones more flexible and conducive to innovation (Burns and Stalker, 1961). These results, however, are contingent, varying strongly with the environment, goals, capabilities of the actors, and other moderating variables. Centralized networks are in general better performers in stable and homogeneous environments, whereas decentralized networks are better adapted to volatile and heterogeneous environments.

Another recent study by Mahmood and colleagues (2013) uses a measure of centralization in the ownership network to predict profitability (return on assets) in a sample of Taiwanese business groups. The authors also include as regressors the densities of equity and directorate ties, a measure of family ownership, and a dummy variable for whether the group exhibits the pyramidal form. Of these only the centralization variable related significantly to return on assets, its coefficient being positive. Centralization also interacted positively with the group's industrial diversification (suggestive of a greater coordination burden) and negatively with a dummy for the post-2008 global financial shock (indicative of a turbulent economic environment).

4.3.3.4 *Clustering and Boundaries*

A distinctive structural feature of many networks is "lumpiness." Ties and connections are not spread evenly over nodes but are instead *clustered*, concentrated in some regions of the network and absent or sparse in others. At the extreme of clustering, the network is fragmented into separate subnetworks or "islands," each tight-knit in density, connectivity, and multiplexity terms. As noted earlier, networks that are highly clustered but well connected via inter-cluster links display the informationally efficient "small world" structure (Watts, 1999).

Mani and Moody (2014) report a blockmodel clustering of ownership ties in the Indian corporate network in 2001 and 2005. They analyze 44,528 pairings of Indian firms and domestic shareholders, the latter comprising firms as well as individual shareholders. Their unit of analysis, however, is the interfirm dyad, which may thus be connected either directly by a firm-to-firm equity tie or indirectly, as when two firms have a third-party shareholder in common. Their cluster analysis empirically revealed a distinct three-level tiering of the network, each tier of which was organized around a different network principle. They describe it as comprising:

> ...a disconnected periphery that conforms to the disconnected networks implied by classical transactional models; a semiperiphery characterized by small, dense clusters with sporadic links, similar to that predicted in "small world" models; and finally a nested core composed of deeply reconnected clusters that echoes the unequal involvement insights of the scale-free literature.

Assigned to the "nested core" of their mapping of the network were the large Indian groups such as Tata. Positioned at the periphery as often isolated dyads and triads were small, regionally based groups.

4.3.3.5 *Clustering Criteria: Cohesion versus Structural Equivalence*

An alternative lens on how groups correspond to network clusters views them as positions or "blocks" whose member firms are "structurally equivalent." Actors are structurally equivalent to the extent that they are similarly positioned in networks; i.e., their direct and indirect ties to others are the same. A pair of nodes may be structurally equivalent yet not directly tied, although indirect ties are necessarily implied. In the business-group literature, firms' ties to third-party actors such as the state, founding families, and foreign investors reveal groups as positions in structural equivalence terms (e.g., Siegel, 2007).

Japan's horizontal keiretsu derived their definition less from internal cohesion than from structural equivalence clustering. The interrelations among industrial firms were mostly sparse and weak compared to the dense and strong equity and director ties flowing to them from such financials as banks, brokerages, and insurance companies. Lincoln and Gerlach's (2004: ch. 3) clustering of large Japanese firms in the 1980s by the structural equivalence of their trade, lending, director, and equity ties accurately reproduced the horizontal and vertical keiretsu socially constructed categories—the names and affiliate lists supplied by institutional archives.

4.3.4 Capturing Group Evolution: Dynamic Clustering

An oft-noted limitation of network analysis is its static portrayal of structure. Networks are rendered as snapshots rather than motion pictures of an unfolding process. Clearly, the speed and trajectory of such dynamic processes matter for a full understanding of the business group form.

An example of business-group evolution is that of Japan's keiretsu networks over the decades following the bubble's burst, such that they are of mostly historical interest today. Lincoln and Gerlach (2004: ch. 3) address the "withering away" hypothesis with a series of blockmodel-type cluster analyses from 1978 to 1998 of the trade, lending, board, and equity ties among large Japanese financials and industrials. They observed clear declines across this period in the cohesion and definition of empirically derived clusters corresponding to the "socially constructed" groups.

A cluster analysis of business groups that takes the modeling of the dynamics of cohesion and dissolution farther is Vedres and Stark's (2010) interesting work on Hungarian business groups. Using longitudinal data, they study "lineages of cohesion" to detect how groups "reproduce[e] and exchange members across generations and maintain their coherence through interwoven lineages." They further ask how entrepreneurial effort and success by affiliate firms feed back to diminish or enhance the cohesion of the group. Their inquiry evokes Schumpeter's "creative destruction" theory. Some affiliate firms pursue innovations that deviate from the mainstream strategies of the group and in so doing undermine its long-term cohesion and viability.

Dynamic network analyses of the Vedres and Stark sort enable a researcher to grapple with the "groupness" in a set of interfirm relations with a temporal depth that cross-sectional snapshots cannot provide. The authors' thoughtful framing bears repeating here:

> The conventional graph snapshot of network analysis does not distinguish robust and stable collectivities from transitory alignments; it only enables the distinction between denser or sparser network regions.... Once we think of groups as histories of cohesion, however, ... [w]e can recognize groups despite temporary losses in density. In fact, we often find that the strategic separation between groups within larger units is only recognizable through historical analysis.

Network measures and models such as those discussed above have considerable power for the network analysis of business groups. Yet it is not always easy to tell from the network data and analysis alone whether a group is vertical or horizontal or within the groups which firms are in controlling positions and which are not. An example is La Porta, Lopez-de-Silanes, and Shleifer's (1999) demonstration using the Toyota Group of their methodology for mapping firms' vertical positions within a pyramidal group. By their coding rule, Mitsui financial institutions "controlled" Toyota Motor Corporation as they collectively held greater than 10 percent of Toyota's stock. That portrait is quite at odds with the common knowledge and evidence at the time that the Mitsui, Sanwa, and Tokai banks were more dependent on and under the control of TMC than the other way around. Sakura Bank (Mitsui) was in fact forced into a de facto acquisition by Sumitomo Bank in 2001 when TMC under then president Hiroshi Okuda spurned the bank's pleas for a financial rescue (Ahmadjian and Lincoln, 2001; Lincoln and Gerlach, 2004). The example makes clear that "control" in the narrow corporate governance sense of voting rights bestowed by ownership is not the same as general strategic and financial dependence in an interorganizational network (Pfeffer and Salancik, 1978).

4.4 BUSINESS GROUPS AS NETWORK FORMS

We shift now to a more focused discussion of business groups as network forms. By "network form" we mean a mode of organization that is more distinctive in structure and performance aspects than "network" or "network-type" as we and others use those terms to describe horizontally linked groups. The concept of network form is much discussed in organization theory and in the business press as well (Kanter, 1989; Powell, 1990; Perrow, 1992; Byrne, 1993; Ancona et al., 1996; Podolny and Page, 1998). It is portrayed as an effective mode of governing and orchestrating transactions that stands in contrast to the "market" and "hierarchy" dichotomy famously articulated by Oliver Williamson (1975). In his later work, Williamson (1999) himself embraced the general concept ("relational contracting") as a governance hybrid able to avert not only market failures but bureaucratic diseconomies as well. Network-form theorists such as Powell (1990), however, resist the suggestion that the network form is subsumed by the "hybrid" governance idea of late-stage transaction-cost economics. Neither markets nor hierarchies display network properties, such theorists argue, so no mere composite of the two can be said to constitute a network form.

Powell (1990) describes the network form as follows:

> Horizontal patterns of exchange, interdependent flows of resources, and reciprocal lines of communication.... Transactions occur neither through discrete [i.e., market based] exchanges nor by administrative fiat but through networks of [agents] engaged in reciprocal, preferential, mutually supportive actions ... Complementarity and accommodation are the corner stones of successful production networks. The entangling strings of reputation, friendship, interdependence, and altruism become integral parts of the relationship.

The network form as here defined is held to be an evolutionary advance in economic organization, superseding the sharply bounded, vertically integrated "command and control" hierarchies of the economic past. In network-form theory, such clusters of legally and often managerially independent companies are quite different from the family-controlled, regionally specific, emerging economy institutions to which business-group research has given so much empirical attention. Nor can they be dismissed as cultural/historical anomalies or legacy holdovers from an "adolescent" phase of economic development as Katz (1998) has claimed in regard to Japan. Business groups exhibiting the "network form" are, on the contrary, theorized as positioned at the forefront of economic evolution (Dore, 1983; Piore and Sabel, 1984; Perrow, 1992).

Much business in the modern global economy is organized in network forms. Today's ideally adapted global corporation is claimed to be a lean, specialized, and nimble player that satisfies its resource needs through flexible partnering with external providers, not by absorbing them into its administrative hierarchy as wholly owned divisions. Apple Computer and its supplier and other allied companies constitute a frequently cited case in point (Varian, 2007). Other global firms, notably Fiat and Corning Glass, operate more as coordinating nodes in strategic alliance clusters than as stand-alone firms (Nanda and Bartlett, 1990; Mitchell and Hohl, 2008). Even such large, diverse, and globally distributed corporations as IBM and Unilever have been portrayed as network forms, the autonomy and flexibility of their divisions approximating those of stand-alone firms (Ghoshal and Bartlett, 1990; Palmisano, 2006) and their interdivisional and functional coordination resting more on flexible intergroup and interpersonal networking than formal rules and executive fiat.

4.4.1 What Kinds of Business Groups Display the "Network Form"?

Our concern is with business groups, so the foremost question for us is: How prevalent among them is the "network form" defined in Powell's terms as a horizontally linked and flexibly coordinated cluster of interacting companies? An extreme view is that the "network form" is the dominant mode of business-group structuring. As webs of specialized, often small-to-medium scale, and separate but interdependent enterprises groups represent a functional alternative to the diversified and divisionalized but centrally controlled and coordinated "M-form" corporation (Colpan and Hikino, 2010; Lincoln and Shimotani, 2010). The reality, however, is that while all or most business groups are indeed networks in the structural sense of interlinked firms, many groups are as hierarchically configured and centrally controlled as any stand-alone corporation. Even among groups described as "network- or alliance-like," as we have done in the preceding pages, many do not meet the organization and performance criteria of the "network form." Thus, while some groups display the connectivity, symmetry, flexibility, synergy, and creativity that Powell and others ascribe to the ideal-type "network form," most other groups, whether pyramidal or otherwise in their outward morphology, clearly do not. In the following sections we consider several kinds of business groupings that appear to embody the "network form."

Many real-world business groups are conspicuous, not for their flexibly lateral coordination, but rather for their (often family-based) control. Yet we would also suggest that a surface appearance of pyramidal structuring and apex control may sometimes mask an underlying reality that is more subtle, flexible, and dynamic. A case in point is the Tata Group, whose interfirm network is explored in a detailed Indian School of Business case (Chittoor et al., 2013). Over the course of a restructuring spearheaded in the 1990s by incoming chief executive Ratan Tata, the Tata Group shifted from a loose horizontal keiretsu-like structure of sprawling cross-shareholdings and board interlocks to a less symmetric, vertical form in which most horizontal equity relations were eliminated. Under the new structure, most equity ties to member companies flowed downward from the group's two holding companies, Tata Sons and Tata Industries, the latter majority-owned by the former.

The new structure corresponds closely to the pyramidal form, but, as in the treatment of the Toyota case by La Porta et al., the appearance is deceiving. The reorganized Tata Group was, in fact, a fluidly coordinated "network form," a configuration that substantially improved alignment of strategies and operations across its many affiliated firms. The holding company coordinated the group through a combination of carrot (e.g., discounted HR, strategic, and legal services) and stick inducements (e.g., denial of use of the Tata name). Strong identity and reputation in India and a shared culture centered on social responsibility helped as well. But affiliate firms retained autonomy and could and did resist pressure from the holding companies to do the bidding of the group. A recent *Financial Times* article underscores the networking style of management exercised by the leadership of the group (Hill, 2011).

> Thanks to Ratan Tata's untangling of internal fiefs over the past 20 years, the Tata empire is doing well. The structure is still idiosyncratic. Tata's chairman exercises moral suasion, mainly through minority stakes, over 100 Tata companies, run by professional managers and independent boards. . . . As Ajay Bhalla of Cass Business School puts it, " . . . he has to be a good steward, rather than a hands-on manager, and stewardship is implemented through connection with various stakeholders."

The lesson to be drawn from these examples is that relative power in a business group is not reducible to the magnitude, connectivity, and sequencing of equity ties, useful as these relational dimensions are to an analysis of the structure of the group. The formalism of the network paradigm has its limitations. In reducing a range of distinct and complex social and economic structures to the common denominators of points and lines, the researcher can bring to bear on the analysis of those structures the leverage of a common conceptual framework and a rich set of methodological tools. The dilemma, however, is that formal network structures, however intriguing the patterns they display, may not be interpretable without a road map drawn from deep and nuanced contextual and institutional knowledge.

In the following sections (4.4.2–4.4.4), we discuss what we believe to be some distinctive examples of "network form" business groups.

4.4.2 The Industrial District as a Network-Form Business Group

There is wide agreement that vibrant industrial districts and technology clusters, of which Silicon Valley is the most celebrated example, instantiate the network form. In Piore and Sabel's (1984) influential theory of regional economic development, such systems of "flexible specialization" represent a "second industrial divide," one sharply distinct from the First Industrial Revolution that ushered in "Fordist" mass production and the large integrated, hierarchically coordinated corporation. Beyond Silicon Valley (Saxenian, 1996), Germany (Herrigel, 1994), Italy (Perrow, 1992), and Japan (Dore, 1983) afford famous examples of localized business clusterings whose network properties render them flexible, entrepreneurial, and dynamic but also conducive to economies of scale and scope.

Saxenian's (1996) comparison of the American high-tech districts of California's Silicon Valley and Massachusetts' Route 128 provides a colorful narrative of how the former enclave outperformed and outlasted the latter. Silicon Valley's configuring as a dynamic cluster of adjacent and connected but managerially autonomous producers, capital, and service providers, as well as universities and think tanks, infused the region with more diverse information flows, faster competitive response, and more innovative product and process development than the self-sufficient and inwardly focused Route 128 corporations (DEC, CDC, Data General) could achieve.

Schröter's chapter on Germany and Colli and Vasta's chapter on Italy in this volume further discuss how the enclaves of small- and medium-sized firms in southern Germany and northern Italy contributed much to the regional and national competitiveness of those countries.

4.4.3 The Keiretsu as a Network-Form Business Group

Japan's postwar horizontal and vertical keiretsu are often identified as loosely knit network groupings subject to little top-down control. Postwar Japan as a whole has in fact been portrayed in scholarly and journalistic writing as network-based. Not only the economy, but Japanese politics and civil society as well appear configured by thick networks of strong ties unguided by any "visible hand" of state or corporate or ruling-class control (Van Wolferen, 1990). In Lockwood's (1968: 503) memorable phrase, Japan is a "web with no spider." Relationships abound and networks layer upon networks, but no one hegemonic actor pulls the strings. An interesting if hard-to-test hypothesis, then, is that the loose interfirm linkage that distinguishes the keiretsu from business groups elsewhere both mirrors and derives from the network makeup of Japan as a whole.

A difficulty with this hypothesis is that the zaibatsu—the large, diversified business groups that dominated the modern Japanese economy until the end of World War II—were as centrally managed and imperatively coordinated as the family-led Korean chaebol of today (Hamilton and Biggart, 1988; Gerlach, 1992; Morck and Nakamura, 1999; Lincoln and Shimotani, 2010). The postwar transformation of the tight-knit zaibatsu into loose-knit keiretsu was an unintended consequence of American occupation efforts, first to democratize and decentralize Japan, and then, as Cold War tensions escalated, to unify and fortify it as a bulwark against communist expansion (Lincoln and Shimotani, 2010). The holding companies coordinating the groups were outlawed, the lead firms were broken up, controlling families lost their stakes, and top executive ranks were purged. Like business groups everywhere, then, the emergence of the keiretsu was grounded in some very specific historical and institutional circumstances (Guillén, 2000).

At the peak of Japanese economic prowess—the mid-1980s to early 1990s—admiring observers imputed many of the ostensible virtues of the network form to the horizontal and vertical keiretsu groupings. The horizontal group firms' stable equity and director interlocks were explained as efficient solutions to the classic corporate governance problem of how to monitor top management when shareholders are small, numerous, and dispersed (Thurow, 1993). The standout production efficiency, product quality, and development speed exhibited by Japanese automakers and their affiliated suppliers were cited as evidence for the organizational superiority of the vertical keiretsu mode of supply chain structuring over the time-honored American system of arms-length and adversarial supplier relations (Womack, Jones, and Roos, 1990).

Toyota is particularly famous among Japanese automakers for the organization of its suppliers into flexible networks able to take quick and decisive action in a bottom-up coordinated way (Dyer and Hatch, 2004). The Toyota keiretsu's network capabilities have been prominently displayed in times of crisis. In the late 1980s a fire on February 1, 1997, at a factory in Aichi Prefecture operated by Toyota Group affiliate Aisin Seiki, halted production of a critical brake component, the p-valve, which brought most Toyota domestic production to a standstill (Nishiguchi and Beaudet, 1998). Yet within days the Toyota keiretsu firms had revamped supply chains, shifted p-valve production to other plants, and through similar collaborative efforts restored output to normal levels. As Nishiguchi and Beaudet (1998: 49) conclude, much of this activity took place without the direct supervision of Toyota Motor itself:

> The Toyota model... involves more than a set of long-term relationships between a firm and a few select suppliers. As the Toyota group's collaborative response to the destruction of a key supplier's plant suggests, the relationships among the suppliers are equally important. More generally, a complex mix of institutions permits self-organization during crisis with little need for a leader's direct control.

A similar spurt of seemingly spontaneous yet finely tuned, coordinated action by Japanese supplier networks in response to a disaster transpired in the wake of the Tohoku region earthquake and tsunami in 2012 (Olcutt and Oliver, 2014). Key plants of several manufacturers in the region were shuttered. Horizontally orchestrated action by a diverse array of firms—some keiretsu partners, others direct competitors—restored production in a short period of time.

In our view, the close cooperation shown by keiretsu groupings in time of crisis and uncertainty dramatically illustrates the self-organizing capabilities attributed to the network form.

4.4.4 Strategic Alliance as a Network Form of Business Group

Strategic alliances appear to epitomize the network form. They are distinctive for their voluntarism—the freedom of the partners to enter and exit at will—but also for their putative cultures of sharing, mutual commitment, and support. These attributes are what theorists of the network form find progressive and attractive in the alliance idea. Collaboration and sharing replace the "fiat" and surveillance that mark divisional relations within the administrative hierarchy of a unitary firm. Strategic alliances also reduce the haggling and opportunism that mar the operation of arms-length markets. This is not to say that strategic alliances are devoid of opportunism. Alliances between competitors, for example, are prone to failure for this reason.

Strategic alliances are generally specialized affairs. They have well-defined and usually explicitly stated goals: joint R & D, consolidated production, coordinated marketing and distribution, and so on. Firms join in them because they believe that they lack the resources, skills, or connections to pursue such aims on their own.

Many strategic alliances are little more than public announcements by two or more firms that they will work together on common goals. The extent to which the firms are bound to one another through the kinds of links that build cohesion in business groups—equity ownership, director interlocks, family connections, resource and personnel transfers, and administrative bodies—is variable. Some highly formalized strategic alliances—joint ventures—lock the partners in through legal rules and common ownership and governance. Others are structured by written contracts and reciprocal equity stakes. Alliance teams and alliance managers are additional devices for coordination. Many alliances, however, get by with none of these.

Thus, the ideal strategic alliance is one rationally and deliberatively entered into by two or more firms that have conscientiously scanned the partner prospect pool and made a careful choice based on the assessed capabilities of the other and the potential for synergy. Yet the evidence is abundant that firms tend to choose alliance partners with whom they have preexisting direct or indirect ties (Gulati, 1998). Such ties include prior alliances, interlocking boards, co-location, family and school connections, and so on. These foster trust and reduce uncertainty (Keister, 1998), although they also reduce the size and diversity of the partner pool and thus the choice set for synergistic matching (Beckman, Haunschild, and Philips, 2004).

The majority of strategic alliances are dyadic—a partnership between a single pair of firms. Given this dyadic nature, the strategic alliance is perhaps best regarded as a type of tie, not in itself a cluster or group. Strategic alliances often function as a flexible governance structure that overlays a set of bilateral transactions (Williamson, 1999). They are thus akin to cross-shareholdings, director interlocks, friendship and kinship bonds, and other "relational contracting" ties.

These, of course, are the kinds of ties that engender cohesion and coordination within a business group, and certainly strategic alliances are prevalent among firms within groups. Co-affiliation is the kind of prior tie that strategic alliances need in order to launch and operate from a platform of trust and compatibility. Strategic alliances in the Japanese electronics industry, for example, were mostly done within, not across, the boundaries of the horizontal and vertical keiretsu groups until the turbulent post-bubble 1990s. Thereafter, R & D alliances in the industry were about as common outside as inside the keiretsu. Within-group alliances for other purposes, however—many aimed at consolidation and cost reduction—surged in numbers often at the behest of group lead firms (Lincoln and Choi, 2010; Lincoln, Guillot, and Sargent, 2017).

Strategic alliances are also a vehicle whereby whole business groups conduct transactions or pursue cooperative ventures with one another. A large-scale multilateral undertaking of this sort was the series of alliances that Japan's Mitsubishi Group pursued with Germany's Daimler companies in the 1980s (Lincoln and Gerlach, 2004).

Strategic alliance activity is prevalent in high-tech industrial districts, among firms whose production processes are intertwined in a supply chain, and among affiliates of an established business group. The prevalence of alliance ties is much of what distinguishes such clusters as "network forms." Apple Computer, a relatively lean corporation that for many years did none of its own manufacturing, is regularly portrayed as a leading-edge practitioner of alliance-style supply-chain management (Kanter, 1994; Varian, 2007).

Similarly, high-tech enclaves such as Silicon Valley and Cambridge, UK, display high rates of alliance activity. The proximity of the firms to one another and to supportive institutions such as venture capitalists, business service providers, and universities render alliances easy to form and to operate. Moreover, the participating firms in many cases are spin-offs of one another or of university research programs.

What kinds of strategic alliance clusters exist, and can they reasonably be characterized as business groups? Most such clusters revolve around a central node and in that respect appear closer in form to vertical or pyramidal than horizontal network groups. Often that node is a firm that is particularly active in alliance formation. Companies such as Cisco, Corning, and Fiat are well-known central nodes in large and active alliance clusters.

Several recent papers use the kinds of analysis reviewed above to detect clusters in strategic alliance network data. As in Rosenkopf and Padula's (2008) longitudinal CONCOR analysis of alliance ties in the mobile communications industry, the resulting clusters are mostly composed of individual firms and their pairwise partnerships. Bridging links do, however, appear across clusters such that the industry network as a whole displays "small world" properties, which are conducive to knowledge-sharing and open innovation (Fleming and Waguespack, 2007). But the kind of dense, decentralized, and lateral networking implied in the concept of "network form" is not evident in these studies.

Japanese supplier associations—or *kyoryoku-kai*—represent another kind of multi-firm yet centralized alliance in which an "apex" firm orchestrates the network. The most effective ones, such as Toyota's *kyoho-kai* or Panasonic's *kyoei-kai,* cultivate horizontal and indirect ties among suppliers. These are useful in mutual learning and problem-solving activities (Dyer and Hatch, 2004; Guillot and Lincoln, 2005).

A similarly centralized cluster distinctive to Japan is the R & D consortia organized by MITI, Japan's then Ministry of International Trade and Industry, which were prevalent in the 1980s and early 90s. Branstetter and Sakakibara (2002) conclude that, without MITI's pressure to participate, few Japanese firms would have done so. On the US side, the semiconductor R & D consortium, SEMATECH, is similarly a multi-member alliance of manufacturers set up and supported by the US government until 1996, when the federal funding was withdrawn.

Our general view is that strategic alliances as such have many of the organizational qualities attributed to the "network form." They are voluntary pacts that firms choose to enter or withdraw from; they are in general governed by flexible, lateral, and reciprocal ties; and they are cooperative and synergistic. They are capable then, as Powell, Williamson, and others suggest, of overcoming both the failures of arms-length market contracting and those of bureaucratic control. That said, we would not characterize strategic alliance clusters as "network-form" business groups. Such clusters are generally made up of networks that are centralized and vertical, not decentralized and horizontal. Strategic alliance is better thought of as a critically important inter-firm *tie* that facilitates cooperation, learning, and synergistic innovation in such network-form business groupings as the Japanese keiretsu, industrial districts such as Silicon Valley, and well-articulated global supply chains.

4.5 CONCLUSIONS

The pervasive global economic form known as "business groups" continues to draw close attention from researchers, journalists, and policymakers. A weakness of this otherwise rich and interesting literature, in our view, is that it fails to address with clarity and precision the internal organization or structuring of groups. In general, research has focused instead on strategic and financial outcomes such as the diversification, competitiveness, and performance of the affiliate firms and how the group allocates capital and other resources among them. The internal organization of the group—the configurations of ties and flows among its constituent firms—is clearly implicated in these concerns but in and of itself has received less close and systematic scrutiny. We propose that business groups are fruitfully conceived as interorganizational networks, and we have attempted to demonstrate the utility of the concepts, logic, and methods of network analysis for making sense of the internal structuring of groups. We are not the first to apply a network lens to the problem of group organization, but we believe that our effort here is broader in scope and perhaps more foundational in its treatment than is true of prior such efforts. We strongly recommend to other scholars that they leverage in their studies of business groups the richness and rigor of the network paradigm.

PART II

NATIONAL EXPERIENCES OF BUSINESS GROUPS

HISTORICAL FRONT RUNNERS IN WESTERN EUROPE

CHAPTER 5

BRITAIN

global legacy and domestic persistence

GEOFFREY JONES

5.1 INTRODUCTION

BUSINESS groups, defined as a constellation of legally independent companies bound together with formal and/or informal ties, used to play no role in the standard accounts of the business history of Britain.[1] In the classic story told by Chandler (and others), the United States raced ahead of Britain as the world's largest economy in the late nineteenth century because it created large industrial corporations which separated ownership from control, created managerial hierarchies and eventually the multidivisional form (hereafter M-form), and undertook the necessary investments in the new capital-intensive investments of the Second Industrial Revolution such as machinery and chemicals. The British, in contrast, remained committed to family ownership and management, which preferred short-term income to long-term growth in assets, and had a bias for small-scale operations which contributed to failures to invest and modernize. Consequently, the British economy was seen as "failing." The major research question was why Britain did not follow the American path of creating big firms with professional managers which was assumed to be the "one best way" (Hannah, 1976; Elbaum and Lazonick, 1987; Chandler, 1990).

Today little remains of this interpretation. The alleged story of British "decline" has become an in-joke among economic historians. The United States had higher productivity than Britain (or anywhere else) by the mid-nineteenth century, for reasons other than business structures, while Britain had a clear productivity lead over its European counterparts until the 1950s, and again between the 1980s and the 2000s.

---

[1] This chapter covers three different types of business groups that have been active in the British economy: international diversified business groups centered around overseas trading companies, holding-company-type business groups, and conglomerates as a variety of diversified business groups.

Nor would many scholars now view family ownership as inherently inferior to professional management. There appears to be no correlation between the adoption of US-style managerial hierarchies and productivity performance in the interwar years. (Broadberry and Crafts, 1992; Jones, 1997).

In any case, revisionist research has suggested that it was in the United States rather than Britain that large industrial corporations clung to family business. In 1900, according to Hannah, it was US business corporations that were dominated by plutocratic family owners, while British quoted companies showed higher levels of divorce of shareholding owners from management controllers (Hannah, 2007b). In 2012 Foreman-Peck and Hannah showed that the divorce of ownership and control in British public companies was far ahead of any other country, and especially the United States (Foreman-Peck and Hannah, 2012).

During the interwar years, and again during the 1960s, there were major merger waves in British industry. By 1958 the share of the 100 largest enterprises in manufacturing net output was higher in Britain than in the United States (32 versus 30 percent). By 1970 Britain was far more concentrated by this measure than the United States (41 versus 33 percent). By that year the M-form was also almost as widespread as in the United States (Jones, 1997; Whittington and Mayer, 2000). Although the 1970s saw a period of structural dislocation, as major industries such as automobile manufacturing experienced major crises, subsequently there was a major renaissance of British business and the British economy, based fundamentally on an embrace of globalization and a strong shift from manufacturing to higher value-added services (Owen, 2009). It was only during and after the global financial crisis beginning in 2008, which adversely affected an economy which was extremely exposed to global financial flows, that some downsides of this shift were observed. Certainly the British-owned manufacturing sector was quite small. In 2014 the four British-headquartered companies among the largest firms were the oil company BP (no. 6), the retailer Tesco (no. 63), and the banks HSBC and Lloyds (nos. 77 and 94, respectively). The largest manufacturing company was the Anglo-Dutch consumer products company Unilever, ranked no. 140 (Fortune, 2014).

It is within these radical shifts in the overall interpretation of what happened to British business from the nineteenth century that the role of business groups has surfaced. The first mention of business groups in the British business history literature appears only in the 1990s (Jones, 1994; Jones and Wale, 1998). However, it is now understood that much British foreign direct investment (hereafter FDI) before 1914 was conducted by business groups which had a striking resemblance to the business groups found in Asia and Latin America today, debunking any view that they were the exclusive preserve of post-colonial developing countries. Much less research, however, has yet been done on the role, if any, of diversified business groups in the domestic economy. However, this chapter shows that they were also not entirely absent.

For the sake of clarity, the following sections separate out the international and domestic stories of British business groups, while noting some commonalities in their growth and development.

5.2 BRITISH BUSINESS GROUPS IN GLOBAL BUSINESS: 1850S–1970S

From the mid-nineteenth century the world economy globalized. Thousands of firms, mostly based in Western countries which had experienced the Industrial Revolution, crossed borders and established operations in foreign countries. In 1914 world FDI amounted to $14.6 billion ($362 billion in 2017 US dollars), or the equivalent of 9 percent of world output, a ratio not seen again until the 1990s. Britain alone was the home economy of nearly one half of this FDI (Jones, 1994; Jones, 2005a; Dunning and Lundan, 2008).

British FDI took a variety of corporate forms. In manufacturing, modern-style multinationals were the dominant form. Firms such as Dunlop in rubber manufacturing and J & P Coats in cotton thread, first built businesses at home and then established wholly owned manufacturing affiliates in other European countries and/or the United States. They were single-product firms (Jones, 1986). In contrast, much FDI in natural resources and services took the form of large diversified business groups organized around core merchant houses or trading companies (Jones, 2000; Jones and Colpan, 2010).

British trading companies grew rapidly to exploit commercial links between their home country and the colonies as well as other developing countries. They perceived that large profits were to be earned from the exploitation of, and trade in, natural resources. The lack of infrastructure and local entrepreneurship in developing countries meant, first, that trading companies had to invest themselves rather than rely on others to create complementary businesses and, second, that there were numerous profitable opportunities which could be exploited as the borders of the international economy and of empires advanced.

The general pattern of diversification before 1914 was from trade to associated services such as insurance and shipping agencies, to FDI in resources, and processing in developing host economies. The British trading companies made the largest investments in tea, rubber and sugar plantations, and teak. Chilean nitrates, Indian coal, and petroleum were also the recipients of considerable investment. As merchants, they were not especially interested in "locking up" capital in manufacturing, but they did make substantial investments in cotton textile and jute manufacture, sugar refining, and flour milling.

Multiple factors exercised systematic influences on the diversification strategies of the British trading companies in this era. The opportunities for scope economies and the incentive to reduce transactions costs formed the first one. The boom in commodity prices in the first global economy created lucrative entrepreneurial opportunities. A third influence was the expansion of imperial frontiers which reduced the political risk of investing in Africa and Asia (Jones, 2000).

Finally, and importantly, there was capital availability arising from Britain's booming capital exports from the 1870s. As the merchant houses expanded, they floated on the stock exchange legally independent firms, subsequently described by the business historian Mira Wilkins as "free-standing firms, which they continued to control through small equity holdings, management contracts and other means in the established tradition of 'agency houses'" (Wilkins, 1988). They functioned, then, as venture capitalists identifying opportunities and placing potential British investors in touch with them.

Retrospectively, it might seem surprising that they could access equity. The legal structure for shareholders was not robust by later standards, as basic financial statements were unavailable even to shareholders, and minority shareholder protection was inadequate. It was not until the Companies Act of 1929 that it was stipulated in the case of British public companies that balance sheets should be sent to all shareholders prior to the annual general meeting, and not until 1948 that the profit and loss account also had to be circulated. However, despite such information asymmetries, as Cheffins has shown there were sufficient mitigating factors, including stock-market regulations and extensive public financial information in the news media, to provide the assurances that enabled a large growth in individual share ownership. The number of individual investors in holding securities on the London Stock Exchange grew from 250,000 to 1,000,000 between 1870 and 1914. There were also institutional investors, as commercial banks, insurance companies, and investment trusts shifted their portfolios into stocks and shares. Overall Britain had by far the largest equity market in the world (Michie, 1999; Cheffins, 2008). Insofar as companies engaged in commodities and other businesses in distant countries might be considered as particularly risky, the association of a reputable trading company with a new company provided some assurance to investors of honest and competent management (Jones, 2000).

Table 5.1 shows the geographical spread of some of the British international business groups in 1914. It also provides the estimated size of the capital employed by the parent company in that year.

Table 5.1. Geographical location and parent capital employed of selected large British international business groups, 1913.

Parent Merchant House	Estimated Capital Employed (£000s)	Major Host Countries Regions	Other Operations
Jardine Matheson	2,500	China	Japan; USA; South Africa; Peru
Balfour Williamson	2,000	Chile; USA	Peru; Canada
Wilson Sons & Co	1,728	Brazil; Argentina; UK	Tunisia; Senegal; Egypt
James Finlay	1,500	India; UK	Ceylon; USA; Canada; Russia
Anthony Gibbs	1,500	Chile; Peru; Australia; UK	USA
Harrisons & Crosfield	1,226	Malaya; Dutch East Indies; India	Ceylon; USA: Canada; Australia; New Zealand
Dodwell & Co	225	China; Canada; USA	Ceylon; Japan

Source: Jones (2000): 54, 55, 58–61.

5.2.1 Organizational Forms of International Business Groups

In the diversified business groups which emerged around the British merchant houses, the merchant house itself would act as the core firm within each group, usually responsible through its overseas branches for trading and agency business, while separately quoted or incorporated affiliates—often not wholly owned—were engaged in plantations, mines, processing, and other non-trading operations. Consequently, although reinvested profits continued to be an important source of funds for the British merchant groups, after 1870 they also drew substantially on outside funds to finance expansion into new activities.

There were several organizational forms. First, there were "unitary" business groups in which activities were wholly owned, although this did not mean that they were integrated in the sense of a modern corporation. A second, "network," form consisted of a core trading company with multiple wholly owned branches surrounded by a cluster of partly owned firms linked not only by equity, but also by debt, management, cross-directorships, and trading relationships. Balfour Williamson was one example. It is this type that most resembles the business groups in today's emerging economies. Table 5.2 shows the organizational structure of Balfour Williamson in 1914.

Table 5.2. Balfour Williamson Group, 1914.

Wholly Owned Partnerships	Country	Date Opened	Activities
Balfour Williamson	UK	1851	Head office
Williamson Balfour	Chile	1852	Selling and managing
Williamson & Co.	Chile	1911	Nitrates, grain milling
Milne & Co	Peru	1912	Oil company agents
Balfour Guthrie	United States	1869	Selling, managing, land
Balfour Guthrie	Canada	1911	Trading fish, newsprint, wood pulp

Principal Affiliates	Country of Registration	Date Started	% equity held by parent	Activities
Pacific Loan and Investment Co,	UK	1878	Majority	Mortgage loans; farms in California
Balfour Guthrie Investment	USA	1889	Majority	Investment company
W.F. Stevenson	Philippines	1904	25	Trading
Lobitos Oilfields	UK	1908	Minority	Peruvian Oil
Sociedad Comercial Harrington Morrison	Chile	1910	75	Trading in north Chile
West Coast Oil Fuel	USA	1911	30	Oil storage in Chile
Olympic Portland Cement	UK	1911	1	Cement Plant, Washington state, USA
Crown Mills Corporation	USA	1911	100	Flour Mills, Portland, Oregon USA
Santa Rosa Milling Co	UK	1913	45	Flour Mills, Chile and Peru
Sociedad Molinero de Osorno	Chile	1913	100	Flour Mill, Chile

Source: Jones (2000): 168–9.

A variant of this type, which might be called a "loose network," had no corporate core beyond family shareholdings. This was the case of a cluster of trading and shipping firms owned by the Inchcape family, which only began to consolidate after 1948 (Jones, 2000; Munro, 2003).

The choice of organizational form was determined in part by the business portfolios of companies. Trading operations and acting as agents for shipping, insurance, and manufacturing firms were generally internalized. These activities required either a large knowledge base on the part of firms, or the maintenance of a sound reputation among actual or potential clients. Trading companies whose business consisted primarily of trading and shipping agency and other agency work were mostly organized on a unitary basis. Within "network"-type business groups, these activities were also the responsibilities of wholly owned branches, but investments in plantations, mines, and other diversified activities were typically placed in independent companies. Merchants made their profits from commissions on trade and agency business. As a result, they sought access to trade flows and information, and to prevent being denied access by being bypassed by parties they had brought together. Outright ownership of mines and plantations was, as a result, unnecessary as sufficient access was secured by non-equity modes.

If ownership of non-core activities could be shared, there were other advantages. It limited the risks of the parent trading companies, while enabling outside capital to be introduced into ventures. This permitted the use of other people's money to undertake entrepreneurial investments designed to generate new sources of income for them through commission and fees.

5.2.2 Competences and Longevity of International Business Groups

How can the competences of these business groups be assessed? Evidently they were initially the beneficiaries of a home country advantage. They developed at a time when Britain dominated world trade flows and, by the late nineteenth century, world capital flows. They were able to access the world's largest equity markets. Many of their investments were located within the British Empire or parts of Latin America under British informal influence. In the interwar years the merchant firms were able to protect their business through extensive collusive cartels supported by the colonial authorities. Although Britain's relative importance in the world economy began to decline from the late nineteenth century, British trading companies in Asia and Africa continued to benefit from the umbrella of British colonial rule until the 1950s, and even later in the case of Hong Kong, Bermuda, and other offshore financial territories including the Cayman Islands and the British Virgin Islands.

The historical longevity of the trading companies in their host regions and the colonial status of many of these countries resulted in multiple "contacts" which provided a major competitive advantage. British colonial officials were frequently critical of the merchant firms, and certainly did not protect them against competitors. But if colonial administrations had their own agendas, they were still sufficiently close to the merchant firms in their ideological and cultural outlook to provide an immensely supportive context. However, business groups also established long-standing "contacts" with local business elites in Asia, Africa, and Latin America, which gave them a "quasi-local" status. They also had core competences centered on the areas of knowledge, information, and external relationships. Management systems which involved staff spending their entire careers abroad generated extensive tacit knowledge about regions, products, and marketing channels (Jones, 2000; Jones and Colpan, 2010).

The constellation of firms around the trading companies were linked by multiple institutional and contractual modes, with flows of managerial, financial, and trading relationships among those. The business groups possessed advantages related to imperfections in capital, labor, and product markets, and in the area of property-rights enforcement. There were numerous conflicts of interest and potential for opportunist behavior, but in practice rent-seeking was restrained. The external relationships surrounding the trading companies were also important elements of their architecture. These networks often relied on trust rather than contracts and were extremely durable. British merchants emerged from hubs such as London, Liverpool, and Glasgow and clustered in hubs overseas, and this provided one support for the high trust levels which facilitated such networks. Long-term relationships with banks provided a source of credit for routine operations, and support during crises (Jones, 2000; Jones and Colpan, 2010).

The overall robustness of the business groups created before 1914 was demonstrated by their longevity. The subsequent decades were a difficult time for international business in the face of the exogenous shocks of world wars and the Great Depression, and the resulting policy responses in the shape of tariffs and exchange controls. After 1931 the global economy disintegrated. There was reduced diversification, yet most of the business groups persisted, sometimes because family and other shareholders were prepared to sustain companies paying low or no dividends. Many of the firms had all or most of their business within the sheltered confines of the British Empire. They sometimes still benefited from fiscal and other privileges from colonial governments, while collusive cartels were permitted and usually supported (Jones, 2000).

After 1945 British business groups continued to diversify and reinvent themselves. General and produce trading gave way to more specialized trading and sales agencies. Firms diversified geographically, while the Inchcape group relocated itself out of India towards the faster-growing and more open economies further east. New business groups emerged. After Tiny Rowland became chief executive of Lonrho, a company which began operating in Africa in 1909 as the London and Rhodesian Mining Company, he transformed the company into a major business group. By 1995 Lonrho's African non-mining businesses had expanded into fifteen sub-Saharan

African countries, with ninety operating companies involved in a wide range of business activities.

In the postwar decades, constraints were often more political than financial. Leaving aside such havens as Hong Kong, where two important merchant houses established in the nineteenth century—John Swire and Jardine Matheson—were based, the general thrust of public policy in most developing host economies was to restrict or prohibit FDI, especially in natural resources and services. Among the most successful trading companies were firms which had suffered traumatic shocks as a result of the Pacific War and the Chinese Revolution. British merchants in the Far East and Southeast Asia acquired new premises and facilities which probably improved their efficiency compared with the prewar period, but more importantly their losses stimulated an entrepreneurial urge to rebuild and renew their businesses. Motivation of this type was lacking perhaps among the British business groups active in India and South America, whose owners and managers seemed resigned to slow decline because of political hostility.

For the most part the basic organizational pattern of the network form of business groups as they had developed by the early twentieth century remained in place until at least the 1960s. The creation of new affiliate firms to undertake non-trading activities continued. After 1929 British exchange controls on investments outside the sterling area as well as the perceived risks of international investment effectively ended the flotation of new firms on the British capital markets. However, well before then the trading companies had begun to make more use of locally registered firms or other types of institutional arrangement. The growing burden of British taxation on companies whose profits were earned largely abroad after World War I was initially an important consideration, and this led to the registration of several affiliated firms being shifted. It was really only in the 1960s that changes to this organizational form began to occur as improvements in corporate reporting and the emergence of organized capital markets in many countries meant that investors no longer needed the brand of a British trading company to guarantee that their savings would be "safe." Indeed, complex groups with cross-shareholdings and internal transfers of commission and fees within the group looked less attractive as shareholders changed from being atomistic individuals to institutional investors (in Britain) or powerful business elites (in Asia and elsewhere) (Jones, 2000).

The postwar fate of the business groups was in part correlated with their main host regions. Some regions became hostile to foreign firms or imposed penal rates of taxation. This happened to the British business groups in South Asia and Latin America. East and Southeast Asia and West Africa—at least through to the 1970s—offered much greater prospects. From the 1950s Hong Kong, which combined fast economic growth with low taxes and a British legal system, offered especially favorable conditions. However, strategic choices were possible. Swire's and Jardine's survived the loss of their Chinese investments in 1949. Inchcape and Booker McConnell both successfully escaped from difficult host countries to more attractive areas. And while overall political and economic conditions in Africa deteriorated from the perspective of Western firms from the 1960s, Lonrho developed as a large business group in this period (Jones, 2000).

The fate of the business groups was also related to the stability of their shareholding structure. In a considerable number of cases, the decision by family shareholders to sell their shareholding was the catalyst which ended the independent existence and/or British ownership of firms. The development of a more fluid market for corporate control in Britain from the 1950s meant that the vulnerability of firms to takeover was much greater (Jones, 2000). Regulatory changes, especially the London Stock Exchange's 1967 code on takeovers, which required anyone acquiring 30 percent of a listed firm to buy 100 percent, also made it much more difficult to retain a networked, or pyramidal, corporate structure (Morck, 2009).

Against this background, in the 1970s especially, diversification strategies focused on "redeployment" from high-risk developing to developed countries such as the Commonwealth countries, including Britain, and the United States. In retrospect, it is apparent that British managements were prone to exaggerate the risks caused by political change in the developing world, while some firms also misjudged their core competences by acquiring firms in new industries and countries where they had no advantage and could add no value. Yet successful transitions were made from traders and plantation owners in developing economies to manufacturers or distributors in developed countries. The British merchant houses in the Far East and Southeast Asia rose from the ashes of the wartime destruction of their assets and built vibrant new businesses, becoming large-scale automobile distributors—and even the owner of a major airline in the case of Swire's and Cathay Pacific. However, British business groups in India and Latin America were notably unsuccessful in finding new strategies to fit changing circumstances.

5.3 THE DISAPPEARANCE OF THE INTERNATIONAL BUSINESS GROUPS

During the 1980s the major British business groups continued to be quite successful. A study of the post-tax returns on net capital employed between 1980 and 1989 showed Booker at 21.3 percent; Inchcape 12.9 percent; Swire's 12.7 percent; Jardine Matheson 10 percent; and Lonrho 9.2 percent. The equivalent figures for BP were 12.1 percent, and for Unilever 10.7 percent (Jones, 2000: 328). Yet by the following decade many of these long-standing business groups had begun to be transformed into focused food companies (Booker Group), automobile distributors (Inchcape), or chemical companies (Harrisons & Crosfield, now Elementis). Of the surviving British trading companies,

Swire's and Jardine Matheson continued in business as large and ultimately British-controlled multinational business groups primarily active in Asia.

What caused the overall decline of most of these business groups? The first challenge arose from further changes in the economic and political environment of important host economies. Jardine Matheson and Swire's continued to draw enormous advantage from their position in Hong Kong. Conversely, the fate of the giant United Africa Company (UAC), owned by Unilever, was all but sealed by the economic and political turbulence of the West African, and especially the Nigerian, economies from the 1970s, as well as the growing level of corruption which was increasingly difficult for its parent Unilever to control (Fieldhouse, 1994). In Malaysia and elsewhere, the British business groups were driven out by government determination to take local ownership of natural resources (Yacob and Khalid, 2012).

Secondly, some business groups fell victim to failed attempts to diversify into regions and industries where they lacked expertise. Returns on capital employed in the 1990s fell at Inchcape, Swire's, and Lonrho, though they rose at Jardine Matheson and Harrison's & Crosfield. The "merchant adventurer" ethos and the desire to escape from their traditional developing-country hosts had led firms in some cases far away from core competences, however widely defined. During the 1980s many of these diversification strategies ran into great difficulties. The competence in region-specific knowledge and know-how was thus both a competitive advantage and disadvantage for the business groups, in that it provided a constraint on diversification options outside the host region. Extensive diversification outside core activities also proved to be detrimental thanks to the escalating costs from managerial constraints and diminishing benefits from the exploitation of established and proven expertise.

The final and the ultimate arbiter of the fate of the diversified business groups was, however, the British capital markets. The capital markets which had made the creation of the diversified business groups possible before 1914 proved their nemesis from the 1980s. It was the declining share price of the publicly quoted firms which led to their ultimate demise as diversified trading companies. This was not due on the whole to poor performance, but rather to changed perceptions and priorities. The changed nature of British equity holders, which was different from before 1914 as individuals had been largely replaced by institutional investors such as investment banks and pension funds by the 1980s, played a major role in that end (Cheffins, 2008). While the individual shareholders before 1914—and indeed arguably through to the 1970s—were passive and often long-term holders of stock, the institutional investors that replaced them later on viewed shares increasingly as short-term investment vehicles. They were responsible to the owners of the funds that they invested, and as such had a duty to maximize investment returns. Consequently, the main preoccupation of the institutions was short-term financial performance and share prices. Institutional investors held their own diversified portfolios, and since the 1980s preferred individual firms to focus on their core areas, enabling their performance and prospects to be more efficiently monitored (Jones, 2000, 2005b).

The language of "core competence" and "sticking to one's knitting" began to be spread by business schools and management consultancies after the 1980s, and in a sense became a self-fulfilling prophecy which reduced the share prices of diversified firms in a way which the managers of publicly quoted firms ignored at their peril. From the 1980s financial analysts became a major influence on corporate strategies. As Unilever, for example, discovered, they disliked complexity and acted as advocates of these fashionable management theories (Jones, 2005b: 347–51). Analysts and fund managers benchmarked against industrial categories to compare price/earnings ratios. Business groups, like the conglomerates discussed below, did not fit this model. The chairman of Inchcape in the mid-1990s noted:

> I would not say the market was that confused about the businesses that Inchcape was in, but we were still seen as a bit of a conglomerate and conglomerates were completely out of fashion. Therefore, the market just refused to accept the intrinsic value of the company.[2]

The ultimate family control of Swire's and Jardine Matheson ensured their survival. Both firms were sheltered from hostile host governmental pressures for localization during the 1980s, as the laissez-faire British colonial government in Hong Kong shared none of the protectionist and nationalistic sentiments of its neighbors in South Korea and Taiwan. The controlling families also took steps to consolidate their ownership of their multiple affiliates in response to occasional attempts by outside groups to take large equity stakes. As early as 1974 Swire placed most of its Hong Kong affiliates into a partly owned but publicly quoted (in Hong Kong) holding company—Swire Pacific—which in turn held equity in the principal affiliates, including Cathay Pacific and Swire Properties. At that time John Swire & Sons directly held 50 percent of the China Navigation Company, the major shipping subsidiary which was British-registered, and in 1976 the firm acquired the remaining 50 percent of the equity. Most of the other affiliates remained partly owned, different classes of shareholding meaning that full control remained in the hands of John Swire & Sons, itself still wholly owned by the founding families. John Swire & Sons employed 122,000 people in 2014.

Swire's "twin," Jardine Matheson, employed 240,000 people by 2014, and controlled businesses with $61.5 billion in revenues. The firm's interests ranged from the Mandarin Oriental hotel chain in Hong Kong to property development in China, supermarkets, construction, and car dealership. It owned more than half of Astra, the largest listed company in Indonesia, which itself has more than 170 companies. Jardine Matheson was noted for opaque governance and complex organizational arrangements. In 1984, following the announcement that Britain would return China to Hong Kong in 1997, it moved its domicile from Hong Kong to Bermuda. Ten years

---

[2] Butler and Keary, 2000: 300.

later, after Hong Kong refused to allow Jardine Matheson to use the protective takeover code of Bermuda, Jardine's relisted its companies in Singapore.

5.4 BUSINESS GROUPS AND DOMESTIC BUSINESS: 1850S–1970S

The diversified business-group organizational form was found much less frequently in British domestic business. The relatively well-developed capital markets and the commercial banking system allowed single-product firms, as the capital-intensity of industries at that time were not great. As firms grew in size, there were large-scale merger movements from the late nineteenth century. These were primarily horizontal. The fragmented cotton textiles industry, for example, saw numerous mergers: textiles accounted for 330 of the 895 firms affected by mergers between 1887 and 1900 (Hannah, 1976: 22). The Calico Printers' Association Ltd was formed in 1899 from the amalgamation of forty-six textile printing companies and thirteen textile merchants. The company at its inception accounted for over 80 percent of Britain's output of printed cloth. In cotton thread, Britain's largest producer—J & P Coats—went public in 1890, and six years later acquired four large competitors to create Britain's largest industrial firm. Other mergers created the Salt Union, controlling 90 percent of the domestic market, Associated Portland Cement (45 percent of the market), Imperial Tobacco (90 percent), and Distillers (75 percent of the whisky market).

These firms sometimes did not closely integrate merged firms, which were often managed as independent fiefdoms. In the literature they have often been described as federations of many specialized companies loosely presided over by holding companies, or "holding-company"-type business groups,[3] which were frequently dominated by families and concentrated on certain industries. Imperial Tobacco, for example, remained a federation of family firms with little central direction (Hannah, 1980: 53). In textiles, the leading firms Calico Printers Association, Bradford Dyers, and Fine Spinners and Doublers were seen by Alfred Chandler as characteristically loose federations of firms throughout the interwar years, although Hannah has recently denounced this view as one of Chandler's many "grotesque misclassifications" of British business history. In the case of Calico Printers, Hannah notes, the inefficient management organization was corrected within two years of the firm's formation (Hannah, 2009: 33).

This dominance of specialist companies in the domestic economy contrasts with the unrelated diversification seen in some economies in Europe, and indeed with the British-based international trading companies. Compared to other countries at the time, institutional voids in financial and trading markets were low. The large equity

---

[3] See Chapter 1 in this volume.

market made it relatively easy and cheap for companies to raise capital. Whatever the risks arising from informational asymmetries, there was a large demand for shares, not least because shares in British-based companies outperformed returns in government bonds for 34 out of the 43 years before 1914. Many local industrial companies floated their shares on provincial stock exchanges, where knowledge about the individuals involved and the industry was well known, greatly reducing the need for formal disclosure in company documents and annual reports (Cheffins, 2008: 205–20). Commodity markets were as well developed as financial markets.

The domestic market was compact and high-income, and many firms were also prolific exporters in the highly globalized British economy. Absent any anti-trust legislation before 1948, specialist combinations could exercise substantial market power in their industries, so the financial incentives for unrelated diversification were hardly compelling, even if it was theoretically possible that they could reinvest the money earned from such monopolies to grow in unrelated industries. While international trading companies formed the core of the overseas business groups, Britain's domestic banking system, which had become highly concentrated by 1914, did not provide an equivalent organizing driver for domestic business groups. In the highly developed and specialized British financial system, the equity and bond markets were perceived as the appropriate source of long-term funding, while the commercial banks provided short-term financial accommodation. This was also the strong preference of the Bank of England, which promoted market-type relationships between banks and industries. Unlike in bank-orientated economies such as Germany or Sweden, British banks did not take or hold large equity stakes in industrial firms, but instead focused on the provision of short-term finance or the floating of stock. It was striking that even for larger enterprises capital came from many sources, including reinvested profits, stock-market issues, private placements with stockbrokers and insurance companies, and family (Hannah, 1980: 55).

The handful of business groups which did emerge typically had substantial international businesses. A large group developed around the engineering contractor Weetman Pearson, which became one of the longest lasting of such businesses in Britain. This began as a purely domestic business, but from the 1880s Pearson developed his business into a global contractor, undertaking massive infrastructure projects in the United States and Mexico. In 1901 he also began securing large oil concessions, and in 1909 found a hugely prolific oil well. Initially the main corporate vehicle was the contracting firm of S. Pearson and Son Ltd. After the discovery of oil, however, the Mexican oil assets were put into the Mexican-registered company Mexican Eagle Oil Company, which had a primary listing in Mexico and a secondary listing in London. In 1912 the Eagle Oil Transport Co. was registered in Britain to control the transportation and distribution of oil outside Mexico. Another British company, Anglo-Mexican Petroleum Company, marketed oil outside Mexico. A fourth company, Whitehall Securities Corporation, was founded in 1908 to manage S. Pearson and Son's other investments. Weetman Pearson closely controlled S. Pearson and Son, which wholly owned Whitehall Securities. Mexican Eagle had substantial outside shareholders in

Mexico and Britain. Eagle Oil's ordinary shares were owned fifty-fifty by Mexican Eagle and S. Pearson, but the preference shares were listed. Anglo-Mexican was a private company. A recent study has estimated the market value of the entire group in 1919 at £79 million, which would have made it Britain's largest business (Spender, 1930; Bud-Frierman, Godley, and Wale, 2010; Garner 2011).

Pearson sold the Mexican oil business in 1919, but the business group expanded and continued to diversify both internationally and domestically. In Mexico and Chile it retained substantial electricity and tramway businesses, which were consolidated into a private British company, Whitehall Electric Investments Ltd, in 1922. These were sold seven years later, but the company established new electricity businesses in Britain, and between 1925 and 1970 operated electricity and tramway business in Athens, Greece. It also established a new company, Amerada, for oil production in the United States. Although this was sequestrated by the British government during World War II, other oil investments were subsequently made in the United States and Canada. In 1969 these were rolled into a US oil company, Ashland Oil and Refining Company, in which Pearson held a substantial equity stake. In 1919 the firm acquired a 45-percent stake in the London branch of merchant bankers Lazard Brothers, and this became a majority stake in 1932. In 1921 Pearson purchased a number of local newspapers in Britain, which it combined to form the Westminster Press. This became the basis of a large publishing group. In 1957 the Group bought the *Financial Times* and acquired a 50-percent stake in *The Economist*. It purchased the publisher Longman in 1968. Meanwhile, in the early 1950s it acquired the Lawley Group—manufacturers, wholesalers, and retailers of china and glass in Britain. Further acquisitions led in 1964 to the formation of Allied English Potteries. During the 1960s the firm also bought a large shareholding in the French winemaker Château Latour. Pearson remained a family-owned private company until 1969, when it floated 20 percent of its equity on the London Stock Exchange and became a public listed company. It had five divisions of roughly equal profit contribution: banking and finance, investment trusts, newspapers and publishing, oil, and industrial. Table 5.3 lists the principal activities of the Group in 1969.

Pearson diversified much further after the public flotation, buying the famous London wax museum Madame Tussauds and amusement parks, and investing in satellite broadcasting and much more. The Cowdray family trust retained a large, though no longer controlling, shareholding through the 1980s, and a family member remained as chairman as late as 1997. The diversification and the family investment by then made the business "an anomaly on the British scene," albeit one that did not prevent it running large and successful businesses, including being "one of the world's leading financial publishers" (Hill, 1985; Whittington and Mayer, 2000: 100–1). It was only in the late 1990s that diversification began to unravel, as financial analysts and markets increasingly looked with disfavor on unrelated diversification. Madame Tussauds was sold in 1998, and the shareholding in the merchant bank Lazards in 2000. The company focused on educational publishing, newspapers, and the

Table 5.3. Pearson Group, c.1969.

Company Name	Sector	% Shareholding by Parent
Whitehall Securities	Management and Financial Services	100
Lazard Brothers	Investment Bank	80
S. Pearson Publishers	Newspapers, *Financial Times*	51
Westminster Press	Provincial British newspapers	51
Longman Group	Book publishing	Majority
Ashland Oil	Oil and chemical production, transport and distribution in US, Canada, Indonesia, Brunei, Ghana	Minority
Standard Industrial Group	UK manufacturing, including pottery, glass, engineering	59
Château Latour	French wines	Majority
Athens Pireas Electric Railways	Athens trolley services	Majority

Sources: Hill (1985), Whittington and Mayer (2000); http://timeline.pearson.com; http://www.gracesguide.co.uk/S._Pearson_and_Son

media. In 2000 Pearson spent $2.5 billion to acquire National Computer Systems, the largest American commercial testing and educational testing company, and within a decade controlled three fifths of the US educational testing market. Overall, by 2015 Pearson had revenues of $8 billion, 60 percent of which were earned in the United States, and was the world's largest educational publisher (Reingold, 2015). In that year the company decided to concentrate entirely on educational publishing, and sold the *Financial Times* and its part-ownership of *The Economist*.

Overall, during the post-World War II period the structure of British business changed radically. Family firms and family directors slowly disappeared (Franks, Mayer and Rossi, 2005). Concentration increased at a rapid pace during the 1950s and 1960s, with major merger waves. Large British companies adopted the M-form, frequently as a result of employing the services of management consultants, notably McKinsey. Channon's study traced the evolution of the M-form of organization for a sample of the ninety-two largest British companies from 1950 to 1970 (and ninety-six companies for the period 1960–70). In 1950 he found that only twelve companies in his sample had adopted a multidivisional structure. By the end of the 1950s some 30 percent of the firms in the sample had such a structure, and by 1970 the M-form was the dominant organizational form, with sixty-eight of the ninety-six sample large British corporations adopting it. The spread of the M-form signaled the rapid expansion of product diversification in large British companies. By 1970 the M-form was almost as widespread in Britain as in the United States, and it had been more widely adopted in Britain than in any other large European economy (Channon, 1973; Jones, 1997). Arguably that form served as a precondition for the growth of conglomerates.

5.5 THE RISE AND FALL OF
CONGLOMERATES: 1960S TO THE PRESENT

5.5.1 The Growth of Conglomerates

Table 5.4 shows the rapid rise in the share of unrelated diversified firms in the top 200 industrial firms in Britain after 1970.

The growth of acquisitive conglomerates occurred in several waves. During the postwar decades a number of highly diversified conglomerates emerged, including Sears, Slater Walker, Thomas Tilling, and Reckitt & Colman. The Rank Organisation was particularly interesting. In 1937 Joseph Arthur Rank formed the Rank Organisation, bringing together a number of motion-picture businesses acquired in previous years, including Pinewood Studios and Denham Films. Subsequently he added the Odeon chain of cinemas, the Gaumont-British Picture Corporation, and the noted film studios at Elstree and Lime Grove. During the 1940s and 1950s the Rank Organisation produced numerous films, but also engaged in unrelated diversification. In 1956 Rank entered into a joint venture with the Haloid Corporation of the USA to manufacture and market photocopying equipment under the name Rank Haloid. The company, which subsequently became known as Rank Xerox, was hugely successful (Rank finally sold its share in 1997). Rank also owned a record company, Top Rank Records (sold in 1960 to EMI) and manufactured radios and televisions through Rank Bush Murphy Group (sold in 1978 to Great Universal Stores). During the 1980s and 1990s Rank made numerous acquisitions in the leisure retail sector, including theme parks, pubs, restaurants, nightclubs, hotels, holiday camps, timeshare developments, and camping grounds, as well as bingo clubs and casinos. The company owned a portfolio of famous leisure brands, including Butlins holiday camps, Odeon cinemas, and Hard Rock Café; and it was associated with Universal Studios in theme-park joint ventures in Florida and Osaka, Japan (Channon, 1973: 62–3, 188–92; Whittington and Mayer, 2000).

The real momentum in the growth of the conglomerates began in the 1960s and was intensified in 1970s. It was enabled by the fluid market for corporate control which had opened up after Sigmund Warburg had introduced the concept of the hostile takeover

Table 5.4. Diversification of top 100 industrial firms in Britain (%).

	1950	1970	1983	1993
Single Product	24	6	7	5
Dominant Product	50	32	16	10
Related Diversified	27	57	67	61
Unrelated Diversified	–	6	11	24

Source: Whittington and Mayer (2000): 139.

when he facilitated the takeover of British Aluminum in 1956 (Ferguson, 2011: 183–99). During the 1960s the tightly regulated British financial system began to be liberalized, enabling a new range of funding opportunities for acquisitions as the subsequent decade of oil-price hikes and extensive industrial strikes weakened long-established firms. They were also weakened by high inflation, while rapidly rising price levels also facilitated the claims of conglomerates to be able to turn around poorly performing firms, as nominal revenues rose sharply.

A new type of financier emerged, engaged in buying and selling companies, and taking advantage of the internationalized financial system. High-profile figures included "Jimmy" Goldsmith, who with the financial backing of Isaac Wolfson bought up a series of bakeries in 1965 and founded Cavenham Foods. He used this as a vehicle to buy and asset-strip established firms like Bovril, using a network of private companies and the Cayman Islands-registered General Oriental Investments, and allied with the controversial finance house Slater Walker, which eventually went bankrupt in 1975. Although Goldsmith sold many of his diversified investments in the early 1980s, he was immortalized as the distasteful British financier Sir Lawrence Wildman in the classic Hollywood movie *Wall Street* in 1987. Meanwhile, in the 1980s, with deregulation and liberalization in full swing under Thatcher in Britain and Reagan in the United States, there were many acquisition opportunities for other "corporate raiders" who could finance acquisitions by borrowing from the financial markets and banks and maintained a self-sustaining earnings growth by the constant accumulation of companies.

Hanson Trust was a classic example. James Hanson, the scion of a long-established family business, and Gordon White built Hanson Trust into Britain's ninth-largest company by the early 1990s with sales of £10 billion. It started in 1964 when James Hanson and Gordon White set up a small company called Welbecson, which imported greetings cards from the United States. In the following year they took over Wiles Group, a small animal byproducts, sack hire, and fertilizer firm, and in 1968 bought a brick maker called Butterley. Hanson Trust was formed in 1969. White settled in New York in 1973 and started building a US business, but Hanson Trust remained a modest affair until the takeover of a struggling British company called Lindustries, which made locks, safes, and security equipment, in 1979. There followed a swath of large acquisitions, including the battery maker Berec, the renamed British Ever Ready in 1982, the Imperial Group in 1986, and Quantum, an American plastics specialist, in 1993. The Imperial Group was bought for £2.5 billion, of which Hanson recouped £2.4 billion in subsequent asset sales, leaving Hanson in control of Imperial's large and profitable tobacco operations. Hanson's activities came to include tobacco products, forest products, coal mining, chemicals, and bricks and construction. Hanson was closely connected to the Conservative Party, which ruled Britain under Prime Minister Margaret Thatcher during the 1980s, and was made a peer in 1983 (Brummer and Cowe, 1994).

Hanson grew using a simple business model: buy asset-rich companies with good cash flows, often in low-risk stable industries such as cigarettes and bricks, and manage them for cash and return on capital. The business was almost entirely based in Britain and the United States, reflecting the active markets for corporate control which made acquisitions and asset stripping far easier than in continental Europe or elsewhere. A key feature of the business model was the payment of as little tax as possible. Until a change in British tax laws in 1987, Hanson employed the device of dual-resident companies—incorporated in the United States but with a trading address in Britain—which enabled the venture to claim tax relief on interest payments in both countries. During the 1980s Hanson had up to twenty companies incorporated in the tax haven of Panama, through which many transactions passed. It was further more complicated in its structure than the usual conglomerates that wholly owned their subsidiaries. For instance, Kidde, a business acquired by Hanson in 1987, was not only retained as an entity but was owned by numerous other Hanson entities, all of them private and many registered outside the UK. The ultimate owner, Hanson Trust, was several tiers distant in ownership terms (Brummer and Cowe, 1994). Figure 5.1 shows the ownership and control of Kidde by Hanson Trust in 1987.

BAT (British American Tobacco) grew out of a single-product firm making tobacco products. In 1952 it acquired the paper manufacturer Wiggins Teape. In 1964 it ventured into entirely new pastures when it acquired both an ice-cream company and a one-third stake in the Lenthéric fragrance house, which became wholly owned within three years. While the ice-cream company was divested within four years, BAT's adventures in beauty proved to be more sustained. Over the following two decades BAT spent $120 million acquiring small and medium-sized cosmetics and fragrance businesses, usually from the descendants of founding families. Acquisitions included Morney (1966), Yardley (1967), and US-based Germaine Monteil (1969), all of which owned well-established brands which had become tired. During the 1970s major investments in retail were made, including the Argos catalogue chain and the Marshall Field's department stores in the United States. In 1984 financial services were added when the firms acquired Eagle Star insurance, followed by Allied Dunbar and Farmers in the United States (Whittington and Mayer, 2000: 141).

From the 1970s BTR grew rapidly from a modest firm in the rubber industry to a diversified industrial conglomerate. This growth was based on a series of acquisitions of once-famous names in British industry, including Thomas Tilling in 1983, Dunlop in 1985, and Hawker Siddeley in 1991. By then the firm had sales of $11.3 billion, operated 600 plants worldwide, had subsidiaries in twenty-four countries, and was one of the ten largest companies on the London Stock Exchange (Elderkin, 1997; Jones 1997).

To some (at the time and subsequently) these conglomerates represented the worst excesses of "financial capitalism." They adopted a particularly decentralized form of organization. Headquarters were often primarily concerned with financial matters; in other matters, managers in divisions were given considerable autonomy, with most production and sales decisions delegated to subsidiaries. While supporters of such conglomerates pointed to their role in disciplining inefficient managements,

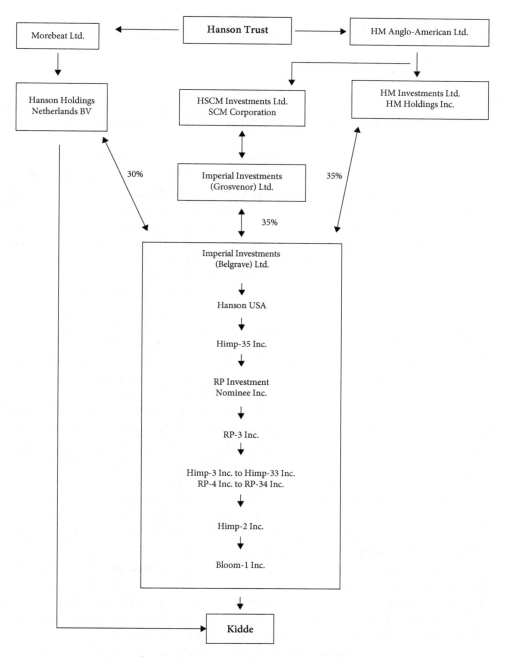

FIGURE **5.1.** Ownership and control of a Hanson Trust subsidiary, Kidde, in 1987.

Source: Redrawn based on Brummer and Cowe (1994): Appendix 5, 319.

their critics questioned both their interest in, and their ability to sustain, long-term strategies centered on innovation rather than the payment of high dividends to shareholders.

5.5.2 Capabilities and the Decline of the Conglomerates

The fact that from the late 1990s many of the conglomerates were unwound would support the view that their organizational capabilities were not sustainable. BAT sold off its diversified businesses. In 1996 Hanson broke itself up into four separate companies focused on tobacco, chemicals, energy, and building materials. In the same period BTR sold off many peripheral activities and restructured itself around four principal global product groups in which the firm held an advantage, either in superior technology or low-cost production. In 1999 it merged with Siebe to form Invensys. It subsequently went through years of divestments to avoid bankruptcy, restructured as an engineering and information technology company, and was acquired by France's Schneider in 2013.

However, the view that the conglomerates were dismantled because they were inherently inefficient, although frequently asserted, is not entirely convincing for several reasons. First, Whittington and Mayer have shown that the financial perform-ance of unrelated diversified firms in aggregate was quite good. Indeed, the financial performance of individual firms was impressive. BTR, for example, started the 1980s with a return on equity of 21.5 percent and ended it with an even higher return of 39.3 percent as it expanded its level of diversification (Whittington and Mayer, 2000: 150–3). In Cassis's study of the profitability of British, French, and German companies for 1987–9, Hanson impressively tops the list of the most profitable British industrial companies with a rate of return of 54.1 percent, although the use of complex account-ing measures raise some questions about the nature of these earnings; BTR was in third place with 36.2 percent, and another conglomerate, Grand Metropolitan, seventh with 28.7 percent. Hanson and BTR were impressively more profitable than any German or French industrial company in his list (Cassis, 1997: 99).

Second, individual case studies point towards real managerial capabilities. Take the apparently odd case of BAT's acquisitions of small cosmetics and fragrance firms. In 1970 the individual acquisitions were merged into a single subsidiary, British American Cosmetics. A former Procter & Gamble manager was recruited as managing director. He hired managers from other consumer-products companies, rather than the tobacco parent. However, synergies were achieved with other parts of the BAT group; in particular, information was shared about consumer marketing and retailing trends at group-wide training sessions. Over two decades a substantial and well-managed business was created out of what had been a random collection of tired brands. There was substantial innovation. Lenthéric successfully developed a mass-market fragrance business sold through drugstores, and became a market leader in Britain by 1977.

BAC slowly grew its business through further acquisitions, although the small size of the business compared to its parent meant that there was a constant struggle to get funds. During the early 1980s a major restructuring of Yardley, its merger with the more successful Lenthéric business, and the creation of a worldwide marketing operation created a viable and profitable company.

By 1984 BAC was the largest British-owned cosmetics firm, if still a modest player in world terms, which manufactured in 37 countries and sold in over 140, with a product range which spanned fragrances, men's products, luxury toiletries, makeup and skincare products. The sale of the business in that year was not because it had failed, but because BAT had other priorities. Beauty products never exceeded 2 percent of overall corporate revenues, 1 percent of the profits of what had become Britain's third-largest company by the 1980s. As BAT shifted into financial services, BAC simply did not fit. (Jones, 2010: 253–4).

Third, it is noteworthy that the conglomerates left substantive legacies. Take Hanson Trust. This company certainly ran into trouble in the early 1990s through a poorly managed hostile acquisition attempt of the chemical company ICI. The purchase of this firm would have made Hanson the biggest British company and secured the hidden jewel within ICI, the pharmaceuticals business that would later become Zeneca. ICI's management, advised by investment bank Goldman Sachs, responded astutely by unearthing some embarrassing facts about Hanson, such as the millions of dollars squandered on racehorses by Gordon White. The company's well-deserved aura of maximizing shareholder value was damaged, the company no longer looked like the shareholders' friend, and the whole episode sparked skepticism about the value of the Hanson corporate structure. Yet the successor businesses survived for some time when the firm broke itself up in 1996. The Hanson name went with the building materials company and continued until 2007, when it was acquired by a large German cement company, which ten years later sold to a US private equity firm. And the quality of its management cadre was demonstrated by the numerous Hanson alumni in senior positions in British industry over the following decade (Pratley, 2004).

The plausible explanation for the winding-up of many of the conglomerates is the same capital market pressures which ended the diversified international business groups: they were simply unfashionable and their share prices came under pressure as a result. Unfashionability resulted in low ratings, which raised the cost of capital. Among other things, this made it increasingly hard to find acquisitions that could maintain earnings growth. This particularly disrupted the business model of the conglomerates, which rested on acquisitions. As the cases of Berkshire Hathaway, News International, and GE in the United States showed, stellar returns and charismatic leadership could enable the bullet of the conglomerate discount to be dodged. However the British conglomerates only seem to have made good financial returns rather than stellar ones, and they were short of charismatic chief executives. Lord Hanson came closest in that regard, but the failed ICI acquisition and the horse-racing scandal wrecked his aura of success.

In contrast, the Virgin Group had charismatic leadership, and developed and survived as a diversified business group, holding majority and minority stakes in its companies. The group originated when 15-year-old Richard Branson established a student magazine in 1965. This finally failed, but it provided the launch pad for a mail-order record business that soon expanded into Virgin Megastore, a chain of popular record stores in Britain. Virgin Records, a lucrative music-production business, was launched in 1973. In 1984 Branson launched Virgin Atlantic, initially offering a service between London and New York that provided "first class tickets at business-class prices." The Virgin Group went public in 1987, but Branson soon realized that the British capital markets were already struggling to understand highly diversified businesses. He took the business private again in 1988. Branson sold the very profitable Virgin Records in 1992, and used the money to expand into new small ventures, including Virgin Cola, Virgin Brides, Virgin Clothing, and Virgin Cosmetics. Many failed. There was further diversification in transport. In 1997 Virgin took over the franchise of part of Britain's rail system and launched Virgin Trains, and in 2000 he launched the Australian airline Virgin Blue. The group entered financial services in 1995 when it partnered with an insurance company to create Virgin Direct. In 1998 Virgin backed a start-up team in the health and fitness sector to launch Virgin Active. In 1999 it launched Virgin Mobile, the first British virtual cell-phone network operator. Typically, Virgin's start-up model involved the use of private financing alongside another equity investor, combined with a large amount of debt to Virgin Group Holdings, the parent holding company (Gordon, 2014).

The Virgin Group was organized in a hierarchical structure but with some especially distinctive features. In 2014 at least eighty companies had the Virgin name, and a small number of them, including Virgin Atlantic and Virgin Media, were large businesses. Virgin Group Holdings, whose portfolio was valued at more than £5 billion (US $7.5 billion) in 2014, fully owned only a few of the companies. The Holdings were run on a private equity model, employing cash or stakes in other firms to support the growth of other Virgin-branded businesses (Gordon, 2014). It held both majority and minority shares in Virgin companies, while other companies were joint ventures. Most of the companies in the portfolio were private, although some, like the Australian airline Virgin Australia, were publicly listed. Some, such as most of the Virgin Mobile companies, were linked to the group only by a licensing agreement, as Branson had sold all the equity. Virgin Mobile Canada, for example, was owned by Bell, and Virgin Mobile Australia was owned by Optus. Virgin controlled the operating companies primarily by having people on their boards and through licensing agreements which stipulated the terms and conditions of the use of the brand (MacCormack, 2001; Pisano and Corsi, 2012). Table 5.5 lists the twelve largest Virgin companies by revenues in 2014 and gives their relationship to Virgin Group Holdings.

It is not straightforward to describe either the performance or the capabilities of Virgin, as the group was opaque. The business was intimately connected to the charismatic founder Richard Branson and a brand that symbolized fun, innovation, rebellion, value for money, and good customer service. In an interesting twist on organizational design, the brand identity serves as the primary means of coordinating disparate companies. The Virgin brand also played an important role in recruiting

Table 5.5. Largest Virgin companies and relationship to Virgin Group Holdings, 2014.

Virgin Company	Annual Revenues (£ million)	Virgin Group Holding share of equity (%)
Virgin Media	4,300	0. Royalty income only
Virgin Australia	2,600	10
Virgin Atlantic	2,600	51
Virgin Mobile USA	1,300	0. Royalty income only
Virgin Trains	946	51
Virgin America	911	22
Virgin Active	631	48
Virgin Holidays	535	Owned by Virgin Atlantic
Virgin Mobile France	362	50
Virgin Mobile Canada	359	0. Royalty income only
Virgin Mobile Australia	343	0. Royalty income Only
Virgin Money UK	299	47

Source: based on Gordon (2014).

management talent, as the group was considered an attractive place to work (Pisano and Corsi, 2012: 8). There were also less flattering explanations. As in the case of other business groups and conglomerates with powerful founder entrepreneurs, such as Lonrho and Tiny Rowland and News Corporation and Rupert Murdoch, there were allegations by investigative journalists that Virgin's growth rested on fragile ethical foundations (Bower, 2008).

It is also possible to see the private equity industry as a successor to the conglomerates. While the two models differ radically in some respects, including the former's use of independent funds organized as limited partnerships to carry out buyouts rather than holding direct ownership stakes, they also share considerable similarities, including the use of acquisitions and unrelated diversification, and perhaps even, as Cheffins and Armour suggest, "a capacity for capturing the public imagination" (Cheffins and Armour, 2007: 27). The industry association claims that Britain in 2015 was "one of the leading centers for private equity in the world."[4] The largest houses included Apax Partners, which traced its history back to Patricof & Co. founded in 1969, Permira (1985), Alchemy Partners (1997), and Phoenix Equity (2001). In 2015 these companies had funds under management of $40 billion, $22 billion, $2.2 billion, and $1.3 billion, respectively. However, the industry appeared to lack the legitimacy of its American counterpart, and was subject to a British public enquiry in 2007 (Cheffins, 2008: 397–401; De Cock and Nyberg, 2014). The British firms also encountered multiple funding and other issues after the 2008 financial crisis (Ebrahimi, 2013). It was too soon to tell, however, whether British private equity firms would recover their dynamism, or eventually follow the path of their predecessors, the conglomerates.

---

[4] http://www.bvca.co.uk/AboutUs.aspx, accessed February 15, 2015.

5.6 Conclusions

During the nineteenth century British merchant houses established business groups with diversified portfolio and pyramidal structures overseas, primarily in developing countries, both colonial and independent. These business groups were often resilient and successful until the late twentieth century. A number, especially Swire's and Jardine Matheson, survive today, albeit with their public companies quoted on stock markets outside Britain. By contrast, in the domestic economy the business-group form had a more limited role. Large single-product firms were the norm, which over time merged into large combines with significant market power. This reflected a business system in which a close relationship between finance and industry was discouraged, but there were few restrictions on the transfer of corporate ownership. Yet large and successful diversified business groups did emerge, such as Pearson and Virgin, which had private or closely held shareholding and substantial international businesses. After World War II, and especially between the 1970s and 1990s, large diversified conglomerates also flourished.

The evidence presented here certainly demonstrates that diversified business groups can add value in mature markets. They proved a highly successful and flexible organizational form for conducting international business over a very long period. In the domestic economy, Pearson and Virgin created well-managed and performing businesses. The much-criticized acquisitive conglomerates of the 1970s–1990s were also quite successful forms of business enterprise. While they were obviously not perfect and capable of major missteps, the demise of many of them appears to owe more to management fads than to serious underperformance.

CHAPTER **6**

....

BELGIUM

*the disappearance of large
diversified business groups*

....

MARCO BECHT

6.1 INTRODUCTION

....

BELGIUM became an independent country in 1831 following the "Belgian Revolution" of 1830 and the installation of Leopold I as monarch embedded in a constitutional parliamentary democracy. The Belgian economy experienced rapid growth in the nineteenth century. The country was at the forefront of the Industrial Revolution in continental Europe and the expansion of capital-intensive industries like mining, iron, steel, glass, armaments, canals, railways, steam, chemistry, and electricity (Van der Wee, 1996).

The Belgian banks combined commercial and investment banking (Houtman-De Smedt, 1994), together with the holding of participations in the capital of industrial and commercial companies—a phenomenon termed "the mixed bank." The dominant institution was the Société Générale de Belgique (SGB), which is credited with being the first financial holding company or "universal bank" (Liefmann, 1921) in the country.[1] The SGB provided a full range of corporate financial services and took equity stakes in the companies it funded. It also maintained a network of dependent banks. The SGB also had close ties with government: it started off as the government's bank, the monarch was a shareholder, it had former government officials on its board, and its headquarters was deliberately chosen to overlook the Royal Park in Brussels (*Parc Royal* or *Warande*) that connects the Belgian parliament, the prime minister's office, and the Royal Palace. In many ways it was a "state within the state."

---

[1] See Cottenier et al. (1989), Kurgan-van Hentenryk (1996), Maville et al. (1997), and Brion-Moreau (1999) for company histories.

The history of business groups in Belgium falls roughly into three periods:[2] first, the Industrial Revolution through World War I to the Great Depression, when the Belgian government imposed the separation of banking from industry (1934–5); second, the rise and fall of the diversified holding company that ended with the takeover of the SGB by the French Suez Lyonnaise des Eaux group (1988); and third, the accelerated sale of the holding-company portfolios to foreign groups and the implosion of the banking sector during the 2007–8 financial crisis.

In the first period the dominant institutions were the aforementioned Société Générale de Belgique and the Banque de Belgigue, founded in 1822 and 1835, respectively. The latter was considerably weakened during the banking crisis of 1876 and had to be rescued by a consortium of its competitors, led by the SGB. In the latter half of the nineteenth century the Banque de Bruxelles, founded in 1871, developed into the SGB's principal rival.

The second period started off with the SGB as the dominant group, but it soon had to share control of key sectors with Groupe Bruxelles Lambert (GBL). GBL was formed in 1972–5 and has its origins in the Banque de Bruxelles. The group was successively controlled by the Launoit family, by the Lambert family, and by the self-made businessman Albert Frère.

The beginning of the second period in 1934–5 was marked by the forced separation of industrial assets and banking that resulted in four institutions evolving in parallel. The SGB became a pure holding company that retained the old name, while the banking interests were placed in a new company called Banque de la Société Générale de Belgique (BSGB). BSGB evolved through a series of mergers to become Générale de Banque/Generale Bank.[3] The industrial holding SGB continued to hold a minority stake in the bank that amounted to 29.7 percent in 1998 (Vincent and Tulkens, 1998). This would become relevant in the third period, which marked the end of history for the bank and the holding company.

In 1935 the Banque de Bruxelles changed its name to Société de Bruxelles pour la Finance et l'Industrie (Brufina) and transferred its banking activities to a new company that kept the old name. Brufina ,along with the Compagnie financière et industrielle (Cofinindus), came under the control of the Launoit family (group), which as a result controlled approximately 50 percent of the Belgian coal industry; the other half was controlled by the SGB (Hannecart, 2010). The Launoit or "Banque de Bruxelles-Cofindus-Brufina" group also rivaled the SGB in steel and electricity and was the second-largest business group at the outbreak of World War II (Gillingham, 1974).

The Banque Lambert, controlled by Baron Léon Lambert, acquired shares in Brufina and the related Compagnie financière et industrielle (Cofinindus). In 1972 they merged

---

[2] This chapter covers the two important forms of diversified business groups in Belgium: bank-centered business groups, and their transformed variety—which we term "holding-company"-centered groups—that controls financial and industrial companies.

[3] See Van der Wee and Verbreyt (1997) and Buyst et al. (1998) for full accounts of the bank's history.

to form the Compagnie Bruxelles Lambert pour la Finance et l'Industrie (CBLFI). The French Paribas, through its Belgian holding Cobepa, could have blocked the merger but was seen off with stakes in the steel and electricity industry. The Banque de Bruxelles merged with Banque Lambert in 1975 to form Belgium's then second-largest bank, the Banque Bruxelles Lambert (BBL). Together these entities formed the Groupe Bruxelles Lambert (GBL) with significant industrial interests controlled by the Lambert family.

The final years of the second period are also marked by the acquisition of control of GBL by Albert Frère over the period 1982–7. GBL was in financial difficulties and the Belgian Banking Commission recommended a "Belgian solution." Albert Frère seized the opportunity and together with a number of allies acquired a 33-percent stake, a blocking minority under Belgian law. The outside investors subsequently diluted the stake of the Lambert family to 5 percent through capital increases. The takeover was final when the sick Baron Lambert (born 1928) died in 1987 and Frère advanced to the position of chairman.

In the third period the attitude of Albert Frère was decisive. The traditional controllers of Belgian industry had generally favored "Belgian solutions" for corporate restructuring. Frère was willing to sell companies he controlled or influenced to the highest bidder, and became a billionaire in the process. The acquisition of control over GBL by the Frère-Bourgeois Group allowed Albert Frère to initiate or broker many of the transactions that resulted in the disappearance of the large business group in Belgium.

GBL shared control over important companies and sectors with the SGB. In 1988 these arrangements were broken. The Italian industrialist Carlo De Benedetti launched a hostile takeover bid for the SGB that shocked the Belgian corporate and political establishment. The SGB and its traditional allies organized a white-knight defense around the French Suez group. The declared intent was to ensure the continuation of the SGB, but this arrangement quickly unraveled. Suez was interested in absorbing the SGB's utility assets, while the Belgian parties to the "rescue" wanted to acquire the SGB's banking assets. In rapid succession the SGB portfolio was restructured or sold. In 2003 Suez completed the absorption of the SGB's utility interests, marking the end of Société Générale de Belgique. GBL participated actively in this restructuring and took full advantage of the shifts in the traditional balance of power between the SGB spheres of influence, Belgian families, foreign interests, and its own. Major transactions included the sale of the Royal Belge insurance company to the French AXA Group and of Petrofina to the French Total. The initial exception was the banking sector. Albert Frère (GBL) sold BBL to the Dutch ING group, but control over the SGB banking interests remained in Belgian hands. In 1998 the SGB (Suez) sold Generale Bank to the Belgian Fortis AG headed by Count Maurice Lippens, one of the architects of the 1988 "rescue." The Fortis AG board installed itself in the former SGB building on Rue Royale. Fortis AG was hailed as a worthy successor to the SGB's banking and insurance tradition that embraced the new strategy of "bancassurance." There were great expectations about the future development of the group, which continued to expand through corporate acquisitions. Belgium was under shock again when

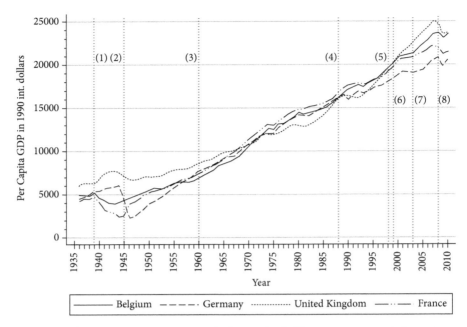

FIGURE **6.1.** Belgian GDP per capita growth during the holding company period 1936–2010.

Source: Drawn based on Maddison (2013).

Fortis AG imploded during the financial crisis of 2008. Its banking interests were sold to BNP Paribas to become BNP Paribas Fortis, a wholly owned subsidiary of the French BNP Paribas group.[4] At the end of the third period the only surviving diversified Belgian business group of historic and economic significance is Groupe Bruxelles Lambert (GBL) controlled by the Frère family, albeit in simplified form.

There were no obvious consequences for economic growth. Figure 6.1 plots GDP per capita growth for Belgium compared to Germany, the United Kingdom, and France as reported in the Maddison Database (Bolt and van Zanden, 2014) after the Belgian banks were forced to place their industrial stakes into holding companies. (1)–(2) mark the beginning and end of World War II; (3) the independence of the Congo; (4) the battle for corporate control of the SGB initiated by Carlo De Benedetti; (5) the complete takeover of the SGB by SLE and delisting; (6) the takeover of Generale Bank/Générale de Banque by Fortis; (7) the merger of the SGB with Tractebel to become Suez-Tractebel; and (8) the forced sale of Fortis Bank to the French BNP Paribas.

The remainder of this chapter is structured as follows. Section 6.2 provides a short history of the mixed banking period (1830–1934); Section 6.3 covers the holding company period (1935–88); Section 6.4 the foreign takeover period (1988–2016); and Section 6.5 concludes.

---

[4] The French Paribas group played a major role in Belgian affairs via its subsidiary Cobepa before it was taken over by its rival Banque Nationale de Paris (BNP) in a hostile takeover.

6.2 The Rise and Transformation of Bank-Centered Business Groups, 1830–1934

6.2.1 The Société Générale de Belgique and the Emergence of Bank-Centered Business Groups

The early history of Société Générale de Belgique (SGB) and the banking and industrial development of Belgium is well documented (Chlepner, 1930; Van den Wee, 1996). The SGB was headquartered between the Belgian parliament and the Royal Palace and is widely credited with bringing about rapid economic growth in the nineteenth century that propelled per-capital income in close range to the United Kingdom.

Figure 6.2 plots GDP per-capita growth for Belgium compared with Germany, the United Kingdom, and France, as reported in the Maddison Database (Bolt and van Zanden, 2014) for the bank-centered business group period when the Belgian mixed banks held major stakes in industrial corporations. Significant events are marked by vertical lines: (1) the creation of the d'Algemeene Nederlandsche Maatschappij ter Begunstiging van de Volksvlijt by William I of the Netherlands; (2) Belgian independence and emergence

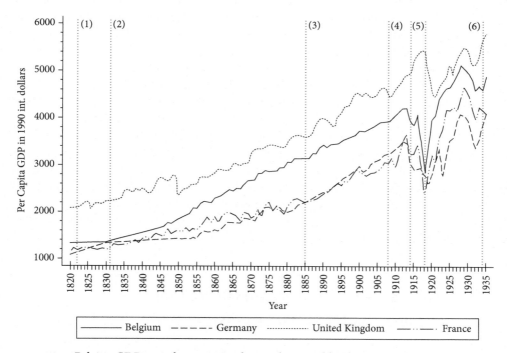

FIGURE 6.2. Belgian GDP growth per capita during the mixed banking period 1820–1935.

Source: Drawn based on Maddison (2013).

of the Société générale pour favoriser l'industrie nationale (which adopted the name Société Générale de Belgique at the beginning of the twentieth century); (3) creation of the "Independent State of the Congo" (État indépendant du Congo) under the personal control of Leopold II, King of Belgium; (4) creation of the Belgian Congo by transfer of control from the king to the state; (5) the beginning and end of World War II; and (6) royal decrees of August 22, 1934, which forced the separation of banking and industrial holdings and the end of the bank-centered period.

During this initial period of industrial development Belgium successfully copied the British development model, taking advantage of its rich endowment of natural resources and ideal geographic location at the crossroads between Germany, France, and Britain. The Belgian Industrial Revolution could build on a long tradition of craftsmanship in Flanders (lace, paintings, cloth) and iron processing in Wallonia. In addition, there was trading through ports such as Antwerp and the opportunity to build canals. In this environment, it was the Societé Générale de Belgique that fueled this industrial development.

Liefmann (1921), in his classic work on industrial and financial holding companies, describes the SGB as the "mother of all universal banks." The ownership structure of the SGB evolved gradually over the nineteenth century and through a number of large capital issuances the company became very widely held.

The early rival of the SGB was Banque de Belgique, founded in 1835. It did not last and was brought down in 1876 by the entrepreneur Simon Philippart, who had established a private rail network that was supposed to compete with the state network in the south of Belgium and in France (Kurgan-van Hentenryk, 1982). It was Banque de Bruxelles, established in 1871, that would grow into the main rival of the SGB. It did so through the systematic acquisition of regional banks, forging links with industry, and taking industrial participations.

The emergence of the mixed bank goes back to the 1850s when the above-mentioned commercial banks had to accept stocks in exchange for the bad debts of several self-standing industrial companies. The banks had originally granted long-term loans to these companies to support the rapid industrialization of the country, and especially the capital-intensive industries of mining, iron and steel, and railroads (Daems, 1977). Nevertheless, due to the economic crisis of the late 1830s and 1840s, many of the industrial companies could not fulfill their duties to pay back the banks. As banks had to accept industrial assets in exchange for the bad debts, they got to hold a controlling interest in many industrial companies in the country. Once those industrial companies were under bank control, however, the banks' influence went beyond pure financial control to technical expertise and commercial guidance, especially in overseas markets (Daems, 1977).

6.2.2 The 1930s Crisis and Transformation of Bank-Centered Business Groups

The world economic crisis of 1929–33 brought the period of mixed banking in Belgium to an end. Financial markets were put into turmoil by the Wall Street Crash of 1929, the inability of Germany to service its foreign debt, and the devaluation of the British pound and the US dollar. In Belgium there was an outflow of funds from the banks. Mixed banks had particular difficulty in meeting this demand because they transformed short-term deposits into long-term loans and equity investments. In normal times they could have borrowed against their industrial portfolios but in crisis the value of these portfolios declined. There were no dividend payments either to bolster liquidity. In addition, the industrial clients were demanding short-term loans to continue operations. Banks could not refuse because bankruptcies would have posed a further threat to the value of the industrial portfolios.

As a result there were a series of debt-to-equity swaps that led to a further rise in the share of equity security holdings in the balance sheets of Belgian banks. At the same time the volume of deposits was falling (Vanthemsche, 1991: 110). The SGB managed the situation well and continued to extend credit to its industrials clients. By contrast, two of its smaller rivals, the Banque Belge du Travail and the Algemeene Bankvereeniging, struggled. In 1934 the government was forced to step in and support the banks. It also extended credit to industry through the Société Nationale de Crédit à l'Industrie ("National Company for Credit to Industry," created in 1919). The measures were designed to prevent a panic and bank runs.

On August 22, 1934 the government also passed a law that prevented deposit-taking banks from investing in commercial or industrial securities. The banks were also to hold a minimum amount of capital. The existing groups like the SGB were forced to split their operations into a pure holding company and a bank. The forced reorganization did not come as a complete surprise. Société Générale de Belgique and Banque de Bruxelles had already created holding companies to manage their industrial holdings (Vanthemsche, 1991: 110). The SGB had several holding companies organized by industry; the BdB had created one large company, the Compagnie Belge pour l'Industrie, in 1928. The link with the banks was not abolished, but they changed position. As a result, the banks no longer controlled the holding company but the holding companies controlled the banks.

6.3 THE EVOLUTION OF THE BELGIAN "PURE HOLDING COMPANY," 1935–88

Belgium was occupied by German troops from May 1940 to September 1944, and its diversified business groups centered around holding companies became linked to the German wartime economy.[5] Wartime industrial production followed the "Galopin

---

[5] The term "holding company" is used here to denote diversified business groups in Belgium that involve a pure holding company that controls financial and industrial companies. It is, however, different from the usage of the term by Williamson (1975) in the sense that the internal control apparatus is provided.

Doctrine" formulated by the Galopin Committee, "a shadow-government in the field of social and economic policy" (Luyten, 2010). The committee was named after the governor of the Société Générale, Alexandre Galopin, whom the occupational forces often referred to as the "uncrowned King of Belgium" (Gillingham, 1974). The doctrine foresaw that industrial production would continue but only at a reduced level. It precluded the production of weapons or ammunition. The Belgian business-group structure made it relatively easy to integrate with the German wartime economy that was based on the country's interwar cartels (Gillingham, 1974: 17). As a result, the main business groups survived World War II and their balance sheets suffered surprisingly little damage.

In 1956 a left-wing report documented the main groups after World War II and their influence on the Belgian economy (FGTB, 1956). The dominance of Société Générale de Belgique was confirmed. Empirically, Daems (1977) arrived at a similar conclusion to the FGTB by analyzing holdings data from the Belgian Banking Commission. His well-known work contributed significantly to the classification of Belgium as a country dominated by diversified business groups in the postwar period organized around pure holding companies.

Daems (1977) focused on the largest holdings companies in Belgium in 1971 (Table 6.1). Société Générale de Belgique was the largest group in terms of assets, followed by Traction et Électricité (which changed its name to Tractionel), Electrobel, Sofina, and Cie Bruxelles-Lambert. The listing masks the fact that the SGB and Cie Bruxelles-Lambert jointly dominated the electricity industry and many of the other holding companies on the list: Sofina was controlled by the SGB, and jointly the SGB and Sofina controlled Tractionel; Electrobel was dominated by Bruxelles-Lambert but the SGB had a shareholding. Cofinindus, Brufina, and Cie Bruxelles Lambert would merge to form Groupe Bruxelles Lambert (GBL). GBL was controlled by the Lambert family with 51 percent in 1983 but also had shareholding ties with two other groups that would become very important in the years to come, the Frère-Bourgeois Group and Cobepa, the Belgian industrial holding controlled by the French Paribas bank (Figure 6.3).

Figure 6.4 shows the joint influence over the electricity sector by Société Générale de Belgique, Groupe Bruxelles Lambert, and Cobepa in 1981–2 (Vincent and Lentzen, 1983). Electrafina was acquired by Groupe Bruxelles Lambert in 2001. Intercom, Ebes, and Unerg were restructured to form Electrabel that was taken over and delisted by Suez in 2005 after a squeeze-out.

Figure 6.5 shows the joint influence over the petroleum sector by Société Générale de Belgique and Groupe Bruxelles Lambert, also in 1981–2 (Vincent and Lentzen,1983). Petrofina was sold to the French Total Group after the Frère-Bourgeois Group had acquired control of Group Bruxelles Lambert.

Figure 6.6 shows joint influence over the retail sector by Société Générale de Belgique, Groupe Bruxelles Lambert, and Cobepa in 1981–2 (Vincent and Lentzen, 1983). GIB-Inno-BM was sold to the French Carrefour in 2000 and Inno to the German Metro retail group in 2001. Delhaize merged with the Dutch Ahold in 2016 to form the

Table 6.1. The twenty largest Belgian holding companies in 1971.

	Assets		Net Worth		Portfolio	
	1971	1975	1971	1975	1971	1975
1. Soc. Générale de Belgique	15,127	22,515	8,570	9,589	8,236	12,565
2. Traction et Electricité	8,506	14,381	3,326	6,369	5,605	9,651
3. Electrobel	9,160	9,386	5,351	5,652	5,680	6,948
4. Sofina	7,147	7,854	5,767	6,079	6,324	6,640
5. Cie Brussel-Lambert						
a) Lambert Mij	5,108	13,704	2,709	6,206	3,549	6,261
b) Brufina	2,208		1,621		1,323	
c) Cofinindus	1,787		1,423		1,545	
6. Glaverbel-Mecaniver	n.a.	8,073	n.a.	6,154	n.a.	6.221
7. Financière Eternit	3,479	4,517	3,223	3,539	3,154	4,011
8. Cobepa	3,451	4,241	3,233	3,683	1,907	3,832
9. Electrorail	2,695	3,323	2,321	1,998	2,565	2,725
10. Contibel	3,747[4]	5,407	2,433[4]	1,722	2,780[4]	2,676
11. Finoutremer	2,017	2,952	1,735	2,357	1,735	2,464
12. Almanij	1,752	2,533	905	1,232	1,063	1,871
13. Financière du Kuau	934	2,135	414	1,843	377	1,814
14. Electrafina	1,552[4]	1,658	1,426[4]	1,491	1,487[4]	1,620
15. Socfin	815	1,305	681	1,215	635	1,130
16. C.D.I.	666	2,196	444	1,254	341	1,099
17. Tabacofina	1,869	1,884	1,035	1,097	1,049	1,016
18. Ibel	257	1,206	240	844	190	879
19. Cie Générale Cond. d'Eau	2,490	1,694	2,175	1,445	757	826
20. Cie Grands Lacs	720	1,173	355	804	458	664

Source: Daems (1977) Tab. 3.

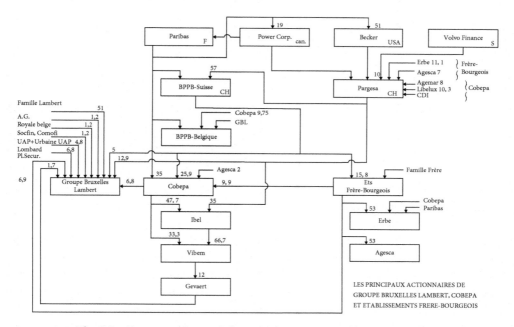

FIGURE **6.3.** The Frère-Bourgeois Group, Cobepa, and Groupe Bruxelles Lambert (GBL) in 1981–2.

Source: Vincent and Lentzen (1983).

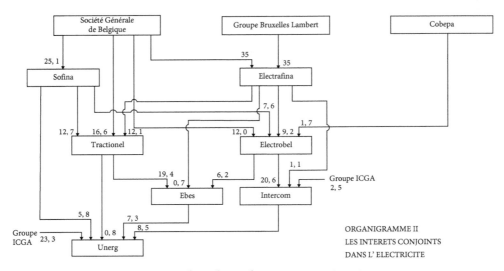

FIGURE **6.4.** The Belgian electricity sector in 1981–2.

Source: Vincent and Lentzen (1983).

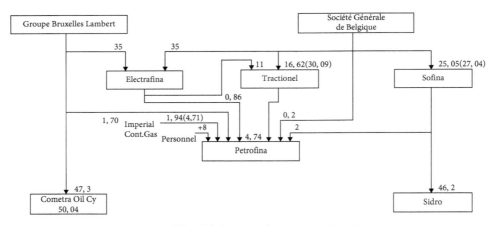

FIGURE **6.5.** The Belgian petroleum sector in 1981–2.

Source: Vincent and Lentzen (1983).

Ahold Delhaize Group. Colruyt has become completely independent and is controlled by the Colruyt family.

At the end of the second period in 1987 the SGB controlled 1,261 companies—487 in Belgium, 468 in the rest of the European Union (or European Economic Community, as it was then), and 306 elsewhere (Société Générale de Belgique, 1988). At the annual general meeting in June 1987 its governor, René Lamy, confirmed that the management saw the future of the SGB as a diversified business group actively engaging in the

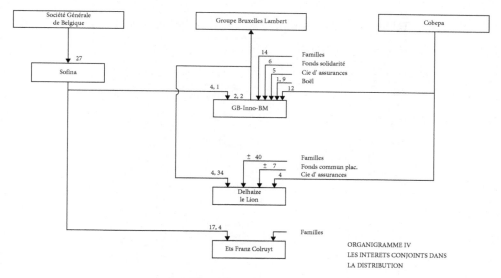

FIGURE **6.6.** The Belgian retail sector in 1981–2.

Source: Vincent and Lentzen (1983).

development of its industrial companies and not as a simple vehicle for financial investment.

He asserted that "Société Générale is foremost an active holding company, not a simple investment vehicle for financial investment.... We have chosen to make Société Générale the head of an entrepreneurial group that is characterized by the pursuit of the following objectives: (1) unification basic policies; (2) control of strategic choices; (3) unification of managerial language and strategic methods; (4) executive mobility; (5) unification of training." The events of the following year would take the SGB down a different path.

6.4 THE DECLINE OF THE BELGIAN HOLDING COMPANY AMID FOREIGN TAKEOVERS, 1988–2016

European integration had already had an impact on the development of Belgian groups in previous years, in particular in the mining and steel sectors, the two industries the European Community was founded on. However, it was the Single European Act of 1986, which aimed to complete the European single market by 1992, that accelerated developments. The defining moment for the third period of Belgian business-group history was the 1988 hostile takeover contest for control of Société Générale de Belgique. The outcome was transformational not only for the SGB but for business

Table 6.2. Evolution of the SGB shareholder structure.

Shareholder structure before 1987	
Boerenbond	0.70%
Assubel	1.00%
A.G.	3.10%
Royal Belge	3.20%
Total "stable" shareholders	*8.00%*
Shareholder Structure September 8, 1987	
(extraordinary shareholder meeting)	
Boerenbond	0.70%
Assubel	1.00%
A.G.	3.10%
Royal Belge	3.20%
Artois-Piedbbeuf	1.90%
Gevaert	1.00%
Total "friendly" shareholders	*10.90%*
Lazard	4.00%
CGE	1.00%
Dumenil-Leble	2.90%
Sumitomo	1.00%
Cerus	1.00%
Total "raiders"	*9.90%*
Shareholder structure April 14, 1988	
Cerus and allies	31%
Europe 92 Group	16%
Total De Benedetti	*47%*
Suez, AG and supporters	*51%*
Shareholder structure June 26, 1989	
Suez	51%
AG and Belgian partners	16%
Cerus	15%
Institutional investors	5%
Retail investors	12%

Source: Cottenier et al. (1989).

groups in Belgium more generally. The events of January to April 1988 are well documented, and since the main purpose of this section is to discuss the resulting restructuring, they are only recounted briefly.[6] The hostile raid was possible because the SGB was widely held and relied on small cross-shareholdings of 7.3 percent with Assubel, A.G., and Royal Belge—three Belgian insurance companies (Table 6.2)—and

---

[6] See Boelaert and Bonucci (1988) for a short summary in English; comprehensive accounts in French include Maville, Tulkens, and Vincent (1997): 136–84.

Table 6.3. BEL20 index evolution.

ISIN	Name	SGB	GBL	1991	1999	2007	2016	Destiny/Comment
be	GIB Group	1	1	19.7	1.6			Taken over by French Carrefour in 2000; delisted 2002
be	Société Générale			9.8				Taken over by the French Suez in 1998 & delisted
be	Recticel pref.	1		9.8				Cie du Bois Sauvage & mgmt buy SGB stake in 1998
be	Electrabel	1		7.4	2.5			Taken over by Suez in 2005
be	Umicore			7.4	1.5	0.8	3.5	Independent
be	Delhaize	1	1	4.9	3.0	3.1	7.9	Acquired by Ahold in 2016
be	GBL			4.9	1.3	2.6	4.9	Part of the Frère-Bourgeois group
be	Barco			4.9	0.7			Independent
be	Royale Belge	1	1	4.9				Taken over by the French AXA-UAP
be	Generale Bank	1		4.9				Taken over by Fortis in 1998
be	CBR	1		3.7	1.3			Taken over by the German Heidelberger Cement
be	PetroFina	1		2.9				Taken over by the French Total in 1999
be	Fortis			2.5	40.8	23.1		Forced restructuring in 2008 after state intervention
be	Solvay			2.5	4.8	1.9	5.4	Independent
be	Tractebel	1	1	2.5	3.3			Taken over by Suez in 1999
be	Bekaert			2.0		0.4	1.1	Independent
be	Sofina	1		2.0				Independent
be	Tessenderlo			1.2	1.6			Independent
be	Gevaert			1.2				Drops out of index in 1994
be	UCB			1.0	8.3	3.2	7.0	Independent
be	KBC				10.9	5.9	9.4	State intervention during financial crisis
be	Agfa-Gevaert				8.0	4.2		Entered index after merger and IPO; restructuring
be	Almanij				5.0			Holding company that controls KBC
be	Dexia				2.1	22.2		Nationalized during the financial crisis
be	Cobepa				2.0			Squeeze out by controlling BNP Paribas in 2000
be	Real Software				0.8			Trading today under RealDolmen after restructuring
be	D'Ieteren				0.3			Independent

(continued)

Table 6.3. Continued

ISIN	Name	SGB	GBL	1991	1999	2007	2016	Destiny/Comment
be	Colruyt				0.2	0.5	2.9	Independent
FR	Suez CR					15.9	12.1	replaced by GDF Suez renamed ENGIE in 2015
be	AB Inbev					6.9	12.8	International brewing group
be	Belgacom/Proximus				5.3	3.8		Partially privatized telecoms company
be	CNP					1.3		Part of the Frère-Bourgeois group
be	Mobistar					1.0		France Telecom Group
be	Ackermans v. Haaren				0.8	2.4		Conglomerate
be	Omega Pharma					0.6		Acquired by Perrigo Plc in 2014
be	Cofinimmo					0.3	1.8	Independent
be	Ageas						5.8	Insurance assets of the Fortis Group
be	Bpost						2.0	Privatized mail company
be	Elia						1.0	Belgian electric grid company
NL	Galapagos						1.2	Dutch, independent
NL	ING Groep						11.4	Dutch banking group
be	ONTEX Group						1.6	GBL Investment
be	Telenet Group						1.9	Independent
	Total			100	100	100	100	

its size as guarantors against a hostile takeover. In a purely Belgian context a hostile takeover of the the SGB appeared unimaginable.

6.4.1 The 1988 Change of Control at the SGB

On Monday, January 18, 1988 Carlo De Benedetti, an Italian financier and industrialist, announced that Cerus, a company controlled by him, and its allies commanded 18.6 percent of the voting shares of Société Générale de Belgique and that he intended to boost the stake to 33.6 percent (a blocking minority) via a tender offer. At a press conference held in Brussels, De Benedetti explained that he was motivated by the fact that the SGB was one of the oldest holding companies in the world, that it was of sufficient size "to be the foundation for the construction of a truly European holding company," and that it had no large shareholders.[7]

The announcement did not come as a surprise to the SGB board. Cerus was a known 1-percent shareholder since 1987 (Table 6.2), when the stake was acquired with full knowledge of the chairman of the SGP board, René Lamy, who called the operation a "friendly exchange." During the week prior to the announcement, on just three days (January 13, 14, and 15) 12 percent of the outstanding shares and warrants of the SGB had changed hands. There was speculation as to the identity of the buyer. On Saturday, January 16 Lamy learned that Cerus had been buying and informed the president of the Banking Commission, the stock-exchange regulator Walter Van Gerven. Lamy also started making phone calls to friends and allies. Sunday, January 17 was decisive. Carlo De Benedetti called Van Gerven and informed him that his group held a 18.6-percent block. The same evening he visited Lamy at the latter's residence.[8] Immediately after the meeting Lamy went to another private residence to meet the SGB board that had been brought together for an extraordinary board meeting. The board decided to increase the capital of the SGB by 43 percent from 35,254 to 50,278 million Belgian francs by creating 12,000 new shares, significantly diluting the block acquired by Cerus.

The capital increase was problematic and controversial: (1) the shares were issued at a price of 3,350 Belgian francs but only partially paid up; (2) the shares were purchased by Sodecom, a subsidiary of the SGB; (3) the funding came from a credit line opened by Générale de Banque, the bank controlled by the SGB; and (4) the credit line constituted more than 50 percent of Générale de Banque's own funds. The timing of the transaction, the use of what were essentially treasury shares, the related party transaction, and the prudential regulation aspect would make the operation impossible under more recent rules. At the time Belgian and European corporate law, securities, and banking regulation were sufficiently unclear to create legal uncertainty that allowed the SGB to look for a white knight.

---

[7] See http://www.sonuma.be/archive/la-saga-de-la-société-générale for a video of the press conference.

[8] It was at this meeting that De Benedetti offered Lamy a box of Italian chocolates.

The initial white knight was a group of Belgian and foreign shareholders headed by the Flemish industrialist André Leysen, who on January 29 announced that he held 32.2 percent of the SGB's capital. This group officially fell apart on February 15. Instead, another group led by Maurice Lippens, the managing director of the AG insurance group, emerged around the French public utility company Suez. A group around AG and Lippens was said to hold around 16 percent, while Suez held 27 percent of the SGB shares.

The case was resolved on April 14, 1988, at an extraordinary general meeting. The company headquarters at 30 Rue Royale was packed and a tent had been erected to accommodate the shareholders. The votes were counted and the De Benedetti Group could only muster around 47 percent of the votes, while a majority of 51 percent was held by the Franco-Belgian group around Suez. The hostile bid had failed. A second general assembly was called on June 21 and a third on July 5. The final outcome was a shareholder agreement between Suez, which was to hold 50 percent, and the "Belgian anchor" coalition, which held 16 percent. The Cerus stake was reduced in a series of exchange and other operations, mostly against shares in Suez.

6.4.2 The Post-1988 SGB Restructuring

The board of Société Générale de Belgique was restructured to reflect the new control structure. The new chairman was Etienne Davignon, a former head of the International Energy Agency and a former European Commissioner. His initial mission was to make good on the promises that had been made to the different parties involved in the "rescue."

Under Suez, the first wave of divestments in the SGB portfolio occurred between 1988 and 1989. The aim was to reduce the SGB from twelve "strategic sectors" to twelve strategic holdings (Maville, Tulkens, and Vincent 1997: 208). The vision was to turn the SGB into "a Belgian center of industrial excellence with a European calling" ("centre d'excellence industrielle belge à vocation européenne").

Suez tightened its control over the SGB in 1991 when it appointed Gérard Mestrallet as chief executive officer. The new mission was to transform the SGB from a business group actively engaged in the development of its industrial companies into a pure holding company engaged in financial investments only. In an important symbolic move the emblematic company headquarters at 30 Rue Royale was sold to Générale de Banque in 1992 and the remainder in 1995. A small part of the building was leased back by the SGB from the bank.

6.4.3 Six Weddings and a Funeral

In the eighteen months between November 1997 and April 1999 there were six mergers that paved the way for the dissolution of the SGB, preceded by its 175th anniversary, the funeral.[9] In short succession GBL (Albert Frère) sold its remaining 12.5-percent stake in BBL and turned the successor of the Banque de Bruxelles into a 100-percent subsidiary of the Dutch ING. GBL also orchestrated the sale of Royal Belge, the insurance company, to the French AXA-UAP (1999). Albert Frère facilitated the sale of Petrofina to the French Total group. The Frère group became a 9-percent shareholder in Total. The Frère group also sold a 25-percent stake in Tractebel, the SGB's Belgian utility holding company, to the SGB (1999). Tractebel has remained a listed subsidiary.

The most significant transaction in this context was the sale of Générale de Banque to Fortis AG, one of the SGB's largest minority shareholders (1999). In a complex transaction the SGB's 30-percent stake in Générale de Banque ended up with Fortis AG, while Fortis's 12-percent stake in the SGB ended up with Suez. As a result of the operation, the SGB became a 100-percent subsidiary of Suez. After the conclusion of the Tractebel operation, the SGB became a largely empty shell. In 2003 the SGB and Tractebel, its listed subsidiary, were merged to form Suez-Tractebel. The name Société Générale de Belgique thus disappeared.

6.4.4 The Transformation of the BEL20

The transformation during the third period is also reflected in the composition of the BEL20, the Belgian blue-chip performance index introduced in 1991. Table 6.2 shows the evolution of the BEL20 benchmark index on its official starting date (March 18, 1991), after the first set of major merger and acquisition transactions that tilted the index heavily to banks (June 14, 1999), before the financial crisis (September 25, 2007) and after the restructuring that followed (March 31, 2016).

At the outset the index was dominated by two business groups: the SGB and GBL, and their portfolio companies. The portfolio companies had disappeared as their sale progressed. The index also tracks the rise and fall of Fortis AG. After the Generale Bank takeover in 1999, Fortis AG had an index weight of 40 percent. The weight is somewhat lower in 2007 through the inclusion of Suez after the merger with Tractebel and the disappearance of the SGB. However, the index is no longer purely "Belgian" since Suez is included with its French ISIN number. The 2016 index composition confirms the disappearance of the large diversified business group in Belgium, with the sole exception of Groupe Bruxelles Lambert.

---

[9] *Six Weddings and a Funeral* is the English translation of the Dutch title of Delvaux and Michielsen (1999), *Zes huwelijken en een begrafenis*, a detailed journalistic account of events. The title is a pun on the 1994 British romantic comedy *Four Weddings and a Funeral*. The title of the French edition (*Le Bal des Empires* or "Dance of the Empires") is itself a pun on the 1967 Polanski parody *Dance of the Vampires*. In 1999 SGB published a voluminous Festschrift to mark its 175th anniversary (Brion and Moreau, 1999).

6.5 CONCLUSION

The diversified holding companies and the associated business groups that long dominated the Belgian economy have largely disappeared. The timing of their disappearance coincides with European integration but also with the decline of the industries they had helped to build: mining and steel. The corporate sector of Belgium in 2016 is dominated by independent family-controlled companies, in particular the brewing giant AB Inbev, and the subsidiaries of foreign groups. The disappearance of the large Belgian diversified business groups is almost complete.

CHAPTER 7

THE NETHERLANDS

the overlooked variety of big business

FERRY DE GOEY AND ABE DE JONG

7.1 INTRODUCTION

UNTIL fairly recently, economic and business historians argued that the Managerial Enterprise, modeled after American big business, with professional managers and having a multidivisional form (M-form), was the final stage of development of big companies. This idea—convergence on one dominant model—is no longer accepted, because there are and always have been a variety of business models (Lamoreaux, Raff, and Temin, 2003; Langlois, 2013). Each of these models offers advantages and disadvantages for entrepreneurs. One major alternative form is the business group.[1] These groups are hardly novel and often grew out of family firms globally active in trade and transport from the nineteenth century. Many started in the colonies of Western countries in South America, Asia, and Africa (Jones and Wale, 1998; San Román, Fernández Pérez, and Gil López, 2014).

Different explanations have been offered for the existence of business groups, including the development or lack thereof of the market (transaction costs perspective), political factors, social relations (network theory), institutional voids, and corporate governance (agency problems) (Smångs, 2006; Yiu et al., 2007; Colpan and Hikino, 2010). These explanations either stress negative factors (e.g., underdevelopment of the capital market) or positive features of business groups (e.g., flexibility). While these factors may offer an explanation for the existence of business groups in late-industrializing or emerging economies, they are mostly not convincing in the case of mature Western countries. Yet business groups exist in today's Western countries as

---

[1] The coverage of this chapter encompasses diversified (and mostly family-owned) business groups and holding-company-type groups that have been active within the Dutch economy, as well as diversified business groups centered around trading companies active overseas.

well, even in such highly developed countries as Sweden or Belgium (Kurgan-van Hentenryk, 1997; Smångs, 2008). Entrepreneurs in these countries prefer business groups because they are flexible with regard to training and reshuffling of managers, facilitating internal or cross-financing, spreading innovation and new technologies, disseminating knowledge on marketing and sales, and sharing experiences (Sköld and Karlsson, 2012).

The focus of this chapter is on business groups in the Netherlands during the twentieth century. The existence of business groups in a highly developed economy like the Netherlands confirms the need to develop alternative explanations. Business historians and management scholars alike have largely disregarded Dutch business groups until now. This could mean that either there have been no significant business groups in the Netherlands or they have simply ignored them because the preferred unit of analysis, especially in business history, is the company. Because of this lack of previous studies, our research on business groups in the Netherlands is exploratory and introductory.

Despite the lack of research from business historians, some scholars—mostly economists and business researchers—have discovered numerous business groups in the Netherlands. The multi-country study by Belenzon and Berkovitz, for instance, records the prevalence of business groups in the Netherlands compared to stand-alone firms: on average 43.9 percent of firms in their sample of countries were part of a business group (Belenzon and Berkovitz, 2008, 2010). In the Netherlands this was even 67 percent, one of the highest scores in their data (the highest was Sweden at 74 percent and the lowest the United States at 0 percent). The data used by Belenzon and Berkovitz consists of 1,922 private and public companies in the Netherlands as of 2005: 634 (33 percent) were counted as stand-alone and 1,288 (67 percent) as affiliates belonging to a business group (Belenzon and Berkovitz, 2008: 26). Heugens and Zyglidopoulos also compare business groups around the world, but their data on the Netherlands is taken from Belenzon and Berkovitz (Heugens and Zyglidopoulos, 2008). The high score of the Netherlands is perhaps not surprising given the widespread existence and importance of family firms in a sample of large companies in the Dutch economy (La Porta, Lopez-de-Silanes, and Shleifer, 1999: 492–3).

The limited amount of research on business groups in the Netherlands is related to the availability of data. Information on share ownership in listed companies prior to the 1992 Wet Melding Zeggenschapsrecht (Law Reporting Majority-Ownership) is almost completely lacking. The law obliged legal entities to report share holdings of 5 percent or more. Shareholders of listed companies before 1991 were not registered but bearer only. Existing company histories thus rarely provide information on the identity of the shareholders (De Jong and Röell, 2005: 481). Furthermore, until 2008 national statistics bureaus recorded mainly legal entities, where business groups are enterprises consisting of many interlinked legal entities. After 2008 the European Union (EU) instructed national statistical bureaus to start collecting information on business groups. According to Statistics Netherlands, in 2010 there were 1,604 non-financial business groups, called "enterprise groups," in the Netherlands. Two years later their number had risen to 1,891.[2] This includes Dutch groups and foreign-owned groups in the Netherlands. Most of these business groups were in agriculture and manufacturing (758), followed by trade and catering (653), transport and ICT (229), and personal and business services (251).[3]

Before jumping to conclusions, we must carefully look at the data used by these scholars and especially their definition of a business group. The data they present usually offers no information on the historical development of business groups: they are snapshots in time (usually the past few years). Most authors use different definitions when investigating business groups. For example, Belenzon and Berkovitz define a business group very broadly as "an organizational form in which at least two legally independent firms are controlled by the same ultimate owner."[4] The literature on business groups is in general hampered by a lack of consensus on a definition (Cuervo-Cazurra, 2006: 420–2). For our research we have used the definition and typology of Colpan and Hikino (Chapter 1, this volume): "An economic coordination mechanism in which legally independent companies utilize the collaborative arrangements to enhance their collective economic welfare."[5] This broad definition includes two main types of business groups: hierarchy and network. The focus in this chapter is on the hierarchal business groups, and especially their diversified variety.

Section 7.2 presents an overview of the history of big business, including the development of banking, in the Netherlands in the twentieth century. In Section 7.3 we construct a Top 20 of publicly listed firms for eleven benchmark years in the period 1903–2003. We next analyze the prevalence and importance of business groups in the Top 20, including the types of business group. To clarify the evolution of business groups, we provide two case studies: a bank-centered and a trading-company-centered business group. Our data on the Top 20 includes only listed companies, but there are also unlisted large companies in the Netherlands, many of which are family-owned. For Section 7.4 we thus exploit a different source to trace these family business groups. This section again contains two case studies. We end in Section 7.5 with some concluding remarks on the prevalence and resilience of business groups in the Netherlands during the twentieth century.

---

[2] Netherlands Statistics uses the following definition of an enterprise group: "An association of enterprises bound together by legal and/or financial links. Explanation: A group of enterprises can have more than one decision-making center, especially for policy on production, sales and profit. It may centralize certain aspects of financial management and taxation. It constitutes an economic entity which is empowered to make choices, particularly concerning the units which it comprises." The number of enterprise groups included Dutch business groups active in the Netherlands and foreign countries, but also foreign business groups in the Netherlands and other countries. See https://www.cbs.nl/en-gb/our-services/methods/definitions?tab=e#id=enterprise-group (last accessed May 27, 2015).

[3] *http://statline.cbs.nl/StatWeb/publication/?VW=T&DM=SLNL&PA=80262ned&D1=0&D2=a&D3=a&D4=10-12&HD=140225-0923&HDR=T,G1&STB=G2,G3* (last accessed May 27, 2015).

[4] This definition is based on Almeida and Wolfenzon (2006a).

[5] See the contribution of Colpan and Hikino in this volume.

7.2 BIG BUSINESS IN THE
NETHERLANDS: AN OVERVIEW

In every country the absolute number of big companies is small compared to the number of small and medium-sized enterprises (SMEs). In 1888–90 there were just 98 companies in the Netherlands with more than 200 employees, which is considered big in the Netherlands; in 1930 this was 709 (or 0.2 percent) of a total of 395,357 registered companies. In 1950 the number of big companies had increased to 3,580, or 1.1 percent, of the total number of companies. Fifty years later this was about 4,000, or just 1 percent (Van Gerwen and De Goey, 2008). Despite their small absolute number, big companies were important contributors to national employment, gross domestic product, and value added.

Company histories on most big businesses in the Netherlands are readily available, but systematic research is limited. In 1993 Bloemen et al. investigated the development of big manufacturing companies, using asset size as a criterion, between 1913 and 1990 (Bloemen, Kok, and Van Zanden, 1993; Bloemen, Fransen, Kok, and van Zanden, 1993). Their study therefore does not include the important service sector. They used the same methodology as business historian A. D. Chandler Jr. in his 1990 book on big business in the United States, Great Britain, and Germany (Chandler, 1990). According to Bloemen et al., Dutch big business in the twentieth century was dominated by a few very large companies: Royal Dutch Shell (oil), Unilever (food), Philips (electronics), AKZO (chemicals), Hoogovens (steel), and DSM (chemicals). To these six big companies we could add others, such as KLM, Fokker, Elsevier, and Heineken (see Appendix, this chapter).

New companies, especially in manufacturing, are usually single-product firms. In the course of their history, through mergers and acquisitions, they diversify in related and unrelated activities. Some become a classic multinational, others form a conglomerate or business group. This development is, however, not a linear process, as companies can follow very different paths. A short history of the six largest Dutch companies will demonstrate this.

Two family firms, Jurgens and Van den Bergh, began producing margarine in the 1870s. The fierce competition forced both firms to incorporate as a joint-stock company and in 1927 they merged to form the Margarine Union. Two years later the Margarine Union merged with the British soap manufacturer Lever Company to form Unilever. Unilever had a unique management structure, with two holdings in each country of origin, two chairmen, and two head offices in London and Rotterdam. In the 1960s Unilever's main business was still in food and soap, but about one third in unrelated activities: specialty chemicals; paper and packaging; transport and trucking; advertising and market research; plantations, logging, and trading. It kept a decentralized structure with a large number of subsidiaries in manufacturing and services (Wilson, 1954; Wilson, 1968; Jones, 2005b). After the discovery of oil in the

Dutch East Indies, several Dutch entrepreneurs applied for a mining concession. In 1890 they founded the Royal Dutch Petroleum Company, which sold petroleum in East Asian markets. In 1907 Royal Dutch merged with the British company Shell. Royal Dutch Shell developed into an international oil company, with interests in mining, manufacturing, transport, and retailing. Like Unilever, it had a dual nationality and organizational structure (Jonker and Van Zanden, 2007). In 1891 Gerard Philips started to manufacture incandescent lamps. Cut off from his main suppliers during the First World War, when the Netherlands remained neutral, Philips was forced to invest in a large number of factories, including glass manufacturing, paper, and packaging. After the war Philips became an international electronics company, producing light bulbs, radios, televisions, shavers, and a growing number of electric consumer products (Heerding, 1980, 1986). The artificial fiber company ENKA was established in 1911 by a number of wealthy industrialists, including F. H. Fentener van Vlissingen (see Section 7.4). In 1929 ENKA merged with the German company Glanzstoff to form AKU. AKU merged in 1969 with the Dutch firm KZO (chemicals and pharmaceuticals) to form AKZO, and in 1994 it merged with the Norwegian firm Nobel becoming AKZO Nobel. The main business of AKZO Nobel was in pharma, coatings, and chemicals, until the pharma business was sold. The First World War convinced Dutch industrialists to establish a blast furnace and steel company to become less dependent on foreign supplies. In 1924 Hoogovens began producing iron and steel. It concluded several joint ventures with other large Dutch companies, including fertilizer (to utilize its byproducts) and steel barrels (De Vries, 1968; Dankers and Verheul, 1993). The last big company is De Staatsmijnen (DSM), originally a state-owned coal-mining company. Before the Second World War DSM produced fertilizer and chemicals, byproducts related to coal. After the closing of the coal mines in the 1960s, DSM became a manufacturer of bulk and fine chemicals (Homburg, 2004). These companies all started as single-product firms in a limited number of sectors typical for the Second Industrial Revolution (Van Zanden, 1998). This was no coincidence, because the Netherlands industrialized late in the nineteenth century.

The First Industrial Revolution (coal, iron, and steam) had little impact on the formation of business groups in the United Kingdom of the Netherlands (1814–30), except in the industrialized southern Netherlands (later Belgium). The separation in 1830 of Belgium most likely reduced the number of business groups. While in Belgium after 1830 the Société Générale de Belgique[6] and some wealthy families (including Solvay, Coppée, and Boël) actively collaborated to develop the country through investments in mines, iron and steel, railways, manufacturing, and colonies (Congo), such close cooperation was almost absent in the Netherlands in the nineteenth century. The relatively late industrialization of the Netherlands compared to the UK and Germany cannot be attributed to a lack of capital, a preference to invest in trade and services or

---

[6] Founded in 1822 by King William I. After the separation of Belgium in 1830 it functioned as the Belgian national bank until 1850 when de Nationale Bank van België (National Bank of Belgium) was established.

foreign bonds and securities. In the early nineteenth century the Netherlands was one of the wealthiest countries in the world. This was the legacy of the Golden Age of the seventeenth century when the Dutch created a global empire based on trade and spices. It led to the development of the stock exchange in Amsterdam and trading companies such as the Dutch East India Company, better known as VOC (Vereenigde Oostindische Compagnie, 1602–1799). However, following the Napoleonic Wars (1803–15) the Dutch economy stagnated until the 1870s. Most companies were small-scale and family-owned. Their demand for external financing remained very modest and they preferred retained earnings and private loans to finance business activities (De Jong and Röell, 2005: 468–72). This allowed them to maintain control of the family business.

Because industrialization occurred relatively late and demand for investment capital remained small, modern banking did not develop until the late nineteenth century. Before the 1860s there were various financial intermediaries: commission traders and merchant houses, cashiers ("kassiers"), Jewish banks, and the Nederlandsche Bank (established in 1814). Except for the latter, these were also small-scale family-owned businesses providing financial services, including insurance, brokering, changing money, and short-term credit. In the period 1860–90 the banking sector witnessed several structural changes: the establishment of new commercial joint-stock banks and the creation of a national network of agencies by these banks. These changes reflect the growing demand for investment capital from manufacturing companies. However, even in the 1880s most manufacturing firms started on a modest scale with families, relatives, and business associates providing the necessary start-up capital. The Amsterdam stock exchange was one of several ways to finance a company. In rare cases Dutch companies used the London stock market to float shares, including the margarine company Van den Bergh (later Unilever) and the Rotterdam-based company R. S. Stokvis (Jonker, 2009).

In the period 1890–1920 the Dutch banks grew rapidly through mergers and acquisitions. By 1925 five banks dominated the Dutch banking sector, including the Amsterdamsche Bank, Rotterdamsche Bank, Twentsche Bank, Incassobank, and Nederlandsche Handel-Maatschappij (NHM, see Section 7.3.2.1). Increasingly these banks made long-term investments in manufacturing companies and often initiated the establishment of new enterprises. In return they occupied seats on the supervisory boards (Raad van Commissarissen). However, after the short but severe crisis of the early 1920s the banks gave up their seats and a more conservative attitude towards financing returned. Many Dutch companies, even large enterprises, continued to prefer internal financing (De Jong and Röell, 2005; Van Zanden, 2009). In the early 1960s a second merger wave led to the establishment of large banks, including Algemene Bank Nederland (ABN, a merger between Twentsche Bank and NHM) and AMRO (a merger of Amsterdamsche Bank and Rotterdamsche Bank). In the 1970s and 1980s rising wages, declining profits, new national legislation, the development of the European Economic Community (EEC, later European Union), and growing international competition forced Dutch companies to adapt their strategy (Barendregt and Visser,

2009). They either disappeared completely from the Amsterdam stock exchange or applied for official quotation to issue shares in order to finance their (international) expansion. They preferred related diversification, while unrelated diversification, according to De Jong et al., "was a sparsely used strategy in the Netherlands, but as far as it happened, it happened in the 1970s" (De Jong, Sluyterman, and Westerhuis, 2011: 72). This was followed by a third merger wave in the early 1990s, this time involving banks and insurance companies, after the legal ban on this type of merger was lifted. This created several large financial companies: ABN AMRO, ING, RABO, AEGON, and Reaal.

7.3 Big Business and Publicly Listed Business Groups

To investigate the prevalence of business groups we collected balance-sheet data on Dutch companies between 1903 and 2003, with ten-year intervals, listed on the Amsterdam stock exchange.[7] For each benchmark year we constructed a Top 20 of the biggest companies. There are several criteria to determine the size of companies: market value, book value of assets, turnover, and number of employees or added value. All these criteria have advantages and disadvantages. Unfortunately data for most of these criteria are not available for the whole of the twentieth century. We therefore decided to collect information on the total asset size. The data is taken from *Van Oss Effectenboek*, an annual guidebook for investors on the Amsterdam stock exchange.[8] We supplement this data with others sources, including the Orbis database, the *Gale Directory of Business Histories*, and several company histories. In contrast to the previously mentioned research by Bloemen et al., our data includes manufacturing companies and the service sector, mainly transport and trade. These were important throughout Dutch economic and business history (Van Zanden and Van Riel, 2000).

The data includes companies established in the Netherlands and which expanded to other Western and non-Western countries. There were also many firms whose focus was mainly on the Dutch colonies in the West Indies and East Indies. The company seat was in the mother country, but their main field of operation was in the colonies. Business historians have labeled them "free-standing companies" (FSCs) (Gales and Sluyterman, 1998). This is similar to Great Britain and her colonies, although the

---

[7] The year 1942—rather than 1943—is selected because until then the effect of the German occupation on the Dutch economy was still relatively small, but thereafter German exploitation of the economy increased.

[8] The data in *Van Oss Effectenboek* is not complete. For some benchmark years no information was available for several companies, including Royal Dutch Shell in 1913 and 1923.

British Empire was much larger and geographically more dispersed.[9] In 1913 there were about 632 Dutch FSCs (Sluyterman, 1998: 40). Although part of the Kingdom of the Netherlands, the political, social, and legal conditions in the colonies differed markedly, and this may have stimulated the formation of business groups (Sluyterman, 2005). We can call them "colonial business groups." However, decolonization after the Second World War forced these companies to adapt their strategy and structure and find new markets. Thereafter the label "colonial business group" no longer applies.

It is imperative to note what is *not* included in our data. The Top 20 is a small part of the universe of large Dutch companies, because not all companies are listed on the stock exchange in the period 1903–2003. In addition, we use the criterion of total assets for company size, because this is available for the whole of the twentieth century and included in *Van Oss Effectenboek*. Because the assets of the financial firms (banks, investment companies, insurance firms) are of a completely different nature when compared to non-financial firms, we exclude the former from our data. Furthermore, the data does not include the hundreds of FSCs in the Dutch colonies, except for a few firms that were also important for the Dutch economy.

Van Oss Effectenboek only contains information on public corporations (in Dutch, Naamloze Vennootschap, abbreviated to NV) listed on the Amsterdam stock exchange. Until the early 1970s the listed companies included two types: those with widely held shares ("open corporations") and closely held shares ("closed corporations"). The latter were mostly family businesses and, although listed, their shares were not actively traded, because the family owners did not accept any foreign influence. In 1970 the Dutch government introduced a new law on annual company reports (Wet op de Jaarrekening van Ondernemingen), which no longer made a distinction between these two types of corporation. According to the old law (1928), the "open corporations" were obliged to disclose information on only twelve different items; the 1970 law increased this number to eighty for all listed corporations. Furthermore, the annual reports had to be certified by chartered accountants. The new law was the result of the First Directive (1968) of the EEC requiring all European corporations to publish their annual reports according to harmonized accounting standards. Because the First Directive did not recognize the existing difference between "open" and "closed" Dutch corporations, the government introduced a new legal entity in 1971 besides the NV: the Besloten Vennootschap (BV). These BVs do not publish annual reports and in general provide little financial and other information on their business activities. Many listed "closed corporations" decided to become a BV: between 1971 and 1974 about 43,000 Dutch NVs were restructured into BVs (Maijoor, 1990). The very large international retail company C&A, owned by the family Brenninkmeijer, is a well-known example. The BVs disappeared from the Amsterdam stock exchange and were also no longer included in the *Van Oss Effectenboek*. To trace potential business groups in these BVs, we used a different research method and other data (see Section 7.4).

---

[9] See Geoffrey Jones, this volume.

7.3.1 Business Groups in the List of Top-20 Enterprises in the Netherlands

Our data reveals 91 unique companies in the Top 20 for the selected benchmark years between 1903 and 2003. Some companies are present for only one benchmark year, while others appear more frequently. Several companies still exist, but many have disappeared because of mergers and acquisitions or were liquidated. The list includes well-known companies like Royal Dutch Shell, Unilever, Holland America Line (HAL), Heineken, AKZO Nobel, DSM, and Philips. It furthermore contains unfamiliar companies, like Deli Spoorweg-Maatschappij (a colonial railway company), Stoomvaart-Maatschappij Zeeland (shipping), and Wester Suikerraffinaderij (sugar refinery). Looking at their industrial classification, the Standaard Bedrijfsindeling (SBI, comparable to the Standard Industrial Classification or SIC), clearly reveals the dominance of product-focused enterprises in transport, trade, food, oil, and chemicals. Between 1903 and 2003 the dominance of transport and trade declined: the Top 20 becomes more varied in terms of the industries. In 1903 the Top 20 numbered thirteen companies in transport, and in 2003 just one. This reflects the declining importance of shipping and shipbuilding after the 1970s. Their place was occupied by companies in other sectors, such as construction, printing and publishing, and chemicals.

Bloemen et al. (2003) investigated how many manufacturing companies disappeared from the Top 100 in the years between 1913 and 1990 and how many were newcomers. They concluded that there was much dynamics, although the Top 10 was rather stable. Most dynamics concerned newly established smaller companies. Our data on manufacturing and service companies shows that on average 34.5 percent in the Top 20 were new in each benchmark year. The highest percentage was in 1942: 70. This was probably caused by the incompleteness of the *Van Oss Effectenboek* in that year, as well as by several very large companies, like Philips and Royal Dutch Shell, transferring their capital to the United States or other places before the beginning of World War II. A second shift occurred at the end of the twentieth century with the arrival of ICT companies and large media companies (Reed Elsevier, Wolters Kluwer) following mergers and acquisitions in the 1990s.

For each company in the Top 20 we determined whether it was a business group (of the hierarchy type) for the years it was in the Top 20 (see Appendix, this chapter).[10] It may well be that some companies were a business group before or after they were listed in the Top 20 in one of the benchmark years. Because the strategy, structure, and scope of companies change, certainly over the period of a hundred years, they may at one time be classified as a business group but in a later benchmark year perhaps better as a classic multinational corporation. Determining the subtype of the business group (diversified, holding, or pyramidal) for such a long time period is even more problematic.

---

[10] We would like to thank Prof. Dr. K. E. Sluyterman for her comments and help.

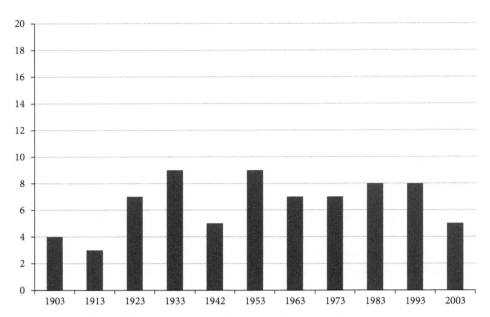

FIGURE 7.1. Number of business groups in the top 20 (1903–2003).

Note: Business groups considered here are the hierarchy-type business groups covering diversified and holding type of groups.

Source: own dataset based on Van Oss Effectenboek.

The Appendix presents an overview of the business groups in the Top 20 between 1903 and 2003. Of the 91 companies, 23 were identified as a business group at least once when they were in the Top 20. For several companies the information is too sparse to draw conclusions and they were conservatively classified as non-business groups. There are a number of companies whose classification is debatable. An example is Heineken, which because of its legal structure (a holding company) is often seen as a business group. In our view the holding only serves to protect the shares of the Heineken family to maintain control of their company, and we have thus decided to classify the company as a non-business group (Sluyterman and Bouwens, 2014: 380–1).

Figure 7.1 shows the number of business groups in the Netherlands for each benchmark year; on average there were 6.5 business groups in the Top 20. Their number increases until the 1930s, then declines, but recovers after the Second World War. Since the 1950s, however, the number of business groups in the Top 20 has slowly declined. The decline of business groups during the Second World War is perhaps related to fiscal measures taken by the German occupiers. Before the war double taxation was explicitly prevented in the Wet op de Dividend- en Tantièmebelasting (Law on Dividend and Royalty Tax) of 1917 by an article stipulating that taxes on dividends paid in a (fully or partially owned) subsidiary firm could be deducted from the tax bill (Schaafsma, 1946: 87). In April 1940—just before the beginning of the five-year occupation by the Germans—a new tax regime based on corporate profit taxes was introduced to replace dividend taxes. Although the new regime also, and even with broader definition, prevented double taxation, in 1941 and 1942 the Nazis took several fiscal measures to discourage holding structures. In the Liquidatiebesluit (Liquidation Order) of 1941 firms could apply fiscally attractive arrangements to dismantle the holding structures (Schaafsma, 1946: 86). Subsequently, in the Besluiten Vennootschapsbelasting (Corporate Tax Order) of 1942 a strict ruling on exemptions for double taxation was introduced, i.e., only for 100-percent ownership, which was highly restrictive (Schaafsma, 1946: 88). In 1945 these rulings were reversed. Morck (2005) incorporates the Dutch case in an international overview on double taxation and also finds that this was not the case in the Netherlands in 1997 (Morck, 2005: 147).[11] Yet pyramids have rarely been seen in Netherlands, even after the war, as the country allows for other control-enhancing mechanisms such as certificates and "golden shares," which make the use of pyramidal structures unnecessary (De Jong and Röell, 2005). Certificates are constructions where a trust office (administratiekantoor) owns the shares of the company and issues non-voting certificates to financiers. As the management of the trust office normally acts in the interest of firm management, an effective device against shareholder influence and hostile takeovers is created. These certificates were initially created to enhance the liquidity of shares, but were used from the 1930s increasingly as a control-enhancing mechanism (Westerhuis and De Jong, 2015). "Golden shares" were not only used by private companies, but also by the Dutch government to protect wholly or partly state-owned enterprises against hostile takeovers. This was particularly the case with economically important and politically strategic companies, including mining (DSM), metallurgy (Hoogovens), electricity companies, the postal services (PTT), defense, and transport (KLM). In the Netherlands these specific measures were implemented in laws, such as the Elektriciteitswet (1998, concerning electricity companies) or the Mijnwet Continentaal Plat (1965, Mining Continental Shelf in the North Sea), and included in company statutes. Other EU countries like Portugal, France, and Belgium used similar instruments. The Treaty of Rome (1957), when the EEC (later EU) was founded, opposed these measures, because they severely hindered the free flow of capital across borders (Article 58). Certificates and "golden shares" were very effective instruments and as such we found no such pyramidal business group in the list of our enterprises in the Appendix.

Figure 7.2 shows the share of the assets of business groups (of the diversified and holding-type variety) in the total assets of all Top-20 companies. Despite the small number of business groups for each benchmark year, the share of assets in total assets is rather large. This is related to the inclusion of several capital intensive companies like Royal Dutch Shell, Unilever, Philips, and AKZO Nobel. The share of assets of business groups increases until the 1960s, but then declines slowly.

Classifications and typologies work best on paper, but in the real world "pure types" are much harder to find. The typology of business groups devised by Colpan and

---

[11] Morck (2005) demonstrated that out of thirty-three countries in his study only the US levies an effective tax on intercorporate dividends, of 7 percent. He argues that this taxation is detrimental to the occurrence of business groups in the US.

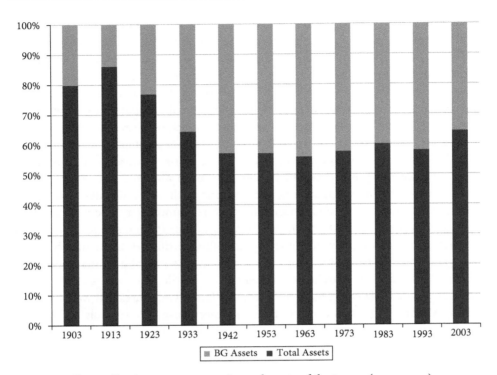

FIGURE 7.2. Share of business group assets in total assets of the top 20 (1903–2003).

Note: Business groups considered here are the hierarchy-type business groups covering diversified and holding type of groups.

Source: own dataset based on Van Oss Effectenboek.

Hikino consists of a large number of variables: ownership, control unit, top management, and administrative control, operating units, growth patterns, and product portfolios. While on some variables firms at some time may resemble a multidivisional enterprise or conglomerate with internal divisions, on other variables they appear as a business group. This is not surprising. Big companies were mostly also multinationals, and although originating in mature Western economies, had to cope with a variety of business environments, markets, and institutional settings, requiring flexibility and ingenuity with regard to organizational forms, management, and strategy. In certain environments they more resembled a classic multinational enterprise, but in others took on the form of a business group. This certainly applies to companies like Royal Dutch Shell, Unilever, Philips, and AKZO Nobel.

It becomes even more difficult to apply a strict typology of types of business groups when we consider the many political, economic, and social changes that occurred during the period 1903–2003. Modern company histories written by business historians clearly exemplify when, why, and how big businesses responded to changes. These studies, however, seldom present sufficient and reliable data on all variables to distinguish (sub)types of business groups for a period covering a century. As already

Table 7.1. Business groups in the largest enterprises between 1913 and 2003: types and subtypes.

Type	Number of enterprises
Diversified:	20
Bank-centered	*1*
Family-owned	*7*
State-owned	*0*
Cannot be classified	*12*
Holding	9
Pyramidal	0

Source: own Dataset based on *Van Oss Effectenboek.*

explained, before 1991 reliable information on shareholders of listed companies is almost absent. Keeping these observations in mind, we have further classified the twenty-three business groups in subtypes (see Table 7.1). Most business groups were diversified in unrelated industries, the majority of these with strong family connections. Because we have excluded the financials, bank-centered business groups are absent, except for the NHM that by 1903 had become a bank. Our sample does not contain a pyramidal business group, partly because we have excluded the financial companies. The total number of types in Table 7.1 of business groups is higher than twenty-three because some companies changed their outlook between 1903 and 2003 and were accordingly reclassified. A number of diversified business groups could not be classified in one of the subtypes—family-owned, bank-centered, or state-owned—because of lack of reliable information.

Our overview of business groups (of the hierarchy-variety, as discussed earlier) demonstrates that their number is smaller than other scholars have assumed, but their prevalence in big business in the Netherlands is nevertheless clear. Most business groups trace their origin to the late nineteenth century, but it took several years or decades before they became a business group.

7.3.2 Case Studies

In contrast to Great Britain, it is not possible to distinguish between unrelated diversified international/colonial business groups and more focused business groups in the home market. From the 1870s we can identify the beginning of some unrelated diversified business groups in the Dutch colonies, mainly the Dutch East Indies. Several trading companies invested in plantations (coffee, tea, sugar), factories, and shipping, and offered some financial services. After the 1890s new industrial companies were started in the Netherlands. These were initially typical single-product firms (oil, margarine, light bulbs), but given the relatively small size of the Dutch home market they soon expanded internationally in related and unrelated business activities and some eventually formed a business group. The decolonization of Indonesia in 1949 forced the colonial business groups to restructure and adapt their business strategy. Many decided to focus on the Netherlands, but further expansion in the 1960s and 1970s was again international.

7.3.2.1 *NHM: A Bank-Centered Business Group*

The second largest company in 1903 was the Nederlandsche Handel-Maatschappij (NHM, or Dutch Trading Company). The NHM remained a very large company and developed mostly into a bank-centered business group from a trading-company-based origin.[12] The NHM disappears from the Top 20 after 1903 because it is reclassified as a financial institution and our data does not include that type of company.

The NHM was founded in 1824 to stimulate the Dutch economy by increasing trade in the Netherlands (until 1830 including Belgium) and the Dutch East Indies and West Indies (Jonker and Sluyterman, 2000; De Graaf, 2012). From the beginning the NHM developed a close relationship with several Dutch shipping companies, owning shares in Koninklijke West-Indische Maildienst (KWIM, 1882), the Koninklijke Paketvaart Maatschappij (KPM, 1888), the Java-China-Japan Lijn (JCJL, 1902), and a seaport (Zeehaven en Kolenstation Sabang). In the East Indies, the NHM was mainly a trader in the beginning, besides acting as sole agent for the Dutch government. From the 1860s, the NHM lost its privileged position when the market in the Dutch East Indies was further liberalized. The NHM not only diversified in terms of its business activities, but in addition expanded geographically by opening agencies in Singapore, Japan, and the United States. Some of these proved successful, at least for a while, but others failed after a short period (De Goey, 2013). As one of the largest companies in the East Indies, the NHM provided several financial services to other Dutch companies, although the company charter did not allow pure banking activities until it was adapted in 1874. Thereafter banking gradually became more important, while trading activities were reduced. In the 1870s the NHM invested in the oil business and mining companies, including coal, bauxite, and gold. It also participated in a distillery, an indigo factory, and two tobacco factories, but most of these investments were discontinued in the early 1880s. More profitable were investments in tobacco and coffee plantations. The NHM developed its own plantations, besides participating in others, either directly by buying shares or indirectly through a hypothecation ("relatie maatschappijen"). Through this system the NHM attained the characteristics close to a network-type business group. The NHM also invested in the Dutch West Indies, particularly Surinam. These investments included plantations, a sugar refinery, and exploration to mine gold, but this venture was stopped after five years.

---

[12] De Graaf (2012): Appendix 2 (on the CD-ROM in the book) contains an overview of all known affiliates, participations, and takeovers of the NHM until 1964.

Table 7.2. NHM enterprises in 1902 and 1916.

	NHM owned		Related through hypothecation		Total	
	Sugar	Other products	Sugar	Other products	Sugar	Other products
1902	14	3	22	7	36	10
1916	16	0	23	46	39	46

Source: De Bree (1918): 421.

The NHM shifted its strategy in response to conditions on world markets. After 1900 the coffee plantations were terminated and replaced by investments in natural rubber and tea, but mainly sugar plantations and sugar refineries (see Table 7.2).

In the early twentieth century the NHM was a trader (on its own account, for the Dutch state and other private companies), a general merchant bank, and an investment bank, besides owning a number of plantations and factories, mainly in the Dutch East Indies. After the First World War, however, the NHM became a major bank and participated in the establishment of many new companies, including Hoogovens (iron and steel) and Royal Dutch Airlines (KLM), Holland-Zuid-Afrika Lijn (shipping), and a dry-dock company in Amsterdam (Amsterdamse Droogdok Maatschappij). During the economic crisis of the 1930s the NHM was forced to restructure its business, particularly because of heavy losses in the East Indies. From 1935 the NHM expanded its banking activities in the Netherlands and developed a new activity—insurance.

The independence of Indonesia in 1949, and more importantly the nationalization of all Dutch property after 1956, meant that the NHM lost most of its banking activities, plantations, and factories there. The financial loss was about 134 million guilders, but only 19.5 million guilders was compensated by the Indonesian government. From the 1960s the NHM focused primarily on further developing its banking activities in the Netherlands and other areas, including Pakistan, Saudi Arabia, the United States, Uruguay, and Brazil. In June 1964 the NHM merged with the Twentsche Bank to form Algemene Bank Nederland (ABN). A week later two other Dutch banks announced their merger: the Amsterdamsche Bank and Rotterdamsche Bank became AMRO. In 1991 ABN and AMRO merged.

7.3.2.2 *Internatio (Internatio-Müller): A Trading-Company-Centered Business Group*

The Internationale Crediet- en Handelsvereeniging "Rotterdam," better known as Internatio, started in 1863 as an import and export business located in Rotterdam. According to its original charter, Internatio was to work as a trader, shipping company, and bank, and invest in agriculture (plantations) (Mees, 1939). In the beginning Internatio appointed agents to trade with British India, China, Japan, and Chile, but this business was stopped because of financial losses, and from 1865 Internatio focused mainly on the Dutch East Indies. Besides trading, Internatio invested in coffee, tobacco, sugar plantations, and several factories. At the turn of the twentieth century Internatio had become one of the largest companies in the Dutch East Indies. Increasingly Internatio felt the competition from foreign producers (e.g., Japan). During the crisis of 1920–1 several trading houses in the Dutch East Indies went out of business, but Internatio survived thanks to its large hidden reserves amassed during the war. In the 1920s Internatio further diversified, investing in several manufacturing companies: paper, sugar, textile, cigars, and heat-resistant materials. In all these joint ventures Internatio handled distribution and sales.

The decolonization of Indonesia, and particularly the nationalization of Dutch property in 1956, forced Internatio to reorient its business activities. Besides a stronger focus on the Netherlands and Europe, this included Australia, Africa, and South America. After 1955 it acquired a number of Dutch companies specialized in engineering and technical services. In 1960s Internatio continued to diversify by investing in factories producing metal wares, industrial gasses, lead, and tin products.

In 1970 Internatio merged with Wm. H. Müller & Co. (founded in 1878), itself a diversified business group in mining, trade, stevedoring, transport, and shipping. In 1972 Internatio-Müller had about 14,500 employees, mostly in Europe, and turnover was 2,100 million Dutch guilders. The main area of investment was Europe (88 percent), the remainder being in the United States (6 percent) and Australia (5 percent). Its diversified activities allowed Internatio-Müller to weather the economic crisis of the 1970s. According to Sluyterman, the spread in activities "did enable losses in one sector to be compensated by the profits of another" (Sluyterman, 1998: 193). In 1990 Internatio-Müller consisted of about a hundred companies in a variety of industrial sectors. Three years later about thirty-five technology and engineering subsidiaries were regrouped in a new company called Imtech. Internatio-Müller next sold all port-related activities (originally owned by Wm. H. Müller & Co.) and the distribution of pharmaceuticals. The remaining chemical and agribusiness subsidiaries were regrouped in a new company: Internatio-Müller Chemical Distribution (IMCD). This company was sold in 2003.

After 2001 Internatio-Müller was no longer listed on the Amsterdam stock exchange but replaced by Imtech. Between 2001 and 2010 Imtech acquired about fifty-five European technology and engineering companies (IMTECH, 2010). Imtech, since 2012 called Royal Imtech, had become a large business group with about 23,000 employees and an annual turnover in 2010 of 4 billion euros. However, the very rapid expansion, several failed investments, and the rising costs of projects in Germany and Poland forced a reshuffling of the board of directors and a restructuring of the company in 2014. In early August 2015 the company filed for bankruptcy. The holding was quickly dismantled, while the receiver looked for potential buyers of the many independent subsidiaries. After August 14, 2015, Imtech was no longer listed on the Amsterdam stock exchange.

Our dataset on listed big companies includes several other diversified business groups, besides NHM and Internatio, such as Wm. H. Müller & Co. (until the merger with Internatio). In some of these business groups family owners were important, like R. S. Stokvis & Zonen (general merchants and manufacturers), Machinefabriek Gebr. Stork & Co. (machinery), and Phs. Van Ommeren Scheepvaartbedrijf (shipping). Several business groups started or were closely related to the Dutch colonies, notably the Dutch East Indies: Royal Dutch Shell, Handelsvereeniging Amsterdam, and Borneo Sumatra Handel Maatschappij (Borsumij). These colonial business groups often started as trading firms, but because of the specific conditions in the colonies diversified their business. Others, including many companies in transport and shipping besides manufacturing, were largely active in the Netherlands and other Western countries, like Unilever, Philips, Rijn Schelde Verolme, Koninklijke Pakhoed, and Koninklijke Nedlloyd Group. They expanded internationally through direct investments (FDI) and mergers and acquisitions.

7.4 CLOSELY HELD FAMILY BUSINESS GROUPS

In this section we discuss closely held family business groups. According to Masulis et al. (2011), Dutch family business groups are either horizontally or pyramidally structured. In horizontal groups the family directly or through a holding controls the equity of group firms. Limiting their research to listed firms in the year 2002, Masulis et al. find only five family business groups out of a sample of 183 listed Dutch firms (their total dataset consists of 28,635 firms in 45 countries). Of these five family business groups, two were horizontal and three pyramidal (Masulis, Kien Pham, and Zein, 2011: 3569–70).

Family business groups exist in mature and emerging markets and often have a long history. Their origin is frequently related to the family firm they once owned. After selling the family firm, they used the proceeds to invest in other companies, often through a holding at the apex. The closely held family business groups in the Netherlands are indeed usually organized as holdings, making it difficult to get a good overview of their investment strategy, legal structure, and management (see Table 7.3). The business group allowed the families to spread risks, acquire knowledge and managerial experience, and try out new product or geographical markets. The group structure in addition facilitated the financing of new investments. Not all family business groups are listed on the stock exchange. As we have previously discussed, after 1971 many listed Dutch family firms opted to restructure as a BV to avoid outsider influence. Unfortunately, no information is available covering the whole period 1903–2003. To trace some of these large family business groups we have used the Dutch magazine *Quote*. Each year it publishes a list of the 500 wealthiest Dutch individuals and since 2013 also the 50 wealthiest families. In Table 7.3 we list the ten wealthiest Dutch families and their business activities in 2014.[13]

---

[13] *Quote* magazine, "Quote 500" (2014).

Table 7.3. Top 10 wealthiest families in the Netherlands, 2014.

Rank	Family (or families)	Core entity	Original sector(s)	Estimated wealth	Business group*
1	Brenninkmeijer	C&A (1841); Cofra Holding	Confection retail	€22 b	Yes
2	Van der Vorm	HAL (1873 sold in 1988); HAL Trust (investment fund)	Shipping, investment fund	€6.2 b	Yes
3	De Rijcke	Kruidvat (1975, sold in 2002); De Hoge Dennen (investment fund)	Retail, cosmetics, toys	€1.9 b	Yes
4	Dreesman	V&D (1887); Commonwealth Investments (investment fund)	Retail	€1.6 b	Yes
5	Van Oord	Van Oord (1868)	Dredging, off-shore, marine engineering	€940 m	Yes
6	Van Oranje-Nassau	(Royal family)		€900 m	N.a.
7	De Pont	AGAM (1956); Janivo Holding (c. 1985) (investment fund)	Automobiles retail	€800 m	Yes
8	De Heus	Royal De Heus (1911)	Compound feed (animal feed)	€700 m	Yes
9	Salzer Levi, Drake and Mayer Wolf	Nidera (1920); Nidera Capital (investment fund); majority shares sold in 2014 to Cofco (China)	agricultural commodities (oilseeds, grains and biofuels), producer of seeds and crop protection products	€600 m	Unknown
10	Van den Broek	Van den Broek (1942)	Food retail, self service	€580 m	Yes

Source: *Quote* magazine (2014): 262–74.
* This covers all types of hierarchical business groups.

The wealthiest family in 2014 is the Brenninkmeijer family, the founders and owners of the C&A retail company. C&A is notorious for a lack of disclosure and does not, for example, provide revenue information for the C&A stores. The main headquarters is located in Zug (Switzerland) and the holding company of the legally independent, privately owned firms since 2001 is Cofra Holding AG Group (retail, real estate, private equity, and financial services). For this family business it turns out not to be feasible to describe its holding structure and affiliated firms. Undoubtedly the family holdings qualify as a diversified business group, because of the holding structure and unrelated-diversified activities. Some of these family-owned holding companies started in the late nineteenth century, but others acquired their capital more recently after the sale of their family business. The notable exception in Table 7.3 is no. 6, the Dutch royal family, where *Quote* estimates its wealth to be in real estate, art, and investments. The families in Table 7.3 typically control their assets via investment funds (holdings) and must be classified as unrelated-diversified business groups.

7.4.1 Case Studies

7.4.1.1 *HAL Trust and the Van der Vorm Family*

The second wealthiest family in 2014 mentioned by *Quote* is that of Van der Vorm. Willem van der Vorm (1873–1975) was an employee of the American Petroleum Company (APC), a subsidiary of Standard Oil (Esso). APC was founded in 1891 in Rotterdam to sell petroleum in the Netherlands and Belgium. In 1896 APC established the Scheepvaart & Steenkolen Maatschappij (SSM) to sell British coal. It competed fiercely with the dominant coal trader SHV (see Section 7.4.1.2). In 1905 Van der Vorm bought a number of SSM shares and was appointed director. He kept this position until 1944, although APC sold SSM to SHV in 1928. However, the takeover was kept secret for many years to maintain the illusion of two competing companies. Van der Vorm, while still director of SSM, invested in a large number of companies: Argolanda (1926, general trading company), Spoorijzer (1927, rail wagons), and Scheepvaart Maatschappij Frederika (c.1930, shipping). To these were later added various other non-related businesses: Mennens & Company (rope), Nederlandse Gasmaatschappij (gas), Nederlandse Fotografische Industrie (photography), Holland-Electro N.V. (consumer electronics), and Apparatenfabriek Thermion (light bulbs). In Sumatra (Dutch East Indies), Van der Vorm in addition owned a tea plantation until it was handed over to the Indonesian government in the 1950s.

Van der Vorm made perhaps his most important investment in 1933. He participated in a financial syndicate to save the Holland America Line (HAL, 1873) from bankruptcy. After the Second World War, HAL became a typical diversified company with interests in shipping, stevedoring, and tourism. In 1971 the freight division was sold and it ceased operating a regular passenger service from the Netherlands to the USA, leaving only the tourism division, including cruise ships, hotels, and tour operators. Furthermore, the headquarters of HAL was moved from Rotterdam to Seattle (USA).

In 1988 the Van der Vorm family sold the cruise business for approximately 1.4 billion Dutch guilders to the American company Carnival Cruise Lines (De Goey, 2005). The revenues were largely invested in the exchange-listed company HAL Trust, itself a subsidiary of HAL Holding, registered in Curaçao (Netherlands Antilles). Although it is generally assumed that members of the Van der Vorm family hold a majority of the shares, the only two disclosed shareholders are First Eagle Investment (mutual fund, 0.82 percent) and Invesco (0.29 percent). The strategy of HAL is "focused on acquiring significant shareholdings in companies, with the objective of increasing long-term shareholder value." When selecting investment candidates, HAL emphasizes, in addition to investment and return criteria, the potential of playing an active role as a shareholder and/or board member. HAL does not confine itself to particular industries.[14] HAL Trust owns three subsidiaries: holdings that invest in domestic and foreign companies in a variety of sectors (including transport and shipping, optics, orthopedic devices, media, hearing aids, credit management, insurance). Many of the domestic companies have a long history, like Royal VOPAK, Royal Boskalis Westminster, and SBM Offshore. In 2014 HAL also became the sole owner of the Dutch design furniture maker Gispen. Although HAL selects its investments with the potential of playing an active role as shareholder, the subsidiaries remain relatively independent. HAL has opted for a "decentralized management approach," with each company remaining "responsible for evaluating and managing its own risks" (HAL Trust, 2014: 17).

7.4.1.2 *SHV and the Fentener van Vlissingen Family*

The Dutch family of Fentener van Vlissingen owns the Steenkolen Handels-Vereniging (SHV: Coal Trading Company). The asset size of SHV Holdings in 2012, numbering 565 domestic and foreign subsidiaries, was 4 billion euros. After the death in 2006 of brothers Paul and Frits Fentener van Vlissingen, the shares were divided among their children. SHV is a diversified business group with a technologically unrelated portfolio, but through the wholly owned NPM Capital, a Dutch investment bank, in 2000 it also attained the characteristics of a bank-centered business group.

SHV was founded in 1896 in Utrecht by seven Dutch coal traders; the shares were non-tradable and remained in the hands of the participating families, although the company was legally structured as a corporation. Two families played a major role in the history of SHV: Fentener van Vlissingen and Van Beuningen (Van Wijnen, 2004; Van der Zwan, 2006). In the head office in Utrecht, F. H. Fentener van Vlissingen (1882–1962), son of the founder, was the main figure between 1911 and 1945, while D. G. van Beuningen, son of another founder, was director of the Rotterdam office from 1902 until 1941. In 1954 the families split and SHV was managed by the Fentener van Vlissingen family. Until the early 1970s it was a typical "closed corporation" (see Section 7.3) and thereafter became a BV to exclude control by outsiders (Wennekes, 1993). Throughout its history SHV disclosed very little information about investments, structure, and business strategy. Newly acquired companies were given very general names, making it hard to link them to SHV.

In 1896 SHV secured a monopoly from the Rheinisch-Westfälisches Kohlen-Syndikat (RWKS, 1893) to trade German coal in the Netherlands. The major competitors were

---

[14] *http://www.halinvestments.nl/*

SSM, managed by Willem van der Vorm (see Section 7.4.1.1) and after 1902 the NV Staatsmijnen (DSM, Dutch State Mines). Besides trading in coal, SHV supplied bunker coal to ships in the ports of Rotterdam and Amsterdam. To handle the large supplies of coal, SHV used technologically modern stevedoring firms and owned a large fleet of Rhine barges. The barges were operated through two legally independent companies: the Nederlandsche Transport-Maatschappij and the Nederlandsche Rijnvaart-Vereeniging (NRV). To supply the Rhine barges, SHV also established the NV Rotterdamsche Victualiënhandel, later renamed NV Handelscompagnie. SHV not only traded in coal, but additionally in petroleum and Liquefied Petroleum Gas (LPG). In cooperation with Standard Oil (Esso), it established the Trading Oil Service with storage facilities in Rotterdam, Flushing, and Antwerp. A new activity after 1938 was fish flour. SHV bought a number of companies to produce fish flour that were combined in Vereenigde Exploitatie Maatschappij (VEM). SHV also invested in phosphate factories, shipyards and towage services, electricity, the KLM (Royal Dutch Airlines), Fokker (airplane manufacturer), iron and steel (Hoogovens), and artificial fibers (ENKA, later AKZO Nobel). Several of these investments were financed through its own subsidiary, Administratiekantoor Unitas.

After the Second World War the two Rhine-barge companies merged in the NRV, making it the world's largest inland-waterway shipping company. SHV and Caltex established a joint venture, called Calpam, for the sale of fuel oil in the Netherlands, Belgium, Luxembourg, and Denmark. This signaled a shift from traditional interests in solid fuels (coal) to liquid fuels (oil); from 1963 SHV started trading in Liquefied Petroleum Gas (LPG) through its subsidiary Dyas. It constructed storage tanks in Dutch ports managed by its subsidiary the Nederlandse Opslag Maatschappij (NOM). SHV diversified still further by investing in a number of fitters and engineering firms. These companies merged in 1970 to form Groep Technische Installatie (GTI). GTI was sold to the Belgian company Fabricom in 2002. From 1968 SHV developed a self-service wholesale grocery business called Makro, with shops in the Netherlands and several foreign countries including South Africa. This was followed by other Dutch retail businesses like Xenos and Kijkshop. By the early twenty-first century SHV had become a very large unrelated-diversified business group. According to Van der Zwan, in 2004 turnover was 13.7 billion euros and profit was 317 million euros. It employed about 30,000 people all over the world (Van der Zwan, 2006: 384).

7.5 CONCLUDING REMARKS

Our research into Dutch business groups for the period 1903–2003 is exploratory and introductory because, as noted earlier, we lack important data for most of our period and existing research is scarce. Furthermore, our analysis is primarily based on the Top 20 (based on assets) enterprises in the country for a number of benchmark years. The

Table 7.4. Current standing of Dutch Business Groups (as of 2015).

Group Name	Standing in 2015
Nederlandsche Handel-Maatschappij (NHM)	Is now ABN AMRO
Koninklijke Nederlandsche Maatschappij tot Exploitatie van Petroleumbronnen in Nederlandsch-Indie (Royal Dutch Shell)	Royal Dutch Shell
Handelsvereeniging Amsterdam	No longer exists
Internationale Crediet- en Handels-Vereeniging Rotterdam (Internatio, after 1970: Internatio-Müller)	Is now IMTECH
Wm. H. Muller & Co. Algemeene Mijnbouw-Maatschappij (after 1970: Internatio-Müller)	Is now IMTECH
Anton Jurgens' Vereenigde Fabrieken(Unilever)	Unilever
Van den Bergh's fabrieken (Van den Bergh's en Jurgens' Fabrieken) (Unilever)	Unilever
Hollandsche Vereeniging tot Exploitatie van Margarinefabrieken(Hovema) (Unilever)	Unilever
R.S. Stokvis & Zonen Limited	No longer exists except as trade mark
Unilever (Lever brothers & Unilever)	Unilever
Philips Gloeilampenfabrieken	Philips
Algemeene Kunstzijde Unie (AKU) (AKZO) (AKZO Nobel)	Is now AKZO Nobel
Machinefabriek Gebr. Stork & Co.	Still exists, different name
Phs. van Ommeren's Scheepvaartbedrijf	Still exists, different name: VOPAK
Borneo Sumatra Handel Maatschappij (Borsumij)	Sold to Hagemeyer, since 2008 owned by Rexel (French company)
Koninklijke Zwanenburg-Organon	No longer exists under this name
DSM	Still exists
Rijn Schelde Verolme (RSV)	Liquidated
Ogem	Liquidated
Koninklijke Pakhoed	Is now VOPAK (see Phs. van Ommeren's Scheepvaartbedrijf, above)
Koninklijke Nedlloyd Groep	Sold to Maersk (Denmark) in 2005
Koninklijke Bols-Wessanen	Still exists called Royal Wessanen NV
Hagemeyer	Sold to Rexel (French company) in 2008

Source: own data; company websites; published company histories; *Gale Directory of Business Histories.*

Top 20 includes only listed companies, but excludes listed financial companies (banks, insurance, and investment companies). Because of these limitations we have added a section on family-owned business groups that are non-listed. Our concluding remarks are based on this sample of companies, although we add some more general tentative conclusions. (The current—2015—status of the most important business groups mentioned in the text is listed in Table 7.4.)

Business groups existed in the Netherlands from at least the late nineteenth century and still existed at the beginning of the twenty-first century. However, this structure has never been and currently is not the dominant business form in the large enterprise economy of the country. The total number of business groups in the Top 20 increased until the 1950s, but then declined. The share of assets of business groups in the total assets of the Top 20 likewise increased until the 1910s, but then dropped to about 60 percent. This is mainly the result of classifying some of the largest companies in the Netherlands as a variety of business group (e.g. Royal Dutch Shell, Unilever, and Philips). These companies are all highly capital-intensive.

This, however, is not the total number of business groups in the Netherlands in the period 1903–2003. As Section 7.4 shows, there are large family-owned business groups that are not listed. They use the business group organizational model to invest family capital in other companies. The case studies highlight the strategy and structure of some of these family-owned business groups. Given the dominance of family firms in the Dutch economy during the twentieth century, there are probably more family-owned business groups. Nevertheless, the huge number of business groups mentioned in some of the existing studies are, in our view, caused by an unrestrictive definition. This conclusion is interesting for two reasons. First, Dutch business historians and other researchers have paid little attention to this organizational form, despite its relative importance to the Dutch economy, and this calls for additional research. Second, while in many other countries the business group structure is either virtually absent (as in mature economies) or dominant (in emerging economies), this does not apply to the Dutch setting, at least since the early twentieth century.

What explains the rather moderate importance of business groups in the Netherlands? We have found no evidence of financial, legal, societal, or political developments that hindered their formation. There were also few factors that would strongly favor the formation of business groups, including an unstable political climate or highly volatile capital markets, neither of which was the case in the Netherlands during the twentieth century. Apparently, Dutch companies could choose freely between the business-group form and many alternatives. The latter include the use of various forms of cooperation; the widespread use of cartels, particularly, is well known in the Netherlands (Bouwens and Dankers, 2010). Our case studies also demonstrate that mainly firm-specific micro-level explanations determine why, when, and how business groups develop. These historical or idiosyncratic explanations offer no generalizations, but they do point towards the many specific factors contributing to the development of business groups in the Netherlands. It is an intriguing challenge for future research to disentangle firm-specific motivations among Dutch firms for the choice of organizational forms, including the business group.

APPENDIX

....

Business Groups in Largest Enterprises

between 1903 and 2003

Compiled from the Top 20 enterprises in 1903, 1913, 1923, 1933, 1942, 1953, 1963, 1973, 1983, 1993, and 2003.
Business groups in italic.

Company name	SBI[1]	Number of times in Top 20	Diversified BG	Holding BG	Pyramidal BG
			Subtypes: - Family-owned (F) - State-owned (S) - Bank-centered (B)		
1 Maatschappij tot Exploitatie van Staatsspoorwegen (SS)	30	2			
2 *Nederlandsche Handel-Maatschappij (NHM)*	28	1	X (B)		
3 Nederlandsch-Indische Spoorweg-Maatschappij	30	3			
4 Dordtsche Petroleum Industrie-Maatschappij	12	1			
5 Nederlandsche Centraal Spoorweg-Maatschappij	30	2			
6 Koninklijke Paketvaartmaatschappij (KPM)	30	6			
7 *Koninklijke Nederlandsche Maatschappij tot Exploitatie van Petroleumbronnen in Nederlandsch-Indie (Royal Dutch Shell)*	12	7	X	X (after 1907)	
8 Stoomvaart-Maatschappij Nederland (SMN)	30	6			
9 Noord-Brabantsch-Duitsche Spoorweg-Maatschappij Boxtel-Wesel	30	1			
10 Deli Spoorweg-Maatschappij	30	4			
11 *Handelsvereeniging Amsterdam*	39	5	X	X (after 1958)	

Business Groups in Largest Enterprises Between 1903 and 2003 (Continued)

12	Samarang-Joana Stoomtram- Maatschappij	30	2		
13	Semarang-Cheribon Stoomtram- Maatschappij	30	4		
14	Petroleum-Maatschappij Moeara Enim	12	2		
15	Stoomvaart-Maatschappij Rotterdamsche Lloyd (RL) Koninklijke Rotterdamsche Lloyd (KRL)	30	5		
16	*Internationale Crediet- en Handels-Vereeniging Rotterdam (Internatio, after 1970: Internatio-Müller)*	28	7	X	X (after 1970)
17	Petroleum Maatschappij Sumatra-Palembang	12	1		
18	Stoomvaart-Maatschappij Zeeland (Koninklijke Nederlandsche Postvaart)	30	1		
19	Rotterdamsche Tramweg- Maatschappij (RTM)	30	2		
20	Madoera Stoomtram Maatschappij	30	2		
21	Nederlandsche Scheepvaart Unie (NSU)	30	5		
22	Nederlandsch- Amerikaansche Stoomvaart- Maatschappij (HAL)	30	4		
23	Koninklijke Nederlandsche Stoombootmaatschappij (KNSM)	30	4		
24	*Wm. H. Muller & Co. Algemeene Mijnbouw- Maatschappij (after 1970: Internatio-Müller)*	12	2	X	X (after 1970)
25	Fransch-Hollandsche Oliefabrieken (Nouveaux Etablissements Calve- Delft)	13	2		
26	Hollandia Hollandsche Fabriek van Melkproducten en Voedingsmiddelen	13	1		

(continued)

Business Groups in Largest Enterprises
between 1903 and 2003 (continued)

Company name	SBI	Number of times in Top 20	Diversified BG	Holding BG	Pyramidal BG
27 Nederlandsche Tramweg Maatschappij	30	1			
28 Wester-Suikerraffinaderij	13	1			
29 Hollandsche IJzeren Spoorweg- Maatschappij (HIJSM)	30	2			
30 *Anton Jurgens' Vereenigde Fabrieken(Unilever)*	13	2	X (F)		
31 *Van den Bergh's fabrieken (Van den Bergh's en Jurgens' Fabrieken) (Unilever)*	13	5	X (F)		
32 Deli Maatschappij	35	2			
33 Centrale Suiker Maatschappij	13	3			
34 Koninklijke Hollandsche Lloyd (KHL)	30	1			
35 *Hollandsche Vereniging tot Exploitatie van Margarinefabrieken (Hovema) (Unilever)*	13	2	X (F)		
36 *R.S. Stokvis & Zonen Limited*	28	1	X (F)		
37 *Unilever (Lever brothers & Unilever)*	28	8		X	
38 *Philips Gloeilampenfabrieken*	22	7	X (F)	X	
39 *Algemeene Kunstzijde Unie (AKU) (AKZO) (AKZO Nobel)*	18	8	X		
40 Dok en Werf Maatschappij Wilton-Fijenoord	23	2			
41 Koninklijke Maatschappij De Schelde (KMS)	23	2			
42 Rotterdamsche Droogdok Maatschappij	23	2			
43 Heineken's Bierbrouwerij Maatschappij	13	6			
44 Nederlandsche Scheepsbouw- Maatschappij (NSM)	23	1			
45 Vereenigde Koninklijke Papierenfabrieken der Firma van Gelder Zonen	16	4			
46 Werkspoor	23	1			
47 P. de Gruyter & Zoon	13	1			

BUSINESS GROUPS IN LARGEST ENTERPRISES
BETWEEN 1903 AND 2003 (CONTINUED)

48	Nederlandsche Gist en Spiritusfabriek	18	1		
49	*Machinefabriek Gebr. Stork & Co.*	22	5	X (F)	
50	Haagsche Tramweg-Maatschappij (HTM)	30	1		
51	Gemeenschappelijk Eigendom Maatschappij tot Exploitatie van Woon en Winkelhuizen	35	1		
52	Nederlandsche Kabelfabriek (NKF)	22	2		
53	Nederlandsche Dok Maatschappij (NDM)	23	1		
54	Koninklijke Nederlandsche Hoogovens en Staalfabrieken (KNHS)	20	4		
55	*Phs. van Ommeren's Scheepvaartbedrijf*	30	4	X (F)	
56	Koninklijke Java China Paketvaartlijnen	30	2		
57	*Borneo Sumatra Handel Maatschappij (Borsumij)*	28	1	X	
58	Koninklijke Luchtvaart Maatschappij (KLM)	30	5		
59	Exploitatie Maatschappij Scheveningen (EMS)	40	1		
60	Koninklijke Zout-Ketjen	13	1		
61	Koninklijke Nederlandse Vliegtuigenfabriek (Fokker)	23	2		
62	*Koninklijke Zwanenburg-Organon*	13	1	X	
63	Koninklijke Nijverdal Ten Cate	14	1		
64	*DSM*	18	3	X	X (after 1973)
65	*Rijn Schelde Verolme (RSV)*	23	1		X
66	*Ogem*	25	1		X
67	Koninklijke Boskalis Westminster	26	2		
68	*Koninklijke Pakhoed*	39	3	X	
69	Verenigde Bedrijven Nederhorst	26	1		
70	Bührmann-Tetterode	16	2		
71	Koninklijke Ahold	29	4		

(continued)

BUSINESS GROUPS IN LARGEST ENTERPRISES
BETWEEN 1903 AND 2003 (CONTINUED)

	Company name	SBI	Number of times in Top 20	Diversified BG	Holding BG	Pyramidal BG
72	Koninklijke Gist-Brocades	18	3			
73	*Koninklijke Nedlloyd Groep*	30	2	X		
74	Hollandsche Beton Groep	26	2			
75	Koninklijke Volker Stevin	26	1			
76	Océ-van der Grinten	18	3			
77	Ballast Nedam	26	1			
78	Koninklijke KNP BT (merged with Bührmann-Tetterode in 1993)	16	1			
79	PolyGram	40	1			
80	Elsevier	17	1			
81	*Koninklijke Bols-Wessanen*	13	1	X		
82	Koninklijke KPN	32	1			
83	VNU	17	1			
84	TPG	32	1			
85	Reed Elsevier	17	1			
86	Wolters Kluwer	17	1			
87	Buhrmann	37	1			
88	Koninklijke BAM Groep	26	1			
89	ASM Lithography Holding	22	1			
90	*Hagemeyer*	28	1	X		
91	Vedior	39	1			

[1] SBI (Standaard Bedrijfsindeling) is the Dutch version of the international Standard Industrial Classification (SIC).

Source: own dataset based on *Van Oss Effectenboek*.

CHAPTER 8

··

GERMANY

an engine of modern economic development

··

HARM G. SCHRÖTER

8.1 INTRODUCTION

··

BEFORE industrialization mines were the only large enterprises found in German Central Europe. In the late Middle Ages mines with around 2,000 employees existed. In the nineteenth century more large enterprises emerged. Some grew slowly out of artisan workshops (e.g., Krupp), and a very few were large from the outset (Deutsche Bank, Mannesmann). Industrialization offered many opportunities for economic growth. The largest firms were concentrated in iron and steel, mining, and later in electrotechnology and chemicals. The concentration process is reflected in production statistics: in the 1880s two-thirds of industrial output in the German Empire were created in small enterprises; some thirty years later this proportion was achieved by the country's large enterprises (Fischer, 1986). A few examples illustrate the change in scale. Before World War I the electrical giant AEG had more employees than the USA's General Electric. In the interwar years IG Farben's size was matched only by DuPont (USA) and ICI (UK), while in steelmaking only United Steel (USA) was larger than Germany's Vereinigte Stahlwerke. In 2016 Volkswagen was the world's largest car-maker, and the premium sector in that industry was dominated by Audi, BMW, and Daimler. In short, for more than a century Germany's largest firms have been among the largest 100 companies in the world. Thus Germany, though famous for its agile medium-sized enterprises ("Mittelstand"), always had some very large firms, and it is worth discussing how they relate to the enterprise structure of business groups.[1]

---

[1] Three varieties of diversified business groups, which have been the most important players among large enterprises in Germany, are the focus of this chapter. They are bank-centered groups, family-owned groups, and state-owned groups.

This chapter is organized as follows. Section 8.2 summarizes the development of big business in Germany. Section 8.3 gives a quantitative estimate of the importance of business groups in the German economy in the long term. Section 8.4 then focuses on the changing attractiveness of the diversified business group as an enterprise form in the country. Section 8.5 examines the earlier research on German business groups. Section 8.6 discusses the different varieties of business groups found in Germany. Section 8.7 concludes.

8.2 The Development of Big Business in Germany

Big business developed parallel to industrialization after 1850.[2] The largest firms concentrated on mining, iron and steel, and above all on railways. After the 1860s railways were taken over by the state, and consequently a good deal of the organizational capabilities Alfred Chandler pointed to were learned in the state-owned railway, postal, and telephone services, which were probably the largest economic organizations in Germany before the First World War (1990, 1992, 1997). Though Germany registered at that time with Hapag and Norddeutscher Lloyd, one of the largest shipping lines in the world, its main strength was in metal and mining. Enterprises such as Krupp, Thyssen, and GHH (Gutehoffnungshütte, see Section 8.6.2) represented big business with several tens of thousands of employees before 1914. As a reaction to the much larger American big business, enterprises in many countries merged in the interwar period. This applied also to a large part of German iron-and-steel production, out of which VSt (Vereinigte Stahlwerke) emerged in 1926. A similar merger created IG Farben (see Section 8.6.3.2), which was a match for the two other world players, DuPont of the USA and ICI of the UK. In Germany heavy industry dominated large enterprise until the 1950s (Dammers and Fischer, 2016), while in 2010 only two of this sector were counted in the top 100 (Süddeutsche Zeitung, 2011). Big business fared differently in the "new industries" (characterized by the application of science to industry, such as chemical or electric/electronic enterprise). AEG (Allgemeine Elektricitäts Gesellschaft) was, based on employment, even larger than General Electric of the USA before 1914, and Siemens has stayed within the first league in that sector to this day. According to the *Forbes* (2012) annual listing, Siemens ranked no. 50 in the world's largest firms in that year. The three large chemical companies—BASF, Bayer, and Hoechst—showed even more resilience. Merged into IG Farben in 1925, the company was broken up by the Allies after the Second World War. Subsequently the three firms re-merged. Since about 2000 BASF represents the largest chemical enterprise in the world. Bayer got out of chemicals and concentrated entirely on

---

[2] New literature on German large enterprise includes Fiedler (1999, providing a full list of other compilations) and the *common database* in Cassis, Colli, and Schröter (2016).

pharmaceuticals. Measured by shareholder value, it became the most valuable enterprise in Germany in 2015, while Hoechst first merged with the French Rhone-Poulenc (1999), with registration in Strasbourg, and was finally taken over by French Sanofi in 2004. In the transport sector, big business emerged fairly late: before 1914 it was dominated by shipbuilders and since the 1970s by the automobile sector. In 2016 *Fortune Global 500* listed Volkswagen (at no. 7), Daimler (16), BMW (51), Bosch (87), and Continental (213).

Before 1914 Germany's financial sector was relatively strong, with four big banks, which were also engaged abroad, for instance with Deutsche Überseeische Bank (see Section 8.6.1). While entirely German-owned, foreign direct investment (FDI) was sequestered during World War I, and super-inflation weakened the financial sector during the early 1920s. In 2015 only two of the "big four" survived (Commerzbank and Deutsche Bank), while only the latter acts as a world player. Insurance fared a bit better: for 2016 *Fortune* listed Allianz at no. 34 and Munich Re Group at 106. The respective size of the largest sectors remained fairly stable during the thirty years 1980–2010: within the top 100 firms, service was represented by 46 enterprises in 1980 (49 in 2010), manufacturing industry by 42 (43 in 2010), enterprises with unrelated diversified operations by 7 (5 in 2010), and construction by 5 (3 in 2010). Compared with other countries this is quite interesting, as deindustrialization started in the UK during the 1960s and in Germany a decade later. Germany is known for its bias towards manufacturing, but that this sector should remain stable within the largest 100 enterprises is still quite remarkable.

A certain industrial profile, sunk costs of investment, and so-called soft factors such as the above-mentioned organizational capabilities create path dependency. When looking at the manufacturing sector, path dependency is dominant in big business. While the service sector offers many more jobs than manufacturing industry in Germany today, we do not see a corresponding change reflected in the top 100. This is a strong indicator for solid path dependency. Also, path dependency is reflected generally in German industry. By world standards and compared with other established industrialized countries, the manufacturing sector is greatly oversized within Germany's economy and its exports. Is the country's economic profile fossilized in consequence? If one has a closer look at manufacturing industry, the longevity of a particular single enterprise in big business is not particularly impressive. Of the fifty largest firms in 1913, only eight still registered in that group in 2000 (Cassis, Colli, and Schröter, 2016: database). We find a strong path dependency only at the first glance at sectors; however, inside the sectors there has been a considerable change among firms.

Ownership of German big business was and is different from the Anglo-Saxon patterns and even from most European countries. While quoted joint-stock companies represented the majority of companies, the amount of non-listed ones, limited corporations, business partnerships, foundations, or other forms of enterprise is much more widespread in Germany. At the same time ownership has been more concentrated. Large blocks of shares were usually owned and traded, and banks owned such blocks; large investors and cross-holding were widespread. In contrast, small private shareholding was much less represented than in other countries. Pension funds used to be absent, because state-governed insurance based on PAYGO provided the usual protection. Large banks traditionally did not care about small private shareholders, or even despised them. Before the First World War Karl Fürstenberg, one of the most influential German bankers, illustrated this attitude: "Shareholders are stupid and fresh. They are stupid because they hand over their money to others without adequate control, and fresh because they ask for dividends—which means that they ask to get rewarded for their stupidity!"[3] Barca and Mayer showed (2001: 22) that in Germany, regardless of low or high ownership concentration, blockholder power was always above the European and US average.

Enterprises that diversified into unrelated businesses, which are important for this chapter concerning diversified business groups, fared differently: those that grew slowly, such as Oetker, Haniel, Werhahn, or Freudenberg, stayed resilient, while others which had grown fast and large within just one generation often fell apart, e.g., Stinnes or Flick. Foreign enterprise was never dominant in Germany. Relatively strong after 1945 (Prizkoleit, 1963), its participation within the group of top 100 firms shrank afterwards; in 1980 twenty foreign direct investments were represented (Frankfurter Allgemeine Zeitung, 1981), while in 2010 this number was down to just twelve (Süddeutsche, 2011). Concerning return on investment, a long-term comparison of European big business showed German firms above average before World War I. But afterwards they consistently underperformed (Cassis, Colli, and Schröter, 2016).

8.3 How Important Were Business Groups? a Quantitative Estimate

One of the purposes of this chapter is to evaluate the impact of large business groups on economic development. For that we need robust quantitative information—which unfortunately is not to hand. In Germany the largest contribution to GNP has always come from small and medium-sized enterprise, which also accounted for the bulk of employment, exports, and so on. However, large enterprise also played an important role, about which some information is available. There are several important compilations of historical value. However, while these databases provide information on what these enterprises owned, there is little information on *our* crucial question: *who owned them*? Therefore, stock-exchange yearbooks and other compilations represent additional sources of information: Commerzbank (1954–2000); Liedke (1993–2006); Prizkoleit (1953–63), Salings Börsenjahrbuch (1882–1932); Handbuch der Aktiengesellschaften (1950–2012); Handbuch der Großunternehmen (1950–2012).

---

[3] Even if this famous quote has no real reference, it reflected the attitude perfectly. And that was the very reason for it becoming famous.

Based on this collective information, we estimate that a third of German big business was organized as business groups during the 1950s, while as we will argue later, in the 1990s about a quarter of the largest firms were organized as business groups.

The definition of business groups is a key issue here. Provided we apply the *wide* definition mentioned by Colpan and Hikino (2010) as a starting point—"Business groups in their broadest sense characterize an economic coordination mechanism in which legally independent companies utilize the collaborative arrangements to enhance their collective economic welfare"—most large companies in Germany, as the authors correctly suggest, fall under this definition because they are mainly organized with legally independent subsidiaries rather than internal divisions (Colpan and Hikino, 2010: 17). Furthermore, considering diversified business groups per se, we believe that unrelatedness is a difficult but necessary concept.

The problem of identifying business groups in Germany can be illustrated by the example of Siemens (see Feldenkirchen, 1997). The company's core business was always electrical and electronic goods. During the 1990s its mostly dependent divisions were energy, industry, communication, information systems, traffic, medical technology, electrical components, lighting, and financial services. However, this last division and parts of others represented legally independent enterprises. All divisions except the last one produced machinery, not services. Its divisions were statistically labeled under ISIC Number C 26 (electrics and electronics), rail vehicles (H 49), and—legally independent—financial services (K 64). This qualifies Siemens as a business group, since we find legally independent entities in unrelated industries in terms of their ISIC codes. However, since all activities were not only related to but also derived from the core business, and also since we observe a strategic control of operating units by the headquarters unit, one might prefer to call Siemens a diversified enterprise rather than an unrelated-diversified business group. This kind of argument could go on: the German post office (Deutsche Post) included at that time both mail and telephone business; it furthermore owned a large institute for basic electrotechnical research. In the interwar period the giant chemical enterprise IG Farben invested in coal mines in order to reduce its energy costs, and so on. In other words, if a definition in the broadest sense is applied, virtually all large German enterprises since at least the 1960s would be labeled "business groups." Consequently, in the German case a rigid application of this kind of definition would make the concept of business groups too ambiguous for academic analysis and blur all possible insights. Therefore, we suggest excluding even highly vertically integrated enterprises from our list of business groups as well as from lists of pyramids. In other words, we suggest using *all* available information, statistical *and* supplementary, before evaluation.[4]

---

[4] This is also the approach with Deutsche Bundesbank (German Central Bank) concerning FDI. Generally an investment abroad is counted as FDI when 10 percent or more of the capital of the respective firm is acquired. However, when investors indicate their intention to consider such a move as portfolio investment, it is counted as the latter. Otherwise, insurance companies, especially, would turn into business groups. A purely statistical approach would not reflect reality.

Furthermore, we prefer not to look exclusively at the juridical form of an enterprise, but also, even primarily, to consider the organization of enterprise management. When an integrated firm with legally independent subsidiaries is understood by its own management as a single entity and directed, also beyond strategic decisions, by a single body of decision-making, we would not call it a business group. However, when this firm starts to spin off parts of its enterprise because they are no longer regarded as part and parcel of the core firm, then we see the definition of business group fulfilled, because management then separates the entities from each other. Again Siemens can provide an example. The firm used to be a highly integrated Chandlerian enterprise, but during the last decade it has spun off large parts of its business, such as *healthcare* and *lighting*, while keeping these legally independent enterprises within its portfolio. Consequently, Siemens is now going in the direction of becoming a business group, but it exemplifies how difficult it is to correctly identify business groups in Germany.

We will use the same categorization of business groups as Colpan and Hikino in Chapter 1: diversified business groups. This also accords with Nathaniel Leff's definition: "The [business] group is a multi-company firm which transacts in different markets but which does so under common entrepreneurial and financial control" (quoted in Colpan and Hikino, 2010). The advantage of this definition is that it focuses on how the firm is run, how management acts, and not on legal constructions or mechanisms. We understand "diversified" as a real unrelatedness of enterprises within the group. In this definition several legally independent enterprises owned by a holding company or parent company are a necessary condition but not a sufficient one; only the combination of separate management and independent entities adequately defines a business group. Consequently, enterprises such as Volkswagen (VW) are excluded in spite of the fact that they own a bank as well as several other legally independent car- and truck-making firms, such as Skoda and Scania. Excluding VW from the category of the business group is not because its different enterprises are related to each other, although all are indeed in the automotive industry. The decisive factor is that VW understands and manages all its constituent firms in an integrated way, including transfer of personnel, managers, technical know-how, and so on. The legally independent entities are understood to be directly related and supplemental to each other. In spite of its legal construction, therefore, we do not consider Volkswagen to be a business group.

Applying this definition, we have identified between 10 and 15 percent of the 100 largest German enterprises in the twentieth century as business groups, especially its diversified variety—including nearly all large banks. This is a substantial amount! However, after the turn of the millennium the picture changed and the number of business groups declined. Also, most banks sold out their non-financial investments and could no longer be regarded as business groups (see Section 8.6.1 for more reasons). The above-mentioned percentages are only an estimate, but for the years 1992 to 2005 there is definite information. Looking at the 100 largest German enterprises (by turnover) in 1992 and 2005, we found a sizable number of business groups (see Table 8.1).

Table 8.1. Diversified business groups in Germany, as part of the 100 largest enterprises.

(measured by turnover)	Amount of unrelated sectors in 1992 (ownership >10%)	Amount of unrelated sectors in 2005 (ownership >10%)
AGIV	5	No longer in largest 100
Allianz	6	3
BASF	5	6
Bayerische Hypo- & W.-bank	4	No longer in largest 100
Bayerische Vereinsbank	3	No longer in largest 100
Benteler	2	2
Commerzbank	4	2
Deutsche Bank	8	3
Dresdner Bank	7	No longer in largest 100
E.ON (1992: Veba, VIAG)		1
Freudenberg	2	2
Hochtief	not in largest 100	2
Haniel	2	2
Krupp	8	Merged into ThyssenKrupp
Linde	2	2
MAN	4	2
Mannesmann	4	No longer in largest 100
Metallgesellschaft/GEA	5	1
Munich Re	5	3
Oetker	3	3
Philip Holzmann	4	4
Preussag/TUI	6	1
Rethmann	not in largest 100	2
RWE	2	1
Ruhrkohle/RAG	4	4
Schörghuber	not in largest 100	3
Tchibo	3	3
Thyssen/ThyssenKrupp	12	7
Veba	5	Merged into E.ON
VIAG	8	Merged into E.ON
West LB	6	No longer in largest 100
Number of busines groups	*27*	*18*
Number of sectors accumulated	*128*	*58*

Note: "Ownership >10%" means 10 or more per cent of share capital were owned by the respective business group.

Source: Commerzbank, *Wer gehört zu wem?*, Frankfurt, several years; Liedke, Rainer, *Wem gehört die Republik? Die Konzerne und ihre globalen Verflechtungen in der globalisierten Wirtschaft*, Eichborn Verlag, Frankfurt/M., 1996 and 2006.

Table 8.1 shows that a quarter of Germany's 100 largest firms in the 1990s were organized as (diversified) business groups. However, the table also shows a clear trend of enterprises reducing this organizational form (Allianz, Commerzbank, Deutsche Bank, Krupp, MAN, Munich Re, Thyssen) or even leaving it (AGIV, VEBA, Viag, E.ON, Metallgesellschaft, GEA, Preussag/TUI, RWE). At the apex of these business groups there were frequently operating holding companies (in nineteen cases); but a large part used to represent pure holding companies (in ten cases). This changed over time, of course. However, it is interesting that pure holding companies figured more prominently than the traditional perception of large German enterprise would suggest. What was the situation before the 1990s and what caused organizational changes during the twentieth century? We will try to answer these questions below.

8.4 Swings in the Attractiveness of the Diversified Business Group as a Form of Enterprise

Up to World War II the leading idea in Germany was to create integrated enterprise in a single industry or around related industries. Steel firms such as Krupp or Thyssen, which owned facilities covering the whole product chain (coal and ore mines, transport, iron- and steelmaking, rolling mills, shipyards, machine building) were perceived as embodying the best corporate structure. In the interwar period IG Farben, which had divisionalized at the same time as DuPont, was still seen and managed as one big entity. In Germany business groups, especially its unrelated diversified variety, historically remained less important, except for the 1880s to 1920s when bank-centered business groups grew to prominence; and were found primarily among state-owned enterprises, family firms, banks, and electrotechnical enterprises.

The "golden age" of 1950–73 was especially golden for West Germany, with above-average high growth rates. Firms started to invest outside their traditional core business. In 1954 only 17.1 percent of 300 large German enterprises were engaged outside their original branch of industry, while in 1960 the respective figure was 23.3 percent (Weder, 1968: 176ff.). That might be an indicator of business groups becoming more important. However, this trend stopped in the 1960s when the American practice of divisionalization was introduced into almost all large firms (Wengenroth, 1997). The change represented a clash of business cultures between the traditional German one, focused mainly on stability and security, and the American one, focused primarily on profit. Many German firms still tried to do both: pay a high and a stable dividend. A combination of different investments, one in a highly volatile area and one in a stable economic field, was deemed to help realize this goal. A 1992 AGIV brochure explained: "AGIV optimizes the policy of her daughter-companies without interference into their principal independence. Thus AGIV tries to improve the balance of risk of the whole group. . . . For our investors we balance the risk by structuring AGIV in a way which combines different branches of industries, firms, and sized of enterprises" (quoted in Liedke, 1993: 23). It was precisely these reasons of risk aversion that caused Dr. Oetker to invest in shipping as well as home-baking products (see Table 8.1). Cases such as Dr. Oetker can explain the substantial number of business groups in 1992, but not their contraction by 2005. That trend is exemplified by Metallgesellschaft, which stayed in the group of 100 largest firms but refocused itself on a single core business and therefore no longer qualified as a business group. Other firms, such as Linde or MAN, also reduced their diversification to what they defined as their core competence, and after 2010 no longer qualified as business groups.

To date there has been no evaluation of the causes of this trend away from business groups. But when the statements given by the respective enterprises are taken together, one reason dominates: the wish to play in the top league of their branch of enterprise at a world level, even if this meant reducing diversification. Linde provides a good example here. In 1992 and 2005 Linde had two separately managed divisions that produced technical gases and materials handling equipment such as forklifts. In order to become one of the world's top technical gas companies, Linde sold its forklift division in 2006, acquired its UK-based competitor BOC, and transformed itself into a one-product-line enterprise. Many large German banks likewise sold out industrial investments to focus on their core business of financial services. Table 8.1 shows that only Deutsche Bank and Commerzbank still qualified as business groups in 2005, and a few years later both had divested their industrial activities entirely.

How can we explain the falling attractiveness of the diversified business group model? Studies of American enterprise have shown substantial discounts of share-holder value on diversified enterprise (Berger and Ofek, 1995; Campa and Kedia, 2002; Graham, Lemmon, and Wolf, 2002). Up to the 1980s this issue was not discussed in Germany. But a new wave of Americanization in the 1990s, which especially changed financial matters in German enterprise (Schröter, 2005), brought it to the fore: did diversification lower the stock-market value of an enterprise? At first the economic media tended to say yes. In 1999 *Focus* magazine ran an article called "The end of conglomerates"; a report in *Manager Magazin* in 2002 was also more negative than neutral. But only two years later, *Handelsblatt* published a headline "Conglomerates offer chance," while in 2007 *Frankfurter Allgemeine Zeitung/Wirtschaft* wrote of "Phoenix from the ashes: the return of conglomerates." It seems that after the millennium better times had come for business groups. Still, the German economic media were largely not a proponent of business groups. How did German economists deal with this question? Their discussion focused on the question of whether in Germany diversification led to a discount in stock-exchange value of the firm or not. After 2000 several books and articles investigated this question. In contrast to the United States, the results were inconclusive. Some researchers found evidence of the discount; others came up with counter-evidence (Szeless, 2001; Schwetzler and Reimund, 2003; Weiner, 2005; Beckmann, 2006). In 2006 Glaser and Müller presented a compromise position.

At first glance there was indeed a diversification discount, but a deeper analysis revealed that it was related to those enterprises within business groups that carried a large burden of debt and not to diversified business groups as a whole. In other words, there was a debt-related discount on the value of business groups in Germany but not a general discount.

8.5 HISTORICAL EXPLANATION AND EARLIER RESEARCH ON GERMAN BUSINESS GROUPS

The sections above left open a couple of questions, such as "Why are there not more business groups?" or "Why does Table 8.1 not provide information over the long term?" Researching large business groups in Germany is problematical because of definitional uncertainties. Whichever formal definition is applied greatly affects the scope of the phenomenon. A wide definition of business groups and pyramids would encompass nearly all large enterprises in the country; a narrow definition, only a small handful. Both approaches make little sense; as so often, the truth lies somewhere in the middle. Below we will argue for the use of a more historical and content-oriented definition rather than a formal one. However, the case of Germany is not clear-cut. Of course business groups existed, but at the same time the role of families as the center of large business groups was considerably less important than in many Asian economies. Business groups in Germany had, and still have, many different types of owners: families, the central state, federal states (Länder) and municipalities, large banks, and so on.

The conditions that have stimulated the organization of business groups in emerging economies were largely absent in Germany. Since the Middle Ages German Central Europe has had a relatively well-developed economy in which product markets were relatively well developed. Consequently, there was little incentive for businesses to become engaged in products or services unrelated to their core activity. The car industry may be used as an example. During its formative years the German car industry was related to machine building; a lot of machine builders came up with their own cars. In most cases they concentrated on the production of the core element—the engine. Everything else could be bought from other German companies: tires (e.g., from Continental), electrical components (e.g., from Bosch), and so on. Even today the workforce of these suppliers considerably outnumbers that of the car producers. When investment in sidelines and necessary supplies is not needed, the enterprise can concentrate on the core of the business. In such a situation, why organize a diversified business group? The same applies to finances: German banks have long supported the country's product market through equity and credit at all levels. From the start of the German Industrial Revolution in the mid-nineteenth century, banks supported manufacturing and railway companies, while at the same time special institutions for helping farmers and artisans were founded in the form of co-ops and state-guaranteed savings banks. Together these two institutions still accounted for a third of the German capital market in 2015. Consequently, even in times of stress German financial markets were never as shallow as those in contemporary developing countries. A developed market for both goods and financial products reduced the incentive to form business groups.

Traditionally there has been very little research on German business groups, and therefore quantitative evidence cannot be provided. We know neither the number of business groups as a percentage of all enterprise at any given time nor their quantitative contribution to economic growth. Takashi Hikino's statement (2014) that "academic research on business groups still remain[s] within the boundaries of emerging markets" is entirely true for Germany. There is extremely little literature on German business groups by either economic historians or economists.[5] Many German business groups of the hierarchy type and diversified variety (see Chapter 1) were either family-owned or bank-centered (see Section 8.5). In the last few years research on family enterprises has increased (for instance, Lubinski, Fear, and Perez, 2013); however, only a few German family firms represent *large* business groups and, at the same time, there are quite a number of business groups which were *not* family-owned. Thus, large family enterprise is not the main starting point for business groups in Germany.

Furthermore, in Germany we find more literature on company law concerning business groups than on the economic issues involved. Indeed, law might be one reason why there are so few business groups of the hierarchy type in Germany. In contrast to US or UK law, German jurisprudence has recognized a special "group law" (Organschaft) for more than a hundred years (Cahn and Donald, 2010: 681ff.). This law treats business groups as one single "de facto" enterprise. There are no incentives to form "pyramids," "cascades," or "Chinese boxes." Thus, as a legal form the business group generates few advantages in Germany, a fact that is also reflected in the lack of indigenous literature.[6] If the juridical advantages of forming diversified business groups are few, then the advantages of organizing related and integrated enterprise come to the fore. La Porta et al. (1999) showed that pyramids were important among the largest twenty listed firms in the country (La Porta, Lopez-de-Silanes, and Shleifer, 1999).[7] Unfortunately, they applied their definition in a rigid and formal

[5] In business history we found only one contribution targeting the issue (Feldenkirchen, 1997). This lack of research is also reflected at the European and general level; research on ownership structure or theories of corporate governance used to omit the issue of the "business group" (see, for instance, Thomsen and Pedersen, 1994; Clarke, 2007).

[6] The catalogue which lists all printed material on economic matters written in German gives two hits for "Pyramiden," five for "Schachtel" (box), and none for "Kaskaden" (http://www.gbv.de; see Schröter, 2011). The problem is, once again, with the definition: if we apply the definition used by La Porta et al. and others—"chains of publicly listed companies"—nearly all medium-sized and all large German enterprises qualify. That inflates the concept of pyramids to a meaningless category.

[7] When a formal definition is rigidly applied, nearly all large and medium-sized enterprises in Germany represent pyramids as they own subsidiaries, some of which are publicly listed. Quite a number of these are majority-owned but not up to 100 percent; for instance Bertelsmann, one of the

way. For instance, they point to Allianz, whose shares they call "widely held" in spite of the fact that Munich Re owned 25 percent. In questioning Munich Re as a business group, their reasoning is absolutely right (p. 483), because Allianz also owned 25 percent of the shares of Munich Re. However, this fact applies to many other cases as well. Until the 1990s, when "Deutschland AG" (see Section 8.6.1) disintegrated, owning large blocks of shares as well as cross-shareholding were widespread. The common reason for establishing pyramids used to be a lack of financial means, because pyramids enable a relatively small investment to govern a larger enterprise; consequently, for their own advantage investors like to form business groups. But in Germany there was no such lack of capital on the one hand, while on the other the aim of separating cash flow from ownership could also be met by cross-shareholding. Thus, in this regard also there was no special incentive to form business groups specifically in pyramidal structures. Barca and Böhmer (2001: 135) also found widespread structures which looked like pyramidal groups. However, they doubted that "they serve the purpose of collecting outside capital"; instead, Barca and Böhmer suggested that such structures enhanced security: "The holding companies (Vorschaltgesellschaften) seem to act in lieu of voting contracts or other forms of formal coalition." This view is also supported by Franks and Mayer (2001: 943): "In a study of the ownership of German corporations, we find . . . only limited evidence that pyramid structures can be used for control purposes."

8.6 VARIETIES OF BUSINESS GROUPS IN GERMANY

8.6.1 Bank-Centered Business Groups

Germany's universal banks[8] used to be known for their long-term investment in industrial enterprise. While other long-term investment institutions, such as real-estate

largest media enterprises in the world, included 342 firms registered in Germany and 1,038 firms registered abroad in its 2005 annual report, all of which were owned 50 percent or more. These included large investments such as RTL Group SA, Luxembourg, and Sony BMG Music Inc., New York, a 50-percent joint venture with Sony. It also included Random House Inc., New York, which in turn owned many subsidiaries abroad. Among them was Random House Mondadori SA, Barcelona, a joint fifty-fifty venture of Random House and Mondadori SA. In spite of this fact (which is just an example, of course), I would not call Bertelsmann a pyramid because of different intentions. Pyramids are constructed in order to govern with little investment of capital. Bertelsmann wanted to rule and agreed to joint ventures for strategic not financial reasons. In this respect the company is representative of German big business. Furthermore, in Germany it is normal to organize enterprise with different legal entities, because it provides legal protection: legally independent parts of any firm can go bankrupt without hurting the owner. Such affiliates used to be owned up to 100 percent by the parent company, a situation inconsistent with the idea of pyramids.

[8] Universal banks offer *all* kind of services at the same time: investment banking, commercial banking, retail banking, etc.

banks, were not interested in the decision-making of their clients, universal banks were supposed to do exactly that, which of course turned them into business groups. However, while we have clear evidence for bank-centered business groups in the case of other countries (for instance, in Sweden), for Germany the picture is less clear. The thesis that large banks directed German industrial enterprise was first published in 1910 by the Marxist economist Rudolf Hilferding. Lenin and others elevated it to party dogma, while a third group, including Alexander Gerschenkron, made it a cornerstone of an ideal typology of industrialization (Hilferding, 1910; Gerschenkron, 1962). Many modern scholars have taken the thesis as part of their accepted knowledge (for instance, Porter, 1990: 154). By owning a substantial part of share capital in addition to providing operating credits, universal banks had the ultimate say in the running of big business, and the banks themselves became business groups.

The power of the banks was sanctioned by law and tradition. Shareholders typically kept their shares with a bank they trusted. Each year before the company general assembly, banks asked these owners if they wanted to take part in the assembly or transfer their vote to the bank (Depotstimmrecht). Most owners chose the latter. Consequently, a bank with many deposited shares could acquire many more votes than its own shareholding entitled it to.

Hilferding's and Gerschenkron's thesis that large German banks represent business groups has been questioned by modern research. Not even Marxist historians in eastern Germany claim any longer that banks turned into business groups (except for the period when bank-centered business groups were formed in the latter phases of the country's industrialization before World War I); Kurt Gossweiler, for instance, spoke of "families" but not of enterprises (Gossweiler, 1975: 328ff.; Büschgen, 1983; Wellhöner, 1989; Gall, 1995; Dammers and Fischer, 2016). Gerald Feldman has even proposed the anti-thesis: the independence of large industry from large banks (Feldman, 1995: 232ff.). Since the question has not been entirely settled, we will evaluate some of its aspects here.

Today's Deutsche Bank has long been the largest of all universal banks in Germany. One of its oldest engagements was with Thyssen, a large coal and steel producer in the Ruhr. A careful look at this relationship reveals that Thyssen jealously guarded its independence from the investment bank. After 1918 Thyssen owed Deutsche Bank 140,000 pounds sterling in prewar debts, which it refused to repay (Wellhöner, 1989). It took Deutsche Bank to court and managed to get its debt reduced to £20,000 based on political considerations. In 1926, when Thyssen had merged into the steel-making giant Vereinigte Stahlwerke (VSt), VSt asked a consortium of the four large German universal banks (Deutsche Bank, Dresdner Bank, Danat Bank, and Disconto Gesellschaft) for a huge credit of 120 million Reichsmarks. The credit was granted on condition that the consortium would be the exclusive provider of all VSt's banking services during the loan's duration and that any other advances could be taken up only with the consortium's consent. Though VSt did not like these conditions, it signed in the end, but since it never used the credit, the conditions never came into force.[9] VSt successfully defended its independence in spite of the fact that eight top bankers were on its supervisory board. The proponents of the anti-thesis argue that such company independence was typical rather than exceptional. With regard to electrotechnical giants Siemens and AEG, Hugh Neuburger has maintained: "The banks were in no position to dictate a merger policy to the industry. In any case one did not dictate to either the Siemens family or to Emil Rathenau" (Neuburger, 1977: 198).[10]

Still, in a few cases the closeness of the bank–industry connection corroborated the Hilferding–Gerschenkron thesis. From the 1920s through the 1990s Daimler (Mercedes) was dominated by Deutsche Bank. Up to the beginning of the twenty-first century, Daimler could not take major decisions regarding investment or management personnel without Deutsche Bank's consent. In 1993 Deutsche Bank still owned more than a quarter of Daimler's shares and in 1998 24.4 percent, but in 2005 it owned no more than 4.4 percent of (then) DaimlerChrysler.[11] According to Liedke (1993), in its history Deutsche Bank "had influence on numerous important industrial enterprises such as Mannesmann, BMW, Daimler, Rheinische Braunkohle, Reemtsma," but by 2005 its non-financial investments were substantially reduced to "DaimlerChrysler (4.4%), Linde AG, Wiesbaden (10%), Deutsche Interhotel Holding GmbH & Ko KG, Berlin (45.51%), Fiat S.p.A., Turin, Italien (0.8%)" (Liedke, 1993:136; 2007: 123). Liedke is right: Deutsche Bank owned and/or at least influenced major industrial enterprises in Germany, which made it a bank-centered business group. And yet, though the largest of its kind, Deutsche Bank could draw only a few industrial enterprises truly into its orbit. No German bank ever had such a great influence on German national industry as the two big Swedish banks exercised in their country.

Still, the story is incomplete. Scholarly debate has not taken into account the engagement of German banks outside the country and, via subsidiaries, in special utilities. For instance, Deutsche Bank owned a large daughter company, Deutsche Überseeische Bank (DÜB), which was heavily engaged in many South American railways and municipal utilities. Its focus was investment banking, while keeping much of such investments in its own portfolio. Deutsche Bank also had a minority stake in Bank für Elektrische Unternehmungen in Zurich, which was associated with AEG. This Zurich-based bank acted as a holding company for electric utilities, as did the Berlin-based Elektrische Licht- und Kraftanlagen AG. We could enumerate a large number of financial holding companies for electrical utilities in and outside Germany which were dominated by German electrical enterprises (AEG, Siemens) and major

---

[9] Instead, VSt took a credit from Dillon Read (USA) (Reckendrees, 2000: 370ff.).

[10] Wellhöner (1989) underlines this thesis in his book on the relation between banks and nine large enterprises before 1914: "Though in five of nine cases (Siemens, Mannesmann, Rheinstahl, Hibernia, Deutsch-Lux) a quite stable nexus between an enterprise and one or two banks was established, the latter could never feel safe of their position because of competition" (p. 238); "The hypothesis of a general dictate by the banks is clearly to be dismissed" (p. 240).

[11] In 1993 exactly 28.13 percent (Commerzbank, 1994: 211; Liedke, 2006: 123).

banks, the most important of which was the Belgian-registered Sofina.[12] Large banks and AEG and Siemens were linked by interlocking directorates. Though interlocking shareholding was not significant, the resultant sharing of information was, indeed, important. Such arrangements qualify perhaps as business groups in the form of networks, while in a couple of cases (e.g., Deutsche Bank and DÜB) we can point to a business group based on ownership. However, World War I and the subsequent hyperinflation in Germany ended most of this; FDI was sequestered during the war, and the inflation cut banks back to their core.

In 1992 Deutsche Bank owned minority stakes in 250 industrial enterprises worldwide, but only exceptionally did the bank itself own more than 10 percent of the share capital. In important enterprises, such as Daimler, the stake was owned directly; in lesser companies it came via the bank's participation in the Munich-based Allgemeine Verwaltungsgesellschaft für Industriebeteiligungen mbH or similar holding companies. Deutsche Bank's majority or minority participation in such holding companies was in many cases organized jointly with other large German banks or investment companies. At first glance these cases remind one of pyramids. However, while pyramids are designed to direct with little financial resources, these holding companies were either straightforward financial investments or the result of financial problems;[13] if situated abroad, one would talk about portfolio investments not direct ones, because of the lack of intention to manage. We find similar structures with all major German universal banks. The structure of such a holding company is very well exemplified in La Porta et al. (1999: fig. 7), where "Stella" collects the influence of many investors, including banks, though none with a decisive influence.[14]

In the period 1992–2005 the following banks were among the 100 largest enterprises by turnover in Germany: Bayerische Hypotheken- und Wechselbank, Bayerische Vereinsbank, Commerzbank, Deutsche Bank, DG Bank, Dresdner Bank, and West LB. Table 8.2 shows their non-banking portfolio was massively reduced from 1992 to 2005 from seventy enterprises to just seven. At the same time their investment in finance-related firms (banks, financial services, insurance, and real-estate banking) grew

---

[12] This "B2B," called "Unternehmensgeschäft," was created in large scale by AEG. AEG's business was in equipment for electricity generation and distribution. Most customers (municipalities) could not pay for it. With the help of banks, AEG set up enterprises for electricity supply, owning these facilities, and sold their shares on the market. AEG and the bank(s) kept a decisive minority stake. Later a financial holding company (such as Sofina) owned these utilities, while AEG and the bank(s) kept a decisive minority stake in these holding companies. Consequently AEG, as well as Siemens, which followed a similar policy, became business groups (see Hertner, 1986)).

[13] For instance, if an enterprise cannot repay its loan, it may be turned into participation.

[14] La Porta et al. (1999): 487. Their Figure 7 illustrates in an organogram the ownership of Daimler. Large shareholders were Deutsche Bank (24.4 percent), Kuwait Government (12.96 percent), and Stella (12.3 percent). Stella had eight owners, each of which stood for 12.5 percent: Dresdner Bank, Commerzbank, Südwest Star, Allianz, a group of state banks, Star, the Voith family, and the Bosch family. Both Star and Südwest Star were owned by four different owners, among them six banks. This means a substantial investment of banks, but no decisive influence. These were neither cascades nor business groups because of the total lack of control. There had been many such companies like Stella.

Table 8.2. Banks in the 100 largest enterprises (by turnover) and their investment in non-financial enterprises, 1992 and 2005.

Name	1992	2005
Bayerische Hypo- und Wechselbank	No. of firms: 5; No. of firms of largest 100: 0	not included in 100 largest
Bayerische Vereinsbank	Firms: 7; of largest 100: 0	not included in 100 largest
Bayern LB	not included	Firms: 1, of largest 100: 0
Commerzbank	Firms: 11; of largest 100: 2	Firms: 1, of largest 100: 0
Deutsche Bank	Firms: 11; of largest 100: 5	Firms: 2, of largest 100: 0
DG/DZ Bank	Firms: 5; of largest 100: 0	Firms: 0, of largest 100: 0
Dresdner Bank	Firms: 12; of largest 100: 5	merged into Commerzbank
HypoVereinsbank	not included in 100 largest	Firms: 1, of largest 100: 0
Landesbank Baden-Württemberg	not included in 100 largest	Firms: 0, of largest 100: 0
West LB	Firms: 18; of largest 100: 1	Firms: 2, of largest 100: 0
Sum	*Firms: 70; of largest 100: 13*	*Firms: 7, of largest 100: 0*

Note: Non-financial investment excludes banks, insurance companies and real estate, threshold for counting: minimum stake of 5 per cent of shares.
Source: Liedke (1993–2006).

considerably. Parallel to this shift, many banks founded common holding companies for the rest of their industrial investment, which is illustrated by the case of the above-mentioned holding company "Stella."

We also need to point out one more issue which supports the perception of an abundance of business groups in the German economy: namely, the concept of "Deutschland AG" ("Germany Ltd."), which emerged in postwar West Germany. As Barca and Mayer have shown (2001), Germany is the country in Europe with a maximum bias towards large-block private control in contrast to a management- or market-control bias. "Deutschland AG" refers not only to a national system of mutual information and support, but also to cross-shareholding, interlocking directorates, and large bank credits for long-term investment. Its mindset and associated practice was a bulwark against hostile takeovers. Within this, Deutschland AG banks used to be the most active and flexible part, which underlined the perception that bank-centered business groups were widespread. But Deutschland AG was dismantled from the second half of the 1990s. Around 2000 two-thirds of the shares of all large German firms were owned by Germans; in 2011 56 percent were owned by foreigners (Thomsen and Pedersen, 1994: 3; Ahrens, Gehlen, and Reckendrees, 2013: 7).[15] The main reason for this change was Americanization: the neoliberal model suggested by Anglo-Saxon advisors was thought to be superior. The banks sold their shares in industry in order to

[15] By contrast, during the early 1990s foreign ownership stood at no more than 22 percent (Thomsen and Pedersen, 1994: 3).

invest in financial activities, which performed better than industry. Two events illustrate the one-time strength of Deutschland AG and its decline: the first was the unsuccessful hostile takeover of Continental by the Italian firm Pirelli in 1991; the other was the successful hostile takeover of Mannesmann by British Vodafone in 2000. Mannesmann could have been sheltered even against the high sum offered ($180 billion), but at that time it was explained openly that the old model of Deutschland AG was too rigid and had too little potential for growth. Consequently, the old Deutschland AG model was terminated. During the period of Deutschland AG's existence, it was the banks which through common action prevented unwanted takeover bids. However, even though such intervention underlined the power of the banks, they did not act as single business groups. The myth of Deutschland AG explains the perception of the power of German banks, but the reality is different from the myth.

An exceptional case in the discussion of German banks as business groups is the special bank Kreditanstalt für Wiederaufbau (KfW), which was founded in 1948 to support the reconstruction of West Germany. Owned entirely by the federal state, its task was, and is, to facilitate growth in sectors which the government designates to be strategically important. Thus, from the beginning KfW was a political instrument. While at first it handed out credits to bottleneck sectors such as energy and transport, from the 1960s it also invested in individual enterprises. In 1971 the instrument for strategic investment (Beteiligungsfinanzierung) was enlarged into a whole "program." Since then KfW has been by definition a bank-centered business group. However, the idea is not to keep such investments but to sell them as soon as the development of the respective enterprise, the market, and the government allows. For instance, in the 1990s the government sold the German postal service (Deutsche Post) to KfW. It was KfW's task to keep these shares and sell them further only in small quantities. Another example of KfW's special position was Daimler's sale of its shares in EADS (Airbus and other firms). Since the government wanted to retain a certain say in EADS's activities, Daimler's shares were bought by KfW. Due to these peculiarities, KfW qualifies as a bank-centered business group in formal terms, but since it is neither a normal commercial bank nor does it intentionally interfere in the management of the firms it owns, we would suggest it not be labeled as such.

When both sides of the debate about universal banks being business groups are considered, we find that the truth lies somewhere in the middle. In the case of a few large enterprises, such as Daimler, banks have clearly operated as business groups. Regarding many other enterprises, they have executed similar but borrowed power (by providing credits, using Depotstimmrecht, and other means) during certain periods for a few years, after which that power ceased. A third group of enterprises cannot be labeled as being part of a bank's business group. Each case has to be considered on its own; it is by no means sufficient to look into a bank's portfolio to point to the existence of a business group. The situation can be puzzling and even bewildering, but in any case to generalize that German banks are heads of large business groups without looking at the underlying operational mechanism is misleading.

8.6.2 Family-Owned Business Groups

In this section we will consider examples of traditional and recent family-owned business groups. A number of German entrepreneurial families own substantial investments in the economy. In most cases these enterprises represent the holding-company type of business group. One of the most distinctive is represented by the Porsche-Piëch family. It controls Porsche Automobil Holding SE, which in 2013 owned 32.2 percent of Volkswagen's stock and 50.73 percent of the votes in VW's stockholders' assembly. Thus it is not far-fetched to suggest that this particular family occupies an extremely influential position, not only in that company but in the whole of the German economy. The same applies to the Schwarz family (Lidl) and the Albrecht family (Aldi). Also, their enterprises (all in the retail trade) belonged among the largest ten German businesses by turnover in 2014. But all the enterprises mentioned focused on one single product line—however differentiated that might be.

By contrast, there are many other family firms representing business groups of the *diversified* type. One of the most powerful and controversial of these was owned by the Flick family. Friedrich Flick made his fortune in the interwar years by speculating in heavy industry, and then branched out into paper. After World War II he was sentenced to seven years' imprisonment for war crimes. His son, Friedrich Karl Flick, sold parts of the family holding's investment in heavy industry and focused on chemicals and Daimler. In 1985 he sold out completely to Deutsche Bank (DM5.4 billion, or €2.7 billion) and retired to his country estate in Austria. The 1972 organogram (Figure 8.1) depicts Friedrich Flick KG as a heavily diversified group with investments in machine building, iron and steel, and paper, as well as other branches of industry.

The Werhahn family started in the first half of the nineteenth century in the timber trade. Up to 1914 the group grew quickly, investing in several other branches such as mills, brewing, and banking. In 2013 its turnover was €3.2 billion, and the range of activities was considerable: construction materials, financial service, flour, real estate, and cutlery (the famous Zwillingsmesser, or "twin knives"). The business group is characterized by a relatively quick change in its investments as well as by a family contract, which holds the group together in spite of the family's increase in numbers. The group has always been led by a family member (in 2015 its CEO was Anton Werhahn).

Roechling represents another family-based business group, founded in 1822 as a coal-trading enterprise. Hermann Roechling enlarged the firm by exploiting the opportunities presented by World War II. Consequently, like Friedrich Flick he was sentenced as a Nazi war criminal to ten years' imprisonment. But the firm survived. Today the Roechling group produces mainly heavy-duty plastics and automotive parts.

The Quandt business group started in 1883 with the production of garments, especially uniforms. As with the Flicks and the Roechlings, the Quandts experienced an upswing during the Nazi years and a downswing afterwards. Today their

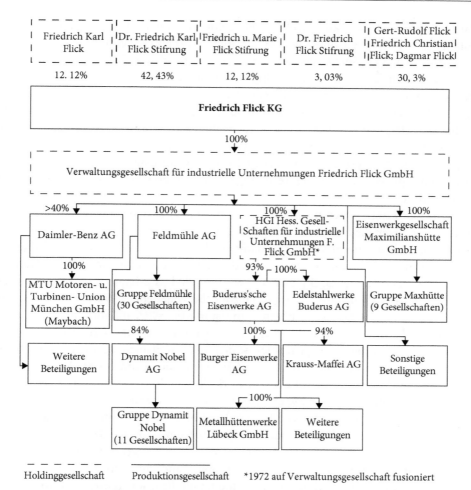

Holdinggesellschaft   Produktionsgesellschaft   *1972 auf Verwaltungsgesellschaft fusioniert

FIGURE 8.1. Organization of the Flick Group, 1972.

Source: Priemel(2007).

ownership is based on the decision to save BMW from bankruptcy during the 1960s. In 2012 they owned 46.7 percent of the car producer, making the Quandts one of the richest families in Germany. At the same time their investment in the pharmaceutical firm Altana, as well as other companies, makes the Quandt family one of the largest business groups.

One of the other best-known family-based business groups is Dr. Oetker, founded in 1891 to produce baking powder. In 1936 the enterprise expanded into shipping (Hamburg-Süd), and after 1950 into hotels and breweries. In contrast to other business groups, Dr. Oetker is known for its long-term investments. The group has never changed from its focus on food and shipping. Two of today's sizable family-based business groups—Herz and Jacobs—were refounded after 1945. In 1949 Max Herz established the Tchibo Company in Hamburg to roast and sell coffee. By the 1970s the Herz family had become Germany's largest coffee retailer, and in the same decade it became a business group by acquiring stakes in Beiersdorf (adhesives, cosmetics— NIVEA) and Reemtsma (tobacco). The Bremen-based Jacobs family also grew rich from coffee. These interests were sold in 1990 in order to buy out several family members. In the following years the Jacobs family invested in Barry Callebaud (chocolate), Adecco (temporary staffing agency), Minibar (hotel room fridges and safes), and others. All the family-owned business groups mentioned here have in common that they represent sizable enterprises but do not figure among the 100 largest German firms—and most of them never did.

In the following we present a short case study of Haniel, one of the oldest and biggest of the large diversified business groups in Germany. In 2010 it stood at no. 20 in the list of the largest enterprises in Germany, while it figured in *Fortune Global 500* at no. 359 (Fortune, 2014). For many decades it was one of the 100 largest German enterprises. The Haniel family business was founded as a haulage and warehousing firm in Ruhrort (Duisburg) in 1756. During the Napoleonic Wars Haniel profited from large-scale smuggling and began to invest in iron, steel, and machinery, which in due course became its main products. During these years the family management established a few business principles which have remained in force until today: diversification of economic activities and independence from banks. Between 1805 and 1808 the Haniels acquired three ironworks located in the environs of Oberhausen in the Ruhr valley. They were the nucleus of a large engagement which not only lasted for more than 150 years but was a key contributor to German industrialization—the Gutehoffnungshütte (GHH). Throughout the nineteenth century GHH expanded very fast and all profits generated were reinvested. For many years the Haniel family's personal prosperity was sustained by its shipping and commercial activities, which had been kept apart from GHH. In 1917 the family firm was reorganized into Franz Haniel & Cie. GmbH (FHC), its present form and name (James, 2005; Franz Haniel & Cie, 2006). The commercial activities were continued, but FHC's main focus was GHH.

FHC was engaged in river and overseas transport, the coal trade, collieries, and, last but not least, in GHH. Though FHC clearly owned GHH, the family's role in the business group became blurred for two reasons: the prominence of GHH's long-standing CEO (Paul Reusch, 1909–42), and the fact that GHH was many times larger than FHC. The imbalance caused even high-ranking GHH managers to perceive the world upside down: when in 1939 coal was short, GHH wanted more coal from the coal trader FHC; a leading GHH manager wrote, "Neither at GHH nor at another concern would it be possible for a subsidiary to follow other lines than the parent company!" (James, 2005: 222).

A strategic step for Haniel was the contract signed by family members after World War II. First, members agreed not to put their shares on the open market before they had been offered to the family. Second, an advisory council containing exclusively family members was established. Today, one feature distinguishes Haniel from most

FRANZ HANIEL & CIE. GMBH

Bekaert Textiles	CWS-boco	ELG	TAKKT	METRO GROUP
Bekaert Textiles is the world's leading specialist in the development and manufacturing of woven and knitted mattress textiles and bed cover materials.	CWS-boco ranks among the leading international service providers of washroom hygiene products, dust control mats, workwear and textile	ELG is one of the world's leading specialists in trading and recycling raw materials, in particular for the stainless steel industry.	TAKKT is the market-leading B2B direct marketing specialist for business equipment in Europe and North America.	METRO GROUP is among the premier international retail groups.
100.00%	100.00%	100.00%	50.25%	25.00%

As at juni 2015

FIGURE **8.2.** Haniel Group, 2015.
Source: courtesy of Franz Haniel & Cie.

other family-owned groups: the separation of ownership and management was introduced. Corporate management has been entrusted entirely to external professional managers; entrepreneurial decisions could thus be taken without regard to family commitments in order to achieve optimal business results. In 1964 Haniel sold its engagement in the energy and gasoline trade, and in 1985 it disposed of all interests in GHH. Instead, Haniel started its engagement in Metro, a German wholesaler of consumer goods. In 1971 Haniel Holding AG in Switzerland became the center of FHC's international engagement. Step by step Haniel became an international investment management firm. Since the 1980s the speed of FHC's transformation has been breathtaking: in 2002 less than 5 percent of Haniel's turnover was generated by enterprises which it had owned twenty years before. In 2014 Haniel—which calls itself a family equity company today—had controlling stakes in: 1) CWS-boco, a worldwide provider of washroom hygiene, dust-control mats, and textile services; 2) ELG, the leader in trading and processing of raw materials; 3) TAKKT, a leading B2B mail-order specialist for business equipment; and 4) Metro, one of the most important international trading groups (see Figure 8.2).

In 2014 FHC had about 11,500 employees in 30 countries; however, the holding company in Duisburg employed only about 200 people. Today the Haniels can look back on more than 250 years as a successful family-based business group. Though on a much smaller scale, Haniel's behavior reminds one of Warren Buffett the American billionaire and main owner of Berkshire Hathaway:

> In effect, Mr. Buffett is arguing that he and his vice chairman, Charlie Munger, and their 25-person team in Omaha are better at deciding allocation of capital among different potential investments than the entire infrastructure of the modern financial system—banks, stock and bond markets, buyout funds and so on. The big advantage that Berkshire may have are that the company decides how to allocate capital with neither the self-interested decision-making of many operating executives—most people don't want to dismantle the company they lead—nor the high

fees and short-term of private equity and other buyout artists. If you believe
Mr. Buffett Berkshire combines the long-term perspective of the former with the
analytical rigor of the latter.[16]

The sentence on managers not wanting "to dismantle the company they lead"
reminds one very much of the embarrassing power of the manager Paul Reusch over
the Haniel family and their holding company FHC. Also the—for German
conditions—swift change of investment by FHC may be compared to Buffett's
Berkshire Hathaway. There are, however, only a few German business groups that
behave like FHC or even more quickly like Berkshire Hathaway.

8.6.3 Other Types of Business Groups

8.6.3.1 *State-Owned Business Groups*

Quite a number of business groups in Germany were created when state-owned
enterprises were reorganized as holding companies during the interwar period. Initially
the operations of these firms were a part of the state budget. Income and expenditure
were the only figures obtainable, preventing a realistic economic calculation. Therefore,
they were transferred into quasi-private holding companies, a process which started
during the First World War. The largest ones—Preussag, Veba, and Viag—were
established in the 1920s and were huge business groups combining mining, glassmak-
ing, transport facilities, the generation and distribution of energy, as well as many other
activities. Most state-owned enterprises remained in this form until the 1990s. However, a cautious and stepwise privatization started in the 1960s. Veba was not listed on
the stock exchange before 1988. Even the Liberal Party did not press for a profound
privatization. However, the attitude changed under the influence of neo-liberalism,
which became dominant in Germany during the 1990s. In consequence most state-
owned firms were privatized. The organogram of Veba (Figure 8.3) illustrates in detail
the diversification of business groups such as Preussag, Viag, or Veba. 1999 was the
year before it merged with Viag in order to create E.ON. The picture shows three
large divisions—energy, chemicals, real estate—and a remainder. The largest division,
energy, was divided into electricity supply and oil, each with several independent
enterprises representing various legal forms. Since the 1980s these state-owned firms
have been privatized step by step. During this process important private firms such as
E.ON (one of the world's largest enterprises in electricity generation and distribution)
emerged. Most of them have subsequently reorganized their operations to focus on one
core business, becoming integrated enterprises, and thus have ceased to be a diversified
business group.

---

[16] Irwin (2015: 18).

Konzernübersicht · Stand: 1.März 2000

VEBA AG
Düsseldorf, Kapital 1.307 Mio €

Energie

Gesellschaft	Anteil
PreussenElektra AG, Hannover, Kapital 1.250 Mio DM	100%
PreussenElektra Kraftwerke AG&Co. KG, Hannover, Kapital 500 Mio DM	100%
PreussenElektra Kernkraft GmbH&Co. KG, Hannover, Kapital 400 Mio DM	100%
PreussenElektra Netz GmbH&Co. KG, Hannover, Kapital 500 Mio DM	100%
PreussenElektra Engineering GmbH, Gelsenkirchen, Kapital 22 Mio DM	100%
Avacon AG, Helmstedt, Kapital 45,7 Mio €	54,7%
e.dis Energie Nord AG, Fürstenwalde/Spree, Kapital 175 Mio €	70%
Schleswag Aktiengesellschaft, Rendsburg, Kapital 200 Mio DM	65,3%
Pesag Aktiengesellschaft, Paderborn, Kapital 33 Mio DM	54,7%
EWE Aktiengesellschaft, Oldenburg, Kapital 300 Mio DM	27,4%
Energie- Aktiengesellschaft Mitteldeutschland EAM, Kassel, Kapital 120 Mio DM	46%
Thüga Aktiengesellschaft, München, Kapital 320 Mio DM	56,5%
Gelsenwasser AG, Gelsenkirchen, Kapital 171,9 Mio DM	52,1%
Veag Vereinigte Energiewerke AG, Berlin, Kapital 1.000 Mio €	26,3%
Bewag Aktiengesellschaft, Berlin, Kapital 1.120 Mio DM	23%
Hamburgische Electricitäts-Werke Aktiengesellschaft, Hamburg, Kapital 460 Mio DM	15,4%
Electriciteitsbedrijf Zuid-Holland N.V., Voorburg (Niederlande), Kapital 20 Mio NLG	100%
Sydkraft AB, Malmö (Schweden), Kapital 1.910 Mio SEK	20,7%
BKW FMB Energie AG, Bern (Schweiz), Kapital 132 Mio CHF	20%

Gesellschaft	Anteil
VEBA Oel AG, Gelsenkirchen, Kapital 488 Mio DM	100%
VEBA Öl&Gas GmbH, Essen, Kapital 697 Mio DM	100%
VEBA Oil Supply and Trading GmbH, Hamburg, Kapital 6 Mio DM	100%
Ruhr Oel GmbH, Düsseldorf, Kapital 602 Mio DM	50%
Aral AG, Bochum, Kapital 300 Mio DM	98,9%
VEBA Wärmeservice GmbH, Gelsenkirchen, Kapital 45,7 Mio €	100%
AFC Aviation Fuel Company mbH, Hamburg, Kapital 8 Mio DM	50%
VEBA Erdöl -Raffinerie Emsland GmbH&Co.KG, Lingen, Kapital 0,05 Mio €	100%
VEBA Oel Verarbeitungs GmbH, Gelsenkirchen, Kapital 0,05 Mio DM	100%

Chemie

Gesellschaft	Anteil
Degussa-Hüls AG, Frankfurt/Main, Kapital 399 Mio €	64,7%
Asta Medica AG, Dresden, Kapital 100 Mio DM	100%
Stockhausen GmbH&Co.KG, Krefeld, Kapital 84 Mio DM	99,9%
Röhm GmbH, Darmstadt, Kapital 119 Mio DM	99,5%
Oxeno Olefinchemie GmbH, Marl, Kapital 35 Mio DM	100%
Phenolchemie GmbH&Co.KG, Gladbach, Kapital 100 Mio DM	99,5%
Cerdec AG Keramische Farben, Frankfurt/Main, Kapital 30 Mio DM	100%
Creavis Gesellschaft für Technologie und Innovation mbH, Marl, Kapital 0,1 Mio DM	100%
Infracor GmbH, Marl, Kapital 45 Mio DM	100%
Degussa-Hüls Antwerpen N.V., Antwerpen/Belgien, Kapital 1.100 Mio bfr	100%
Degussa-Hüls Corporation Ridgefield Park, New Jersey/USA, Kapital 20.400 US-$	100%
Degussa-Hüls China Ltd. Hongkong, Kapital 1 Mio HKD	100%
Degussa-Hüls Ltda. Guarulhos/Brasilien, Kapital 123 Mio BRL	100%
Allgemeine Gold-Und Silberscheideanstalt AG Pforzheim, Kapital 20 Mio DM	90,8%
Degussa-Hüls Japan Co. Ltd. Tokio/Japan, Kapital 495 Mio JPY	100%
Algorax Pty. Ltd. Port Elizabeth/Südafrika, Kapital 1,8 Mio ZAR	55%

Immobilien Management

Gesellschaft	Anteil
Viterra AG, Essen, Kapital 350 Mio DM	100%
Viterra Wohnen AG, Bochum, Kapital 0,5 Mio DM	100%
Viterra Wohnpartner AG, Bochum, Kapital 5,05 Mio DM	100%
Viterra Baupartner AG, Bochum, Kapital 33,6 Mio DM	100%
VEBA Wohnen GmbH, Gelsenkirchen-Buer, Kapital 15,3 Mio DM	83,66%
VEBA Urbana GmbH, Düsseldorf, Kapital 31,9 Mio DM	58,17%
Deutschbau- Holding GmbH, Eschborn, Kapital 20 Mio DM	50%
WBRM-Holding GmbH, Essen, Kapital 1 Mio €	50%
Viterra Energy Services AG, Essen, Kapital 7 Mio DM	100%
Viterra Sicherheit und Service GmbH, Essen, Kapital 5 Mio DM	100%
Viterra Gewerbeimmobilien GmbH, Essen, Kapital 1 Mio DM	100%

Gesellschaft	Anteil
Stinnes AG, Mülheim a.d. Ruhr, Kapital 371 Mio DM	65,3%
VEBA Electronics LLC, Santa Clara, Kalifornien/USA	100%
VEBA Telecom GmbH, Düsseldorf, Kapital 250 Mio DM	100%
MEMC Electronic Materials Inc. St. Peters, Missouri/USA, Kapital 508 Mio US-$	71,8%

FIGURE 8.3. Organization of the VEBA Group, 1999.

Source: VEBA AG, Annual Report (1999).

8.6.3.2 *Special Cases of Business Groups: Cooperatives, Cartels, and Konzerne*

One sector that contains several large enterprises has not been mentioned up to now: cooperative business. These enterprises used to be rather small and local, but they were unified by a strong common ideology: cooperatives claimed not to exploit other human beings. The German co-op movement experienced its peak after the Second World War, especially in food retailing, supplying about 5 percent of the market. German co-ops founded two major wholesale companies, BayWa and GEG. Because of their organizational structure and the ideology of mutual aid, German co-ops can be seen as business groups of a network type. German co-ops flourished during the postwar "golden" decades but, following a wave of demutualization in the 1980s, they no longer play a major economic role except in housing and banking (Battilani and Schröter, 2012).

Cartels are another form of alliance that can form business groups. Again the definition is both decisive and difficult. Cartels differ from the standard type of business group by having no ultimate owner and representing a cooperation which, based on its contract, is limited in time. However, in certain types of cartels members hand over one or several functions of their enterprise to the cartel. Some even form their own permanent organizations: for instance, during the 1930s the Nitrogen Syndicate had a bureaucracy of several thousand employees, which represented the sole sales outlet and allocated and monitored production quotas. Such cartels could be called business groups because central parts of decision-making were allocated to a superior institution and not located within the members' firms. Such special cartels, called syndicates, were important in Germany, governing the entire markets for coal, fertilizers, and other goods up to 1945. Like cartels, "communities of interest" can form business groups, at least in theory. Such communities of interest are organized frequently, especially when construction firms join forces to complete a large project, such as an airport. These communities establish their own legal bodies and have command authority over the entire project or parts of the constituent enterprises. If the community intends to continue cooperation beyond the lifespan of a single project, we surely have a business group. But such communities of interest are by law bound to one single task.

The German term for "community of interest" is "Interessengemeinschaft," often abbreviated to "IG." German history has included several such organizations, the most important being the large chemical firm "IG Farben." However, the abbreviation "IG" has no legal meaning; it is just another expression for "group." An IG can represent a cartel, an enterprise, or just a group of persons with a common interest—in wine tasting, for instance. Consequently, IG Farben took the legal form of a normal stock company.[17] Like Interessengemeinschaft, the meaning of the German term "Konzern," often translated as "combine" or "trust," is extremely vague. A Konzern is nothing but a

---

[17] Its full name was "*Interessen Gemeinschaft Farben*industrie Aktiengesellschaft."

firm which owns and directs other enterprises as legally independent units. Thus a Konzern can represent a business group, or it may represent a Chandlerian integrated enterprise operating in related industries as well as others. The term is still used in law, but much less frequently in everyday life. For a century up to the 1970s it was a politically loaded term that evoked the populist struggle between big business and small-scale producers (shopkeepers, artisans, farmers). Regardless of its size, a state-owned enterprise was never called a Konzern because the state was seen as neutral.

8.7 CONCLUDING REMARKS

The contribution of this chapter is limited to business groups as part of large enterprise, in which we found evidence of a substantial number of this type of organization in Germany: about a quarter of the largest 100 firms by turnover represented business groups during the 1990s! For German scholars this result is extremely surprising, if not breathtaking, because the question and what it might entail for the country's economic history and future performance have been largely overlooked by economists and historians. Relevant literature is almost non-existent. This situation has two implications: 1) our findings presented here are not secured by literature, and thus they must be considered preliminary; and 2) there is huge potential in a new field of research related to the better understanding of German enterprise, its history, and its future.

However, the result can be looked at the other way round: why was only a quarter of German big business organized as business groups? Would not the influence of the famous universal banks entail a much larger presence? Since the financial and product markets were relatively well developed since the industrialization of the country, the main management idea of German big business was vertical integration in order to control as much of the value chain as possible for reasons of quality control and to internalize profit. Horizontal integration could be obtained by cartels, which were legal and widespread until the end of World War II (e.g., IG Farben, Siemens, and Thyssen). When the instrument of cartelization was interdicted by the Allies in 1947, German big business sought safety through diversification. That trend was interrupted by two waves of Americanization in the 1960s and 1990s. From the 1980s the perception of the prevailing Anglo-Saxon business model discouraged diversification, with a consequent decline in the number of business groups. The collapse of that model's influence after 2008 has resulted in a renewed trend to diversify and thus to create business groups.

The role of large universal banks has been overestimated to a large extent. Also, German banks were looking for security. During the industrial crisis of the 1880s it was the banks, not industrial enterprises, which pressed firms into cartels, because banks were afraid that their industrial borrowers might default. They also accepted the transformation of credit into ordinary stock. Both sides learned from these moves: from then on industrial enterprises promoted security through cartelization, while banks achieved a much better control—or security—through investing in their customers than by extending them credit. Though industry tried to ward off banks' intervention, banks succeeded in their policy to a large extent until World War I. During that period Marxist writers pointed out the special influence of German banks on industry. These writings shaped a perception of the enormous power of German banking, which has been challenged in Germany only since the 1990s and which still remains widely accepted in the Anglo-Saxon world. In any case, the First World War and subsequent hyperinflation terminated the influence of German banks over big business, except in a few cases. However, a prominent case for the banks-as-business-groups thesis, and usually the only example the literature provides, is Deutsche Bank's investment in Daimler. The engagement was, indeed, stable and turned Deutsche Bank into an industrial business group, until it divested itself of Daimler in several steps from the 1990s. Other bank stakes in big business were rather insignificant as regards the managerial influence obtained (see Table 8.2).

Of course, all the above-mentioned results are decisively affected by the definition used. When a business group is defined by the existence of a holding company and several legal entities, then almost all German large and medium-sized firms fall into that category. In Germany legal provisions create a high degree of security when several entities are joined; if one fails, the rest can continue unharmed. We therefore looked predominantly for groups of legally independent enterprises active in unrelated markets, owned and directed by a superior organization. But our main concern is how these enterprises were understood and managed by their parent company: as independent entities or closely supportive units. If the second applied, we did not count them as a business group. Still, things can change: for most of its history Siemens did not qualify as a diversified business group, but in recent years it does. Management practice is decisive here. Finally, the relationship of the state and families to business groups is similarly checkered. From the 1920s to the 1990s the central state, federal states, and municipalities owned business groups more by chance than by choice. After World War I they removed their utilities, mines, and so on from their general budgets and set them up as holding companies. During a third wave of Americanization (in the 1990s) these public holding companies were privatized, which entailed the termination of this kind of business group. Today there are quite a number of business groups dominated by families, but few of them are found among the country's 100 largest firms.

In short, the number and economic influence of business groups in Germany have been much greater than hitherto assumed. At the same time their history shows a considerable variability. At first universal banks dominated the form of enterprise, but their position was undermined by the First World War. After 1945 the emergence and growth of business groups were hampered by waves of American influence in business management. Lately the business-group form has been expanding again, especially in terms of family firms which are fairly big yet still smaller than any of the 100 largest German enterprises. In any case, business groups have played an important role in the development of German big business for more than 150 years. To perceive them as an outdated and dying species would be utterly wrong and misleading. This type of enterprise was important, is important, and may be even more important in future.

Acknowledgments

I would like to thank those who directly or indirectly helped me in writing this contribution: the participants of our Kyoto workshop in 2013 and of the session at the WEHC, also in Kyoto, and, above all, Asli Colpan, whose comments were extremely helpful. I extend my warmest thanks to the personnel of enterprises who gave information, such as Dr. Oetker, but above all to Christine Erz of Haniel and Reinhard Frost of the Historical Institute of Deutsche Bank.

APPENDIX 1

Diversified business groups in Germany, as part of the 100 largest enterprises (measured by turnover; International Standard Industrial Classification (ISIC, Rev. 4), core business field in italics—the amount of numbers indicates the size of diversification

Name	investment in sector, ownership >10% in 1992	investment in sector, ownership >10% in 2005
AGIV	C 27; C28; D 35; F 41, H 49	No longer in largest 100
Allianz	D 21, D 35, F 41, K 64, *K 65*, L 68	C 28, K 64, *K 65*
BASF	B 08; D 35; *C 20*; G 46; H 52	B 06, B 08; D 35; *C 20*; G 46; H 52
Bayerische Hypo- & W.-bank	C 13, D 35, I 56, *K 64*	No longer in largest 100
Bayerische Vereinsbank	C 13, D 35, *K 64*	No longer in largest 100
Benteler	*C 28; G 46*	*C 28; G 46*
Commerzbank	C 28; C 30; G 47; *K 64*	C 28; *K 64*
Deutsche Bank	A 01; C 29; F 41; G 47, H 50; *K 64*; M 69; R 90	C 28; I 55; *K 64*
Dresdner Bank	B 08; C 13; C 20; C 30; F 41; *K 64*; K 65	No longer in largest 100
E.ON (1992: Veba, VIAG)		*D 35*
Freudenberg	*C 15, C 19*	*C 15, C 19*
Hochtief	*not in largest 100*	*F 41, F 42, F 43, N 81*
Haniel	*C 23*; H 50	*C 23*; H 50
Krupp	C 19; *C 24*; C 27; C 28; C 29; F 42; G 46	Merged into ThyssenKrupp
Linde	*C 28; C 20;*	*C 28; C 20*
MAN	C 26 *C 28*; C 29; C 30	C 28; *C 29;*
Mannesmann	*C 25;* C 27; C 28; G 46	No longer in largest 100
Metallgesellschaft/GEA	B 08; C 19; *C 24*, C 28; G 46	*C 24*
Munich Re	*C 20, C 25, C 28, K 65, M 70*	A 2, *C 25, C 28, K 65*

(*continued*)

Name	investment in sector, ownership >10% in 1992	investment in sector, ownership >10% in 2005
Oetker	C 10; C 11; H 50	C 10; C 11; H 50
Philip Holzmann	C 23; D 35; F 41, L 68	C 23; D 35; F 41, L 68
Preussag/TUI	B 08; C 24; C 28; F 41, G 46; N 79	N 79
Rethmann	not in largest 100	E 47; H 50
RWE	C 27; D 35; E 47,	D 35
Ruhrkohle/RAG	B 05; C 19; C 23; G 46	B 05; C 19; C 23; G 46
Schörghuber	not in largest 100	C 11; F 41, L 68
Tchibo	C 10; C 12, C 20	C 10; C 12, C 20
Thyssen/ThyssenKrupp	B 08; C 19; C 23; C 24; C 28; C 29; C 30, F 41, G 46; H 49, H 50; H 52	C 19; C 24; C 27 C 28; C 30,; F 42; G 46
Veba	B 08; C 19; D 35; G 46, H 49	Merged into E.ON
VIAG	C 19; C 23; C 24; C 28; D 35; G 46; G 47, H 52	Merged into E.ON
West LB	B 05; C 15; C 27; I 55; K 64	No longer in largest 100
Number of busines groups	27	18

Note 1: "Ownership >10%" means 10 or more percent of share capital was owned by the respective business group.

Note 2: The above codes denote the ISIC codes (revision 4). For individual codes see Appendix 2.

Source: Commerzbank, *Wer gehört zu wem?* Frankfurt, several years; Liedke, Rainer, *Wem gehört die Republik? Die Konzerne und ihre globalen Verflechtungen in der globalisierten Wirtschaft*, 1996 and 2006, Frankfurt am Main: Eichborn Verlag.

APPENDIX 2

Excerpt from the International Standard Industrial Classification of All Economic Activities, Rev. 4 (only those numbers listed in Appendix 1 are included)

- *A*—Agriculture, forestry and fishing
  - *01*—Crop and animal production, hunting and related service activities
  - *02*—Forestry and logging
- *B*—Mining and quarrying
  - *05*—Mining of coal and lignite
  - *06*—Extraction of crude petroleum and natural gas
  - *08*—Other mining and quarrying
- *C*—Manufacturing
  - *10*—Manufacture of food products
  - *11*—Manufacture of beverages
  - *12*—Manufacture of tobacco products

- ○ *13*—Manufacture of textiles
- ○ *15*—Manufacture of leather and related products
- ○ *19*—Manufacture of coke and refined petroleum products
- ○ *20*—Manufacture of chemicals and chemical products
- ○ *21*—Manufacture of basic pharmaceutical products and pharmaceutical preparations
- ○ *23*—Manufacture of other non-metallic mineral products
- ○ *24*—Manufacture of basic metals
- ○ *25*—Manufacture of fabricated metal products, except machinery and equipment
- ○ *26*–Manufacture of computer, electronic and optical products
- ○ *27*—Manufacture of electrical equipment
- ○ *28*—Manufacture of machinery and equipment n.e.c.
- ○ *29*—Manufacture of motor vehicles, trailers and semi-trailers
- ○ *30*—Manufacture of other transport equipment
- ○ *33*—Repair and installation of machinery and equipment
- • *D*—Electricity, gas, steam and air conditioning supply
- ○ *35*—Electricity, gas, steam and air conditioning supply
- • *F*—Construction
- ○ *41*—Construction of buildings
- ○ *42*—Civil engineering
- ○ *43*—Specialized construction activities
- • *G*—Wholesale and retail trade; repair of motor vehicles and motorcycles
- ○ *46*—Wholesale trade, except of motor vehicles and motorcycles
- ○ *47*—Retail trade, except of motor vehicles and motorcycles
- • *H*—Transportation and storage
- ○ *49*—Land transport and transport via pipelines
- ○ *50*—Water transport
- ○ *52*—Warehousing and support activities for transportation
- • *I*—Accommodation and food service activities
- ○ *55*—Accommodation
- ○ *56*—Food and beverage service activities
- • *K*—Financial and insurance activities
- ○ *64*—Financial service activities, except insurance and pension funding
- ○ *65*—Insurance, reinsurance and pension funding, except compulsory social security
- • *L*—Real estate activities
- ○ *68*—Real estate activities
- • *M*—Professional, scientific and technical activities
- ○ *69*—Legal and accounting activities
- ○ *70*—Activities of head offices; management consultancy activities
- • *N*—Administrative and support service activities
- ○ *81*—Services to buildings and landscape activities
- • *R*—Arts, entertainment and recreation
- ○ *90*—Creative, arts and entertainment activities

Source: http://unstats.un.org/unsd/cr/registry/isic-4.asp, accessed 30 August 2015

CHAPTER 9

....

FRANCE

a complement to multidivisional enterprises

....

YOUSSEF CASSIS

9.1 INTRODUCTION

....

THE discussion of business groups in France has long been intrinsically linked to the broader issue of the country's "economic backwardness," especially with regard to the development of large corporations, which appeared to have somewhat lagged behind that of other advanced economies, namely the United States, Britain, and Germany.[1] French companies were judged to have been not only smaller in overall size, but also to have suffered from a presumed inferior form of organization. The dominant form in French large firms—the holding company based on layers of *participations* and often called groups (*groupes* in French)—was considered deficient in comparison to full ownership and a multidivisional structure, especially in the key industries of the Second Industrial Revolution, such as electricity, steel, or chemicals.[2] Admittedly, such views of French big business have been discarded by historical research undertaken in the last thirty years or so. Despite some corporate singularities, French big business was in most respects comparable to its British and German counterparts (Cassis, 1997; Smith, 2006). However, with the reappraisal of the role of business groups in business and economic development, should we go one step further in the reappraisal of French business performance? France is no longer seen as a laggard, but should it actually be seen as a leader in business organization, having pioneered the development of "business groups"?

---

[1] The focus of this chapter is on the varieties of diversified business groups. However, other types of groups are also taken into consideration when relevant.

[2] For a discussion of the issue, see Levy-Leboyer, 1980.

Whether France should be seen as a leader or laggard is, of course, of minor interest. A far more important question is how to assess the significance of business groups in France, not least in comparison with other forms of business organization, and their contribution to France's economic and business development. It must be said from the outset that the type of company that has long dominated French big business was not the diversified business group, as conceptualized by Colpan and Hikino in Chapter 1— whether of the conventional or emergent variety.[3] The main characteristic of France's leading *groupes* (Saint-Gobain, Thomson, Compagnie Générale d'Electricité, Schneider, Renault, and many others) was that a number of their activities—which were mostly in single or related industries—were undertaken through legally independent units, in which the parent company held a majority or a controlling minority stake. Vertical integration, whether backward or forward, usually involved the creation of a new company, which often shared its registered office and senior management with the parent company. In some respects, especially their legal structure, they resembled the "holding company" variety of hierarchy-type business group. However, in terms of business organization, there was not always a fundamental difference between legally independent and partially owned units, fully owned subsidiaries, and internal subdivisions. From this perspective, despite a lesser development of managerial hierarchies, the French *groupes* were more akin to business enterprises, including, in some cases, Chandlerian firms, whether functional or multidivisional, depending on their degree of related diversification and control styles.

Only a few of France's largest businesses can thus be considered to be diversified business groups—even taking into account all their different varieties. The object of this chapter is to identify them, assess their position among the country's largest companies, and discuss some issues related to their development and longevity, strategy, ownership and governance, and economic significance. Amongst the conventional varieties of diversified business groups, only bank-centered groups and a few family-owned groups existed before the First World War. Family-owned business groups have been a persistent though minority component of French big business since the 1920s. And unlike Italy, Spain, and indeed Germany, state-owned business groups have, perhaps surprisingly, not properly featured in France. As for the emergent varieties, neither conglomerates in the 1960s and 1970s nor private equity since the 1980s really took off in France, though there are exceptions that prove the rule.

---

[3] Colpan and Hikino establish three main conceptual distinctions. First, in terms of organizational models, they distinguish between multidivisional enterprises and business groups. Second, they identify two types of business groups: the "authority-type" and the "alliance principle." The former includes "diversified business groups," "holding companies," and, from a governance and finance perspective, "pyramidal business groups," while the latter is made up of "network-type business groups." And third, they differentiate between five main varieties of "diversified business groups"—the main topic of the present volume. Three are described as "conventional"—the "family-controlled business group," the "state-owned business group," and the "bank-centered business group"; and two are described as "contemporary"—the "conglomerate" and "private equity." For more details about the main characteristics of business groups, see Chapter 1.

One problem is, of course, that ideal types are rarely found in the actual business world. The frontier between the Chandlerian multidivisional enterprise, the diversified business group, and even the "holding company" is not always clear-cut, especially in France. The degree of diversification of a business group can also be a matter of contention. The main characteristics of a business group can change over time. Some flexibility is thus necessary when dealing with the long-term history of business groups in France—or indeed any advanced economy. For this reason, while the focus of this chapter will be on the five varieties of diversified business groups, "holding companies" as well as pyramidal business groups, which often overlap, will also be taken into consideration.

The chapter is divided into four chronological periods: the pre-1914 years, the interwar years, the "Golden Age," and the turn of the twenty-first century. Greater emphasis has thus been put on historical than on contemporary developments. While fairly uncontroversial, the chronological subdivision is well suited to the analysis of business groups, with their emergence in the nineteenth century, rise between the two world wars, persistence during the Golden Age, and decline—but possibly also revival—at the end of the twentieth century. There is thus both a degree of continuity and discontinuity, as some groups went through two or more periods, while most of them appeared or disappeared according to the prevailing conditions of the moment. A conclusion will reflect, over the long term, on business groups' ownership, governance, strategy, and longevity, as well as their contribution to France's economic and business development. Beforehand, a brief survey of the development of big business in France will provide some landmarks for the discussion of the specific position and role of business groups.

9.2 THE DEVELOPMENT OF BIG BUSINESS IN FRANCE

In the decade preceding the First World War big business in France, while displaying the same characteristics as in other leading industrialized countries, also reflected the specificity of French industrial capitalism.[4] The largest French firms were, by a wide margin, the railway companies—the PLM (Paris-Lyon-Méditerranée), Europe's largest company, with total assets in excess of $1,200 million, followed by the Paris-Orléans, the "Est," the "Nord," and the "Midi," all with total assets ranging between $400 million and $600 million (Caron, 1997–2005). The other firms making up the top

---

[4] This survey is based on the database established for the project on "The Performance of European Business in the Twentieth Century." See Cassis, Colli, and Schröter (2016) and the chapter on France in that volume. Companies' size is measured in assets before the 1960s and in turnover thereafter. Figures are in US dollars in order to gauge the size of France's largest firms in an international comparative perspective.

ten non-financial companies were transport (two shipping companies, Messageries Maritimes and Compagnie Générale Transatlantique) and utility companies (Compagnie Parisienne de Distribution d'Electricité, Compagnie Centrale d'Eclairage par le Gaz, and Compagnie Générale des Eaux), with assets between $30 million and $60 million (Beltran, 2002; Berneron-Couvenhes, 2007; Williot, 2010).

No manufacturing company thus ranked among the country's top ten, the two largest (Saint-Gobain in glass and chemicals and Thompson-Houston in electrical engineering) being respectively twelfth and thirteenth, with assets around the $25 million to $30 million mark, followed by the metallurgical concerns Marine Homécourt and Schneider, with assets just above $20 million (Rust, 1973; Lanthier, 1988; Daviet, 1989; Moine, 1989). Because of their huge assets, mostly made up of deposits, the large commercial banks (Crédit lyonnais, Société générale, Comptoir national d'escompte de Paris) all ranked amongst the country's ten largest companies, but this was also the case when using such criteria as share capital and market capitalization (Desjardins et al., 2003).

French big business was thus clearly dominated by finance and services, which made up fourteen out of the country's twenty largest companies. This trend was reinforced by the emergence of large enterprises in commercial activities, especially department stores: Le Bon Marché, which featured in the top twenty with $26 million in assets, but also Printemps and Nouvelles Galeries. Within the manufacturing sector, the heavy industries (coal, iron and steel, and shipbuilding) held sway (Cassis, 1997). Apart from Saint-Gobain and Thomson, large companies in the major industries of the Second Industrial Revolution (chemicals, electrical engineering, mechanical engineering) remained on the fringe of big business and were only fractionally larger than firms in food or textiles.

The structure of French big business altered after the First World War. The railway companies remained the country's largest. More significant, however, was the rise of the industries of the Second Industrial Revolution, which had taken off fairly slowly before 1914. Their rise was not as strong as in Britain, but still significant and particularly noticeable in automobiles, where France enjoyed an early lead before being overtaken by the US in 1906, though still retaining first place in Europe until the depression of the 1930s. By 1929, Citroën was France's largest manufacturing company (with assets reaching $67 million) and Renault was not far behind, though data is unavailable because the company remained in family ownership (Fridenson, 1972; Schweitzer, 1982; Loubet, 2009). It was followed by Saint-Gobain ($51 million) and two newcomers—Michelin in rubber ($42 million) and Produits chimiques et métallurgiques d'Alais (Pechiney) in aluminum and chemicals ($41 million). In electrical engineering, the largest firm, CGE ($33 million), just about made it in the top twenty, with Thomson-Houston ($25 million) a little behind.

Nevertheless, big business was still dominated by the heavy industries, with the large collieries of northern France—such as Mines de Lens ($55 million) and Mines de Vicoigne-Noeuds & Drocourt ($44 million)—on the one hand, and the iron-and-steel concerns—such as Nord Est ($38 million) and Longwy ($36 million)—on the other.

Forward integration for the former and backward integration for the latter mainly took place through cross-shareholding or joint ownership of subsidiary companies—a type of business group to which we will come back later in the chapter.

In finance and services, shipping companies—such as Compagnie générale transatlantique ($54 million)—and utility companies—such as Lyonnaise des Eaux ($38 million), Energie électrique du littoral méditerranéen ($35 million), and Union d'électricité ($34 million)—remained prominent. Taken individually, they were now smaller than the largest industrial concerns. However, especially in electricity, they were at the heart of vast business groups, which will be discussed in Section 9.4. With the odd exception, such as Saint-Frères in textiles and Galeries Lafayette in distribution, other industries, both traditional and new, such as oil, were left behind. Banks, for their part, were weakened by war and inflation, but in spite of their decline remained an integral part of French big business.

Perhaps surprisingly, French big business was not fundamentally transformed by depression, war, occupation, and reconstruction. It is rather its organization, in particular its form of ownership, that was altered through the nationalization of some of its key components. The railway companies and armaments industry had already been nationalized by the Popular Front in 1937.[5] They were followed in 1945–6 by the Banque de France, the big four commercial banks (though not the investment banks), insurance companies, coal mining, gas and electricity (though not water) companies, air transport, and the carmaker Renault, following accusations of collaboration with the German war effort made against its head and founder, Louis Renault (Andrieu, Le Van, and Prost, 1987).

Leaving aside the state-owned monopolies—SNCF (railways), EDF (electricity), GDF (gas), and Charbonnages de France (coal mining)—French big business was henceforth dominated by the industries of the Second Industrial Revolution. Oil finally took off with the Compagnie Française des Pétroles (CFP), created in 1924 on the state's initiative and France's largest industrial company by 1956 (with $248 million assets), as well as the subsidiaries of the two "Anglo-Saxon" giants, Esso-Standard ($170 million) and Pétroles BP ($132 million). Concentration in the iron-and-steel industry led to the formation of two groups of European dimensions: Sidelor ($207 million) and Usinor ($208 million), on top of Le Creusot ($181 million) and de Wendel ($168 million), the latter still largely in family hands (Marseille, 2004; Godelier, 2006; James, 2006). Saint-Gobain ($164 million), Pechiney ($161 million), and Ugine ($104 million) in chemicals, Alstom ($141 million) and CGE ($106 million) in electrical engineering, Renault ($188 million) and Citroën ($131 million) in automobiles, SNECMA ($98 million) in aerospace, and the Messageries Maritimes

---

[5] The Popular Front, a left-wing electoral alliance between the Radical, Socialist (SFIO), and Communist parties, came to power in May 1936. Its main reflationary measures included salary increases (7 to 15 percent), the forty-hour week, and two weeks paid holidays. It also introduced collective bargaining, and nationalized the railway and armament industries. However, these measures, together with the devaluation of the franc, failed to revive the French economy.

($190 million) in shipping completed, together with the four leading banks, the group of the country's twenty largest companies. Commercial banks, however, now in state ownership, continued their decline. In terms of capital (though not, of course, of assets), not a single one featured in the top twenty. Only the privately owned Banque de Paris et des Pays-Bas (investment banks had not been nationalized) still managed to do so.

By the early 1970s, after thirty years of sustained economic growth, French big business had reached a new dimension, both in quantitative and qualitative terms. Quantitatively, the size of the leading French companies was comparable to that of their main European competitors in Britain and Germany (Cassis, 1997). Qualitatively, in each of the main sectors of the Second Industrial Revolution, which reached full maturity during the three decades following the Second World War, France had one or two companies capable, or supposedly capable, of competing in world markets: Renault (with a turnover of $2,429 million in 1972), Peugeot ($2,134 million), and Citroën ($2,089 million) in automobiles; Total ($2,806 million) and Elf ($1,854 million) in oil; CGE ($2,164 million) and Thomson ($1,521 million) in electrical engineering; Pechiney-Ugine-Kuhlmann ($2,651 million) and Rhône-Poulenc ($2,479 million) in chemicals; Usinor ($1,046 million) and Wendel-Sidelor ($1,099 million) in iron and steel; Michelin ($1,681 million) in tires; Saint-Gobain-Pont-à-Mousson ($2,690 million) in building materials—all of fairly comparable size. These companies, with the state owned monopolies (SNCF, EDF, GDF) and the big commercial and investment banks (BNP, Crédit lyonnais, Société générale, Paribas), made up the bulk of France's big business.

In terms of corporate identity, the core of French big business did not change very much during the last thirty years of the twentieth century. The giant firms which dominated the field in 1970 were still present in 2000: Total, now merged with Elf (and Petrofina of Belgium), the country's largest firm measured by turnover ($115 billion); Peugeot, now merged with Citroën ($41 billion); Renault ($37 billion); CGE, now called Alcatel ($29 billion); Générale des Eaux, now called Vivendi ($42 billion); Saint-Gobain ($27 billion); BNP and Paribas, now merged ($51 billion); EDF ($34 billion); Rhône-Poulenc, now called Aventis following its merger with Hoechst of Germany ($21 billion).

Three major changes, however, best characterize the profile of French big business at the turn of the twenty-first century, shaped by the globalization of the world economy and the advent of the Third Industrial Revolution. First, with or without a change of name, a shift took place in the domains of activity of the country's leading firms, usually as a result of mergers and/or demergers. The best-known examples are those of Alcatel focusing on telecommunications, Vivendi on media and telecommunications, and Aventis on pharmaceuticals and biotechnology. Second, a number of newcomers, all in services, emerged at the top: Axa in insurance ($94 billion); Carrefour ($60 billion), from a large company in commercial activities to one of the giants of French and European business; France Telecom ($31 billion); Adecco ($27 billion) in business services (temporary employment); Pinault-Printemps-Redoute ($23 billion), the commercial and luxury-goods group set up by François Pinault. And third, a change took place within the hierarchy of French business, with a number of big names (Usinor, Michelin, Danone, Pechiney, L'Oréal, Thalès, and others) no longer in the top twenty, though still large and influential.

9.3 THE EMERGENCE OF BUSINESS
GROUPS BEFORE 1914

Business groups were the natural form of organization of French big businesses and were commonly named *groupes*. However, these *groupes* were not diversified business groups active in unrelated business fields, but were either holding companies or, from an organizational rather than a legal perspective, business enterprises. All large industrial companies had fully or more often partly owned subsidiaries—in France and often also in other European countries—in lieu of and sometimes in combination with internal units. This was, for example, the case with such companies as Thomson-Houston in electrical engineering, with a myriad of participations in tramway companies; Schneider in iron and steel, armaments, shipbuilding, construction, and engineering; or Saint-Gobain in glass and chemicals—France's three largest industrial companies at the turn of the twentieth century (Daviet, 1989; Marseille and Torres, 1992; D'Angio, 2000). The degree of control over partly or jointly owned subsidiaries varied considerably, though the relationship with the parent company was clearly hierarchical, and their product portfolio was mainly focused, with the exception of Saint-Gobain.

A form of diversified business group did emerge in mid- to late nineteenth-century France, mostly around trading firms and investment banks. Some were family-owned, others bank-centered; most, however, were of the hybrid type between the business enterprise, the "holding company" (in the Chandlerian sense of the word), and the diversified business group.

One type of diversified business groups common to most European countries were the trading companies, though nowhere were they as numerous, diversified, or powerful as in Britain (Chapman, 1985; Jones, 2000). One French group stood comparison with its British competitors: Louis Dreyfus & Co., one of the world's leading grain merchants, with a capital of £1.9 million at the turn of the twentieth century—comparable to Bunge & Co. and second only to Ralli Brothers (Chapman, 1992). The firm was founded in 1851 in Alsace by Léopold Louis-Dreyfus and, after being based for a while in Switzerland, moved its headquarters to Paris in 1875; Louis-Dreyfus opted for French citizenship after the incorporation of Alsace-Lorraine into the German Empire in 1871. Around this period, he began to take an interest in Russian wheat, setting up an agency in Odessa, in Imperial Russia. In 1875 his activities had already started to diversify and were described as "chartering, shipping, arbitrage, and banking." Later in the century, with the loss of attractiveness of the Russian grain trade (partly because new Russian inland dealers found it easier to forge their own connections with Western European markets) Louis-Dreyfus moved to the Balkans, supported by his small fleet of steamers, and became a close friend of King Carol I of Romania, exporting the best and highest yielding grain in Europe, and soon dominating the grain trade along the Danube (Chalmin, 1987). After the death of the founder in 1915, his heirs decided to move the core of the grain business from Eastern Europe to South America (Louis Dreyfus, 1951).

There were probably other trading companies featuring, on the British model, some of the characteristics of the diversified business groups—colonial companies such as the Société Commerciale de l'Ouest Africain (SCOA), the Compagnie Française d'Afrique Occidentale (CFAO), the Compagnie des Phosphates et des Chemins de Fer de Gafsa, the Société Mokta-El-Hadid, with their involvements in trade, mining, railways, and finance. However, they were much smaller and less diversified than their British counterparts.

The largest family-owned and diversified (both in France and overseas) business group was undoubtedly De Rothschild Frères, Europe's foremost bankers—with their cousins in London, Frankfurt, Vienna, and for a while Naples—between 1815 and 1870 and still a formidable financial power up to the First World War. Despite being organized around a private bank, the Rothschild group was more characteristic of a family-owned than a bank-centered business group—in terms of ownership, of course, but also top management, administrative control, operating units, and growth pattern. The formation of the group corresponded to a restructuring of the bank's activities in the last quarter of the nineteenth century, as it was facing stronger competition from the ever more powerful joint-stock banks (Banque de Paris et des Pays-Bas, Crédit lyonnais, Société générale, Comptoir d'escompte), especially in the issue of government loans, where the Rothschilds had been reigning supreme.

Besides government loans, where they remained a major force until 1914, the strength of the Rothschilds increasingly lay in their investments. They were still involved in railway companies, first of all with the Chemins de Fer du Nord, the most profitable French railway company, which they had established in the 1840s and where they held five directorships in 1869 and six in 1933 (Gille, 1965–7; Ferguson, 1998). In the 1880s and 1890s, in connection with the London house, they acquired extensive interests in minerals, especially in nonferrous metals and petroleum (Bouvier, 1983; McKay, 1986; Ferguson, 1998). In 1880 and 1881 the French house took part in the formation of the Société minière et métallurgique de Peñarroya, taking 40 percent of its capital, fixed at 5 million French francs on its official foundation in Paris in October 1881; in 1913 Peñarroya produced 80 percent of Spain's silver and 60 percent of its lead, and by 1917 its capital had grown to 73 million francs. A second area of interest in nonferrous metals was in the company Le Nickel, which had been established in Paris in May 1880 with a capital of 6.25 million francs, in order to develop rich nickel deposits in the French-owned island of New Caledonia in the Pacific Ocean; the Rothschilds were not among the founders, but had advanced funds to its initiator, the Australian John Higginson, taking a 25 percent stake in the 1880s. The third area was copper: in 1885, they took a 37.5 percent interest in the Compagnie du Boléo, formed with an initial capital of 6 million francs in order to exploit deposits in Mexico. In oil, the Rothschilds' interests were mainly centered on Russia: in 1886 they purchased the Batum Oil Refining and Trading Company, known from its Russian initials as Bnito, and proceeded to market Russian kerosene, linking Russian suppliers with Western European distributors. In 1912 they sold their entire oil interests in Russia to Royal Dutch, becoming the company's largest shareholders.

This represented a vast, diversified, family-controlled business group, with interests in banking and finance, railways, and minerals essential to the nascent industries of the Second Industrial Revolution. By 1900 the Rothschilds had invested some 58 million francs in their Russian oil operations and a combined minimum of 11.5 million francs in Peñarroya, Le Nickel, and Boléo. All in all, the Rothschild capital invested in oil and non-ferrous metals might have been as high as 100 million francs, nearly a sixth of the capital of the Paris house (McKay, 1986). The bank, for its part, could rely on huge resources and was by far the largest buyer of bills on the Paris financial market, with a portfolio reaching 500 million francs.

On a smaller scale, the family-owned private bank Mirabaud & Cie. was actively engaged in company promotion, especially mining, where they had gained expertise through their early association with the Rothschilds (Peñarroya, Boléo) and through the Société Française d'Etudes et d'Entreprises, a fully owned consulting engineering company. They struck gold in 1904 when they bought the concession for a copper mine in Serbia and formed the Compagnie Française des Mines de Bor, with a capital of 5.5 million francs, where they held a minority controlling stake, which entitled them to a 1-percent commission on the gross proceeds of the sales of copper and other products, including gold, extracted from the mines (Plessis, 2000).

The group formed around the Banque de Paris et des Pays-Bas (Paribas), France's leading *banque d'affaires* (investment bank), was more typical of a bank-centered business group—Paribas was publicly owned, run by salaried managers, and exerted financial control over the listed companies in which it was involved. In addition to its activities as an issuing house, Paribas held controlling (and historical) stakes in Forges et Aciéries du Nord et de l'Est, one of the country's leading iron-and-steel concerns, with its own subsidiaries. The bank was similarly involved in the electricity industry with, in particular, joint interests in two major holding companies—the Société Générale des Chemins de Fer Economiques in Belgium and the Société Franco-Suisse pour l'Industrie Electrique in Switzerland—and in the chemical industry with Norsk Hydro, a Norwegian company (Bussière, 1992).

Diversified business groups were thus little developed, though far from totally non-existent in France before 1914. Network-type business groups, on the other hand, were far more popular, especially alliances of product-focused companies operating through a variety of channels, such as equity stakes and joint ventures, but also family connections and overlapping directorships. Within the world of big business, or on its fringes, this was especially the case in the iron-and-steel and the textile industries.

9.4 THE RISE OF BUSINESS GROUPS
IN THE INTERWAR YEARS

Despite the physical damage caused by the First World War, especially in the industrial north, and the country's weakened financial position, at any rate until 1926, French economic growth was comparatively strong in the 1920s and early 1930s, and certainly stronger than in any of the large European economies. France was hit by the Depression later than other advanced economies, though recovery was also slower, because of the decision to remain on the gold standard until 1936 and the unsuccessful reflationary policy of the Popular Front. This was thus a period of modernization, especially of the industries of the Second Industrial Revolution, which partly caught up with their American, German, and British competitors.

Business groups played a role in this modernization process, though not necessarily the "pure" type of family-owned diversified business groups. The structure of France's large enterprises, with their amalgam of legally independent units and the widespread adoption of various sorts of holding companies, lent itself to the transformation of some of them into a more or less conventional type of diversified business group, more often of a hybrid form with many of the characteristics of the "holding company."

Two of the country's leading businesses—those of the Schneider and Gillet families—bore some resemblance to the model of family-owned business group, though their affiliates/subsidiaries were not in entirely unrelated industries. Schneider & Cie, established in 1836, was still family-owned and -controlled, being headed by the third generation family heir, Eugène Schneider II, grandson of the founder Eugène Schneider. Schneider & Cie had started as ironmasters in Le Creusot and had soon integrated—backwards into coal mining and forwards into heavy engineering and armaments, where they were Krupp's and Vickers's chief competitors in the global markets. The firm had started to diversify into construction and electrical engineering before the First World War, but the movement amplified in the 1920s and extended to new activities, such as electricity distribution and automobiles. Diversification was thus not entirely unrelated. The main objective of this strategy was to facilitate and increase the possibility of raising funds, not least through the borrowing capacity of the subsidiary companies.

The group was formed by a constellation of firms around the mother company, linked by a complex web of subsidiaries, affiliates, and participations. The group's main components included Schneider & Cie, the vertically integrated metallurgical concern with its main works in Le Creusot; the Energie Electrique du Rhône et Jura (EERJ), in electrical distribution;[6] Schneider-Westinghouse, in electrical equipment, headed by

---

[6] Formed in 1917, the EERJ formed the basis of Schneider's undertakings in electricity, usually in association with an old allied firm, the Mines de Blanzy, a coal-mining company which had diversified into the production of hydro-electricity (D'Angio, 2000: 186–90).

Duke Pierre de Cossé-Brissac, Eugène Schneider's son-in-law;[7] the Ateliers et Chantiers de la Gironde, established by Schneider in 1882, in shipbuilding; the Union Européenne Industrielle et Financière, in banking; and Skoda in Czechoslovakia, with a similar product portfolio as the mother company—mechanical engineering, tractors, locomotives, and later automobiles, where Schneider itself had never been successful. Each company had its own set of subsidiaries and joint ventures. While these relationships within what could be called the "inner group" were based on the "authority principle," the broader Schneider group also included relationships based on the "alliance principle," not least with the Banque de l'Union Parisienne, France's second investment bank after Paribas, which supported several of the group's ventures.

The Gillet Group, though less known than the Schneider group, was hardly less important. Its foundations were laid in the nineteenth century: Gillet & Pierron, later Gillet & Fils, a silk dyeing company, was founded by François Gillet in 1843 and soon diversified into chemicals. But the group really expanded and further diversified, though not in a totally unrelated way, in the 1920s. It was principally involved in chemicals, cotton, and synthetic fibers. In chemicals, the Produits chimiques Gillet (Progil) was founded in 1918 to bring together under the same roof all their activities; in cotton, the group's various interests were gathered in 1932 into the firm Gillet-Thaon; and in synthetic fibers, Givet-Izieux was created in 1936 with the merger of two companies, the Soie artificielle de Givet and the Soie Artificielle d'Izieux (set up in 1904). As in the case of Schneider, each company had its own *participations* and joint ventures. The Comptoir des textiles artificiels (CTA), for example, had been jointly established in 1911 by Givet-Izieux (Gillet group) and the Société française de la Viscose (controlled by the Carnot family) in order to market artificial fibers (Cayez, 1989). The group remained family-owned and was controlled by Joseph Gillet, the founder's son, his three sons (Edmond, Paul, and Charles), and his son-in-law.

The business groups that were established in the electricity industry were somewhat different: closer to the "holding company," with little if any diversification, and more pyramidal in their governance and financial structure. They were primarily a financial combination linking a number of legally independent companies. Some were family-controlled, others publicly owned—though more often than not ruled by an all-powerful entrepreneur. The group itself was usually organized at three levels: a leading company at the top; a first tier of main affiliates, each heading the subgroups (usually at regional level); and a second tier of companies, made up of the main affiliates' subsidiaries. Beyond these three levels, the influence of the group could extend to a fourth tier of minority stakes, joint ventures, and allied companies, and even to a fifth tier of personal and corporate relationships. While organized on the "authority principle,"

---

[7] The Matériel électrique Schneider Westinghouse was founded in June 1929 with a capital of 100 million francs in order to use Westinghouse patents in heavy electrical engineering. Schneider took 55 percent and Westinghouse 5 percent. With the capital increase to 150 million francs later in the year, the shares were respectively 80 and 20 percent (Lanthier, 1994: 1057).

business groups in the electricity industry thus also extended their influence through networks based on the "alliance principle."

By the late 1930s the production and distribution of electricity in France were concentrated into eight such groups. The largest was the Mercier Group (from the name of its managing director, Ernest Mercier), also known as the Messine Group (from the address of its headquarters). It was in public ownership and controlled by the Société Lyonnaise des Eaux et de l'Eclairage, a water and light company created in 1880. The group's head company was the Union d'électricité, founded in 1919 in Paris through the merger of six suburban electricity companies. Its share capital reached 275 million francs in 1929. In 1941 the Mercier Group had fifteen "direct subsidiaries," in which it held "preponderant interests" and "controlled the management."[8] They were mostly electrical utility companies located in the Paris region, central France, and North Africa. Some ten other companies were "further removed," in other words the group "possessed important interests" and "shared in the management" (Kuisel, 1967). They included the Compagnie Parisienne de Distribution d'Electricité, one of the country's largest electricity distribution companies. All in all, by 1949 the Mercier Group probably had links with as many as seventy-five companies (Morsel, 1981).

Close behind the Mercier Group was the Durand Group, which was controlled by Pierre-Marie Durand and his brothers Louis and Pierre-Louis. Its head company was the Énergie industrielle, established in 1906 with the modest capital of 3 million francs, of which 70 percent was in the hands of Pierre-Marie Durand. Its capital had grown to 50 million francs in 1925 and to 200 million francs in 1934. As Pierre-Marie Durand had subscribed to more than half of all the capital issues, he remained the sole majority shareholder of the firm, a majority further strengthened by the contributions of his family (Vuillermot, 2001). By 1945 the Énergie industrielle was linked to ninety-two companies (though the number might have been overestimated), with several tiers of subsidiaries, and distributed 16 percent of electrical energy sold in France, serving 18 percent of its population. Interestingly, the leaders of the Durand Group considered adopting the conglomerate form of unrelated diversification. They did venture into mining, construction, and tramways, though this remained marginal to their main business and was abandoned in favor of horizontal integration (Vuillermot, 2001).

The main purpose of the groups in the electricity industry—and elsewhere—was to enable the head firms to access the capital market more easily and through multiple ways. Each subsidiary company had the possibility to independently raise equity or debt capital, while the parent company could keep control over a chain of subsidiaries with only a series of minority stakes. In that respect the groups were undoubtedly successful: the industry raised huge amounts of capital in the interwar years, its assets growing from 1.6 billion to 19.6 billion francs between 1919 and 1939. Despite the persistence of thousands of companies, the industry became very oligopolistic, yet in a highly politicized climate the group structure offered a degree of flexibility and

---

[8] This is how Mercier himself described the relationship between head company and subsidiaries (Kuisel, 1967: 12–13).

Table 9.1. Share of the securities of large corporations held by holding companies and investment banks (%).

	Holding companies	Investment banks
1919	5.9	27.6
1932	15.5	12.7
1937	14.0	8.6

Source: Levy-Leboyer (1980): 140–1.

autonomy at regional level. In any case, electricity production increased more than fivefold between the wars (from 4 to 22 kWh), and France caught up with other industrialized countries (Lévy-Leboyer and Morsel, 1994).

Bank-centered groups were less influential in the interwar years. The Rothschilds were clearly weakened by the First World War. The Paris house remained a financial power but with the coming of the third generation they showed obvious signs of entrepreneurial decline, contenting themselves with managing more or less passively their industrial interests in railways, mines, electricity, or oil (Bouvier, 1983). The *banques d'affaires*, for their part, especially Paribas, had to rethink their strategy and increasingly turned towards financing the national economy. Purely banking activities, including the collection of deposits, became increasingly important in the banks' business to the detriment of more financial specialties (Bussière, 2003).

As a result, the influence of holding companies increased considerably during this period. Their share of the securities of large corporations became far larger than that of investment banks, as can be seen from Table 9.1.

Finally, network-type business groups should not be entirely dismissed from the corporate landscape during this period. As indicated above, hierarchy-type business groups could extend their influence by forming a broader network-type business group. Moreover, the "alliance principle" dominated in other industries. A complex network of joint ownership characterized the heavy industries, for example, especially with regard to the German mining and industrial properties in disannexed Lorraine. They were sequestrated and divided into five coal, iron, and steel concerns, each acquired by a group of several companies (Prêcheur, 1959). Marine-Homécourt, Micheville and Pont-à-Mousson, for example, were linked by cross-shareholdings and joint interests in various companies, forming a powerful group known as Mar-Mich-Pont. In 1919 they jointly acquired (together with the Forges d'Alais and the Aciéries de France) for 125 million francs the Société Lorraine des Aciéries de Rombas, which included mines and plants formerly belonging to Rombacher Hütte and Deutsch-Luxemburg. Network-type business groups also existed in the electricity industry, for example those linking equipment manufacturers with construction companies and electricity power companies, as was the case with Thomson-Houston, the Société des Grands Travaux de Marseille, and the Énergie Électrique du Littoral Méditerranéen (Morsel, 1981).

9.5 THE PERSISTENCE OF BUSINESS GROUPS IN THE GOLDEN AGE

The thirty years or so that followed the end of the Second World War are called the Trente Glorieuses in France—the thirty glorious years known as the "Golden Age" in the Anglo-American literature. Between 1950 and 1973 annual growth rates averaged 5 percent for GDP and 4 percent for GDP per capita. By 1973 France's level of productivity, as measured by GDP per man-hour, had reached 70 percent of that of the United States (up from 40 percent in 1950), ahead of both Britain (67 percent) and Germany (64 percent) (Maddison, 1991). The transformation of French big business, in terms of size,[9] ownership and control, and forms of organization, was at once a cause and a consequence of this period's rapid growth. From the perspective of business groups, and more generally business organization, two episodes are of particular significance: the postwar nationalizations and the merger wave of the 1960s.

The nationalization movement was due to a combination of economic, political, and ideological reasons—the deep-rooted conviction that business leaders had failed the country, and the role of communists in the Resistance (Andrieu, Le Van, and Prost, 1987). Some of the interwar business groups disappeared as a result of nationalization, above all those in the electricity industry, while others lost some of their constituent parts—the Rothschilds, following nationalization of the railways, and Schneider following that of the armament industry. The nationalizations of the Liberation did not lead to the formation of state-owned diversified business groups. Public utilities and transport were organized in separate state-owned entities: Gaz de France for the gas industry, Electricité de France for the electricity industry, SNCF for the railways, and Charbonnages de France for the coal industry. The commercial banks (Crédit lyonnais, Société générale, Comptoir national d'escompte de Paris, Banque nationale pour le commerce et l'industrie) retained their corporate identity, as did Renault. There was little in the way of unrelated diversification within these state-owned entities, unlike IRI in Italy, or Veba and VIAG in Germany.

The growth of giant companies was largely the result of far-reaching mergers, often encouraged if not prompted by the state and aimed at creating companies sufficiently large to compete successfully in world markets—a policy of "national champions" carried out most spectacularly, though by no means exclusively, in France in the late 1960s and early 1970s (Bauer and Cohen, 1981). Accordingly, mergers took place between firms which already were among the very largest in their respective sectors: the merger between Kuhlmann and Ugine in 1966, joined by Pechiney in 1971 to form Pechiney-Ugine-Kuhlmann (PUK) in chemicals; between Saint-Gobain and Pont-à-Mousson in building materials in 1970; between de Wendel and Sidelor in 1968 in the steel industry; the takeover of Citroën by Peugeot in 1974 in the automobile

[9] The number of companies employing 10,000 people or more rose from 20 in 1953 to 62 in 1972 (Cassis, 1997: 63). The figures are respectively 65 rising to 160 for Britain, and 26 to 102 for Germany.

Table 9.2. Structure of the French leading industrial companies, 1950, 1970.

	Holding	Multidivisional
1950	24%	5%
1970	16%	42%

Source: Dyas and Thanheiser, (1976): 184.

industry. These new giant enterprises increasingly adopted a multidivisional structure of organization, at the expense of the more informal "holding" traditionally favored by French big business (Table 9.2). Some business groups thus became increasingly integrated into multidivisional companies. The Gillet Group, in particular, linked to Rhône-Poulenc from its beginnings, was eventually absorbed into it when its holding company, Progil, was taken over by the chemical giant in 1969—though Renaud Gillet was chairman of Rhône-Poulenc between 1973 and 1979 (Allard et al., 1978; Daumas, 2010).

As in the interwar years, unrelated diversification remained limited in most French businesses. Seven of the top 100 industrial companies in 1970 have been described as "unrelated business companies" (not including the subsidiaries of foreign firms, such as ITT France).[10] Yet it is doubtful that many of them could be classified as a diversified business group, whether of the conventional or the emergent variety. Take Saint-Gobain-Pont-à-Mousson, one of the country's largest enterprises. It was involved in iron, steel, tubes, various types of glass, plumbing, packaging, and other areas. This might look like unrelated diversification, yet Roger Martin, chairman and chief executive of Pont-à-Mousson and later of the merged company (it was a reverse takeover of Saint-Gobain by Pont-à-Mousson), was at pains to underline the industrial logic of a merger between a glass and an iron tubes company and the creation of a world leader in building materials. In any case, there was no conglomerate logic in Saint-Gobain-Pont-à-Mousson (Martin, 1980). The same can be said of the Schneider group, which became Empain-Schneider in 1969.[11] As in the interwar years, its product portfolio may have been unrelated, but only to a limited extent—heavy industry, heavy engineering, electrical engineering, atomic energy, construction, and so on. The group was organized as a holding company, with limited control over fairly autonomous subsidiaries. As for Ferodo, its products were overwhelmingly centered on automobile accessories, above all brakes and clutches.

Some, however, came nearer to the model of family-owned business groups, even though unrelated diversification hardly went beyond two products. One was

[10] Béghin, Boussac, D.B.A., Ferodo, Groupe Floirat, Schneider-Empain, and Saint-Gobain-Pont-à-Mousson (Dyas and Thanheiser, 1976).

[11] Schneider experienced serious problems following the death of Charles Schneider in 1960 and the decline of the iron-and-steel and shipbuilding industries, leading to the merger with the Empain group.

Béghin, a sugar company that had belonged to the Béghin family since the early nineteenth century and had diversified into paper. In 1972 Béghin merged with an equally old sugar refiner, Say, to form Béghin-Say. The Agache-Willot group was the result of a more predatory strategy. The Willot brothers belonged to a family of small textile manufacturers established in the north of France since the beginning of the twentieth century. Through a series of bold amalgamations they built a group extending from cotton and linen (with old-established names such as Agache, Boussac, and Saint-Frères) to distribution (with famous Parisian department stores Le Bon Marché and La Belle Jardinière) and real estate (Foncière immobilière du Nord Est). It had become the thirtieth-largest industrial company in France by 1972, before being wound up in 1981 (Battiau, 1976; Boussemart and Rabier, 1983).

A handful of large-scale family-owned business groups appeared on the French corporate scene. The Groupe Floirat, ranked no. 46 in 1970 (Dyas and Thanheiser, 1976), was a holding company gathering the interests of the self-made entrepreneur Sylvain Floirat, in armaments, aerospace, telecommunications, sports cars, electronics (with Matra, a company he joined after World War II and developed in partnership with the founder, Marcel Chassagny, and later with Jean-Luc Lagardère), radio stations (with Europe 1, which he bought in 1955 and turned into one of the most popular stations in France), television equipment (with the Compagnie française de télévision, which developed SECAM, the color-television system), and tourism (with Hotel Byblos in St.Tropez) (*Les Echos*, March 16, 1993). Floirat was able to seize the opportunities presented by technological innovation, but also use his contacts with the French government, who asked him to buy Europe 1, and was always involved in the armaments and aerospace industries. Other groups were the result of the diversification strategy of a particular family. This was the case with the group Chargeurs Réunis, controlled by the Fabre family, a shipping dynasty from Marseilles. On the basis of their shipping interests (Compagnie Maritime des Chargeurs Réunis), they diversified into air transport (founding UTA in 1949), tourism (Commerciale et immobilière des chargeurs réunis), as well as civil engineering (with a minority stake in Grands Travaux de Marseille) and trade and industry (SAFIC ALCAN in rubber, SEPPIC in chemicals) (Allard et al., 1978).

The *banques d'affaires* had little room for maneuver in a domestic market controlled by the big nationalized banks, but they were still able to exploit certain niches and to innovate. In particular, they established a vast network of *participations* in, and privileged relationships with, a number of leading French companies. In this way the bank-centered groups they had formed since the late nineteenth century, through financial control over a number of companies, extended into broader financial groups, more akin to network-type than hierarchy-type business groups.[12]

---

[12] The Paribas network, based on participations and overlapping directorships, included, among the largest French companies, CFP, Thomson-Brandt, BSN-Gervais-Danone, Générale des Eaux, Rhône-Poulenc, PUK, and Hachette; while that of Suez extended to SGPM, Lyonnaise des Eaux, Béghin-Say, CGE, Lafarge, Pernod-Ricard, and Wendel (Allard et al., 1978).

While Paribas remained the leader in the game, it was joined by a newcomer, Suez, born after the nationalization of the Suez Canal in 1956. With the indemnity paid by the Egyptian government, the Compagnie financière de Suez diversified into banking and finance, building France's second investment bank and financial group (Bonin, 1987). As for the Rothschilds, they were able to reconstitute their group after World War II[13] through the Compagnie du Nord (constituted following the nationalization of the railways in 1937) as holding company of a group involved in banking (Banque Rothschild), mining (with Imétal, a holding company combining its various interests, not least in Peñarroya, Le Nickel, and Mokta), but also transport (SAGA, CEGF), real estate (SFGP, SFGC), and tourism, with Club Méditérranée, as a result of the reconciliation with the branch of the family headed by Edmond (Allard et al., 1978; Bouvier, 1983; de Rothschild, 1983).

9.6 The Decline of Business Groups in the Late Twentieth and Early Twenty-First Centuries

On an economic and business level, three major characteristics, closely linked to each other, have defined the last thirty-five to forty years. The first is the new wave of globalization marked, in particular, by a resumption of international capital flows; the second is the widespread movement of deregulation, in which one should include privatizations; and the third is what has commonly been called the Third Industrial Revolution, in other words the rise of the "knowledge industries," primarily in information technology and biotechnology. While these general characteristics of the "new economy" could be found in all advanced economies, they did not necessarily develop in the same way in all countries.

France has at once been among the world's largest capital exporters and importers of capital. It went against the grain in the early 1980s, with the nationalization of the country's largest companies during the early part of the Mitterrand presidency—though most of them had been privatized by the mid-1990s.[14] However, the state did not surrender all control and retained a minority stake in a number of companies. Moreover, a 1993 law allowed the government to keep a "golden share" in privatized companies, in order to protect "national interests," especially in strategic industries. In the same way, the state often relied on core shareholders in order to prevent the

---

[13] The Rothschild bank was liquidated under the Vichy regime, but did not suffer confiscations and re-emerged after the War (Dreyfus, 2003).

[14] The following companies were nationalized: CGE, St Gobain, Pechiney-Ugine-Kuhlmann, Rhône-Poulenc, and Thomson-Brandt. In addition, the state took a controlling stake in Matra, Avions Dassault, Usinor-Sacilor, ITT-France, CII-Honeywell-Bull, and Roussel-Uclaf.

Table 9.3. Structure of the French leading industrial companies, 1983, 1993.

	Holding	Multidivisional
1983	18%	69%
1993	14%	76%

Source: Whittington and Mayer (2000): 164.

division of some companies or encourage the gathering of others. Such moves could be favorable to the formation of business groups. However, they did not fundamentally alter the strategy and structure of French big business. Despite the advent of the network organization, the multidivisional form has continued to spread amongst the country's largest companies, to the detriment of the holding form (Table 9.3).

Conversely, unrelated diversification remained the strategy of only a small minority among them.[15] And as in previous periods, the degree of product diversification remained comparatively limited. Take Schneider, the perennial French business group: having shed what remained of its interests in heavy industries, it focused on electrical and instrument engineering, an activity it had been involved in since the early twentieth century, and called itself Schneider Electric in 1999. Its product portfolio included electrical distribution, automation and control, building management, critical power and cooling service, installation system and control, and solar power.

For all its diversification, the Arnault Group (Financière Agache, Christian Dior, LVMH) has primarily been centered on luxury products. The group was created in 1984 by Bernard Arnault when he bought Financière Agache and then took control of LVMH (formed in 1987 by the merger of Louis Vuitton with Moët-Hennessy) in 1989. In 2015 the group was still managed by its founder and engaged in five main lines of luxury products: fashion and leather goods (with Louis Vuitton, Celine, Givenchy, Dior, and others); watches and jewelry (with Tag Heuer, Ebel, Zenith, Chaumet, and others), wines and spirits (with Moët-Hennessy, Dom Pérignon, Château d'Yquem, and others), perfumes and cosmetics (with Guerlain, Dior, Givenchy, and others), and retailing (Le Bon Marché, Sephora, and others, including, for a brief period, the auctioneer Phillips), as well as other activities, not least the financial newspaper *Les Echos.*

At the Compagnie Générale des Eaux, renamed Vivendi in 1998 and headed by Jean-Marie Messier between 1996 and his fall in 2002, unrelated diversification only prevailed during a transitory period. The group focused on communication (Canal+, Universal Music Group, EMI), into which the venerable water company had started to

---

[15] Nine of them have been described as such in 1993: CGIP, Fimalac, Financière Agache, LVMH, Matra-Hachette, Schneider, Strafor Facom, Taittinger, and Thomson (Whittington and Mayer, 2000).

diversify in the early 1980s, after demerging its activities in water environment (Veolia) in 2000. In the same way, the Lagardère Group (led by Jean-Luc Lagardère, succeeded by his son Arnaud), originally involved in publishing (with Hachette) and defense and aerospace (with Matra), turned itself into a media group—though the process was slow and convoluted. Jean-Luc Lagardère had been Sylvain Floirat's right arm at Matra in the 1960s before taking control of the company and then buying Hachette in 1981. Following Matra's nationalization, Lagardère centered its activities on Hachette and diversified into television, but regained control of Aerospatiale-Matra, the outcome of the merger and privatization of the two companies in 1999. The group remained involved in defense and aerospace after Aerospatiale-Matra was integrated into EADS (later reorganized as Airbus Group) in 2000, but decided to sell its entire stake in 2013. By then the Lagardère Group's activities centered on book publishing; media, radio, TV, and advertising; travel retail and local distribution; and sports and entertainment.

In the end two large French businesses could be considered as diversified business groups in the early twenty-first century. Both were family-controlled. The first was Bouygues, founded in 1951 by Francis Bouygues, the "concrete king." Thirty years later, the company had become the world's number one in the building industry and one of the ten largest French industrial companies (Barjot, 1992). From related diversification into civil engineering, Bouygues moved into media and telecommunications by buying France's largest television channel, TF1, when it was privatized in 1987; and in 1994, under Francis Bouygues's son Martin, by successfully bidding to become France's third mobile-phone operator through its newly created company, Bouygues Telecom. A further step was taken in 2006, when Bouygues bought the French government's 21-percent stake state in Alstom, the energy and transportation group. Despite some possible synergies with Bouygues's construction business, in particular in power stations, the deal has been seen as a way for the French government to sell its stake in Alstom while guaranteeing the company's independence.[16] Bouygues's political connections have been a central feature of its development as a business group. The other diversified group was Fimalac, founded by Marc Ladreit de Lacharrière in 1991. It was centered on financial services (with a 50-percent stake in the rating agency Fitch) and real estate (North Colonnade in London), leisure activities and hotels, entertainment, and a digital division.

9.7 CONCLUSION

The most common type of business group in France has been the holding company, commonly called *groupe*. The term has primarily been used to describe a constellation of firms hierarchically gathered around a parent company, usually a holding

---

[16] General Electric bought Alstom's energy activities in 2014, with the French state deciding to acquire a 20-percent participation in Alstom on the market or from Bouygues.

company, owning majority or minority stakes in other companies, which were themselves often organized along the same lines. These were hierarchical-type business groups, undiversified but often with related diversification, and mostly of a pyramidal type. These links were often reinforced by networks of personal relationships, through family links and/or interlocking directorships. Such groups are best exemplified by the holding companies in the electricity industry in the interwar years, which undoubtedly contributed to the strong development of the sector. However, they were not the type of diversified business groups that this chapter tries to identify in particular.

Another, more recent feature of French big business has been the continuous spread of the multidivisional structure of organizing since the 1960s, rising from 5 percent in 1950 to 42 percent in 1970 and 76 percent in 1993. Holding companies did not turn themselves into diversified business groups, whether family-owned or conglomerates, but into Chandlerian enterprises with internal divisions and related diversified businesses.

Diversified business groups have formed a small but not insignificant part of French big business. Those that have emerged on the French corporate scene have presented a number of specific features. One was their degree of diversification. On the whole, French diversified business groups have not been very broadly diversified, the dividing line between related and unrelated diversification being, in most cases, fairly difficult to perceive. This was especially the case with the Schneider Group, the longest-living French business group, whose diversification, however unrelated, appears to have retained a fairly clear industrial logic (heavy industry and mechanical engineering, including transport equipment and armament; mechanical engineering, electrical engineering, electrical distribution, and construction; and banking and finance to cement the whole). The same can be said of the Gillet Group from the 1920s to the 1960s (chemicals, dye products, and textiles), and of the Arnault Group in more recent decades (luxury products). To be sure, the diversification of some groups was more clearly unrelated, though not before the 1960s—the Lagardère Group, for example (defense and publishing), or Vivendi (environment and media). However, both of them refocused around one core activity, in both cases communications and media. Unrelated diversification has persisted only in a handful of cases, most prominently with Bouygues (building industry, media, telecom, energy, and transport) since the 1990s.

Most French business groups have been family-owned, and from this perspective have closely corresponded to the ideal type of diversified business groups discussed in this volume. The Rothschild, Louis-Dreyfus, Schneider, Gillet, Durand, Fabre, Floirat, Lagardère, Arnault, and Bouygues families have all owned France's most important business groups. In the few cases of publicly owned groups (Mercier Group, for example, or Vivendi), a strong entrepreneurial figure was at the helm. Some were able to become owners (Lagardère took over from Floirat and then passed the reins to his son). Interestingly, despite the interventionist nature of the French state, no state-owned diversified business groups were formed in the wake of nationalization, whether in the mid-1940s or early 1980s: state-owned companies remained confined to single or closely related products or activities. Bank-centered business groups have also been little developed in France, despite the strong position of investment banks (*banques d'affaires*) within the banking system. While the French investment banks have held controlling stakes in some companies, they have mostly operated on the basis of the "alliance principle," forming network-type business groups to finance joint ventures with industrial and other companies. Conglomerates, for their part, have hardly made any mark in France, and a number of private equity companies have developed in recent years (Ardian, Butler Capital Partners, Eurazeo, PAI Partners), often the offspring of large financial institutions (PAI with Paribas, Ardian with Axa), though the industry is far less developed than in the United States.

Before 1945 a main rationale behind the creation of business groups (other than the trading-company-centered ones in the prewar period) was to better access the capital market. Holding companies increased the capacity of the group's head company, or companies, to raise finance, whether through debt or equity capital; they also offered a high degree of flexibility for the allocation of resources within the group. This, of course, did not only apply to diversified business groups. After the Second World War diversified business groups were formed by entrepreneurs keen to seize the new business opportunities offered by technological innovation (in defense, electronics, IT, media, and communication), market restructuring (in declining industries, such as textiles), or state intervention (nationalization and privatization). Business groups offered a more suitable corporate structure than the increasingly common multidivisional enterprise—a case of "societal choice" that explains apparently deviant corporate structures (Whittington and Mayer, 1996). All business-group leaders had close relationships with political power, though not necessarily closer than those of their counterparts in large multidivisional companies.

Being mostly family-owned, business groups in France have not been entirely free of the rule of three generations—a rule that has nevertheless been found wanting for many a French family firm! With the exception of Rothschild and Schneider, arguably France's two most famous business dynasties, no business group has remained in the hands of the same family beyond the second generation. Schneider did not survive the death of Charles Schneider in 1960, but the group was already in trouble as a result of its commitments to the iron-and-steel industry; while Gillet was absorbed into Rhône-Poulenc. The Rothschilds have survived but are too atypical a case to be discussed in this context.

A few diversified business groups emerged in the interwar years and, interestingly, their number has remained more or less stable until the present day. Their proportion of French big business is difficult to assess—less than 5 percent in terms of the number of large companies, with their share of assets or turnover of the country's largest companies still having to be estimated. However, the most significant groups, such as Schneider, Gillet, or Arnault, were present in highly significant industries. So, despite their small number, their position within the country's corporate world should not be dismissed nor their contribution to France's economic development underestimated. Business groups have not been an alternative to the multidivisional enterprise in France, but they have provided it with a necessary complement.

CATCH-UP NATIONS IN WESTERN EUROPE

....

CHAPTER 10

SWEDEN

tradition and renewal

....

MATS LARSSON AND TOM PETERSSON

10.1 INTRODUCTION

....

SWEDEN is a small, open economy, depending heavily on a rather small number of large and internationally oriented companies. Both in a historical and a contemporary perspective the dominance of "big business" in Sweden is apparent, especially when it comes to employment, product and technological innovations, and investments (Fellman et al., 2008). Another distinct feature of the Swedish economy, especially apparent from the interwar years up to the late twentieth century, is a very high level of concentration of control of the private business sector.

Business groups, defined as constellations of legally independent but in other ways intertwined companies, have been a major factor of Swedish business since the late nineteenth century, i.e., when Sweden underwent its Industrial Revolution.[1] But business groups in Sweden were not only a phenomenon in the early phases of economic development. During the twentieth century, especially from the 1930s to the 1970s, as Sweden became one of the most industrialized and richest countries in the world, some business groups heavily increased their influence over the private business sector. Business groups still today, at the beginning of the twenty-first century, in several aspects dominate Swedish business, especially as control-owners of the largest listed companies.

Two business groups stand out as especially persistent and seem to have the capability of both adaptation and dynamism in the long term. The first is the

---

[1] This chapter focuses on the dominant form of business groups in the Swedish economy, which is the diversified (family-owned and bank-centered) business groups that are often pyramidal in terms of their ownership arrangements.

Wallenberg group, controlled by the Wallenberg family. One of the basic fundaments of the Wallenberg group since the late nineteenth century has been the ownership of a large commercial bank—Stockholms Enskilda Bank/SEB—which was able to function as financiers for the business group. Being the dominant business group in Sweden at least since the late interwar years, and with roots back to the latter half of the nineteenth century, the Wallenberg group and its entities, as well as family individuals, have been the subject of numerous studies (Lindgren, 1994; Olsson, 1997; Olsson, 2002; Nilsson, 2005; Carlsson, 2007; Lindgren, 2009; Lindgren, 2012). The second contemporary major Swedish business group is the Handelsbanken banking group, which in contrast to the Wallenberg group has had a much more anonymous existence, often in the shadow of the high-profiled Wallenberg family.[2]

The Wallenberg group and the Handelsbanken group have some obvious similarities. The core of each group consists of a holding company (closed-end investment fund)—Investor (Wallenberg group) and Industrivärden (Handelsbanken group). The holding companies exercise their ownership mainly through controlling equity blocks in listed companies, largely exploiting the advantages of dual-class shares with differentiated (higher) voting rights. Over the years both the Wallenberg and the Handelsbanken group have clearly adopted a diversification strategy, broadening their economic activities from the financial sector to almost every other major industrial sector, including service industries (Lindgren, 1994; Collin, 1998).

They differ in some important aspects, however: the Wallenberg group is a family-controlled business group, and the Handelsbanken group is a managerial-controlled business group, as it has not had a controlling owner in the last century. The Wallenberg family controls Investor through family funds, while the Handelsbanken group is held together by an intrinsic system of cross-shareholding in combination with strong personal networks and pension funds. The Wallenberg group thus has a pyramidal structure, where blockholding in one company in turn gives control of other listed firms, and so on.

For much of the twentieth century the two groups dominated Swedish business. However, in recent decades there are some signs that the Wallenberg group is perhaps losing its predominant position. At the end of the 1990s the Wallenberg group held controlling positions (control defined as the ownership of at least 10 percent of the votes) in companies accounting for 42 percent of the total market value of the Stockholm stock exchange (Agnblad et al., 2001; Högfeldt, 2005). In late 2010 their control had declined to 17 percent of the total market value (Henrekson and Jakobsson, 2011: 10). There are several explanations for the seemingly declining power of the Wallenberg group. One is the deregulation of the financial markets in the 1980s, which opened the Swedish stock market to foreign capital. Another explanation is that private equity companies, working outside the traditional capital markets, replaced established

---

[2] Despite their family motto being *Esse non videri* ("To be, not to be seen"), some members of the Wallenberg family, for example Marcus Wallenberg Jr. (1899–1982), have been active in the public economic debate.

financiers, and with new methods and little interest to maintain the traditional ownership structure they challenged the Wallenberg group.

Both the Wallenberg and the Handelsbanken business groups were founded on the inclusion and use of commercial banks. Sweden was a relatively poor and undeveloped country in the late nineteenth century and the commercial banks played a decisive role in the accumulation of capital, which was necessary for the industrialization and urbanization processes. The upper and middle classes in the cities, especially, placed their savings in commercial banks, while the working class, both in urban and rural areas, more often used savings banks. Since there were no investment banks established in Sweden, the commercial banks also played a crucial role in financing the growing industrial sector. Hence, the commercial banks were in a strong position by the late nineteenth century, and during the early decades of the twentieth century Sweden's financial system became increasingly bank-oriented in this respect.

This chapter is not solely dedicated to describing and analyzing the two present-day dominating business groups in Sweden. Since the late nineteenth century there have been numerous business groups, especially family-controlled, that have proved to be at least as successful, in economic terms, as the two major business groups. Several of these groups have also proved to be more open to new ideas, innovations, and markets, and to be more prompt in adapting to changes in demands and general market conditions. Recently, business groups such as the Stenbeck group have successfully moved from traditional basic industry into "new" and fast-growing economic sectors within, for example, the media and entertainment industries.

10.2 BUSINESS GROUPS IN SWEDEN: AIM AND SCOPE

In this chapter we analyze the establishment and long-term development of the major business groups in Sweden, giving special attention to the Wallenberg and Handels-banken groups. The history of Swedish business groups from the 1870s to the early twenty-first century can be divided into four chronological periods, each having distinct features.

We are especially interested in explaining how and why some business groups, such as the Wallenberg and Handelsbanken groups, have been able to stay at the center of Swedish industry and business for such a long time. In international comparisons, Sweden often stands out as an extreme case as regards the high levels of concentration of control and ownership of the private business sector. This can be explained by the historically low importance of the stock market. Since the late nineteenth century Sweden has had a bank-dominated financial system in which commercial banks not only have acted as financiers of large ownership groups but also have entered as direct owners in industry and trade. It was not until the 1980s that the concentrated ownership structure in larger Swedish companies began to be questioned. However, one important exception is Handelsbanken, which since the late nineteenth century has lacked a large controlling owner.

A glance at the twenty-five largest Swedish companies in 2015 shows that both the Handelsbanken and Wallenberg groups play an important role in the contemporary Swedish economy. The Handelsbanken group and the Wallenberg group controlled six and five of the twenty-five largest companies, respectively (see Table 10.1). One company stands out as an interesting example—Ericsson, formerly producer of telephones and telecommunications systems, which today defines itself as a service company within the IT sector. Since the early 1930s—when it was taken over from the liquidated Kreuger group—Ericsson has been jointly owned by the Wallenberg and Handelsbanken groups, as two equal partners. During the last couple of years the Handelsbanken ownership in Ericsson has been considerably reduced. Ericsson is, however, an exception to the rule, as the two groups have in most aspects been fierce competitors for nearly a century.

Aside from the two dominant owner groups, only the Johnson group, controlled by the Johnson family, is comparable in size, as it has long-term interests in three of the twenty-five largest Swedish companies. The Johnson group has considerable interests in shipping and trade as well as construction and building. However, compared to the two largest business groups the Johnson group is comparatively small, and its interest in the Swedish economy remains stable within these companies.

In order to understand why Sweden is still dominated by a few business groups, what the long-term driving forces behind Swedish development are, and why it is that the dominating business groups are so generally accepted within Swedish society, we focus our description and analysis on four aspects of the business groups' long-term development. The first aspect has to do with the institutional setup, basically the construction of official regulations, especially the tax system as regards the creation of hidden reserves and the handling of profits in private companies. If the institutional setup facilitates private wealth-building and capital accumulation, it makes it easier for owners to consolidate and to develop business groups. An institutional structure, or setup—for example, inheritance taxes—can thus be designed to favor some specific ownership groups, for example those owners that are considered vital for the long-term development of the industry, business, and even the nation's entire economy. In this aspect the track record of the business groups, especially in times of turbulence and crisis, is important for continued support in terms of favorable institutional setup.

The second aspect deals with the construction of the Swedish financial system. By the late nineteenth century banks, especially the large commercial banks, came to play a dominating role in the long-term development of Swedish industry and trade. However, from the late 1970s this situation gradually changed as the financial markets were deregulated and opened to foreign capital. As a consequence Swedish commercial banks encountered greater competition from other financial actors as well as the stock market. As a result, the previously bank-oriented, and bank-dominated, Swedish financial system became much more market-oriented (Zysman, 1990; Larsson, 1998).

Table 10.1. The 25 largest companies in Sweden 2012, ranked according to turnover.

Company	Sector	Turnover, M. EURO	Founding year	Ownership category	Rank in 1968
Volvo	Trucks	33,805	1927	Bank, Handelsbanken	1
IKEA	Trade	27,628	1943	Family, Kamprad	
Ericsson	IT and communications	26,305	1876	Bank, Handelsbanken/Family, Wallenberg	4
Vattenfall	Energy	19,785	1909	State	
Skanska	Building	14,479	1887	Bank, Handelsbanken	5
Volvo car group	Car	14,034	1927[1]	Foreign	1
Tetra-Laval	Machinery	13,580	1951	Foreign/Family, Rausing	
H&M	Trade	13,422	1947	Family, Persson	
Telia Sonera	Telephone operator	13,308	2003	State. Diversified	
Electrolux	Household and professional applicances	12,230	1919	Family, Wallenberg	12
Preem	Energy	11,726	1996	Foreign	
Sandvik	Engineering	10,975	1862	Bank, Handelsbanken	17
ICA	Trade	10,861	2000	Bank, Handelsbanken	
Stora Enso	Paper, pulp	10,350	1357 (1998)[2]	Foreign/Family, Wallenberg	13
Atlas Copco	Engineering	10,112	1873	Family, Wallenberg	16
Nordea Bank	Banking	9,895	2000	Foreign. Diversified	
SCA	Paper, pulp	9,507	1929	Bank, Handelsbanken	9
Scania	Trucks	9,369	1891	Foreign	15
Securitas	Service	7,386	1934	Family, Schörling	
Nordstjernan	Conglomerate	7,311	1890	Family, Johnson	
SKF	Engineering	7,247	1907	Family, Wallenberg	2
ABB Norden	Financial services	7,151	1883 (1988)[3]	Foreign.	3
Axel Johnson group	Financial services	7,029	1873	Family, Wallenberg	
NCC	Building	6,360	1988	Family, Johnson	
Astra Zeneca	Pharmaceuticals	6,309	1913 (1999)	Foreign	

Note: Tetra-Laval and IKEA have been added to the original 25 largest companies. They are formally owned by family foundations situated outside Sweden but controlled by Swedish interests. 1. Volvo trucks and Volvo cars separated into two companies in 1999. 2. Merger between Swedish Stora and Finnish Enso in 1998. 3. Merger between Swedish ASEA and Swiss Brown-Boveri. 4. Merger between Swedish Astra and British Zeneca.

Source: https://www.va.SE/nyheter/2016/11/29/det-har-ar-sveriges-500-storsta-foretag-2016; Sundin and Sundqvist (2016); annual reports, respective companies.

The third aspect is the business groups' access to, and good relationship with, the leading political spheres. This can often be seen as a mutual dependence and deep acceptance of one another. However, in the Swedish case the mutual relationship between business and politics should not be confused with the negative term "crony capitalism," where corruptive friendship is a prerequisite for long-term success and sets aside basic market principles.

A fourth aspect has to do with the organizational structure of business groups. As Colpan and Hikino (2010) point out, the diversified business group often has a headquarters unit responsible for the long-term allocation of resources and monitoring operations, with the operating units primarily organized as legally independent subsidiaries. In this paper we analyze what kind of structure has been used in Sweden and how this can help explain the long-term survival of Swedish business groups.

We will also stress the fact that financial and economic crises have played a significant role in the development of both the Handelsbanken and the Wallenberg business groups, i.e., their ability to handle such turbulent situations. As will be shown later in this chapter, both business groups have actually gained from the problems of other companies and business groups. Hence, they have been able to increase their influence and strengthen their position within the Swedish economy through mergers and acquisitions during and after times of turbulence and crisis.

10.3 EARLY BUSINESS GROUPS, 1870S–1910S

Sweden's industrialization developed sharply from the 1870s. The international boom during the Franco-Prussian War in the early 1870s opened the way for the export of traditional Swedish products, such as iron, steel, and wood products. Within these industries there were several—often family-controlled—companies established during the seventeenth century. However, the 1870s meant a more general promotion of industrial activities and thus the creation of new companies (Larsson, 1991; Magnusson, 2010).

New companies were established both as family-owned companies and joint-stock limited liability companies with families as the largest owners. A special joint-stock company regulation had been accepted in 1848. But the general breakthrough for this type of owner construction was not immediate. Initially the establishment of joint-stock companies was hampered—probably by a lack of confidence in this type of company construction with limited liability. The early joint-stock companies did not exhibit any large diversification of ownership (Broberg, 2006). Instead, the old owners often used the new ownership structure to transfer ownership between generations rather than to provide capital to the company. However, during the latter decades of the nineteenth century this gradually changed.

The first industries that more frequently used the joint-stock company structure were those in need of capital for large-scale investments, often established by families or groups of people with the help of private financiers or commercial banks. Among these companies were the steel industry and the fast-developing paper industry, where new technology required large investments. The new engineering industry, including such companies as telephone company Ericsson established in 1876, electrotechnical company ASEA established in 1883 (merged with ABB), electric-tool producer Atlas Copco established in 1873, and construction company Skanska established in 1887, all used the joint-stock company structure. All these companies were among the twenty-five largest Swedish business groups—measured by turnover—in 2012 (see Table 10.1) (Glete, 1994). In some of these new companies—for example, ASEA and the mining company LKAB—the Wallenberg family entered as owners, but the actual development of the Wallenberg group did not start until the 1910s.

However, the use of the stock-company structure did not solve all the financial problems in the late nineteenth and early twentieth centuries. On the contrary, industrial and trading companies established increasingly closer relations with the Swedish commercial banks. This was primarily done through bank credits for investments but also through rescue credits for companies in distress during the 1880s. This resulted in a breakthrough for the commercial banks towards the late nineteenth and early twentieth century, and they consolidated the central position of the financial system. In 1900 50 percent of institutional lending was handled by the commercial banks, but in 1919 this share had increased to 71 percent (Nygren, 1985: 140).

As a result connections between the industrial/trading companies and banks increased both in economic terms—credits from banks and company savings in the same bank—and as personal networks. During the last decades of the nineteenth century several of the largest Swedish companies had established house-bank connections—with one bank both lending capital and handling all other financial activities of the company—which limited their use of market solutions. These close connections were boosted after 1911 when commercial banks were allowed to own and trade with shares of both listed and non-listed companies. House-bank connections were then supplemented by ownership relations, making it even more difficult to break established contacts (Lindgren, 2011). The right to own shares became a crucial institutional fundament for bank-industry development in the 1910s, which had an effect for several decades to come. The Stockholm stock exchange became a functioning market for shares towards the late 1890s, and from World War I the development of the stock exchange could be characterized as euphoric and speculative. The commercial banks together with bank-owned special investment companies, created for trade with shares, became large owners in industry. These investment companies were owned by the commercial banks, which also financed their activities with credits. Thus the banks had a direct risk through shareholding and credits to industrial companies, but also an indirect risk through credits to investment companies. The increase in share values was therefore important to avoid losses, and during the 1910s the development was positive for the banks (Östlind, 1945, Larsson, 1998: 87–90).

The industrialization process during the period 1890–1919 had been built on the introduction of new techniques and the establishment of joint-stock companies in all major industries. This process was largely finished by the end of 1910s. During this period the initiatives in economic as well as industrial development changed considerably. Up to the late nineteenth century trade-based capital had dominated economic initiative. This capital was often connected to the old industrial tradition in Sweden of the production and export of iron. However, neither trade capital nor the iron barons were at the center of the industrialization process in the late nineteenth and early twentieth century. Instead, the combination of finance capital and industrial capital was the driving force behind economic development and the creation of new companies. These new companies were often established by entrepreneurs with the financial support of commercial banks, and in local markets also by savings banks. During those thirty years, economic development in Sweden was impressive and ahead of most competitive states (Glete, 1987: 134–8; Iversen and Thue, 2008).

The extensive use of natural resources was an important part of economic development, but the larger part of this development was connected to the dominant urban areas of Stockholm, Gothenburg, and Malmö. In Gothenburg, for example, new entrepreneurs entered the scene: the Broström family with the establishment of the Götaverken shipyard, and the Mark and Carlander families, who were controlling owners of the Swedish ball-bearing company SKF. However, since these activities were quite capital-intensive, the companies needed the support of the Skandinaviska Banken. This bank was also heavily involved in the development of building company Skanska and the Kockums shipyard in Malmö (Glete, 1994).

In Stockholm the turn of the twentieth century resulted in the development of three new business groups which originally had been established around the middle of the nineteenth century but started to expand considerably during the industrialization of the early twentieth century. These three business groups were dominated by the families of Bonnier, Söderberg, and Johnson.[3] The diversification in all these business groups can simply be explained by a wish to reduce the risks connected with their main industries. During the first decades of the twentieth century the Bonnier group developed into a dominating media company, while Johnsons became one of the largest family-owned business groups in Sweden. Both families used an active ownership control in their business groups, and could act without external capital or interest from banks or the joint-stock market (Glete, 1987; Larsson, 2001). The relative smallness of the Swedish economy made it possible to develop these companies into dominating positions within their industries in Sweden, with the help of annual profits and short-term capital from commercial banks. These companies were good examples of the survival of the traditional family business, and even in the early twenty-first century they are organized in much the same way as a hundred years ago.

The Söderberg family were active owners not only in the companies where they had a dominant position, but also in businesses where they had minority interests.

---

[3] During the twentieth century the Bonnier group diversified their business into media, printing, the chemical industry, and engineering; the Söderberg group into trade, iron, and engineering; and the Johnson group into trade, iron, and shipping.

If we analyze the business groups established in both Gothenburg and Malmö, we see the same pattern of development. Before 1920 the owners played an important role in the progress of the companies, while the financier—in this case Skandinaviska Banken—was represented on the board.

In the early twentieth century a similarity between family business groups and business groups controlled by banks was that they organized as diversified business groups, with independent companies coordinated by a business group headquarters. This could either be an investment company or a trading or industrial firm.

The Wallenberg group, with the Stockholms Enskilda Bank, used another strategy. The majority of companies within this group were controlled with minority interests through bank-owned investment companies, combined with commercial credits from the bank. Their position as controlling owners during this period was seldom questioned despite an ownership share of sometimes not more than 20–30 percent—the rest of the shares were spread among a large number of shareholders. The Wallenberg family were known for their long-term engagement, both in ownership and credits. But this also meant a close monitoring of the development in the companies and an active ownership control from the bank or investment company (Lindgren, 1988; Lundström, 1999). Towards the end of the 1910s the Wallenberg group, with its holding-company structure, was probably the best-organized business group with the largest potential for development.

While the banks developed a diversified interest in different industries, the large industrial and trading companies wanted to make use of economies of scale. During the 1910s a large number of mergers and acquisitions were carried out. From 1915 to 1919 around 200 mergers were carried through by companies on the Stockholm stock exchange—or close to two mergers per registered company. In 1918 alone, seventy-nine mergers were carried out. Looking at the period 1913–38, nearly 70 percent of the mergers were horizontal, more than 20 percent were vertical, while less than 10 percent were diversifying. The engineering industry dominated, with over half of the mergers (Larsson, 2002).

This development confirms that diversification was of marginal importance and hardly the basis for the development of the large companies' strategies during the interwar period 1919–39. The concentration on horizontal mergers could, to some extent, be an effect of an unwillingness in family companies to enter new areas of activity.

10.4 CONSOLIDATION, 1920S–1940S

The deflation crisis in the early 1920s changed the ownership situation radically. In the first place, it meant the establishment of integrated bank groups. Large parts of the banks' interest in industrial companies were owned by the special investment companies that had been established in the 1910s. But the deflation crisis meant large losses, the companies had to be liquidated, and the shares which were used as securities were taken over by the commercial banks—which were the original creditors. Thus the immediate effect of the crisis was that the control of Swedish industry was to a large extent transferred directly to the commercial banks—especially the four largest ones. In order to avoid long-term bank control over industry, the right to own and trade with shares was limited in the 1920s and totally abolished in 1933. Shares controlled by banks had to be realized within five years, provided this could be done without losses. However, three of the four largest commercial banks chose another way. Through the establishment of holding companies connected to the banks and owned by the banks, foundations, pension funds, and reliable people, i.e. the banks' owners and managers, the control of these holding companies remained with the bank. The introduction of dual-class shares with differentiated voting rights was also important for retaining control over the investment companies (Larsson, 1998).

Two of the major commercial banks were exceptionally successful in their business—Handelsbanken and Stockholms Enskilda Bank (after the merger with Skandinaviska Banken in 1972, the name was changed to Skandinaviska Enskilda Banken, SEB). These two banks created long-term ownership with their holding companies, which allowed them to expand their interest in industry and closely monitor their companies. However, there were also important differences between the two banking groups. Stockholms Enskilda Bank had a strong personal ownership by the Wallenberg family, both in the bank and the holding companies, and chose to control their operating companies directly from those companies, which also suggests that this group should be defined as a family business group rather than a financial business group. Handelsbanken, on the other hand, had no strong owners but was instead controlled by the bank's management. The holdings in industry were not only handled through the holding company but through a network of shareholdings between the companies of the banking group and the holding company at the center of the banking group (Lindgren, 1988; Larsson, 1998).

However, both banks had a wish to establish large, stable business groups and develop their interest in industry. In this they were also successful. In 1924 a total of 15 percent of industrial workers were employed in industries controlled by the banking groups. By the mid-1940s this share had increased to 31 percent, by 1979 to 40 percent, and by 1985 to 53 percent (see Table 10.2) (Lindgren, 2011). However, the investment company Custos was by then quite independent of the Skandinaviska Enskilda Banken and had instead increased its contacts with the industrial companies Skanska and Volvo.

The Wallenberg and Handelsbanken business groups were, during the interwar period, the two most important diversified owner groups in Sweden. Together with these business groups, a few family-controlled companies diversified their activities during the 1920s and 30s. Both the Johnson group and the Söderberg group, with the investment company Ratos, continued their diversification. However, the most spectacular example of a diversified business group during this period was the Kreuger empire. Ivar Kreuger had begun his career as one of the owners of a building company

Table 10.2. Industrial workers in different business groups as share of total industrial employment in Sweden, 1924–85.

	1924	1945	1963	1979	1985
SHB/Industrivärden	6	6	8	13	15
SEB/Wallenberg	4	11	16	23	24
SKAB/Custos	5	14	7	4	14

Note: SHB=Handelsbanken, SEB= Stockholms Enskilda Bank, SKAB=Skandinaviska Banken. After the creation of Skandinaviska Enskilda Banken—a merger between Skandinaviska Banken and Stockholms Enskilda Bank—in 1972, the ownership group centered around the investment company; Custos gradually became more independent and cannot therefore be included in the Wallenberg group.
Source: Lindgren (2011): 118.

(Kreuger & Toll). But by the early 1910s he showed an interest in the production of safety matches. He established the company Swedish Match, which soon obtained a monopoly situation on the Swedish market. Ivar Kreuger's efforts to create an international monopoly for safety matches are well known. Less attention has been given to Kreuger's work in creating a business group with diversified activities. During the 1920s he took advantage of the low valuation of shares in several Swedish companies and soon had large holdings in the Swedish wood industry, iron production, as well as in the Swedish metal company Boliden and the telephone company Ericsson. After the financial crash in the USA in 1929, Ivar Kreuger's economic situation became increasingly problematic, and after his suicide in March 1932 his financial empire fell apart and a large part of his shareholdings was taken over—as securities for credits—by the banks that had previously sold these shares to him. Another consequence of the Kreuger crash was that the right of commercial banks to own and trade with shares was totally abolished. The right to trade with shares was regarded as one reason for the economic problems that hit the Kreuger bank connection Skandinaviska Banken in 1932. The problems for the Kreuger group meant that the shares of several companies were sold by the Kreuger group's trustee. This meant that Handelsbanken became the controlling owner of several wood and paper companies. At the same time Handelsbanken and Stockholms Enskilda Bank jointly became controlling owners of Ericsson (Glete, 1994; Lindgren, 2011). The Kreuger crash is unique in Swedish business history and its result was far-reaching compared with other company failures in Sweden.

Thus the financial crises in the 1920s and 1930s resulted in a consolidation of the two banking groups, to some degree at the expense of family ownership. During this period the banking groups managed to increase and diversify their ownership in industry, which in the longer run made them increasingly important. Traditional companies within the Wallenberg group, which controlled Stockholms Enskilda Bank group during this period, were regarded as entrepreneurially governed companies, while companies in the Handelsbanken group had a more managerial tradition (Glete, 1994: 285). Gradually and especially from the 1930s, the two holding companies controlled by the Wallenberg family—Investor and Providentia—became centers exercising ownership and control of the entire group. Later, Investor took over as the one important center. Another essential part was played by Stockholms Enskilda Bank, which had been a veritable profit machine for several decades and had the capacity to finance many of the mergers, takeovers, and other structural processes (Glete, 1994: 122). However, the more concentrated ownership, with a strong bank as owner, facilitated the structural changes which had started in the 1910s, making some companies—especially in the engineering industry—internationally competitive. Four important companies can be given as examples of this development.

In the ball-bearing company SKF the Wallenberg family entered as a controlling owner beside the old family owners Mark and Carlander. A few mergers were realized in order to vertically integrate the production of high-quality steel with the production of ball bearings. The Swedish market was too small for this specialized product and efforts were made to increase the international market. During the interwar period SKF became the international leader in the production of ball bearings (Fritz and Karlsson, 2006).

Another company concentrating on the international market was Separator (later the Alfa-Laval company), producing milk separators and other mechanical equipment for the agricultural sector. During the interwar period horizontal mergers were made with other Swedish producers of milk separators. This helped consolidate the company but it did not result in any spectacular development during the interwar years.

The Wallenberg family gradually increased their ownership in both Separator and ASEA during the interwar period. But compared to other companies within the Wallenberg group, management in both ASEA and Separator had a relative independence in relation to the Wallenberg family during the interwar years. During this period ASEA developed quickly to become an international actor in electrical engineering, with some vertical integration in the engineering sector. The number of employees increased from 7,000 in the mid-1920s to nearly 25,000 in the mid-1940s (Glete, 1987).

Telephone company Ericsson exhibited international development during the interwar period, but a large part of the company development was also dependent on governmental orders for the establishment of the national telephone system and for the development of military communication equipment. As a result, the Ericsson company diversified its production within the area of communications.

The development of these four companies demonstrates the internationalization process of the Swedish engineering industry, which started during the interwar years and accelerated in the late 1940s. A similarity between these companies was their concentration on a limited number of products—especially compared to the early engineering companies that developed in the mid-nineteenth century. None of these companies were family-owned in the strict sense, but they had a strong interest from owners connected to the financial sector, which in the case of Wallenberg also included a family interest.

The interwar years were a turbulent political period. But the struggle for political power between the Conservative, Liberal, and Social Democratic parties was to a large extent halted in the 1930s when the Social Democrats came to power. Over the following decades the Social Democrats held the position of prime minister, and though they sometimes cooperated with other political parties, including in government, they largely set the political agenda. With the more stable political situation, it became increasingly important to have good contacts with politicians and to have the opportunity to affect the development of new regulatory measures.

10.5 COOPERATION, CONCENTRATION, AND DIVERSIFICATION, 1945–1970s

The postwar period to the early 1970s is widely considered a "golden age" for the Swedish economy in general, with relatively high annual growth rates, only minor economic downturns, and steadily growing living standards in general. The internationally oriented industries within engineering, shipyards, forestry, mining, etc. were able to expand their businesses in the early postwar years, as many of the fiercest competitors were either temporarily eliminated by the war (especially German companies) or mostly concerned with satisfying their home markets (especially American companies). Then, in the 1960s, annual growth rates between 6 and 8 percent for the industrial sector significantly contributed toward making Sweden one of the most industrialized, and wealthiest, countries in the world (Dahmén and Carlsson, 1985: 49).

Alongside the continuous growth of the private industrial sector, the public sector expanded most intensively from the 1960s, creating the Swedish welfare state. This consisted of a comprehensive and universal social security system of flat-rate and income-related benefits, by international standards generous provision of social assistance, and a wide range of tax-funded social services provided by public organizations. Healthcare, primary and secondary education, care services for children, the elderly, and disabled were all part of the public sector's responsibility (Vartiainen, 1998; Blomqvist, 2004).

During these decades the Swedish economy has been labeled, especially within the varieties of capitalism debate, a coordinated market economy. In contrast to the liberal market economies, such as the UK and USA, employers in coordinated market economies had supported the development of a tax-based, general welfare system in order to have access to specialized, high-skilled labor (Hall and Soskice, 2001: 19). However, others have emphasized that the Swedish labor force, like those of the UK and USA, was also characterized by a high level of mobility, especially in the 1950s and 1960s. Furthermore, the Swedish educational system was actually much more general than that of other coordinated market economies, for example Germany (Korpi, 2006).[4] Nevertheless, during that period one aspect of the Swedish economy with implications for the increased importance of some of the large business groups was

---

[4] See Fellman et al. (2008) for a contrasting view on the historical development of Swedish, and Nordic, capitalist systems.

that large private employers and the unions developed a common agenda that benefited both parties, and they also had the blessing of the government.

In postwar Sweden the Social Democrats had evolved as the dominating political party. They assumed power in 1932 and continued to govern the country without interruption, though for short periods in coalition with one of the right-wing parties, for forty-four years, until 1976. The Social Democrats and the labor unions, which were very closely linked to the Social Democratic Party, continued to develop a very pragmatic view on the private business sector in general and on the dominating business groups in particular. Experiences from the deep interwar crises had convinced both the economic elite and the labor movement (Social Democrats and labor unions) that cooperation, not conflict, could favor their mutual interest. The result was an explicit tripartite negotiating culture, which in the postwar period constituted a cornerstone of the Swedish corporatist model (Smångs, 2008). One result was that very few measures were taken to socialize the ownership of private firms, at least up to the 1970s. Another consequence was that the export companies—often owned by the large business groups—became leaders in wage negotiations through the so-called "solidarity wage policy." This promoted the larger companies, as the small and medium-sized companies had difficulties in paying the same wages.

But not all private companies were considered equally important in this private–public arrangement. Clearly the "private business sector" was interpreted as the large industrial companies and their major owners, i.e., the large business groups. In practice the dual Swedish model meant that the private sector was responsible for creating enduring economic growth, and the government was to distribute the increased economic wealth by implementing various social welfare reforms, creating a social welfare state.

A number of legislative measures were taken which in practice also favored established big business. The corporate tax system was designed, perhaps not entirely intentionally, to benefit well-established, incumbent companies and institutional owners, such as the bank-owned holding companies like Investor (part of the Wallenberg group) and Industrivärden (part of the Handelsbanken group). For example, the use of hidden reserves made it possible for the companies to postpone the taxation of profits and dividends. New private wealth creation was in general discouraged and obscured. Foreign ownership of Swedish companies was almost entirely precluded by a number of restrictions. In combination with strict credit-market regulations, which effectively excluded small and medium-sized companies from getting access to risk capital, the result was a further concentration of power in the established business groups (Glete, 1994: 98; Reiter, 2003; Smångs, 2008). To sum up, the general domestic political, economic, and legal conditions in the postwar era were thus in favor of the established business groups.

10.5.1 The Wallenberg Group

The established business groups, not surprisingly, grasped this opportunity to expand. The Wallenberg group was the most successful of them all. The two Wallenberg brothers, Jacob (1892–1980) and Marcus Jr. (1899–1982), had by the late 1920s started to engage in the restructuring and development of large, internationally oriented industries, such as ASEA and Alfa-Laval. In the postwar period, after the death of their father and head of the Wallenberg dynasty, Marcus Sr. (1862–1943), the two brothers exercised dual leadership of the group. Jacob Wallenberg had a number of companies that he was responsible for (e.g., Swedish Match, SKF, Separator, Astra), and Marcus had others (e.g., ASEA, Atlas Copco, Scania, Saab, SAS). With time, however, the younger but much more expansionist (and charismatic) Marcus stepped up as the family's leading figure. During the 1960s and 1970s Marcus Wallenberg Jr. was more or less considered the godfather of Swedish business, becoming legendary for his working capacity, his sometimes brutal authority, and his ability to carry through complicated structural industrial solutions. He recruited new, 100-percent loyal CEOs to the growing number of companies in the group, but he was also known for his ability to negotiate with, and not least to charm, businessmen of all kinds as well as politicians of both the left and right (Glete, 1994; Lindgren, 2009; Olsson, 2002).

Marcus Wallenberg Jr. was also the driving force behind the merger of the old family bank, Stockholms Enskilda Bank, and Skandinaviska Banken in 1972. The Wallenberg group had to find a way to expand its capital base (in order to continue its industrial expansion), and a merger with Skandinaviska Banken, with its nationwide network of branch offices and much bigger deposit base, seemed logical. In addition, Skandinaviska Banken had no obvious controlling owner, and a merger would make it possible to add even more industrial companies to the Wallenberg group. At the same time, the holding company Investor gradually took over as the governance center of the group, replacing the old family bank (Thunholm, 2007).

The strategies of the Wallenberg group were highly successful. In 1925 two of the twenty-five largest industrial companies in Sweden were controlled by the group. In 1945 they controlled six and in 1967 ten of the twenty-five largest companies. The severe industrial crisis in the 1970s struck hard at some Swedish business groups, but the Wallenberg group, just as in the turbulent interwar years, managed to hold, if not enhance, their position. In 1990 they had control blocks in nine of the twenty-five biggest Swedish industrial companies (Glete, 1994: 286–90).

10.5.2 The Handelsbanken Group

In comparison with the Wallenberg group, the postwar period for the Handelsbanken group was characterized more by careful and gradual growth and diversification. The Wallenberg group diversified intensively and eagerly into new business sectors, while the Handelsbanken group concentrated first and foremost on the paper and pulp industry in the north of Sweden, thus sticking to its traditions. The most important industrial company within the group—still today, together with Sandvik, Volvo, and Skanska—was SCA (Svenska Cellulosa AB), established in cooperation with Ivar

Kreuger in 1928. Other major industries belonging to the group in the postwar period were AGA, Sandvik, and Ericsson.

In contrast to the family-controlled Wallenberg group, the Handelsbanken group has since the 1910s been dominated by professional managers, with the exception of the period 1927–32, when Ivar Kreuger owned a major block. The holding company Industrivärden was established in 1944, but in contrast to the pyramidal structure of the Wallenberg group (with the holding company Investor at the top), the Handelsbanken group was (and is) held together by an intricate system of crosswise holdings between companies within the group. In combination with strong personal networks, primarily consisting of professional top managers—who had proven their competence and loyalty over many years of service within the group—there has also been an informal, but still important, mechanism of holding the group together.

10.5.3 Other Groups

Thus the guiding principle and key to success for the established business groups in postwar Sweden, especially the Wallenberg group, was diversification. Withheld profits were invested in new ventures and new lines of business. The Söderberg and Johnson groups, both family-controlled, are good examples of successful diversification. The Söderberg family followed the example of the Wallenberg group and established a holding company called Ratos in 1947, which it has controlled since 1960 through two family foundations. Ratos in turn had a twofold strategy in the postwar period, partly investing in large, well-established listed industrial companies, and partly by getting control holdings in companies within dissimilar sectors such as paper and pulp (Holmen), engineering (Bulten-Kanthal), and printing (Esselte).

The Johnson group had already diversified from trade to iron and shipping in the late nineteenth and early twentieth century, and it continued to chase synergy effects between the group companies in the postwar period. The shipping business, which was partly started to support the trading business, expanded enormously and initiated investments in oil refineries that had the Johnson shipping company as one of their major customers. The oil refineries also produced asphalt, and the Johnson group consequently engaged in building roads, eventually diversifying into the building industry (Glete, 1994; Sjögern, 2011).

Even the Bonnier group, with its roots in publishing and newspapers, made a serious attempt to diversify into more traditional industries. From the late 1940s large investments were made in the paper and pulp industry (Billingsfors-Långed), an example of vertical integration motivated by the fact that the group was the biggest buyer of paper in the country. In the 1950s investments were made in engineering, shipping, and the chemical industry (Larsson. 2001, Sjögern, 2011).

As mentioned above, one extremely important explanation regarding the success of the major business groups in postwar Sweden, and their ability to control a large proportion of the country's major industries, was the introduction of dual-class shares

Table 10.3. Number of listed companies on the Stockholm stock exchange and percentage with dual-class shares, 1950–81.

Year	No. of listed firms	Percentage with dual-class shares, %
1950	91	18
1963	112	29
1968	146	32
1972	134	36
1977	130	44
1981	128	54

Source: Henrekson and Jakobsson (2011): 6.

with differentiated voting rights. This innovation, first introduced by Ivar Kreuger, was becoming more and more widely used, especially in the Wallenberg and Handelsbanken groups. In several of the largest companies, such as Ericsson, Electrolux, Swedish Match, Alfa-Laval, and SKF, the holding companies mainly held class-A shares (with one vote per share), while class-B shares (with one tenth of a vote per share) or even class-C shares (with one thousandth of a vote per share) were widely distributed among the public and institutional investors such as pension funds and insurance companies. The prospect of issuing these "golden shares," i.e., shares with a thousand times the voting weight of the "standard" share, was abolished by the Swedish Company Act of 1944. However, companies that had already introduced this form of vote differentiation—such as those mentioned above—were allowed to hold on to the old system (Table 10.3) (Reiter, 2003: 108).

In the late 1960s there was an intense political debate, with the radical parts of the labor unions and sections of the Social Democrats questioning the increasing concentration of ownership within Swedish business. Business groups such as the Wallenberg group and capitalist families such as the Wallenberg family stood right at the center of the controversy. In-depth studies of the distribution of ownership revealed and made very clear to the public that a small number of business groups—many of them under family control—dominated major parts of Swedish industry. The notion of the "fifteen families," referring to the leading families, was established, and this contributed to a spread of indignation and annoyance. A couple of implications of this debate are worth mentioning.

Firstly, the consensus character of the relations and negotiations between the labor movement on one side and big business and its representatives on the other changed into one of controversy and conflict. Secondly, this led to demands for increased state ownership of companies. As a result, a state-owned business group, with the holding company Statsföretag at the core, was established in 1970. Initially companies within mining, steel, forestry, and shipyards formed the business group. However, during the industrial crisis of the 1970s Statsföretag's main objective was changed to take over and manage large, often private, industries in need of new capital. Unsurprisingly, Statsföretag suffered severe losses, and something had to be done. During the 1980s and early 1990s most parts of the business group were sold to private domestic or foreign interests, while some of the companies, such as the mining company LKAB, remained state-owned. Thirdly, in the mid-1970s the labor unions launched a proposal for setting up union-controlled wage-earner funds, aiming to eventually take over the bulk of the share majority in Swedish listed companies. In the 1980s a modified version of wage-earner funds was introduced by the Social Democratic government, despite massive protests from Swedish business in general. However, over a period the consensus- and growth-oriented part of the labor movement recaptured the initiative in its relationship with major business interests. The clash between the labor movement and the employers was thus swiftly overcome. One of the first measures that the new non-socialist government undertook when it came to power in 1991 was to dissolve the wage-earner funds, and in fact this decision caused little debate (Glete, 1994; Henrekson and Jakobsson, 2003:85–6; Smångs, 2008: 906).

In contrast to the large and well-established business groups that were able to increase their influence on and dominance in the Swedish economy, very few new major business groups were established in the postwar period. However, some of the true twentieth-century success stories of Swedish business—companies such as IKEA and H&M, both established in 1943—began to grow intensively from the 1960s. Both IKEA and H&M were, however, very much dedicated to one line of business—furniture and clothes, respectively—and only in recent years diversified into new businesses.

To sum up, from 1945 to the late 1970s a number of the largest Swedish business groups, and the Wallenberg group in particular, were extremely successful in increasing their influence in Swedish industry and business. They were able to exploit advantages of having close, reciprocal, and long-term relations with the dominant political spheres. Changes in the institutional setup, especially the tax system, were clearly in favor of the large and established companies and business groups. Having a large commercial bank within the business group, access to necessary financial capital and to the financial markets in general was guaranteed. As far as access to human capital, i.e., managerial capacity, was concerned, both the Wallenberg and Handelsbanken groups intentionally built up their own pools of such capacity. Lastly, during the deep industrial crisis of the 1970s both groups proved to be trustworthy co-partners when the Swedish government felt obliged to intervene. Some attempts to save, and then restructure, large industrial companies were indeed successful (within the iron-and-steel industry, for example), not least due to the fact that private and public interests were able to cooperate.

10.6 GLOBALIZATION AND NEW CHALLENGES, 1980–2010

Over the last three decades circumstances for the traditional business groups and for ownership of Swedish companies in general have undergone profound changes.

Table 10.4. The distribution of ownership of listed shares on the Stockholm stock exchange, 1983–2010.

Year	Swedish households	Swedish institutions[1]	Foreign owners
1983	30	62	8
1985	28	64	8
1990	18	74	8
1995	15	55	30
2000	13	45	42
2005	15	50	35
2010	13	49	38

Note: Both private and public institutions and organizations.
Source: Statistics Sweden, statistical database; shareholder statistics.

The Swedish financial markets were, as in many other Western countries, deregulated from the late 1970s. Many of the instruments and regulations that the Swedish government had introduced in previous decades and used for control of the financial markets were gradually dismantled. Sweden ended up having one of the most liberated systems, instead of, as earlier, one the most regulated financial systems. For example, allocation and price of credits were no longer under governmental control. Another important measure was to open the domestic market to foreign capital, in order to increase competition and efficiency. The banking market was opened to foreign banks in 1986, when they were allowed to open subsidiaries, and in 1990 they were allowed to set up branches.[5] Foreign exchange control was lifted in 1989, and in 1992 the restrictions on foreign ownership of listed Swedish companies were abolished, and foreign capital virtually flooded the Swedish stock market (see Table 10.4) (Larsson, 1998; Reiter, 2003).

10.6.1 Established Business Groups

One cornerstone of the Swedish corporate governance model, and an absolute prerequisite for the major business groups' ability to continue to exercise their ownership—dual-class shares with differentiated voting rights—was, however, maintained. This time the major business groups, especially the Wallenberg group, had almost unreserved support from most of the political parties. Even the Social Democrats, who had been somewhat inconsistent in their attitude towards Swedish "big business" in the 1970s and 1980s, now showed their full support for the system of differentiated voting rights. It was important to keep the largest companies in Swedish

---

[5] Foreign banks still at present (December 2016) hold only about a 10-percent market share on the Swedish deposit and lending markets; see Swedish Bankers' Association (2017).

Table 10.5. Number of listed companies on the Stockholm stock exchange and percentage with dual-class shares, 1981–2010.

Year	No. of listed firms	Percentage with dual-class shares, %
1981	128	54
1986	217	74
1992	202	87
1998	304	63
2006	295	46
2008	299	46
2010	255	49

Source: Henrekson and Jakobsson (2011): 6.

possession (Table 10.5) (Reiter, 2003: 111; Holmén and Högfeldt, 2009; Sjögern, 2011; Sjögern, 2012).

Nevertheless, one aspect of the system of differentiated voting rights has been abandoned—the extreme version, the so-called "golden shares," which gave owners of class-A shares 1,000 times the votes of class-C shares. This system, which was most prevalent within the Wallenberg group, was gradually abandoned, mostly due to pressure from foreign owners and new, domestic financial actors. Even if many of the foreign investors on the Swedish stock market, especially pension funds and globally oriented investment funds, were not interested in stepping in as active owners, they could not accept the system of "golden shares," giving them no possibility whatsoever to influence the companies they invested in. The Wallenberg group and others gave up the system of golden shares "voluntarily," for example in Electrolux in 1998, in SKF in 1999, and as late as 2012 in Ericsson.

The traditional major business groups have thus faced a number of challenges since the early 1980s. Institutional investors, both foreign and domestic, have put pressure on the traditional owners, perhaps not so much regarding corporate governance but more by having high-yield requirements. In combination with the ever-present conglomerate discount that business groups such as Handelsbanken and Wallenberg have been forced to deal with, it is fair to say that pressure from the capital market increased severely. The long-term investment and development strategy, which has been a feature of both the Wallenberg and Handelsbanken groups as well as some of the other old business groups, has thus been confronted with more short-sighted demands from institutional investors. Heavily increased turnover on the stock exchange over the last decades, along with some large-scale domestic and international mergers and acquisitions, have made it very hard, especially for the Wallenberg group, to keep business groups intact. For example, Investor has sold parts of or its entire holdings in SKF, Scania, and AstraZeneca. The closed-end investment funds' authority over the Swedish stock market reached its peak in the 1990s, when they controlled more than 60 percent of the total value on the

Table 10.6. Closed-end investment funds' control of the Stockholm stock exchange, 1986–2010.

Year	Total value of the Stockholm stock exchange, billion SEK	Share of total value under CEIF control, %	Share of total value under control of Investor (the Wallenberg group) & Industrivärden (the Handelsbanken group), %
1986	405	70	48
1993	832	83	63
2000	3135	57	49
2005	3077	51	44
2010	3680	48	36

Source: Henrekson and Jakobsson (2011): 11.

Stockholm stock exchange (Table 10.6). Since then, their share has decreased to about 30–35 percent.

The two largest business groups have also been challenged from within. From the late 1970s and through the 1980s and early 1990s car manufacturer Volvo and its CEO Pehr Gyllenhammar made a serious attempt to create a new dominant and highly diversified business group, alongside the Wallenberg and Handelsbanken groups. Ever since its establishment in the 1920s, Volvo had been connected to Skandinavbanken. However, in the 1960s Volvo, having immense success with both their trucks and cars, marked its independence as regards the existing business groups by electing the chairman of Handelsbanken to its board. When Gyllenhammar took over as CEO in 1971, replacing his father-in-law Gunnar Engellau, Volvo soon started to diversify, and from the 1980s especially into groceries and pharmaceuticals—lines of businesses that weren't affected by dramatic changes in demand in the same way as the car and truck industries. Marcus Wallenberg Jr. was so impressed by the young, bold Gyllenhammar that in the early 1980s he moved to merge the Volvo group with the Wallenberg group. However, after Marcus Wallenberg's death in 1982, the merger plans were abandoned. Volvo continued to grow (and diversify), but after 1993, when Gyllenhammar had left Volvo, a process of concentration started, once again making Volvo an outright car and truck manufacturer (Glete, 1994: 321–3). In the late 1990s Volvo Trucks was separated from Volvo Cars, which was then sold to Ford, who in 2010 sold Volvo Cars to the Chinese company Geely.

10.6.2 Newly Established Business Groups

The revival of the Swedish stock market in the early 1980s, together with a number of tax reforms that facilitated private wealth accumulation, boosted the wealth of a large number of capital owners—both old and new capital. Some new business groups have evolved, though perhaps not on the same level as the Wallenberg and Handelsbanken groups. The major reason behind this development was the establishment of new business segments (e.g., media and IT)—in which the traditional companies had no interest or knowledge—along with the development of the Swedish financial system and regulations—such as tax laws—promoting large-scale enterprises.

The Lundberg group, controlled by the Lundberg family, started with real estate in the 1940s, but diversified in the 1970s into paper and pulp (Holmen), construction (NCC), and banking (Östgöta Enskilda Bank). It is interesting that in the early twenty-first century its main strategy has been to invest in companies belonging to the Handelsbanken group. Today, the Lundberg group is a major owner in Handelsbanken, Industrivärden, and Sandvik—three major components of the Handelsbanken group. So far the head of the family, Fredrik Lundberg, has not been totally accepted within the group, with its very long and strong traditions of being run by professional managers rather than major owners.

The Stenbeck group is yet another business group that has strengthened its position enormously in recent decades. Having its industrial and stable economic base in the forestry and paper industry (Korsnäs), from the 1980s the Stenbeck group—under the leadership of Jan Stenbeck (1942–2002)—successfully diversified into media and communications. Both the Lundberg and Stenbeck groups, and many other family-controlled Swedish business groups, have a listed holding company as the control center. Thereby they get access to the capital market, but still can, through block holdings, keep control over the group.

Within the category of old wealth, the business groups of Bonnier, Johnson, and Söderberg remain major players among Swedish groups. The Söderberg group has mainly stuck to its long-term strategy, i.e., investing in large listed companies but not taking much active part in their day-to-day business. The Bonnier group has returned to its focus on media and communications. The Johnson group has, after a severe crisis in the 1970s and 1980s, sold many of its industrial companies and returned to its roots, once again concentrating on trade.

In brief, the major business groups continue to play a significant role within Swedish business, even if they are not as dominant as in the decades after World War II. The major business groups have still been able to interact with the national political sphere, not least in safeguarding Swedish interests from institutional challenges stemming from the European Union. The market challenges have, on the other hand, led to some strategic reorientation. The Wallenberg group has been somewhat on the defensive, letting some of its long-term core investments go—after hostile takeovers of companies from capitalists using money from the globalized financial market—in order to keep control of the remaining ones and at the same time setting capital free for investments in new lines of business. The Handelsbanken group appears to have been less vulnerable to both institutional and market changes. However, during times of turbulence, such as the crisis for the Swedish IT industry at the turn of the twenty-first century and during the global economic crisis starting in late 2008, both business groups once again proved their stability.

To understand the long-standing success of the Handelsbanken and Wallenberg groups it is important to stress once again their ability to gain and keep the confidence of the general public, the political sphere, and the financial markets in general. One obvious example concerns the possibilities of tunneling, i.e., transfer of wealth from minority shareholders to controlling shareholders (Johnson et al., 2000). Considering the wide use of dual-class shares and the historically strong position of control-owners such as the Handelsbanken group and the Wallenberg group, one could have expected such tunneling to have existed in Sweden. However, studies point out that tunneling is not a widespread phenomenon within Swedish business, at least during the 1980s and 1990s. It should be stressed that in Sweden it is not socially acceptable to exploit minority shareholders in this way (Agnblad et al., 2001; Holmén and Knopf, 2004). For the dominant business groups it has thus been important to live up to the social norms set up jointly by the business community and society.

10.7 THE RESILIENCE OF BUSINESS GROUPS IN SWEDEN

The ownership structure of the two most important business groups in Sweden exhibits both important differences and similarities. In a comparison the Wallenberg group and Handelsbanken group can be used as illustrative examples of the dynamism and resilience of Swedish business groups.

The Wallenberg group is hierarchical, with the family on top of the pyramid and with investment companies and a commercial bank as tools for the execution of ownership. While the companies of the Wallenberg business group are mostly owned and controlled directly by the investment companies, ownership in the Handelsbanken business group is based on a network of equity ownership between the companies within the group (Figure 10.1). Therefore, the Handelsbanken group has been much more protected from outside, "hostile" attempts to take control of companies within the group, at least in comparison with the Wallenberg group (Figure 10.1). This became especially obvious in the 1980s and 1990s when entrepreneurs, with the help of the globalized financial market, were able to challenge the Wallenberg group—and often with success.

Several, but not all, large Swedish business groups have had a pyramidal organizational structure. The family business groups have had a strong tradition of centralized control, and representatives of the family have often taken positions as CEO and chairman of the board. In the family-controlled business groups—such as Wallenberg, Bonnier, and Söderberg—the ownership control and the performance of active ownership originate from family representatives. As a consequence of ownership the families have been represented on—and have controlled—the board of directors.

However, as the Wallenberg group increased in size and scope over time, it became increasingly difficult—both for the bank and the investment company Investor—to

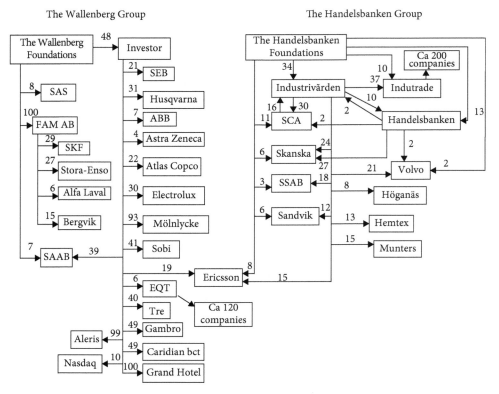

FIGURE 10.1. The Wallenberg and Handelsbanken business groups in 2009 (companies that are owned and controlled, and companies where the business groups have large interests).

Note: The Handelsbanken Foundations are owned and controlled by Handelsbanken, while the Wallenberg foundations are owned and controlled by SEB. The numbers represent the owners' vote percentage. These percentages are often higher the capital invested due to the differentiation of voting rights between shares.

Source: Sundin and Sundqvist (2009), Investor, Annual report 2009, Industrivärden, Annual report 2009.

maintain direct control of the companies within the group. From the 1930s the group developed into a diversified business group, with both companies listed on the Stockholm stock exchange and with smaller development companies. However, through ownership of Investor the Wallenberg family also held central positions in companies within the group. This caused the business group to embrace a more pyramidal organizational structure and at the same time allowed members of the family to execute active ownership in practically all of the companies within the group and sometimes in the subsidiaries of those companies. Governance activities were not limited to the boardroom. There are several examples from both the Wallenberg and Bonnier groups that representatives from the owner family would turn up more or less unannounced at the site of a controlled company to inspect and control its activities and effectiveness (Larsson, 2001; Larsson, Lindgren, and Nyberg, 2008; Sjögern, 2012).

However, the execution of control of the individual companies within the Wallenberg group was not homogeneous. Instead, the involvement in daily operations of the companies was adjusted to the specific situation and varied according to levels of trust in the company's management and especially the trust in, and performance of, the CEO. A managing director who had demonstrated knowledge and ability would be given more space and opportunity to develop the company than an untried CEO. This was the case in ASEA (later ABB), where for several decades in the early twentieth century Sigfrid Edström held a very strong position in the company and was trusted to develop it more or less on his own (Tell, 2008).

The Handelsbanken group also developed into a diversified business group, especially during the 1920s and 1930s, and as in the Wallenberg group a specialized investment company was established—Industrivärden. Compared to governance in the Wallenberg group, however, Industrivärden was relatively more independent from the bank and the Handelsbanken foundations. In fact Handelsbanken, the Handelsbanken foundations, and Industrivärden, together with the forestry-industry company SCA, became the basis for the Handelsbanken business group (Figure 10.1). Together, these companies coordinated their governance activities within the business group. This resulted in a pyramidal organization where the control activities towards the groups' companies seem to have been less active than in the Wallenberg group, but instead more reactive if a company was in some kind of trouble.

Both the Wallenberg and Handelsbanken groups include core investments, especially in large listed companies, which are too valuable to lose control over. Other companies are of less importance, or are seen as financial investments. Both business groups also include ownership in companies with the aim of developing production and economy in small and medium-sized companies. The Wallenberg group holds a smaller share in EQT with the aim of investing in companies with growth potential. The Handelsbanken group, on the other hand, has a considerable ownership in the investment company Indutrade, which has holdings in around 200 high-tech companies in 27 countries (Figure 10.1 and Table 10.7).

Neither the Wallenberg nor the Handelsbanken group was strategically coordinated with other companies in the business group. Both business groups were diversified, which probably hampered the coordinating activities. However, on special occasions, such as the introduction to a new foreign market, companies within a business group could cooperate in order the make the establishment more successful.

Why have the two business groups—Wallenberg and Handelsbanken—managed to survive and develop for more than a century? Obviously, the existence of a consolidated bank within the group has been of great importance. The banks have been used as financiers for the companies within the business groups, which has also helped to protect the groups' ownership interest.

The business groups have today become accepted within Swedish society—after a period of wide, politically motivated criticism, especially in the 1960s and 1970s. They are (in many cases) considered as long-term, responsible owners, whom the general public can trust. Their legitimacy and trustworthiness are important explanations. They have worked closely with the political spheres and thus have had and exploited the opportunity to affect the institutional setup of, for example, tax regulation. For

Table 10.7. Major companies in the Wallenberg and Handelsbanken groups.

Wallenberg group	Handelsbanken group
Holding companies	*Holding companies*
Investor	Industrivärden
Fam AB	Indutrade
EQT	
	Engineering industry
Engineering industry	Volvo
SKF	Sandvik
Alfa-Laval	Ericsson
Saab	Munters
Husqvarna	
ABB Ltd	*Wood and paper industry*
Atlas Copco	SCA
Electrolux	
Ericsson	*Building industry*
	Skanska
Wood and paper industry	
Stora-Enso	*Iron & steel industry*
Bergvik	SSAB
Tele com	*Chemical industry*
Tre	Höganäs
Pharmaceuticals & Medical equipment	*Commercial activities*
Caridian bct	Hemtex
Gambro	
Aleris	*Financial companies*
Sobi	Handelsbanken
Mölnlycke	
Astra-Zeneca	
Commercial activities	
Grand Hotel	
SAS	
Financial companies	
SEB	
Nasdaq	

Source: Sundin and Sundqvist (2009); Investor, annual report, 2009; Industrivärden, annual report 2009.

most of the twentieth-century representatives of the Wallenberg family had continuous contacts with Swedish governments and prime ministers, despite the fact that Sweden had left-wing governments. The Wallenberg family's direct involvement in international politics during the two world wars can also help explain the family's legitimacy.

Both business groups have been interwoven with the Swedish innovation system, in which private and public parties cooperate to make the Swedish economy more internationally competitive. The Wallenberg and Handelsbanken groups have been controlling owners of several of the largest Swedish companies, and therefore directly involved in these companies' innovation activities. But even though the core of both business groups' ownership has been in large companies, they have also been active as both direct and indirect owners in smaller companies in developing industries, as, for example, the above-mentioned EQT and Indutrade. The concentration on ownership of larger companies—or even "national champion"[6] companies—was more evident after the Second World War, when companies within the engineering and paper-and-pulp industries developed especially fast. Among these companies we today find Volvo, SCA, Skanska, ABB, and Ericsson (Figure 10.1).

The Wallenberg and Handelsbanken business groups exhibit two different forms of corporate governance. The Wallenberg group—with the bank SEB and the holding company Investor—demonstrates that family ownership can also be developed in large international and diversified business groups. The control of companies and active ownership is performed in the boardrooms, through the selection of loyal CEOs and coworkers. But the Wallenberg business group also performs both a proactive and reactive ownership, dealing with specific problems in companies.

Both the Wallenberg and Handelsbanken groups have been organized as diversified business groups, as have other larger Swedish business groups. Ownership within the business groups has been kept together with the help of investments or holding companies, but also with an ownership structure based on personal relationships. The construction of ownership structures within the Wallenberg group has been more hier-archical and centralized, which has made it more difficult to keep them together.[7] This became obvious after the deregulation of the financial markets in the 1980s and 1990s, when it became easier to borrow money on the market. New entrepreneurs challenged ownership in the Wallenberg group and purchased large blocks of shares in these companies on the Stockholm stock exchange. Since the Wallenberg companies were controlled by minority holdings, the investment company Investor had to sell off some of their holdings—which resulted in a concentration of the Wallenberg group in fewer companies, where the group had a larger part of the companies' shares. Thus the concentration of holdings by Investor made it both costly and difficult for the Wallenbergs to retain their ownership positions compared to the Handelsbanken group, where several companies (Industrivärden, SCA, Handelsbanken, and Handelsbanken Foundations) jointly owned both each other and the other companies within the group—also with minority shareholdings.

---

[6] The designation "national champions" is understood as the dominant companies in a specific branch, which also have a position in the international market.

[7] The capital limitations in SEB and the holding companies have made it difficult to protect the ownership in several companies. A network construction of ownership between the companies within the business group would have reduced the pressure on SEB and the holding companies and distributed the costs of protecting the ownership more equally among companies in the group.

The long-term allocation of capital in both the Wallenberg and the Handelsbanken group has been of vital importance, not only as a means to prioritize activities, but also to perform consequent monitoring. However, both business groups—and especially the Wallenberg group—have been active owners, interfering in the group companies' activities, sometimes on a daily basis. This organizational structure has proved to be a well-functioning form in Sweden, and has also probably helped the business groups' long-term survival.

The majority of large family business groups and, of course, company groups and banking groups have been listed on the Stockholm stock exchange. This has been important for raising capital, but also for creating a general acceptance and legitimacy for the companies.

10.8 CONCLUSIONS

Sweden presents a striking illustration of the importance of large business groups over the long term. In our examples we have stressed their ability to adapt to changes in market conditions and institutional restructuring. Among Swedish business groups the Wallenberg group and the Handelsbanken group stand out. They have been able to expand and retain their positions as owners in Swedish industry and trade since the early twentieth century.

The Swedish business groups have been of vital importance for the development of the Swedish economy. This is shown, for example, by the role of the Wallenbergs and Handelsbanken in industrial employment. These two business groups have, together with a handful of other family groups, been especially important for the long-term development and stability of the Swedish export industry. But these companies have also made up the bulk of investment in research and development. The combination of financial strength and long-term engagement has made it possible for some large companies in the engineering and paper-and-pulp industries to develop into world-leading companies. Hence, the Swedish state and the large business groups have had mutual interests. After the Second World War export industries were given the role of trendsetters, for example in terms of wage levels, promoted by favorable legislation. It was also easier for the business groups to use and reinvest their accumulated investment funds.

As long as the Swedish financial system was basically bank-oriented—i.e., up to the middle of the 1980s—both the Handelsbanken group and the Wallenberg group could easily defend their owner positions. But with the growing access of capital and new market solutions for financing it became more difficult, especially for the Wallenberg group, to maintain their position, and the group had to concentrate on fewer but important companies in their portfolio.

CHAPTER 11

··

ITALY

enduring logic and pervasive diffusion

··

ANDREA COLLI AND MICHELANGELO VASTA

11.1 INTRODUCTION

··

BUSINESS groups (that is, clusters of legally independent companies connected together through formal and informal linkages) have been a constant presence in the Italian economy since the beginning of the process of industrialization in late nineteenth century.[1] Since those times, companies in a vast array of sectors followed a pattern of growth and expansion by means of the acquisition of partial control of other companies in the same or closely related areas of activity, followed later on by unrelated diversification. The purpose of these strategies was seldom risk diversification. Indeed, from time to time entrepreneurs chose the pattern of growth based upon the creation of business groups for various reasons. Additionally, this was a process which, contrary to predictions in the dominant literature largely based upon East Asian experiences, continued to prosper well after the country reached a level of development that can be considered truly modern. Business groups were in sum not a temporary measure in order to accelerate the process of growth by diversifying risk. In the case of Italy, their steady presence was motivated by a vast array of reasons which varied in different periods. This chapter offers a long-term analysis of the diffusion, relevance, and rationales of business groups in Italy over the long term. The next section will frame their diffusion in the context of the industrial modernization of the country, a process that lasted for almost all the twentieth century. Section 11.3 will assess the impact of their presence on economic analysis through a review of the existing literature, in order to identify the main explanations for their existence, proposing a taxonomy that

---

[1] This chapter takes an approach that examines business groups in two dimensions: ownership (state- and family-owned) and strategy (diversification and specialization).

will be fully presented in Section 11.4. A relevant issue is also to understand the quantitative relevance of the phenomenon, which in the long term has been possible only through the use of inductive methodology provided by the use of network analysis based on interlocking directorship: Section 11.5 proposes such measures. In Section 11.6 we finally put forward some of the main rationales accounting for the stubborn presence of business groups in the Italian corporate landscape. Section 11.7 concludes.

11.2 THE DEVELOPMENT OF BIG BUSINESS AND BUSINESS GROUPS IN ITALY

Italy reached, rather early after its political unification in 1861, a level of industrial development that granted her a position among the advanced nations in the Western world. This was achieved from humble beginnings: in 1861 Italy was still more a kind of "geographical concept" than a modern, unified, and developed country. Notwithstanding a persistent lack of economic, social, and cultural integration between the northern and southern part of the Italian peninsula that persistently affected the economic dynamics of the country's economic growth, Italy fought successfully in the First World War. This remarkable success was the consequence of a modernization effort concentrated over a relatively short time span. After all, Fiat, the automotive company destined to be the most important symbol of the Italian manufacturing industry for almost a century, had been founded only in 1899. However, before the 1890s and in the years immediately following unification, the country had created the essential premises for industrial takeoff, starting from the basis of a virtuous relationship between a dominant primary sector and the artisanal creativity present among peasants and in the dense web of commercial activities and competencies dating from the Middle Ages.

Post-unification economic policies aimed to create an efficient administrative sector, an improvement of the transportation network (railways above all), and the attraction of foreign direct investments in technologically intensive industries such as urban transportation, gas, water, and electricity production and distribution, which witnessed the full involvement of the country in the first wave of globalization. Together with this, the state put in place a mix of protectionist policies both for agriculture and industry from the end of the 1870s,[2] followed by the creation of a banking system modeled on the German system of the universal bank that put financial resources at the disposal of entrepreneurs willing to grow through a process of intense investment. The result of such a process of growth was that, on the eve of the First World War, Italy could be considered one of the world's industrial nations. Its manufacturing industry included a section of large companies, specialized in capital, and technology-intensive industries

---

[2] For a recent account of protectionism in Italy, see Federico and Vasta (2015).

such as automotive, shipbuilding, steel, building materials, heavy mechanics, and electromechanics, along with other mass-production industries such as cotton. The degree of concentration in these industries was very high and in line with what was happening in other leading economies (Giannetti and Vasta, 2006), although the weight of the top 200 manufacturing firms, measured by their total assets as a proportion of GDP, was only 11.6 percent in 1913 (Giannetti and Vasta, 2010: 29). As was the case in other European countries, if one looks at the dominant forms of business enterprise, particularly in the fast-rising industries such as steel and mechanics, a clear tendency emerges to self-regulate the process of expansion through the creation of collusive agreements, sometimes shaped in the form of trusts and cartels, as for instance happened in the case of the steel industry, which grew under the umbrella of a horizontal trust characterized by a dense network of cross-shareholdings (Bonelli, 1982). The First World War introduced another variable in this process. Companies started an intense process of vertical and horizontal growth, and carried on reinvesting their huge returns, particularly in industries most affected by war procurement. Companies like Fiat in automotives and Montecatini in chemicals, for instance, expanded their boundaries during the war years and immediately after, acquiring major stakes in other companies, sometimes competitors and in other cases strategic suppliers. At the same time, the largest firms accumulated shares in the main banks, acquiring their stakes in order to gain control over the source of financial resources. In their turn, banks were progressively increasing their shareholdings in the most important customers, becoming at the same time lenders and owners. In the case of the country's largest bank, the Banca Commerciale Italiana, one can see it at the end of World War I as a sort of financial holding with shareholdings in a wide range of equity stakes—in some cases conspicuous—in many companies in almost all the relevant industries (Confalonieri, 1982).

The basic guidelines of this process of growth and consolidation of big business went on during the interwar period, characterized by two relevant phenomena. The first was the full consolidation of technology and capital-intensive industries of the Second Industrial Revolution, in particular chemicals—even though with a marked specialization in fertilizers—electromechanics, electricity production, steel and shipbuilding, and, of course, the automotive industry. Even in a declining phase of globalization, foreign presence remained relevant in advanced industries, such as electromechanics and oil refining. A relevant aspect of the consolidation of big business was, however, its tendency to stick to the domestic market enjoying monopolistic positions, something which further strengthened its relations with the political power—i.e., the Fascist dictatorship—but also put a structural limit on the dimensional growth of big business. In addition, the financial system continued to be shaped in the German way, influencing heavily how large corporations were getting their own resources. Universal "German-style" banks provided significant financial support and qualified managerial advice to the major industrial companies of the country, especially in modern capital-intensive sectors such as steel, heavy engineering, electricity, shipping, and so on. The stock exchange was seriously weak and unattractive for both companies and investors, due also to a frail regulatory framework. This resulted in a marked incentive for the main blockholders to leverage on control-enhancing mechanisms and low transparency in order to keep high control levels with limited investment. Looking more closely at this process of expansion, in contrast to what theory predicts (and historical experience shows) in the case of developing countries (Khanna and Palepu, 2010), even if with some notable exceptions, business-group growth appears to be driven by instances of vertical and horizontal growth in the same, or related, industries. One standard case is that of the electrical industry. Here the main companies carried on a process of horizontal growth, acquiring majority stakes in other smaller firms, consolidating their geographic presence, and creating a sort of regional or macro-regional monopoly. At the same time they were actively pursuing a process of vertical, forward integration, acquiring controlling stakes, for instance, in local transportation networks, such as tramway companies. In sum, in all the main capital-intensive industries the pursuit of growth in order to reach a minimum standard scale of operations prevailed over strategies of risk diversification, confirming the relevance of technological stances over other strategic purposes.

A second relevant event was the massive intervention of the state in the economy, following an emergency situation created by the Great Depression. In the early 1930s the largest universal banks found their balance sheets heavily burdened by toxic assets: credits to the distressed industrial systems, plus the shares of failing big business. The solution, a giant bailout of the nation's three largest banks—Banca Commerciale, Credito Italiano, and Banco di Roma—put a considerable portion of the whole share capital of Italian stock companies into the hands of a state agency, the Istituto per la Ricostruzione Industriale (IRI). In 1936 a new banking law allowed banks to provide only short-term credit to the industrial sector, explicitly prohibiting them from acting as shareholders and from providing long- and medium-term credit to industrial firms, which was left to state-owned agencies set up with this explicit purpose. Since, as mentioned above, the main banks had amassed a huge portfolio of minor, and often major, stakes in the countries' most significant companies, in the end the agency—originally designed as a temporary bailout measure, which soon became permanent—resembled a sort of giant group, which was internally reorganized through a system of specialized sub-holdings (see Figure 11.2).

The state's intervention marked a major event in the nation's industrial history. From that moment on, and in particular after the Second World War, a huge complex of state-owned enterprises speeded up the growth of industries of the Second Industrial Revolution. As a result, the weight (as a share of total industrial output) and sector composition of Italian big business converged with those of most industrialized countries. Private, mostly family-owned big business prospered as well, even if always in a clearly monopolistic situation on the internal market. At the beginning of the Golden Age, in 1952, the weight of the total assets of the top 200 manufacturing firms on GDP was doubled compared to 1913, reaching 25.7 percent. This ratio showed a rising curve and reached its highest point at the beginning of the 1970s, with a value of 38.5 percent (Giannetti and Vasta, 2010: 29). At the peak of the *economic miracle* in the early 1960s, the top Italian manufacturing industry was thus composed of a number of large companies. They were shaped in the form of both well-structured business groups—such as the state-owned ones—and in loosely associated hierarchy-type business groups characterized by a certain degree of related diversification, in general the consequence of strategies of vertical integration. Two of the largest companies in the country were shaped this way. As for the public group, ENI (a state-owned agency for energy, created in 1953) was shaped as an operating holding company controlling a vertical chain of operation from drilling to refining and distribution, with a very limited diversification process in non-related fields. In the private sector, Fiat (automotive) had completed a process of vertical integration and related diversification (with some degree of diversification in related as well as unrelated business fields). The 1960s, however, also witnessed a new phenomenon—the undertaking of technologically unrelated strategies of growth, due also to a willingness to expand in profitable industries, particularly when the growth process started to slow down after 1963 and in the second half of the decade.

The general framework changed progressively after the oil crisis of the 1970s and the first signs of the ICT revolution. Since then, the weight of big business—both in terms of total assets and employment—decreased in Italy more than in the other advanced economies, with a much smaller weight of ICT-related industries than in other developed countries. The decline of big business since the 1970s was accompanied by the rise of other forms of enterprise, already existing but less relevant than big business in terms of contribution to GDP formation. These were small firms (often clustered in industrial districts), cooperative firms, municipalized firms, medium-sized enterprises (the Italian Mittelstand), and foreign-owned firms, which increased their share of both total employees and manufacturing output. Notably, as we will see in detail in the following sections, these forms of enterprise also showed a strong tendency towards the progressive agglomeration of companies, that is the formation of different typologies of business groups. Indeed, hierarchy-type business groups can today be found almost everywhere in the Italian industrial landscape, and they include companies of different sizes, legal status, ownership, and sectors. Instead of vanishing or weakening, the business group—as a governance and organizational device—seems to be further rooted and to diffuse among Italian enterprises as time goes by and over the nation's whole industrial history.

11.3 Business Groups in Italy: a Review of the Literature

As the most recent literature about the forms of enterprise in emerging markets stresses, the early phases of Italian industrialization were characterized by the widespread presence of business groups, defined as clusters of independent companies linked together, or to a major holding, by significant share ownership enough to exert some control on the strategic behavior of the companies themselves. However, a significant trait of Italian industrialization—which has been quite surprisingly taken for granted by even the most recent studies on Italian corporate development (see, for example, Colli and Vasta, 2010)—has been the fact that the group, as a form of corporate development, has established itself as a *permanent* feature of business enterprises of every size and sector over the country's whole industrial history right up to today. Of course, the tendency of Italian companies—and, up to the early 1930s, of the country's main banks—to establish control linkages through share ownership in order to expand their borders was well known, for instance, to contemporary commentators, worried by the fact that such "unregulated" behavior would lead simultaneously to monopolistic situations and to the exploitation and expropriation of minority shareholders (see, for instance, Zorzini, 1925). The existence of business groups which resulted in monopolistic or oligopolistic positions in almost all the strategic, technology, and capital-intensive industries of the Second Industrial Revolution (from steel to chemicals, from electricity production to shipbuilding, and from automotives to heavy mechanics) became clear—and scrutinized in detail—immediately after the Second World War, when the presence of such positions, both in private and state-controlled business, became an overheated issue in the political debate concerning the concentration of economic power (Radar, 1948; Rossi, 1955). From a completely different intellectual perspective, at the beginning of the 1970s other scholars started to become interested in the diffusion of business groups, particularly among large firms in Italy. Italy was one of the countries analyzed by a group of Harvard Business School researchers led by Bruce Scott and supervised by Alfred Chandler at the end of the 1960s and the beginning of the following decade. The purpose of the research group was to verify the degree of diffusion of the multidivisional, or M-form, organizational structure, widespread among US enterprises, on the Continent. Italy was just one of the cases analyzed, along with France, Germany, and the UK (Channon, 1973; Dyas and Tanheiser, 1976). The analysis made clear that in Europe, and in Italy in particular, the privileged way to grow was through the creation of legally independent subsidiaries. The creation of internal divisions dependent on a central headquarters was far less common practice, incentivized both for legal and strategic reasons. Fiscal arrangements avoiding double taxation emphasized the benefits of the creation of groups instead of centralized M-Form organizations, while the presence of partially controlled subsidiaries both allowed the decentralization of power and the exploitation of leverage (Pavan, 1976, 1978). The present status of our research does not allow us to assess the issue of the degree and quality of the administrative control exerted by headquarters over subsidiaries. An analysis like this can be done in different ways with different degrees of precision. For instance, careful prosopographical research could illuminate the intensity of control exerted by headquarters over some of the companies of a group. A recently published research study on the history of the IRI group described in detail the control practices which occurred between the main holding, the sectorial holdings, and the operating companies in the pyramidal structure which characterized the group since its very beginning in the 1930s, concluding that the nature of the control was basically financial and not strategic, leaving the operative companies largely free to decide on their policies (Colli, 2013). Another, more feasible, way could be the identification of proxies for the intensity and direction of these linkages. For instance, the size of the shareholding is a clear indicator of the willingness to establish close control, which could probably also be translated into a strategic influence of the controlling over the controlled company. In this case, however, and particularly in the long run, the identification of the size of ownership quotas is not easy to achieve on a homogeneous scale. Again, network analysis could be a way to solve the problem, assuming that some typologies of interlocking directorship links indicate a willingness to exert strategic control, more than a merely financial one. With the data available, however, it is difficult to provide even superficial insights. One impression derived from the analysis of the existing literature in Italy is that the overall intensity of systematic financial control, instead of purely strategic control, grew progressively, reaching its maximum level in the early 1980s when the principal purpose of the creation of business groups was the maximization of stock-exchange listings and thus of opportunities for tunneling resources from the market.

Business historiography, which started to flourish in Italy at the beginning of the 1970s and immediately became interested in the contribution that big business made to the country's economic growth, became aware of the existence of the dominant organizational arrangements, that is the creation and consolidation of large firms through the creation of legally independent subsidiaries. The first studies on the steel industry (Bonelli, 1975), electricity industry (VV.AA, 1992–4), chemical industry and the dominant player, Montecatini (Amatori and Bezza, 1990), banking industry (Confalonieri, 1974–1976, 1982. 1992), cotton industry (Romano, 1992), and on other capital and technology intensive industries—both private and state-owned—clearly showed the dominant pattern of growth through hierarchy-type business groups mostly in focused or related industries. Very little, if anything, was devoted to an understanding of their administrative functioning, partly in consequence of the fact that this was rarely integrated and centrally planned.

In sum, Italian manufacturing industry, after its first takeoff before World War I, flourished during the conflict and consolidated during the interwar period, expanding its range of activities in all the industries of this technological wave, in order to prepare its definitive affirmation in the years of the economic miracle after the Second World War. No differently from other advanced nations, large firms shared a marked tendency to grow, even if, in comparison with other European and American counterparts, they showed a weaker approach to internationalization. Growth was achieved through a process of consolidation (i.e., taking over competitors in the same industry), through a policy of internal expansion, and, more often, through the acquisition, spin-off, or ex-novo creation of legally independent companies which enlarged the boundaries of the company itself. Even if quite well known, and common to *all* companies in *all* capital-intensive industries, however, this phenomenon has not been systematically studied in terms of its nature, determinants, and outcomes.

One of the first attempts to treat the issue of business groups in a more systematic way was by Amatori (1997), who, explaining the peculiarities of the process of growth among the largest Italian companies over the long term, stressed the policy of group creation as a way to hyperinflate the company's dimension in an expansionist strategy aimed at achieving a strong bargaining position towards political power than at pursuing rational strategies of growth in order to exploit scale and scope economies.

Even if well aware of the existence of business groups as a dominant form of organization and control in the history of Italian capitalism, business historians and management scholars have limited themselves to reconstructing their composition and formation over time, avoiding any systematization of the issue. In particular, four questions still remain to be answered:

i. Which are the main typologies of business groups in the Italian context? Are they all the same, or do they display different characteristics, both in a cross-sectional and longitudinal way?

ii. What has been their relevance (in terms of sales, assets, employment, and other size measures) on the whole economy?

iii. Are these organizational forms diffused only among big business, or do they affect other forms of enterprise?

iv. Last but not least, does historical analysis allow us to say something more about the rationale behind their existence and persistence in the long term, i.e., not only in the initial phases of the country's development but also when Italy reached a sort of "industrial maturity," if that is indeed the case?

Since the 1990s there has been a revival of interest in the presence of business groups, especially of the pyramidal variety, in the process of Italian industrialization. Research in the area of corporate governance, both contemporary (Barca et al., 1994; Bianchi, Bianco, and Enriques, 2001) and oriented toward the longer term (Brioschi, Buzzacchi, and Colombo, 1990; Amatori and Colli, 1999; Aganin and Volpin, 2005), have highlighted the role played by the *pyramidal* business groups as mechanisms set up in order to leverage control by relevant shareholders. In this respect the analysis follows a precise logic in terms of corporate finance, and again concentrates on listed private and state-owned big business; the diffusion and persistence of business groups are explained by the presence of weak governance institutions, allowing the exploitation of minority shareholders and the magnification of the logic of pyramidal control. Controlling shareholders—families, individuals, but also the state—were thus able to retain a firm control on their business empires, recurring to multiple listing of companies inside the same groups.

Another, even more recent stream of research tries to provide a more detailed answer to the questions outlined above, suggesting an approach to the issue of business groups which explicitly takes into account the variety of the forms of enterprise which can be found in the process of Italian industrialization (Colli and Vasta, 2010). Quite recently, Colli and Vasta (2015) offered a taxonomy of business groups—basically referred to as large firms—distinguishing between coalitional and vertical business groups, family- and state-owned, specialized or diversified, showing how in different periods of the country's economic history in the twentieth century business groups were always resilient, but progressively changing their rationale and "demography." The same authors, recurring to a proxy determined by the analysis of interlocking directorship, also try to measure the size, and thus the impact, of the fifteen largest groups across six benchmark years in the twentieth century, concluding that their weight in terms of share capital and total assets on the population of joint-stock companies was consistently very large. This research, which confirms the persistence of the organizational forms based upon a holding controlling legally (and sometimes de facto) independent units during the whole process of growth, maturity—and eventual decline—of the Italian economy, and not only in the initial phases of development, paved the way even more recently for further research, which started to deal with the diffusion of the form of the group not only among large companies, but also among other legal and dimensional typologies of enterprises in Italy. Colli, Rinaldi, and Vasta (2016) have thus extended the study of business groups including the diffusion of this organizational form among small and medium-sized enterprises, municipalized companies, and, last but not least, cooperatives. This research has highlighted the fact that the instrument of the group as a way to manage the process of growth and expansion (both geographical and dimensional) is common to various business forms despite their legal structure and orientation, and not only to "traditional" big business (see Figure 11.1). The institutional environment—that is, the basic rules of the game—had, in the course of time, played a role in facilitating the application and consolidation of

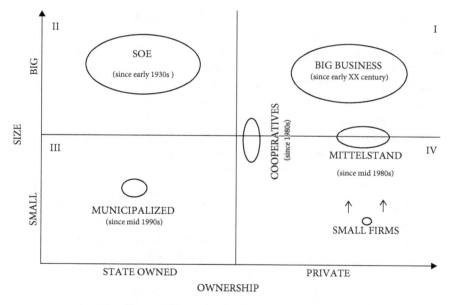

FIGURE 11.1. Forms of Business Groups in twentieth-century Italy.

Note: circles' size represents a broad estimate of their relevance.

Source: Colli, Rinaldi, and Vasta (2016): Fig. 2.

this organizational device to different business forms and situations, showing how over time the rationale behind the decision to adopt the business-group form based on a controlling holding company (H-form)—instead of other, more centralized structures, such as the U-form or the M-form—has varied according to different situations and contexts. This concept will probably constitute the basis for future research into what could be defined as the "variety of business groups" within a defined domestic environment.

11.4 THE VARIETY OF BUSINESS GROUPS IN ITALY

In order to fully understand the characteristics and mechanisms of business groups in the Italian context, we introduce a taxonomy that emphasizes two main dimensions, namely ownership and strategy. Although these dimensions are not exclusive and can be reconstructed mainly by stylized facts, they are crucial in shaping business groups. Of course, in this reconstruction a single business group can simultaneously belong to more than one typology, or transform over time from one to another. According to ownership, we can identify two main categories: family-controlled groups and state-owned and -controlled groups.

11.4.1 Family-Controlled Business Groups

Family-controlled groups represent one of the most important typologies within Italian capitalism. Accordingly, it is possible to include some of the "long survivor" groups, such as Fiat, Pirelli, and Falck, controlled by founding families in almost all the crucial phases of the economic history of the country. By World War I all three companies were already important first movers in their respective industries. Fiat, founded in 1899, immediately emerged as a first mover, totally different from the small workshops which crowded the automotive industry at the beginning of the twentieth century. Founded in 1872, Pirelli quickly developed as a domestic leader in the production of caoutchouc, establishing operations abroad, and benefiting to a significant extent from public and military procurement, especially in the case of cables. Falck, incorporated in 1906, rapidly became the national leader in steel production from scrap iron with the electric smelting technique. All three companies took advantage of the increase of procurement due to World War I and were able to reinvest their profits in order to finance a process of horizontal and vertical expansion in related fields. During the interwar period this process continued steadily for all the largest private business groups, including another leader in chemicals, Montecatini, under the leadership of the Donegani family. For instance, in the case of Fiat, the number of companies belonging to the group grew in the different branches of the mechanical industry, or in components such as glass or aluminum, or in related activities such as controlled-access highways. The number of Pirelli's affiliates also increased in the same period, in a logic of vertical downward integration—for instance, in telephone and telegraph cable communication companies. The expansion of Fiat and Pirelli is so relevant that, in both cases, the founding families already felt the necessity to increase their control leverage through the creation, during the interwar period, of pure holdings (IFI in the case of Fiat, Pirelli & C. in the case of Pirelli), a process which, however, did not happen in the case of Falck, despite its growing dimensions and diversification. The trend of the enlargement of the dimensions of family-controlled groups continued during the 1950s but declined in the following decades. The renewal of the expansion of private groups in the most recent period has been underlined by some studies (Brioschi, Buzzacchi, and Colombo, 1990; Bianchi et al., 2005). During the 1980s private groups expanded their boundaries through acquisitions both by the holdings and by the operating companies. The expansion was often driven by financial goals and speculative purposes, as in the case of the Fiat group or that of Cofide, the holding of Carlo De Benedetti, a tycoon aggressively active in the market since the beginning of the 1980s (Borsa, 1992). In the case of family-controlled groups, the dynamic of their expansion was quite linear. The operating companies, which were already established leaders by World War I, started to accelerate their expansion during and after the war, pursuing a process of both vertical and horizontal integration, a process which continued at least until the first half of the 1960s. The process was carried on through the creation of subsidiaries, controlled by the operating company and progressively by pure financial holdings. During the crisis of the 1970s, and in the first half of the 1980s, these groups shrank in size, expanding again in the second half of the 1980s and in many cases benefiting from the vibrancy of the stock market.

11.4.2 State-Controlled Business Groups

The tradition of state intervention goes far back in the history of Italian capitalism: immediately after the country's political unification in 1861, the state played an important and supportive role in fostering Italian economic development, building the necessary infrastructures, providing military procurement, and introducing protection. In some strategic industries, such as steel, state intervention went further, when companies in difficulty were rescued by the central bank in order to ensure their survival (Amatori and Colli, 1999). But state involvement in the direct ownership of companies started in 1933 with the creation of the IRI. This was basically an emergency measure, but the IRI ended up representing the permanent, direct involvement of the state in the ownership of companies for nearly seventy years, until its dissolution in 2002. In the mid-1930s the IRI took over the banks' shareholdings at book value, becoming the majority owner in a vast array of companies in different industries, from real estate to steel, from shipbuilding to mechanics, and from textiles to utilities. The IRI was

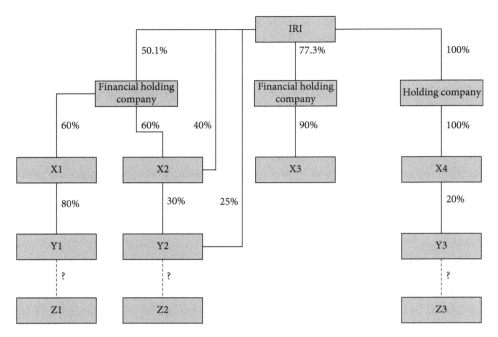

FIGURE 11.2. The structure of Istituto per la Ricostruzione Industriale (IRI) group (schematized and simplified).

Source: Toninelli and Vasta (2010): 56.

originally conceived as a temporary measure, but it soon became clear that private domestic capitalism was unable to repurchase what the state had bought. Thus, four years after its creation, the IRI was declared permanent. It was enormous: according to some recent estimates, it controlled around 12 percent of the total share capital of Italian joint-stock companies (Toninelli and Vasta, 2010: 74). In addition, after the bailout the three largest banks in the country also belonged to the state-owned group. A complex architecture was designed in order to give some order to the vast array of companies under the IRI's control (Figure 11.2): the group was based on a head company, a "super-holding" (IRI) under the direct control of the government. The super-holding controlled (by statute, with at least 50.01 percent of the capital) some financial holdings which were characterized by sectorial specialization: for instance, Finsider (steel), Finmeccanica (mechanics and engineering), and Finelettrica (electric energy). These financial holdings—some of which were listed—were, in their turn, controlling companies (in some cases, with less than the 50 percent of the share capital) belonging to that specific industry (in Figure 11.2, for example, X1–X4 and at a lower level Y1–Y3 and Z1–Z3), some of which were listed as well.

This pyramidal structure built progressively over time and took a definitive shape in the second half of the 1950s, allowing the IRI not only to benefit from the leverage effects of the pyramidal control, but also—more importantly—to start a process of rationalization in some industries and of expansion in others. During the late 1950s, and especially during the 1960s, the IRI played a key role in the country's fast economic growth and modernization, through the creation of infrastructure and a pervasive investment policy in capital-intensive industries such as steel and heavy mechanics, also trying to put in place some synergies and interdependencies across companies in different industries. Behind the pyramidal architecture, however, the IRI was characterized by a peculiar kind of governance and distribution of power inside the organization.

Another relevant example of state-controlled business groups is provided by the Ente Nazionale Idrocarburi (ENI), created in 1953 to manage the country's needs in the fields of oil and gas, which already had some active companies such as Agip. The ENI was much smaller than the IRI, but with a similar vertical organization, reinforced by interlocking ownership across the companies of the group: Agip Mineraria (drilling), ANIC (refining), Agip (distribution), Snam (gas), and other minor companies such as Nuovo Pignone and Saipem (engineering).

Beyond some obvious similarities (including an intensive use of leverage and other control-enhancing mechanisms), state-controlled groups also show at least three main differences from private groups. First, the use of multilevel organizational architectures (longer chains of company control), more sophisticated than those of groups under family control—also due to their much larger dimensions. Second, the presence of strong links with the country's largest banks, which put the companies of the group in a better position than the private enterprises regarding access to credit. The third difference is the propensity of state-controlled groups (both the IRI and ENI) to build resilient links with private firms (Rinaldi and Vasta, 2005; 2012; 2014). Indeed, there were a large number of cross-participations between different groups—both private and state-owned—achieved through bridging companies. More generally, private companies and SOEs were induced to have strong links, because they play an essential function in ensuring strategic coordination and stabilization of managerial control. More generally, we can observe another relevant difference related to different origin: while private groups expanded progressively from the interwar period onwards, the state-controlled groups were largely the effect of the reorganization of companies already in the hands of the state, which were assembled in order to give them a more rational structure, particularly in the period after World War II. In the mid-1950s, the IRI and ENI controlled a little less than a quarter of the total share capital of Italian joint-stock companies, but this share rose to a third in the early 1980s (Toninelli and Vasta, 2010).

11.4.3 Specialized Business Groups

The strategy of business groups is the second part of our classification to be investigated. In this sense, Italian business groups refer to their degree of specialization/diversification in terms of core production activities. Specialized (single-product, or characterized by a low degree of production diversification) groups without integrated administrative mechanisms were widely present in the period before World War II.[3] Its epitome can be found among the producers and providers of electricity, which, until the nationalization of the whole industry in 1963, were dominant among Italian joint-stock companies. The process of the expansion of business groups in the electricity industry followed a relatively standard procedure, based on a progressive expansion both before and after World War I through acquisition of the relevant shareholdings in smaller electricity producers. The process of horizontal expansion continued throughout the 1920s and 1930s, when the largest companies also started diversification initiatives in utilities, or downward integration in local transports, tramways, and narrow-gauge railways. The progressive aggregation of smaller companies on a regional basis led to the creation of regional monopolies, each under the control of a single large business group (Galasso, 1993). Until the 1960s the dominant business groups in the electricity industry progressively enlarged their boundaries through the acquisition of companies operating in the same industry, or in closely related fields. The "specialization" of the groups in the electricity industry changed, however, on the eve of nationalization of the industry, basically in two directions. The first concerned shareholdings in the portfolios of the electricity companies: many of them, foreseeing the nationalization of their core business, started to invest in non-related or only partially related activities. For instance, during the 1950s Edison, the largest and most powerful Italian electricity company, started a process of diversification into chemicals and retail distribution by opening a supermarket chain (Pavan, 1976). The second direction concerned share-holdings in the main companies of the groups. There was a relevant presence of linkages among groups, particularly with the major role played by the electricity companies. The high profitability of electricity providers, which was due to various reasons, including their monopolistic position, had a relevant effect on their govern-ance. After the interwar years, these companies had an increasing number of share-holders, many of which, including those central to the groups concerned, were apparently public companies, characterized by concentrated ownership. However, in reality the fragmentation of share capital was accompanied by the practice, followed by minority shareholders, of delegating their administrative rights to top management, and led to a unique situation in which top management basically controlled itself. Specialized groups, similar to those in the electricity industry, were prevalent, as already stated, in the interwar years and the period of the *economic miracle*. Manufacturing companies such as Fiat, Pirelli, and Falck also showed a low tendency towards diversification. Clearly, a notable exception is the state-owned IRI, which was characterized by an overall high degree of diversification. However, if one takes into account the level of control *below* the super-holding IRI (Figure 11.2) and focuses on the sectorial sub-holdings heading the activities of the IRI in the various

[3] Here we use the term specialized business groups to label holding companies that are mostly pyramidal in their ownership arrangement and that somewhat loosely control autonomous subsidiaries involved in product-related activities.

industries, a high degree of specialization clearly emerges. This was surely due to the real reason for the existence of the IRI, which was conceived more as an instrument for industrial policy than as a standard business group free to undertake strategies of diversification.

11.4.4 Diversified Business Groups

Apart from the state-owned business groups such as the IRI and ENI, diversified groups began to appear in the 1970s, and increasingly in the 1980s, enlarging their boundaries through a policy of acquisitions, pursued through the use of control-enhancing mechanisms going from different categories of shares to pyramidal structures based on several listed companies, and, albeit to a minor extent, cross-shareholdings. One example is Fiat, which, after the 1970s, started a progressive diversification in fields that were markedly different from its core business, such as distribution (La Rinascente), insurance, synthetic fibers, and even food.[4] The availability of legal control-enhancing mechanisms, such as the creation of pyramidal groups composed of several listed companies and an increasing separation between ownership and control through the issuance of privileged stocks with limited administrative rights, provided further incentives for the creation of complex architectures designed to gain resources from the stock market, which was characterized by an unusual vibrancy during the 1980s (Siciliano, 2001; Consob, 2011). This process of related, but increasingly unrelated, diversification can be seen, in some ways, as an Italian version of the conglomeration wave occurring at international level. The available qualitative evidence suggests that the process of diversification through the addition of companies continued throughout the 1990s, partly due to the privatization program that allowed private Italian companies to take over activities previously under state control (Goldstein, 2003; Barucci and Pierobon, 2007). In some cases this promoted a process of related and unrelated diversification, as, for instance, in the case of the Benetton group, which from an original core in textiles expanded into retail distribution and expressways through the acquisition of the former state-owned SME and Società Autostrade.

As stated, all these forms of business group play a crucial role in the Italian process of economic growth, at least since the last decade of the nineteenth century when Italy started its transition from the periphery to the center of the European economy. Starting with evidence provided in a related work (Colli and Vasta, 2015), we sum up the main phases which characterized the dynamics of Italian business groups in the period under investigation in Table 11.1. Comparing the evidence emerging from the taxonomy described above, it clearly appears how the strategies and structures of

---

[4] The case of Fiat, however, is something of an exception; from early on the company invested in unrelated businesses, including agriculture, cement, and tourism, between the 1930s and 1950s. Yet the relevance of these unrelated businesses was limited within the firm's total portfolio (in terms of assets).

Table 11.1. Dynamics of business groups in Italy.

Phase	Period	Strategy	Tactics	Main actor	Prevalent group type
1 (collusive logic)	Prior to 1914	Collusion and coordination	Cross-shareholdings among companies belonging to the same cartel	Single companies of the cartel; cartel HQ	Coalitional groups; banking groups
2a (expansionistic logic)	1914s–1920s	Horizontal and vertical integration among privately held companies and banks	Acquisition of companies in related activities; joint ventures	Operating companies	Vertically integrated groups; banking groups
2b (Leviathan's logic)	1930s–1960s	Horizontal and vertical integration especially among state-owned companies	Acquisition of companies in unrelated activities; joint ventures	Operating companies	Vertically integrated groups
3 (re-structuring logic)	1970s	Decentralization with some degree of control	Spin-offs	Operating companies	De-centralized and unrelated diversified groups
4 (opportunistic logic)	1980s	Acquisition of financial resources from the stock-market; financial speculation	Multiple listing of old and new subsidiaries	Holdings	Pyramidal groups
5 (consolidation logic)	1990s and afterwards	Consolidation; diversification (in some cases)	Acquisition of privatized companies	Holdings	Pyramidal groups

Source: Based on Colli and Vasta (2015).

business groups dynamically changed over time. Accordingly, the relevance of the different forms followed the nature and the evolution of national and international frameworks.

The five phases presented in Table 11.1 require brief clarification. The first phase (*collusive logic*) sees the rise of relatively large companies in the early beginnings of the industrial sectors of the Second Industrial Revolution. The best example is the cartel-type agreement of the so-called "steel trust" created in 1903 by the main iron and steel producers of the country (Amatori, 1997). The logic was for a large part of the country's steel production to adopt a collusive behavior aiming at the coordination efforts prevailing over competitive attitudes. The second phase (*catching up* with the Second Industrial Revolution) can be divided into two sub-phases: *expansionistic logic* and *Leviathan's logic*. In the former phase, groups are mainly formed through a process of progressive aggregation of companies, listed and not listed, active largely in the same industry or in related fields, very often under a logic of technologically driven vertical integration. In this phase, the logic was clearly to pursue growth, market control, and control over critical inputs. Examples can be found in the process of the expansion of companies of the electricity industry, as shown previously. The phase of the *Leviathan* is mainly characterized by the formation and consolidation of the two main state-owned groups, the IRI and ENI, as described above. In this phase the attempt for a latecomer country to close the gap with the technological frontier represented by both the technological waves of electricity and steel and that of oil, automobiles, and mass production emerged clearly (Freeman and Soete, 1997; Freeman and Louçã, 2001). The third phase (*restructuring logic*) is the period of the oil crisis of the 1970s, which resulted in a large process of restructuring of large companies. In several cases, the creation of business groups was the outcome of a strategy of decentralization and the downsizing of vertically integrated firms in order to enhance their flexibility, minimize control costs, and dilute tensions in industrial labor relations. The process of disintegration went on until the beginning of the 1980s and found a sort of "institutional" justification in the system of incentives to investments provided by the state in the economically backward areas of the country, which encouraged companies to create several spin-offs and subsidiaries, each entitled to access public funds for investments. The epitome of this behavior was Società Italiana Resine (SIR), a chemical company run by a tycoon, Nino Rovelli, who created hundreds of companies in order to obtain state resources for investing in Sardinia (Zamagni, 2007). The fourth phase (*opportunistic logic*) took place during the 1980s and was characterized by the process both of creation of new groups and of the expansion of the boundaries of those already existing. These processes were incentivized by two concurring phenomena: first, the abolition of double taxation on inter-corporate income of transactions inside a group eliminated a powerful incentive towards merging subsidiaries into a multidivisional structure (Coltorti, 1988);[5] and second, a sudden vibrancy, after years of stagnation, in

---

[5] The issue of the impact of double taxation as a disincentive to the formation of business groups, and its subsequent progressive abolition by a series of laws starting at the end of the 1970s, is still debated. In

the stock market, which made it possible to obtain financial resources by listing subsidiaries. This strategy was followed by all the major groups, both private and state-owned, such as Fiat, De Benedetti, Ferruzzi, and the IRI (Brioschi, Buzzacchi, and Colombo, 1990). Thus there was a generalized diffusion of the pyramidal structure jointly with a process of both related and unrelated diversification, carried out mainly during the 1990s, when global leaders (famously, for example, General Electric) were, in contrast, moving in the opposite direction—that of refocusing and deconglomeration (Amatori and Colli, 2011). In the fifth phase (*consolidation logic*), private groups further enlarged their activities, also following the intense wave of privatization which, during the 1990s, brought a massive sell-off of state-owned companies. In some cases acquisitions were made in related activities—for instance, in steel (Lucchini, Riva, and Marcegaglia), chemicals (Mapei), construction, and publishing. In other cases opportunities stemming from the privatization process caused existing groups to enhance their degree of diversification, as in the case of Benetton with the acquisition of the Società Autostrade (expressways) and Autogrill (mass distribution).

11.5 THE BOUNDARIES OF BUSINESS GROUPS IN ITALY

The empirically historical research on business groups in Italy—their typologies and structures, their composition and relevance—has always been problematical due to a scarcity of information. Until the mid-1980s (when a change in the legislation concerning corporate information disclosure occurred), it was extremely uncommon to find consolidated statement accounts, or detailed information about the effective composition of a group, in terms of the companies belonging to it. If we return to the interwar period, this kind of information is totally absent, even if the phenomenon of business groups was, as stated above, known and discussed from the 1920s (Zorzini, 1925; Luzzatto Fegiz, 1928). Valuable, but random and non-homogeneous, information is available for the post-World War II period (Zerini, 1947; Radar, 1948; Benedetti and Toniolli, 1963).

---

theory, double taxation of the dividends of the companies belonging to a group—present, as stated, until the end of the 1970s—should have acted as a powerful disincentive to the formation of business groups, something that, as described in this chapter, did not happen. The reason for this apparent contradiction is probably the result of a mix of elements, among which the most relevant was the possibility for controlling owners to leverage on the resources invested by minority shareholders. To establish a multidivisional enterprise means that entrepreneurs need full control of the incorporated assets, and therefore that owners have to provide all the necessary resources. In the case of partially owned subsidiaries, they can get the same result (that is, control over the subsidiary's activity) but without committing themselves for the entire amount of the resources needed. This possibility probably made the disincentives implicit in double taxation strategically much less important than the incentives embedded in the possibility of enjoying the benefits of the business group as a mechanism for enhancing the dominant shareholders' control.

The introduction of the European directive concerning large holdings (Large Holdings Directive 88/627/EEC) made new information available, but it is limited to the most recent years (Barca et al., 1994; Barca and Becht, 2001; Bianchi et al., 2005). Recently, the availability of a comprehensive dataset (Imita.db) on Italian joint-stock companies has allowed us to extend the systematic analysis of Italian big business from different perspectives.[6] Starting from this source, and by using the network analysis approach (e.g. Wasserman and Faust, 1994), which is a new tool, we can understand better the dynamics of business groups in Italy and, more generally, in different institutional contexts.[7]

By focusing on six benchmark years (1921, 1936, 1951, 1961, 1971, and 1983), we can offer a (rough) estimate of the boundaries and relevance of the largest fifteen manufacturing-centered business groups of the country.[8] After having identified the fifteen largest companies, by total assets, for each of the benchmark years, our (strong) hypothesis (also corroborated by recent qualitative business-history literature) is that each of them was leading a group, the extension of which had to be reconstructed.[9] We thus take interlocking directorates as a proxy of the existence of a formal link between two companies.[10] Clearly, this methodology has some limitations, mainly because it allows us to identify the existence of relationships among different firms but cannot provide the exact representation of the ownership structure of a business group. However, we consider it to be the only possible way of obtaining precious and reliable information about the shareholdings of single companies.

In order to find a proxy measure of the weight of each single group, we identified two methodologies, both based on the network analysis, which allow us to estimate a lower and an upper boundary of the group extension. When the presence of a possible link between the companies belonging to the group has been identified, the Imita.db database enables us to identify the relevance of the group, by number of companies, total assets, and share capital, on the universe of Italian joint-stock companies. We do this in two ways: first we consider a firm as "controlled" by a group if at least one board

---

[6] Imita.db is one of the largest datasets on joint-stock companies from a historical perspective in the world. In particular, it contains information regarding companies, boards of directors, and balance sheets for a very large sample of Italian joint-stock companies for several benchmark years covering a wide time span of the twentieth century. Overall the set contains data on more than 38,000 companies, almost 300,000 directors, and more than 100,000 balance sheets. Representativeness, in terms of capital, is very high as the sample covers well over 90 percent of the total corporate universe in all but the first two benchmark years (1911 and 1913) and the last year (1983), for which the proportion is around 85 percent. For a detailed description of this dataset, see Vasta (2006a). The dataset is available online at imitadb.unisi.it/en.

[7] For a comparative study of fourteen different countries, see David and Westerhuis (2014).

[8] The rest of this section is an abridged version of Colli and Vasta (2015).

[9] The full list of the business groups we have selected is presented in Appendix 1, where a rough measure of their boundaries is also provided.

[10] The interlocking directorates technique is based on the analysis of the links created between two units (i.e., two firms) when an individual belongs to both; that is, a director of two or more companies in the case of ownership structure. The analysis comprises the reconstruction of the articulation of inter-company links by quantitative techniques of varying complexities.

Table 11.2. Average number of companies belonging to a group, by benchmark year, 1921–83.

Years	AR		LR	
	All shares (As)	Weighted shares (Ws)	All shares (As)	Weighted shares (Ws)
1921	58.1	36.9	35.7	26.5
1936	71.7	38.8	49.1	31.8
1952	74.2	39.8	43.1	27.9
1960	79.3	42.5	56.7	36.7
1972	57.8	37.7	39.0	29.2
1983	33.8	24.9	21.7	17.9

Source: Colli and Vasta (2015).

member is shared by the group and by the firm (all roles—AR); secondly, in order to identify the lower boundary of the networks' boundaries, the whole exercise is repeated on the sub-network when two firms are linked if, and only if, they share at least one "qualified" board member, that is president, vice president, or CEO, on one of the two boards (leading role—LR).

Table 11.2 presents the average number of firms belonging to a group for the two methods we have illustrated. As appears clearly in all periods, the average boundaries of each group are always large, showing an inverted U-shape form with an apex reached in 1960. In order to provide a rough estimate of the relevance of the top fifteen business groups, we have chosen to use total assets, information which is available for each single company included in the dataset. In order to define the size of the single group, we first calculated its boundaries with the two methodologies described above: namely, all roles (AR) and leading roles (LR).

However, this method, which takes into account all shares (As), suffers from double counting because the same firm could be controlled by more than one group. For this reason, and to solve the double-counting problem, a second approach has been developed. It allows us to split the firm into as many equal shares as the board members that are also in the holding, and then assign one share to each group (for example, if group 1 has two board members, and groups 2 and 3 have one board member each, group 1 will get one half of the firm, while the other two groups will get one quarter each). We call this latter approach weighted shares (Ws). This reduced approach will give us a lower boundary to the previous one, because now each firm that was previously controlled by one or more groups may be controlled by fewer.

Figure 11.3 reports the average weight by total assets of each of the first fifteen groups as a percentage of the total of the joint-stock companies included in Imita.db, by each benchmark, calculated with the two different methodologies described above and both for all shares (As) and, in order to avoid duplication, for weighted shares (Ws).

After illustrating the average weight of the groups, in Figure 11.4 we report the total weight of the top fifteen groups, for total assets and share capital, on the Italian

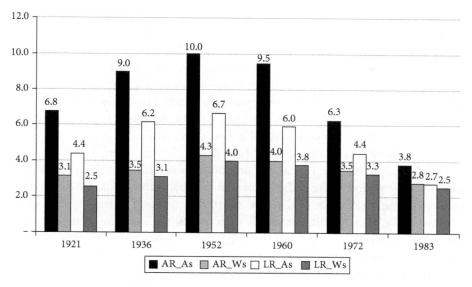

FIGURE 11.3. Average weight (percent) of the total assets of the first fifteen groups on the total of joint-stock companies in Imita.db.

Source: Colli and Vasta (2015): Fig. 4.

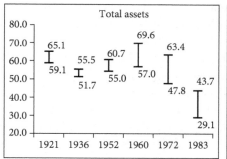
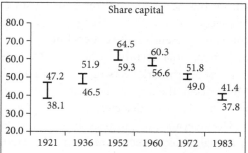

FIGURE 11.4. Weight of the top fifteen groups on the total capital and assets of companies included in Imita.db.

Source: Colli and Vasta (2015): Fig. 6.

joint-stock companies for the lower and the upper boundaries. It is worth noting that the values are calculated following the weighted-share method, which allows us to avoid duplication. The trend is quite evident. The relevance of business groups in the Italian economy is confirmed: both private and under the control of the state, they grow steadily in the interwar period, and again after World War II until the 1960s. This is the phase of catching up to Second Industrial Revolution trajectories in which the strategy is to reach the minimum efficient size following the technologically driven vertical integration. This is particularly true both for the private electrical business groups—including Sade and Edison—which proceeded through the aggregation of smaller companies previously operating upon a local basis and for state-owned business groups which, being active in a wide variety of sectors, followed "Leviathan's logic." In the following years this relevance steadily vanishes, although its weight still remains considerable. Whatever the calculation methodology used for 1983, the incidence of the first fifteen business groups on the universe of joint-stock companies considered is lower by 30–40 percent of that registered in 1960. The crisis and restructuring processes of the late 1960s, 1970s, and early 1980s definitely impacted heavily on business groups, weakening the internal cohesion of companies.

More specifically, we can observe that before World War II private, family-controlled groups, such as Fiat and Montecatini, prevailed both in terms of capital and assets. The period between the 1950s and the end of the 1960s is characterized by the overwhelming relevance of the state-controlled groups, particularly of the largest and most articulated, the IRI. From the early 1970s, the situation changes again. As seen above, the overall relevance of the largest groups diminishes, while that of state-controlled groups remains higher than average—also due to the fact that the crisis caused them to enlarge their boundaries through rescues and acquisitions.

The dynamics of the largest business groups allows other considerations—for instance, the longevity of the leading enterprises in the sample. The overall number of leading companies present at least once in the sample is forty-three (see Appendix 1). Of them, twenty-five are present only once, which suggests a relative instability and turbulence in the top ranks of Italian capitalism, where big business seems to be relatively unstable in the long run, whatever the reason for this may be. The sole company present in all six benchmark years is Fiat, followed, with fewer occurrences, by Pirelli, Snia (synthetic fibers), Stet (telephones), and Edison (electricity, in the last two benchmark years merged with another big group, Montecatini, giving birth to Montedison, the largest chemical group in the country). This picture is fully consistent with the dynamics detected among the top 200 Italian firms (Vasta, 2006b: 99ff).

The relevance of business groups in Italian capitalism has emerged clearly above. Although it decreased throughout the period, its crucial role is still evident in the 1980s. Moreover, it must be said that the empirical analysis has offered a prudential estimate of the relevance of business groups in the Italian economy. Indeed, we have always only considered, with different methodologies, the link at distance one between the holding and other firms. The capacity of a holding to influence the strategy of the firms in the holding goes well beyond the direct link, and thus it must be considered that the influence of business groups is probably larger than our estimate. In order to offer a case of the pervasiveness of the influence of the groups, in Figure 11.5 we present an example of the boundaries of the Fiat group. In particular, Figure 11.5a shows the network between one of the most important groups in the country throughout the period under consideration, Fiat (holding), and its "neighborhood," i.e., those firms which share at least one member on their board with Fiat. This is the method used in this chapter so far. In Figure 115b we add to these "direct" links those firms which share at least one member on their board with a firm in Fiat's "neighborhood." In the language of network theory, this set of nodes (i.e., firms) is

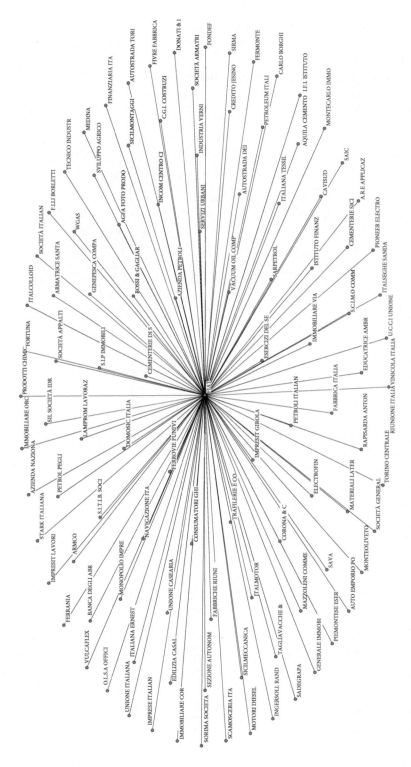

FIGURE 11.5A. Fiat and its "neighborhood" (distance 1) in 1960.

Source: Colli and Vasta (2015): Fig. 7.

called the "neighborhood" of distance two of the Fiat node. It clearly emerges how the influence of the business group could be larger than what we have offered in our "prudential" estimates.

The importance of business groups in Italian capitalism is still considerable today. Table 11.3 presents the top fifteen non-financial Italian business groups for turnover

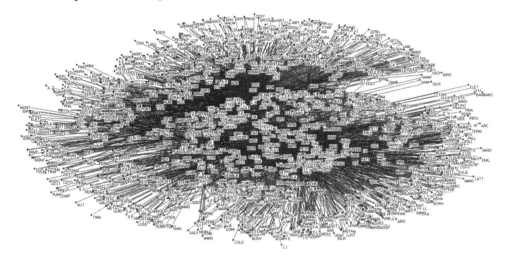

FIGURE 11.5B Fiat and its "neighborhood" (distance 2) in 1960.
Source: Colli and Vasta (2015): Fig. 7.

Table 11.3. Business groups (non-financial) by turnover, 2013.

#	Group's name	Sector of main activity	Type of owner	Turnover (billions of euro)	Number of employees
1	Eni	Petroleum fuels, natural gas, mineral oils, and petrochemicals	State-controlled	114.7	82,289
2	Exor	Vehicles, and several others	Private	113.7	305,963
3	Enel	Production, distribution, and trade of electricity and gas	State-controlled	78.1	71,394
4	GSE - Gestore dei Servizi Energetici	Production, distribution, and trade of electricity and gas	State-controlled	34.3	1,277
5	Telecom Italia	Telecommunications	Private	22.9	59,527
6	Finmeccanica	Aerospace, defense, and security	State-controlled	16.0	63,835
7	Edison	Production, distribution, and trade of electricity and gas	Private	12.3	3,250
8	Edizione	Miscellaneous industries, mainly manufacturing, services, and distribution	Private	12.3	71,257

9	Saras - Raffinerie Sarde	Petroleum fuels, natural gas, mineral oils, and petrochemicals	Private	11.1	1,837
10	Poste Italiane	Public services	State-controlled	9.4	145,431
11	Kuwait Petroleum Italia	Petroleum fuels, natural gas, mineral oils, and petrochemicals	Private	7.8	904
12	Ferrovie dello Stato Italiane	Airlines, shipping, road, and rail transport undertakings and ancillary services	State-controlled	7.6	69,425
13	Luxottica Group	Eyewear, frames, and lenses	Private	7.3	73,415
14	Prysmian	Rubber, cables, and allied products	Private	7.3	19,374
15	Supermarkets Italiani	Retailing and wholesale in general	Private	6.8	20,605

Note: The above list includes the different varieties of business groups analyzed throughout this chapter, which include diversified and specialized as well as state- and family-owned groups.

Source: Compiled from Mediobanca (2014): Tab. 1.

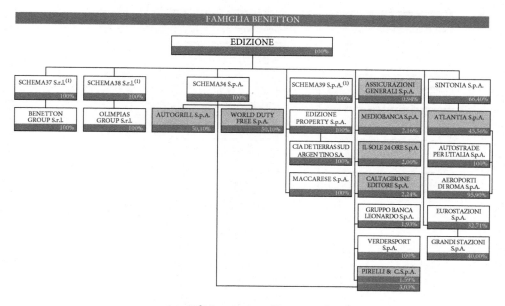

FIGURE 11.6A. Edizione group (Benetton family group).

in 2013. First of all we see that all the main, most important private firms are represented: Fiat (controlled by the holding Exor), Benetton (Edizione), Moratti family (Saras), Del Vecchio family (Luxottica), Pirelli (Prysmian), and Caprotti family (Italiani supermarkets). Secondly, the huge importance of state-controlled business groups is clear considering that they are the majority in the list (eight out of fifteen) and

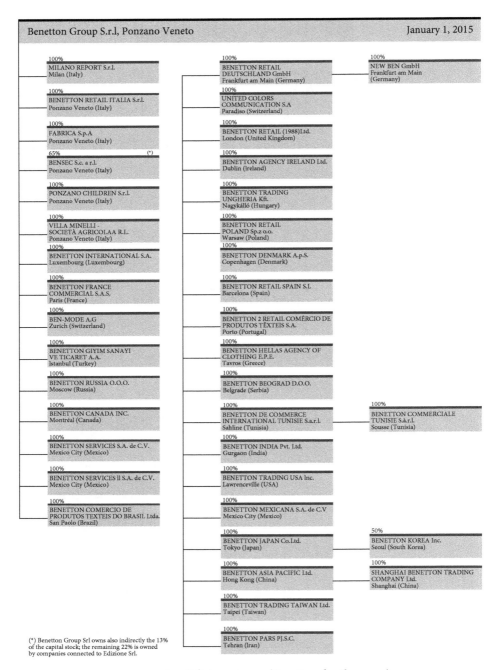

FIGURE **11.6B.** Edizione group (Benetton family group).

Source: www.edizione.it and www.benetton.it. Accessed April 9, 2015.

that, among the top six, there are four public enterprises. Moreover, their size is impressive in comparison with other private groups, apart from Exor.

The case of the business group related to the Benetton family (shown in Figure 11.6) looks particularly effective in explaining the recent process of growth of business groups in Italy. Benetton started as a family-run small business in the early 1950s and rapidly expanded and consolidated, particularly in the 1980s when it began a process of related diversification in the field of apparel and sports gear accompanied by a strategy of horizontal and vertical integration, which resulted in the creation of subsidiaries, partially or fully controlled (Figure 11.6b). Towards the end of the 1980s the Benetton family started a strategy of non-related diversification, investing in very different areas. This strategy was boosted by the privatization process introduced by the Italian government at the beginning of the 1990s. The Benetton family acquired control of former state-owned enterprises, in food retail and distribution (Autogrill), controlled-access highways (Società Autostrade), and infrastructures (Aeroporti di Roma). Initially, the diversification process was managed through a holding company (Edizione Holding), which acted as a final "strongbox" of the various investments undertaken by the company. More recently, Edizione Holding changed its name to Edizione (Figure 11.6a) and a process of reorganization took place. Edizione now controls a series of sub-holdings, each in charge of a segment of the whole group's activity, ranging from clothes retailing (Benetton Group), textile production (Olimpias Group), duty free and retailing (Autogrill and, until very recently, World Duty Free), real estate, infrastructure (Sintonia spa), and miscellaneous minority holdings.

11.6 Why are Business Groups so Resilient in the Italian Economy?

After proposing a taxonomy of different business groups, and a very rough estimation of their relevance over the whole national economy in the long term, this section discusses the reasons why Italian entrepreneurs (in all forms of enterprise) preferred to grow by creating business groups with legally independent subsidiaries rather than trying to develop large M-form corporations with integrated internal divisions. A longitudinal analysis of the persisting diffusion of business groups in Italy highlights at least *six* relevant determinants of the diffusion and persistence of business groups in Italy during the twentieth century and at the beginning of twenty-first century.

A *first* reason refers to the business group as an instrument to enhance the control of dominant shareholders with a limited investment of their own resources through pyramidal arrangements, an explanation which, in turn, is connected to institutional determinants, among which is the presence of favorable legislation, or at least the absence of rules limiting some kind of leverage effect. Above all—and in the case of Italy this seems particularly evident—limits to the dimension and quality of the domestic financial markets, and the absence of specialized financial institutions, play a relevant role in incentivizing the formation of business groups through which the dominant shareholders obtain resources from the stock market without losing much of their decision power. This happened several times in the course of the history of Italian capitalism. Initially, up to the Second World War, private big business created multi-layered enterprises to catch up with the technological paradigm of the Second Industrial Revolution, a strategy which was also followed after the war by state-owned enterprises (Colli, 2013). Similarly, benefiting from a sudden vitality of the stock market during the 1980s, many private corporations—such as Fiat—spun off divisions and listed them in order to collect financial resources from a vibrant stock market (Brioschi, Buzzacchi, and Colombo, 1990).

Secondly, business groups provide more freedom and incentives to the subsidiaries' management, something which is more difficult in an integrated organization in which the headquarters has a strong grip on the divisions and in which the management's decision power is severely constrained. This is a crucial point, which deserves a more detailed explanation. The existence of this potential incentive to the formation of business groups was already noted by one of the components of the above-mentioned Harvard group, Robert J. Pavan, in a piece following up his major research on the strategies and structures of the Italian corporations (Pavan, 1978). Extending his longitudinal analysis, which originally covered 1945 to 1970, to the period up to 1977, he found that the trend towards diversification of the activities among large firms, which led to an increasing (even if still insufficient) adoption of divisional structures, was creating a new situation, which saw divisions progressively transformed into legally independent subsidiaries coordinated by a corporate office (in its turn, the holding company). On its side, the fiscal and legal system allowed and incentivized the process; but behind this, according to Pavan (1978: 5–6), "It was necessary to proceed beyond divisions, entrusting to separate companies the management of most important sectors, with the aim of attaining a major level of productive and sales efficiency, through an autonomous management, more flexible and sensitive to the specific market problems and their tendencies." The creation of legally independent subsidiaries, sometimes specialized and of smaller dimensions, was the Italian solution to the problem of coping with diversification, flexibility, and management independence. What Pavan pointed out was, to a certain extent, a sort of global trait: independence of divisions was ensured by separate legal status more than a mature managerial culture resulting in a real autonomy of professional management, at least in the Italian case. The trait of management independence is also a leitmotiv in the case of medium-sized companies, quite recent protagonists in the Italian corporate landscape which, as recalled before, largely use group forms to manage their business. In this case, a determinant element is the presence of an owner family: the creation of a group makes it possible to separate power and responsibilities across members of the family, thus avoiding conflicts among them and, at the same time, providing a sort of equal "endowment" to siblings.

Thirdly, the group structure is simply the only possible structure when, for some reason, it is necessary to maintain a legal separation among companies. A couple of examples will clarify this point. The first example refers to the case of the family firm Luigi Fontana Spa, a bolts-and-screws producer which progressively became, since the 1960s, one of the most important suppliers to the expanding automotive industry (Colli and Merlo, 2006). Together with a strategy of internal growth, the company started to make a number of acquisitions, taking over smaller, entrepreneurial companies in the same industry. These companies were, however, not merged into the main one, nor transformed into divisions. Luigi Fontana SpA transformed itself into a sort of "operating holding company," at the same time exerting the role of producer and that of central office of the subsidiaries, each one characterized by a high degree of independence which largely reflected their previous status as independent companies. The reasons put forward to explain this behavior were basically twofold: to preserve the autonomy of the acquired company's management (in some cases, the former owners transformed into managers); and to approach the automotive companies with different brands and products, which were not to be perceived as part of one single company. A second example refers to the creation of joint ventures among different companies. Joint ventures involve, by definition, a partial share-ownership quota in companies which are independent and not divisions. The more a country is characterized by the presence of joint ventures (for instance, between local domestic companies and more technologically advanced foreign companies), the more this will result in the creation of partially owned subsidiaries. Looking, for instance, at the history of the most important Italian oil and gas producer, the state-owned ENI, it becomes clear how a large section of the ENI's subsidiaries are de facto joint ventures with foreign companies in order to get new technologies, for instance in the field of chemicals, plastics, and polymers. A third example of "forced" creation of a group is the case of cooperatives expanding their boundaries. The incorporation of new activities into the boundaries of the cooperative with a simple process of merger, integration, and internal growth would mean that the new activities were subject to the corporate regulation of the cooperative sector: for instance, the fundamental pillar that one vote corresponds not to a share but to a head. With the progressive dilution over recent decades of a strong ideological push, both of socialist/communist and catholic inspiration, the incentive for the top management of the most important cooperatives—sometimes of a relevant size to get a firm control over the new activities—becomes high.[11] This, added to the presence of favorable legislation which from the early 1970s allowed cooperatives to own shares, led to the progressive creation of business groups, composed of a cluster of joint-stock companies headed by a holding/operative company, i.e., the former original cooperative.

A *fourth* possible explanation for the diffusion of business groups lies in the fact that this form proved very effective in accommodating the pressure of both local

---

[11] In 2010 co-ops accounted for 10 percent of all Italian enterprises with more than 500 employees. Larger co-ops have become market leaders in Italy in some sectors, e.g., large-scale retailing, construction, and agri-food. For further details, see Battilani and Zamagni (2010; 2012).

shareholders and stakeholders. This was particularly the case for specialized business groups that were formed in the public utilities from the aggregation of the former municipalized companies. In this case the setting-up of a separate subsidiary—with its own staff and board of directors—in each local context (a province or a union of municipalities) is used by the business group to create new offices for individuals connected with local politics and, in a wider sense, for the interaction between the business group and the local community.

Fifth, fiscal policies play a relevant role, especially when they neutralize the difference between a business group and other forms of organization (such as the M-form). Large business groups can have better access to credit than large integrated organizations, leveraging on and redistributing the resources and value created by the most profitable subsidiaries. Moreover, the business group structure better allows, both for private and public business groups, the tunneling of resources from companies where the holding has low cash rights to companies where it has high cash rights. Another peculiar situation is where the multiplication of subsidiaries is due to the opportunity to obtain resources in the form of incentives and subsidies from public institutions. In Italy, the policies aimed at fostering the industrialization of the south were largely based on the concession of tax exemptions, loans, but also of direct subsidies. This led some private entrepreneurs to create business groups characterized by a wide number of subsidiaries, each one separately asking for public support, as happened in the case of the Rovelli group, a chemical company which invested in Sardinia and over a few years opened hundreds of subsidiaries, each receiving funds from the state.

A *sixth*, far less unplanned, case occurs when a company is acquired, or becomes part of an existing group by chance or following an unplanned event, and in particular when the buyer is allowed to buy only a partial, even significant, stake in the company, something which does not allow a full integration of the acquired company into a division. This was quite frequent in Italy in the case of banks, which up to the early 1930s frequently became controlling shareholders after taking over a distressed company (Confalonieri, 1992), or in the case of larger companies called to rescue minor ones thanks to their close *do ut des* relationships with the political power interested in such rescues for social reasons—as happened in the case of a chemical company Montecatini, which in the 1930s transformed itself into a group after having rescued (under pressure from the government) companies in the mining and textile industries (Amatori and Bezza, 1990). The problem with this process was the presence of a variable number of minority shareholders in the acquired company, something which could in principle create some governance problems and which finally made a full takeover of the rescued company more complex so that it had to be left as an independent legal entity. Probably the most obvious example of this practice was the above-mentioned creation, almost overnight, of the largest Italian business group, the IRI, under the control of the state. As already mentioned, the strategy at the basis of the creation of the IRI was to manage the emergency situation of the financial crisis of the three largest banks in the country. In short, the state acquired all the shares of companies in the banks' portfolios, in this way de facto rescuing the banks and putting them into one single large portfolio—that of the IRI. In this way the IRI directly controlled, as has been calculated, a quarter of the nominal capital of Italian joint-stock companies. This was rarely, however, a full ownership, which made it impossible to create a standard-type M-form with internal divisions. In addition, it was soon clear that this situation allowed the IRI to leverage control, in particular of listed companies, exactly as happened to private companies. Of course, the IRI formula, which started as a sort of emerging strategy, soon became a standard for almost all the large State-owned concerns in many sectors.

11.7 CONCLUSION

This chapter has shown that business groups are not a static component of the Italian industrial landscape, even if the rationale for their existence constantly modifies over time according to institutional and technological changes. Notwithstanding the changes in the rationale for their existence, the relevance of business groups within Italian capitalism, measured by the network analysis, has been constant and significant whatever proxy measures (companies involved, share capital, and assets) are taken into account, even if a declining trend is certainly evident in recent decades.

Even if the different streams of literature were well aware, at least since the 1930s, of the existence of the business group as a dominant form of organization and control in the history of Italian capitalism, many of these studies have mainly provided blurred pictures or detailed reconstruction, avoiding any systematization of the issue. Starting in the 1990s, with the diffusion of a new theoretical approach to corporate governance, some studies of Italy have also highlighted the role played by pyramidal groups as mechanisms set up in order to leverage control by relevant shareholders. Following this pattern, and adopting an approach which explicitly takes into account the variety of the forms of enterprise, in this chapter we have introduced both a taxonomy and a periodization of business groups within Italian capitalism.

Finally, this chapter shows that business groups are present not only among large firms but in almost all the dimensional and juridical forms of Italian firms. This challenges the conventional wisdom that assumed that business groups are (more or less) simply an *alternative* to the M-form characterizing big business around the world.

In conclusion, we can sum up this chapter by stating that, in the case of Italy, business groups as an organizational model look particularly flexible, adapting themselves to different ownership and market conditions. In the absence of hurdles of a legal or fiscal nature, this flexibility is probably the main reason for its resilience. This suggests further investigation of the institutional determinants of its adoption, i.e., if, why, and how policymakers incentivized, or at least did not hinder, the formation of business groups instead of integrated, divisional structures. An analysis of this is beyond the scope of the present chapter.

Acknowledgments

We would like to thank Asli Colpan and Takashi Hikino for their comments and help along the whole research project. This paper has also benefited from the comments of all participants of the Conference "Business groups in the West: the evolutionary dynamics of big business" (Kyoto, March 2014), and of the Session "Diversity in the evolution of big business: business groups in mature industrial economies" at the XVIIth World Economic History Congress (Kyoto, August 2015).

APPENDIX

List of Italian business groups with their boundaries for number of companies (leading roles [LR]—left side—and all roles [AR]—right side—methods).

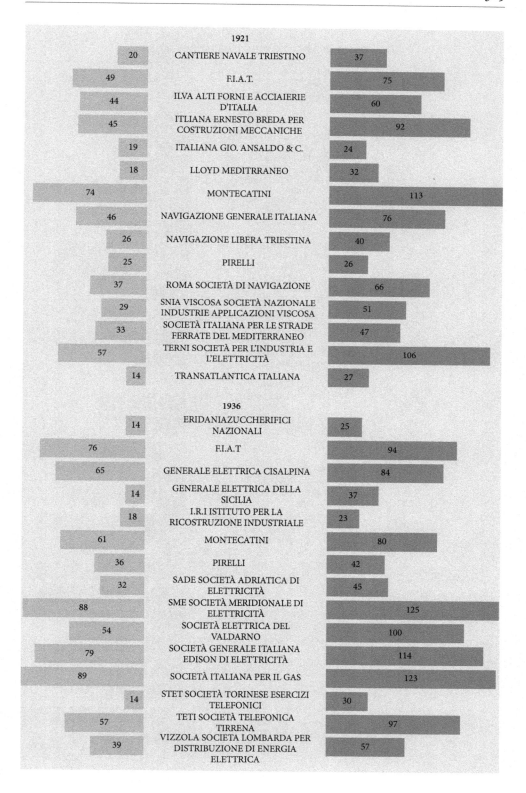

1921

20	CANTIERE NAVALE TRIESTINO	37
49	F.I.A.T.	75
44	ILVA ALTI FORNI E ACCIAIERIE D'ITALIA	60
45	ITLIANA ERNESTO BREDA PER COSTRUZIONI MECCANICHE	92
19	ITALIANA GIO. ANSALDO & C.	24
18	LLOYD MEDITRRANEO	32
74	MONTECATINI	113
46	NAVIGAZIONE GENERALE ITALIANA	76
26	NAVIGAZIONE LIBERA TRIESTINA	40
25	PIRELLI	26
37	ROMA SOCIETÀ DI NAVIGAZIONE	66
29	SNIA VISCOSA SOCIETÀ NAZIONALE INDUSTRIE APPLICAZIONI VISCOSA	51
33	SOCIETÀ ITALIANA PER LE STRADE FERRATE DEL MEDITERRANEO	47
57	TERNI SOCIETÀ PER L'INDUSTRIA E L'ELETTRICITÀ	106
14	TRANSATLANTICA ITALIANA	27

1936

14	ERIDANIAZUCCHERIFICI NAZIONALI	25
76	F.I.A.T	94
65	GENERALE ELETTRICA CISALPINA	84
14	GENERALE ELETTRICA DELLA SICILIA	37
18	I.R.I ISTITUTO PER LA RICOSTRUZIONE INDUSTRIALE	23
61	MONTECATINI	80
36	PIRELLI	42
32	SADE SOCIETÀ ADRIATICA DI ELETTRICITÀ	45
88	SME SOCIETÀ MERIDIONALE DI ELETTRICITÀ	125
54	SOCIETÀ ELETTRICA DEL VALDARNO	100
79	SOCIETÀ GENERALE ITALIANA EDISON DI ELETTRICITÀ	114
89	SOCIETÀ ITALIANA PER IL GAS	123
14	STET SOCIETÀ TORINESE ESERCIZI TELEFONICI	30
57	TETI SOCIETÀ TELEFONICA TIRRENA	97
39	VIZZOLA SOCIETA LOMBARDA PER DISTRIBUZIONE DI ENERGIA ELETTRICA	57

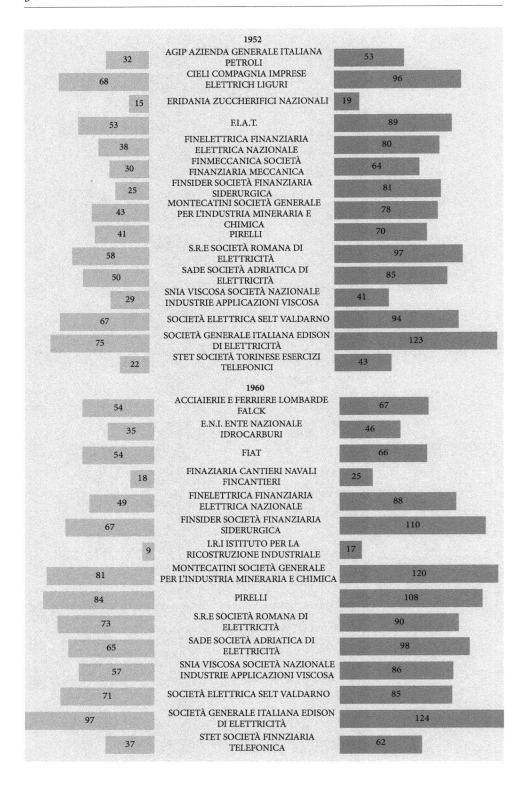

1952

32	AGIP AZIENDA GENERALE ITALIANA PETROLI	53
68	CIELI COMPAGNIA IMPRESE ELETTRICH LIGURI	96
15	ERIDANIA ZUCCHERIFICI NAZIONALI	19
53	F.I.A.T.	89
38	FINELETTRICA FINANZIARIA ELETTRICA NAZIONALE	80
30	FINMECCANICA SOCIETÀ FINANZIARIA MECCANICA	64
25	FINSIDER SOCIETÀ FINANZIARIA SIDERURGICA	81
43	MONTECATINI SOCIETÀ GENERALE PER L'INDUSTRIA MINERARIA E CHIMICA	78
41	PIRELLI	70
58	S.R.E SOCIETÀ ROMANA DI ELETTRICITÀ	97
50	SADE SOCIETÀ ADRIATICA DI ELETTRICITÀ	85
29	SNIA VISCOSA SOCIETÀ NAZIONALE INDUSTRIE APPLICAZIONI VISCOSA	41
67	SOCIETÀ ELETTRICA SELT VALDARNO	94
75	SOCIETÀ GENERALE ITALIANA EDISON DI ELETTRICITÀ	123
22	STET SOCIETÀ TORINESE ESERCIZI TELEFONICI	43

1960

54	ACCIAIERIE E FERRIERE LOMBARDE FALCK	67
35	E.N.I. ENTE NAZIONALE IDROCARBURI	46
54	FIAT	66
18	FINAZIARIA CANTIERI NAVALI FINCANTIERI	25
49	FINELETTRICA FINANZIARIA ELETTRICA NAZIONALE	88
67	FINSIDER SOCIETÀ FINANZIARIA SIDERURGICA	110
9	I.R.I ISTITUTO PER LA RICOSTRUZIONE INDUSTRIALE	17
81	MONTECATINI SOCIETÀ GENERALE PER L'INDUSTRIA MINERARIA E CHIMICA	120
84	PIRELLI	108
73	S.R.E SOCIETÀ ROMANA DI ELETTRICITÀ	90
65	SADE SOCIETÀ ADRIATICA DI ELETTRICITÀ	98
57	SNIA VISCOSA SOCIETÀ NAZIONALE INDUSTRIE APPLICAZIONI VISCOSA	86
71	SOCIETÀ ELETTRICA SELT VALDARNO	85
97	SOCIETÀ GENERALE ITALIANA EDISON DI ELETTRICITÀ	124
37	STET SOCIETÀ FINNZIARIA TELEFONICA	62

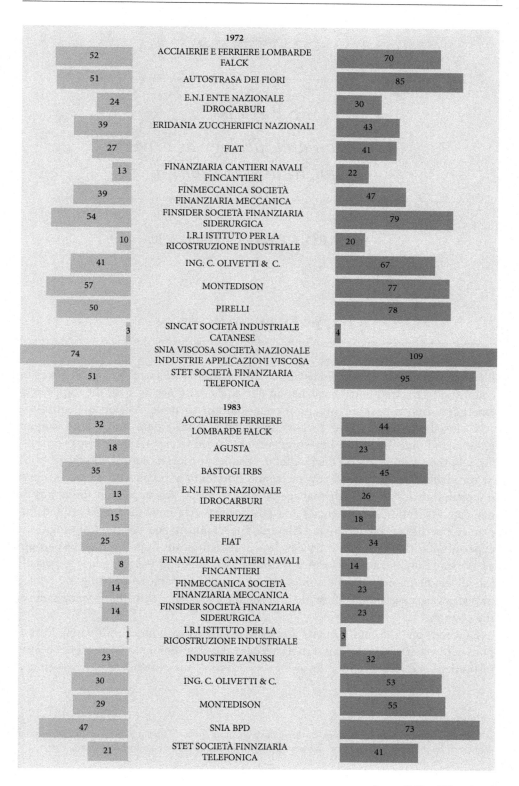

1972

52	ACCIAIERIE E FERRIERE LOMBARDE FALCK	70
51	AUTOSTRASA DEI FIORI	85
24	E.N.I ENTE NAZIONALE IDROCARBURI	30
39	ERIDANIA ZUCCHERIFICI NAZIONALI	43
27	FIAT	41
13	FINANZIARIA CANTIERI NAVALI FINCANTIERI	22
39	FINMECCANICA SOCIETÀ FINANZIARIA MECCANICA	47
54	FINSIDER SOCIETÀ FINANZIARIA SIDERURGICA	79
10	I.R.I ISTITUTO PER LA RICOSTRUZIONE INDUSTRIALE	20
41	ING. C. OLIVETTI & C.	67
57	MONTEDISON	77
50	PIRELLI	78
3	SINCAT SOCIETÀ INDUSTRIALE CATANESE	4
74	SNIA VISCOSA SOCIETÀ NAZIONALE INDUSTRIE APPLICAZIONI VISCOSA	109
51	STET SOCIETÀ FINANZIARIA TELEFONICA	95

1983

32	ACCIAIERIEE FERRIERE LOMBARDE FALCK	44
18	AGUSTA	23
35	BASTOGI IRBS	45
13	E.N.I ENTE NAZIONALE IDROCARBURI	26
15	FERRUZZI	18
25	FIAT	34
8	FINANZIARIA CANTIERI NAVALI FINCANTIERI	14
14	FINMECCANICA SOCIETÀ FINANZIARIA MECCANICA	23
14	FINSIDER SOCIETÀ FINANZIARIA SIDERURGICA	23
1	I.R.I ISTITUTO PER LA RICOSTRUZIONE INDUSTRIALE	3
23	INDUSTRIE ZANUSSI	32
30	ING. C. OLIVETTI & C.	53
29	MONTEDISON	55
47	SNIA BPD	73
21	STET SOCIETÀ FINNZIARIA TELEFONICA	41

Source: Colli and Vasta (2015).

CHAPTER 12

....

SPAIN

regulation and ideology as drivers
for transformation

....

ALVARO CUERVO-CAZURRA

12.1 INTRODUCTION

....

BUSINESS groups have been discussed as an organizational form typical of emerging countries.[1] The traditional explanation for their existence is that they appear in emerging countries as an organizational solution to underdeveloped institutions and closed economies (see reviews in Khanna and Yafeh, 2007, and Colpan, Hikino, and Lincoln, 2010). Entrepreneurs are forced to expand their firms vertically because they cannot rely on the market to ensure appropriate supply and distribution or on institutions to defend contracts; and horizontally because there are business opportunities for those with managerial and financial resources and the ability to navigate institutional deficiencies and government relationships under limited foreign competition (Ghemawat and Khanna, 1998; Guillen, 2000). Under this logic, the expectation is that as the country develops and institutions improve, business groups as a distinct organizational form will decline (Khanna and Palepu, 2000), especially the diversified ones, transforming into focused companies operating in related industries because the logic for their existence disappears with the development of the country.

However, one can find business groups in advanced economies with strong institutions and open markets. This fact challenges the conventional explanation of weak institutions and closed economies as the sole drivers of the existence of business groups.

---

[1] This chapter covers four types of diversified business groups (that are present in the Spanish economy) by their ownership: state-owned, bank-owned, family-owned, and labor-owned.

Therefore, to understand this apparent contradiction in the literature, I analyze the evolution of business groups in Spain since the middle of the twentieth century, separating them into four types according to their ownership (Cuervo-Cazurra, 2006): state-owned, bank-owned, family-owned, and labor-owned. The four types of business groups show behavioral differences that challenge the universalistic explanation for the existence of business groups. First, state-owned business groups expanded as a result of the ideology of import substitution and social stability and continued to exist, although reduced in scope, after the implementation of pro-market reforms, following the ideology of social stability and strategic development. Second, bank-owned business groups expanded as a result of regulatory incentives, but declined and in some cases disappeared with the deregulation that accompanied pro-market reforms. Third, family-owned business groups emerged to take advantage of growth opportunities in a closed and regulated economy, refocused their activities with the deregulation and competitive pressures of pro-market reforms, but maintained some diversification to benefit from business opportunities. Finally, labor-owned business groups emerged as a result of an ideology of social development and solidarity, and continued in existence after pro-market reforms.

Thus, the analysis of business groups in Spain reveals two additional drivers of the existence and transformation of business groups—regulation and owner ideology—that complement the traditional explanations of weak institutions and closed economies. First, regulation of the industry by the government leads to the creation of business groups as owners and managers face a limited scope of activities and are forced to diversify their firms into other industries in search of growth and opportunities to use excess entrepreneurial and financial resources. However, pro-market reforms and the associated deregulation result in the transformation of business groups, initially expanding diversification as they are allowed entry into new industries, and later reducing diversification as they face increased competition. Some business groups may even disappear as distinct organizational forms, with the individual firms continuing their activities as independent ventures or as parts of other firms. Second, owner ideology leads some business groups to expand and diversify activities to achieve social and economic development. Although pro-market reforms may lead to a reduction of diversification because some businesses are unable to remain competitive, the business groups nevertheless continue in existence as diversified ventures because owner ideology rather than financial returns dictates the continued diversification.

In the next section I provide an overview of the development of Spain in the twentieth and twenty-first centuries, and then I present some statistics on the importance of business groups. After this I discuss the four types of business groups and their differing objectives. I illustrate each type by reviewing the history of selected groups. I conclude with a review of how the analysis of business groups in Spain provides new insights that advance theory.

12.2 THE EVOLUTION OF THE ECONOMY AND BUSINESS IN SPAIN

In the early twentieth century Spain suffered from political instability and economic weakness (more detailed historical explanations appear in Nadal, Carreras, and Sudria, 1991; Tamames, 1992; and Tortella, 1994). The early industrialization wave of the late nineteenth century, funded in part by foreign capital and the repatriation of capital from the former colonies, resulted in the establishment of some industrial poles in extractive and heavy industries, but Spain suffered from weak human capital (Tamames, 1992). Political upheaval and aristocratic control of the economy that benefited a few slowed its economic development (Tortella, 1994). Although the country benefited from its neutrality during the First World War, it experienced a crisis after the end of the conflict and during the Moroccan wars in the 1920s. The dictatorship of Primo de Rivera (1923–30) adopted a nationalist and interventionist economic policy with public works (railroads, roads, ports, hydroelectric dams), regulation of industries (national councils of rice, resin, gasoline, economy), monopolies (gasoline distribution, telecommunications), and state-owned banks. The global crisis of 1929 created additional upheaval, and the country became politically polarized during the Second Republic of 1931–9.

The destruction of the economic and human infrastructure during the Civil War of 1936–9, which led to the dictatorship of Francisco Franco until 1975, and the subsequent autarchic period of the 1940s resulted in a poor country with a weak industrial base. During the autarchic period, the state took a leading role in the development of the country, creating state-owned firms, regulating competition, and inducing banks to invest in the capital of industrial firms. The opening of the country to foreign investment and trade after 1959 ignited a period of rapid industrialization and the economic miracle of the 1960s. This period resulted in the entry of many foreign-owned firms as well as the growth and diversification of family-owned firms, while the government changed its participation in the economy from engine of economic development to support of private investors.

In the 1970s Spain suffered a deep economic crisis while dealing with the political transition from dictatorship to democracy, which led to a deep transformation in the economic model. The economic crisis of the 1970s that accompanied the oil embargoes of 1973 and 1979 proved fatal to many firms, and the government ended up intervening and nationalizing many to support employment and development. At the same time, the country had to manage a political transition after the death of dictator Franco in 1975, which added political upheaval. The new, democratically elected government embarked on a program to achieve economic stability in support of the political transition from dictatorship to democracy. A socialist government gained power in 1982 and—despite its socialist rhetoric—started a program of pro-market reforms that dismantled the state-led economy via the deregulation of industries, liberalization of prices, and privatization of state-owned companies. This was done partly to deal with the crisis and partly to adjust to the requirements imposed by Spain's impending entrance into the European Economic Community in 1986. Although the deregulation and privatization of state-owned firms provided additional opportunities for diversification and growth for business groups, the increase in competition countered this and led many business groups to rethink their operations. As some of the groups expanded abroad, they further streamlined their operations to achieve the necessary size and competitiveness for global competition, becoming leading multinationals (Guillén and García-Canal, 2010).

The high growth of the boom years of the 1990s and 2000s supported the growth, improvement, and expansion of firms abroad. However, the 2008–16 economic crisis questioned the viability of many business models. Some leading firms even went bankrupt, weighted down by high leverage levels incurred during the boom years. Despite the crisis, by 2016 there were still large business groups operating in the country.

12.3 LARGE FIRMS AND BUSINESS GROUPS IN SPAIN

The identification of business groups in Spain is notoriously difficult. This is partly because their complex cross-ownership and pyramidal structures complicate their analysis, and partly because there is limited historical information on firms (Crespí-Cladera and García-Cestona, 2001). In this study I define business groups as collections of legally independent firms linked by ownership and operating in unrelated industries under some degree of strategic coordination.

One indirect way to identify business groups is to start with a list of the largest companies in Spain. Although not all large firms are business groups and not all business groups are large, many business groups are large. Thus, given the paucity of data, I start the identification of business groups in Spain by studying large firms. One systematic listing of the largest firms in Spain, which provides the longest historical coverage, appears in the biweekly economic magazine *Fomento de la Producción*. This annual list, which began with a list of the 200 largest companies by sales in 1970, was gradually expanded to include the largest 2,500 after 1975. The list includes foreign, state-owned, and private companies operating in Spain, ranked by sales, and provides some basic information such as sales, assets, employees, profits, industry, and a brief description of the firm and its activities.

Table 12.1 presents the twenty-five largest firms operating in Spain in selected years, ranked by sales. The list illustrates the transformation of companies in the country. In the 1970s most of the largest firms were either state-owned or foreign-owned. In the 1980s and 1990s private firms started to supplant state-owned firms as the latter were privatized. In the 2000s state-owned firms were almost absent among the largest firms,

Table 12.1. Largest firms in Spain ranked by sales, selected years.

	1970				1980				1990			
	Company	Industry	Revenue, billions of pesetas	BG	Company	Industry	Revenue, billions of pesetas	BG	Company	Industry	Revenue, billions of pesetas	BG
1	Seat	Automobiles	30	s	Campsa	Petroleum	832	s	Telefónica de España	Telecom	852	s
2	CEPSA	Petroleum	23	b	E.N. de Petroleos	Petroleum	358	s	El Corte Inglés	Retail	662	F
3	Dragados y Construcciones	Construction	21	b	CEPSA	Petroleum	267	b	Repsol Petróleo	Petroleum	571	s
4	Altos Hornos de Vizcaya	Steel	21	s	Compañía Telefónica Nacional de España	Telecom	219	s	Campsa	Petroleum	549	s
5	Unión Explosivos Río Tinto	Chemicals	21	s	Rumasa	Diversified	180	F	Tabacalera	Diversified	530	s
6	Ensidesa	Steel	19	s	Unión Explosivos Río Tinto	Chemicals	145	b	Seat	Automobiles	452	s
7	Repesa	Petroleum	19	s	Petronor	Petroleum	134	s	Fasa Renault	Automobiles	429	
8	Astilleros Españoles	Shipyard	16	s	FASA Renault	Automobiles	134	F	E. N. Electricidad	Electricity	387	s
9	Butano	Petroleum	15	s	El Corte Inglés	Retail	121	s	Iberia	Transport	375	s
10	Standard Eléctrica	Electronics	14	F	Iberia L.A.E.	Transport	121	s	General Motors España	Automobiles	365	
11	FASA Renault	Automobiles	12	s	Seat	Automobiles	117		Ford España	Automobiles	364	
12	Hidroeléctrica Española	Electricity	11	s	Ensidesa	Steel	115		Iberdrola II (Hidroeléctrica Española)	Electricity	332	

#	Company	Sector	Value		Company	Sector	Value		Company	Sector	Value	
13	Iberduero	Electricity	11		Ford España	Automobiles	93		Cepsa	Petroleum	318	b
14	E.N. de Autocamiones	Automobiles	10	s	Dragados y Construcciones	Construction	84	b	Iberdrola I (Iberduero)	Electricity	298	
15	Agromán E. Constructora	Construction	10		Iberduero	Electricity	84		Centros Comerciales Pryca	Retail	295	
16	Nestlé A.E.P.A.	Food	9		Petrolíber	Petroleum	81		Union Eléctrica Fenosa	Electricity	267	
17	Entrecanales y Tavora	Construction	9		Hidroeléctrica Española	Electricity	80		Dragados y Construcciones	Construction	259	b
18	Ebro, Azúcares y Alcoholes	Food	8	s	Renfe	Transport	78	s	Sevillana de Electricidad	Electricity	258	s
19	E.N. Calvo Sotelo	Petroleum	8	s	Butano	Petroleum	75	s	Citroen Hispania	Automobiles	234	s
20	Chrysler España	Automobiles	8		Hispanoil	Petroleum	72		Centros Comerciales Continente	Retail	227	s
21	Sevillana de Electricidad	Electricity	7		Tabacalera	Diversified	66		IBM España	IT	218	s
22	E.N. Bazán	Shipyard	7	s	E.N. Electricidad	Electricity	62	s	Petróleos del Norte	Petroleum	196	s
23	General Azucarera	Food	7		Cía. Sevillana de Electricidad	Electricity	59		Peugeot Talbot España	Automobiles	193	
24	Fuerzas Eléctr. de Cataluña	Electricity	7		Automóviles Talbot	Automobiles	59		Fuerzas Electricas de Cataluña	Electricity	191	
25	S.A. Cros	Chemicals	7		Citroën Hispania	Automobiles	59		E. N. Siderurgica	Steel	185	s

(continued)

Table 12.1. Continued

	2000			2010				2012				
	Company	Industry	Revenue, billions ofpesetas	BG	Company	Industry	Revenue, billions of pesetas	BG	Company	Industry	Revenue, billions of pesetas	BG
1	Repsol-YPF	Petroleum	7328	b	Telefónica	Telecom	10,106	b	Telefónica	Telecom	10,375	b
2	Telefónica	Telecom	4739	b	Repsol-YPF	Petroleum	9240	b	Repsol-YPF	Petroleum	9807	b
3	Endesa	Electricity	2491	b	Iberdrola	Electricity	5063		ACS	Construction	6389	
4	TI Telefónica Internacional España	Telecom	2094	b	Endesa	Electricity	4918		Iberdrola	Electricity	5691	
5	Cepsa	Petroleum	2026	b	Cepsa	Petroleum	3675		Endesa	Electricity	5372	
6	El Corte Inglés	Retail	1797		Gas Natural Fenosa	Petroleum	3266		Cepsa	Petroleum	4460	
7	Altadis	Tobacco	1266		Mercadona	Retail	2743		Repsol Petróleo	Petroleum	4146	
8	Renault España	Automobiles	1209		El Corte Inglés	Retail	2731		Gas Natural Fenosa	Petroleum	4144	
9	Iberdrola	Electricity	1158	b	ACS	Construction	2559		Repsol Comercial Prod. Petrolíferos	Petroleum	2995	
10	Centros Comerciales Carrefour	Retail	1146		Mondragón Corporación Cooperat.	Diversified	2455	L	Mercadona	Retail	2916	
11	Seat	Automobiles	1057		Industria de Diseño Textil	Apparel	2084		International Consolidated Airlines Group	Transport	2760	
12	Peugeot Citroën Automóviles España	Automobiles	962		Grupo Ferrovial	Construction	2025		Inditex	Apparel	2653	
13	Telefónica Servicios Móviles	Telecom	873	b	FCC	Construction	2016		El Corte Inglés	Retail	2421	
14	Opel España	Automobiles	818		Loterías y Apuestas del Estado	Gambling	1596	s	Mapfre	Insurance	2159	

#	BG	Firm	Sector	Value	BG	Firm	Sector	Value	BG	Firm	Sector	Value
15		Gas Natural SDG	Petroleum	814	b	Telefónica Móviles España	Telecom	1421	L	Mondragón Corporación Cooperat.	Diversified	2147
16		FCC	Construction	743		Mapfre	Insurance	1407		FCC	Construction	1856
17		Volkswagen Audi España	Automobiles	726	s	Grupo Eroski	Retail	1377	I	Endesa Energía	Electricity	1830
18		Iberia Líneas Aéreas España	Transport	718	s	Ford España	Automobiles	1364		Distribuidora Int. de Alimentación (Dia)	Retail	1685
19		Grupo Dragados	Construction	715	b	Centros Comerciales Carrefour	Retail	1349	s	Loterías y Apuestas del Estado	Gambling	1540
20		Eroski	Retail	700	l	Grupo Villar Mir	Diversified	1082	F	Gas Natural Aprovisionamientos	Petroleum	1360
21		Ford España	Automobiles	687		Vodafone España	Telecom	1061		Abengoa	Construction	1295
22		Aceralia Corporación Siderúrgica	Steel	666		Acciona	Construction	1042		Grupo Ferrovial	Construction	1279
23		Petróleos del Norte	Petroleum	601	b	VidaCaixa Grupo	Insurance	938		Centros Comerciales Carrefour	Retail	1253
24		Peugeot España	Automobiles	600		Abengoa	Construction	926		Acciona	Construction	1167
25		Grupo Ferrovial	Construction	599	F	Peugeot Citroën Automóviles	Automobiles	919	F	Grupo Villar Mir	Diversified	1132

Note: In 1999 the Spanish peseta was set at the rate of 166.386 pesetas to 1 euro, and was replaced by the Euro in 2002. Data for 2010 and 2013 were converted at that rate to facilitate comparisons across time.

Key: (BG) Business Group: (S) State-owned business group; (s) firm that belongs to state-owned business group; (B) Bank-owned business group; (b) firm that belongs to a bank-owned business group; (F) family-owned business group; (f) firm that belongs to a family-owned business group; (L) labor-owned business group; (l) firm that belongs to a labor-owned business group. Firms are considered part of a business group at participations above 5 percent of capital. Information from Fomento de la Producción, corporate websites, and newspapers.

Source: Fomento de la Producción (1972, 1981, 1991, 2001, 2011, 2013).

and foreign firms also started to disappear from among the largest firms in the country as private domestic firms grew in size thanks to their foreign expansion. By 2012 the largest firms in Spain were private companies, and most were leading multinationals.

In Table 12.1 I include an indication of whether the firm is connected to a business group, or is a business group, using qualitative information from the above-mentioned magazine. This is a tentative classification of companies since there are no lists of business groups available, and thus will likely underreport their existence. The table suggests a decline in the role of business groups among the largest firms in Spain, as a result of multiple factors. Whereas in the 1970s the state-owned business-group affiliates dominated the list of the largest firms, these lost importance from the 1990s onward with the privatization of state-owned firms. Similarly, some of the bank-owned business-group affiliates of the 1980s and 1990s stopped being affiliated with bank-owned business groups as banks reduced their holdings in industrial firms to concentrate on gaining global size in banking. Table 12.1 also shows the presence of some family-owned business groups, such as Rumasa in 1980. However, by the 2010s there were still business groups among the largest firms, such as the family-owned Villar Mir, and the labor-owned business group Mondragón Corporación Cooperativa.

It is challenging to identify the boundaries of business groups. First, for example, the economic magazine *Actualidad Económica* provides a list of the largest 1,000 groups in Spain (Actualidad Económica, 2012). However, many of these operated in related industries and their classification as diversified business groups was questionable. Second, some firms are tied together by common personal ownership and control even though they are not commonly considered business groups. For example, among Spain's billionaires one could find Alicia Koplowitz with a diversified portfolio of investments in steel, electricity, and banking as a result of investing the proceeds of the sale of her stake in the construction group FCC; Florentino Perez was the CEO of the construction group ACS and also president of the football club Real Madrid; while Isak Andik was the founder of the fast-fashion retailer Mango and also had a significant stake in the bank Banco Sabadell (Forbes, 2015). Third, there is a complex web of ownership connections among the largest publicly traded firms, but it is unclear whether this could be considered a business group, given the lack of coordination among firms.

Figure 12.1 illustrates the cross-shareholding among the largest Spanish firms and banks on the stock market in 2013. This network of cross-shareholdings, although similar in shape to a business group, rather reflects a different logic. The web of shareholdings is the result of the promotion by the government of the *núcleo duro* (hard core) of Spanish owners among former state-owned firms. This was promoted as an alternative to the golden shares that the government had in the privatized firms to prevent their takeover by foreign firms, because such golden shares were deemed uncompetitive by the European Union.

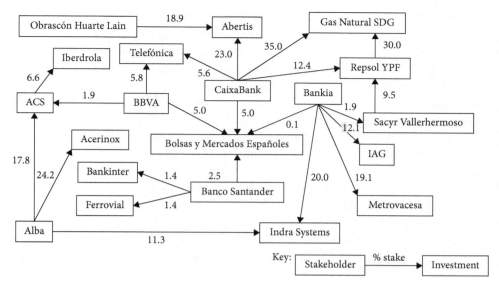

FIGURE 12.1. Ownership relationships among companies on the Spanish stock market, 2013.

Source: Created using information from Johnson (2013).

12.4 TYPES OF BUSINESS GROUPS BY OWNERSHIP: DIFFERENCES IN OBJECTIVES

Business groups are not a homogeneous type of organization. I consider four types of business groups by their ownership: state-owned, bank-owned, family-owned, and labor-owned. The classification of business groups by their ownership is important because different owners face diverse agency challenges that affect behavior (Cuervo-Cazurra, 2006). I now analyze each of the types in more detail within the historical context of the transformation of Spain since the middle of the twentieth century, focusing on understanding the reasons for their existence and their transformation with the pro-market reforms and development of the country.

12.4.1 State-Owned Business Groups: Industrialization and Social Objectives

State ownership of firms in Spain has a long tradition. One noticeable example is the trading monopoly with the colonies in the form of the *Real Casa de Contratación de Indias* in 1503. In the nineteenth century the government created firms, but as it was unable to fund their development some were sold to foreign investors, like the mining complex at Rio Tinto. During the dictatorship of Primo de Rivera (1923–30), the government increased its control of the economy following a nationalist and development ideology, regulating industries and creating monopolies like the gasoline distribution CAMPSA in 1929. However, state-owned business groups began in earnest in 1941 with the creation of the *Instituto Nacional de Industria* (INI, National Institute of Industry), modeled after the Italian IRI created by Mussolini in 1933, to facilitate the industrialization of the country. INI had four main phases of existence in terms of its objectives (Martin Aceña and Comín, 1991; SEPI, 2014): development of the country from 1941 to 1963; support of private industry from 1963 to 1976; support of social stability as a hospital for firms from 1976 to 1983; and restructuring and privatization from 1983 to 1995. It grouped firms that were directly created by the state as well as firms that were nationalized.

In 1981 the *Instituto Nacional de Hidrocarburos* (INH, National Institute of Hydrocarbons) was separated from INI, grouping companies in the oil industry in response to the oil crisis of the 1970s and the need for coordinating activities. In 1987 INH grouped the oil firms into Repsol as a requirement of the end of monopolies by the European Economic Community, and privatized it via an IPO and subsequent sales of shares.

The 1990s resulted in a large restructuring of the state-owned groups in response to limitations from the European Union on the provision of subsidies to firms. In 1992 Teneo was created to incorporate all companies that could be run as private firms; companies' debts were reduced and their managers were given independence. Companies that needed state support were restructured and continued under INI. In 1995 *Sociedad de Estatal de Participaciones Industriales* (SEPI, State Society of Industrial Participations) was created and INI and INH disappeared. Teneo became part of SEPI until it was dissolved in 1996 and its firms transferred to SEPI. SEPI also incorporated state ownership of Repsol, Enagas, and Gas Natural from INH until the sale of these firms on the stock market. Also in 1995, the *Agencia Industrial del Estado* (AIE, State Industrial Agency) was created to group uncompetitive companies from INI and with the competencies to coordinate industrial policy and manage privatizations. AIE was dissolved in 1996 and its assets transferred to SEPI. In 1996, the *Sociedad Española de Participaciones Patrimoniales* (SEPPA, Spanish Society of Patrimony Investments) was created to group entities that were under the *Dirección General del Patrimonio del Estado* (*General Directorate of State Patrimony*); it was integrated into SEPI in 2001. The government continued to privatize firms in the 1990s and 2000s, either via direct sale to other firms (like the automobile firm Seat, sold to the German Volkswagen) or via IPOs and sales of participations on the stock market (like the telecom operator Telefónica or the petroleum firm Repsol).

Despite the privatization drive, by 2012 SEPI was still an important state-owned business group. The industrial holding, which was a public law entity with a separate budget and which reported to the Ministry of Finance and Public Administrations, had direct majority participation in sixteen firms and one foundation, minority participation in nine, and indirect participation in over a hundred, with 74,000 employees.

Firms were grouped into four activities (SEPI, 2013): energy (Ensa, Grupo Cofiva-casa, Grupo Enusa, and Grupo Hunosa, and minority participation in Enagas, Enresa, and Red Eléctrica Corporación); defense (Defex, Izar Construcciones Navales, and Grupo Navantia, and minority participation in EADS NV, Hispasa, and Indra); food and the environment (Cetarsa, Hipódromo de la Zarzuela, Mayasa, Grupo Mercasa, Saeca, Grupo Tragsa, Alimentos y Aceites, and Sepi Foundation); and communications (Grupo Correos, Agencia EFE, Corporación RTVE, Ente público RTVE, and Grupo Sepides, and minority participation in International Airlines Group (IAG) and España Expansión Exterior). The logic was a combination of economic and social achievement, with some firms supporting employment or providing public services.

12.4.2 Bank-Owned Business Groups: Investment and Regulation Objectives

For most of the twentieth century bank-owned business groups were the norm in Spain. The country was classified as a bank-led financial system, like Germany and Japan, in contrast to the market-led system of the US and UK (Berglöf, 1990), and the stock market played a minor role in the funding of firms until the 1990s. Bank ownership of industrial firms was encouraged to provide industrial firms with the capital needed to grow.

The banking industry was highly regulated, with banks constrained in their ability to offer different financial instruments or charge different interest rates for deposits, and operated under conditions of oligopoly until the 1970s (Tortella and García Ruiz, 2013). The banking law of 1946 established stringent controls on bank behavior, imposing a ceiling for interest rates for deposits, as well as minimum and maximum interest rates and commissions for loans. The law also limited the creation of new branches, a restriction which was slightly relaxed after the stabilization plan of 1959 and the banking law of 1962, which redirected banks to support development, a role that had been filled by state-owned banks until then. The central bank dictated interest rates and commissions. As a result, the seven largest banks acted in effect as an oligopoly, coordinating actions and limiting competition. Competition was achieved by providing convenience in the customers' access to the bank, resulting in Spain having one of the largest bank-branch densities in the world. Profitability was achieved via loans, although interests were regulated, and via participation in the stock of industrial firms. Addition-ally, the large number of savings banks, which were non-profit and did not have to return dividends to shareholders, provided additional competition in lending. Savings banks were nominally owned by the depositors, constrained to operate locally or regionally, and controlled by local politicians who directed them to invest in local development, including participating in local firms or firms with local importance for development and employ-ment. As a result, Spanish banks had large incentives to participate in the stock of industrial firms (Tortella and García Ruiz, 2013), as an avenue not only to fulfill regulatory mandates, but also to obtain high returns on their deposits.

Nevertheless, there was a wide diversity in banks' industrial holdings. Whereas Banco Santander tended to have a relatively small industrial group, other competitors like Banco Central and Banesto had very large holdings. However, the banking industry was progressively deregulated in 1974, 1977, and 1981, setting the basis for the transformation of the industry and its internationalization. The deregulation of the industry led to the breakup of the collusion among banks, which Banco Santander ignited with the creation of high-yield deposit accounts. This period also witnessed a deep crisis in the industry as a result of the economic crisis of the 1970s, which resulted in the disappearance of many banks (Cuervo, 1988). The combination of all of these factors, which also resulted in the concentration of the industry into what were eventually the two leaders, Banco Santander and BBVA, led to the reduction of bank-owned business groups. Many banks sold participations in industrial firms to obtain capital to deal with the crisis and acquire local competitors, and in some cases to fund international expansion.

Some banks created separate holdings to manage the industrial groups. For example, Banesto created *Corporación Industrial y Financiera de Banesto* (Banesto's Industrial and Financial Corporation) in 1990 by grouping the industrial holdings of Banesto and its affiliated banks Bandesco and Banco de Vitoria. The Corporación became a separate business group with over 200 companies, representing close to 1 percent of Spain's GDP. Among these firms, the largest nine constituted two-thirds of the value of the group and had 150,000 employees among them (El País, 1990). However, Banesto was intervened by the Central Bank in December 1993 after the discovery of growing losses and the disappearance of funds, and was subsequently sold at auction to Banco Santander in 1994. The holding company was reabsorbed by Banesto in 2007, when the bank was part of Banco Santander.

In the 1980s and 1990s banks increased their industrial participation as the government privatized state-owned firms. These purchases offered good investment opportunities and banks were encouraged to form the hard core of Spanish investors in the privatized firms. At the same time, however, the government discouraged participation in industrial companies for fear that such participations could lead to collusion among firms in one industry that were partially owned by the same bank (Belmonte, 1999). Thus, in the 1990s and 2000s banks continued selling their industrial groups, in part to fund their foreign expansions. The crisis that started in 2008 partly reversed this trend, as banks again became owners of industrial firms when they converted troubled companies' debts into shares, in the hope of recovering some of the investments by recapitalizing the firms.

12.4.3 Family-Owned Business Groups: Opportunity and Legacy Objectives

Family-owned firms dominate the Spanish economy in terms of the number of firms, with an estimate of 85 percent of firms being family-owned and generating about

70 percent of GDP and private employment in 2009 (Instituto de la Empresa Familiar, 2009). Most small and mid-size firms and many of the largest firms are family-owned or family-controlled; some of the family-owned largest firms include the construction firms FCC, Ferrovial, ACS, and Acciona; the clothes makers Inditex and Mango; the automobile component firm Gestamp; the retailer Mercadona; and the security firm Prosegur (Forbes, 2014).

The evolution of family-owned business groups in Spain is typical of many countries that underwent import substitution policies before embarking on pro-market reforms. Under the import substitution regime in Spain, the economy was dominated by state-owned firms and industries were highly regulated in terms of activities and output (see a review of import substitution in Bruton, 1998). As a result, many family firms remained relatively small and those whose owners wanted to grow had to achieve growth by diversifying in other industries (Cuervo-Cazurra, 1999). Some of the diversifications were done to ensure access to supply or distribution channels, while others were done opportunistically. The result was some noticeable family-owned business groups like Rumasa, which by 1982 controlled close to 2 percent of GDP, had 700 companies and sales of 350 billion pesetas, and employed 65,000 people. However, the group was nationalized in 1983 because of the danger of bankruptcy as a result of fraudulent accounting (Cinco Días, 2003). Despite nationalization, the family recreated a business group in 1986, which by 2005 operated in food, hotels, beverages, real estate, and clothing (El Múndo, 2005), but in 2011 went bankrupt for fraud.

The pro-market reforms of the 1980s changed the incentives of families to maintain business groups. The initial deregulation of industries and the privatization of state-owned firms offered opportunities for family-owned business groups to expand into new businesses, which became very profitable ventures as the country achieved high levels of growth in the 1980s. Thus, for example, many of the large construction firms, such as ACS, FCC, and Acciona, grew via acquisitions of competitors and diversified from construction and real estate to services, infrastructure, and energy as the government retrenched from the direct ownership or operation of services and privatized state-owned firms (Cuervo-Cazurra, 1999).

At the same time, however, the opening of the country to foreign competition exposed many domestic firms to foreign competitors that were not only larger but in many cases technologically more sophisticated. Some family-owned firms were sold to foreign competitors as families perceived that their firms could not compete and were offered attractive purchase prices by foreign multinationals. However, others reacted to foreign competition by reinvesting and improving their capabilities, acquiring domestic competitors to dominate the local market, and some even became leading multinationals (Guillén and García-Canal, 2010). In the process, some of these groups changed from being family-owned to family-controlled. The domestic and then global expansion required many firms to sell shares to partners or become more widely quoted on the stock market. However, the families remained in control with significant, although not always majority, participation in the stock of the business group, in many cases via pyramidal structures that enabled control of the firms (Faccio and Lang, 2002).

Despite the transformation, some notable family-owned business groups remained by 2014, such as Grupo March, which controlled the financial holding Corporación Financiera Alba with investments in construction, food, real estate, manufacturing, healthcare, steel, apparel, the bank Banca March, and the foundation Fundación Juan March; or Grupo Villar Mir, with investments in construction, services, real estate, chemicals, metals, mining, and energy.

12.4.4 Labor-Owned Business Groups: Social and Development Objectives

Although cooperatives have a long tradition in Spain (see a historical overview in Guinnane and Martínez Rodríguez, 2010), most have remained relatively small and focused on one industry. Agricultural cooperatives emerged in the late nineteenth century to provide support for the use of collective resources and achieve scale (Beltrán Tapia, 2012), with a 1906 law providing a framework for their development.

Credit cooperatives have had a long history, starting at the end of the nineteenth century as credit unions linked to farmer's cooperatives and called *cajas rurales* (rural savings banks). People's and professional cooperatives appeared later, but in the 1970s their numbers fell via mergers with other rural savings banks (to form the Grupo Caja Rural) and via absorption by *cajas de ahorro* (savings banks) (Chaves, Soler, and Sajardo, 2008). By 2014, and as the result of the crisis and excess debt accumulated during the boom years, many of the saving banks had merged into larger groups and transformed into banks even though they maintained their old names.

Producer cooperatives have been for the most part small in scale, represent a small percentage of economic activity, and tend to be clustered in particular sectors. An explanation for the limited development of cooperatives and labor-owned business groups may be the restrictive legislation imposed during the Franco regime. Although cooperatives had been promoted in the 1931 cooperative law, the 1942 law subjugated them to the national interest and official unions. With the exception of Mondragón in the Basque Country, which had a widely diversified portfolio of activities and grouped hundreds of cooperatives, most cooperatives remained small and in areas that were not deemed viable by private investors. However, the political transition resulted in more favorable legislation and the expansion of cooperatives, especially with the 1999 cooperative law that facilitated not only the creation of cooperatives, but also the creation of cooperative groups acting as holdings for other cooperatives (Comos Tovar, 2004). As a result, the number of cooperatives expanded and grew, and although many remained focused on one industry, some decided to group together to achieve economies of scale in services, such as purchasing, finance, and distribution. Among these, Mondragón Corporation received most of the attention, given its long history and size (Bonin, Jones, and Putterman, 1993).

However, there were other smaller diversified labor-owned groups, such as Tagente in Madrid with seventeen cooperatives. Nevertheless, the norm seemed to be cooperative groups operating in related industries. One example was Coren, which was created in 1959; headquartered in Galicia; operated in beef, pork, poultry, and egg and milk production; and had sales of 982 million euros in 2013, of which 30 percent were exports to over fifty countries. Another was Grupo AN, which was created in 1910; headquartered in Navarra; operated in cereals, meat, and fruit and vegetables; and had sales of 672 million euros in 2013. Despite their size, these groups were still minnows in comparison to the much larger European cooperative groups (Blázquez, 2014). Although many labor groups operated in one industry, even within these groups there was a degree of diversification as the group provided diverse services. In the previous examples these included insurance, training, research and development, petroleum, replacement parts, or fertilizers.

12.5 SELECTED EXAMPLES OF BUSINESS GROUPS IN SPAIN

I now go deeper into the study of business groups in Spain and provide brief analyses of selected example groups. The selection of these groups was done in part because they are some of the largest firms in the country, and in part because of data availability. Hence, I study the state-owned business group INI, which was by far the largest business group in Spain even though it disappeared in 1995; the bank-owned business group BBVA; the family-owned business group Grupo Villar Mir; and the labor-owned business group Mondragon Corporation.

12.5.1 State-Owned Business Groups: INI

Of all the state-owned business groups, INI was the most notable in terms of both size and importance in the Spanish economy. (The history of INI appears in Martín Aceña and Comín, 1991, and in SEPI, 2014, which I summarize here.) Table 12.2 lists some of the largest firms under INI over time.

INI was established in 1941 with the main objective of promoting the development of the country, focusing especially on the industries of electricity, coal, and steel, although it participated in multiple other industries such as transport, automobile production, and oil refining. In the period 1941–63 the focus was on being the main economic driver of the country, facilitating industrialization and substituting imports (Schwartz and Gonzalez, 1978). It depended directly on the president of the government and its budget was dependent on the state. This period coincided with the autarchy of Spain and the need to achieve self-sufficiency, and INI focused on

Table 12.2. Largest firms by revenue in the state-owned business group INI, selected years.

	1960			1970			1980			1990			1993		
	Company	Industry	Sales, billions of pesetas	Company	Industry	Sales, billions of pesetas	Company	Sector	Sales, billions of pesetas	Company	Sector	Sales, billions of pesetas	Company	Sector	Sales, billions of pesetas
1	Refinería de Petróleos de Escombreras	Petroleum	6.1	Enpretrol	Petroleum	87.4	Enpretrol	Petroleum	356.1	ENDESA (Grupo)	Energy	572.8	Grupo Teneo	Diversified	1,767
2	Empresa Nacional Siderúrgica	Steel	3.5	Ensidesa	Steel	63.8	Iberia	Transportation	120.0	INESPAL (Grupo)	aluminum	104.9	Grupo CSI, Gupo Sidenor and Productos Tubulares	Steel	320
3	Sociedad Española de Automóviles de Turismo	Automobiles	3.2	Seat	Automobiles	55.8	SEAT	Automotive	117.8	CASA	Aerospace	102.8	Hunosa, Figaredo, Presur	Mining	103
4	Empresa Nacional de Autocamiones	Trucks	2.3	Iberia	Air transport	43.7	Ensidesa	Iron and steel	111.0	AESA	shipyard	77.6	Grupo Aesa, Astano, Barreras	Shipyard	83
5	Empresa Nacional Bazán	Defense	1.7	Aesa	Shipyard	34.6	Butano	Gas	75.9	ENASA	automotive	66.7	Grupo Santa Barbara, Bazán	Defense	66
6	Empresa Nacional Calvo Sotelo	Petroleum	1.7	Butano	Natural gas	27.1	Hispanoil	Petroleum	72.1	Bazán	Defense	55.4	Grupo Musini	Insurance	40
7	Iberia, Líneas Aéreas de España	Air transport	1.5	Enasa	Automobiles	20.5	ENDESA	Power	62.3	Auxini (Grupo)	Construction	48.9			
8	Empresa Nacional Elcano de la Marina Mercante	Sea transport	0.9	Bazán	Defense	15.5	UESA	Power	43.8	Aviaco	aviation	45.5			
9	Fabricación Española de Fibras Textiles Artificiales	Chemicals	0.8	Hispanoil	Petroleum	15.4	AESA	Shipbuilding	41.3	Hunosa	Mining	40.5			
10	General Eléctrica Española	Electronics	0.8	Hunosa	Mining	9.1	ENASA	Automotive	33.8	ENUSA	Energy	39.2			
11	Empresa Nacional de Aluminio	Aluminum	0.7	Enfersa	Chemicals	7.8	Bazán	Defense	32.2	Iberia	aviation	38.0			
12	Empresa Auxiliar de la Industria	Construction	0.6	Enher	Energy	7.8	ENDASA	Aluminum	30.3	Musini	finance	34.0			
13	La Maquinista Terrestre y Marítima	Transport	0.5	Endesa	Energy	7.5	Enher	Power	25.9	BWE	Constrution	32.2			

14	Astilleros de Cádiz	Shipyard	0.4	Endasa	Steel	7.3	Mevosa	Automotive	22.7	INISEL (Grupo)	Defense	27.2
15	Empresa Nacional Hidroeléctrica de Ribagorzana	Energy	0.4	Ence	Pulp	6.4	Hunosa	Coal	21.7	Ence	Pulp	26.5
16	Marconi Española	Electronics	0.4	Fosbucraa	Mining	6.4	Enfersa	Fertilizers	20.1	Carboex	commercial	20.0
17	Frigoríficos Industriales de Galicia	Food	0.4	Casa	Aerospace	4.7	AHM	Iron and steel	19.4	Ensidesa	Steel	19.3
18	Industria Frigorífica Extremeña	Food	0.3	Aviaco	Air transport	4.6	CASA	Defense	16.9	Santa Bárbara	Defense	16.3
19	Empresa Nacional de Electricidad	Energy	0.3	Cacersa	Food	4.3	ENCE	Various	16.7	Infoleasing	finance	14.9
20	Sociedad Anónima de Construcciones Agrícolas	Machinery	0.2	Auxini	Construction	4.1	Aviaco	Transportation	14.8	Elcano	shipping	13.6

Source: Martín Aceña and Comín (1991), INI (1980, 1990, 1993).

achieving production over profitability. The position of the president of INI, Juan Antonio Suanzes, as minister of industry enabled him to implement his desired policies (Carreras, Tafunel, and Torres, 2008). INI created companies in leading industries such as petroleum (Encaso, E.N. Repesa, E.N. Petróleos de Aragón, Petróleos de Navarra), aluminum (Endasa), electricity (Enher, Gesa, Eneco, Unelco), air transport (Iberia, Aviaco), trucks (Enasa), shipbuilding (Bazán), defense (Santa Bárbara), steel (Ensidesa), automobiles (Seat), coal (Encasur), and chemicals (Celulosa de Huelva, de Motril, de Pontevedra). The management of firms within INI varied over time as the objectives of the institute changed with the needs of the country, but INI maintained influence in the firms in both their strategies and their financing (Martín Aceña and Comín, 1991). Figure 12.2 shows the firms within INI in 1963 and the relationships among them.

As the economy opened with the Stabilization Plan of 1959, the role of INI changed. In 1963–76 it adopted a subsidiary role in support of private initiative. Nevertheless, it continued to create companies, such as in tourism promotion (Entursa), oil exploration (Hispanoil), coal (Hunosa, via the nationalization of companies in crisis), pulp and paper (Ence), and shipbuilding (Efsa). At the end of the period, although INI restructured its portfolio and closed or sold over twenty firms, it also continued to incorporate or create new firms.

The economic crisis that started in 1973 as a result of the oil embargo, and which in Spain coincided with the political transformation from dictatorship to democracy, continued throughout the 1970s and changed the role of INI toward helping private firms in difficulties in the 1976–83 period. The rescue of private firms in difficulties, such as the nationalization of coal mines in Asturias, was done to facilitate social stability and support the nascent democracy, but resulted in a period of large losses for INI. At the same time, firms in the oil and gas industry were separated to create INH.

In the period 1983–95 INI changed its role with the pro-market reforms that induced the government to privatize firms. To facilitate the privatization of firms, INI restructured the loss-making companies and reorganized them. In 1989 INI was converted into a Public Law Entity and was required to focus on profitability and efficiency. Because in 1992 the European Union planned to restrict subsidies, INI separated firms that could be run profitably without subsidies into TENEO, while those that needed continued government support, such as those in defense, mining, shipbuilding, or steel, continued to depend on INI. In 1995 INI was dissolved as its companies were transferred to AIE and later SEPI.

12.5.2 Bank-Owned Business Groups: BBVA

In 2013 BBVA was the second largest bank in Spain and a multinational operating in forty countries. Here I focus on its industrial group, or investments in non-financial companies. The industrial group of BBVA and its component banks were noticeable

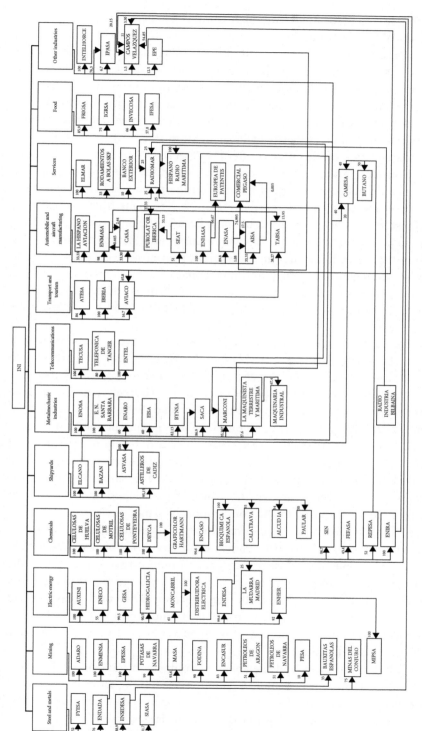

FIGURE 12.2. Relationships among companies in the state-owned business group INI, 1963.

Source: Martín Aceña and Comín (1991).

throughout the twentieth century. Although diminished in significance in recent times, in 2012 BBVA still had significant investments in firms in telecommunications, media, electricity, oil, gas, and finance, with a book value of almost 3 billion euros (BBVA, 2013). Table 12.3 summarizes the investments in non-consolidated subsidiaries in 2002 and 2012. Although some of these subsidiaries are in financial services and investment vehicles, there are other significant direct participations in industrial firms as well as in service companies in telecommunications, hotels, and real estate.

The bank started operations as Banco de Bilbao in the northern city of Bilbao in 1857 thanks to the deregulation of the industry after the 1856 law. (The history of BBVA is presented in González, Anés, and Mendoza, 2007, of which this section is a brief summary.) Banco de Bilbao was created by local businessmen seeking new business opportunities with the right to issue currency and provide loans (this right to issue currency was lost in 1876 when the Bank of Spain became the only issuer). The bank expanded its operations and its relationship with industry as it lost the issuance rights, benefiting from the expansion of mining, steel mills, shipyards, hydroelectric power, and industry in the region. The entry into the capital of firms sometimes took the form of loans that were provided with the shares of the firm as collateral; companies that entered into difficulties were then partially owned by the bank by converting loans into shares.

Banco de Vizcaya, the other main component of BBVA, started operations in 1901 in Bilbao as a commercial bank, with a more focused strategy of participating in industry and especially in energy and chemicals. Banco de Vizcaya participated in the creation of numerous hydroelectric power firms such as Hidroeléctrica Española in 1907, the acquisition of Eléctrica de Viesgo in 1908, Electra de Besaya in 1912, Sociedad de Electricidad de Mongemor in 1913, Union Eléctrica Vizcaína in 1908, and Cooperativa Eléctrica Madrid in 1910. By 1925 it participated not only in over a dozen energy firms, but also in deposits and loans; despite its initial focus, it had become a universal bank. In the 1920s it expanded nationally, and in 1920 it participated in the Sociedad Explotadora de Petróleos Begoña, which explored and produced oil in Mexico. Banco Bilbao responded to the competition of Banco de Vizcaya with the acquisition of Banco de Comercio in 1901, and the opening of subsidiaries in Paris in 1902 and London in 1917 to support Spanish exporters. Both banks shifted their investments towards public debt during the 1920s to reduce risk in the face of the crisis and bankruptcy of some competitors. The Civil War of 1936–9 created a challenge because both banks operated in the Republican and National areas and had to deal with a war economy with the expropriation of funds and two currencies. The regulation of the industry in 1946 and 1962 limited operations in banking and led to a continued relationship with industry.

The deregulation of the 1970s and the ability to compete in the banking industry, as well as joining the European Economic Community, led to the acquisition of other banks to gain size. Thus, in 1988 Banco de Bilbao and Banco de Vizcaya merged to form BBV. In 1999 they acquired Argentaria, the third largest bank in what is now BBVA, which was the result of the 1991 merger of state-owned banks (Banco Exterior,

Table 12.3. Firms in the bank-owned BBVA business group (excluding consolidated subsidiaries), 2002 and 2012.

Companies, 2002	Location	Sector	Direct, %	Indirect, %	Total, %	Book value, thousand euros	Companies, 2012	Country	Sector	Direct, %	Indirect, %	Total, %	Book value, thousand euros
Acerinox,S.A.	Madrid	Industrial	4.68	5.01	9.69	187,815	ACA, S.A. Sociedad de Valores	Spain	Financial Services	-	-	37.5	5397
Banca Nazionale del Lavoro, S.P.A.	Italy	Banking	14.61	0	14.61	510,373	Adquira España, S.A.	Spain	Services	-	40	40	2443
Banco Atlántico, S.A.	Barcelona	Banking	24.37	0	24.37	141,266	Almagrario, S.A.	Colombia	Services	-	35.38	35.38	5013
Banque de Credit Lyonnais, S.A.	France	Banking	3.73	0	3.73	341,696	Altitude Software Sgps, S.A.	Portugal	Services	-	31	31	8856
Brunara Simcav, S.A.	Bilbao	Portfolio	0.46	13.61	14.07	28,180	Aurea, S.A. (Cuba)	Cuba	Real Estate	-	49	49	3690
Cementos Lemona, S.A.	Bilbao	Industrial	6.54	0	6.54	7094	BBVA Elcano Empresarial II, S.C.R., S.A.	Spain	Venture Capital	45	-	45	23,774
Grupo Auxiliar Metalúrgico, S.A. (Gamesa)	Vitoria	Industrial	0.91	18.89	19.8	88,109	BBVA Elcano Empresarial, S.C.R., S.A.	Spain	Venture Capital	45	-	45	23,787
Iberdrola, S.A.	Bilbao	Services	2.75	6.39	9.14	853,568	Camarate Golf, S.A.	Spain	Real Estate	-	26	26	2232
Iberia Líneas Aéreas de España, S.A.	Madrid	Services	9.41	0	9.41	152,828	China Citic Bank Corporation Limited CNCB	China	Bank	15	-	15	5,372,496
Repsol YPF y Empresas Vinculadas	Madrid	Services	7.86	0.29	8.15	1,566,824	CITIC International Financial Holdings Limited CIFH	Hong Kong	Financial Services	29.68	-	29.68	592,988
Sogecable, S.A.	Madrid	Services	0.16	5.01	5.17	17,073	Compañía Española de Financiación del Desarrollo S.A.	Spain	Financial Services	18.81	-	18.81	15,166
Telefónica, S.A.	Madrid	Services	2.51	4.02	6.53	1,584,191	Compañía Mexicana de Procesamiento, S.A. De CV.	Mexico	Services	-	50	50	5849
Terra Networks, S.A.	Madrid	Services	0.18	1.38	1.56	70,680	Corporación IBV Participaciones Empresariales, S.A.	Spain	Holding	-	50	50	135,312
The Argentine Investment Company	Argentina	Portfolio	0	5.24	5.24	10,720	Ferromovil 3000, S.L.	Spain	Services	-	20	20	5886
Tubos Reunidos, S.A.	Bilbao	Industrial	0	24.26	24.26	19,031	Ferromovil 9000, S.L.	Spain	Services	-	20	20	4379
Vidrala, S.A.	Llodio-Alava	Industrial	15.66	1.53	17.19	22,045	I+D México, S.A. De CV.	Mexico	Services	-	50	50	15,423
Wafabank	Morocco	Banking	0	9.99	9.99	30,801	Las Pedrazas Golf, S.L.	Spain	Real Estate	-	50	50	2013
							Metrovacesa, S.A.	Spain	Real Estate	17.34	0.02	17.36	317,122

(continued)

Table 12.3. Continued

Companies, 2002	Location	Sector	Direct, %	Indirect, %	Total, %	Book value, thousand euros	Companies, 2012	Country	Sector	Direct, %	Indirect, %	Total, %	Book value, thousand euros
Compañía Española de Financiación del Desarrollo S.A.	Madrid	Services	21.82	0	21.82	10,225	Occidental Hoteles Management, S.L.	Spain	Services	-	38.53	38.53	67,207
Concesión Sabana de Occidente, S.A.	Colombia	Services	0	47.2	47.2	8234	Redsys Servicios de Procesamiento, S.L.	Spain	Financial Services	16.08	1.16	17.24	2477
Conservas Garavilla, S.A.	Bermeo–Vizcaya	Industrial	0	41.17	41.17	20,891	Rombo Compañía Financiera, S.A.	Argentina	Financial Services	-	40	40	17,052
Grubarges Inversion Hotelera, S.L	Madrid	Services	33.33	0	33.33	98,233	Servicios de Administracion Previsional, S.A.	Chile	Pension Fund Management		37.87	37.87	7534
Hilo Direct Seguros y Reaseguros, S.A.	Madrid	Insurance	0	50	50	20,883	Servicios Electrónicos Globales, S.A. de CV.	Mexico	Services		46.14	46.14	4937
Holding de Participaciones Industriales 2000, S.A.	Bilbao	Portfolio	0	50	50	21,798	Servicios on Line para Usuarios Múltiples, S.A. (Solium)	Spain	Services		66.67	66.67	4808
Iniciativas de Mercados Interactivos, S.A.	Madrid	Services	0	40	40	7543	Servired Sociedad Española de Medios de Pago, S.A.	Spain	Financial Services	21.06	1.53	22.59	8356
Landata Payma, S.A.	Spain	Services	0	50	50	38,600	Telefónica Factoring España, S.A.	Spain	Financial Services	30		30	4319
Onexa, S.A. de CV.	Mexico	Finance	0	49.8	49.8	6531	Tubos Reunidos, S.A.	Spain	Industrial		24.12	24.12	53,686
Promotora Metrovacesa, S.L.	Madrid	Real Estate	0	50	50	11,532	Vitamedica S.A de CV.	Mexico	Insurance		50.99	50.99	2666
Sociedad Administradora de Pensiones y Garantias Porvenir	Colombia	Pensions	0	20	20	10,051	Other companies						88,275
Técnicas Reunidas, S.A.	Madrid	Services	0	25	2500	37,779	TOTAL						6,803,143
Other companies						99,581							
TOTAL						6,024,175							

Source: BBVA (2002, 2012).

Instituto de Crédito Oficial, and Caja Postal). This process of acquisition was encouraged by the Spanish government and sought by the banks in search of size to compete in the European and global markets. The bank continued with an active participation in industry, boosted by the privatization of firms in the 1990s and the encouragement by the government to have domestic banks become the hard core of national champions. However, as the bank grew and the industry was deregulated, BBVA disposed of investments, partly to fund its expansion in banking. Despite this, the disposal was done gradually and in 2013 it still had some participation in the capital of non-financial firms, though this was minor in the company's total portfolio.

12.5.3 Family-Owned Business Groups: Grupo Villar Mir

Grupo Villar Mir was in 2013 one of the leading family-owned business groups, with operations in construction, services, and real estate, as well as chemicals, metals, mining, and energy. In 2012 it had sales of 6.76 billion euros and 25,491 employees, operated in 35 countries representing 67 percent of sales and 82 percent of EBITDA, and managed assets worth 16.61 billion euros. Despite the crisis in Spain, the group achieved record profits of 746 million euros in 2012. Table 12.4 summarizes the distribution of sales across sectors.

The group was created in 1987 by Juan Miguel Villar Mir (information on this section comes from Sanchez Montes de Oca and Saavedra Acevedo, 2008, Grupo Villar Mir annual reports, and the group and affiliate websites). In 1968 Juan Miguel Villar Mir was asked to restructure the chemical and energy firm Hidronitro Española by three banks that owned it. His success led the banks that owned the steel company Altos Hornos de Vizcaya to ask him to restructure it in 1970. In 1987 he purchased the highly indebted and loss-making construction company Obrascón, which was part of Altos Hornos de Vizcaya, for one peseta from the Banco de Bilbao and other Basque banks, and the real-estate company Espacio. He restructured Obrascón and issued an IPO in 1991. To achieve the necessary size to operate nationally, Obrascón engaged in a series of acquisitions of construction companies that were facing difficulties, purchasing eleven firms in the construction industry between 1996 and 1999 (e.g., Cuarzos Industriales in 1996 from the Portuguese Cimpor, Sato in 1997, Huarte in 1998, Padadar in 1998, Ferroven in 1998 from the Venezuelan government, Laín in 1999, and Ramsa [Rocas, Arcillas, y Minerales SA] from the Norwegian group Elkem in 2000). Obrascón, Huarte, and Laín were integrated to form the construction company OHL. Grupo Villar Mir continued acquiring participations in OHL to achieve majority control in 2006.

The group continued to expand via the acquisition and restructuring of firms in difficulties. In 1992 it purchased the chemical and energy firm FerroAtlántica, which was the electrometallurgy and energy division of Carburos Metálicos, from its US owner Air Products. In 1995 it purchased the fertilizer firm Fertiberia, which was part

Table 12.4. Evolution of the sales across divisions in the family-owned Grupo Villar Mir, 2003–12.

	2003	2004	2005	2006	2007	2008	2009	2010	2011	2012
Electrometallurgy division	307.9	405.1	491.3	662.6	848.1	1,171.30	641.4	1,085.40	1,217.10	1,098.90
Energy division	41.3	32.6	31.4	44	44.4	60	52.7	118.6	333.1	407.2
Fertilizer division	451.6	487.9	685.4	605.5	726	876.5	586.6	897.7	1,041.70	1,231.10
Real estate division	126.7	107.4	123.6	178.8	60.3	81.1	112.9	109.8	62.2	70.9
Prefabricated division	67.4	45.7	59.3	94.5	75.1	69.5				
OHL	2,111.80	2,230.50	2,442.70	3,278.20	3,764.40	4,008.80	4,780.20	4,771.50	3,702.00	4,029.60
Consolidated accounts	3,047.90	3,267.80	3,836.60	4,862.90	5,538.60	6,288.00	6,256.60	7,021.10	6,362.10	6,760.40

Source: Grupo Villar Mir (2004, 2012). Figures in millions of euros.

of Ercros, which was in difficulties and was being sold by its owners, the Kuwaiti fund KIO.

Grupo Villar Mir internationalized via acquisitions. With the profits from the restructuring of FerroAtlántica, in 1996 it purchased Hidro from its French owner Pechiney, which was part of the Canadian group Alcan; in 2005, it purchased its electrometallurgy division, Pechiney Electrometallurgie, which had plants in France and South Africa, thus internationalizing the group further. Also in 2005 Grupo Villar Mir acquired the fertilizer firm Fertial SPA from the Algerian government, and in 2008 it purchased metal operations from Rand Cardbide PLD in South Africa, created the Brazilian subsidiary FerroAtlántica Brasil Mineracao Ltd., and purchased the Portuguese fertilizer firm Adubos de Portugal. In 2010 it purchased the silicon metal plant Sinice Silicon Industries in China, and in 2012 it purchased the solar silicon assets of the Canadian firm Timmincon, and the quartz mine Sam Quarz in South Africa.

Additional diversification was also achieved via acquisitions. In 2007 the group's real-estate complex Torre Espacio Castellana entered into service. In 2009 it purchased the renewable energy firm Céntrica Energía, S.L., which became Eenrgya VM. In 2012 it bought the fertilizer and agricultural product firm Fercampo and 15 percent of the highway, airport, and telecommunication management firm Abertis.

Unlike other family-owned business groups in which owners tend to maintain a high degree of coordination of the actions of companies, Villar Mir was coordinated in a very decentralized manner, allowing managers a high degree of autonomy. For example, in 2008 the holding firm had only fourteen people who coordinated finance and investments. The companies were run by Juan Miguel Villar Mir from their acquisition until solvency, and then a new manager was brought in to run the firm (Sánchez Montes de Oca and Saavedra Acevedo, 2008). Figure 12.3 illustrates the companies and the relationships among them in 2012. It is worth noting the indirect control that the group has achieved over OHL, which is larger than the rest of the group combined.

12.5.4 Labor-Owned Business Groups: Mondragón Corporation

The Mondragón Corporation is one of the largest groups in Spain, and a leading multinational. By 2012 it included 110 cooperatives and 147 companies; employed 80,000 people, of whom 85 percent were cooperative members in the industrial area; had revenues of 14 billion euros; and had operations in 29 countries. Table 12.5 lists the cooperatives in the Mondragón Corporation.

The group traces its origins back to the work of the priest Jose María Arizmendiarrieta, who promoted the creation of cooperatives in the town of Mondragón. (This section draws from Ormaechea, 1993, Cancelo Alonso, 1999, Elio, 2004, and the group's

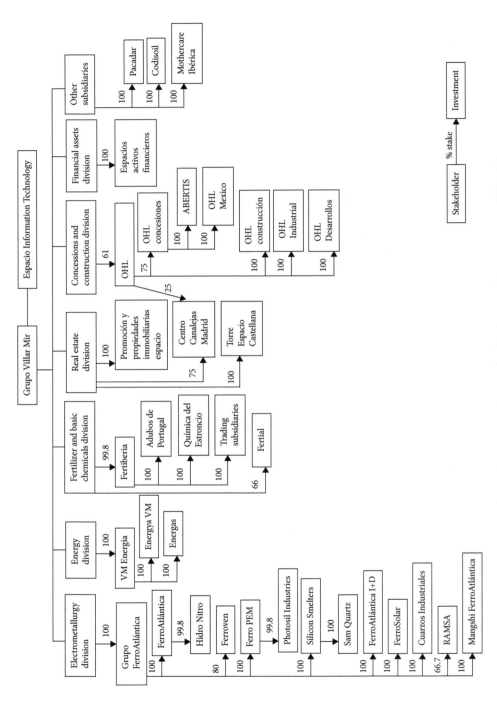

FIGURE 12.3. Relationships among firms in the family-owned business group Villar Mir, 2012.

Source: Created using information from Grupo Villar Mir (2012).

Table 12.5. Firms in the labor-owned business group Mondragón Corporation, 2013.

FINANCE

Laboral Kutxa	Banking
Lagun Aro, EPSC	Social protection for cooperative members
Langun Aro Servicios	Social security and medical management for members
Osarten	Hazard prevention service

KNOWLEDGE

Aotalora	Training
Aotek	Automation and optics
Arizmendi	Education
Ategi	Purchasing
CS Centro Stirling	Sustainable energy
Escuela Politécnica Superior	Technical school
Etic Microsoft	Innovation center
Facultad de Ciencias Gastronómicas	Food school
Facultad de Empresariales	Business school
Goierri Goi Mailako Eskola	Education
IK4-Ikerlan	R&D
IK4-Lortek	R&D
Koniker	Forming and assembly technology center
Leartiker Polymer R&D	Technical education
Leartiker Tecnologia de Alimentos	Technical education
MIK (Mondragón Innovation and Knowledge)	Innovation and knowledge center
Mondragón Centro de Promocion	Promotion of new activities
Mondragón Lingua	Language training and translation services
Mondragón Unibertsitatea	Univeristy
Otarola	Cooperative and business training
Txorierri Politeknika Ikastegia	College

RETAIL

Auzo-Lagun	Refurbishment and cleaning services
Barrenetxe	Vegetable production
Behi-Alde	Dairy milk production
Eroski Sociedad Cooperativa	Commercial distribution
Forum sport	Sporting goods distribution
Grupo Ausolan	Catering (refurbishment and cleaning services),
Grupo Eroski	Retail (supermarket, hypermarket, petrol stations) and specialist (perfume, sport, travel, leisure, culture)
Miba	Animal fodder
Unekel	Rabbit meat production

INDUSTRY

Agantail	Design
Aleco	Education and training

(continued)

Table 12.5. Continued

Alkargo	Transformers
Aurki (LKS)	Training
Aurki SL (LKS TSI)	Recruitment and training
Aurrenak	Moldings
Batz	Automotive systems
Biurrarena	Construction machinery and underground containers
Cikautxo	Polymer parts
Coinalde	Nails and wire for construction
Copreci	Appliance components
Danobat	Machinery
Dikar	Rifles and barrels
Domusa	HVAC
Ecenarro	Anchorage elements
Ederfil-Becker	Copper wire
Edertek	Chassis and powertrains
Efficold	Catering equipment
Eika	Resistances
EKO3R	Cooking oil recycling
Electra Vitoria	Lifts and escalators
Embega	Metal parts, condensers, and sealing
Eredu	Outdoor furniture
Etorki	Wood products
Fagor Arrasate	Presses and stamping
Fagor Automation	Machine automation and control
Fagor Ederlan	Automotive components
Fagor Ederlan Tafalla	Cylinder blocks and heads for engines
Fagor Industrial	Catering equipment
FGM	Commercial furniture
Goiti	Sheet metal transforming
GRS Gestion de Servicios Residenciales	Senior housing management
Hertell	Vacuums
Ibai sistemas	IT services
IK4-Ideko	Technology center
Kide	Cold rooms
Lana	Timber boards
Latz	Metal cutting tools
LKS	Professional services
LKS Ingeniería	Consulting
LKS Tasaciones	Property valuation, advice, and management
Loramendi	Foundry equipment
Maier	Automobile components
Mapsa	Aluminum wheels
Matrici	Automobile components
Matz-Erreka	Automation, plastic
mccgraphics	Marketing and graphic services
Mcctelecom	Telecom and IT services

MEI	Education and training
Mondragón Assembly	Automation technologies
Oiarso	Disposable medical material
Ondoan	Engineering
Orbea	Bicycles
Orkli	Heating components
Orona	Lifts and escalators
Osatu	Electro-medical equipment
Polo de Innovación Faraia	Innovation and knowledge center
Prospektiker	Consulting
Soraluce	Machine tools
Tajo	Plastic components
Ulma Agrícola	Greenhouse materials
Ulma Architectural Solutions	Construction materials
Ulma Carretillas Elevadoras	Forklifts
Ulma Construcción	Scaffolding
Ulma Conveyor Components	Conveyor components
Ulma Embedded Solutions	Engineering services
Ulma Handling Systems	Logistics
Ulma Pipping	Flanges
Urola	Blowmoulding machinery
Urssa	Steel construction
WinGroup	Fitness and camping gear

Source: Mondragón Corporation (2014).

website.) In 1943 Fr. Arizmendiarrieta created the Professional School (Escuela Profesional) to complement the training provided by the Unión Cerrajera, which gave a selected group of students the opportunity to study and work. In 1947 he convinced the Engineering School in Zaragoza to allow the students to continue their university education at a distance, combining their work and studies at the Escuela Profesional.

In 1956 five of the students created the company Talleres Ulgor (using the initials of their names), manufacturing appliances because they had purchased a company in Vitoria that had a license for producing these. In 1957 they moved the company from Vitoria to Mondragón, and in 1959 the company was transformed into a labor cooperative.

In 1959 Ulgor and three other cooperatives—Funcor, Arraste, and San Jose Consumer Cooperative—joined together to form the credit cooperative Caja Laboral Popular (CLP). The idea of CLP came from Fr. Arizmendiarrieta, who thought that the cooperatives needed the financial support of a bank to promote future development and additional cooperatives. To enable the growth of CLP, the cooperatives agreed to create it, contribute to its capital and managers, and work only with CLP for their financing needs. In 1971 CLP came under the supervision of the Bank of Spain after the new regulations in the banking system. In 1989 the new regulations allowed credit cooperatives to serve nonmembers.

Other cooperatives were created in the early 1960s. In 1959 Lagun Aro was created within CLP to provide social security for its members, because since 1958 cooperative members were excluded from the social security system. With changes in legislation, Lagun Aro became independent from CLP in 1973. In 1961 the steel construction company Urssa was created by people from Mondragón in Vitoria, in 1962 the wood product company Lana was created with capital from CLP, and in 1963 Vicon was created using the ideas from Mondragón in San Sebastian.

Cooperatives were created using four alternative methods. One was the promotion from CLP, which provided technical and financial support and intervened in the appointment of management. Another was the conversion of limited liability companies into cooperatives, in some cases as a result of crisis in the company. The third method was the merger and split of existing cooperatives. The fourth method was the independent creation of cooperatives by themselves, using the statutes in place of the Mondragón cooperatives but without direct intervention from CLP; these cooperatives later joined CLP. Some cooperatives ceased existence as a result of the crisis of 1974–85 and more recently as a result of the 2008–14 crisis, with Fagor's 2013 bankruptcy being the most notable case for its size and significance.

In terms of organization, cooperatives joined the group initially by establishing an association with CLP. In 1975 a contract of association was created which established the conditions under which new cooperatives would join the group and CLP, which would audit the accounts. In 1964 cooperatives in the Leniz Valley were grouped in the Ularco Industrial Complex, which was intended to provide them with common services and scale, becoming Ularco in 1975 and Fagor in 1986 to make use of their best-known trademark. In the late 1970s such geographic groupings spread elsewhere, partly as a result of the crisis of the 1970s, which led to the creation of groups that provided mutual support.

In 1984 the General Council and the Congress of the Mondragón Cooperative Group were created to coordinate, promote, and serve the cooperatives, partly in response to Spain joining the European Economic Community in 1986, and to a perceived need for increasing scale to take advantage of market opportunities in Europe. The result was a transfer and centralization of decision-making from the cooperatives to the groups and from the groups to the General Council, merging sectors and replacing the geographical groups that had a social basis with industry-based groups. In 1991 the group was reorganized by industry instead of geography, leading to the creation of Mondragón Corporation. Figure 12.4 illustrates the industrial structure.

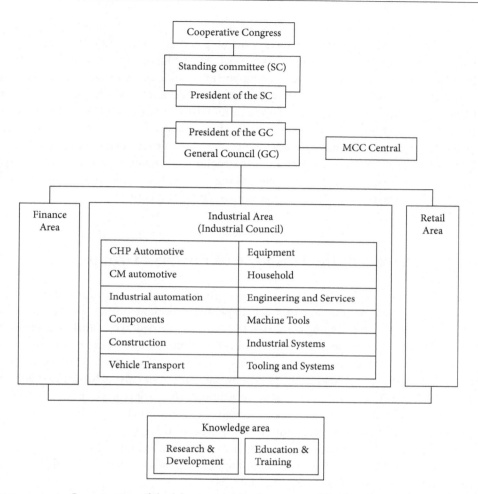

FIGURE 12.4. Organization of the labor-owned business group Mondragón Corporation, 2012.

Source: Created using information from Freundlich, Grellier, Altuna (2009) and Mondragon Corporation (2012).

12.6 CONCLUSIONS: DRIVERS OF THE EXISTENCE OF BUSINESS GROUPS

The analysis of the emergence and transformation of business groups in Spain in the twentieth and twenty-first centuries leads to two conclusions. First, business groups do not emerge only in response to the characteristics typical of emerging markets: weak institutions and closed economies. Other drivers explain the existence and resilience of business groups, and the analysis of business groups in Spain points to the regulation of industry and the ideology of owners as additional drivers explaining the existence of business groups.

Second, there are important differences among types of business groups. The separation of business groups by their ownership reveals important differences driven by the nature of the owner. Whereas state-owned and labor-owned groups are driven by ideologies of development and employment, bank-owned groups are driven by regulation and the search for return opportunities, while family-owned groups are driven by entrepreneurial capabilities and the search for return opportunities. Although some of the founders may take an active role in the firm, many of these business groups are actually run by professional managers, especially as the groups expand in size and age. Some of the groups have used pyramidal structures to maintain control over a large number of companies with limited financial stake, especially as the groups grow and the family no longer has the financial clout to maintain direct control.

12.6.1 Drivers of the Existence of Business Groups

The traditional explanation for business groups—weak institutions and closed economies—needs rethinking. Although these are important drivers for the existence of business groups in emerging countries, they need refinement when analyzing business groups in advanced economies with stronger institutions and open economies. The analysis of business groups in Spain reveals a more complex reality. Abstracting from the particularities of Spanish business groups, I identify four drivers for the existence of business groups (closed economy, weak institutions, industry regulation, and ideology) and explain how these change over time with the transformation of the country after pro-market reforms. Table 12.6 summarizes these four drivers.

The first two drivers (closed economy and weak institutions) have been explained elsewhere (Khanna and Yafeh, 2007), but the two original contributions of this chapter (industry regulation and ideology) need further explanation.

First, the regulation of industry induces entrepreneurs to create business groups to achieve growth. In a regulated industry, the entrepreneur may find that there are no growth opportunities because competition is limited and there is little ability to expand and generate additional revenue. The regulation may limit not only the number of competitors but also the level of competition and the actions that competitors can take. Hence, the entrepreneur may use the cash generated in the regulated industry and invest in other industries with higher growth opportunities even when the entrepreneur has limited knowledge of those industries, relying on managers with the expertise to run the new operations. Additionally, in some cases industry regulations mandate entrepreneurs to diversify and invest in other firms. Pro-market reforms reduce the incentive to expand across industries because the deregulation of the industry enables the entrepreneur to expand within the same industry and use the excess cash to build size, buying weaker competitors and investing in improving the competitiveness of the operations to face new entrants and challengers. Thus, the entrepreneur can reduce

Table 12.6. Four drivers of the existence of business groups.

Driver of the existence of business groups	Driver of unrelated diversification	Objective	Impact of pro-market reforms on unrelated diversification
Closed economy	Vertical integration to ensure supply and distribution in the face of limited local suppliers and channels. Unrelated diversification to achieve growth opportunities in the face of limited foreign competition	Increase revenues from excess managerial and financial resources	Initially increase diversification to take advantage of privatization and deregulation opportunities and later reduce diversification in the face of strong foreign competition
Weak institutions	Vertical integration to ensure supply and distribution in the face of opportunism and inability to ensure the implementation of contracts. Unrelated diversification to benefit from trust relationships with business partners and government officials, and to exploit gaps in product markets	Reduce opportunism in economic relationships	Reduce vertical integration and diversification in non-core activities to benefit from a stronger contractual system
Regulation	Invest in growth industries using funds from regulated industry as expansion within the industry is constrained by regulation	Comply with norms and search for returns from excess funds	Reduce diversification and use funds from sales of unrelated operations to gain size and competitiveness in deregulated industry
Ideology	Invest in activities that support the development of a location	Economic and social development	Continue diversification if owner is willing to cross-subsidize operations to achieve non-business objectives. Reduce diversification if owner changes ideology with pro-market reforms

diversification and sell investments to generate funds to invest in gaining size and competitiveness in the original industry.

Second, the ideology of the entrepreneur drives the creation of business groups. Some owners have non-business objectives that drive their diversification into multiple activities. Thus, the entrepreneur may encourage the creation of multiple companies in diverse activities to promote the economic and social development of particular locations, placing more emphasis on the achievement of the non-business objectives over the business ones, or being more willing to accept lower levels of return on the businesses. Pro-market reforms have a limited influence on these business groups unless the entrepreneur changes ideology with the pro-market reforms. The increase in foreign competition may induce the exit from certain businesses which are no longer viable economically, but the ideology may dictate against such exit and the business group may continue to operate in non-viable areas as long as there is cross-subsidization among operations and the overall group is viable.

12.6.2 Differential Existence and Evolution of Types of Business Groups

Differences in ownership among business groups result in diverse transformations over time. I abstract from the specific experiences of particular business groups in Spain and venture a proposal for the evolution in the complexity of business groups over time with changes in the economy. Figure 12.5 illustrates this evolution. The x-axis represents changes in the economy from the early industrialization typical of many countries at the end of the nineteenth and beginning of the twentieth century to the closed economy and import substitution and state-led industrialization-period characteristics of many countries in the middle of the twentieth century; to the implementation of pro-market reforms and the associated deregulation, privatization, and liberalization in the 1980s; to the global integration of the country which was usual from the 1990s onward. The y-axis represents the level of diversification and complexity of the business group, with higher levels representing higher degrees of unrelated diversification and complexity in managing a diverse set of businesses within one organization. The proposed shapes of the evolution in the level of complexity of each type of business group are merely an abstraction and are not intended to represent particular companies. Specific measures and particular evolutions can be analyzed in future research.

Abstracting further from the experience of business groups in Spain, in Table 12.7 I summarize a proposal of the drivers of the existence and transformation of the different types of business groups. First, state-owned business groups grow significantly during the closed-economy and import-substitution period, as the government takes a leading role in the development of the country. With the advent of pro-market reforms, these groups reduce in complexity, either as a result of the privatization or closure of their component firms. Nevertheless, they continue in existence with firms that were

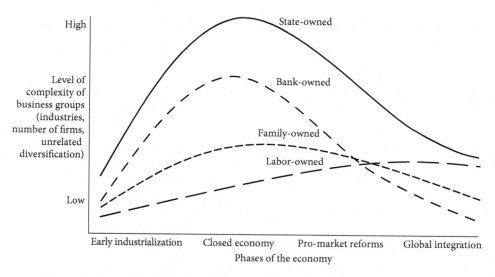

High

Level of
complexity of
business groups
(industries,
number of firms,
unrelated
diversification)

Low

State-owned

Bank-owned

Family-owned

Labor-owned

Early industrialization   Closed economy   Pro-market reforms   Global integration
Phases of the economy

FIGURE 12.5. Evolution in the complexity of business groups with changes in the economy (based on the Spanish experience).

deemed to be of either strategic or social importance. Second, bank-owned business groups also grow during the early industrialization and later closed-economy periods in response to regulation and the search for yields. With the pro-market reforms, however, their complexity diminishes significantly. They are no longer required to invest in industrial firms, and they therefore reduce their exposure to industrial firms. However, they may maintain an industrial portfolio for the investment value, but with increasingly low levels of stockholdings to benefit from diversification and reduced exposure to any particular company. Third, family-owned business groups expand their complexity as the economy remains closed and they reach growth limits within their industries, using their abilities and funds to undertake new business opportunities. While the pro-market reforms offer new investment opportunities and family-owned business groups expand their complexity, the increase in foreign competition leads to the restructuring of these groups and the focus on the areas in which they can operate at an advantage. Fourth, labor-owned business groups emerge with the development of the country and expand as the economy grows, maintaining high levels of diversity despite the pro-market reforms to ensure social development. The logic of solidarity and the grouping of cooperatives to achieve economies of scale in purchasing and distribution limit the need to reduce complexity with pro-market reforms.

12.6.3 Final Conclusions

Business groups in Spain emerged in the twentieth century and dominated much of the economy during the development and industrialization of the country. As the

Table 12.7. Types of business groups and drivers of their existence and transformation.

Type	Existence	Transformation	Theoretical driver
State-owned	Import substitution ideology induces investments in multiple industries to facilitate industrialization. Acquisition of private firms in difficulties to avoid social unrest	Change to pro-market ideology leads to privatization and reduction of diversification Unrelated diversification remains for strategic and social reasons	Closed economy Economic development Ideology
Bank-owned	Regulation of industry induces investment in industrial firms to obtain a return	Deregulation of industry leads to large reduction of industrial groups	Regulation Excess resources and search for returns
Family-owned	Closed country induces unrelated diversification to ensure supply and distribution Use of management, finance, and government relationships for growth opportunities	Opening to foreign competition induces reduction of unrelated diversification Use management and finance to grow abroad, but still diversified	Weak institutions Closed economy Entrepreneurial capabilities Excess resources and search for returns
Labor-owned	Ideology induces investment in multiple industries to facilitate employment Diversification provides flexibility for employment	Pro-market reforms induce internationalization Diversification maintained to ensure social objectives	Closed economy Social development Ideology

economy opened and the government implemented pro-market reforms, state-owned and bank-owned business groups reduced their size and diversification. However, family-owned and labor-owned business groups continued to exist and in some cases expanded, becoming leading multinationals. The differences in behavior among business groups reflect different drivers. Thus, in addition to the usual explanations for the existence of business groups of weak institutions and closed economies, this chapter proposed additional drivers in the form of regulation and owner ideology that future research can explore in detail.

ACKNOWLEDGMENTS

For providing very detailed and useful suggestions for improvement to this chapter, I thank Asli Colpan and Takashi Hikino, as well as Marcelo Bucheli, Youssef Cassis, James Lincoln,

Harm Schröter, and the audience at the Kyoto International Conference at Kyoto University on March 8–10, 2014. For financial support to conduct this research, I thank the Patrick F. and Helen C. Walsh Research Professorship and the Robert Morrison Fellowship from the D'Amore-McKim School of Business at Northeastern University. For financial support to present this research, I thank the Mizuho Securities Co., Ltd. Endowment at the Graduate School of Management at Kyoto University and the Hakubi Center for Advanced Research at Kyoto University.

CHAPTER 13

....

PORTUGAL

changing environment and flexible adaptation

....

ÁLVARO FERREIRA DA SILVA AND PEDRO NEVES

13.1 INTRODUCTION

....

THE development of Portuguese business groups over the last century has much to thrill historians and management scholars alike. Their relevance in the business structure is indisputable. Although a crude measure of their relative importance—the market capitalization of the largest family-controlled groups as a fraction of total market capitalization—reveals Portugal to be in second place in Europe, surpassed only by Sweden, a country always referred to as a stronghold of family business groups (Morck, 2010: Fig. 21.1). Major structural changes dictated different contexts for their advent and transformation. Unexpectedly, the largest business groups were victims of sudden elimination due to decisions by the government, which at other times was a vital partner, protector, and promoter of their development. Intrigues and struggles within the family dynasties that ruled these groups add an extra air of drama.

As clusters of firms bound together by block shareholders exercising administrative control and operating in widely diversified business fields, business groups emerged in Portugal between the late nineteenth and early twentieth centuries.[1] They prospered after the mid-twentieth century in the context of an emerging and protected economy. The 1974 revolution dictated their nationalization and disappearance in 1975, after two decades during which they expanded in scale and scope. A new institutional framework emerged in the late 1980s, after a period of restrictions to private business activity in economic sectors previously regarded as strategic. A quick and massive privatization

---

[1] Throughout this chapter, business groups are defined as above. As such, the focus of this chapter is on diversified business groups, as all large Portuguese business groups discussed here have been organized in this manner—although the extent of diversification has varied across different time periods.

process went along with the emergence of new groups. At the beginning of the twenty-first century this process was complete, and new business groups occupy the top of the Portuguese business structure.

This brief historical outline explains why the Portuguese case is so interesting for the investigation of some of the riddles raised in the study of business groups. It is true that their abrupt end in 1975 precludes answering the question of what would have happened to these groups in a new institutional and economic framework. Would they have perished, as happened to the Spanish groups after the Franco period, unable to withstand the double impact of the economic crisis and new institutional context (Guillén, 2001; Cuervo-Cazurra, this volume)? Would they have been able to adapt to new conditions, as happened in Asia and Latin America (Carney, 2005)?

What is lost in the impossibility of answering these questions is gained, however, in creating a situation similar to a laboratory experiment. More than an expression of rhetoric, the fact that the pre-revolution business groups were nationalized in 1975 created the conditions for isolating the emergence and expansion of groups in different institutional and economic contexts. It allows the control over factors that so often introduce confounding elements in the comparative analysis over time and across space. Nationalization removes what is sometimes regarded as a source of causality deflected by path-dependency in the evolution of groups over time, which could be summarized in the following way: they persist because they use their political influence to maintain institutional voids which should disappear with economic modernization (Khanna and Palepu, 1999; Carney and Gedajlovic, 2002; Schneider, 2008). The structural shock represented by the 1975 nationalization interrupts the flow of continuity in the evolution of business groups in Portugal and isolates two different historical contexts. The most important question turns out to be the persistence of groups as a form of business organization in different economic and institutional contexts rather than the resilience of individual groups. This shift in the research question allows—one may assume—a clearer analytical approach.

13.2 BUSINESS GROUPS IN DEVELOPING AND MATURE MARKETS: THE PORTUGUESE CASE AND THE RESILIENCE CONUNDRUM

The success of business groups in emerging economies is commonly attributed to contextual explanations related to the economic, institutional, political, and cultural environment (Morck, Wolfenzon, and Yeung, 2005; Khanna and Yafeh, 2007). Two main limitations cast doubt on this interpretation, identified in the most perceptive reviews (Colpan and Hikino, 2010, and this volume). On the one hand, they are so focused on contextual reasons (Yiu et al., 2007) that do not consider intra-group-generated resources and advantages as potential explanations for groups' success. On the other hand, they fail to explain why business groups persist and prosper in contexts with mature market, governance, and political institutions.

The resilience of business groups has been a clear conundrum in management studies. Over time and across space business groups appear as a favorite organizational design for big business, contradicting any version of the modernization theory applied to the evolution of business structures. This chapter argues that business groups have been more than a second-best organizational form, typical of developing economies with rudimentary market and business institutions. They prospered in advanced Western economies, reinvented themselves in the transition from developing to developed countries, and survived serious financial crises. In this sense they can no longer be understood as some kind of poor substitute for the multidivisional form, typical of less developed countries.

The evolution of business groups in Portugal represents a good case for discussing their persistence and success in different economic and institutional contexts, as the historical outline briefly presented in Section 13.1 reveals. The period studied in this chapter could also be the motive for reviewing the literature on Portuguese business groups and its public perception. Ignored during much of the twentieth century, groups became the subject of studies and debate in the early 1970s, following their increasing prominence in the Portuguese business structure (Martins, 1973). A similar phenomenon occurred in neighboring Spain, where a mix of academic and political literature was dedicated to the business groups that had developed during the Franco period (Tamames, 1967, 1977; Muñoz, 1969). The 1975 nationalization curtailed such literature. Only recently did similar studies appear, marking the re-emergence of groups after the 1990s (Caeiro, 2004; Costa et al., 2010). The recent difficulties experienced by the Espírito Santo group placed this topic at the center of the political debate and public scrutiny (e.g., Fernandes, 2014; Esteves and Jesus, 2015).

Neither the older nor the newer streams of this literature explore a comprehensive reconstitution of these groups and ignore any comparative and theoretical studies on business groups. Their evolution, strategies, and configurations are still to be traced and understood. Advocating the continuity between the pre-nationalization groups and those emerging after the end of the twentieth century (Costa et al., 2010) stems from these methodological and theoretical weaknesses.

This analysis is based on the reconstruction of the seven largest business groups over time, ending the story at the time when the 2008 financial crisis hit the Portuguese economy. In some cases this evolution started in the late nineteenth century (Burnay group). For other groups their development began later, especially in the case of some of the most important groups in the present-day Portuguese economy.

The groups' corporate networks and equity ties were reconstructed, turning to a wide variety of sources, including the annual reports of public companies, equity reports for firms nationalized in 1975, and commercial databases for the most recent periods (Amadeus, DB Informa). Membership of a given group was assumed when direct or indirect shareholdings in one firm's equity were at least 10 percent, with a few exceptions (Silva and Neves, 2018b). In addition, a study on corporate networks for the same period permits another level of control on the clusters of firms identified by equity ties (Khanna and Rivkin, 2006). More qualitative information (yearbooks, monographs, company histories, and biographies, for instance) complemented these sources.

In the next two sections the largest Portuguese business groups are put into context: firstly, with the presentation of the economy, institutions, and political regimes over the period analyzed (Section 13.3); secondly, comparing the largest business groups with other forms of big business (Section 13.4). Two complementary approaches comprise the remainder of this chapter. On the one hand, using a comparative perspective we distill into taxonomic categories what one may consider as the anatomy and physiology of business groups in Portugal, in two snapshots: 1973 and 2010. The first date corresponds to the peak of the development of business groups within the framework of the corporatist economy (*Estado Novo*), just before the severe shock of the 1975 nationalization. In 2010 a new wave of business groups stabilized, following the end of the privatization process and before the impact of the financial crisis, whose most severe effects started in 2011. Sections 13.5 and 13.6 favor this first approach. On the other hand, the second approach is eminently dynamic, seeking to understand the problems related to the emergence, growth, and crises of business groups. Section 13.7 addresses these issues.

The historically grounded analysis of Portuguese groups over a long period of time is our contribution to the debate on the emergence, strategic dynamics, and organizational configurations of business groups. This study not only places Portugal on the map of international comparative studies of business groups in developing and developed countries, it uses new sets of data and a quasi-experimental research design to understand the resilience of groups as an organizational form. Yet another contribution of this study is to understand how different historical contexts affect groups' taxonomical categories, organization, and strategies. The role of groups at the top of the business structure is the third issue raised in this study, identifying the weight of groups as an alternative form of big business and following their relative importance over time.

13.3 Business Groups and Structural Change in Portugal

Four major structural changes provided different economic and institutional contexts for the development of business groups in Portugal: the impact of the Great Depression; the "golden age" of Portuguese economic growth in the 1950s and 1960s; the 1975 nationalization of big business and the financial sector; and finally, the economic liberalization and privatization process starting in the late 1980s (Table 13.1).

Table 13.1. Political regimes, institutions, and economy in Portugal, 1910–2010.

Period	Political regime	Economic overview	Economy: growth and structural change	Institutional environment
1910–1926	First Republic	Inflation and currency depreciation (1918–24) Economic growth (1920–24) Deflationary policy (after 1924)	*Annual growth rate GDP per capita* 1910–26: 1.01% *Employment in agriculture* 1911: 57% *GDP per capita as % of developed countries* 1910: 33%	Inheriting changes in institutional framework from the nineteenth century 1925 banking law
1926–1974	*Estado Novo,* Authoritarian and single party regime	Mild impact of the Great Depression, with the exception of colonies High economic growth, 1950s–1970s	*Annual growth rate GDP per capita* 1950–60: 3.88% 1960–73: 6.54% *Employment in agriculture* 1950: 48% 1970: 32% *GDP per capita as % of developed countries* 1950: 33% 1973: 54%	1935 banking law Corporatism (regulate and contain competition; creation of cartelized structures) Industrial licensing
1974–1986	Democratic revolution (1974) Consolidation of democracy (1974–82)	Economic recession (1975) Financial crises (1975–78 and 1983–85)	*Annual growth rate GDP per capita* 1973–86: 1.73% *Employment in agriculture* 1981: 18% *GDP per capita as % of developed countries* 1985: 52%	Decolonization and confiscation of firms in the colonies 1975 nationalizations Abolition of corporatist institutions Social and political turmoil (1974–76)
1986–2010	Democracy	High economic growth (1986–92) Low economic growth and stagnation (mid-1990s on)	*Annual growth rate GDP per capita* 1986–2000: 3.95% 2000–2007: 0.45% *Employment in agriculture* 2010: 11% *GDP per capita as % of developed countries* 2007: 60%	Entering in the EEC (1986) Constitutional revisions and laws opening up public sectors to private investment (1982–89) Privatization (late 1980s on)

The Great Depression had a relatively mild effect on the Portuguese economy when compared with other countries, but it affected the economic policy and institutional environment for business activities (Cardoso, 2012). After the 1930s the corporatist regime created mechanisms and institutional bodies intended to regulate and contain competition (Confraria, 2005; Garrido, 2005), using administrative-sponsored cartelization, price controls, and administrative profit margins to regulate the market (Lucena, 1976; Madureira, 2002). Free entry or mergers and acquisitions in many industries depended on an administrative licensing process (Brito, 1989; Confraria, 1992). In addition, the new political regime (*Estado Novo*) assumed a more interventionist and import-substitution economic policy. Even without the creation of state-owned firms, the state sometimes directly supported some business ventures, becoming a shareholder in firms created in what were considered strategic sectors (oil, paper pulp, energy, basic metals) or using the state-owned banks to award credit under favorable conditions.

The financial impact of the Great Depression and the previous deflationary policies to control the financial imbalances inherited from the early 1920s created a new regulatory framework for the banking industry (Amaral, 2013). The new legislation prevented banks from acquiring stock of other firms to a value higher than 20 percent of their own capital, seeking to curtail excessive exposure to long-term credit and investment in securities, in line with similar legislation intended to regulate the banking industry worldwide (Cassis, 2011), without assuming drastic measures, such as the separation of commercial and investment banking.

The corporatist institutions nurtured a new environment for business activities. Industrial conditioning not only limited the entry of firms, but also favored the creation of oligopolistic or monopolistic markets supported by corporatist arrangements. Import-substitution policies also accommodated closer ties between government and business. The restriction in the creation of state-owned enterprises, in contrast with what occurred in other European corporatist regimes (Toninelli, 2000), led to more opportunities for big business to assume the group form. The opportunities of growth based on scale and related diversification remained scarce, and diversifying across unrelated industries thus became an effective strategy.

Therefore, the development of business groups characterizes the *Estado Novo* period (Silva et al., 2015). Some of these groups, bank-centered and with close relations to colonial businesses (BNU and Burnay groups), have their roots in the late nineteenth century. Another group (CUF) was born in the early postwar period, when the inflationary surge allowed the rapid expansion of some business ventures. However, it was after World War II that groups gained more importance. State intervention in the economy supported the development and economic resilience of those groups. Policy signals guided private investment and in certain cases the administration played a discretionary role in the promotion of business initiatives. Involving the state, directly or indirectly, in certain projects and limiting the entry of foreign capital also provided Portuguese firms with a brokering role for accessing domestic and overseas markets.

After the 1950s and until 1974, Portugal witnessed the best growth record in its history and was transformed from a backward agricultural economy into a medium-developed industrialized economy (Table 13.1). At the end of World War II GDP per capita in Portugal was just 30 percent of that of richer European countries; by 1973 it had reached a level of more than 50 percent, a notable progression not just for the figures involved, but also for its consistency. From 1960 on the regime opened the economy to the world market, being one of the founding members of EFTA. By the end of the *Estado Novo* period (1974) the degree of openness of the economy was not far from the European average (Lopes, 1999; Amaral, 2010).

In the aftermath of the 1974 revolution a new institutional and economic period began. The end of the *Estado Novo* regime opened a tumultuous process of democratization. Unlike other political transformations in the past, the 1974 revolution triggered profound changes in the business environment. Firstly, the *Estado Novo*'s corporatist institutions were abolished. Next, a rapid process of decolonization with the confiscation of property and assets affected business interests with investments in Africa (Ferreira, 2002). Thirdly, the withdrawal of earlier restrictions on the exercise of trade-union activity set off a wave of industrial and political turmoil, increasing labor costs and creating a legal framework limiting labor redundancies. In short, the country became less business-friendly, especially to foreign investment, which after 1975 fell sharply (Leite et al., 2001). Finally, the existing large business groups were nationalized in 1975, just when they were expanding at their fastest rate, constituting the most profound transformation of the business environment.

A new institutional change occurred in the 1980s—the end of the state-led economy and the beginning of privatization. Finance and basic sectors remained closed to private initiative for a decade after 1975, but from the early 1980s the restrictions on investment in several sectors of the Portuguese economy began to fall away. The 1982 constitutional revision and the 1983 law for the delimitation of economic sectors allowed private investment in previously closed business activities, namely in banking and insurance. The negotiations for Portugal's entry to the EEC (1985) would also be responsible for changes in the institutional framework, in order to reduce direct and indirect state intervention in the economy. The financial sector was privatized first. In the mid-1990s, with the exception of CGD, which remains a state-owned bank, all banks were in private hands. The privatization of non-financial state-owned enterprises started in the mid-1990s, and some of them passed into private ownership only in the early twenty-first century. At the beginning of the 2010s, the state still controlled railway, air, and urban transport, water supply, waste management, electricity, and postal services. At the time of writing some of these industries are being privatized.

The last two decades also display a powerful tendency toward economic and financial integration within the European Union, market deregulation, and participation in global capital flows. It was in this new institutional and economic environment that a new wave of business groups emerged. Some of them descended from groups nationalized in 1975, but their characteristics were different.

13.4 Large-Enterprise Economy in Portugal: The Role of Business Groups

From a long-term perspective groups were not marginal players in Portugal when looking at the top of the large-enterprise economy (Table 13.2). In banking, business groups dominated the industry in 1973, occupying seven of the top ten places. The other three banks were state-owned, this being one of the industries where state capital had an evident weight. The presence of business groups in the insurance industry is less overwhelming, but they dominate the top of the industry—the three largest insurance firms belong to groups, which also own other less important insurers.

The dominance of groups in the banking industry derives, firstly, from banks heading several business groups created after the late nineteenth century, the earliest being Burnay and BNU. The 1920s and 1930s banking legislation, as well as the gloomy economic environment of the period, limited their potential for expansion. By contrast, the booming economy of the 1960s increased the scale and scope of banking groups.[2]

Table 13.2. Top 125 firms and business groups, number of firms by industry.

Industry	1973		2010	
	Top125	belonging to BG	Top125	belonging to BG
Non-financial firms				
Agriculture	2	0	0	0
Manufacturing	47	22	26	8
Electricity, water supply, waste management	8	1	9	1
Construction and real estate	9	1	22	3
Wholesale and retail trade	9	1	11	2
Transportation and storage	5	1	16	2
Colonial business	13	4	0	0
Others	7	2	16	5
	100	*32*	*100*	*21*
Financial firms				
Banking	15	9	14	2
Insurance	10	3	8	1
Financial holdings	0	0	3	2
	25	*12*	*25*	*5*

Source: 1973: compiled and calculated from database constructed for the project "Business Groups in the *Estado Novo* period," funded by Fundação para a Ciência e Tecnologia (PTDC/HIS-HIS/099683/2008). 2010: Amadeus and DB Informa databases; annual reports.

---

[2] The banking groups could become more active in industrial investment in the 1960s and early 1970s, as legal limitations on banks' investment in securities became less strict, and banks also created a complex web of financial holdings to overcome legal restrictions.

The industrial policies promoted by the *Estado Novo* sought to direct private capital to what were regarded as strategic investments in sectors such as energy and heavy industry. This created another opportunity to expand industrial investments based on banks.

The second driver for this dominance in the banking industry came from business groups with non-financial origins (CUF and Champalimaud). Manufacturing-born business groups internalized banking as soon as they started to move to unrelated diversification: the CUF group with the acquisition of Totta banking house in the 1920s, and Champalimaud buying Banco Pinto & Sotto Mayor in the 1960s. Organic growth in each of these banks was followed by a further strategy of mergers and acquisitions. This was sometimes successful, as when Totta merged with Banco Lisboa & Açores in 1969; in other cases there was evident failure, as when the CUF group tried to control Banco Fonsecas & Burnay or when António Champalimaud moved to acquire BPA.

The dominance of Portuguese business groups in the banking sector points to one conclusion about their strategy during the *Estado Novo* period. Although these groups included some listed companies, the capital market was an insignificant source of corporate finance. The banks within business groups created capital flows internal to the group, financing its organic growth, greenfield investments, and acquisitions. The combination of a bank and an insurance company within the group is also typical of a bancassurance model (Fields et al., 2007), mutually leveraging the banking and insurance activities and contributing to the attraction of more financial resources.

In non-financial industries there was a more varied business landscape. Stand-alone firms dominated among the largest 100 firms, but at the top of the ranking the number of enterprises belonging to groups matched the number of stand-alone firms. Groups' firms led in capital-intensive manufacturing activities: tobacco, petroleum, chemicals and pharmaceuticals, cement, electrical equipment, basic metals, and transport equipment. In this sense they seemed to have the same historical role that the integrated enterprise had in Chandler's interpretation of the rise of big business (Chandler, 1990).

In 2010 groups withdrew from the financial sector. The pre-nationalization rule that every group had a bank no longer exists in the twenty-first century. Banks are no longer at the head of business groups (see Table 13.3, col. 2), and these cease to internalize banking, despite the repeated attempts by the large business groups created after the 1990s to recreate the internal capital flows that existed before 1975. The Mello group started its process of reconstruction by acquiring two banks in the privatization of the financial sector (UBP and Sociedade Financeira Portuguesa) and also creating the Banco Mello, which could act as the pivotal financial arm in the new group. They were sold in 2000, and the Mello family maintained only a small holding in Banco Comercial Português until 2007 (BCP is one of the largest Portuguese banks, which acted as a confederation of several business interests [Silva and Neves, 2014a]). Américo Amorim, leading the group with his name, had been an important shareholder and founder of several banks (BCP, for instance) and had an important stake in

Table 13.3. The largest Portuguese business groups, an overview.

Group	Sector of origin	Date of formation	Ownership	Generational depth	Diversification (# of sectors)	Turnover A 2010 M€	Turnover B 2010 M€
1973							
CUF	Manufacturing	1920s	Family	3rd	46	4,765	3,000
Champalimaud	Manufacturing	1950s	Family	1st	20	2,268	1,812
Espírito Santo (ES)	Banking	1940s	Family	2nd	11	1,917	978
Banco Borges & Irmão (BBI)	Banking	1940s	Family	2nd	19	804	706
Banco Português do Atlântico (BPA)	Banking	1960s	Federation	-	17	749	606
Banco Nacional Ultramarino (BNU)	Banking	1890s	Federation	-	17	883	437
Banco Fonsecas & Burnay (BFB)	Banking	1880s	?	-	16	668	316
2010							
Sonae	Manufacturing	1980s	Family	2nd	14	7,652	7,652
Américo Amorim	Manufacturing	1980s	Family	1st	11	18,701	5,434
José de Mello (ex-CUF)	Manufacturing	1920s	Family	4+	11	6,223	1,505
Mota-Engil	Construction	1990s	Family	2nd	12	2,596	2,229
Semapa	Manufacturing	2000s	Family	2nd	6	1,688	1,688
Jerónimo Martins	Retailing	1940s	Family	3rd	8	8,691	8,691
Espírito Santo (ES)	Banking	1940s	Family	4+	12	9,888	6,518

Ownership: nature of the group's ultimate owner (federation: federation of business interests, represented by several families and entrepreneurs as owners of the bank). In 1973 the GUO of Burnay is not clearly defined due to the struggle for control of the bank taking place at the end of the 1960s.

Generational depth: number of generations at the head of the group.

Diversification: number of industrial branches where the group has operations, using the International Standard Industrial Classification (ISIC) classification at the 2-digit level.

Turnover: turnover of groups' affiliates—(A) Total turnover of the firms at 2010 constant prices; (B) Turnover weighted according to the group's stake at 2010 constant prices.

Source: 1973: compiled and calculated from database constructed for the project "Business Groups in the *Estado Novo* period." 2010: Amadeus and DB Informa databases; annual reports.

Banco Popular, the fifth-largest Spanish bank in 2010. However, none of these ventures in banking recreated the internal capital markets characteristic of the *Estado Novo* business groups. The SONAE group also moved into the financial sector, first creating a small investment bank with SG Warburg (EFISA, 1987), next fighting for control of the privatization of two former state-owned banks (BTA, 1991, and BPA, 1995), and finally trying to launch a new bank, the Banco Universo. Belmiro de Azevedo, the founder of the group, emphatically assumed the cross-participation between industrial and financial interests as a strategic move "to create business groups with European dimension and competitive power" (cit. in Fernandes, 2008: 59). This strategy was eventually abandoned in the late 1990s. In short, the new business groups renounced internalizing banking activities to boost their internal capital markets.

The only exception was the Espírito Santo group, in which the bank flagging the name of the founding family had, since its privatization in 1992, been the pivotal enterprise in the group's re-emergence and expansion, attaining a clearly larger size when compared with the family group that existed before 1975. An investment bank and several financial subsidiaries across different continents (banks, investment societies, and other vehicles) completed the banking portfolio of the Espírito Santo group in 2010. It also reconstructed the bancassurance model existing during the *Estado Novo*, having one of the largest Portuguese insurance companies (Tranquilidade). In 2010 the Espírito Santo group was the only one maintaining the intra-group capital flows sustained by its financial enterprises, either directly through credit and investments or indirectly through their banks' clients, who bought debt and equity issued by companies belonging to the group. The group's vulnerability to the recent financial crisis derived from the dark side of this internal capital market, as well as from the poorly managed and highly leveraged banking operations in Angola through a group affiliate (with a loans-to-deposit ratio of 210 percent). The financial holding (ESFG) and the ES bank became increasingly exposed to the debt from the group's non-financial enterprises. Debt instruments were sold to the banks' customers, and funds managed by the different financial arms of the group had great exposure to the ES non-financial sector. This cascade of liabilities eventually led to the group's disappearance.

Even though less pronounced than in the financial sector, the importance of Portuguese groups in other industries also decreased in 2010: from a third of the top firms, their relative share dropped to a fifth. Manufacturing continues to attract more affiliate firms, especially in the same branches as in 1973. Some services have an even greater importance—particularly health, tourism, construction, and real estate. From 1973 to 2010 the Portuguese economy became markedly more complex and heterogeneous, favoring specialization and the rise of stand-alone firms.

A final conclusion emerges from this comparison of the relative importance of business groups at the top of business hierarchy. The 1975 nationalization process not only dismantled the largest business groups. It was also the largest and fastest consolidation process in several major industries, e.g., transport, cement, pulp paper, oil, electricity, and chemicals. Therefore, former private competitors were consolidated into single and larger state-owned enterprises for each business sector. This was another major transformation in the business landscape—one that was impossible to attain within the earlier framework of the corporatist state or so rapidly through the competitive processes of a market economy.

This consolidation process might imply that privatizations would not lead to the recreation of business groups in these areas, in which the advantages of specialization and further economies of scale and related diversification would prevent their integration into widely diversified business groups. However, this did not happen. Several of these integrated firms (oil, chemicals, paper pulp) moved into the portfolio of the second wave of diversified business groups created after the privatization process. This is another face of the resilience of diversified business groups—they not only re-emerged, but also entered into business areas where a process of former consolidation would predict its disappearance.

13.5 TAXONOMIES: COMPARING BUSINESS GROUPS OVER TIME

A group's ultimate owner may be a family, the state, or a federation of families/ entrepreneurs clustered around a bank. Family largely prevails as the core entity and stands as a long-term characteristic of Portuguese business groups. Exceptions do exist, as some banking groups are federations of interests (BPA and BNU in 1973, see Table 13.3), and there is even a cluster of state-owned enterprises, but without the mechanisms of intra-group coordination and control. Family ownership is the major commonality characterizing Portuguese business groups over time. In fact, when one compares the two periods (pre-nationalization and post-1990s), most characteristics are shared within each period but not between the two periods.

Before the 1975 nationalizations groups relied on the domestic market, taking advantage of the protectionist framework characterizing the *Estado Novo* policy (see Section 13.3). Expansion beyond the mainland borders took place only in the Portuguese colonies in Africa, firstly through the exploitation of the natural resources in these territories (foodstuffs and agricultural raw materials in the CUF and Espírito Santo groups; mineral resources in the case of the Burnay group). Later, in the 1950s and 1960s, the colonial expansion followed path-dependent investments in industries where groups were already dominant on the mainland: Champalimaud, cements and steel; CUF, chemical products and transport services. By contrast, after the 1990s internationalization became an objective pursued by every group. Only one group has its internationalization strategy based only on exports (Semapa, pulp and paper). The other groups moved most of their manufacturing and services operations abroad (Sonae, JM, Amorim, and Mota being the most exemplary cases).

Size (number of enterprises or turnover) and level of diversification are also widely different (Table 13.3). Again, there is a clear divergence between the *Estado Novo* period and the groups emerging after the 1990s. Average diversification is greater at the end of the first period than at the beginning of the twenty-first century. Before nationalization only one group (Espírito Santo) operated in a number of industrial branches similar to what became the norm after 1990.

The sectorial origin of the Portuguese groups shows identical diversity. In 1973 banking groups prevailed, even if the two manufacturing groups (CUF and Champalimaud) had the largest scale and scope of activities. The banking legislation of the 1920s and 1930s limited the potential for growth of groups headed by banks, which did not happen in the case of the manufacturing groups. In these groups the sector of origin—chemicals for CUF and cements for Champalimaud—was already surpassed by the importance of new ventures. On the contrary, groups headed by banks continued to rely on the financial sector as the main source of their turnover, even after the economic expansion in the 1960s and early 1970s, when the barriers imposed by the banking legislation started to be overcome.

Generational depth is also diverse. The greatest longevity characterizes the Mello and Espírito Santo groups, still among the seven largest groups in 2010, but having their entrepreneurial origins in the nineteenth century. As groups they were in the fourth generation by 2010. The JM group was created in the 1940s, but it was then a small business entity, very far from its current economic importance. In other family groups the generational depth is very short, depending heavily on the presence of the founding entrepreneur. The group created by Henry Burnay is typical in this respect. It survived the death of its founder in 1909, but the family rapidly lost control of the bank and affiliates to the Société Générale de Belgique in the late 1920s. The group founded by António Champalimaud had a similar fate to the old Burnay group. It reemerged after the privatization process, but the large pre-1975 family group disappeared even before its founder's death.

This examination of the ownership, size, diversification, sectorial origin, and generational depth of business groups reveals the possibility of building up taxonomical categories for their study. Taxonomies have the obvious advantage of providing a comparative framework across different countries and over time. Taxonomies of groups have been developed with different epistemological approaches and degrees of success (e.g., Kock and Guillén, 2001; Cuervo-Cazurra, 2006; Yiu et al., 2007; Schneider, 2009). The taxonomy proposed by Colpan and Hikino (2010; this volume) constitutes a major effort in conceptualizing business groups. We built on their effort and introduced several other categories: ownership and control, capturing the shareholding structure of the affiliates and how this introduces different elements of capital control; organizational form, representing the relative importance of vertical/hierarchical equity ties or horizontal ties, based on circular and cross-shareholdings; and corporate finance, seeking to define how the group mobilizes financial resources. Two other categories, already mentioned above, were also added, proposing a time dimension to this taxonomy of business groups: sectorial origin and generational depth.

The results are summarized in Table 13.4. The main conclusion points to the different profiles business groups may reveal. This strong variance is valid not only

Table 13.4. Taxonomy.

Groups	GUO	Generational depth	Sector of origin	Administrative Control	Ownership/control	Structure and control	Organizational form	Corporate finance
1973								
CUF	Family	3rd	Manufacturing	Strategic, budgetary	50% + stake	Operating	Vertical	Intra-group capital market
Champalimaud	Family	1st	Manufacturing	Strategic, budgetary	50% + stake	Personal	Vertical	Intra-group capital market
Espírito Santo (ES)	Family	3rd	Banking	Financial	Smaller	Operating	Vertical	Intra-group capital market
Banco Borges & Irmão (BBI)	Family	2nd	Banking	Financial	50% + stake	Operating	Horizontal	Intra-group capital market
Banco Português do Atlântico (BPA)	Federation	-	Banking	?	50% + stake	Operating	Horizontal	Intra-group capital market
Banco Nacional Ultramarino (BNU)	Federation	-	Banking	Financial	Smaller	Operating	Vertical	Intra-group capital market
Banco Fonsecas & Burnay (BFB)	?	-	Banking	Strategic -> Financial	Smaller	Operating	Vertical	Intra-group capital market
2010								
Sonae	Family	1st	Manufacturing	Strategic, budgetary	Pyramidal	Holding	Vertical	Banking intermediation
Américo Amorim	Family	1st	Manufacturing	?	Pyramidal	Holding	Vertical	Banking intermediation
José de Mello (ex-CUF)	Family	4+	Manufacturing	?	Pyramidal	Holding	Vertical	Banking intermediation
Mota-Engil	Family	2nd	Construction	Strategic, budgetary	Pyramidal	Holding	Vertical	Banking intermediation
Semapa	Family	2nd	Manufacturing	Strategic, budgetary	Pyramidal	Holding	Vertical	Banking intermediation
Jerónimo Martins	Family	3rd	Trade	Strategic, budgetary	Pyramidal	Holding	Vertical	Banking intermediation
Espírito Santo (ES)	Family	4+	Banking	Financial	Pyramidal	Holding	Vertical	Intra-group capital market

GUO: group ultimate owner.

Generational depth: see Table 13.3.

Administrative control: characteristics of the administrative control exerted by the top control unit over the group.

Ownership/control: shareholding structure of the affiliates, representing the level of control by the GUO.

Structure and control: characteristics of the control unit and organizational structure. Personal: no formalized control unit at the top of the group. Operating: control unit and organizational structure based on operating companies. Holding: holding company at the top of the group and financial sub-holdings at the top of different business areas. Mixed: mostly based on operating companies, but with the existence of a few financial holdings.

Organizational form: relative importance of vertical/hierarchical equity ties, based on circular and cross-shareholdings (see Yiu et al, 2007).

Corporate finance: the most important source of corporate finance to the group. Intra-group capital market: capital flows internal to the group, based on its own bank (relational banking), are the most important source for financing its organic growth, greenfield investments, and the acquisition of new companies. Banking intermediation: arm's-length bank relationships between the group and independent banks.

Source: 1973: compiled and calculated from database constructed for the project "Business Groups in the Estado Novo period." 2010: Amadeus database and annual reports.

between periods, but also within periods, and it is so clear that it needs no further development. It emphasizes the inherent flexibility assumed by business groups, evident in the different characteristics presented in terms of ownership and control, financial arrangements, organizational configuration, sectorial origin, and generational depth. This is a hybrid organization, even more plastic than the multidivisional form (Bartlett and Ghoshal, 1993; Hoskisson et al., 1993), explaining why it is so difficult to agree on a standard definition, given the diversity of arrangements the group form may assume.

13.6 OWNERSHIP AND CONTROL: TIES THAT BIND

13.6.1 Business Groups during the Estado Novo

The definition of business groups emphasizes two distinctive features that have organizational consequences. The first is the existence of a core entity (a family or an individual entrepreneur, for instance), giving coherence to the aggregation of different firms. The nature of the ultimate owner of Portuguese business groups was established in the above section—family-oriented, either from banking or manufacturing origins. The second feature refers to the existence of binding ties, linking together the clustered firms (Khanna and Rivkin, 2006). The relationship between ownership and control may take different forms in business groups, a relatively underdeveloped topic in business studies (Boyd and Hoskisson, 2010). The structuring of equity ties within the group addresses the ownership and control mechanisms, which guarantee the central role assumed by the core entity. The configuration of the business group reflects the relative importance of vertical and horizontal ties (Silva and Neves, 2018a).

Before nationalization Portuguese groups sought positions of incontrovertible control, striving to secure about 50 percent of the capital of affiliate firms, either through the direct involvement of the core entity (family or firms acting as holdings) or through cross-shareholdings between different affiliate firms (Table 13.5). For many firms this equity participation exceeded 50 percent, but rarely attained 100 percent of the capital, unlike subsidiaries of present-day conglomerates (Colpan and Hikino, 2010). Even when equity participation remained below 50 percent, it still allowed a controlling stake by the ultimate owner. These positions of large ownership holdings reveal another strategic characteristic of these groups. They were inward-looking and exclusive organizations, segmenting the affiliate firms from more inclusive partnerships with other groups or stand-alone firms (Silva and Neves, 2014a; Silva et al., 2015). Response to specific characteristics of the business system or some Malthusian behavior from the business elite is a question open to investigation.

Groups of banking origin reveal a lower level of equity control over affiliates, always below 50 percent, with the exception of Borges & Irmão. Legal restrictions on the holding of stock by banks explain this common pattern. The Fonsecas & Burnay group

Table 13.5. Number of firms according to group shareholding, 1973–4.

Group	Participation 10–20%	Participation 10–20%	Participation 20–50%	Average group shareholding in %
CUF	4	25	98	69.3
ES	6	5	6	38.6
BBI	0	2	85	85.9
BFB	11	9	8	30.9
BPA	3	12	15	49.0
Champ	7	12	19	54.0

Source: Compiled and calculated from database constructed for the project "Business Groups in the Estado Novo period."

(BFB) presents the lowest average shareholding, as there has been a trend toward decreasing the level of equity participation in several firms. The Espírito Santo and BPA groups remain in higher positions, but still below 50 percent.

At the other end of the spectrum, the CUF group favored large equity control, regardless of the different segments in which the group operated. For instance, in the manufacturing sector the CUF company (the chemical firm at the origin of the group and still its largest operating unit) had always owned more than 50 percent of its affiliate firms, which operated in business areas belonging to the chemical firm's value chain. The equity ties thus corresponded to an operational integration with the CUF company. The same logic was followed in the transportation segment. Two dozen enterprises gravitated around CNN, the group's sea transport company, which was the operating holding for the transport segment. Similar reasoning could be applied to the financial sector (clustered around Banco Totta & Açores and Império insurance company), shipbuilding (Lisnave), and tobacco (Tabaqueira). These large companies acted as operating holdings and gathered together other firms doing business in the same segment. In any of these situations, equity control matched the control of strategic resources by the parent company. In short, the administrative or operating holdings allowed the managerial coordination of sectorial investments. The equity participation they maintained with the segment affiliates formalized the control ties into ownership relationships (Figure 13.1).

The existence of a holding company at the apex of the group exercising equity control over the group was unusual in 1973. The closer situation might be the role some banks had as a financial holding (BFB, BPA, BBI, BNU). In other situations the founding entrepreneur assumed direct control, also without formalizing any holding company (Champalimaud).

The CUF group had more diverse and complex forms of control, revealing the peculiar organizational problems created by its size and scope. Diversity over time, as the group's organization did not remain the same, and organizational complexity culminated in 1973 when about 200 firms belonged to the group.

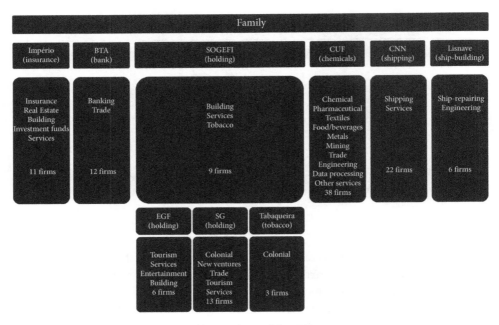

FIGURE **13.1.** Organization of the CUF group, 1974.

Source: CUF archive, equity participation of the firms
nationalized in 1975, and annual reports.

Before World War II the group's nearly two dozen companies could easily be managed from an operating company, CUF, the above-mentioned chemical firm. Outside the chemicals cluster the group was already present in the financial sector, shipping, shipbuilding, and tobacco. The formation of the Empresa Geral de Fomento in 1947 created a firm to act in a similar way to the headquarters staff unit in multi-divisional firms (Chandler, 1991), providing budgetary control and planning to family and professional top managers, but without acting as a strategic or financial holding. In short, EGF professionalized staff support to top management in the family group.

Twenty years later, in the mid-1960s, the situation had changed. The CUF company remained the most important operating unit, but now the group had more than fifty companies in very different business areas. Further expansion was expected, taking advantage of the opportunities created by a booming economy during the 1960s. In 1964 a non-listed financial holding (SOGEFI) emerged to gather the shares held by family members and to support further expansion of the group. However, the pretense of organizational rationality in which SOGEFI would occupy the financial vertex of the business group was more apparent than real. The equity ties shaping the group created a more complex structure (see Figure 13.1). There was a strategy of turning financial or manufacturing firms into administrative holdings for organizing different market segments in which the group operated, as explained above. Horizontal ties were absent between these business silos. They emerged only in the top tier of firms acting as administrative holdings in the different segments in which the CUF group operated or between the firms clustered within a segment holding.

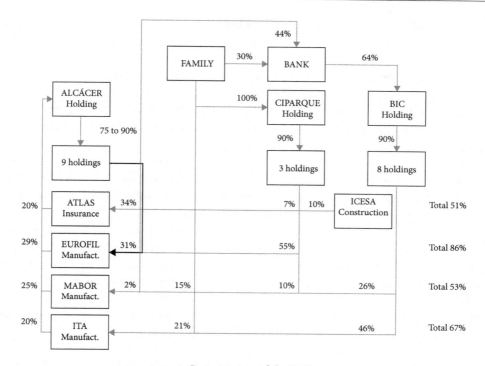

FIGURE **13.2.** Organization of the BBI group, 1974.

Source: Equity participation of the firms nationalized
in 1975 and annual reports.

In other less diversified and smaller groups horizontal linkages were more frequent. Accompanying the increasing expansion of the BBI group, a set of thirty-two small financial holding companies was created. Compared to other banking groups, BBI had exceptionally high levels of equity participation in industrial affiliates, which were supported by this web of small financial holdings. A complex system of cross- and circular holdings linked these companies to each other and to the bank and the main operational companies (see Figure 13.2). The holding scheme set up by the Borges & Irmão group was able to avoid the legal restrictions on banks' equity participation in other companies.

13.6.2 Hierarchical Groups without Financial Pyramids

Groups' configurations based on vertical ties do not imply the existence of pyramidal structures (Morck, 2010). The CUF group is a clear example of a hierarchical organization based not on a pyramid but on some sort of hybrid form in which the hierarchical structure appears only in each business segment (Figure 13.1; Yiu et al., 2007: 1567–9). The resulting configuration is the product of several decades of acquisitions, greenfield investments, and mergers. It is more the result of stratigraphic processes, in which different layers of firms had been added to the group without following a Cartesian logic.

These stratigraphic layers of firms added to the group are very evident in older segments such as the chemical industry. The fragmentation and juxtaposition of affiliates in the same business area pushed profitability down, making coordination difficult and increasing overhead costs. This complexity prompted the first attempt to implement organizational rationalization, resorting to McKinsey & Co. in 1970 to reorganize the cluster of firms in CUF company business areas. The CUF company maintained its position as an operating holding company, and the affiliates were organized according to different business segments, but without ending their status as legally independent firms. (In Figure 13.3 these affiliate firms are listed at the bottom of the figure, within dotted rectangles and under each CUF company division: chemical, consumer goods, textile, metal-mechanical.) McKinsey's reorganization did not merge the different affiliates into an integrated multidivisional firm with internal divisions, as occurred in several other cases across Europe during the late 1950s and 1960s (McKenna, 2006). It laid a rationalized organizational layout, based on four clear business segments and many underlying profit centers across the existing twenty firms acting in the CUF company's value chain (Figure 13.3) (Silva, 2011).

The analytical consequence of the new organizational design implemented by McKinsey may not be immediately perceived, but it supports Colpan and Hikino's assessment of the definition of business groups (Colpan and Hikino, this volume). The legally independent character of the firms alone does not qualify a cluster of enterprises to become a business group. Had the CUF group been restricted to the twenty independent firms in technologically related businesses headed by the CUF company and reorganized by McKinsey (Figure 13.3), this would become an organizational structure close to a (Chandlerian) multidivisional firm.

The type of managerial control affects the organizational configuration and the role of pivotal enterprises within the group. The case of CUF illustrates this situation. The Empresa Geral de Fomento emerged in 1947 to act as a "headquarters staff unit." In the late 1960s the increasingly rapid diversification trend in the CUF group turned the firm into an apex of strategic and budgetary control. In late 1973 the EGF formalized this transition, revising its statutes and expanding its board through the inclusion of the two Mello brothers (the owners of the CUF group), as well as professional top managers in the most important companies of the group. The 1974 revolution and the subsequent nationalization prevent us from assessing the success of that change.

13.6.3 The Rise of Pyramidal Business Groups after 1990

Groups' reemergence after 1990 introduces some changes in the relationships between ownership, control, and organizational configuration. In 2010 every group had a financial holding formalizing the apex of the group equity ties and concentrating the

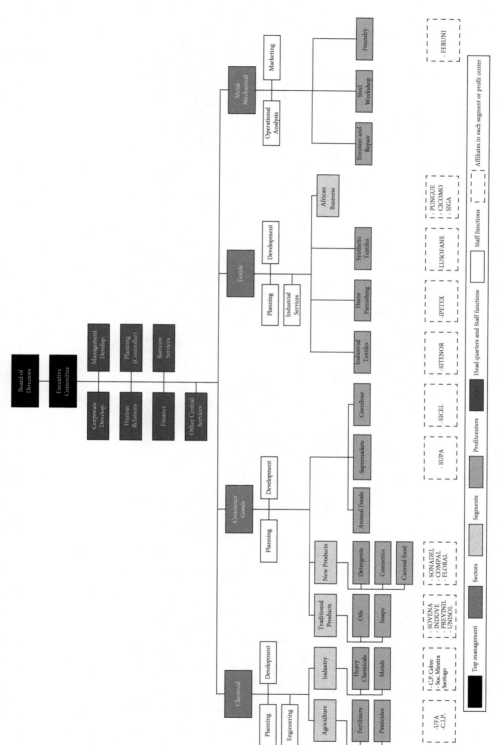

FIGURE 13.3. CUF Company—Organizational structure proposed by McKinsey, 1970.

Source: McKinsey proceedings, 1970 (CUF Archive).

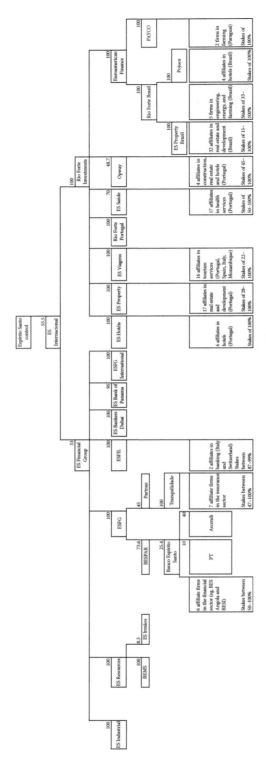

FIGURE 13.4. Organization of the Espirito Santo group, 2010.

Source: Amadeus database and annual reports for 2010.

family shareholdings. They were not listed and remained closed to investors outside the family. They constitute the actual vertex of the pyramidal structures in present-time business groups.

Another major difference is the role of sub-holdings. Before nationalization they were mostly administrative or operating holdings: large enterprises in a business segment, organizing a cluster of firms having value-chain relationships among them. In 2010 they were listed financial sub-holdings, draining financial resources into different business segments, with access to non-family sources (qualified shareholders, capital market, bank loans).

Typical pyramid structures characterize the current business groups: under the family holding, a first tier of listed firms, usually financial holdings, control layers of other listed and unlisted firms. The first tier of listed financial holdings is ultimately owned and controlled by the closed family holding, with the remaining shares sold to other investors. The cascade of control rights depending on the ultimate owner is achieved through the investment of a disproportionately minor proportion of ownership rights (see Figure 13.4 for the Espírito Santo case). Even without dual-class shares (existing only in previously state-owned firms, but where the state maintained minority "golden shares"), the cascade of ownership rights across the pyramid magnifies control rights over a larger amount of the aggregated capital of the entire group (see the stylized pyramidal business group in Morck, 2010: Fig. 21.3; Almeida and Wolfenzon, 2006b).

The emergence of pyramids after the late 1990s has a direct correspondence in the two organizational innovations mentioned above: the top family holding and the financial sub-holdings. It also reveals new characteristics of the economy at the beginning of the twenty-first century when compared with the *Estado Novo* period: the need to mobilize more capital resources for the new ventures that groups are currently involved in and a more active capital market from which funding may be drained.

Different ownership and organizational patterns coexist and evolve over time in Portuguese business groups. More than a parochial conclusion, this may lead to rethinking what business groups are as an organizational form. The holding form is often mentioned as a characteristic of business groups' ownership and coordination mechanisms. However, holdings may perform different organizational functions: family ownership holdings, as closed blocks of shares (early twenty-first century); administrative or operating holdings, acting as a means of polarizing ownership and managerial coordination (pre-1975); financial holdings in pyramidal arrangements to act as financial vehicles for business segments and new ventures, mobilizing third-party funding to family business groups (early twenty-first century). Failing to perceive these distinct types of holdings may lead to analytical confusion and to inadequate understanding of different organizational forms assumed by business groups.

Are some organizational forms more dominant than others in the history of the Portuguese groups? The main conclusion is to stress the multiplicity of arrangements assumed by organizational design. Nevertheless, there is a clear period-specificity in groups' organizational forms. They converged in the late twentieth century to pyramidal structures, with financial holdings in the first and second tiers. The cascade effect of the pyramids in magnifying control capabilities regarding the ownership rights of the ultimate owners is a subsequent result, implying that the extensive shareholdings (50 percent or more) characterizing pre-1975 groups were less frequent in 2010.

Is there any sign of path-dependency when we follow the few pre-1975 business groups which are still present in early twenty-first century? The answer is definitely in the negative. Groups re-emerging in the late twentieth century and descending from pre-1975 large groups adopt the characteristics of the particular period.

13.7 GROWTH DYNAMICS AND STRATEGIES

13.7.1 The Rise and Expansion of Business Groups

Diversification levels are remarkably diverse between pre-1975 and post-1990 business groups. Before the 1975 nationalizations the strategy of expansion moved into more unrelated business areas, rushing to new investment opportunities in an economy witnessing strong growth rates, but with a reduced market size and an unsophisticated competitive environment. One clear example of this diversification trend affecting every group is the tertiarization impetus occurring in the 1960s, the golden age of Portuguese economic growth and the most important period of expansion in both size and scope regarding any business group (Silva et al., 2015: Tabs. 2 and 3). Besides other business segments, every group moved into areas such as tourism, real estate, consulting, and IT services.

The early twenty-first-century groups are much more focused than their predecessors. They display a more reduced scope of activities and in most cases the original sector where the group was created retains a substantial weight in the group's turnover (retailing, JM; pulp paper, Semapa; construction, Mota; cork, Amorim; laminated wood, Sonae). Greater competitive advantages reflect specialization in core sectors and the accumulation of product-based capabilities, in contrast to broad diversification in the past. This new specialization pattern encourages the internationalization strategy followed by every business group during the last two decades. It is the accumulation of product-specific capabilities that maintains their competitiveness in international markets, in contrast to the domestic orientation of pre-1975 groups. Three cases illustrate this point. The Sonae group focus on retailing, IT, media, and shopping-mall construction and management. This last activity is developed abroad, as is the production of laminated wood, the original manufacturing activity of the group and where it is a world leader, with twenty-one plants across three continents. The Amorim group is present in different business segments, but it originated in cork manufacturing. Today it is the world's largest producer of cork products and its manufacturing company is one of the most internationalized of Portuguese firms. Finally, the Mota group originated in construction and public works, which still form its predominant sector. Nowadays, turnover abroad represents the largest part of the group's operations.

The ES group is the polar opposite of this tendency to specialize in core sectors as a driver to expansion and diversification. It abandoned the former reluctance to diversify that it held until nationalization—reluctance in the number of sectors in which it was present, and in the shareholding level in the affiliate firms, mostly minority, but qualified, stakes. In 1973 the ES group was primarily a family commercial bank, with some interests in oil, colonial firms, tires, and tourism. In this self-restraint strategy, the ES group was different from other pre-1975 banking groups, which followed a more active strategy of diversification and expansion, e.g., Burnay (1880–1920) and BBI (after the 1950s).

The resurgence of the ES group after 1990 resulted in a completely different profile. The new group developed a strategy more similar to the processes of expansion and diversification characterizing banking groups before 1975. Espírito Santo did this even more intensively, leveraged in the bank that was the group's center of gravity. At the beginning of the twenty-first century, in addition to the financial sector (banking and insurance) it was present in real estate, hotels, tourism, construction, agriculture, telecommunications, media, and health services.

The role of exogenous environmental factors in the emergence and expansion of groups is usually emphasized, in line with the idea that they are a second-best organizational solution (for a synthesis, see Colpan and Hikino, 2010). It is easy to associate these factors with the development of Portuguese business groups during most of the twentieth century: an interventionist and protectionist regime, highly regulated markets, low development of the capital and labor markets, and domestic insufficiencies in the supply of goods and services (Silva et al., 2015). As an explanation for groups' expansion, the processes of rapid economic growth are less emphasized. In the Portuguese case the period of growth ending in 1974 is a textbook example of the role of economic conditions in encouraging the very rapid growth of every business group, either in terms of the number of companies or in terms of diversification (Silva et al., 2015: Tabs. 2 and 3).

By contrast, periods of economic stagnation hinder groups' expansion. For instance, the Great Depression decreased the fortune of colonial activities, which were more affected than mainland exports by the global slump in demand. Simultaneously, regulatory changes turned banks away from investing in industry. Both factors and the general economic downturn checked business groups' expansion.

The dynamic endogenous factors may have several origins. The gap-filling strategy is commonly used in developing countries (Langlois, 2010) and is also visible in the first phase of groups' creation in Portugal. It takes advantage of market deficiencies in the provision of goods and services. Groups internalize these market failures, creating new product-specific capabilities at the firm level or consolidating generic capabilities at the group level. This process may be more complex than simply the creation or the acquisition of a company for operating in a new business area. Sometimes the new activity starts to be developed in an existing company, for intra-group transactions only (engineering, for instance). Scaling up operations and moving them into the market leads to spinning-off these activities through the creation of a new firm (Silva et al., 2015).

Dynamics of growth may also be different when comparing manufacturing and financial groups (see Section 13.5). But even within manufacturing groups strategies of growth may take different paths, in a complex combination of exogenous and endogenous factors, as exemplified by the evolution of the CUF and Champalimaud groups (Silva et al., 2015). The manufacturing origin of the group dictates more or less potential for growth. CUF comes from the chemical industry, where intersectorial relatedness is greater than in cement, the manufacturing origin of Champalimaud.

Timing in the creation of the group is also critical for exogenous and endogenous reasons. If created in a time of economic dynamism, diversification occurs more rapidly, as happened with the CUF group in the 1920s, contrary to Champalimaud, which started its activity in cement just after World War II. Timing of creation provides generational depth to a group, raising the internal accumulation of resources and capabilities. Being a three-generation family group, as CUF was during the 1960s, provided it with the group-level capabilities that could be mobilized more rapidly and successfully to new ventures in different business areas, which explains the vibrant rhythm of growth experienced by this group in the 1960s and early 1970s. This endogenous function of timing explains the scale and scope of CUF diversification in 1973, when compared with the Champalimaud group still led by its founder.

13.7.2 Haunting Business Groups: Family Succession, Financial Crises, and the State

The dynamic processes of groups' evolution are not only those affecting their formation and expansion, but also those leading to their decline and possible disappearance. Generational devolution is one of the reasons for the demise of business groups (Silva et al., 2015). The demographic lottery may end a family group when succession cannot be assured. The actual process of succession can initiate internal struggles for controlling the group, leading to its implosion, as happened after Henry Burnay's death. Even when the outcome is not so severe, family struggles for power may paralyze the group or reduce the liberty of action of the leader, as occurred with the "Sommer inheritance," the long trial dispute affecting the Champalimaud group (Canha and Fernandes, 2011).

The intervention of the state is usually stressed as a promoter of industrial policies leading to the expansion of groups to new activities. State-led industrialization in developing countries or large public investments in mature economies are common examples (Schneider, 2009 and 2010), and both were important to the consolidation of business groups in Portugal.

The 1975 nationalization constituted a deadly intervention for the largest business groups. The March 1975 legislation nationalized the entire financial sector. As banks, insurers, and investment funds had a substantial presence in the capital of other companies, this meant the indirect nationalization of about 2,000 companies (Pintado and Mendonça, 1989). Between April and August 1975 other industries were also nationalized: energy, steel, transport, media, shipbuilding and repair, cement, paper pulp, chemicals, and petrochemicals. The institutional shock represented by the nationalizations decapitated the business groups and changed the ownership and control of the largest Portuguese companies overnight.

The disappearance of business groups is not only the result of radical-led state intervention. On August 3, 2014, the Espírito Santo bank resolution plan adopted for the first time in the eurozone the EU Bank Recovery and Resolution Directive, approved months earlier (Directive 2014/59/EU). It followed a month of increasing deterioration in the BES market position due to the contamination of the group's debt. Several financial holdings of the ES group located in Luxembourg (ESI and Rioforte, see Figure 13.4) asked for creditor protection in a cascade of default events. In July the holding for the financial sector (ESFG) publicly recognized the exposure to the group's debt and also filed for creditor protection at the end of the month. At the beginning of August BES's stock had fallen 90 percentage points, before being suspended; its deposits had squeezed by €3.5 billion and lost access to the lifeline of European Central Bank funding. The resolution plan in fact terminated the ES group: shareholders were called to bail in the bank and the Espírito Santo family, the bank's largest shareholders, were the ones to lose the most.

This debacle reveals the potential impact of financial crises in pushing business groups into trouble and change (Ghemawat and Khanna, 1998; Ahlstrom and Bruton, 2004; Kim et al., 2004; Hoskisson et al., 2005). The Espírito Santo group was the most dramatic case, but other groups have not gone untouched by the 2008 financial crisis (Silva and Neves, 2014b). Financial and economic crises have many consequences for economic activity, affecting business groups in different ways. The drop in demand and economic activity is one of them, especially the fall in state expenditures and investment. Groups more dependent on public works or generally on public tendering and concessions are more severely affected. Nevertheless, diversification, internationalization, and services-orientation in more insulated sectors (IT, media, and mass retailing, for instance) lower the pressure of the financial crisis in business groups. The same happens with the impact of a credit squeeze, another consequence of financial crises. Small and medium-sized firms are more vulnerable to the sudden reduction of credit access than powerful business groups.

Debt deleveraging is another consequence of financial crises, and business groups suffered its impact in different ways. Although they did not have the dark side effects of the internal capital flows that characterized the ES group, they have to reduce their exposure to debt. A double movement of retrenchment took place: on the one hand, divesting from some business areas (Mota-Engil from energy, Mello from electricity, for instance), refocusing even more on segments where they had more competitive advantages (for similar retrenchment processes see Kim et al., 2004; Hoskisson et al., 2005; Fracchia et al., 2010); on the other hand, reducing family ownership positions and opening the capital of the group to new partners in order to survive (Mota-Engil to Angolan partners, for instance). This is a process still in action and its end cannot be anticipated, but the financial crisis may undermine family ownership, opening the groups to outside investment. As the stock market has never been a major source of corporate finance in Portugal, this process is not achieved through the dispersion of ownership but through the arrival of new important foreign partners, which may challenge the control of Portuguese families in some groups.

13.8 Conclusion: The Rise, Fall, and Resurgence of Groups

The analysis of the rise and expansion of Portuguese groups during the *Estado Novo* period shows the relevance of exogenous factors typical of emerging economies. This study emphasizes two further explanations, absent from previous analyses. The first adds the role of economic growth to the exogenous factors explaining groups' expansion. The 1960s and early 1970s represented the period of most intense growth and convergence of the Portuguese economy. It was also the golden age of the *Estado Novo* groups. The second explanation stresses the role of endogenous factors, tangible and intangible, developed within each group and without the potential to be easily emulated. The importance of generational depth is one of these factors not previously emphasized in the literature. It supports the accumulation of contact capabilities at political and business levels, as well as project management resources, which could be mobilized to new ventures in different industries.

Decline and potential disappearance should be considered as defining moments in the evolution of groups, a topic deserving more attention in the literature. Three motives stand out for the demise of business groups. Generational devolution is a critical moment potentially stressing the family inner circle at the top of the group. The creation of informal or formal governance rules tries to address this issue, gathering together different branches of the family in a common interest and overcoming deadly sources of conflict. Family holdings at the top of the groups and their governance rules are one of these devices. Financial crises constitute the second potential source of difficulties. Large family groups have their own advantages when facing financial crises, protected by diversification and privileged access to sources of financing in periods of credit squeeze. However, they need to decrease their exposure to debt and implement financial deleveraging, divesting and opening their capital to outside investors. When capital markets are unimportant to corporate finance and depressed as a result of financial crisis, the solution is selling part of the stake to external investors, decreasing the participation of the family. In the worst cases, as in the Espírito Santo group, financial crises could destroy them. Finally, the state can be a decisive agent for the ruin of business groups, as the 1975 nationalization or the financial resolution plan applied to the Espírito Santo bank demonstrate.

The resurgence of business groups after the 1990s raises the fundamental question as to why groups thrive and prosper in more mature market and institutional frameworks. The answer to this question benefits from the quasi-experimental opportunity created by the particular historical evolution of Portugal over the twentieth century. Three former groups reappeared after the 1990s: Champalimaud, CUF (Mello family after 1990), and Espírito Santo. For different reasons only the CUF/Mello group exists in 2017: Champalimaud abandoned the reconstruction of his pre-1975 business empire, concentrating his wealth in a foundation dedicated to scientific research in biomedicine (Fundação Champalimaud); ES group was engulfed by the financial crisis. For answering the question as to the reasons for groups' competitiveness in mature economies, this outcome is less important than comparing the strategies and corporate arrangements followed by groups after 1990, trying to establish the reasons for their success. Every group, with the exception of ES, reduced wide, unrelated diversification and focused on a number of core yet still unrelated sectors (see Khanna and Palepu, 1999, for a different view on the evolution of groups in more mature markets). All of them became more active in international markets, moving from domestic-centric to multinational groups. Internationalization acts in a recursive relationship with specialization in core sectors. Competitive resources and capabilities are needed to compete abroad, and simultaneously being exposed to foreign competition strengthens their internal capabilities. Finally, early twenty-first-century groups are more dependent on the capital market than during the *Estado Novo* and, mostly, are more dependent on arm's-length banking intermediation than on banking internalization. By contrast, the internal capital market based on group-owned financial institutions only resurfaces in the case of the Espírito Santo group.

The resurgence of large groups in a more mature and competitive environment does not presume the perennial nature of individual family groups. They may develop Malthusian behaviors to preserve family ownership and control, leading to self-restraining expansion. They may also face very stressful moments when generational devolution occurs, even if family firms are unique in providing long-term orientation to business ventures (Lumpkin and Brigham, 2011), in building up a sense of shared culture (Zahra et al., 2004), and in taking advantage of generic, cross-industry capabilities accumulated over generations. The viability of family groups over time depends on their plasticity to adapt strategy and control structures to different business environments and governance rules, even when they seem to undermine old mechanisms of control.

As an organizational form business groups are endowed with this flexibility, being easily adaptable to different environments. The legal independence of affiliate enterprises may increase overhead costs but also reduce the costs of merging and managing integrated, stand-alone firms. Furthermore, legal independence means that the different enterprises within the group can be easily divested, when a strategic reorientation takes place. Atomization in independent firms constitutes an advantage in integrating, selling, or changing the configuration of business groups.

Flexibility is also extended to what constitutes a business group, explaining the vast array of definitions present in the literature, as well as the diverse taxonomical configurations visible in the case of Portuguese business groups. For instance, the presumed relationship between family, pyramidal structure, and unrelated diversification as inherent to business groups is far from a universal tendency. The evolution of groups in Portugal over a century and in different contexts establishes the multiple configurations this organizational form can assume. Changes in strategic positioning moved business groups along a continuum of more restricted or broader diversification. Different growth strategies over time or across groups generated different organizational solutions. Pyramids represent one of these solutions, visible in the Portuguese case only in the contemporary period, when capital markets become more active and capital intermediation by stand-alone banks substitute intra-group banking relationships.

The advantage of historically grounded investigation of business groups is the possibility of addressing the resilience conundrum in a long-term perspective, assuming that many of the questions about the persistence of business groups benefit from the multifaceted lens of history (Jones and Khanna, 2006). The comparative perspective prevents insular explanations and provides meaning to processes beyond a particular time and place. The combination of these two approaches is very likely the reason why so many of the issues raised in recent reviews of business groups are addressed in this chapter (e.g., Khanna and Yafeh, 2007; Yiu et al., 2007; Colpan and Hikino, 2010).

GROUP 3

WESTERN OFFSHOOTS

CHAPTER 14

THE UNITED STATES IN HISTORICAL PERSPECTIVES

*the strange career of business groups
in industrial development*

TAKASHI HIKINO AND MARCELO BUCHELI

14.1 INTRODUCTION

THE US economy historically represented the critical seedbed for Chandlerian multidivisional enterprises. According to Chandler's synthesis (1962, 1977), the "modern industrial enterprises" that were originally involved in a focused product category and then got expanded into multi-industries with technologically related product portfolios became the core economic organization of US industrial competitiveness since the Second Industrial Revolution of the late nineteenth and early twentieth centuries. The Chandlerian summary theoretically contains two different yet interrelated aspects: the *strategy* of product diversification into related categories, and the *structure* of intra-firm organization with administrative divisions. Although Chandler himself logically integrated those issues by the famous thesis "structure follows strategy," subsequent research, especially that which has taken business groups as the subject of inquiry, has often been preoccupied with the structural aspect of the Chandler thesis without systematically considering the strategy factor.[1]

This emphasis on the structural aspect of business groups has resulted in more logical and empirical confusion rather than solving the puzzle related to the evolutionary shifts in the contributions of different varieties of large business enterprises to long-run US industrial development. If we adopt the broad definition of "business groups" that follows

---

[1] While this chapter surveys the broad range of business groups that have historically developed in the United States, in accordance with the general theme of the present volume it mainly deals with two types of diversified business groups that historically played critical roles in that US economy: the business groups centered around overseas trading and operational firms; and the groups organized around banking institutions.

the classic proposition of Mark Granovetter (1995, 2005), which is the "economic coordination mechanism in which legally independent companies utilize the collaborative arrangements to enhance their collective economic welfare" (Colpan and Hikino, 2010: 17), various types of business group organizations have actually appeared and played their distinctive roles in the historical development of the US economy. In spite of the significant contributions that the varieties of business groups have characteristically made to date, however, scholars in history and management have deliberately or unconsciously fallen into strange contempt for systematically examining this particular form of corporate and organizational design, especially in today's mature industrial economies.

In this chapter we aim to re-examine the Chandlerian interpretation of the historical development of business enterprises in the United States by using an analytical framework that brings diversified business groups into the analysis. These are a particular variety of business groups characterized by a product-wise unrelated diversification and with a structure of multisubsidiary operational organization. In terms of their original operational scope, diversified business groups have historically appeared in two basic varieties in the US economy: (a) business groups with regional orientations, especially international business groups centered around trading firms and operating companies; and (b) business groups organized around banks and other financial institutions, which have played important roles in not only financially assisting entrepreneurs in establishing their own enterprises but also actively reorganizing industries, especially at the time of serious financial troubles and structural turning points.[2]

Following the general theme of this volume, this chapter re-examines the Chandlerian interpretation of the linear and evolutionary progression of modern industrial enterprises and explores the intriguing development of characteristic varieties of business groups in that economy. In this way, the chapter aims to systematically lay down the economic background of the emergence of diversified business groups and then examine the organizational and administrative mechanisms through which the strategy of unrelated diversification and the structure of business groups are integrated.

14.2 REINTERPRETING THE CHANDLERIAN PARADIGM OF THE GROWTH OF LARGE INDUSTRIAL ENTERPRISES

Chandler's interpretation of the core business enterprises in the historical process of US industrial development, which mostly excludes the characteristic contributions of business groups, among everything else, can be summarized as a three-phase model: the first phase up to the 1840s—"traditional" general merchants with diversified

---

[2] A great deal of attention has been given to Chandler's interpretation of large vertically integrated firms. For an approach analyzing the process of creation of large vertically integrated firms using a transaction costs economics lens see Bucheli, Mahoney, and Vaaler (2010).

industry and geography portfolios; the second phase up to the 1920s—"modern industrial enterprises" with the strategy of specialized product portfolio and the structure of functional organization; and the third phase since the 1920s—"modern industrial enterprises" with the strategy of related-diversified product portfolio and the structure of multidivisional organization.

Table 14.1 illustrates the historical evolution and industrial distribution of the 200 largest industrial enterprises in the United States in the twentieth century, ranked by their assets and classified by their Standard Industrial Classification (SIC) code. As is clearly illustrated, most of the largest industrial enterprises throughout the century possessed a strong orientation toward the core industry domain, although the rising significance of conglomerate firms is observed in the 1960s and 1970s. Accompanying these changes in strategy of expanding product portfolio was the representative structure model adopted by large industrial enterprises in the United States. This went from a functional organization up to the 1920s to a multidivisional organization that became firmly established by the 1960s.

This developmental model of the US large firms proposed by Chandler illustrates four distinctive characteristics, two of which are related to the causal mechanism of dynamic growth of strategy and structure adopted by the firms, while the remaining

Table 14.1. The distribution of the largest industrial enterprises in the US.

Group	Industry	1917	1930	1948	1973	1988
20	Food	29	31	27	22	18
21	Tobacco	6	5	5	3	3
22	Textiles	6	4	8	3	2
23	Apparel	3	0	0	0	1
24	Lumber	3	4	2	3	7
25	Furniture	0	1	1	0	1
26	Paper	5	8	6	10	9
27	Printing and Publishing	2	2	2	1	9
28	Chemicals	20	20	23	28	40
29	Petroleum	22	26	22	26	18
30	Rubber	5	5	5	5	1
31	Leather	4	2	2	0	0
32	Stone, Clay, and Glass	5	8	6	8	6
33	Primary metals	31	23	23	18	10
34	Fabricated metals	11	10	6	4	5
35	Machinery	17	19	23	13	13
36	Electrical machinery	5	5	7	15	21
37	Transportation equipment	24	23	29	22	20
38	Instruments	1	2	1	2	4
39	Miscellaneous	1	2	2	1	1
–	Conglomerate	0	0	0	16	11
	Total	200	200	200	200	200

Source: Chandler and Hikino (1997): 40.

two are concerned with the actors that played the role of the main character in US business growth. First, in order to understand the causal mechanism that drove these transformations of strategy and structure, Chandler focused on the dynamic inter-actions between strategy and structure, rather than the simple one-way influence of strategy factors on the structural configuration that firms chose to adopt, which many scholars tend to misunderstand. As a prime factor, then, Chandler underlined intra-firm resources and capabilities, especially technological ones, that generated competi-tive advantages for large industrial enterprises. This would put Chandler squarely in the school of the "resource-based theory of the firm." However, Chandler also empha-sized the critical role played by the economies of scale at the trans-firm market level of products and industries, which would put him in the "positioning school." This is apparent in Chandler's analyses of the critical role played by competitive market forces as determining the large corporations' choice of strategy and structure, particularly in cases of inter-firm rivalry in oligopolistic industries.

Second, by contrast Chandler relatively undervalued the significance of external factors in the firms' strategic choices other than competitive and technology forces such as government price regulations, investment agendas, and priorities of families owning family firms, or the impact of financial and capital markets. Certainly, he discussed the issues related to antitrust policies adopted by the US government and recognized the presence of bank representatives on the board of directors of large industrial enter-prises. Yet he remained skeptical about the long-term influence of those factors on the viability of the strategic decision-making that modern industrial enterprises adopted. Most often, he argued, large industrial enterprises effectively transformed their strategy and structure in responding to changing regulatory regimes. Actually, as was typical in the process of their responses to antitrust enforcement, the large industrial enterprises eventually enhanced their organizational effectiveness by not only converting the legal form of their businesses but also systematizing their administrative design to be operating at tighter and more coordinated levels. Chandler, then, remained skeptical of the instrumental value of the critical influence of financial interest on the strategic management of industrial enterprises. Bank associates may represent the interests of the financial community on the board of directors of industrial enterprises, but their expertise naturally remains the know-how related to financial, rather than industrial, domains, which creates information and knowledge asymmetry on the part of those executives. They may surely oppose the strategic proposal made by insider senior management but ultimately cannot come up with effective alternatives to materialize their potential influence. Chandler's priority of the salaried senior management in *The Visible Hand* basically remained sound as long as the latent effect of financial interest stayed as the potential nature of the *ultimate*, rather than *direct*, control.

Third, from Chandler's viewpoint the basic development of large industrial enter-prises was eventually completed in the interwar years when they adopted the strategy of related diversification that required them to convert their organizational design to multidivisional structure. Except for the temporary disturbance caused by the rise (and subsequent struggle) of conglomerate firms in the 1960s and 1970s, Chandler's heroes—multidivisional enterprises with related product portfolios—have permanently placed themselves at the viable core of US business development.

Fourth, in contrast to the active and positive contributions made by the "modern industrial enterprises" with first focused and then related-diversified product portfolio, Chandler reasoned that diversified business groups, either in the form of general merchants and their successors in the nineteenth century, bank-centered groups at the turn of the nineteenth century, or acquisitive conglomerate firms in the 1960s and 1970s, made only minor (or sometimes even negative) contributions to the US economy as well as individual corporations. For instance, after all, Chandler did not quite acknowledge the self-inflicted troubles in terms of strategic effectiveness and international competitiveness that multidivisional enterprises faced in those decades that resulted in the emergence of conglomerate firms.

In reality, however, we argue that the different varieties of business groups played characteristic and important roles in US industrial development. While Chandler valued the contributions of railroads as the "nation's first big business," his interpretation of US business evolution led him to be dismissive of other forms of large businesses before the railroads. He remained openly critical of such organizations as antebellum plantations in the agricultural sector or was not that positive about the "traditional" operation in manufacturing organized by the community of former mercantile entrepreneurs, the Boston Associates. He belonged to the intellectual orientation toward progressive history, so that the long-term evolution of corporate businesses basically follows the straight and upward line from organizations with marginal effectiveness to those of high productivity (Woodman, 1981; Dalzell, 1987; John, 1997). As long as Chandler narrowly focused on the administrative efficiency of business organizations at their corporate and operational level, then, he eventually excluded many forms of large organizations like various varieties of business groups that do not necessarily fit into the sharply focused analytical framework that he formulated around the intra-firm resources and capabilities mainly in management and technology and the competitive forces of external product markets. In this regard Chandler comes close to the perspective that economists, particularly those belonging to the evolutionary school, customarily adopt (Nelson and Winter, 1977; Nelson, 1991). In order to come up with a broader and more comprehensive picture of the dynamic evolution of business enterprises in the United States, we examine below those business organizations that became sidelined in the Chandlerian story.

14.3 THE MULTIPLICITY OF CORPORATE MODELS IN US INDUSTRIAL DEVELOPMENT

One underappreciated aspect of the dynamics of the US industrial economy is the multiplicity of contributions of various types of corporate and business organizations

Table 14.2. Varieties of business groups in US history.

Type	Representative examples
Network-type business groups	American Iron and Steel Institute, National Association of Manufacturers
Hierarchy type business groups	
Diversified business groups	
(Boston Associates as a prototype)	
International business groups	W.R. Grace and Company, United Fruit Company
Bank centered business	J.P. Morgan & Company (Morgan group), Mellon National
groups	Bank (Mellon group)
Pyramidal business groups	Insull, United Corporation
Holding-company type	Standard Oil Trust
business groups	

to the long-run growth and dynamism of that economy. Chandler's hero of multi-divisional firms may ultimately have taken the significant role of the prime function in the long-run path of the emergence, development, and maturity of large industrial enterprises representing the competitiveness of that economy. While acknowledging the power of Chandler's narrative of progressive history, different types of business organizations, large or small, have certainly appeared and actually played their distinctive roles as an indispensable part of the whole dynamic economy of the United States. Standing as one significant organization model among them are several varieties of business groups. Leaving a detailed examination of the two major varieties of diversified business groups to the next section, below we briefly examine the varieties of business groups, especially in the broad context of the Chandlerian evolution of modern industrial enterprises. Table 14.2 summarizes these different types of business groups that have operated in the US economy with their representative examples. (For the classification and definition of the different categories of business groups, see Chapter 1.)

14.3.1 Network-Type Business Groups

Network-type business groups without the controlling center at the helm of the business organization have appeared in the process of US industrial development in different varieties from classic trade and industry associations to contemporary long-term strategic alliances (including franchising contracts, licensing agreements, and joint ventures). Despite the rising popularity of network research among management scholars, systematic approaches to this issue from historical perspectives remain regrettably limited for the national case of the United States (Galambos, 1966; Tedlow, 1988). Several scholars in organization science have argued that even the enterprises adopting multidivisional structure with related product portfolio have actually exhibited the basic characteristics of network-type business groups, as internal divisions have begun operating as if they are independent and autonomous strategic decision-making units. They point to the underappreciated gap between the conventional understanding (including Chandler's interpretation) that the headquarters exercised over individual internal divisions based on controlling equity stake and the new paradigm of eventual strategic autonomy on the part of those operating units even within the modern industrial enterprises adopting multidivisional structure (see Chapter 4, this volume; also the classic statement of the issue in Wrigley, 1970).

Historically, several trade associations appeared as early as in the eighteenth century. These early cases include a craft-based association organized by house carpenters of Philadelphia in 1724 and a regional association like the Boston Society for Improving Trade and Commerce established in 1761. From the early decades of the nineteenth century, then, local and national trade and industry associations started playing their characteristic roles. The representative associations included single-industry groups such as the National Textile Association (originally established in 1854 as the Hampden County Cotton Spinners' Association); the American Iron and Steel Institute, established in 1855; the American Chemistry Council, 1873; the American Bankers Association, 1873; the Investment Bankers Association of America, 1912; and the American Petroleum Institute, 1919. The multiple-industry and functional groups appeared to include those such as the National Association of Manufacturers, established in 1895; the Association of National Advertisers, 1910; the US Chamber of Commerce, 1912; and the American Marketing Association, 1915. For these associations, especially the industry-wide ones, the individual constituent firms theoretically *competed* against each other in product markets, although they *cooperated* in the other aspects such as lobbying the government, establishing technical standards, and providing insurance cover for employees (Galambos, 1966).

In reality, however, trade and industry associations were sometimes utilized as a practical instrument for the purpose of output or price control, often without a satisfactory outcome. This particular use of trade and industry associations reached a peak from the 1870s to the 1910s, the decades in which the enforcement of antitrust policies by the federal government got tighter and more extensive through such legislations as the Interstate Commerce Act of 1887, the Sherman Antitrust Act of 1890, and the Clayton Antitrust Act of 1914, which will be discussed in detail in Section 14.3.2. Consequently, the focal activities of trade and industry associations got shifted toward lobbying and working with government authorities to influence policymaking to be more conductive to members of the associations.

In the 1870s, to cite concrete historical cases in the Chandlerian evolution of modern industrial enterprises, leading oil refiners consecutively formed two industry associations—the South Improvement Company, and then the Central Association of Refiners under the leadership of John D. Rockefeller, who as president of both associations attempted to control the transportation and wholesale distribution of crude and refined oil. As was the case with these particular associations, however, most often the associations did not possess effective means to enforce agreements among the participating firms as long as they remained not only legally independent but also autonomous in terms of their strategic decision-making (Hidy and Hidy, 1955).

Different practices of horizontal arrangements that are theoretically classified as the network-type business group became popularized, especially in the 1880s, among which the commonly called "Standard Oil Alliance" should be singled out for its significance. It was again founded under the leadership of John D. Rockefeller and actually included forty companies to collectively control more than 90 percent of US refining capacity by the 1880s (Chandler, 1982b). Chandler regarded this control to be still ineffective for the enforcement of the original contract and thus accounted the horizontal contractual arrangements to be inoperative as a practical form of modern administrative design, concluding that hierarchical apparatus for administrative coordination should be a matter of necessity.

14.3.2 Hierarchy-Type Business Groups

Hierarchy-type business groups can be examined under three major varieties: diversified business groups; pyramidal business groups; and holding-company-type business groups. While the three varieties should be separate in terms of their classification, in reality they often overlap. Below we examine each category in the historical context of the United States (following the conceptual arguments made in Chapter 1).

At the outset, diversified business groups can actually be examined under two major categories. First, business groups with regional orientations, especially international business groups centered around trading firms and operating companies, can be comprehended in two subcategories: Boston Associates as a prototype of diversified business groups in the United States; and international business groups that were active mainly in Latin American markets. The second category is made up of business groups organized around banks and other financial institutions, which have caused much controversy among scholars as well as the public regarding their economic welfare effects ever since their development in the second half of the nineteenth century. As we will delve into the case of diversified business groups in detail in Section 14.4, below we examine the cases of pyramidal business groups and holding-company business groups.

The second of the three varieties of hierarchy-type business groups—pyramidal business groups such as Insull Utilities Investment, United Corporation, and Electric Bond and Share—appeared mostly in the public utility and transportation sector in the early twentieth century, and they played a significant role in developing urban infrastructure in major cities.[3] The ownership structures in which controlling entrepreneurs

---

[3] Most of the US pyramidal business groups were generally focused and operated in a narrow set of industries, as mentioned above. There were also, however, widely diversified groups, in particular the bank-centered groups that also included pyramidal arrangements, which are examined in Section 14.4 under diversified business groups.

built layers of publicly listed corporations became a target of criticism for the possible tunneling of profits by the parent firms and their controlling entrepreneurs (Becht and DeLong, 2005; Morck, 2010; Kandel et al., 2015). The general conditions for the creation of pyramidal business groups in the United States during the twentieth century were twofold. First, the scarcity of managerial skills and underdeveloped capital markets encouraged corporations to create their own internal sources by bringing together these two elements from several corporations. Second, bringing multiple firms within a single larger organization acted as a way to create mechanisms of mutual insurance and risk-taking (Kandel et al., 2015). Nevertheless, after the 1930s new regulations controlling big business, including anti-trust legislation, taxation policies on inter-corporate dividends, and laws (including the Public Utility Holding Company Act of 1935 and rising intercorporate dividend taxation after 1935, the Investment Company Act of 1940 against holding companies) brought the eventual demise of US pyramidal business groups (Kandel et al., 2015).

Finally, the business groups that exhibit the "holding-company" character, despite their significance in reality, have regrettably created much confusion among management scholars and thus function as an appropriate testing ground to illustrate the complicated task of classifying different forms of business groups into logically coherent analytical framework. Three categorical uses of the holding company organization should thus be differentiated to make the academic discussion of this corporation model clear and robust. First, in the Chandler–Williamson line of argument, the holding-company structure remains the administrative design that exhibits unsystematic structure with loose control exercised by the apex unit legally formed as a holding company over operating subsidiaries. This characteristic understanding of the holding-company structure is based mainly on the British model that has mostly been operating in single industries and had their shares as influential business organizations especially in the late nineteenth and early twentieth centuries, as detailed in Chapter 1.

Second, in the United States, on legal grounds, the holding company was accepted as a legitimate entity for domestic industrial corporations after the 1880s, when the state of New Jersey legalized them without requiring any special charter or permission. Holding companies in the administrative sense then emerged as a practical response by individual entrepreneurs, especially when the trust arrangements the entrepreneurs had formulated were judged as illegal by the Sherman Antitrust Act of 1890. The administrative use of the holding-company structure became a practical vehicle to achieve effective control of horizontal contractual cooperation and hierarchical enforcement. With the operative apex organ being established by the coming of the holding-company structure, they should now be classified as hierarchy-type business groups since they are now equipped with the headquarters unit that aims to control the functional subsidiaries underneath.

Third, however, the market-controlling use of the holding-company organization was threatened by the decision of the Supreme Court in the Northern Securities case of 1904, which found the monopolistic behavior allegedly shown by the holding-company organization to be illegal. In 1901 James J. Hill, in alliance with John D. Rockefeller, established the Northern Securities Co., a holding company that was supposed to own all the stocks of the three major railroad companies operating in the western United States, creating a regional monopoly. As a consequence of the Supreme Court decision, many enterprises terminated the employment of this particular form of holding-company organization to reformulate themselves into the administrative structure of unitary or multidivisional design, although the court decision never made the holding company itself illegal.

Rockefeller's case of Standard Oil is a telling example of the actual functioning of various varieties of business groups that sought inter-firm market control and intra-firm administrative efficiency. In response to ineffective enforcement of horizontal contractual arrangements (i.e., a variety of network-type business groups), Rockefeller actually had to come up with a new device, which he ultimately found in 1882 in the form of business trusts. In 1890, however, the Sherman Antitrust Act made the arrangements of business trusts illegal, and many of those business trusts were converted into the holding-company structure.

In the case of Rockefeller's Standard Oil, however, the holding company as a *legal* structure remained, although many large industrial enterprises in the United States started adopting the unitary organization or multidivisional form as the *administrative* mechanism, as Chandler persuasively preached. Standard Oil Trust, organized by John D. Rockefeller in 1882, which turned into a holding company in 1899, continued to use the holding-company form as a legal device. After the 1911 Supreme Court decision to break up the Standard Oil Company of New Jersey into more than thirty independent firms, Standard Oil Company (New Jersey), the entity's central body, remained operating as a holding company until well after World War II. During this period the firm achieved administrative efficiency through intra-organizational coordination rather than inter-firm contractual cooperation; and eventually it became one of the prototypes of Chandlerian modern industrial enterprises (Chandler, 1962; 1982b).

Ironically, however, Chandler himself caused confusion regarding the business-group varieties by eventually employing the concept of the "holding company" in two different ways. In his early writings he employed the holding-company concept mostly in a legal sense, as he understood that multidivisional enterprises often employed the legal structure of a pure (or investment) or operating holding company, as the prominent case of Standard Oil (New Jersey) and General Motors illustrated. They, however, exercised administrative control over legally independent subsidiaries in similar ways as they did over internal divisions. For this type of multidivisional enterprise, Chandler did not even refer to the *legal* aspect of the holding-company structure, as the *administrative* design remained the central issue to his framework.

In his later writings, however, Chandler started singling out the categorical concept of the "holding company" as an administrative design for large enterprises with unsystematic structure and loose control that the headquarters unit applied over operating subsidiaries, which Oliver Williamson theoretically popularized in management discipline. Chandler designated the British example of Calico Printers' Association and

Imperial Tobacco as the representative case of the operation which simply dictated the amount of output that individual enterprises produced. While the Chandlerian interpretation of those British enterprises has been empirically challenged by many scholars, the use of the "holding-company" structure is now confused, as many scholars implied the multidivisional enterprises have internal divisions only, while the holding companies consist of legally independent companies.

14.4 DIVERSIFIED BUSINESS GROUPS AS THE PRIME ALTERNATIVE MODEL OF CHANDLERIAN LARGE ENTERPRISES

Among different varieties of business groups diversified business groups should be singled out as the prime alternative to Chandlerian multidivisional enterprises in terms of their contrasting strategy of unrelated product portfolio and the distinctive structure of *administratively as well as legally* independent subsidiaries. Below we examine business groups in the long-term development of the US economy by acknowledging the contributions of major varieties of diversified business groups.

We argue that historically these diversified business groups played distinctive roles in terms of the *generation* or *reorganization* of individual industries as well as enterprises. The industry generation model is represented in US economic growth, first by the Boston Associates as a prototype of business groups, and, then by international business groups controlled by trading or operating companies active in overseas markets. The industry reorganization model, on the other hand, is historically most associated with the business groups organized around investment banks, especially J. P. Morgan, and the so-called "Money Trust" up to the New Deal era when the policies of the Roosevelt administration critically undermined the market power of those groups. Yet financial and capital markets became active again in the late 1950s in supporting the corporation model of acquisitive conglomerate firms, and then in the 1980s in more vigorously engaging in the creation of private equity firms and other forms of diversified business groups such as activist hedge funds. See Figure 14.1 for the characteristic operational mechanism of US international business groups active in developing economies. Figure 14.2 then illustrates the operational mechanism of diversified business groups organized around banks and financial institutions.

Since the following chapter (Chapter 15 by Collis et al.) examines conglomerates and private equity firms as its focused topic, this chapter concentrates on the two earlier historical categories: first, business groups with regional orientations, especially international business groups centered around trading firms and operating companies, which we will examine below in their two subcategories; and, second, business groups organized around banks and other financial institutions.

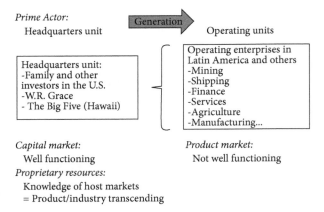

FIGURE 14.1. US corporations and international business groups.

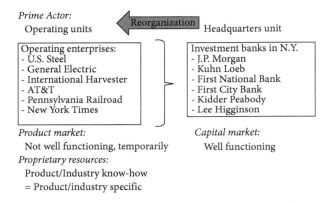

FIGURE 14.2. The "Money Trust" in New York and bank-centered business groups.

14.4.1 Boston Associates as a Prototype of Diversified Business Groups

The first variety of diversified business groups can be argued to have originated as regional groups in which usually family and kin networks, while utilizing their own or local financial and network resources, played critical roles in the process of generating enterprises and industries by expanding their product and industry portfolio into unrelated domains as long as demand for those products was expanding for entering firms. The Boston Associates, which played a significant role in establishing the wide range of enterprises and industries in the early phase of industrialization of the New England region in the first half of the nineteenth century, represents this variety as a predecessor or prototype of diversified business groups in the United States.

Historically, the Boston Associates, a group of local investors and entrepreneurs connected through social as well as financial ties, played a significant role in the early phases of industrialization after the late eighteenth century, as they established many enterprises that collectively developed overseas trading networks, initiated manufacturing activities, and arranged related physical and financial infrastructure. Taken individually, however, those enterprises remained focused in terms of their product domains, and some of them grew to be significant players in their respective industries. In the textile industry the Boston Associates eventually generated the First Industrial Revolution centered around textile production, with the foundation of Boston Manufacturing Company in 1813. Soon after, such towns as Lowell, Lawrence, Chicopee, all in Massachusetts, and Manchester, New Hampshire, were flooded with textile mills established by the investment committed by the Boston Associates. Further, they created other industries extensively in the New England region, such as railroads (Boston & Lowell Railroad, for instance, starting service in 1835); banking and other financial institutions (Suffolk Bank, serving as a clearinghouse bank founded in Boston in 1818); and insurance (Merchants Insurance Company, chartered in 1825). Taken together, in the long run, however, they did not formulate the organized coherence as a diversified business group as they were not equipped with a central headquarters unit or any equivalent controlling and coordinating apparatus at the helm, while they still could not employ the legal device of the holding company to keep the economic unity for investment due to legal restrictions. As the industrial fortunes were transferred from the original entrepreneurs to their subsequent generation, individual entrepreneurs and their families separately evolved as portfolio investors without active involvement in managerial decision-making or systematic coordination between families and started pursuing separate goals, while in the typical fashion of the Buddenbrooks Syndrome those family members took themselves out of the business and became more involved in the world of politics and other non-economic spheres. As such, all of the thirty or so textile firms founded by the Boston Associates, including Boston Manufacturing Company (which filed for bankruptcy in 1930), were liquidated or taken over by other interests (Dalzell, 1987).

Many local and regional enterprises with family and kin network ties have historically developed into groups with diversified portfolios in such major cities as New York, Philadelphia, and Chicago (where the business group controlled by the Pritzker family can be cited as a representative case of diversification into extensive and unrelated industry spheres). As long as those firms possessed some advantage in terms of knowledge of local staples and commodities and also regional markets, product, and/or capital, that knowledge could function as a source of competitiveness. Still, this local and regional character often functioned as a limited boundary of corporate growth, especially when the external environment of product and capital markets shifted to invalidate conventional advantages, or the investment priority or preference changed for the entrepreneurial families and their enterprises to focus on a narrow range of product portfolio and/or to exit from controlling and strategic investment in industries to adopt the non-controlling philosophy of portfolio investors.

The subcategory of these regional business groups is made up of those that emerged as trading and operational businesses in geographically specific markets overseas.

Some of the earliest cases of this particular variety were Hawaii's prominent enterprises, the "Big Five," which started in the 1820s to the 1870s with the agricultural production of staples in plantations. The five enterprises—C. Brewer (founded in 1826 as an international trader), Theo Davies (1845, an international trader headquartered in Liverpool), Amfac (1849, a dry-goods merchant), Castle & Cooke (1851, a local general store), and Alexander & Baldwin (1870, a sugar-cane plantation)—embarked upon plantation agriculture originally in sugar cane and then pineapple. They dominated the local economic scene through their involvement in major businesses covering infrastructure and transportation and all the related and unrelated businesses, as well as through their extensive connections to local Republican Party politics. The Big Five, however, would not grow to become major players as international enterprises, for the local product market stayed relatively moderate for their geographically limited knowledge to sustain their long-term development, and their product-related know-how in agricultural produce remained not viable enough to compete against international players in a globalizing economy (Daws, 1968). The most important cases of this category of diversified business groups, however, can be seen as the overseas enterprises that operated in the regional markets of Latin America, which we examine in detail below.

14.4.2 International Business Groups and the Overseas Expansion of US Economic Interests

An early yet important variety of diversified business groups in the US historical context appeared after the 1880s in the form of multinational enterprises operating in overseas markets, especially those of the developing markets in Latin America. An analysis of the global expansion of US capital in the late nineteenth and early twentieth centuries thus provides us with further insights to understand the creation and consolidation of business groups in the United States in that period. The Chandlerian starting point, with its focus on the multidivisional firm, does not take into consideration the fact that some of the American multinationals of the late nineteenth and early twentieth centuries belonged to larger entities organized as diversified business groups and composed of legally independent firms operating in unrelated industries, often coordinated by a family-controlled apex. In this section, we analyze the operations of such international business groups.

As examined in detail below, those enterprises were originally founded in metropolitan capital centers such as New York and Boston and operated in exploiting specialty commodities, often in mining and agriculture, in regional markets like Hawaii and, more extensively, Latin America. Taking advantage of their knowledge of the local economy as well as their access to financial and capital markets in their home country, those firms extended their industry portfolio into a wide variety of unrelated product categories as long as their demand remained unfulfilled or supply underutilized in those local emerging markets. This characteristic integration of "capital" raised in relatively developed financial and capital markets in high-income economies and "production" in less-developed overseas markets represents a common pattern that has been observed in many large enterprises headquartered in Europe that operated mainly in overseas markets.

As Wilkins (1970, 1988) pointed out, however, the US pattern of overseas business activities differed, especially from that of the UK, in that US direct investment was carried out by multinational enterprises, while in the UK "freestanding" companies that were independently incorporated in London for specified and special overseas ventures played a significant role. In both cases, however, the US and UK enterprises are theoretically categorized as diversified business groups (Jones, 2000, 2005a; Jones and Khanna, 2006). This is because US multinational enterprises mostly incorporated local operating units as legally independent subsidiaries via partial shareholding stakes for legal, tax, and commercial considerations, while many "freestanding" firms were promoted, organized, and managed by London-based trading and service firms which positioned themselves as the core of business groups operating overseas.

We posit that the following two factors played a role in the emergence of US international business groups. First, the expansion of markets created by the consolidation of the United States as a world power and the acceptance of liberal economics by rulers in the western hemisphere; government support of big business, particularly in the 1920s, also surely helped. Second, the development of relational capabilities by the firms, which facilitated expansion through partnerships and the need of partnerships in the host countries due to existing regulations that obliged foreigners to do so.

Developing extensively in different geographical markets from the 1880s, several American firms expanded as business groups in Latin America as a result of these incentives. They played significant roles, mostly in creating businesses in new industries, or sometimes reorganizing traditional ones. W. R. Grace and United Fruit Co. are appropriate examples to cite in this context. The former started its business in the guano trade in Lima, Peru, and in the 1870s from its headquarters in New York City established diverse businesses usually connecting the markets of Latin America with those of the United States and Europe, the most famous of which remained the passenger and freight ocean-shipping service, the Grace Line, which launched its service in 1882. If W. R. Grace is more of a case of the *generator* of new enterprises or even novel industries in emerging markets as the most characteristic of international business groups, United Fruit Co. showed another aspect by functioning as a *reorganizer* of established enterprises to integrate and rationalize the relevant industries. The company was established by a merger of two US-based trading companies of agricultural products (Bucheli, 2003, 2005). Probably the most characteristic and significant example of international business groups, however, is the case of W. R. Grace, which we explore in detail in the following section.

14.4.2.1 *W. R. Grace & Company*

W. R. Grace Company & Co. constitutes a good example of an American business group that was organized as such outside the United States. Not only was it diversified into many unrelated businesses, but also what made Grace a typical diversified business group was the fact that most of its operating corporations in South America were incorporated in the host countries, with locals often owning more than 50 percent of the stock. By the early twentieth century the organization was described as "a parent corporation of about sixty corporations engaged in a wide variety of undertakings. Some of its activities are carried on by the parent company and others by the associated companies" (James, 1993: 317). In Table 14.3 we display the variety of businesses in which Grace invested, and their ownership share. The table shows the evolution of the business and how diversified it remained without attempting to integrate its operations within a single entity.

W. R. Grace traces its origins to the 1870s, when Irish-born American entrepreneur Michael Grace arrived in Peru to develop a business in which he transported foodstuffs from the Peruvian mainland to the adjacent islands where guano was being produced. By the 1930s the Casa Grace (as it was known in Latin America) had investments in a wide range of activities from mining to sea and air transportation, sugar plantations, beverage and clothing factories, and radio stations (Burgess and Harbison, 1954). The firm's founder made an obvious effort to organize his business as a diversified business group. As one biographer put it, "For years, [Michael] Grace had spoken with pride of the fact that the Grace business was not a corporation, but a series of partnerships. . . . This was also a family firm, which did not become a corporate entity until 1899" (Marquis, 1993: 291). The business only went public in 1953 (James, 1993).

The exogenous factors explaining the origins of the Grace group are related to the particularities of Peru's economic development as well as that country's evolution of domestic and foreign politics. A demoralized, bankrupt, and destroyed country with unmanageable obligations to British bondholders and Chilean invading forces provided the Grace brothers with opportunities to build a large diversified business group. Grace had already profited from the war by using its ship transportation line to import weapons for Peru (de Secada, 1985). However, what gave Michael Grace the big push for the creation of the group was how he positioned himself during the war so that he would be in a privileged situation in the postwar period. He became the main negotiator between the Chilean government, the British bondholders, and the Peruvian elite. In 1889 all parties reached a deal by which Grace, the bondholders, and the British business groups created an organization called the Peruvian Corporation (chartered in London) (Clayton, 1999). Through the Peruvian Corporation Grace rapidly expanded his interests to areas beyond his previous maritime trade operations and incipient agricultural ones.

The post-War of the Pacific period created political and economic conditions that stimulated further diversification of Grace's interests. A new long-term mining exports boom started in Chile, while other Latin American countries promoted their own agricultural and mining exports. Grace's New York and Pacific Steamship Company became the continent's major transportation firm for both exports and imports. The Latin American commodity boom continued for the first two decades of the twentieth century, and Grace was the only organization with the transportation capabilities to

Table 14.3. W. R. Grace and Company, 1875–1930.

Name of Subsidiary or Branch	Year of creation	Location of Operations (Country)	Location of Registration (Country)	Industry or Activity	Percentage of Ownership
Compagnie Finnanciere et Commerciale du Pacifique	c. 1880	Peru	France?	Guano	Majority [not specified]
Hacienda Cartavio	c. 1879	Peru	Peru	Sugar plantation	
Cerro de Pasco Railway	c. 1884	Peru	Britain (?)	Railways	3/8
Sears and Company	1877	Brazil	N/A	Rubber plantation	80%
Scott and Company	1877	Brazil	N/A	Rubber	70%
New York and Pacific Steamship Company	c. 1885	Latin America	New York, USA	Transportation	
W. R. Grace & Company	1894	Coordination of global operations	West Virginia, USA	Diverse	Family owned. Old partners with shares in profits for 41%
Nicaragua Canal Syndicate	1896	Nicaragua	N/A	Infrastructure	Majority (unspecified)
Grace National Bank	1915	International	New York	Finance	N/A
Merchants Line (Grace Line in 1914)	1882	International	New York	Transportation (sea)	N/A
Panagra	1928	International	USA	Transportation (air)	50%
Sugar mills	N/A	Peru	Peru	Sugar processing	Majority (unspecified)
Cotton mills	N/A	Peru, Chile	Peru, Chile	Cotton processing	Majority (unspecified)
Nitrate soda	1930	Chile	Chile	Nitrate soda processing	50%
Candy Factory	N/A	Peru	Peru	Food	51%
New York Trading Company	1885–1889	International	USA	Rubber trade	Partial (not specified)
Panama Mail Company	1915	International	N/A	Mail	Wholly owned
Grace Steamship Company	1916	International	USA	Transportation	
North Pacific Division	1903	International	N/A	Transportation	Majority
Compañia Agricola Crabayllo	1917	Peru	Peru	Sugar	Majority
Inca Mill	1902	Peru	Peru	Textile Manufacturing	1/3
Imaco	1912	International	New York	Machinery trade and leasing	N/A
Paposo mine	c. 1930	Chile	N/A	Nitrate mine	N/A
COSACH	1926	Chile	Chile	Nitrate mining	Partial ownership with Chilean government

Source: Information from Grace (1953), Burgess and Harbison (1954), Miller (1976, 1983), Marquis (1993), and Clayton (1999).

operate at the continental level. Grace took advantage of the Chilean export boom not only through transportation and trading activities in partnership with Chilean companies, but also through direct participation in the mining industry (Burgess and Harbison, 1954).

However, it was not only environmental forces that contributed to Grace turning into a diversified group; it also possessed relational capabilities and effectively transferred those from one industry to others, which we can classify as endogenous factors explaining its growth. The Grace brothers developed the organization's relational capabilities very early on when they made a clear and explicit effort to insert themselves among the Peruvian elite and make their businesses as domestic as possible (Grace, 1953). Their role in the negotiations between Chile and Peru allowed them to establish long-term relations with the Chilean elite as well, which translated into joint partnerships in mining with the Chilean government as well as the opening of trading houses in that country. The Graces also built strong relationships with the American elite, when after starting their business in Peru William Grace returned to the US, entered politics, and was elected mayor of New York in 1880 (James, 1993; Bishel, 1996). The relationships built through William's political career were crucial for the Graces to enter the financial sector and consolidate their trade activities (James, 1993).

The rise of the Grace group also reflects its capabilities to transfer skills from one industry to another one. The core of their business was transportation, which they first developed through the New York and Pacific Steamship Company. The high degree of control over the Latin American import and export trade that they achieved through this business led them to open trading houses in most countries. Given the need for coordination of their business activities, they entered the telecommunications industry. Between 1878 and 1879 the Mexican Telegraph and the Central and South American Telegraph companies were created, with the two Grace brothers sitting on the board. By the early twentieth-century they expanded their interests to air transportation when they became half-owners of a newly created airline, Panagra, in 1928. Their early investments in sugar plantations also led them to partner with local producers to invest in sugar mills in the late nineteenth century, a sector in which they gained the experience to invest in cotton mills and later on in food, beverage, and textile factories. Machinery needs led them to become General Electric's exclusive agent in Peru and Chile (Burgess and Harbison, 1954; James, 1993). The Graces also took control of their financial needs by creating the Grace National Bank in 1915, which provided funds to their many businesses and a year later the W. R. Grace & Company Bank, for family and close customer needs.

14.4.3 Bank-centered Business Groups and the Alleged Way to Financial Rule

The two prime varieties of diversified business groups organized around banks and financial institutions that operated mostly in the US economy before World War II should be singled out: the infamous "Money Trust" that the largest banks in New York assembled individually and collectively to "control" a large proportion of US industrial big businesses around the turn of the century; and the banking group that Mellon National Bank organized under the entrepreneurial leadership of Andrew W. Mellon, which functioned as an early provider of venture capital for such significant industrial enterprises as Westinghouse Electric, Alcoa, and Getty Oil. While both of these groups can be cited as appropriate examples of the contribution made by diversified business groups organized by banking institutions, the Money Trust exemplifies the most characteristic and significant case of the reorganization model, while the Mellon group represents an appropriate illustration of the generation model (Cannadine, 2006).

For all of their contributions to the reorganization and rationalization of constituent enterprises and relevant industries, the bank-centered groups that adopted the reorganization model, rather than the generation model, became the major target of federal prosecutors during the heyday of antitrust concerns about the monopolistic market behavior from the late nineteenth century to the New Deal era. The New York banking houses headed by John P. Morgan not only held an equity stake in many of the large industrial enterprises but also handled a substantial portion of their debt financing. Based on these financial relationships, the bankers and their associates representing J. P. Morgan; Kuhn Loeb; First National Bank; First City Bank; Kidder, Peabody; and Lee, Higginson sat on the board of directors of their client firms and ostensibly attempted to influence business transactions in their favor (Carosso, 1970, 1987).

This whole operation of industrial companies financed and administered by banking institutions, interestingly, resembles bank-centered business groups that have also been seen in such continental European nations as Germany, Sweden, and Belgium. Yet, given the different ideological orientations of American society against the concentration of economic, especially financial, power, the "Money Trust" became the target of the House Committee on Banking and Currency that ultimately formed a special committee, as well as the Pujo Committee after its Democrat convener, Arsene Pujo, started investigating the eventual exercise of monopoly power behind the entire setup in 1912. The committee ultimately found that the "Money Trust" constituted "an established identity and community of interest between a few leaders of finance, which has been created and is held together through stock-holding, interlocking directorates, and other forms of domination over banks, trust companies, railroads, public service and industrial corporations, and which has resulted in vast and growing concentration and control of money and credits in the hands of a few men" (Untermyer quoted in *The New York Times*, 1913).

All contemporary allegations aside, as has been summarized above, Chandler remained skeptical about the effectiveness of the control of large industrial enterprises by financial institutions (Chandler, 1977). Even if the banks through their equity and debt financing attempted to "control" those firms to maximize their interest at the cost of the firms' own, or, paradoxically, as some recent studies such as De Long (1991) have suggested, those bank representatives on the board eventually monitored the effectiveness of managerial decision-making to prevent agency problems, asymmetry in terms of information, knowledge, and capabilities prevented the banks from exercising the discretionary control of decision-making of industrial enterprises. Even when bankers and their associates sat on the board and thus had an access to strategic, operational, and financial information, Chandler suggested, they did not possess the industry- and firm-specific knowledge and capabilities to analyze that information. They might criticize the strategic and operational plans proposed by the salaried professional management on various grounds, but such asymmetries prevented banking interests from submitting more effective alternatives. Ultimately, even for the sake of their own interest, banking institutions eventually had to accept managerial decision-making to establish the principle of "managerial capitalism," rather than "financial capitalism." In the United States, thus, both the primacy of Chandlerian managerial enterprises and non-market interventions of antitrust regulations such as the Clayton Act of 1914 and finally the Glass-Steagall Act of 1933 prevented the full development of bank-centered groups.

Next we examine the case of J. P Morgan & Company, which represents the characteristic operational role of bank-centered business groups whose major function was the *reorganization* of industrial companies.

14.4.3.1 *J. P. Morgan & Company*

Historically, the largest, most significant, and certainly most controversial business group organized around financial institutions remains the one assembled by John Pierpont Morgan. The Morgan family had engaged in real estate and insurance agency as a small-scale family business in Hartford, Connecticut, until J. P. Morgan's father, Junius Spencer Morgan, took the family firm into the new territory of banking by the 1850s. Learning the banking business in New York, Junius Spencer started a close working relationship with George Peabody, an American merchant banker who had a new, successful operation in international banking based in London, to become a junior partner at Peabody's firm in 1854. After Peabody's retirement, Junius took over the business and reorganized the firm as J. S. Morgan & Co. In his successful international career organizing and channeling a large amount of investment mostly from Europe, especially its most developed financial hub—London—to the United States, Junius accumulated an enormous fortune and, more importantly for his son Pierpont, an invaluable reputation as a trustworthy financial figure in both financial centers (Carosso, 1987; Strouse, 1999).

After completing his formal education in Europe and the United States, through which he became fluent in several languages and established extensive personal networks, Pierpont Morgan embarked upon a career in financial services in 1857 when he started working at Peabody, Morgan & Co., an Anglo-American merchant bank based in London in which his father was an associate to George Peabody—a partnership that his father originally founded in 1871 when he joined the Philadelphia banker, Anthony Drexel, to jointly form a merchant banking partnership, Drexel, Morgan & Co. Pierpont Morgan took over his father's business when Junius died in 1890, by which time the banking house was the most prominent investment bank on Wall Street. In 1895 Pierpont converted the bank into J. P. Morgan & Co., which became a prime apparatus for him to become extensively involved in the financing of major corporations and industries whenever they gave new opportunities for financial reorganization or restructuring. Morgan expanded his business into diversified product lines by acquiring the equity stake of established industrial firms and reorganizing them into larger enterprises to establish advantageous positions in relevant product markets, which would become the major source of controversy as being monopolistic and harmful to the public interest (Carosso, 1970). Ultimately, he formed a huge diversified business group centered around the investment bank of J. P. Morgan & Co. Figure 14.3 amply illustrates the scope of the influence that Morgan exercised over major industries, especially those with high capital intensity, in the early twentieth century.

Morgan's involvement in the variety of industries became practically possible and ultimately profitable for two basic reasons, one endogenous and the other exogenous. First, he accumulated invaluable resources represented by the extensive personal network of capital market players both in London and New York that remained unique among banking executives of his generation. He partially inherited the original seed of this social and economic privilege from his family background, yet he still deliberately or unconsciously nurtured and further developed that network through his business practices in London, as well as in Boston and New York. Morgan then possessed high capabilities of mobilizing potential investors in capital markets based on his apprenticeship in which he assisted his father with the varieties of railroad financing that remained most capital-intensive in those days. Second, the most critical factor for Morgan to be as extensive as he was in terms of his industry portfolio was the technological shifts in the Second Industrial Revolution of the late nineteenth and early twentieth centuries through which the optimal size of factories suddenly increased, necessitating the commitment of huge amounts of capital resources. Thanks to the long-term investment in production facilities, investment risks also became high, as the substantial proportion of fixed cost, relative to variable cost, should result in fragility and volatility of short-run cost that would eventually be critical to the ultimate financial outcome of investment. Morgan was there at the right time to function as an intermediary between such voluminous demand for investable capital and risk-taking supply of money in Europe as well as the United States. His solid experiences and resulting reputation were naturally reckoned critical as the investment banker to be trusted. Because Morgan's advantages had little to do with the nature of products per se, Morgan could function as an investment banker for such diverse and heterogeneous industries as iron and steel, telecommunications, and railroads. The diversified business group Morgan created was thus a natural and fitting outcome of the characteristic endogenous resources he possessed and capabilities he nurtured, along with the exogenous opportunities that the Second Industrial Revolution provided to industrial entrepreneurs and capital investors.

In order to secure and promote the huge sum of equity stakes in such diverse industrial enterprises, Morgan appointed close associates ("Morgan's men") onto the

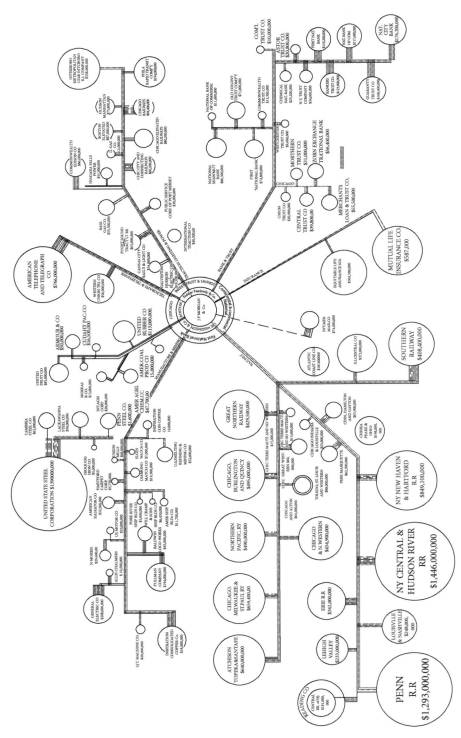

FIGURE 14·3. J. P. Morgan & Co. and its influence on large enterprises.

Source: Brinton (1914): 13.

boards of directors of those enterprises. Through equity stake and board representation Morgan ostensibly aimed to solidify his control over the enterprises. What sort of control he actually exercised over his companies and what the welfare implications of his involvement in those companies were for the interests of the public in general, as well as the general investors and employees, have always been a matter of public and scholarly controversy (Carosso, 1987; De Long, 1991; Chernow, 1993; Strouse, 1999; Hannah, 2007a). Viewing this very issue of his own involvement into the decision-making of industrial enterprises, Morgan himself allegedly stated, from the practical angle of an investment banker: "I always make it a rule, unless something is radically wrong, to follow the wishes of those who are in the management of properties in which I am interested, and refrain from pushing my views unduly" (quoted in Strouse, 1999: 314).

This pattern of expansion into and the apparatus of control over many capital-intensive industries, however, resulted in hostile public reaction. It attracted various government and legal actions against the Money Trust organized by the investment bank and ultimately led to the Glass Steagall Act of 1933, which divided J. P. Morgan & Sons into two separate entities—J. P. Morgan as a commercial bank, and Morgan-Stanley as an investment bank. Thanks mainly to the Glass-Steagall legislation, which would last until 1999, the influence of J. P. Morgan as a whole in the American industries critically declined.

14.5 CONCLUDING REMARKS

Why and how did different business enterprises (mainly business groups and multi-divisional enterprises) develop the characteristic corporate model in the United States at a specific time of history? And why and how could many of the business groups not be viable and survive in the long run in the face of a competitive economic environment? While this aspect has been widely and individually examined at the firm level to date, this chapter aims to present a synthesis of past literature by holding a comprehensive and organized framework of research.

Before reaching any concluding generalization, however, it should be noted that many scholars to date have employed the concept of business groups in different ways. Often they classify an enterprise as a business group as long as it holds two or more legally independent subsidiaries without considering if it is publicly listed or not, without examining its product portfolio, and especially without discussing the administrative design that the headquarters exercises over operating units. The particular case of Standard Oil, which was extensively examined above, gives us a significant warning in that the technical examination and classification of the enterprises and their groups can be confusing and misleading, as the case illustrates the simultaneous adaptation of the holding company as a legal form, which is thus more detectable to researchers, and the administrative design of unitary or multidivisional structure that should be more appropriate to managerial research but difficult to pin down from outside observations.

In discussing the pros and cons of this particular corporate organization, many eventually considered the characteristics of big business in general, rather than those of business groups—diversified, pyramidal, or other varieties—per se. A more systematic approach is now necessary to comprehend this intriguing yet confusing corporate model to reach an analytically robust assessment of business groups, rather than big business as a whole. This sort of systematic research is especially required for the national case of the US economy, where Chandlerian interpretation has been so critically important to undermine the reputation of business groups.

This chapter specifically concentrates on the two varieties of diversified business groups in the US economy in particular: international business groups centered around trading firms and operating companies; and business groups organized around banks and other financial institutions. The formation of American business groups abroad in the late nineteenth and early twentieth century resulted from the general environment in which they exploited market opportunities in underdeveloped economies and *generated* businesses and industries in those local economies. These ventures were realized through transferring necessary capital and business skills that had been mostly nurtured in the more developed home country context of the US economy. Those groups had relational capabilities, which facilitated their expansion through partnerships and networking in host countries and regions. Many of those groups, however, ultimately experienced the relative or even absolute decline of business activities, especially after World War II, as the political environment and economic opportunities shifted against their economic interest and accumulated capabilities. The reformed strategy of focusing on the product market in which they possessed competitive advantages allowed some of the companies to barely survive. The prominent case of W. R. Grace that was extensively examined in Section 14.4.2.1 represents a rare example of those successful transformations in which product-related know-how in chemicals that the company had nurtured rescued it when the market environment started swinging against conventional region-bound advantages in Latin America to reformulate basic strategic orientation to become a modern industrial enterprise with competitiveness in product markets in chemicals.

The formation of diversified business groups organized around banks at about the same time period, on the other hand, shows the different nature of the characteristic contributions that this particular model of corporate organization made to the US economy. Those banks, with their capability to mobilize a huge amount of financial resources, *reorganized* firms and industries in capital-intensive sectors whenever those firms and industries experienced fundamental changes or structural troubles in the shifting context of the Second Industrial Revolution in the late nineteenth and early twentieth century. J. P. Morgan, the most prominent of those investment banks, was instrumental in the formation of such industrial giants as U.S. Steel, General Electric, and American Telephone & Telegraph, transforming the respective industries and eventually establishing the modern-day economic landscape of oligopolistic giants.

These bank-organized groups, similar to the fate of such industrial groups as Rockefeller's Standard Oil, became the target of public outcry and federal prosecution on antitrust concerns after the turn of the twentieth century and ultimately were dissolved thanks to the Glass-Steagall legislation in the New Deal reforms.

In sum, diversified business groups in US business evolution played characteristic roles in generating and reorganizing modern large enterprises to establish the contemporary industrial landscape of oligopoly. These distinctive contributions made by business groups should be recognized as the critical factor that Chandler did not acknowledge to an adequate degree. As long as his heroes in functionally organized firms with a concentrated product portfolio and multidivisional enterprises with related product lines could not internally initiate those mechanisms of generation or reorganization, the characteristic functions that business groups provided whenever necessary should be vital even to the Chandlerian interpretation of corporate developments in the US economy. Such roles played by the diversified business groups should thus be acknowledged, and their contributions should be complemented to Chandlerian multidivisional enterprises to comprehend the whole spectrum of the industrial dynamics of the US economic development in the long term.

Acknowledgments

We thank Asli Colpan for her invaluable editorial and substantive input to this chapter. We also thank Lou Galambos and Franco Amatori for their comments on earlier versions of this chapter.

CHAPTER 15

THE UNITED STATES IN CONTEMPORARY PERSPECTIVES

evolving forms, strategy, and performance

DAVID COLLIS, BHARAT ANAND,
AND J. YO-JUD CHENG

15.1 INTRODUCTION

THE US is often considered to be the originator of many innovations in the management and governance of diversified firms. The late nineteenth century saw the emergence of pools, trusts, and financial holding companies which took over important sectors of the economy. The 1920s and 1930s were the heyday for pyramidal groups (Kandel et al., 2013; Hikino and Bucheli, this volume). The 1960s saw the rise of conglomerates that competed in a wide range of seemingly unrelated businesses. And, the last decades of the twentieth century featured the novel organizational form of leveraged buyout (LBO) firms, subsequently renamed private equity (PE) firms.[1]

Given the attention devoted to business groups as a form of diversifying entity in emerging markets, it is important to understand the historical evolution of diversified firms in the US as a leading indicator of their role in developed countries. Towards this end, it is useful to document the extent and performance of the *different* forms of diversification in the US, and to develop a theoretical explanation for their occurrence, evolution, and performance over time. This chapter attempts these tasks, focusing particular attention on how and why the management of diversification has expressed itself within the US economy since the 1960s.

---

[1] This chapter draws on Anand and Jayanti (2005). It focuses on conglomerates and private equity firms, which have been the primary types of diversified business groups in the US economy since the 1960s.

We wish to highlight three issues. First, even though certain types of diversified entities—notably, the conglomerate form of organization—have declined in import-ance over time in the US, the *presence and importance of unrelated diversification remains important,* with conservative estimates suggesting that conglomerates cur-rently comprise about 5 percent of non-financial corporate assets in the US, and private equity comprises approximately 10 percent. In other words, unrelated diversification is not a phenomenon restricted to developing countries that feature product and factor market inefficiencies (Khanna and Palepu, 1997; Khanna and Rivkin, 2001). Second, the "average performance" of diversified firms as a whole—the question of whether or not there is a diversification discount or premium that receives considerable attention in the academic literature and the popular press—masks considerable *systematic heterogeneity* between diversified firms. While many diversifying firms destroy economic value, many others are exemplars of impressive value creation over long periods of time. The average returns to diversification are in many ways less interesting than the variation in returns across diversified firms, particularly since the requirements for business groups to generate value is likely to become harder over time as erstwhile "institutional voids" are filled.

Third, and as a corollary, we posit that in order for diversified firms to continue to be able to create value over time (even as market failures that characterize early stages of economic development diminish), the management and governance of diversified firms must evolve as well. Simply put, in a more efficient market context, diversified firms (including business groups) must evolve to *develop unique capabil-ities and resources* that generate a corporate advantage across their portfolio com-panies (Collis and Montgomery, 2005; Anand, 2012). We offer a simple theoretical framework to anchor this idea, and to explain the first two facts: why unrelated diversification continues to persist in the US, and how certain unrelated diversifiers in the US continue to create large economic value.

The chapter proceeds by first placing our analysis of diversification in the US against the backdrop, and definition, of business groups as commonly used elsewhere; docu-menting the prevalence and performance of diversified entities over time in the US economy; and then advancing an explanation for their presence in a developed country while utilizing certain popular case examples to illustrate how the framework applies to real-world organizations.

15.2 Definition and Characteristics of US Business Groups

This chapter acknowledges the definition of terms introduced in an earlier volume on business groups in late developing markets (Colpan, Hikino, and Lincoln, 2010, specif-ically Ch. 2), and the terminology agreed upon for this volume (Colpan and Hikino, this volume). Under this classification, most "groups" in the US fall into the category of: (a) "authority" principle, (b) hierarchy type, and (c) diversified (Colpan and Hikino,

2010: Tab. 2.1); and they are primarily differentiated from the classic Chandlerian multidivisional-form organization by a pattern of "unrelated" diversification.

A strict application of this definition is problematic for two reasons. The first concerns the measure of relatedness to adopt, and where to draw a bright line between related and unrelated diversification. As is known, measures of relatedness are varied, and range from simple counts of standard industrial classification (SIC) codes to more complex analyses of input/output tables or patent networks (Silverman, 1999). More than that, and regardless of which measure of diversification is chosen, there is the challenging question of where to partition the set between related and unrelated diversifiers.

The second concern is that most subsidiaries in "US business groups," and, indeed, large US firms in general, are 100-percent owned by the parent or holding company (which itself may or may not be a public company). There is typically also systematic administrative control of the operating units by corporate headquarters. This ownership structure and internal control mechanism is different from the general understanding of diversified business groups in emerging markets, but is similar to related diversifiers in the classic multidivisional-form organization. As a result, it is hard to construct a clear definition of business groups in the US.

Because of the definitional challenges described above, we use the term "unrelated diversification" to anchor our exploration of these types of firms.[2] Substantively, this means that we track diversified firms that compete across multiple businesses, or "conglomerates." We also track the prevalence and performance of private equity firms in the US—entities that can be clearly identified because they have a specific legal form. (The downside of this approach is that, as privately held entities, public coverage, particularly of their performance, leaves a lot to be desired; see Harris, Jenkinson, and Kaplan, 2014.) The latter are formed as a combination of legally independent companies. Some of the former are organized with internal divisions, although many others, like Berkshire Hathaway, do operate as a holding company with legally independent companies.

In the rest of this chapter we therefore examine the evolution of "business groups" in the US—including both conglomerates and private equity firms—since the 1960s.

15.3 Prevalence and Performance of Unrelated Diversification in the US

We begin our analysis in the 1960s, when the first conglomerate merger wave appeared with the rise of unrelated diversification (Servaes, 1996). This was not the first time,

---

[2] Importantly, the resource-based view of the firm that underpins many modern treatments of corporate strategy views all successful multibusiness entities as having a portfolio of companies that are related in the sense that they benefit from the distinctive resources of the parent company, however seemingly unrelated they might be in a product market sense.

however, that "business groups" appeared in the US: the "pools and trusts" during the nineteenth and twentieth centuries can be thought of as earlier expressions of the phenomenon (Hikino and Bucheli, this volume),[3] and were terminated by antitrust legislation, notably the Sherman Act of 1890 and the Clayton Act of 1914. Similarly, as Kandel et al. (2013) noted, traditional, often pyramidal, groups emerged during the "golden age" of business groups in the 1920s—many concentrated in the utility sector—which at their peak in 1932 controlled 35 percent of corporate assets (Kandel et al., 2013).[4] As the authors note, however, this form of group—with a holding company owning stakes in many publicly quoted entities—had largely disappeared from view by 1960.[5]

We pick up the story at this time, and document the emergence and evolution of two primary types of "diversified business groups": the *conglomerate,* which is diversified across many seemingly unrelated businesses; and the *private equity partnership* (including its predecessor, the leveraged buyout firm). Both share the characteristic of (typically) 100-percent ownership of their portfolio companies, and so differ from their immediate predecessors, which featured the traditional group structure, namely, public ownership of the portfolio companies,[6] and private ownership of the holding company. The data presented below draws in part on some of our own research, but predominantly summarizes the extant literature employing public databases. Unfortunately, much of this work relates to the twentieth century, with less information available on more recent trends.

15.3.1 Prevalence of Diversified Business Groups

15.3.1.1 *Degree of Diversification*

We start by examining the extent of diversification in the US. The first observation is that the majority of output comes from firms that operate in multiple businesses. Table 15.1, based on US Manufacturing Census data, shows that while a minority of all US manufacturing establishments in 1997 is multibusiness, the majority of output is controlled by such entities. In other words, multibusiness firms are much larger than their single business counterparts. The extent of diversification does, however, depend on the definition of business in multibusiness. If the definition of diversification applies

---

[3] The British trading companies, like the Hudson's Bay Company, might be thought of as the original business groups operating in North America.

[4] Intriguingly, the 1920s also saw the creation of business groups by investment banks which saw an opportunity to generate fees and speculate in stocks (Kandel et al., 2013)—what goes around, comes around!

[5] By 1950 the share of corporate assets accounted for by pyramidal groups had fallen to just 5 percent (Kandel et al., 2013).

[6] Although, as Kandel et al. (2013) note, the public's ownership stake in most affiliate companies was very small—often below 20 percent.

Table 15.1. Prevalence of firms producing multiple products, operating in multiple industries and sectors, 1997 and earlier years.

Type of Firm	Percentage of Firms	Percentage of Output	Mean Products, Industries, or Sectors per Firm
Multiple Product 1997	39%	87%	3.5
Multiple Industry 1997	28%	81%	2.8
Multiple Sector 1997	10%	66%	2.3
Multiple Product 1972	34%	65%	
Multiple Product 1977	34%	69%	
Multiple Product 1982	30%	66%	

Sources: Bernard, Redding, and Schott (2010); Streitwieser (1991).

Table 15.2. Diversification of firms, by year.

Year	No. of Firms	Pct. Diversified (Compustat, Self-Reported Segments)	Pct. Diversified (BITS, 4-digit SIC Industry Codes)
1989	1,481	41%	82%
1990	1,563	40%	80%
1991	1,762	37%	78%
1992	1,999	34%	74%
1993	1,700	34%	76%
1994	1,549	15%	80%
1995	1,403	35%	82%
1996	1,251	37%	86%

Source: Villalonga (2004).

to the product level (and one of about 1,500 5-digit SIC codes), then 87 percent of output comes from diversified firms. When "diversification" is deemed to imply expansion into another industry (defined at the 4-digit SIC level), then the share of diversified firms is 81 percent. And, when defined as expansion into another sector (2-digit SIC code level), then diversified firms account for 66 percent of output. What this also makes clear, however, is that, regardless of definition, most manufacturing output in the US today comes from diversified firms.

A similar picture emerges from other sources (Table 15.2). Of all publicly listed firms outside the financial and agricultural sectors, roughly 40 percent are diversified at the level of self-reported different segments, and about 80 percent are diversified when defined at the 4-digit SIC code industry level.

The *overall level of diversification* does appear to have gone through two phases during the last fifty years. There was an initial phase of increasing diversification which coincided with the first conglomerate merger wave in the 1960s. Ravenscraft and Scherer (1987), for example, showed that while 18 percent of all manufacturing industry

Table 15.3. Percentage of firms operating in 1 through 6 business segments, by year.

No. of Segments	1961	1964	1967	1970	1973	1976
1	55%	55%	53%	51%	36%	28%
2	26%	26%	25%	23%	29%	22%
3	11%	12%	14%	14%	17%	20%
4	6%	5%	6%	7%	11%	15%
5	2%	1%	2%	4%	7%	10%
6	0%	0%	1%	1%	1%	4%
Total	100	100	100	100	100	100
No. of Firms	266	353	397	445	514	518
Avg. No. of Segments	1.7	1.7	1.8	1.9	2.3	2.7

Source: Servaes (1996).

acquisitions were "conglomerate acquisitions" between 1956 and 1963, this share rose to over 30 percent between 1963 and 1975. Servaes's (1996) work (Table 15.3) shows a similar increase in diversification from the 1960s onwards as the share of publicly quoted firms that competed in multiple segments (where "segment" is defined at the 2-digit SIC code level) rose from being in the minority in 1961 to comprising almost three quarters of all firms by 1976. Even if one were to apply a more conservative definition of diversification by restricting attention to firms expanding into three or more segments, the share of diversified firms increased from 19 to 49 percent during that period, while the average number of segments operated by publicly quoted firms rose from 1.74 to 2.70 (Servaes, 1996).

The increase in diversification during the 1960s and 1970s was followed by a decrease in diversification, at least among the Fortune 500 firms, after the 1980s, regardless of how one defines "segments" (i.e., whether at the 2- or 4-digit SIC code level; see Table 15.4).[7]

Of course, not all diversified firms qualify as business groups. We therefore focus attention on two entities that comprise such "unrelated diversifiers": conglomerates and private equity firms. Here a picture emerges of a shift from traditional conglomerates to private equity as the preferred form of unrelated diversification in the US since 1980. Conglomerates have been on the decline as a share of corporate assets since the early 1970s, while private equity firms (with cycles around a long-term trend that follow stock-market performance) have taken control of an increasing share of corporate assets since their appearance at that time.

15.3.1.2 *Conglomerates*

Extensive longitudinal data on conglomerates is hard to find, in large part because there is no agreed-upon definition. From the 1960s through the 1970s, the increase in

---

[7] This appears to contradict the continuing expansion of scope by all firms at the most disaggregated product level, which rose from 65 percent of total output in 1972 to 87 percent in 1997 (Table 15.1).

Table 15.4. Median levels of diversification among Fortune 500 firms, by year.

	1980	1985	1990
Total Diversification *(4-digit SIC segments)*	1.00	0.90	0.67
Unrelated Diversification *(2-digit SIC segments)*	0.63	0.59	0.35
Number of Firms	468	453	448

Source: Davis, Diekmann, and Tinsley (1994).

Table 15.5. Prevalence of focused firms and conglomerates, by year.

Year	No. of Firms	No. of Focused Firms	No. of Conglomerates	Conglom. Pct. of Tot. Firms
1984	2,499	1,567	932	37%
1985	2,461	1,610	851	35%
1986	2,497	1,711	786	32%
1987	2,665	1,910	755	28%
1988	2,577	1,896	681	26%
1989	2,524	1,886	638	25%
1990	2,538	1,921	617	24%
1991	2,658	2,031	627	24%
1992	2,910	2,256	654	23%
1993	3,257	2,605	652	20%
1994	3,547	2,881	666	19%
1995	3,893	3,209	684	18%
1996	4,287	3,597	690	16%
1997	4,356	3,716	640	15%

Source: Yan (2006).

overall diversification was attributed to the emergence of conglomerates noted above (Ravenscraft and Scherer, 1987; Servaes, 1996). What is notable is that at least one time series for publicly quoted non-financial, non-utilities with sales above $20 million (Table 15.5) shows that conglomerates, defined as operating in two different 4-digit SIC code segments, declined substantially between 1984 and 1997. This data accords with the longitudinal data on overall diversification among larger firms, which shows a decline over the same period. It also coincides with the emergence of LBO (leveraged buyout) firms, which rose to prominence in the 1980s before peaking with the RJR Nabisco ("Barbarians at the Gate") deal in 1988, and subsequently morphing into private equity partnerships. Nevertheless, the data suggest that at their peak conglomerates accounted for nearly 40 percent of larger publicly quoted firms in the US in the late 1970s, and that this share has now fallen to under 20 percent.

15.3.1.3 *Private Equity*

Private equity (PE) firms, and their leveraged buyout predecessors, originated in the late 1960s and came to prominence in the late 1970s at just the time conglomerates appeared to be going out of favor.[8] KKR (Kohlberg, Kravis, Roberts), for example, was founded in 1976. This substitution occurred in part because of the increasing capital market emphasis on shareholder value (Jensen, 1986). The number of these funds, as reported by Preqin[9] (see Figure 15.1), shows a rapid growth through the 1990s, as well as a correlation with stock-market performance as the absolute number of funds declines in the two bear markets after 2001 and 2007.[10]

In order to examine the assets that private equity partnerships control, we start by focusing on total capital commitments to the firms. Figure 15.2 shows funds flowing into PE firms each year. As with the number of firms, these show a huge increase over time, with a cycle correlating with stock-market performance. To understand the total funds under management at a point in time, we need to cumulate the annual

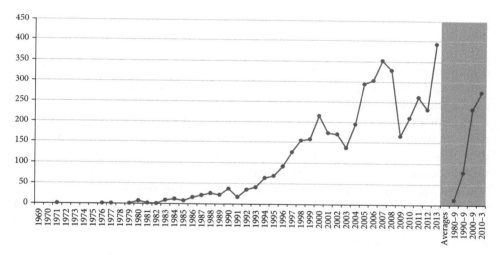

FIGURE **15.1.** Number of private equity funds, by fund vintage year.

Source: Preqin.

[8] We also examined data on venture capital firms that can also be thought of as a variety of diversified business groups. While larger in earlier years, they have been surpassed by private equity since the 1980s.

[9] It should be noted that there are disputes about the accuracy of the databases available on the size and performance of these private entities. We primarily utilize data from Preqin (an independent provider of private equity data) rather than the main alternative (Thomson One), as experts note that the Thomson One database systematically underreports the number of private equity funds and funds' cash flows from around 2000 onward (Harris, Jenkinson, and Kaplan, 2014). Many recent studies have relied on Preqin data in lieu of Thomson One (see, for example, Chung et al., 2012; Acharya et al., 2013; Sensoy, Wang, and Weisbach, 2014).

[10] Some private equity firms will operate more than one fund at a point in time. However, most firms have only one active fund.

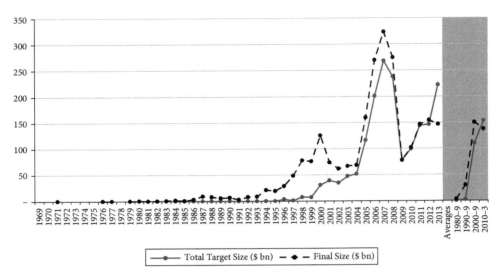

FIGURE **15.2.** Size of private equity funds, by fund vintage year ($ bn).

Source: Preqin.

commitments assuming an average fund life of ten years (Kaplan and Schoar, 2005). This suggests that at its peak in 2007 there was $1.3 trillion in total capital committed to private equity (and $282 billion to venture capital).

To calibrate the share of assets that are under the control of private equity firms, one needs to multiply their capital available by an average leverage ratio of roughly 3:1. At their peak this would mean that they would control over 12 percent (15 percent including venture capital) of all non-financial corporate assets in the US economy, and would have averaged about 7.3 percent of corporate assets during this century. This compares to a share peak of 21 percent for private equity in all global M&A activity in 2006 (TheCityUK, 2012). Relatedly, we can follow the number of investments made by private equity firms that peaked at nearly 1,400 companies in 2007 (Figure 15.3).

These data tell a similar story. When "business groups" (or "unrelated diversification") is taken to include "seemingly unrelated diversifiers present in more than two sectors" as well as private equity partnerships, then "groups" might account for roughly 15 percent of corporate assets in the US even today. In other words, unrelated diversification in the US has not abated as much as one would be led to believe if one restricted attention to conglomerates.

15.3.2 Performance of Diversified Business Groups

We examine performance data of private equity firms and conglomerates separately. We start by highlighting some challenges in performance measurement, and then summarize the findings regarding heterogeneity in performance across firms.

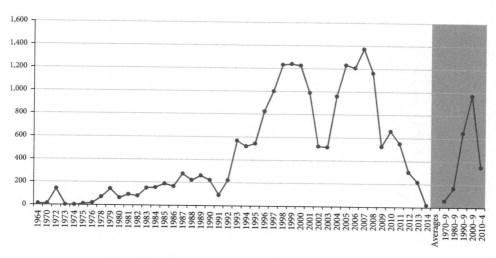

FIGURE 15.3. Number of investments by private equity firms, by fundraising year.

Source: Thomson One (Thomson Reuters).

15.3.2.1 *Private Equity*

Private equity firms generate returns for their general partners (the operators of the partnership) and the limited partners (the providers of funds to the partnership). It is important to recognize that returns to the former are orders of magnitude higher, and less variable, than to the latter. General partners have managed to shape the fee structure—the traditional 2 plus 20 (2 percent of funds raised, and 20 percent of profits after a hurdle rate, often 8 percent, is passed)—and the compensation they extract from portfolio companies in the form of "management" fees, termination fees, and other fees that are largely unrelated to the performance of the underlying fund, with the result that nearly two thirds of their income is independent of fund performance (Metrick and Yasuda, 2010). Because of the asymmetric nature of returns to the two sets of partners, we focus on returns to the limited partner.

Returns to limited partners in private equity are obtained from the Preqin database and remain controversial (Harris, Jenkinson, and Kaplan, 2014). Care needs to be taken to adjust returns for risk and leverage (Table 15.6). While absolute performance might be high, if those returns were achieved simply by "levering up" on a rising stock market, then returns would appear artificially amplified. Swensen, for example, found that between 1987 and 1998 investing in the S & P 500 at similar leverage to LBO firms would have delivered returns 50 percent per annum above their performance (Swensen, 2009)! In addition, as Welch (2014) notes, the reputed benefit of portfolio diversification that private equity appears to offer—its returns have a low correlation with the overall market—might simply be due to private equity firms manipulating the asset values of their portfolio companies through strategic reporting (i.e., not reporting lower values in a bear market and waiting for the recovery to recognize those losses).

Table 15.6. Literature on private equity (buyout, venture capital) performance.

Paper	Performance Relative to S & P 500	Context	Data Source	Method
Ljungqvist & Richardson (2003, WP)	Excess returns of 5–8% per year relative to S & P 500	1981–2002; 1981–1993 vintage years; 73 funds	One of the largest US institutional investors in PE; Thomson Venture Economics	Fund IRR minus S & P 500 IRR; cash flows only, ignores unrealized capital gains
Kaplan & Schoar (2005)	Average fund returns net-of-fees roughly equal to S & P 500 for buyout and VC funds; when weighted by committed capital, VC outperform S & P 500, buyouts do not; strong persistence in returns	1980–2001 (mostly 1995 or earlier vintage years); 746 funds	Thomson Venture Economics	Public market equivalent: comparison of investment in PE fund to equivalently timed investment in S & P 500; does not account for market risk
Swensen (2009)	Buyouts underperform risk-adjusted S & P 500 by 50 percentage points per year (buyouts return 36% per year; comparably timed, sized and leveraged investments in S & P 500 return 86% per year)	1987–1998; 542 buyout deals	Yale Investment Office transactions	Comparison of buyout deals presented to Yale to comparably leveraged investments in S & P 500
Phalippou & Gottschalg (2009)	Average net-of-fees PE fund performance 3% below S & P 500, 6% below when risk-adjusted	1980–2003; 852 funds (US and non-US)	Thomson Venture Economics	Excess IRR
Harris, Jenkinson, & Kaplan (2014)	Buyouts outperform S & P 500 by 20–27% over life of fund (>3% per year); VC outperform S & P 500 in 1990s, underperform in 2000s	1984–2008; 1,400 funds (US only)	Burgiss, Thomson Venture Economics, Preqin, Cambridge Associates	Public market equivalent: comparison of investment in PE fund to equivalently timed investment in S & P 500; potential data quality issues with Thomson Venture Economics
Ghai, Kehoe, & Pinkus (2014)	Private equity funds with vintage years 1995–2006 meaningfully outperformed S & P 500 (even on a leverage-adjusted basis)	1990–2006 fund vintage years	Bloomberg, Cambridge Associates, Preqin	Cash-flow-matching approach: assumes investment into and out of public equities matched the average of cash called and returned by private equity companies

The returns to private equity show that unadjusted average returns to funds since their inception date have cycled (with peak returns being made for funds raised in "down" markets) with a slight downward trend (Figure 15.4). Clearly, early movers before the explosion in the number of funds after the mid-1990s have been more successful than later funds on average (although final returns are as yet unknown for the most recent funds, since they have not yet been closed out). With the exception of the last few years, decade averages for these returns exceed the comparable S & P performance by between a 2- and 5-percent annual internal rate of return (IRR). Again, these *returns are unadjusted for leverage*, but do suggest that, particularly in the early days, private equity was a value creating organizational form. Venture capital, in contrast, was very profitable in the 1970s and 1980s, but has struggled with poor returns since the late 1990s (Figure 15.5).

More interesting for our purposes is the heterogeneity of fund performance. In each decade, the absolute difference in annual IRR between a top and bottom quartile performing fund is close to 20 percent. Top quartile funds have usually earned close to 20 percent annual returns, while bottom quartile funds have always provided returns below 10 percent (Table 15.7). Venture capital shows a similar pattern although with losses, on average, for bottom quartile performers in recent years.

Given this variance, the sustainability of performance across private equity firms is of obvious interest. Research has shown that there is persistence in fund performance over time (Kaplan and Schoar, 2005; Phalippou and Gottschalg, 2009), and that some of the larger funds have been able to maintain above-average performance. Consistent with this (and as seen below), until the most recent period the size of the top-performing funds increases over time as successful firms are able to raise larger funds (Table 15.8).

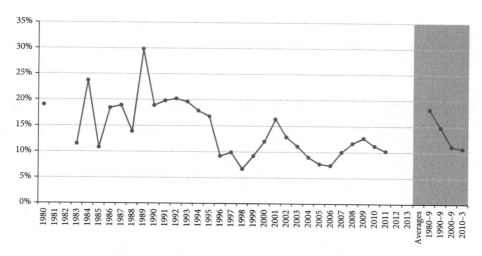

FIGURE 15.4. Net median IRR to private equity funds (percent to date), by fund vintage year.

Source: Preqin.

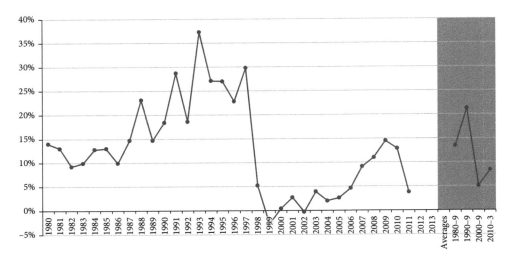

FIGURE 15.5. Net median IRR to venture capital funds (percent to date), by fund vintage year.

Source: Preqin.

Table 15.7. Median and quartile IRR to private equity funds and venture capital funds (percent to date), by decade of fund vintage year.

	Private Equity Funds			Venture Capital Funds		
	Top Quartile	Median	Bottom Quartile	Top Quartile	Median	Bottom Quartile
1980–9	31%	18%	10%	19%	13%	8%
1990–9	25%	15%	7%	46%	21%	3%
2000–9	18%	11%	6%	12%	5%	−2%
2010–3	18%	11%	3%	22%	8%	−1%

Source: Preqin.

Table 15.8. Median IRR to private equity funds (percent to date), by decade of fund vintage year and fund size ($ m).

		Fund Size ($ m)							
	Median	50–100	100–200	200–300	300–400	400–500	500–750	750–1,000	1,000+
1980–9	18%	26%	18%	21%					
1990–9	15%	16%	15%	13%	17%	5%	13%	8%	14%
2000–9	11%	10%	11%	12%	12%	10%	11%	12%	14%
2010–3	11%	16%	12%	2%	10%	16%	9%	14%	10%

Source: Preqin (note: IRR by fund size is not available for years with fewer than three funds).

15.3.2.2 *Conglomerates*

The performance of conglomerates is popularly characterized as suffering from the "conglomerate discount." The discount is typically estimated by "sum of the parts" or "chop-shop" approaches that compare the actual market capitalization of the conglomerate with the sum of its individual businesses valued at the same level as single business firms in those industries. Since the seminal paper by Lang and Stulz (1994), studies have reported that conglomerates typically demonstrate a discount of about 15–20 percent that appears to be relatively unaffected by the degree of diversification (Table 15.9). Wall Street analysts and investment bankers perform similar calculations that show similar results.[11] In sum, these findings resulted in the conglomerate discount being generally accepted as an "established fact" by the finance community for a long time.

More recently, there have been important debates concerning the magnitude and existence of the "conglomerate discount." These debates have largely centered on three sets of issues: (i) whether the discount changes over time; (ii) whether and how the discount varies between countries; and, perhaps most importantly, (iii) whether the discount reflects causal effects rather than correlation. Disagreement with the argument that diversification reduces performance has focused on the empirics surrounding measures and data sources, control groups and survivorship bias, and on the theoretical argument that firms which are performing poorly tend to diversify in the hunt for better returns. Villalonga's is perhaps the most effective critique of the diversification discount (Villalonga, 2004); those that follow her line of research now even speak of a "conglomerate premium" (Hund, Monk, and Tice, 2012).

Beyond these debates concerning the *average effect* of diversification on performance, however, there is another issue that merits greater attention and that has been the implicit focus of much of the corporate strategy literature: namely, the heterogeneity of performance between diversified firms. Studies as far back as Lang and Stulz (1994) showed that some diversified firms create value. However, most studies are based on an analysis of a cross section rather than a more careful analysis of *systematic* heterogeneity in the diversification effect (that is, heterogeneity that is persistent for a firm). More careful research on this subject demonstrates that roughly 30–40 percent of diversified firms create value (Table 15.10) (Anand and Byzalov, 2011). Moreover, this performance heterogeneity appears to be two to three times as large as the diversification discount itself. These findings are qualitatively similar to research findings on private equity funds' performance that illustrate systematic differences across partnerships in their value creation over time, even if

---

[11] The Trefis website (https://www.trefis.com) is useful in this regard, allowing users to alter their estimates for the drivers of business unit performance, which instantaneously adjusts the corporate value and its comparison to the current market capitalization of the firm.

Table 15.9. Literature on the diversification discount/premium.

Paper	Diversification Discount/Premium	Context	Method/Methodological Improvement
Lang & Stulz (1994)	Yearly average discounts ranging 27–73%; statistically significant almost all years 1978–1990	1978–1990; 18,255 firm-years, 2- and 5-segment firms	Chop shop; Tobin's q
Berger & Ofek (1995)	13–15% discount	1986–1991; 3,659 firms, 16,181 firm-years	Excess value (natural log of ratio of firm's total value and sum of imputed values for its segments as stand-alone entities)
Servaes (1996)	45% discount, 1960–70; declined to 7%, 1973–6 (time-varying)	1961–1976; 2,493 firm-years	Tobin's q, sales multiplier (market value to sales ratio)
Klein (2001)	7% mean discount (8% median): not stat. sig. 1966–8; 18% discount (11% median) 1969–71; 20% discount (4% median) 1972–4. With add'l controls: 36% avg. premium 1966–8; not stat. sig. 1969–71; 17% discount 1972–4	1966–1974; 36 large, acquisitive conglomerates, 283 firm-years	Matched benchmark portfolio; Tobin's q; narrowly defined sample of large, highly diversified conglomerates with detailed line-of-business data
Campa & Kedia (2002)	18–30% premium	1978–1996; 8,815 firms, 58,965 firm-years	Accounts for endogeneity in decision to diversify (Heckman selection model, 2SLS)
Villalonga (2004)	11–43% premium (28% average across years)	1989–1996; 12,708 firm-years	More accurate, comprehensive data source with establishment-level data to construct business units (instead of segments)
Amman, Hoechle, & Schmid (2012)	11–21% discount	1985–2005; 18,898 firm-years	Excess value; Heckman selection model, fixed effects, instrumental variables approaches
Hund, Monk, & Tice (2012, WP)	19% average premium over sample period, value-weighted	1977–2009; 79,142 firm-years	Value-weighted to give firms with largest market value more weight

one might argue what their average effect might be (Ghai, Kehoe, and Pinkus, 2014). Together, these results suggest a way forward in the need to examine the factors that make some unrelated diversifiers more profitable than others.

Table 15.10. Performance heterogeneity in diversified firms.

	Asset Multipliers		Sales Multipliers		Industry-Adjusted q-s	
	1978–1996	1998–2008	1978–1996	1998–2008	1978–1996	1998–2008
Mean Diversification Discount	−0.111	−0.101	−0.124	−0.115	−0.137	−0.119
Median Diversification Discount	−0.105	−0.096	−0.130	−0.135	−0.102	−0.082
% Diversified Firm-Years that have Higher Excess Values than the Median Single-Segmented Firm	38%	42%	39%	40%	37%	43%

Source: Anand and Byzalov (2011).

15.3.3 Explaining the Performance of Unrelated Diversifiers

With these findings as a backdrop, Figure 15.6 provides a simple framework with which to examine the value-adding role of diversified business groups, whether in the US over time or across countries at a point in time (Anand and Jayanti, 2005). It emphasizes two issues that merit investigation in any such analysis: first, the role of institutional context and the efficient functioning of markets; and, second, a firm's corporate strategy.

Going back to Coase (1937) and subsequent "theories of the firm," it is well understood that firms in general—and unrelated diversifiers in particular—can be effective in mediating transactions when markets don't work well. As a result, it is important to understand how efficiently markets function within an economy at a given point in time. The degree of development of capital and labor markets, and the types of intermediaries present to allocate resources in these input markets and to enable the functioning of the product markets, can fruitfully explain why conglomerates had a useful role to play both in earlier time periods in the US (for example, during the 1950s and 1960s, when growth financing for small businesses was not available, pools of professional managerial talent that believed that they could manage any business were emerging and were therefore still scarce, and the legislative environment motivated expansion across industries), and in certain countries today, particularly emerging markets, where "institutional voids" are large (Khanna and Palepu, 1997; Khanna and Rivkin, 2001). Thus, "market development" constitutes an important dimension to consider when evaluating the performance of unrelated diversifiers or diversified business groups (the x-axis in Figure 15.6).

However, at any point in time and in any country there also exists a substantial performance difference within the group of companies that compete across multiple

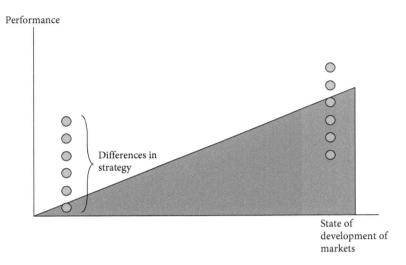

FIGURE 15.6. Explaining business group performance—context and strategy.
Source: Anand and Jayanti (2005).

businesses. In other words, the fact that some markets don't function well is neither a necessary nor sufficient condition for unrelated diversifiers and diversified business groups to create value: weak-functioning markets do not automatically imply that all groups perform well, nor does it follow that in well-functioning markets no unrelated diversifying business groups should exist. Instead, it is important to examine the corporate strategies of individual business groups in order to understand *how* exactly it is that they add value to seemingly unrelated businesses and how the capabilities they build to do so cannot simply be accessed by transacting on efficient markets (Teece, Pisano, and Shuen, 1997).

One framework that has proven useful over time in understanding effective corporate (or multibusiness) strategies builds on the resource-based view (RBV) of the firm (Wernerfelt, 1984; Barney, 1991; Peteraf, 1993; Collis and Montgomery, 2005). Central to this perspective is the argument that every successful corporate strategy which creates shareholder value, whether involving related diversification or seemingly unrelated conglomerate diversification, is ultimately built around (a) a distinctive set of resources (Figure 15.7), and (b) alignment among the three central strategic choices that any multibusiness firm makes: portfolio, organizational design, and ownership structure.

Diversified firms are an efficient organizational form that creates economic value when they possess a corporate advantage such that the sum of the "better-off" and "ownership" tests is positive. "Better off" refers to the presence of a resource (popularly, but incorrectly, described as a core competence) which when deployed in a business improves the competitive advantage of that business either by raising customer willingness to pay, increasing volume, or by decreasing cost. (For the definition of resources and

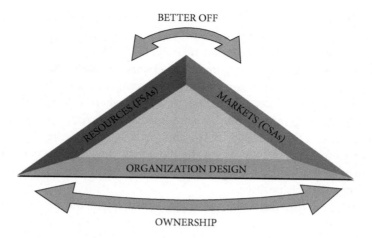

FIGURE 15.7. Corporate strategy framework.

characteristics that make them valuable, see Barney, 1991, and Collis and Montgomery, 2005.) Classic examples are the Disney characters which allow Disney hotels to charge at least a 50-percent premium over equivalent quality hotels a quarter of a mile away while operating at over 90-percent utilization (Rukstad, Collis, and Levine, 2009); or Newell's skills at manufacturing, merchandising, and distributing low-price consumer staples like paintbrushes and curtain rods through mass merchants, which allowed it to create value by acquiring and "Newellizing" over fifty such companies (Collis and Montgomery, 2005).[12] When these pass the VRIN (valuable, rare, inimitable, non-substitutable) tests of valuable resources (Barney, 1991), they can be the source of value creation across markets.[13]

The "ownership" test compares the governance cost of performing activities inside the corporate hierarchy with the transaction costs of some form of market exchange or contract with third parties (Williamson, 1981). Typically the market governance of transactions has the lower cost because of the high-powered incentives independent entities have as residual profit owners. While the corporation must always design its internal administrative context to minimize the costs of retaining the activity inside the hierarchy, typically the ownership test will only be positive when there is some form of market failure which raises market transaction costs inordinately high (Williamson, 1979, 1981). In those instances of market failure, internalizing the activity is more efficient.

---

[12] For completeness, the scale and scope a group creates across different markets can become a valuable resource of its own. It is also true that diversification that destroys value in the new business can still be worthwhile if that new business contributes more back to the corporate parent, e.g., when Merck, a pharmaceutical company, bought Medco, a pharmacy benefit manager, to have access to its data on prescription usage.

[13] Notice that the rarity of a resource depends on the state of the factor market. Institutional voids lead to inelasticity in the factor market supply and so make resources acquired on those "missing" markets valuable.

We therefore have the two arguments typically advanced in favor of diversification: to leverage a distinctive set of resources into additional markets, and to substitute the hierarchy for the market organization of exchange. While related diversification is usually explained by the former argument, diversified business groups have traditionally been justified by the latter argument[14] (for example, when an institutional void raises the cost of the market transaction to a level where internalizing the activity creates value). We suggest that while both arguments are correct, a fuller and consistent treatment recognizes that the scope of the enterprise should be extended *whenever* the sum of the two tests is positive—when the difference between the cost of production inside the firm and by a third party plus the difference between the governance costs of the two arrangements is positive.

An advantage of this framework is that it can explain the presence, and value-creating potential, of several modern diversified business groups in developed countries like the US. Whether private equity or conglomerates, such firms do not solely depend for their existence on market failures that raise external transaction costs. Rather, they operate and succeed by building a set of distinctive resources or capabilities (Teece, Pisano, and Shuen, 1997) which can create value across a broader set of businesses than those of related diversifiers. Rather than thinking of a dichotomy between related and conglomerate forms of diversification, it is more productive to think of a continuum of effective corporate strategies that are characterized by the specificity of a firm's underlying resources and the breadth of their applicability across businesses. These businesses might range from tightly related (e.g., Clorox, or even single businesses), all the way to conglomerates, private equity, or even mutual funds (Figure 15.8).

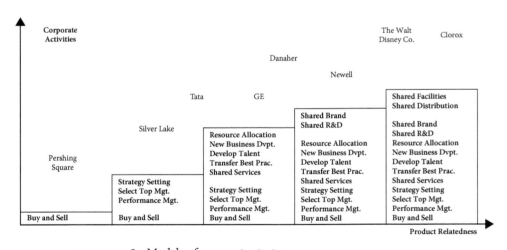

FIGURE **15.8.** Models of corporate strategy.
Source: Adapted from Anand (2005, 2016), lecture on "Strategies of Multibusiness Firms."

---

[14] As has vertical integration.

Why is this framework useful? At first glance, the various corporate strategies referred to in Figure 15.8 appear completely dissimilar—in large part because their scope and organizational design are so different. Firms like Clorox, for example, operate in largely related businesses with centralized corporate structures and large corporate headquarters. Others like Danaher, Berkshire Hathaway, or private equity firms operate across a large range of seemingly unrelated businesses, with lean headquarters.

But focusing on any one of these corporate choices in isolation misses a crucial point: in order for multibusiness firms to successfully create value, they need to employ or leverage distinctive resources; and their scope, organizational structures, and ownership choices need to be aligned. Thus, a tightly related corporate strategy, like Clorox, which leverages a brand name, relationships with retailers, consumer insights, and technology for a set of food products, can *only* operate in a closely related set of businesses, and only with a unified structure and large corporate headquarters. On the other hand, a conglomerate like Danaher, which leverages a set of best practices and a pool of managers trained in those techniques, can spread its domain across portfolio companies that are seemingly quite disparate, with fairly independent business units and a much smaller corporate headquarters (Collis and Montgomery, 2005; Collis and Anand, 2014; Anand, Collis, and Hood, 2015). Success in each case comes from crafting a set of resources that are value-creating given the institutional context that determines the efficiency of product and factor markets, and hence the cost of market transactions, and then aligning corporate scope, organizational design, and ownership structures with those resources.

Thus, at the unrelated end of the continuum, entities can operate with seemingly relatively pedestrian resources, such as stock-picking skill, access to capital, and general management skills, that are fungible across many businesses but which are typically readily imitable and widely available from efficient factor markets. Success in leveraging these resources is more likely in less developed markets where factor or product markets are less efficient, so that even these resources or basic capabilities can be rare and valuable. Indeed, groups in developing countries, like Tata, typically possess a set of what look like general resources—access to capital, managerial talent, government relations, etc.—but can nevertheless create substantial value if relevant markets are missing or failing.

In developed countries, on the other hand, private equity firms (like Silver Lake, TPG, Blackstone, and others) that leverage a set of resources which can in principle be accessed through efficient markets (for example, resources like incentive design, strategic insight, etc.) will only create value across unrelated markets *if* those capabilities are truly distinctive and built internally over time rather than acquired immediately in a market transaction (Dierickx and Cool, 1989; Barney, 1991; Gompers and Lerner, 2001; Teece, Pisano, and Shuen, 1997; Anand, Collis, and Hood, 2015). Similarly, conglomerates like Danaher which build such unique capabilities—for example, the famous "Danaher Business System"—that improve the operating performance of a set of seemingly unrelated businesses, can also serve as efficient organizational forms. We will return to the nature of these capabilities in the next section.

A key point is that in all these cases the businesses, however unrelated they might appear in product market terms, remain related in the important sense of benefiting from the presence of the parent's common resources. Furthermore, these resources are valuable *in the context of the markets in which they operate* at any point in time. As a result, an important distinction is that for resources in developed markets to be rare and hard to imitate they must be more "advanced" than simple management skills.

15.4 RATIONALE FOR, AND EVOLUTION OF, BUSINESS GROUPS IN THE US

With this framework in place, we can now examine the evolving rationale for the continuing presence of diversified business groups in the US since the 1960s and provide specific examples at each stage.

15.4.1 Conglomerates in the US, circa 1960–80

The first conglomerate merger wave in the 1960s has been attributed to the enforcement of antitrust legislation against horizontal acquisitions within a single business.[15] Prevented from growing within an industry and faced with capital markets that rewarded growth, corporations sought to expand across industries (Figures 15.9 and 15.10)—this was the era of the "Nifty Fifty." This environment, in combination with postwar economic optimism, low interest rates, and large corporate cash flows, allowed

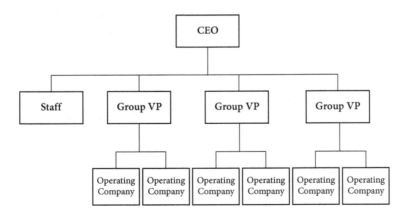

FIGURE **15.9.** Organizational chart for conglomerates.

[15] The definition of industry boundaries always remains contentious.

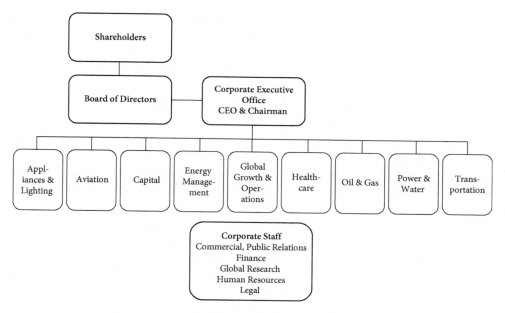

FIGURE **15.10**. Organizational chart for General Electric.
Source: General Electric. "GE Company Organization Chart
(November 2014)."

for unprecedented expansion of firm diversification and the popularity of conglomeration (Sobel, 1984; Shleifer and Vishny, 1991). Early conglomerates in the US succeeded, much as business groups in developing countries currently do, as practitioners of simple managerial skills, allocators of capital, and the decision to compete, where possible, in faster-growing industries.

Companies like Gulf + Western, IC Industries, ITT, and Whittaker spread their boundaries far and wide as they followed perhaps the first true conglomerate, Textron. Among this group, Beatrice Corporation stood out, not only as the most active acquirer in the US during this early period, but also as one of the strongest performers (Collis, 1997). At first glance, Beatrice's functioning appeared simple and not particularly noteworthy: allocate capital (typically at market interest rates) to those businesses that needed it and use the cash flows from high-performing businesses to cross-subsidize others suffering from a cyclical downturn or declining profitability. Normally, one might regard such a company to be a "poorly functioning bank"—lending capital without adequate due diligence or adequate oversight. However, features of both the context and its strategy suggest why the firm may have been quite effective in this role. External sources of growth capital for small businesses were inadequate at the time, creating a role for an internal capital market. In addition, although the corporate headquarters' lack of due diligence when allocating capital appears troublesome when viewed in isolation, it looks quite different in the context of the company's overall strategy. Specifically, Beatrice would look to acquire well-run (but often liquidity-constrained) companies in high-growth industries, where the managers would agree to stay on after the acquisition. In other words, the requisite diligence appears to have been performed not at the time of allocating capital but at the time of choosing to invest in the business.

By the early 1980s many of the original conglomerates, and even those that might not qualify as groups but had diversified beyond their core businesses, were under pressure thanks to their financial underperformance. Coca-Cola had bought Columbia Pictures (the movie company), presumably in the belief that people drank Coke when watching movies! Entrenched corporate management, relatively immune to capital market pressures, built empires that increased their pay (often at this period related more to corporate size than performance) and supported unnecessary corporate overhead (such as corporate aircraft). Entrenchment allowed managers to indulge in businesses they enjoyed—American Tobacco, for example, diversified into the liquor business (Jim Beam), golf (Titleist), and do-it-yourself equipment (Master Lock) allegedly because the chairman, promoted from running the tobacco business, had little to do but play golf, enjoy the nineteenth hole, and potter around fixing up his house!—and led them to subsidize poorly performing businesses rather than make the hard decision to close them down or sell them off.

In contrast to corporations building pathological portfolios with no underlying value creation potential were the conglomerates that operated according to strict ROI investment criteria: allocating resources between businesses according to their current profitability. These conglomerates saw their portfolios gradually shrink as the emphasis on short-term returns led to an erosion of market share, particularly when they confronted the emerging Japanese competition that adopted a long-term market-share objective. The US machine-tool industry, for example, saw several of its leading manufacturers, like Burgmaster and Bridgeport, suffer at the hands of Japanese CNC machine-tool manufacturers through the 1970s and 1980s when owned by the conglomerates Houdaille and Textron, respectively (Holland, 1989).

15.4.2 Private Equity Firms (and their Predecessors— Leveraged Buyout Firms), 1980 to Today

Into this environment came the LBO firms with the support of a new intellectual perspective on the role of the corporation. Building on Milton Friedman's argument that the only valid objective for corporations was to maximize shareholder value, Michael Jensen suggested companies should return free cash flow to shareholders rather than retain it inside the firm, where it would be dissipated in uneconomic diversification or managerial perks and self-aggrandizement (Jensen, 1986). This sense that investors themselves rather than corporations should make diversification decisions, along with the emerging acceptance by Wall Street of efficient capital market theory, led to the breakup of many of the most pathological and underperforming conglomerate portfolios. The term leveraged buyout reflected the form that much of this activity took. An LBO partnership would "buy out" a business from a conglomerate, leverage it up with debt, and then expect the resulting high-powered incentives for its managers to improve performance by relatively obvious cost-cutting.

Most of the transactions involved in these asset divestitures were executed by firms whose business portfolios, at first glance, looked quite similar to (and as unrelated as) those of the conglomerates they had replaced and taken apart. For example, a typical LBO firm, like KKR and Berkshire Partners, might invest in firms as diverse as bakeries, footwear stores, radio stations, underground storage tanks, and polyethylene pipe manufacturers. However, despite similarities in business mix, there were significant differences between the *organizational design* and *ownership structure* of these two "models" that affected their ability to add value to the individual portfolio companies (Baker and Montgomery, 1994). High debt-equity ratios in LBO investments focused managerial attention on cash generation and restricted discretionary expenditures by managers. Legal separation of the businesses in the portfolio, with contractual responsibilities specific to each buyout, eliminated cross-subsidization. It also reduced the monitoring challenges that would otherwise confront a large conglomerate with a diversified portfolio, since each business now had its own distinct board responsible for monitoring that business alone. An added difference came from the fact that "corporate managers"—in this case, the general partners—were typically responsible for contributing between 1 and 10 percent of the total equity from their *personal wealth*, providing powerful incentives to run the businesses effectively. Last, the limited legal life of the partnership fund resulted in forced divestitures of the portfolio businesses, thereby imposing a natural limit on the scope of the organization (Figures 15.11and 15.12).

LBO firms were relatively straightforward in their behavior, relying on leverage to boost returns and the combination of carrot (portfolio company managers were rewarded with an equity share rather than salary) and stick (debt covenants required careful attention to cash flow to prevent bankruptcy) to deliver results, rather than developing any distinctive capabilities. With the ready imitation of this form of corporate organization as many Wall Street executives set up their own LBO firms, and banks subsequently refusing to support the degree of leverage, this strategy failed. In their place, private equity firms, some of them the very same LBO firms, now carefully repositioned to avoid the word leverage, emerged. Essentially the same legal entity, these firms now paid more attention to the strategy put in place by their portfolio companies and to growth rather than just cost-cutting.

While private equity firms appear to retain certain structural advantages over conglomerates, they are far less differentiated when compared with each other—explaining why the rents to these firms have diminished over time as competition and so the price of deals has increased, equity stakes required by general partners (GPs) have increased, and deal sizes have become bigger. Indeed, today most private equity firms are rushing to find ways to differentiate themselves from a crowd of plain vanilla competitors whose skills and capabilities are now in excess supply and available on efficient markets. To remain as superior performers, i.e., on the right side of the

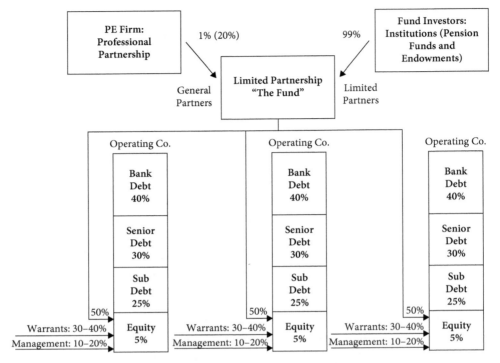

FIGURE **15.11.** Private equity organizational structure.

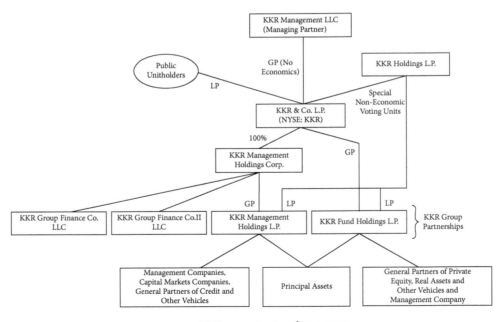

FIGURE **15.12.** KKR organizational structure.
Source: KKR & Co. L.P. SEC form 10-K for fiscal year 2013.

Table 15.11. Performance of major private equity firms (US funds), 1971–2014.

Firm	Average IRR	No. of funds	Pct. funds by quartile			
			1st Q	2nd Q	3rd Q	4th Q
Advent International	11.3%	3	0%	33%	33%	33%
Apollo Global Management	19.8%	7	29%	57%	14%	0%
Bain Capital	18.9%	16	63%	19%	13%	6%
Blackstone Group	20.6%	9	56%	11%	11%	22%
Carlyle Group	13.3%	12	33%	25%	33%	8%
Goldman Sachs Merchant Banking Division	10.7%	12	17%	25%	33%	25%
KKR	21.2%	11	18%	36%	18%	9%
Oaktree Capital Management	17.1%	29	24%	31%	41%	3%
TPG	25.6%	9	44%	22%	22%	11%
Warburg Pincus	16.8%	10	40%	60%	0%	0%

Source: Preqin.

distribution of firm performance (Table 15.11), successful PE firms must build a distinctive capability. Some are attempting to build an industry expertise, like Silver Lake in the technology sector (Collis and Kind, 2014). Others, like TPG, are claiming to have built an operational expertise—though how an in-house team of perhaps fifty "operators" can outperform major consulting firms and a business's own managers is hard to see (Roberts, Sahlman, and Barley, 2008; Kelly, 2011). Others are specializing in particular forms of investing, such as the provision of growth equity. Increasingly, to be successful private equity firms must be able to take a contrarian view of a business's potential, in a way that justifies paying the most in a competitive auction without becoming a victim of the "winner's curse." In this regard, they look more like Berkshire Hathaway, which remains one of the most successful business groups based on Warren Buffett's distinctive ability to spot undervalued companies.

Either way, it is no longer sufficient just to cut the costs of business units that might have been given a cushion to operate inefficiently within a corporate portfolio, or to add capital to a mid-tier growth company. Rather, to be successful, like Silver Lake, they need to build distinctive resources.

15.4.3 Conglomerates, 1980 to Today

In contrast to the commoditization of private equity, many of the conglomerates that remain in the twenty-first century have honed a distinctive set of skills and capabilities over many decades that allow them to create value even in the presence of a more "efficient" institutional and market context. These have included firms like General Electric, Dover, and Danaher, holding companies like Leucadia, and technology conglomerates like 3M. Many of these firms have outperformed the S & P 500 over the past three decades. While some of the mechanisms that allow these firms to "add value" to their businesses are idiosyncratic, each of these conglomerates appears to have crafted its own set of resources as well as put unique organizational processes and coordinative mechanisms in place. At the same time, the design of these firms reveals more general lessons on how conglomerates add value. The first, and perhaps best known among this group, was General Electric (GE).

The example of GE, specifically its twenty-year history under Jack Welch, illustrates several aspects of successful conglomerates. The first point is that, unlike the simple resources and organizational processes that characterized earlier conglomerates (like Beatrice), those at GE were far more nuanced and complex—reinforcing the fact that consistently outperforming market benchmarks requires much more than simply "being a bank" as the corporation built a set of capabilities and a cadre of managers with distinctive skills. (These initiatives are described in detail in Bartlett and Wozny, 2005.) In addition, although the specific initiatives launched by Jack Welch between 1981 and 2000 were both disparate and wide-ranging, their implementation reveals how these initiatives were closely *aligned* with other strategic choices of the firm.

The business scope, for example, was based on the infamous #1, 2, or 3 rule for market rank, which each business had to pass, develop a strategy to "fix" and so achieve this goal, or else be sold. Similarly, market attractiveness was employed as a screen so that GE swapped its global number-1 position in consumer electronics in 1986 for Thomson's much smaller medical electronics business in order to compete in an inherently more profitable industry. Later expansions demonstrated the limit to trying to add value to "just any business," as in the failed diversification into investment banking with Kidder Peabody (Sherman, 1988).

Similarly, the sequencing, not only implementation, of initiatives was important. For example, it is unlikely that "best practice sharing" would have succeeded without each business unit having generated its own set of "best practices" in the first place. Nor is it likely that either of these would have succeeded without first empowering the organization through the Crotonville initiatives (Workout and other programs).

Additionally, a key advantage that Welch, like any GE CEO, enjoyed is the belief that "unless something goes horribly wrong, he's got the job for 20 years" (Useem, 2004). This confidence of both the public markets and the company's own board, in turn, stems partly from the conglomerate's own *past* record of creating an internal pipeline of managers impressive enough to sustain the belief that any CEO chosen from this pack must have the credentials and ability to manage a large, complex, multibusiness organization.

GE has substantially underperformed on the S & P 500 since Jeff Immelt took over from Jack Welch as CEO in 2001. Partly this reflects the deterioration in attractiveness (and valuation) of the financial services businesses that Jack Welch had built and whose performance had correlated with the booming stock market. Partly, however, it reflects the fact that the institutional and market context has also changed since 2000. GE's resources—industry selection, access to capital, managers trained in basic techniques of

Six Sigma, and financial discipline—are now more common (similar to the decrease in value of traditional private equity resources as their supply increases) and therefore inherently less valuable and of more restricted scope.

In its place, *successful conglomerates* today have upgraded their resources and developed novel types of distinctive capabilities. Danaher, for example, a relatively unknown entity with current revenue close to $20 billion, has shown the best total return to shareholders of any conglomerate over the last thirty years (Table 15.12). It has achieved this by developing a unique set of business processes and tools that are collectively referred to as the Danaher Business System (DBS) (Anand, Collis, and Hood, 2015). What were once a set of lean manufacturing tools derived from the Toyota Production System have become an ingrained management philosophy that drives continuous improvement in every activity from manufacturing to new product development, and which can improve performance of acquired companies by 700 basis points in a short period of time. Developed over twenty-five years and deployed by the same management team for that time, the Danaher Business System demonstrates how business process expertise can add value across a wide range of seemingly unrelated businesses—Danaher operates in businesses from dental drills to environmental test equipment and videojet printing.

Table 15.12. Performance of major conglomerates, 1985–2014.

Company Name	Cumulative Returns	Average Annual Compounded Returns
3M	2,944%	13%
AT&T	2,073%	11%
Berkshire Hathaway	13,066%	18%
Comcast	7,278%	16%
Danaher	35,199%	22%
Dover	3,414%	13%
Fortune Brands	2,755%	12%
General Electric	2,322%	12%
Illinois Tool Works	7,063%	16%
ITT Industries	6,695%	16%
Leucadia	6,689%	16%
Nordson	7,506%	16%
Raytheon	1,897%	11%
Teledyne	188%	4%
Textron	1,536%	10%
Time Warner	1,053%	9%
United Technologies	4,942%	14%
Viacom	5,570%	15%
Walt Disney Company	7,517%	16%
S & P 500	1,919%	11%

Source: Calculated based on data from CRSP Stock/Security Files ©2015 Center for Research in Security Prices (CRSP®), The University of Chicago Booth School of Business.

The Danaher Business System (DBS), as its name suggests, is an organizationally complex set of processes that all subsidiaries are required to adopt, including strategic planning, monthly performance reviews of progress towards improvement targets that have been cascaded to the lowest levels of each business, talent management and development, and a set (now over sixty) of process-improvement tools that cover activities from ideation and financial management to traditional manufacturing improvements. The toolbox is itself continuously refreshed and expanded, while senior management of every new acquisition—Danaher acquires at least seven or eight companies a year—are expected to spend a week applying the basic tools to their own business within the first month of ownership. While DBS is operated by a small office, its main teachers are executives who have used the tools themselves. In addition, current performance is visibly displayed outside every office and department. In this way, the accumulated experience and faith in the system are passed on to new managers and embedded within the entire organization.

As this very brief account suggests, DBS is not made up from one or two simple routines, each of which can be easily replicated. Rather, it is a complex capability, acquired over time and embedded in the relationships and accumulated experiences of the entire organization, which becomes hard to imitate or acquire on the market. Other successful conglomerates, like United Technologies (UTC) and Illinois Tool Works (ITW), have developed similar process improvement systems. UTC has ACE, its operating system, to which George David, UTC's former CEO, attributed half the increase in shareholder value during his tenure (David, 2007). ITW has an 80/20 philosophy applied rigorously to every part of its operations, from product line breadth to customer segments, and even the corporate portfolio (ITW, 2013). Importantly, while adoption of the Pareto principle is simple, embedding it in the organizational DNA through relentless and repeated use, training, and monitoring and rewarding its usage and results are what build the distinctive capability over time. This is why it continues to add value in contexts where ready markets now exist for the pedestrian resources and skills, such as lean Six Sigma training, which once were rare.

None of this denies the possibility of the continuing success of a more traditional group, like Berkshire Hathaway in the US context. It does, however, suggest that Berkshire Hathaway is perhaps now the exception that proves the rule. Relying on the stock-picking capabilities of Warren Buffett (and possibly also of one or two other executives), is likely to be increasingly rare as the market for corporate control becomes ever more efficient in developed countries. Berkshire Hathaway is a notable performance outlier, but it is unlikely to serve as a credible strategy for imitation by others.

15.5 CONCLUSION

In this chapter we make three points. First, unrelated diversification, often thought to be a strategic relic of the past in developed markets, is hardly so. Indeed, the phenomenon of unrelated diversification continues to be important even in markets like the US today, as traditional ways of managing these organizations (the conglomerate form) have given way to different ways of doing so (the private equity form). Second, in understanding the performance of these firms we establish the importance of focusing on the heterogeneity in returns across firms, rather than focusing on the "average" discount or premium. Third, we offer a unified theoretical framework that allows one to examine not only why unrelated diversifiers continue to exist today in developed markets, but how they must continue to evolve as market efficiency improves.

The examples in this chapter reinforce a basic point that is common to the study of both unrelated diversifiers in developed markets and business groups in emerging markets: namely, their ability to add value derives not only from what they do, but what their key "competitors"—including markets and market intermediaries—*don't* do. As described, understanding the role of context is critical to examining the performance and function of business groups across countries and over time.

Indeed, while popular debate takes the efficiency and functioning of markets to be excellent in developed economies, in practice they may not be. The reason is that "markets" are themselves intermediated by firms (e.g., accounting firms, investment banks, media firms, venture capital firms, mutual funds) that, as recent events have shown, embody their own set of structural challenges and incentive problems. Over and above this, firms have certain intrinsic advantages over markets as well: the use of authority, superior information about the individual businesses, the ability to create a common culture and informal norms, repeated exchange and trust. As a result, whether or not diversified business groups can add value in these economies is a question whose answer depends critically on their individual corporate strategies, rather than solely on the attributes of the external (market) context.

This also points to the key threats to the viability of business groups in any given setting. Specifically, since a central way that business groups add value is through their internal organizational processes as well as by substituting for "voids" in the external context, it follows that the most salient threats for these entities come not only from rivals and competitors, but from the continued improvement in the functioning of markets and from their own internal organizational challenges.

CHAPTER 16

AUSTRALIA

from family networks to boom-and-bust groups

SIMON VILLE

16.1 INTRODUCTION

WE know relatively little about business groups in Australia and their role in the nation's modern economic development.[1] This stems in part from the belated emergence of business history as a scholarly research field in Australia.[2] It may also be the consequence of their apparent sparseness in the corporate sector and limited contribution to economic development.

In this chapter we seek to summarize the existing work on business groups in Australia, offer some thoughts about why their importance was limited on the whole to specific time periods and types of organization, and look more deeply into their brief importance in the last quarter of the twentieth century. Some pointers to future research are also proffered. In the next section (16.2), we address the economic, business, and political environment in Australia that helped to shape the nature and role of business groups. The evolution of large-scale enterprise in Australia is broadly summarized in Section 16.3. The developmental backgrounds of business groups in Australia since the mid-nineteenth century are described in Section 16.4, including any evidence of diversified business groups, network groups, and cooperation through cross-shareholding and interlocking directorates. A major growth period of business groups in the 1970s and 1980s and their subsequent decline are addressed in Section 16.5. Sections 16.4 and 16.5 also provide greater depth through several case studies that examine diversification strategies and governance structures. Concluding

---

[1] This chapter encompasses diversified business groups (often organized in pyramidal structures) and network-type business groups that have been observed in the Australian economy.
[2] Business history has flourished as a scholarly field in Australia over the last few decades.

comments and an overall assessment of their contemporary role completes the account in Section 16.6.

16.2 The Economic, Political, and Business Environment in Australia

Business groups, like all forms of enterprise, are shaped by their local environment, through broader global trends, and by beliefs in best practice. In this section we briefly sketch relevant local influences on corporate form. Indeed, the implications of divergence theory might suggest that national setting was an important influence on such structures. Moreover, the relationship between setting and form is interactive in that we would also expect corporation practices to shape the local environment. Firms respond to impulses in the environment and in turn seek to mold that environment to suit their needs (Boyce and Ville, 2002: 20–1).

The Australian market has been small and geographically isolated.[3] Externally, geographic distance separated Australia from the key overseas markets in Western Europe and North America in the nineteenth and first half of the twentieth centuries before the more recent economic rise of East Asia. Internally, wide distances also separated a series of highly concentrated urban markets in the colony/state capitals— in spite of its enormous size Australia has long been highly urbanized. These vast lands reflected a comparative advantage in resource-based industries that has provided a distinct development pathway to economic modernization in which manufacturing has played a muted role. Exports of wool, wheat, gold, coal, iron ore, and many other resources have driven economic development for much of the nation's history (Pinkstone and Meredith, 1992). International economic transmissions—principally trade, investment, and labor—have aligned national development to a high degree of synchronicity in cyclical behavior with the global economy (McLean, 2013). Since these were British colonies, imperial influence has been critical in shaping the economic and political environment. Stable government, the rule of law, and a market economy were all imported from the most advanced industrial nation of the early nineteenth century. After the Federation of Australia (1901), a greater plurality of external influences emerged, emanating especially from the USA and, later, Japan.

Finally, government has played an important role in economic development, invoking the epithet "colonial socialism" by Butlin (1959) to describe government investment and ownership of infrastructure in the second half of the nineteenth century. It continued to play an important role after Federation, imposing tariffs to protect infant industries, although for too long. An implicit sense of egalitarianism motivated centralized wage fixing based on fairness more than economic imperatives. Less desirably,

---

[3] The question of isolation was encapsulated in Blainey (1966).

immigration policy actively excluded non-white workers until later in the twentieth century. Microeconomic reform, including financial deregulation and an active competition policy, has been a defining feature of continued government intervention in recent decades (Borland, 2015). In spite of Federation, which created a national government known as the Commonwealth of Australia, individual state governments have continued to play an important role in the economic life of the nation. This has complicated the official influence on business development, particularly through imposing multiple layers of regulation, central and state, and competing jurisdictions among state governments (Kenwood, 1995). For example, each colonial (then state) government built its own railway network designed to foster intrastate traffic and divert trade away from other states (Linge, 1979).

Some general observations can be made about the evolution of the business environment in Australia. Extreme economic uncertainty in the early years of the convict colony (c. 1788–1850) fostered enterprises that had limited capital needs and were spread across multiple functions and products, particularly in shipping, importing, and wholesaling. These strategies were designed to mitigate risk and overcome small markets and a lack of ancillary services (shipping, finance). Economic expansion from the middle decades of the nineteenth century fostered specialization within industries, such as finance, and the emergence of new industries previously constrained by insufficient scale, particularly in the embryonic manufacturing sector. The introduction of incorporation laws after 1860 nourished new and expanded forms of enterprise, especially in mining, as a result of "no-liability" provisions introduced into Victoria in 1871.[4] Economic uncertainty in the 1890s encouraged greater resort to interfirm cooperation (Ville, 1998). Firms had cooperated with each other in the early convict period to share assets and information and continued to do so in response to the economic uncertainty of the 1890s—a financial crisis, labor unrest, and drought conditions. Cooperation continued to be an important part of the landscape of Australian capitalism in the twentieth century, as we shall see in Section 16.4.

16.3 The Development of Large Enterprises in Australia

The growth of large-scale enterprise in twentieth-century Australia has been analyzed in detail elsewhere.[5] A series of factors together shaped the growth of the size and geographical reach of leading firms after Federation. These included nation-building strategies that helped to drive corporate scale by providing access to larger, more

---

[4] In no-liability companies investors were not liable for any unpaid portion of their shares in the case of a firm's bankruptcy, which was a boon for high-risk prospecting activities.

[5] See Fleming, Merrett, and Ville (2004); Merrett (2015).

unified interstate domestic markets and through external trade protection. Some principal factors driving development were: improvements in transport and communications; developments in scale-based production technologies; the expansion of domestic capital markets; the growth of per capita incomes and with it a consumer society; and the tariff protection of some infant industries.

A number of distinctive features of big business in Australia should be noted. The largest firms were more commonly found in, or supporting, resource industries than in many modern industrialized nations due to Australia's powerful comparative advantage in this sector. Dalgety (pastoral agency), Colonial Sugar Refiners (CSR), Broken Hill Proprietary (BHP) (mining), and Burns Philp (South Seas trader and plantation owner) were persistently among the very largest firms for much of the twentieth century. Manufacturing industries were more often dominated by local subsidiaries of foreign multinationals that drew upon their parent's scale and technological reach to compete effectively in Australia. On average, multinationals constituted about a quarter of the top 100 non-financial firms. The opportunity to jump tariff barriers, tap into an expanding market with good levels of per capita income, and utilize a trained, educated workforce were now more appealing than the search for natural resources that had driven the freestanding multinational companies of the nineteenth century. As a result, multinationals clustered in manufacturing, especially from the 1920s, arriving from the United States as the principal industrial nation. By the post-Second World War era increasing numbers of Japanese firms also arrived on the landscape. Multinationals often occupied a central position in industries associated with progressive scientific, administrative, managerial, and technical capabilities that were transferred to Australia. By the 1960s several expanding Australian industries were dominated by global firms such as Shell, BP, Mobil, Esso (oil refining), Ford, General-Motors Holden, Toyota (vehicle production), Nestlé, and Unilever (food processing). Outward flows of Australian enterprise have mostly been of more recent origin—since the 1980s (Merrett, 2002).

It is striking that Australia's largest firms were minnows compared with their counterparts in countries such as the USA or Britain, yet they were comparatively more dominant in their home economy, casting a longer shadow over the local sector than was the case in other nations (Fleming, Merrett, and Ville, 2004: 29). The smallness of the local market and the presence of foreign multinationals are a big part of the reason for this dominance, which has led to the coining of the term the "Big End of Town." The epithet, with its somewhat pejorative and exclusive implications, appears to be quintessentially Australian and has been taken to imply that the largest firms tended to keep themselves apart from the mainstream of corporate Australia and perhaps even that they colluded together. The high degree of concentration, and the fact that some were controlled from abroad or survived in the elite list for a long period of time, lend credence to concerns about their exclusivity.

While local competitors, suppliers, and customers benefited from spillover effects from multinationals, their presence also raised the ire of some contemporaries. It was argued that they suffocated the ability of some local firms, lacking scale and experience, to establish themselves. This may explain, in part, the paucity of Australian firms internationalizing before about the 1980s. However, there were other factors, including the smallness of the local market as a launching pad for international expansion. Australia's comparative advantage, as we have seen, lay predominantly in resource industries for which exporting was often the preferred mode of internationalization. The contentious issue of transfer pricing, wherein "adjusted" internal costs facilitated tax minimization, and the influence of international business on government macro-economic policy, were also hotly debated.

This anti-competitive assessment, however, is challenged by the notion that large firms drew their dominance in the long term from efficiency-driven corporate strategies. Many leading firms were characterized by their longevity at the top of the list of the largest firms. To continue to prosper, these "corporate leaders" needed to be adaptive and agile, responding to changes in their environment. Banks and pastoral agents replicated their branch networks to align with the spread of rural industries focused on exporting. With small local markets supporting only a few efficient scale firms in many manufacturing industries, pursuit of prime-mover advantages was critical. Thus, in the early decades of the twentieth century successful manufacturers aggressively pursued market share by exploiting new mass production technologies that leveraged economies of scale. In some cases, vertical integration followed to pursue up- or downstream growth opportunities or, defensively, to protect against contractual holdups common in small markets. Diversification, related and later unrelated, mostly occurred after the Second World War. This was especially the case for resource-based firms conscious of the need to pursue growth opportunities away from crowded resource markets and in expanding manufacturing sectors such as building materials (CSR) and fabricated steel products (BHP).

Many firms were comparatively slow to adopt the modern governance and organizational structures associated with the divorce of ownership from control and the development of systematic managerial hierarchies. In many cases the governance of Australian firms has historically consisted of light and loose organizational hierarchies. The founding families continued to exert ownership and management influence into the post-Second World War era. There was little evidence of hierarchies of salaried managers outside banks, pastoral companies, or mines. In some cases, such as CSR, organizational structures took on a hybrid form as firms sought to retain their areas of specialization supported by functional departments.[6] In the early 1950s a study of the largest 102 companies in Australia, including financial institutions and subsidiaries of foreign firms, indicated that founding families were able to control the majority of those companies through their positions on boards and through stockholdings. Only a third of domestic companies could be identified as management-controlled (Wheelwright, 1957: 4, 119). The reasons for this are not entirely clear. There were no educational programs to train managers, and the universities and schools of mines

---

[6] For a more detailed discussion of these changes, see Fleming, Merrett, and Ville (2004).

generated only limited numbers of professional engineers, industrial chemists, metallurgists, and the like (Schedvin, 1987; Edelstein, 1988). The smaller size and less diverse sets of activities of many Australian firms may also provide some of the answers, as may the tendency to draw upon British practices and mores in business as in other walks of life. The willingness to embrace interfirm cooperation also meant that some elements of governance were external to the firm. In this general sense, at least, the architecture of the business group was not antagonistic to Australian governance practices.

A final piece of the jigsaw of the corporate landscape has been the important role of state enterprise. Flowing from the colonial socialism era, mentioned earlier, came public enterprise in network industries. Government network monopolies continued to outsize the largest private enterprises for most of the twentieth century: the Postmaster General's office and the state-based rail systems were significantly larger than any private enterprise well into the twentieth century (Fleming, Merrett, and Ville, 2004: 15). Indeed, it was not until the 1980s that BHP had become larger than any government corporation. As in many nations, privatization returned, or shifted, many of the enterprises to the private sector in the last two decades of the twentieth century. The impact of government enterprise was twofold: it closed off opportunities for private business, and it imposed monopoly costs, especially of network industries, on the corporate sector.

16.4 The Long-term Evolution of Business Groups in Australia

16.4.1 Conceptualizing Business Groups

Opinions differ in defining the nature of business groups. For the purpose of this chapter, we are guided by Colpan and Hikino (Chapter 1, this volume). Business groups are situated along a spectrum of transacting frameworks that runs from the autonomy of pure market transactions to the authority of internal hierarchies within a single firm (Boyce and Ville, 2002: 263). They tend towards the hierarchical end of the continuum but can take several forms. Network-type groups consist of firms, in the same, related, or unrelated industries, which cooperate for their mutual benefit such as through the sharing of knowledge, technology, or operations. There is generally no specific controlling entity and thus they are akin in some respects to a network of firms evidenced by Japanese keiretsu, industrial districts (Silicon Valley, Third Italy), or strategic alliances such as the air travel services groups.

The hierarchy type of business group consists of a collection of legally distinct companies controlled by a dominant entity and is closer to the firm end of the transacting spectrum. The dominant authority has traditionally been an entrepreneur or family but may also be a company, bank, investment vehicle, state bureaucracy, or a group of shareholders. A variety of ownership relationships may exist, particularly where the operating units take the form of subsidiaries, affiliates, or listed companies. The pyramidal structure occurs when a shareholding by the control unit facilitates hierarchical control through several vertical tiers of publicly listed companies, each with ownership interests in the next layer. These types of business groups are thus distinguished from conglomerates that operate through fully owned subsidiaries. Some writers have criticized this organizational form for providing excessive power to controlling interests that can "tunnel" economic benefits to themselves out of all proportion to their financial interest in the group (Morck, Wolfenzon, and Yeung, 2005).

In addition to the nature of the authority structure, hierarchical business groups are often diversified in strategy by operating in technologically unrelated industries. This contrasts to the single multidivisional firm described by Chandler that expands into related products to leverage scope economies, and to the type of conglomerate that extends over a diverse range of industries but often in several groups of related products and services. The absence of scope economies suggests unrelated business groups will be less inclined toward careful strategic coordination of operations across the group. On the other hand, it provides opportunities for spreading risk and for financial and budget management that compares the performance of different firms in the group. It also suggests that the group could respond quickly to new opportunities by acquiring shares in emerging companies. As well as domestic market opportunities, the diversified business structure can be well placed to arbitrage between national markets utilizing "fungible capabilities" (Colpan and Hikino, 2010). It is open to debate whether this represents short-term opportunism to exploit imperfect markets or a genuine espousal of growth opportunities that help to propel economies forward and eradicate allocative distortions. Where there is no attempt at operational or budgetary coordination across the group, it is more akin to a "pure holding company" in the Chandlerian sense of the term.

Michael Porter's work provides some insights and clarification here. He distinguishes between three types of corporate strategy relevant to business groups with ascending degrees of active management—portfolio management, restructuring, and the leveraging of resources. Passive portfolio management is where each unit in the group remains entirely separate and management is limited to monitoring and allocating financial resources among them. Restructuring resources occurs where capabilities are reorganized, maybe rationalized through sell-offs, for greater efficiency. This is often a one-off gain after the purchase of a company, or through an occasional strategic reassessment. Finally, leveraging resources among businesses, such as the sharing and transferring of knowledge and skills, provides a more ongoing and integrative strategy for a group to maximize synergies, although arguably less relevant to the highly diversified business group (Porter, 1987).

A broad contrast has been drawn between the life cycle of business groups in early and late developing economies (Colpan and Hikino, 2010: 51). Business groups appeared early in the development of the later industrializers and have remained important to the present. Conversely, with a few exceptions such as Sweden and Belgium, earlier industrializers experienced two waves of corporate development, the first in which diversified business groups were prominent and a later one in which the Chandlerian modern enterprise, featuring internalized related diversification, more commonly drove economic growth. This motivates an important research question— whether business groups were transitionary institutions that helped mitigate imperfections in early markets and served as the government-anointed vehicles of industrial diversification but were eventually supplanted by permanent, more efficient forms of enterprise. On the other hand, the maturing of markets in developed economies, particularly the mitigation of investment rigidities through financial deregulation, may provide greater opportunities for groups able to move seamlessly between product markets.

16.4.2 Diversified Business Groups

We lack an established literature on the history of business groups in Australia, and therefore this section is assembled from a miscellany of sources. Diversified business groups (of the hierarchy type hereafter), while frequently visible, do not appear to have had a major presence in the Australian economy except during the later decades of the twentieth century. The enterprise landscape emerging from the second half of the nineteenth century, sketched above, consisted primarily of one or several dominant firms within their core industry. Horizontal expansion, through acquisition or internal growth, was the battleground for industry dominance among prime movers and challengers. Vertical integration within industry was pursued in some cases; more loosely, BHP worked cooperatively with several downstream metal-fabricating firms through cross-shareholding linkages. New opportunities to diversify into several key growth industries were often seized by the proliferation of multinationals which benefited from greater size and experience to leverage their existing scale economies and research capabilities in a small market—Dunlop (rubber), ICIANZ (chemicals), British Tobacco, Nestlé, Lever, Shell. Several leading Australian firms also pursued related and unrelated diversification in the decades after the Second World War, including CSR, Australian Gas Light, and Burns Philp. In the case of CSR, diversification into building materials was sometimes by internal growth, or by partial or full acquisition of private and listed companies (Campbell, 1963: 124–5).

Governments, while operating network industries and actively facilitating infrastructure, do not appear to have provided the type of support of individual firms and groups commonly associated with Japan or South Korea in the earlier stages of their industrialization. There was no system of "crony capitalism" in the sense of developmental inducements into new industries offered to individual firms on the basis of close ties with officials and state departments. The capital market, while somewhat small and late to develop, may have been sufficiently mature to provide the necessary funds to support the development of new industries rather than rely upon in-house treasuries or constellations of individual families and corporate networks. Merrett and Ville (2009) have shown that, by the interwar period, there was a widening range of shares of recently incorporated companies being traded on the state stock exchanges, a diversification from the focus on mining before the First World War to exploit new opportunities in manufacturing and services. The number of firms listed on the key Sydney and Melbourne stock exchanges doubled from 472 to 950, and their paid-up capital trebled from £166 m to £485 m between 1919 and 1939 (Merrett and Ville, 2009: 569). An active market in new issues was often utilized to launch new products and processes. While the market enabled the largest of these firms to acquire many smaller unlisted firms struggling during the slump years, there was an insufficient range and depth of listed firms to facilitate business pyramids based on controlled subsidiaries. The limits to the interwar capital market were evidenced by the fact that most companies were only listed on a single state stock exchange, and the banks, tarnished by the 1890s financial collapses, were minor players in industrial finance before the Second World War. Finally, British influence had a bearing by providing a blueprint for corporate form and by facilitating rapid maturity of commercial standards and practices that mitigated the use of internalized control mechanisms such as group behavior to avoid excessive transaction costs.

For similar reasons, British domestic firms also remained fairly specialized, yet British business groups trading overseas in the nineteenth century were highly diversified, a fact Jones (Chapter 5, this volume) attributes primarily to their ability to leverage the benefits of mature British capital sources in a world of networked imperial trade. Inevitably, this affected Australia. Bright and Company, a partnership branch of a British firm, began operating out of Melbourne from 1853 (and as Gibbs, Bright and, Company from 1881). It was part of a diversified British business group (Jones, 2000: 103). It grew into a diversified resources enterprise in Australia that included mining, stevedoring, pastoral investment, shipping, importing and exporting, sheep and cattle ranching, timber, a mining company, and a wire netting manufacturer. It evolved many of these activities increasingly at arm's length from its British ownership, acquiring a series of companies in the process and becoming a national firm with additional offices in Sydney, Perth, Adelaide, and Brisbane. Indeed, when the main group was severely affected by the collapse of nitrate prices after the First World War, the Australian partnership continued to thrive.

In spite of an environment generally unconducive to domestic diversified business groups in Australia, there were some notable exceptions. Thomas Mort swam against the tide of corporate specialization in the 1850s to 1870s with a mix of private and corporate interests that were diversified across auctioneering, wool, docks, engineering, food, refrigeration, railways, shipping, and mining. Barnard, his biographer, praises him for his "ability to think in grand terms, his mighty visions, his prophetic inspirations, and his determination to persevere in his efforts . . . despite the immediate sacrifices" (Barnard, 1961: 216). Mort recognized the need to impose a rational structure on his expanding and diverse business interests, dividing the enterprise into two separate entities according to the main areas of activity. In practice this division was incomplete: the affairs of the two continued to overlap, especially in their accounting systems, creating inefficiencies and concern among some staff members. A pioneer in wool broking in Sydney, this developed to become the core business that generated the main profit stream and cash flow to finance industrial experiments such as in refrigeration and the early cultivation of wine, cotton, sugar, and maize. While his interests were wide, there was a degree of technological relatedness among some of his enterprises, particularly the nexus of resource production, marketing, and transport infrastructure.

16.4.3 Network-Type Business Groups

Network-type business groups were more common than hierarchical groups in Australian development in the nineteenth and early twentieth centuries. Although the large-scale enterprise remained the dominant corporate form, networks sometimes included several major players in their ranks, particularly in the mining sector. For the same reasons discussed in the previous section, network groups tended to be product-focused rather than diversified. Many product-focused network groups were formed in response to threats of excess capacity in specific industries in the difficult economic times of the late nineteenth century. By the eve of the First World War, "combines," "trusts," "groups," and "vends" suspected of collusion, or, more positively, as cooperative responses to oversupply, could be found in a number of products and services including the brick, confectionery, sugar, tobacco, dried fruit, fresh produce, mineral oil, coal, and shipping industries (Wilkinson, 1914). Intra-industry groupings were also sometimes the product of a desire to secure upstream supplies or downstream markets.

Typically, those groups did not have a controlling unit at the apex of the group. Several examples of holding companies had existed, only to be restructured into multidivisionals. British Tobacco (Australia), James Hardie Industries, and Australian Consolidated Industries all found that the holding form constrained technology transfer within the group and restructured in response to the emergence of more efficient multinational competitors after the Second World War (Fleming, Merrett, and Ville, 2004: 177, 183). More often, network groups, perhaps best defined as "loose networks" (Jones and Colpan, 2010: 84–5), relied on cooperation, founded on social capital and mutual self-interest, and bolstered in some cases by the leadership vision of a key entrepreneur. Some examples follow.

The Collins House Group is an important example of an early twentieth-century alliance operating largely within a narrow confine of industries. It was centered on three of Australia's leading mining companies—North Broken Hill, Broken Hill South, and the Zinc Corporation—all of whom had their headquarters in the Collins House building at 360 Collins Street in the Melbourne CBD. Initially formed in 1915 to fill a vacuum created when the pre-1914 German domination of base-metal mining and metallurgy was interrupted, it became the most sustained cooperation among a group of leading Australian firms. Among its activities was joint smelting and refining at the Port Pirie works, under the name of Broken Hill Associated Smelters. The Collins House Group continued up to 1951, nourished in part by interlocking directorates, personal friendships, and family, not least those centered on the prominent business family, Baillieu. Although it was mostly an alliance type of group, other firms were periodically involved as partly or wholly owned subsidiaries. While predominantly focused on mining and metallurgy, the group occasionally extended its product reach, famously joining forces in 1936 with BHP, General-Motors Holden, ICIANZ, and P&O to found the Commonwealth Aircraft Corporation. In the same year, it pioneered the manufacture of fine printing and writing paper from eucalyptus through the formation of Associated Pulp and Paper Mills.

A closer look at the Baillieu family is justified by their influence on the formative years of a number of Australia's major corporations. Their business empire was based on William ("Willie") Lawrence Baillieu (1859–1936). His early career was shrouded in doubtful business ethics when he made a personal fortune from the Melbourne property boom of the 1880s. When the inevitable bust occurred, he exploited a little-known provision of the insolvency laws, the notorious "secret compositions," which enabled creditors to be met privately (Cannon, 1966: 117–45; Yule, 2012: 34–46). The result was that he paid only 6 pence in the pound (2.5 percent) to his creditors. This experience must have had a profound impact on his ethics, since his subsequent business rebuilding involved far more careful and considered decision-making. Over the next thirty to forty years Baillieu built a relatively wide-ranging business empire, as part owner and director, focused on mining and property firms but also banking, newspapers, insurance, building materials, and brewing. Key companies he helped to shape included Zinc Corporation, Amalgamated Zinc, the Herald and Weekly Times, and Carlton and United Breweries (CUB).

Baillieu's entrepreneurial flair was evident on many occasions. He had an eye for innovative companies, working with Auguste De Bavay and Herbert Gepp to develop and commercialize the flotation process for separating metallic ores from sulfide impurities, which created value for deeply buried ores at the north and south ends of Broken Hill (Yule, 2012: Chs. 12–13). Of particular importance was his role in the Collins House Group in addressing the loss of wartime smelting facilities through the creation of Broken Hill Associated Smelters. He was the central figure in the development of the Collins House building, which provided a home to around fifty companies and with it the opportunity for networking and the sharing of information that became the watchword of the Melbourne business environment (Yule, 2012: Ch. 14). His descendants—especially his son Clive, who experienced a stellar business career—continued to contribute to the development of Australian "majors," including Dunlop, Rio Tinto, CRA, Comalco, Western Mining, and Alcoa. There were criticisms as well, that their approach was part of a culture where cooperation among large firms became collusive and anticompetitive. Companies like Dunlop and CUB were exposed as lazy, inefficient monopolists when competition policy was tightened in the 1970s.

While Baillieu's business interests took the form of related and unrelated diversification, it is more difficult to judge whether he managed them in a coordinated manner as a controlling entity at the helm. He described himself as an "investor," although clearly, as evidenced above, he was far more than a passive portfolio manager. Although his main expertise focused on mining and metallurgy, he also gave his time and talents to a range of interests in other industries. His was akin to an internalized market in entrepreneurial skills as well as capital. Clive's career, reflecting perhaps the growth of the age of managerial firms and globalization, was focused much more on senior executive positions such as deputy chairman of Rio Tinto and chairman of the Federation of British Industry (Poynter, 1979).

A rather different form of twentieth-century business group, or at least "empire," was that belonging to William Lionel Buckland. While the Collins House Group drew its strength from webs of firms and networks of their entrepreneurs, Buckland was in many respects a lone wolf. Although he recognized the importance of social networking to build business connections, Buckland ran his empire through a meticulous hands-on approach, the "antithesis of a Chief Executive who stood above the detail" (Merrett, 2004: 76). He summarized his philosophy as, "There can only be one captain . . . and he must be on the bridge" (Merrett, 2004: 76). He used every form of communication to keep in regular contact with his firms and, as Merrett notes, became a leading customer of the Postmaster General. The careful attention to detail required extreme hard work, maybe as much as 90 to 100 hours per week, which ultimately had a severe impact on his health. There is no doubting, though, his considerable entrepreneurial talent in recognizing business opportunities and following through on them. He worked mostly through his control of a series of private companies. However, his claims for unrelated diversification are intertemporal, as he divested one set of interrelated business activities for another several times through his business career. His key set of businesses lay in the automobile trade, including service stations, insurance, and finance, particularly during the interwar period. After the Second World War, his focus shifted to ownership of a series of major pastoral and cattle stations. In each case his businesses were managed as a single strategy; thus, for example, his chain of pastoral stations were strategically located on stock routes and near railheads in support of each other. His contribution might be seen as something akin to a late stage venture capitalist by building up the strength of his businesses before selling out to larger public firms, such as Ampol and L. J. Hooker, which were better placed to exploit the major postwar economic expansion. The diversified public and private enterprises (timber, chemicals, glass, pharmaceuticals, oxygen, scientific instruments) of the Grimwade and Felton families from the mid-nineteenth to early twentieth centuries similarly provided the foundations of several important Australian corporations, notably Drug Houses of Australia, Commonwealth Industrial Gases, and Australian Consolidated Industries (Poynter, 1967).

The revival of competition policy in the 1960s and 1970s, described in the following section, contributed to the postwar demise of a number of the network groups believed to be involved in anti-competitive behavior, fostering instead more diversified business groups that were less dominant in specific industries. In addition, the growing scale of enterprises after the Second World War made the entrepreneurial groups of the Buckland type much more difficult to manage effectively as a single strategic concern.

16.4.4 Cooperation through Cross-Shareholding and Interlocking Directorates

Thus, with several notable exceptions, Australia's history has been predominantly one of focused and internalized enterprise converging towards Chandlerian forms consistent with a mature economic environment, overlain in some cases by intra-industry cooperation between firms. However, there is an alternative literature, often the product of writers on the left of politics, which implies broader and more insidious forms of control exercised by elite groups of entrepreneurs and their families. Books, often running to multiple editions, with titles like *Who Owns Australia?*, *The 60 Rich Families who Own Australia*, and *The Controllers,* are, on one level, polemical attacks on the wealthy (Rawling, 1939; Fitzpatrick, 1944; Campbell, 1963; Rolfe, 1967). For our purposes, though, they also reveal much about interlocking directorates, share ownership, and business influence by individuals across groups of firms. One particularly intriguing piece of research by James Rawling produced a complex network diagram for 1939 entitled "The seventy-nine men who controlled Australia" (Figure 16.1). More specifically, Rawling describes the "Kingdom of 360 Collins Street." Seven leading mining companies, including the Collins House group, were occupants of this building. Thirty men occupied the sixty-three directorate seats on their boards, fourteen sitting on more than one of these companies (Rawling, 1939: 26–32). Many of these directors held shares in, or sat on the board of, companies from other sectors including brewing, finance, pastoral agency, textiles, paper, vehicle production, chemicals, glass, rubber, packaging, engineering, and transport.

Ernest Campbell took a somewhat different approach in 1963, focusing on families rather than individuals (Campbell, 1963). He identified key groups of families in Melbourne, Sydney, and Adelaide, and showed how they were intertwined through business (shareholdings and directorships), intermarriage, social ties (religion, clubs), attending the same schools, and living within the same residential areas. Thus, for example, the "Main Sydney Group" consisted of ten families who between them held directorships in forty companies with a total paid up capital of A$155 m that spanned a wide range of industries including sugar, banking, insurance, beer, gas, textiles, chemicals, finance, industrial, pastoral, rubber, and coal (Campbell, 1963: 45–6).

Other studies have adopted a more arm's-length moral standpoint (Wheelwright, 1957; Lawriwsky, 1978; Alexander, Murray, and Houghton, 1994). They were

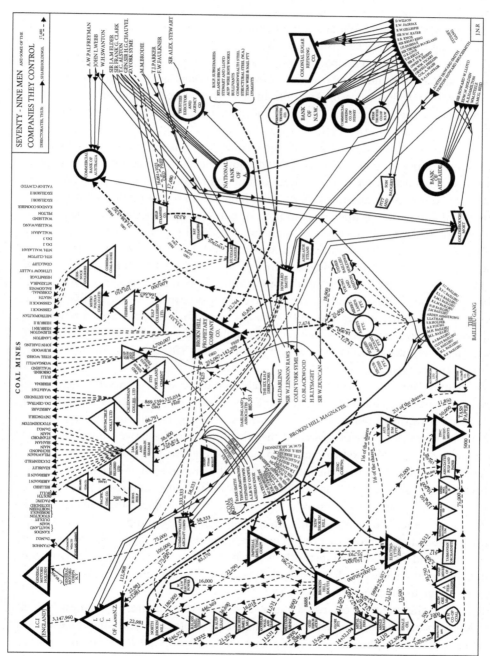

FIGURE 16.1. The seventy-nine men who controlled Australia in 1939.

Source: Rawling (1939): 36–7. Reprinted with permission from the copyright holder Louise Stammers.

interested in broad comparative questions about the separation of ownership from control and the rise of the managerial firm, themes so beloved of business historians. What seems clear is that the influence of elite individual owner/directors and their families concedes ground to management control but slowly and belatedly in Australia. By the mid-1970s financial institutions had become the largest cohesive ownership group, but individuals remained strong (Lawriwsky, 1978: 11). Two decades later, though, argues Alexander, interlocking directorates remained a more concentrated form of corporate influence in Australia than in the United Kingdom or USA, and through them there remained "a fairly cohesive and self-conscious business elite" (Alexander, Murray, and Houghton, 1994: 60).

Consistent with the dominance of big business in Australia, noted above, these related literatures are convincing in showing how concentrated control of large-scale enterprise remained in the mid-twentieth century and how diverse were the economic interests of key families and individuals. The challenge, in revisiting this literature, is to interpret the meaning of this concentration of corporate power. Most of the original authors focused on the question of monopoly. Aided by protective tariffs in many industries, close relations with political leaders, and a lack of competition policy, the country—it is argued—was being run in the collective interests of a small elite of wealthy entrepreneurs and their families and connections at the expense of small firms, consumers, and workers. Motives are imputed from structures. More positively, close cooperation within the business elite through cross-shareholding and interlocking directorates served as devices for the exchange of information and opinion in a manner most effectively achieved in a relatively small society (Rolfe, 1967: 96; Alexander, Murray, and Houghton, 1994: 60).

Our aim is somewhat more specific: to establish if these sets of ownership "tentacles" amount to diversified business empires per se by wealth creators or are little more than the passive investment portfolios of rich rentiers, behaving nonetheless in the interests of their business class when required. If they do amount to the active control of a wide range of firms, we still need to establish whether there was much sense of running a diversified business empire in the forms identified by Porter. Insofar as a pattern can be divined among these controlling families and individuals, it would seem that much of the strategic behavior was intra-industry, with firms recognizing the benefits of the environment described above—tariffs, no competition policy, and political "clientism." Most interlocking and cross-ownership occurred among competitors, with suppliers or consumers, and with financial institutions (Rolfe, 1967: 92–4). Wider investments into unrelated industries were driven largely by portfolio investment considerations—growth opportunities and risk spreading.

Related to the literature discussed above, that the leading figures in business locked up the corporate sector industry by industry, is another strand that focuses on competency levels rather than collusive behavior. Authors such as Hugh Stretton have derided the entrepreneurial skills of Australian managers, suggesting many were inadequately and narrowly educated, cautious in their plans, and prone to blame the workforce whenever performance was poor (Stretton, 1985). In these circumstances, the failure of many to diversify in pursuit of growth opportunities might be viewed as a failure of Australian entrepreneurship. Doubtless this applied to some business leaders, including those for whom corporate inheritance provided easy pickings, but it is less credible as a general thesis. Fleming, Merrett, and Ville provided important examples of leadership and achievement by Australian big business (Fleming, Merrett, and Ville, 2004).

Where genuine family business groups operated, they appear to have been relatively few and came quite late, mostly from about the 1960s. One possible reason may have been the important role of migrant entrepreneurs in Australia. Many of Australia's most successful entrepreneurs have been first-generation or very young migrants arriving just before or after the Second World War. Examples include Frank Lowy (Westfield—shopping centers), Richard Pratt (Visy—packaging), Tan Le (SASme Wireless Communication), Harry Triguboff (Meriton—property development) and John Hemmes (Merivale—leisure and entertainment). By comparison with Britain and continental Europe, Australia lacked established families of great lineage who had acquired wealth, privilege, and power over centuries and with it the ability to extend their social and economic interests widely.[7] Some family business groups were quite short-lived, failing to make an effective intergenerational transfer. In the 1960s and 1970s Reg Ansett's empire was very diverse, spanning an airline, rental cars, resorts, and a television station. His estranged son Bob fought his father by setting up a rival rental-car business. The group effectively died with Reg (Brimson, 1987). Several other family groups opted to reinvest their fortunes in a lavish lifestyle.[8] Somewhat exceptionally, the newspaper barons—Fairfax, Packer, Murdoch—made the intergenerational transition but have largely focused on core industries in the media and entertainment, although tunneling out appears to have occurred through minority family ownership of pyramids.

16.5 Boom and Bust in Diversified Business Groups in Australia

The history of business groups in Australia shifted significantly from the long-term trajectory during the 1970s to early 1990s. Many leading firms had begun to change strategy to favor diversification in the 1950s and 1960s. Global business trends, underpinned by American thinking on business strategies and structures, began to permeate Australia through the local presence of multinationals. This began primarily as related diversification in pursuit of scope economies mainly by individual

---

[7] Dutch group Van Hoboken, for example, stretched back to the mid-eighteenth century (De Goey, this volume).

[8] For example, Nicholas's of Aspro fame or Ramsays with Kiwi shoe polish (Smith and Barrie, 1976).

corporations. Latterly, especially in the 1970s and 1980s, it took the form of unrelated diversification into new products and industries, mostly through the development of business groups of legally separate companies but with cross- and hierarchical partial shareholdings. The earlier generations of business groups, where they existed, were headed by the family and its entrepreneurial leader, but this generation was organized around a head company at the apex, normally under the control of a key entrepreneur. While there were no diversified business groups among the top 100 Australian firms in 1910, by 1986 most of the groups cited in Table 16.1 made the list (Ville and Merrett, 2016). Unlike the scope economies leveraged from related diversification, unrelated growth was prompted in some cases by defensive moves against declining traditional markets and areas. In other instances, growth opportunities in new and expanding industries provided a spur to action as groups served as internal capital markets. Finally, from the 1980s, in a further shift of strategy, Australian firms increasingly internationalized, acquiring foreign businesses in a range of industries.

The revival of competition policy from the 1960s and 1970s in Australia was designed to counter an atmosphere of "all the restrictive practices known to man" and began by attacking collusive behavior perceived to be exercising monopoly power in individual industries (Butlin, Barnard, and Pincus, 1982: 125). The policy mainly served to expose the continued extensive, mostly intra-industry, price agreements among firms if not full-fledged cooperation. The effects of enhanced competition policy have yet to be closely analyzed, but conceivably it may have driven horizontal alliances into mergers or, in some cases, into diversification in new markets to evade competition policy that was increasingly based around market share within an industry.

It would be pertinent to ask why unrelated diversification took the form of business groups of legally independent affiliated companies, rather than through internalized expansion or fully owned conglomerates, and why it occurred somewhat later than elsewhere. While we do not have definitive answers to these questions, it seems that the deregulation of Australian capital and financial markets in the early 1980s was an important watershed that opened up new and larger sources of corporate borrowing, from both domestic and newly admitted foreign lenders, and a more robust domestic market in corporate takeovers (Fleming, Merrett, and Ville, 2004: 116–23; Borland, 2015: 423–6). Foreign banks, well versed in merchant banking and capital-raising services, focused on this market rather than building a retail clientele in competition with locals. Australian banks relaxed their prudential standards in an effort to follow suit. The removal of these potential barriers to acquisition may have made it easier for arbitraging entrepreneurs to acquire assets at good value, although there are numerous examples of "overpayment" for a quick and successful acquisition leading to a massive piling of debts in some of these groups. For those in a hurry, controlling positions in such acquisitions were preferable to slower internal growth or financing full ownership.

Prominent examples of diversified business groups in this period include Adelaide Steamship Company (Adsteam), Elders IXL, and Bond Corporation. Many sought ambitious and overreaching expansion, appropriately captured in the title of Trevor

Table 16.1. Business groups in Australia, 1970s, 1980s.

Business Group	Entrepreneur	Range of Industries	1986 rank, Australian companies	Total assets ($bn)
Bond Corporation	Alan Bond	Brewing, media, mining and minerals, property, retail, car dealerships, airships, education, telecommunications	8	2.8
Brierley Investments Ltd/Industrial Equity Ltd	Ron Brierley	Media, banking, manufacturing (electronic goods, furniture, wood), insurance, publishing, wine and brewing, car dealerships, shipping, retail, textiles, mining and minerals, property development	12	2.4
Bell Group	Robert Holmes à Court	Wool, earthmoving, car manufacturing, construction, media and telecommunications, mining and minerals	16	2.0
Elders–IXL	John Elliot	Pastoral, international commodity trading, shipping, finance (merchant banking, property, rural, investment); materials (hops, malt, timber, building supplies), metals, mining, construction, food and drink	19	1.9
Adelaide Steamship Company	Ken Russell/John Spalvins	Transport, shipping and distribution, commodity imports, mining and minerals, technology, construction, real estate, retail, timber, optical manufacturing, metal manufacturing, engineering, brewing, agriculture, wine, food, leisure	32	1.2
Hooker Corporation	George Herscu	Property, hotels and leisure, trust management, retail, car parks, whitegoods,	46	0.8
Ansett Australia	Reg Ansett	Airlines, resorts, television stations, financial, office supplies, rental cars	13*	2.3
Qintex Ltd	Christopher Skase	Hotels and leisure, media and broadcasting, retail, jewellery, timber, minerals	–	~1.5

Notes: *Owned by TNT whose value is indicated; ~ Estimation due to close ownership of the group.

Sources: Brimson (1987); Sykes (1994). Company rank and total assets from Ville and Merrett (2016).

Sykes's detailed account, *The Bold Riders* (1994). Table 16.1 lists some of the key groups. Their rise and fall has been dramatic. A 1986 list of the top hundred non-financial companies shows four business groups in the top twenty and six in the top fifty. The importance of others was partly concealed by the close ownership of shares (Qintex) or their inclusion as part of another company (Ansett as part of transport company TNT). By the turn of the twenty-first century most had disappeared from the landscape of Australian corporate leadership with the dismantling of the groups.

Frequently, there has been a key entrepreneur controlling and driving the group, such as Alan Bond (Bond Corporation), John Elliott (Elders IXL), John Spalvins (Adsteam), Ron Brierley (Brierley Invesments), Christopher Skase (Qintex), and Robert Holmes à Court (Bell Resources). The verdict on these groups has focused on their speculative nature driven by pragmatic entrepreneurial practices, subsequently revealed to be frequently unethical, if not illegal, in some cases, and earning for this generation of entrepreneurs the epithet "corporate raiders." The verdict has largely been one of a failure to nurture the skills, culture, strategy, and structure that underpin the long-term success of business groups. They overestimated their ability to manage effectively over a diverse range of industries and hold together a large group. In many cases, the group folded in ignominious circumstances or declined to a mere shadow of its former corporate self.

Adsteam was a prominent example of a diversified business group with a pyramidal structure. It had a long history as a pioneer shipping company, dating back to the early days of steam (established 1875) under the name Adelaide Steamship Company. In the 1930s and 1940s it diversified, mainly into related products and services including shipbuilding, towage, and air transport. Its unrelated diversification by the 1970s and 1980s, funded particularly by large amounts of debt, was bold—manufacturing, retailing, real estate, food and drink, and smallgoods. Figure 16.2 shows that the group was developed by mostly minority but controlling interests in a range of firms, sometimes cross-ownership, and sometimes consisting of several tiers of a pyramidal ownership structure. It included many of Australia's corporate leaders of the twentieth century—AWA, Tooth's, David Jones, Petersville Sleigh, and Howard Smith.

As one history of Australian big business has noted of Adsteam, "Here strategy and configuration were one and the same" (Fleming, Merrett, and Ville, 2004: 185). The ability to reach into many markets through a set of minority controlling shareholdings was the key strategy. Unfortunately, the structure was flawed, as Sykes has explained. A number of companies were "ghosts" in the consolidated accounts, since accountancy rules did not require the inclusion of companies in which the ownership share was 50 percent or less. This concealed the true nature of the business group and the likely reverberatory effects if subsidiary firms faced a crisis. Sykes identified an illogical trading structure to the group, for example that its substantial food interests were divided among three companies. Finally, the level of gearing was high and, when combined with rising indebtedness in the group and the opaque condition of the consolidated accounts, made the group as a whole vulnerable to the instability of any individual company. While the debt of each company was non-recourse to others in

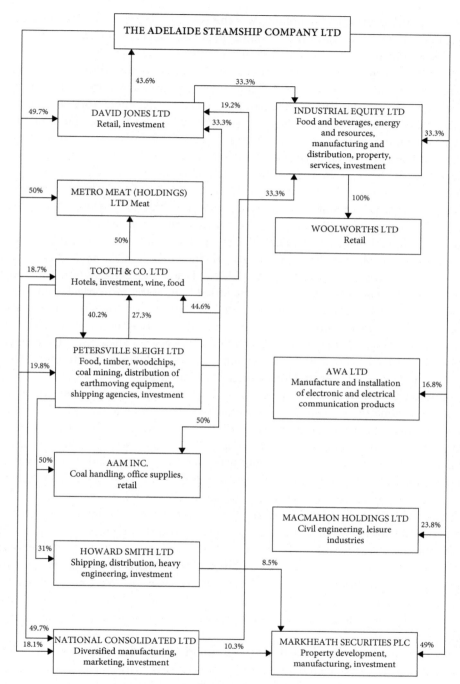

FIGURE **16.2.** Adsteam group structure, 1990.
Source: Fleming, Merrett, and Ville (2004): 186.

the group, the interfirm shareholding was the conduit for group instability. As Sykes concluded, "The chain was only as strong as its weakest link and the weakest link could have been something the analysts couldn't see" (Sykes, 1994: 430).

No story of modern business groups in Australia would be complete without mention of Bond Corporation (see Figure 16.3). The personal story of its "entrepreneur," Alan Bond, adds flavor to the narrative. His is a remarkable story of rise and fall in a couple of decades: from a modest signwriter, he rose to be a multimillionaire entrepreneur and on the journey was Businessman of the Year in 1978, bankrolled the Australian team to a famous victory in the America's Cup in 1983, and became Australian of the Year in 1987. These different facets of his life were inextricably linked—the profile and reputation gained from the America's Cup victory further charged his sense of hubris and effectively gave him a hearing at any financial institution in Australia. Bond's creditors were an impressive who's who of local and international bankers, including the Hong Kong and Shanghai Bank, Standard Chartered Bank, Midland Bank, Barclays Bank, the First National Bank of Boston, the National Australia Bank, and Westpac (Clarke, Dean, and Oliver, 2003: 186). At its peak in about 1989, Bond Corporation reported total assets of nearly $12 bn (Sykes, 1994: 238). However, as the group collapsed he became bankrupt in 1992, and was imprisoned in 1993. Bond acquired debt-funded minority shares in a bewildering number and range of companies in Australia and overseas. These included property, brewing, retail, energy, media, car dealerships, hotels, and telecommunications, which spanned the USA, UK, Japan, Hong Kong, Chile, and Italy.

Bond made many mistakes, particularly paying too much for acquisitions, and behaved dishonestly in many of his dealings, especially by hollowing out the value of public companies in the group in favor of his private firms and by overstating asset values to friendly creditors. Not surprisingly, the group was geared far too highly. When its decline occurred, in the fallout from the 1987 crash and the close investigations behind the group's corporate veil, it was rapid. Most of the research on the Bond Corporation has focused on Alan Bond and his dubious practices (Barry, 1990). There appears to be limited evidence of strategic and operational coordination of the group as a whole. Through all of this Bond was, in some respects, a visionary and indeed a great marketer. He foresaw the future of network television and had a good eye for the development of the property market. In this sense, his access to a diversified range of assets could have brought substantial economic benefits to Western Australia and indeed Australia as a whole. Unfortunately, he also made plenty of poor judgments which, when added to frequent dubious practices, cast a long pall over the history of Bond Corporation.

Between them the diversified business groups controlled large sections of the economy in the 1980s, including all beer production, the largest pastoral companies, the second-largest retail chain, and a similarly substantial presence in industrials, food, textiles, property, mortgages, and car dealers. Researchers have been highly critical of the impact of most of the groups, arguing that they destroyed far more wealth than they created. Between them they lost an estimated A$16 bn in value and inflicted serious

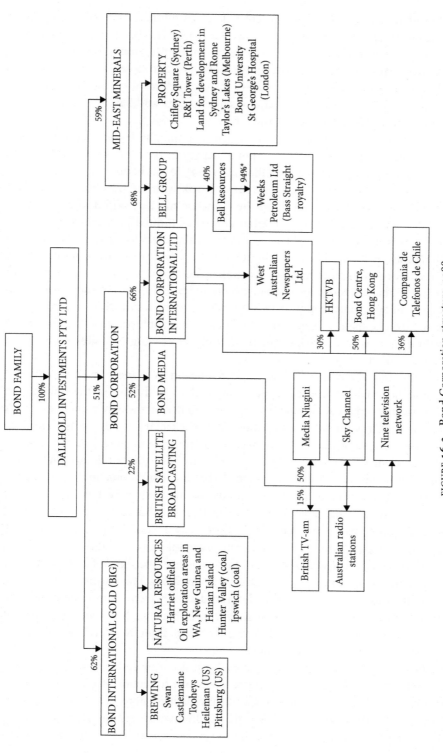

FIGURE **16.3.** Bond Corporation structure, 1988.

Source: Sykes (1994): 190–4, 210–11.
*"Operating loss for Weeks Petroleum,
"*The Canberra Times,* 6 September, 1985: 16.

damage on many Australian corporate icons. They paid little or no tax and siphoned off significant amounts in pursuit of luxury lifestyles. The prudential standards of banks, which lost an estimated $20 bn to these companies, non-executive directors, lawyers, accountants, and brokers have all been brought into close scrutiny. Politicians accepted "donations" and many journalists feared libel cases or merely held these groups in misplaced admiration. Taxpayers, shareholders, and bank customers paid a heavy price for years to come (Sykes, 1994: Ch. 17).

While there are many stakeholders at which to point the finger, it is also worth reflecting on the emphasis placed on corporate legacy in the seminal work of Bartlett and Ghoshal and others (Bartlett and Ghoshal, 1989). What happened in Australia in the 1970s and 1980s, in particular, was a major break with the tradition of a focused strategy and structure located largely in the domestic market. Within the Australian context, Zalan and Lewis have drawn attention to the limited performance of eleven key firms of this era (Zalan and Lewis, 2007). While their focus is particularly on internationalization, it reminds us that heritage matters more broadly. In addition, they criticize the "portfolio mentalities" of Australian enterprises. Zalan and Lewis conclude: "Until managers move away from deeply ingrained portfolio mentalities with little integration and coordination between business units and instead commit themselves to the development of synergies, capabilities and sophisticated mechanisms of coordination, there is little prospect of their firms succeeding in highly competitive international markets" (Zalan and Lewis, 2007: 61).

By the mid-1990s the corporate landscape had begun to change, reverting closer to its long-run shape. La Porta et al. (1999) showed that on the eve of the millennium most of the twenty largest Australian enterprises had become widely owned, and their structure was non-pyramidal. Clearly, the 1987 stock-market crash was pivotal in triggering the collapse of the over-leveraged debt structure of most business groups. The ensuing enquiries brought malpractices directly into the public eye. While the revelations hastened the return to "normal" trading conditions in Australia, the simultaneous introduction of dividend imputation in 1987 may have further, but inadvertently, sounded the death knell of these forms of business groups. Dividend imputation ensured that corporate profits were only taxed at the corporate level, meaning investors paid only the difference to their marginal tax rate on dividends, including a rebate where it was lower than the corporate rate. The effect was to lower the cost of equity by making it more attractive to investors. This further damaged the prospects of the business groups, heavily leveraged as they were on mountains of debt. The absence of other factors sustaining groups elsewhere, such as close government relations, market imperfections, and well-established founding families, made for ephemeral business groups in Australia.

By the beginning of the twenty-first century, most corporations were focused in a particular industry or several closely related areas of production. Nonetheless, while not operating as a business group as specifically defined here, many leading firms possessed some "controlled entities." Mostly wholly owned and unlisted, these were held for a variety of reasons, such as tax-haven vehicles, providing outside investment to smaller firms, or to mitigate risk by creating multiple legal entities for their business (Ramsay and Stapledon, 2001).

Today the Australian corporate sector continues to be dominated by mostly product-focused firms that do not form part of a diversified business group. The top twenty firms listed on the Australian Stock Exchange by market capitalization largely operate in a single or several closely related industries; they are principally found in finance, resources, logistics, retail, healthcare, or telecommunications (*The Australian*, 25 March, 2015: 27). Only one, Wesfarmers, is a highly diverse group with operations across resources, retail, finance, chemicals, and plantations. Many of its subsidiary firms are owned outright, but it retains several partial holdings in resources and chemicals that are mostly unlisted. It is not closely controlled by an individual or entity, its shares being widely owned and traded.

16.6 CONCLUSION: THE ROLE AND LEGACY OF BUSINESS GROUPS IN AUSTRALIA

While diversified business groups have sometimes been concealed from public scrutiny, it seems fair to conclude that their presence in Australia was quite limited until a brief era in the late twentieth century. The growth of large freestanding enterprises, domiciled and multinational, dominated the corporate landscape for most of Australia's history. There are several reasons for this. During the nineteenth century and beyond Federation, the Australian economy lacked breadth, focusing on key exporting resource industries and their service ancillaries. As the economy diversified, particularly into manufacturing after the First World War, well-established multinationals arrived to exploit these opportunities in specific industries, while a maturing capital market supported growth by established domestic corporations and mitigated the need for the in-house treasuries of business groups. The influence of British institutions ensured the rapid maturity of commercial practices, which helped to minimize market imperfections and supported the growth of independent corporations. Following Britain's lead, Australia's banks, after initial setbacks, occupied an increasingly important place in the maturing capital market but never operated business groups in the manner of some of their German counterparts (Schröter, this volume). However, the arrival of overseas banks in the 1970s and 1980s spurred greater industrial investment. Governments provided facilitating infrastructure and networks, especially rail and postal services, but did not diversify their own economic activities. Though susceptible to lobby groups, neither did they support crony capitalism to the benefit of particular diversifying groups and their influential family controllers in the sense experienced in several Asian and Latin American nations, including China, India, Argentina, and Brazil. Finally, the rapidly changing environment of the modernizing Australian economy from the mid-nineteenth century created conditions that were disruptive to the evolution of the type of traditional business groups and their controlling family dynasties that flourished in Europe.

We do know, however, that individuals and leading families built substantial personal and often diverse portfolios and that a highly concentrated business elite cooperated with one another. However, this was rarely akin to the control and active management characteristic of a diversified business empire. Such family empires generally adopted a narrowly focused form and were often ephemeral. Network-type groups also existed, although mostly with a narrow focus as demonstrated by the Collins House Group or the legion of industry-based cartels and agreements. The likes of Thomas Mort, Alfred Buckland, and the Baillieus, while fairly narrow in their core business management, often diversified their groups over time. As we have argued above, however, the business conditions of mid-twentieth century Australia—especially rising minimum scale and revitalized competition policy—increasingly favored large-scale specialist enterprises.

The organic development path of business structures in Australia was severely, if temporarily, disturbed by the major discontinuity of the 1970s and 1980s—the building of very large diversified business groups by charismatic entrepreneurs whose collective display of hubris far outweighed their skills of providing stable and permanent businesses. Competition policy, financial deregulation, and an active corporate takeover market were among the driving forces and provided the opportunity to mimic developments in other nations, but the necessary prudential requirements were regularly flouted and regulation policy was found wanting.

What of the economic impact of business groups? Without being overly reductionist, it is probably fair to say that, most of the time, Australia got the business structures that best suited its environment, which was rarely the business group. Even if they were not of the business-group type strictly defined in this work, the structure of interactions occurring beyond the individual firm—be they networks, agreements, or cooperation among individuals with diverse portfolios—created a fluidity of connections that were a critical part of the business environment in Australia and in the process helped to address the challenges facing a small, remote economy. Those who battled against the tide to form diversified business groups before the last third of the twentieth century were exceptional entrepreneurs. Mort, Buckland, Grimwade, and Baillieu were in advance of their time in experimenting with and initiating new products and services ahead of broader economic trends in Australia. Aided by their determination, insight, and some reliable cash-flow products over time, they initiated or provided the foundations for the formation of a series of major Australian firms, as described earlier. Several innovative entrepreneurs were also at the helm of the business groups of the 1970s and 1980s. However, they also proved to be impatient and extreme risk-takers, whose moral compasses were misdirected and whose business judgments were often far from sound. To date, our assessments of this period suggest they probably destroyed more wealth than they created. While some of the earlier entrepreneurs helped to create iconic Australian firms, this generation destroyed more than a few.

While not without some benefits, therefore, business groups, particularly diversified or possessing a pyramidal structure, in Australia have lacked resilience and viability as a corporate form. They have been small in number and influence for most of Australia's history; while they dominated the corporate landscape for a period towards the end of the twentieth century, their business model was deeply flawed in relation to the Australian environment, as we have explained. When they finally grew in importance, most proved unable to survive the economic impact and regulatory scrutiny arising from the downturn of the late 1980s and early 1990s.

ACKNOWLEDGMENTS

I am grateful to Claire Wright for research assistance in the writing of this chapter and to Professor David Merrett for discussing ideas and sources.

CHAPTER 17

CANADA

the rise and fall, and rise and fall again

RANDALL MORCK AND GLORIA Y. TIAN

17.1 INTRODUCTION

CANADA is a large, open economy that industrialized rapidly around the turn of the twentieth century behind high tariff barriers that subsequently fell away. A French colony for a century and a half and a British colony for over a century thereafter, Canada mixes French and British institutions. Its government is a Westminster-style parliamentary democracy; but its industrial, social, and labor policies have emulated continental European models, especially after Quebec's Quiet Revolution brought French Canadian ideals to prominence. Its legal system is a civil code in Quebec, but common law elsewhere; and a single Supreme Court oversees both systems. Other institutions are similarly hybridized—largely Anglo-Saxon, but with an occasionally heavy French accent.

The importance of diversified and pyramidal business groups (hereafter, business groups) has varied considerably over the decades.[1] In 1910 business-group firms were roughly as important as freestanding, widely held firms. By mid-century freestanding, widely held firms predominated. In the 1970s business groups abruptly resurged in importance, regaining their 1910 prominence within a few years and then fading away again in the 1990s so that, by 2010, Canada's large firms were once again predominantly widely held and freestanding.

The predominance of business groups early in the twentieth century accords with their playing a role in rapid catch-up industrialization by substituting for dysfunctional markets (Khanna and Yafeh, 2007) or centrally coordinating massive capital investment across multiple sectors (Morck and Nakamura, 2007). The business groups of

---

[1] This chapter focuses on the prevalent form of business groups in the Canadian economy in most decades—family- or tycoon-controlled diversified business groups organized in pyramidal structures.

1910 were diversified across many industries, and some contained important instances of vertical integration. For example, the largest business group at the time, controlled by Max Aitken, partially expanded through Royal Securities, his investment bank. The group contained the Steel Company of Canada and Canada Cement Lafarge, both of which provided inputs to its construction projects. A group built around the Canadian Pacific Railway (and the Bank of Montreal) contained Sun Life, Consolidated Mining & Smelting, Ogilvie Flour Mills, Lake of the Woods, Montreal Loan & Mortgage, and CP Hotels. These groups appear to have been organized as pyramids; however, ownership data were not disclosed, so this inference rests on narrative historical records, news archives, and lists of directors. Most groups were controlled by wealthy tycoons or their heirs, though the Canadian Pacific Railway was apparently a widely held apex firm. Unfortunately, this era predates the advent of modern corporate disclosure practices, so available firm-level data are cursory and perhaps unreliable. After the catch-up phase of development ended, these business groups slowly faded away until, at the century's midpoint, about 80 percent of market cap was freestanding widely held firms (Morck, Percy, Tian, and Yeung, 2005).

The resurgence of business groups in the 1970s coincided with a succession of governments led by Prime Minister Pierre Trudeau that countered a surge of Quebecois nationalism with federal bilingualism and biculturalism policies designed to make Canada "more French." French economic policy at the time was *dirigisme*: interventionist industrial policies allocating subsidies to select firms and intensely regulating whole industries, all of which became Canadian policies too. "Canadian control" of natural resources also became politically salient, and regulations and subsidies favored Canadian-controlled firms in those sectors. Business groups expanded by acquiring control blocks in major natural resources firms as these policies were rolled out, but their expansion was not confined to that sector. Their ownership structures, since the mid-1970s, are fully documented in Statistics Canada's *Directories of Inter-Corporate Ownership (ICO)*, and reveal pyramidal structures similar to those of Japanese prewar zaibatsu with member firms spread across many seemingly unrelated sectors (Morck and Nakamura, 2005).

The final decline of business groups, from the late 1980s on, coincides with a succession of governments backing away from dirigiste economics. The Canadian Pacific Railway group reorganized itself into several freestanding, one-industry firms. Member firms of the Edward and Peter (Edper) Bronfman group, one of the largest pyramids of this era, became significantly more highly leveraged than other firms in their industries (Daniels et al., 1995). This group, along with another controlled by the Reichmann family, collapsed when their key firms failed to make interest payments in the 1990s, amid a recession that featured an unprecedented interest-rate spike, in which the prime lending rate for businesses reached 14 percent and the real rate exceeded 10 percent. Another large group, Bell Canada Enterprises, broke up amid the failure of Nortel, one of its major member firms. Yet another, the Hollinger group, collapsed at the turn of the millennium, its controlling shareholder, Conrad Black, having been sentenced to federal prison in the United States for obstruction of justice.

Two family-controlled pyramidal groups survive, and the divested debris of the failed groups and several privatized state-owned enterprises expanded the ranks of free-standing firms.

17.2 THE CHANGING IMPORTANCE OF BUSINESS GROUPS

To assess the economic importance of business groups, we classify each of the largest 100 publicly traded companies in Canada as belonging to a business group or not at intervals from 1900 to 2010, the most recent data available at the time of writing. These lists are from Tian (2006), as summarized in Morck, Percy, Tian, and Yeung (2005), for 1900 through 1998, and from the electronic versions of annual Financial Post (FP) 500 rankings for subsequent years. Because of the ultimate data sources Morck et al. (2005) use, firms are ranked by assets until 1965 and thereafter by revenue. Revenues include dividend income from subsidiaries as well as sales, and assets also include shareholdings in subsidiaries.

Firms that belong to business groups are further partitioned into those belonging to business groups controlled by a tycoon or business family and those with widely held apex firms. Firms not in Canadian business groups are partitioned into freestanding widely held firms, freestanding family-controlled or tycoon-controlled firms, state-controlled firms, and foreign-controlled firms.

Data for assigning firms to these categories are readily available in successive volumes of *Directories of Inter-Corporate Ownership (ICO)*, by Statistics Canada, from 1965 onward. These ICO volumes, especially those of 1975 and thereafter, let us diagram the detailed structures of all business groups, assigning control to the shareholder with the largest voting block over 10 percent or having power to appoint a majority of the board through director constituencies or other control mechanisms. The ICO volumes trace control upwards through successive layers of inter-corporate ownership to identify an ultimate controlling shareholder, if one exists. The FP listings provide the name and stake of controlling shareholders of freestanding firms from the 1970s on. For earlier years, Morck et al. (2005) rely on historical descriptions of business groups provided by Naylor (1975), Francis (1986), Bliss (1987), and Taylor and Baskerville (1994), and searches of historical news archives. We recognize that our classifications for earlier years may be rough, so we focus on the second half of the sample window more intensely.

The large business groups of the mid-twentieth century are all pyramidal in form, and resemble Japan's prewar zaibatsu. None are held together by multiple small crossholdings, as Japanese postwar horizontal keiretsu are. This is perhaps because inter-corporate dividend income on stakes smaller than 20 percent is subject to full double taxation, while that on stakes of 20 percent or more is exempt. The tax law thus

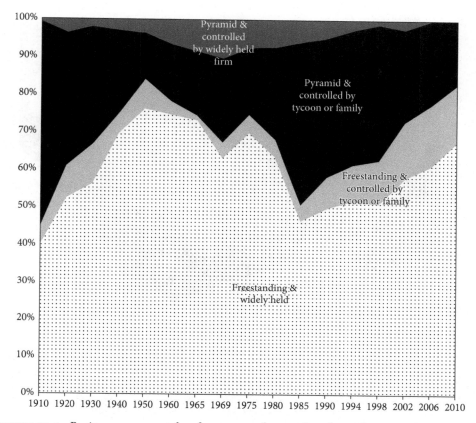

FIGURE **17.1.** Business group member firms versus freestanding firms, domestically controlled private-sector firms among the top 100 firms in Canada in each period, 1910–2010.

Note: The relative importance (by assets until 1965, by revenues thereafter) of domestically controlled firms ranked among the top 100 that are in business groups versus freestanding firms is measured at intervals from 1900 to 2010. Business groups are partitioned into those controlled by a tycoon or business family and those controlled by a widely held firm. Freestanding firms are partitioned into widely held firms versus firms controlled by a tycoon or business family. State controlled firms, foreign controlled firms, and a small number of early years observations for firms whose control structure is unknown are excluded.

Source: This figure is an updated version of Figure 1.7 in Morck, Percy, Tian, and Yeung (2005), with post-1998 data sourced from Statistics Canada's Inter-Corporate Ownership (ICO) directories.

favors large control blocks of the sort that hold pyramidal business groups together, but discourages multiple small crossholdings. Several large business groups of the early twentieth century were likely also controlled via pyramiding, but further research is needed in this area.

Figure 17.1 summarizes this pattern by highlighting changes in the control of domestic private-sector firms only. Figure 17.2 adds context by including state-owned enterprises and foreign-controlled firms as well as a small number of observations for the earliest years in the sample window for firms whose controlling shareholders are uncertain. The major stylized fact—clearest in Figure 17.1, but readily evident in

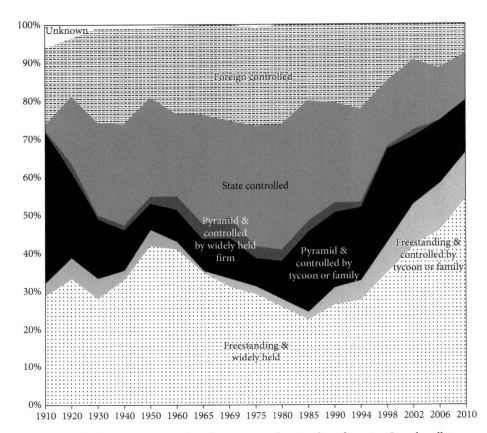

FIGURE 17.2. Business group member firms versus freestanding firms in Canada, all top 100 firms each period, 1910–2010.

Note: The relative importance (by assets until 1965, by revenues thereafter) of the top 100 firms of firms in business groups versus free-standing firms is measured at intervals from 1900 to 2010. Firms with Canadian federal or provincial governments and with foreign individuals or firms as controlling shareholders are distinguished as state-controlled and foreign-controlled, respectively. Business groups are partitioned into those controlled by a Canadian tycoon or business family and those controlled by a Canadian widely held firm. Freestanding firms are partitioned into widely held firms versus firms controlled by a Canadian tycoon or business family. A small number of early years observations for firms whose control structure is unknown are also included. Foreign controlled firms are not separated into foreign group member firms and foreign independent firms.

Source: This figure is an updated version of Figure 1.6 in Morck, Percy, Tian, and Yeung (2005), with post-1998 data sourced from Statistics Canada's Inter-Corporate Ownership (ICO) directories.

Figure 17.2 as well, is that widely held freestanding firms were relatively unimportant at the beginning of the twentieth century, became very prominent by mid-century, declined abruptly in importance from 1975 through the 1980s, and again gained steadily in importance from 1990 through 2010. The importance of diversified business groups with pyramidal structures controlled by tycoons or business families follows precisely the opposite pattern, gaining in prominence whenever freestanding widely held firms decline, losing ground whenever freestanding widely held firms grow in importance.

Freestanding firms controlled by tycoons or families, much less important—at least among the top 100 firms in a given year—than either of the above categories, appear to wax and wane in importance in roughly the same periods as freestanding widely held firms. Inspection of the data shows that the gain in this category's importance in later decades reflects the rise of many relatively new firms with controlling shareholders. These include new high-technology firms, such as BlackBerry (RIM).

A handful of business groups with widely held firms at their apexes become noticeable in the data in the mid-decades of the twentieth century, but these are also far less prominent than either family- and tycoon-controlled pyramidal groups or freestanding widely held firms. The most important among these are a business group controlled by Bell Canada Enterprises, built around a firm initially founded by Alexander Graham Bell in the nineteenth century, that precipitously declined with the collapse of Nortel, one of its major member firms; and the Canadian Pacific group, which contained railroad, airline, hotel, and shipping firms, all associated with the country's first transcontinental railroad, built in the 1870s and 1880s.

Figure 17.2 shows foreign-controlled and state-controlled firms similarly rising in importance in the middle of the twentieth century before falling back in prominence. The major state-controlled groups include Canadian National Railways, formed early in the twentieth century from the bankruptcies of the country's second and third transcontinental railways; Air Canada, an airline; Petro-Canada, an oil company; various public utilities; and several depression-era state-run monopoly marketing companies for various agricultural products. These state-owned enterprises were almost all privatized in the later twentieth century, and all the marketing boards were dismantled—except those for chickens and dairy products, which survived because of intensive lobbying. State-owned French and English radio and television networks survived the privatization era. Foreign capital surged into the country in the 1920s to develop a series of major mineral finds, and again in the mid-twentieth century to develop the oil and gas sector, expanding the ranks of foreign-controlled firms. In the 1970s, and especially the early 1980s, a series of nationalist measures precipitated the takeovers of previously foreign-controlled firms by Canadian firms (Morck and Tian, 2005).

17.3 BRIEF HISTORIES OF SOME MAJOR BUSINESS GROUPS

Figure 17.1 shows the resurgence of family-controlled business groups cresting just prior to 1990. The largest family-controlled business groups identified by Statistics Canada's 1990 ICO are the Edper Bronfman, Desmarais, Reichmann, and Weston groups. This section describes their development prior to this point in time, their structures around 1990, and their subsequent demise or prosperity.

17.3.1 The Edper Bronfman Group

The Bronfman dynasty was founded by Sam Bronfman (1889–1971), a Jewish refugee from tsarist Russia who settled in Saskatchewan.[2] After trying tobacco farming, the family moved to Manitoba and acquired a hotel. Appreciating that much of their profits came from their bar, Sam became a liquor distributor. When the United States illegalized alcohol (1920–33), he began producing whiskey on a large scale, later buying the Seagram's brand and expanding into a broad range of liquor products. The family sold liquor legally in Canada; however, his buyers, Americans who smuggled into the United States, were considered criminals in that country. After Sam Bronfman's death, the family empire was divided between Sam's sons, Charles and Edgar Bronfman, and his nephews, Edward and Peter Bronfman.

Charles dabbled in professional sports teams and ultimately emigrated to the United States. Edgar bought into MGM, a Hollywood studio, and then moved his inheritance out of Canada in 1991, under an initially secret and subsequently highly controversial tax ruling waiving the capital-gains taxes normally due on estates.[3] When his son, Edgar Jr., took over in 1994, the business group controlled by this fraction of the family was largely outside Canada. Two major investments were Warner Music (USA) and Viviendi (France). Edgar Jr., convicted of insider trading in the shares of Vivendi, fined €5 million, and given a suspended fifteen-month sentence, has been a vocal critic of online music piracy. Edgar Jr.'s sisters, Sara and Clare Bronfman, have reportedly invested much of their wealth in NXIVM, an American multilevel marketing and personal development organization that some allege to be a "cult."[4]

Sam's nephews, Edward and Peter, remained in Canada to head the country's largest late-twentieth century business group—the Edper Bronfman group. A huge pyramidal structure, by the late 1980s the group contained twenty-two listed firms and hundreds of private firms, all organized into sixteen tiers of firms controlling firms controlling firms. Its scale and scope are widely accredited to Jack Cockwell, a South African immigrant hired by the brothers to manage their businesses. Cockwell reportedly built up the Edper group along the lines of South African business groups familiar to him.

Figure 17.3 shows the group's pyramidal structure in the early 1990s, at its maximum size. Only major member firms operating in Canada are shown. The layout of Figure 17.3 is also used in the diagrams describing the other three family-controlled pyramidal groups discussed in this section.

In Figure 17.3, the alphanumeric beginning with "c" below each firm's name indicates its main industrial sector. The details of this industry classification, based on an

---

[2] See Taylor (2006) on the family's rise and fall; see Marrus (2000) for a detailed biography of the founder.

[3] See "Angry taxpayer takes on the Bronfmans: Revenue Canada says $2-billion tax loophole is none of his business," by Janice Tibbetts, *Ottawa Citizen*, March 6, 2000.

[4] See "The Heiresses and the Cult," *Vanity Fair* (UK edition), November 2010.

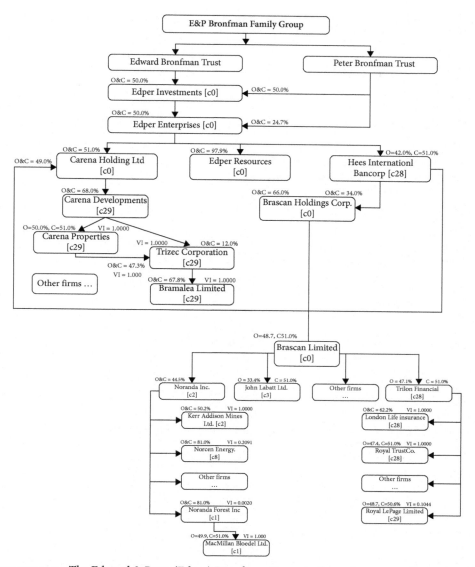

FIGURE 17.3. The Edward & Peter (Edper) Bronfman Group in the early 1990s, at its maximum extent.

Note: The main industry of each firm is indicated by the alphanumeric beginning with "c" below its name (see Table 1). The ownership structure of each firm is indicated by the two numbers above it, with "O" and "C" indicating the cash flow rights and control rights, respectively, of its controlling shareholder. Only major Canadian member firms are shown.

Source: Assembled using data from Statistics Canada's Inter-Corporate Ownership (ICO) directory for 1990.

input-output system from the World Input-Output Database (WIOD), is listed in Table 17.1. For Edper Bronfman in the early 1990s, the firm nearest the bottom of the figure is MacMillan-Bloedel, whose most important line of business is forestry. This puts it in industry category "c1," which Table 17.1 describes as "Agriculture, Forestry, and Fishing."

Table 17.1. Industry codes.

Industry	Code
Agriculture, Forestry, and Fishing	c1
Mining and Quarrying (excluding Crude Oil)	c2
Food, Beverages, and Tobacco	c3
Textiles and Textile Products	c4
Leather, Leather, and Footwear	c5
Wood and Products of Wood and Cork	c6
Pulp, Paper, Paper Products, Printing, and Publishing	c7
Coke, Crude Oil, Refined Petroleum, and Nuclear Fuel	c8
Chemicals and Chemical Products	c9
Rubber and Plastics	c10
Other Non-Metallic Mineral	c11
Basic Metals and Fabricated Metal	c12
Machinery (not elsewhere classified)	c13
Electrical and Optical Equipment	c14
Transport Equipment	c15
Manufacturing (not elsewhere classified); Recycling	c16
Electricity, Gas, and Water Supply	c17
Construction	c18
Sale, Maintenance, and Repair of Motor Vehicles and Motorcycles; Retail Sale of Fuel	c19
Wholesale Trade and Commission Trade, Except of Motor Vehicles and Motorcycles	c20
Retail Trade, Except of Motor Vehicles and Motorcycles; Repair of Household Goods	c21
Hotels and Restaurants	c22
Inland Transport	c23
Water Transport	c24
Air Transport	c25
Other Supporting and Auxiliary Transport Activities; Activities of Travel Agencies	c26
Post and Telecommunications	c27
Financial Intermediation	c28
Real Estate Activities	c29
Renting of Machines & Equipment, and Other Business Activities	c30
Public Administration and Defense; Compulsory Social Security	c31
Education	c32
Health and Social Work	c33
Other Community, Social, and Personal Services	c34
Private Households with Employed Persons	c35
Diversified Conglomerate	c0

Industry classification codes below are based on an input-output system from the World Input-Output Database (WIOD): http://www.wiod.org/new_site/database/niots.htm. *In addition to the original WIOD 35 industries codes, we also add Diversified Conglomerates as a separate industry and code it as c0.*

The ownership and control rights of each firm's immediate parent are indicated by two numbers above and to the left of its name. The number flagged with an "O" is its immediate parent's cash-flow rights and that flagged with a "C" is its immediate parent firm's control rights. Both are calculated as in La Porta et al. (1999). Figure 17.3 shows that MacMillan-Bloedel was 49.9-percent owned by Noranda Forests, which controlled 51 percent of the votes in its shareholders meetings.

The final number, above and to the right of each firm, flagged with "VI," is a measure of its vertical integration with its immediate parent firm. We follow Fan and Lang (2000) in developing a method to assess how vertically integrated the companies in a business group are. The first step makes use of Canada's input-output tables (Leontief, 1986). The annual input-output (IO) table is a 35 by 35 matrix whose rows and columns are labeled with industry names. Each entry in the table is the value of the inputs used by one industry (the one labeling its row) that come from another industry (the one labeling its column). For example, consider the basic and fabricated metals industry (IO industry code c12) and the transport equipment industry (c15). In 2010 total transport equipment industry produced output worth $152.164 billion and used $9.810 billion of basic and fabricated-metals products as one of its inputs. That is, the transport equipment industry used $0.0645 of basic and fabricated metals per dollar of its output. In the same year, the basic metals and fabricated metal industry generated output worth $201.834 billion using, among its many inputs, $234 million of transport equipment industry products. On a per dollar basis, $0.0012 of transport equipment went into each dollar of basic and fabricated metals output. The 2010 vertical integration (VI) coefficient of this pair of industries is the average of 0.0645 and 0.0012, or 0.0328.

The WIOD database provides annual Canadian IO tables over the period 1995 through 2010, based on which we compute the VI coefficients of every possible pair of the thirty-six industries in Table 17.1.[5] The number above and to the right of each firm's name is the VI coefficient of its main industry with the main industry of its immediate parent firm. Thus, MacMillan-Bloedel's parent firm, Noranda Forests Inc., is another forestry firm, also flagged "c1," so the two firms are in the same industry category and MacMillan-Bloedel's VI coefficient is 1.00. However, Noranda Forest's parent firm, Noranda Inc., is primarily a mining company, so Noranda Forest's vertical integration with its parent is only 0.0020, reflecting the fact that mining and forestry use relatively little of each other's products as inputs. For comparison, across the entire economy and all years, mean VI coefficient is 0.0179 and the median vertical integration is 0.0055.

The Edper Bronfman group collapsed in the early 1990s. By then it had aggressively expanded its operations in commercial real estate. Much of this expansion was debt-financed. This left the group's listed member firms far more leveraged on average than they had been in previous decades (Daniels et al., 1995). In the early 1990s Canada experienced a brief but severe recession. The prime commercial borrowing rate spiked to 14 percent in 1990, the real rate reaching an unprecedented 10 percent, all while real

---

[5] Annual Canadian data are retrieved from the World Input-Output Database (WIOD) at http://www.wiod.org/new_site/database/niots.htm. Some firms are conglomerates (single firms with divisions or fully owned subsidiaries operating in more than one industry). In such cases, Canadian financial reporting standards consolidate fully owned subsidiaries into the accounts of the parent firm, and thus consider such structures as single firms, not business groups, from accounting perspectives. There is no single industry in the input-output tables for conglomerates, so we create industry category c0 = diversified conglomerate.

GDP growth dropped to minus 2 percent in 1992. After two of its highly levered group real estate member firms, Bramalea and Trizec, failed, the group was dismantled. Many of its member firms remain in business. Peter Bronfman died in 1996 and Edward in 2005.

17.3.2 The Reichmann Group

A second-largest late-twentieth century business group was the work of Paul Reichmann, who came to Canada by way of France and Morocco as a refugee from Nazi Austria. Paul's brother, Edward, opened Olympia Flooring and Tile in Montreal and sent Paul to Toronto to open a branch there. Paul began organizing tradesmen and soon ran a construction firm, Olympia and York, which became the apex firm of a large and, by the 1980s, highly diversified pyramidal group. The group's major diversification efforts into natural resources included Abitibi-Price Inc. (pulp and paper) and Gulf Canada Resources (petroleum). Controversy surrounded the family's Gulf Canada Resources acquisition because Deputy Finance Minister Marshall Cohen quit the government to manage the acquisition, allegedly structured around a peculiarity in the tax code to sidestep a billion-dollar tax liability. Commercial real estate remained the Reichmann group's core competence, but like the Edper group, it expanded into many industries. Also like the Edper Bronfman group, the Reichmann group reached is maximum scale and scope around 1990. This is shown in Figure 17.4.

One of the group's core firms, Olympia and York, had borrowed heavily to transform London's docklands area with its huge Canary Wharf redevelopment project. A persistently high vacancy rate in the development left Olympia and York unable to meet its interest costs and in 1992 the Reichmann group followed the Edper Bronfman group into bankruptcy.[6]

Their fortune greatly reduced, the family re-entered the fray and succeeded in regaining a stake in the ultimately highly profitable Canary Wharf development. Paul Reichmann died in 2013. The Reichmann heirs remain active in some of the group's core businesses—ceramic tiles and real estate.

17.3.3 The Desmarais Group

Paul Desmarais (1927–2013) brought his venerable French Canadian family to prominence when he bought a near-bankrupt bus company from his grandfather for one dollar. Paul rapidly rebuilt the company into a group of profitable transportation firms. An equity swap in 1968 gave him control of Power Corporation, the apex firm of a business group begun in the 1920s by A. J. Nesbitt and P. A. Thomson, whose member firms were primarily in electric power generation. After many of these were nationalized in the 1960s, the Nesbitt and Thomson heirs had diversified the group into

---

[6] See "Cohen broke conflict guidelines: opposition," *Montreal Gazette*, October 23, 1985, p. B4.

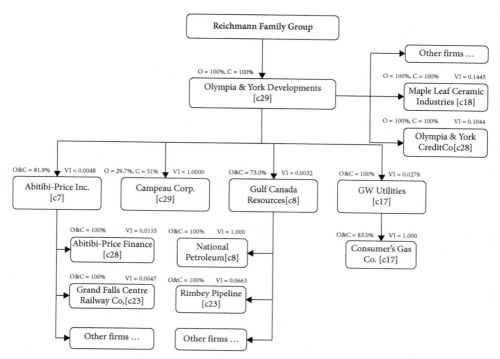

FIGURE 17.4. The Reichmann Group, in the early 1990s, at its largest extent.

Note: The main industry of each firm is indicated by the alphanumeric beginning with "c" below its name (see Table 1). The ownership structure of each firm is indicated by the two numbers above it, with "O" and "C" indicating the cash flow rights and control rights, respectively, of its controlling shareholder. Only major Canadian member firms are shown.

Source: Assembled using data from Statistics Canada's Inter-Corporate Ownership (ICO) directory for 1990.

finance, manufacturing, and real estate. After he gained control, Paul Desmarais diversified the group into yet more sectors—acquiring control blocks in Canada Steamship Lines (transportation), Consolidated-Bathurst (paper products), Investors Group, Great-West Life, and Montreal Trusto (all financial firms), and Gesca and La Presse (both in newspapers). Under Desmarais the group also expanded into Europe, acquiring control of Pargesa (Switzerland), the non-French assets of Paribas, Imétal (France), Totalfina Elf (France), Compagnie Luxembourgeoise de Télédiffusion (Luxembourg), and Suez Lyonnaise des Eaux (France).

In 1996 Paul retired, bequeathing control to his sons Paul Jr. and André. The Desmarais group has attracted considerable attention for its political connections. André's wife France is the daughter of former prime minister Jean Chrétien. Former prime minister Paul Martin worked for the Desmarais as CEO of Canada Steamship Lines. Other prominent federal and provincial politicians also served in various capacities at certain group firms.

Panel A of Figure 17.5 shows the group's structure in the early 1990s, for comparison with the Edper Bronfman and Reichman groups at their maximums; Panel B shows the group in 2010. The Desmarais group remains a major player in Canada and internationally.

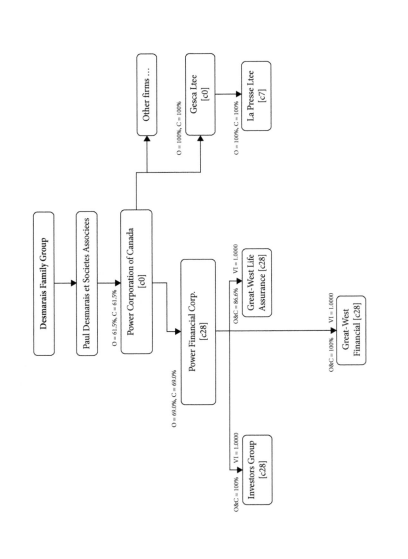

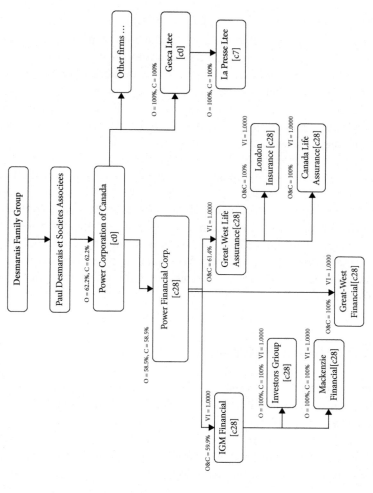

FIGURE 17.5. The Desmarais Group.

Note: The main industry of each firm is indicated by the alphanumeric beginning with "c" below its name (see Table 1). The ownership structure of each firm is indicated by the two numbers above it, with "O" and "C" indicating the cash flow rights and control rights, respectively, of its controlling shareholder. Only major Canadian member firms are shown.

Source: Assembled using data from Statistics Canada's Inter-Corporate Ownership (ICO) directory for 1990 (Panel A) and 2010 (Panel B).

17.3.4 The Weston Group

The Anglo-Canadian Weston family controls the fourth major business group we consider in detail. Garfield Weston (1898–1978) built his father's Toronto bakery into a huge food processing, distribution, and retail empire without running up large debts. This let him assemble a large business group by acquiring troubled firms during the Great Depression of the 1930s. By the 1940s the group had member firms in Canada, Britain, and the United States; and Garfield had a Tory seat in the British parliament. During World War II, the group bought E. B. Eddy, a match company, from former Canadian prime minister R. B. Bennett. After the war the group continued expanding in Canada, the United Kingdom, and other Commonwealth countries.

The group's most publicly prominent firms in the postwar decades were Twinings Tea, the Fine Fare supermarket chain, and Aerated Bread Company in Britain; National Tea in the US; and the Loblaw's supermarket chain in Canada. By 1971 the group was overextended and highly levered. Garfield stood down in favor of his son W. Galen Weston, who began downsizing the group rapidly. With the group still teetering on bankruptcy, Galen brought in his university classmate Eric Nicol, who imposed yet more downsizing and began a major rationalization and reorganization.

Restored to financial health, the group survived the early 1990s recession and interest rate spike, and began expanding again, notably with the acquisition of a control block in Selfridges, a British department store chain. In 2006 W. Galen stepped aside at Loblaw Companies in favor of his son, Galen G. Weston, while still retaining the executive chair at George Weston Limited. The Weston family remains a major presence in the Canadian economy. Figure 17.6 sketches out the major components of the group in 1990 and 2010.

17.3.5 Other Major Business Groups

The Thomson Group expanded internationally, and is arguably no longer primarily Canadian. Its founder, Roy Thomson, built a small-town Ontario newspaper into a large international business group, whose major members include Thomson Reuters, Thomson Financial, Thomson Healthcare, Thomson Legal, Thomson Scientific, and Thomson Tax & Accounting. The group owns EndNote, MedStat, the Web of Science, Westlaw, and other prominent information-technology ventures. Thomson merged with Reuters Group in 2008 and moved its operating headquarter out of Canada. Its Canadian operations, now a minor part of its overall operations, include *The Globe and Mail*, Toronto's largest-circulation newspaper, and CTV, the country's largest private-sector over-the-air television network. The group is currently headed by David and Peter Thomson, Roy Thomson's grandsons. David Thomson, 3rd Baron Thomson of Fleet, inherited the British peerage obtained in 1964 by his grandfather, who then controlled *The Scotsman* of Edinburgh, and *The Times* and *The Sunday Times* of

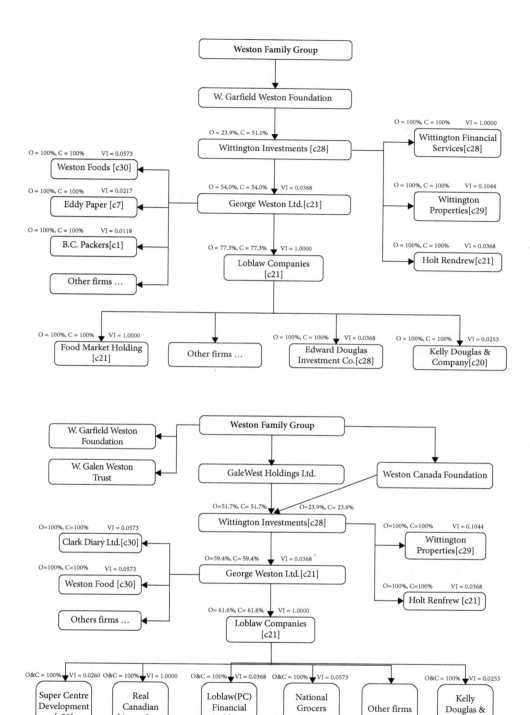

FIGURE 17.6. The Weston Group.

Note: The main industry of each firm is indicated by the alphanumeric beginning with "c" below its name (see Table 1). The ownership structure of each firm is indicated by the two numbers above it, with "O" and "C" indicating the cash flow rights and control rights, respectively, of its controlling shareholder. Only major Canadian member firms are shown.

Source: Assembled using data from Statistics Canada's Inter-Corporate Ownership (ICO) directory for 1990 (Panel A) and 2010 (Panel B).

London. Like his father and grandfather, David surrendered his Canadian citizenship to accept the foreign title. Roy Thomson locked the family's wealth into a legal structure that necessitates family succession, explaining: "David, my grandson, will have to take his part in the running of the organization and David's son, too.... With the fortune that we will leave to them go also responsibilities. These Thomson boys that come after Ken are not going to be able, even if they want to, to shrug off these responsibilities" (Francis, 2008).

A second family-controlled group whose expansion was largely outside Canada was that of Conrad Black. George Black died in 1976, leaving his sons Conrad and Montegu 22 percent of Ravelston, the apex company of the Argus group, the largest business group in Canada in the mid-twentieth century. Argus operating companies included Dominion Stores, Domtar, Hollinger Mines, Labrador Mining, Massey-Ferguson, Noranda Mines, and Standard Broadcasting. Black acquired full control of the group in 1978 by buying up the Ravelston stock his father's partners left to their widows. In a rapid-fire series of spin-offs and acquisitions, Conrad transformed the Argus group into a new Hollinger Group. Ravelston remained its apex firm, but now controlled a worldwide constellation of newspapers at the base of a pyramid of intermediate holding companies controlled with super-voting shares. The newspapers included the The *Daily Telegraph* in London, the *Chicago Sun-Times*, *Jerusalem Post*, *National Post*, and numerous others. In 1999 and 2000 Hollinger International, a lower-level holding company sold its newspapers, whose buyers also made side payments to Black and other Ravelston insiders in the form of "non-compete agreements." Hollinger International's independent directors viewed these side payments as the rightful property of the firm, and their payment to others as a corporate governance problem. Black was convicted of fraud, SEC violations, and obstruction of justice in the US and sentenced to six and a half years in federal prison. On appeal, Black overturned many of these convictions and had his sentence reduced. Although Black surrendered his Canadian citizenship to accept a British peerage, he returned to Canada after his release. He was charged with Ontario securities law violations in 2013 and convicted of tax evasion in 2014. Black maintains his complete innocence, and likens the American justice system to that of North Korea.[7]

Another family-run business group merits mention: that of the Irving family. Kenneth Colin (K. C.) Irving (1899–1992) took over a New Brunswick sawmill his father had owned, and expanded it into a large diversified business group with operating companies in forest products, oil refining, trucking, and heavy industry. In 1972, amid charges of tax evasion, he emigrated to the Bahamas. Shortly before his death, he oversaw the division of the business group's firms among his sons, James (forest products), Arthur (oil refining), and Jack (heavily industry). Irving companies remain dominant throughout the New Brunswick provincial economy, but have little presence elsewhere in the country.

---

[7] See "Conrad Black gets nasty with British interviewers over his US criminal convictions" by Steve Mertl, *Daily Brew*, October 23, 2012.

The late twentieth century also saw the dismantling of two large diversified business groups whose apex firms were widely held: Canadian Pacific and BCE. Canadian Pacific, founded in 1881 as a widely held firm, built the country's first transcontinental railroad. Over the subsequent century Canadian Pacific expanded into hotels, airlines, and numerous other sectors. The group sold its CP Air in 1986 and spun off CP Hotels in 2001 as Fairmont Hotels, an independent company. Canadian Pacific is now a focused railway company. The BCE group was founded by Alexander Graham Bell in 1876. Bell moved to the United States to build a second Bell Telephones in that country, leaving Bell Canada in his father's hands. By the 1990s the widely held Bell Canada Enterprises (BCE) controlled a large business group that included legacy landline telephone infrastructure as well as Northern Telecom (Nortel), a cell-phone company that controlled several other firms in related areas. Bell Canada spun Nortel off in 2000, but remains a major cell phone and internet service provider and has also expanded into cable television and media content production.

17.4 THE ECONOMICS OF BUSINESS GROUPS IN CANADA

Why does the importance of business groups change so extensively over time? Did fundamental economic advantages from the business group structure vary? Or did political, legislative, or regulatory changes drive these changes?

17.4.1 Business Groups as Instruments for Rapid Industrialization

The business groups that dominate today's successful emerging market economies are typically controlled by powerful families and are very broadly diversified (Khanna and Yafeh, 2007). Likewise, the major zaibatsu business groups that drove the rapid industrialization of Taishō Japan in the late nineteenth and early twentieth century, like the major chaebol business groups that powered South Korea's rapid ascent to First World status in the twentieth century, were characterized by "full set" diversification— each business group contained at least one firm in every major industry. Khanna and Yafeh argue that these highly diversified business groups serve as a substitute for weak markets and dysfunctional institutions in developing economies. Thus, a group member firm can rely on intra-group transactions, rather than arm's-length market transactions, to source inputs and financing, hire workers, and place outputs. While market transactions may be impeded by fraud, corruption, or unverifiable quality control, one-group firms do not cheat each other because all are controlled by the same powerful family.

Rosenstein-Rodan (1943) prescribed state-run industrial policies to coordinate rapid economic development, which he correctly characterized as requiring the coordinated and synchronized formation and growth of numerous firms in many different sectors. However, Easterly (2013) notes the near universal government-failure problems associated with state-driven development strategies and disparages Rosenstein-Rodan's ideas and disciples. Morck and Nakamura (2007), drawing on Japanese economic history, suggest that Rosenstein-Rodan was right about the problem but wrong about the solution. They suggest that highly diversified business groups under centralized control, rather than centrally planned economies under bureaucratic control, can best choreograph the allocation of capital and resources to coordinate the synchronized expansion of existing firms and formation of new ones across diverse industries. Competing rival groups, operating under a laissez-faire government that minimizes the returns to political rent-seeking, might then earn higher group-level profits by following more efficient development paths.

Figure 17.7 explores the importance of business groups at different stages of the country's industrialization. More specifically, Panel A addresses the question of how important these business groups are in various industry sectors, and Panel B evaluates the importance of each industry sector to these business groups. We create twelve industry groups, augmented using the United Nation's International Standard Industrial Classification (ISIC) codes, and then aggregate these industry groups into four broadly defined industry sectors: primary, secondary, tertiary, and mixed. In each year of roughly every two decades—1910, 1930, 1950, 1969, 1990, and 2010—we manually check the industry affiliations of the top 100 companies and classify them into different industry sectors.

Consistent with the business groups of the early twentieth century playing a key role in industrialization, family-controlled business groups in 1910 comprised over 60 percent of secondary industry by assets. The presence of these groups in the secondary sector steadily declined over the century. The importance of the natural resources (primary sector) in family-controlled business groups also declined over time, except for a surge in 1990. This spike is attributable to the Edper Bronfman group, which expanded aggressively throughout the 1970s and 1980s.

Family-controlled pyramidal groups are more prominent in the mixed industry sector towards the end of the twentieth century and in the early twenty-first century. This is mainly due to the likes of Brascan Corporation of the Edper Bronfman group and Power Corporation of the Desmarais group, both of which are diversified firms, and investment companies such as Onex Corporation of the Schwartz family group. It is also noteworthy that the oil and gas industry (O&G), for this part of the analysis, has been grouped in the mixed industry sector. The O&G industry was by and large unimportant until the 1970s, largely ignored by old families and left to small entrepreneurs and foreign companies. The 1981 National Energy Program (NEP) was a response to intensive nationalist pressure to "reassert" Canadian control over natural resources, especially oil and gas. After the NEP was repealed

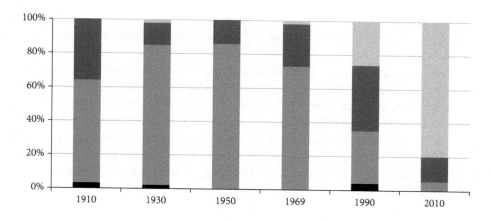

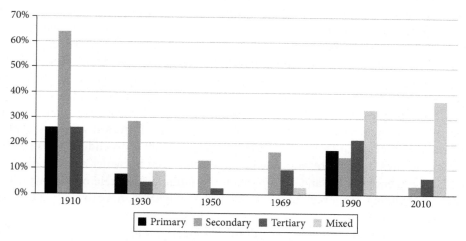

FIGURE 17.7. Industrial configuration of business groups.

Note: This figure depicts the importance of business groups at different stages of Canada's industrialization. We create 12 industry groups, augmented using the United Nation's International Standard Industrial Classification codes (http://unstats.un.org/unsd/cr/registry/regcst.asp?Cl=17), and then aggregate these industry groups into four broadly defined industry sectors. These sectors are: Primary (Agriculture, Forestry & Fishing; Mining & Quarrying other than oil & gas), Secondary (Manufacturing; Utilities; Construction & Civil Engineering), Tertiary (Wholesale & Retail; Transportation, Storage, and Postal Services; IT, Telephone & Other Communications; Finance, Insurance, Real Estate & Related Activities; Arts, Entertainment, and Recreation), and Mixed sector (Oil & Gas, and related Distribution; Conglomerates).

Source: Assembled using data from Financial Post FP100 list for 2010, and earlier data are from Tian (2006). We first manually check each firm's industry using corporate annual reports and other public data sources, and then assign each firm to a particular industry group and industry sector as described above.

in the mid-1980s, many oil and gas firms integrated downstream. As such, the modern O&G industry includes companies or groups that spread across primary, secondary, as well as tertiary sectors. An example of business groups operating in O&G is the Irving family group, in particular the branch of companies controlled by

Arthur Irving, one of the three sons of the group's founder K. C. Irving. Irving Oil Limited operates refineries, a fleet of oil tankers, marine ports, and a network of gasoline stations.

Canada transformed itself from an agricultural to an industrialized economy in a "high growth" period that lasted from the mid-1890s to World War I. During that period, which roughly corresponds to successive governments led by Prime Minster Wilfred Laurier (in office 1896–1911), the economy grew at unprecedented rates year after year as a flood of primarily British capital financed rapidly expanding business groups' expansions into coal mining, steel, cement, insurance, shipbuilding, manufacturing, and other sectors (Bliss, 1987). The larger, early-twentieth century business groups were thus highly diversified, and Laurier governments were untainted by corruption, at least in contrast to many preceding ones.

The largest of the business groups in 1910 was controlled by Max Aitken (Lord Beaverbrook) which was partially expanded through his investment bank Royal Securities, and by then already contained firms in publishing, precision engineering, steel, cement, and hydroelectric power, among other sectors. Vertical linkages are evident: for example, steel and concrete are both needed in major engineering construction projects, such as power dams. Unfortunately, detailed firm-level financial records from the era are sparse, so precisely how these groups formed, how their member firms financed, co-insured, or otherwise interacted with each other, and even how their pyramidal structures formed and changed over time can only be inferred from archival materials, biographies, and other historical accounts. Aitken borrowed money in London to take over numerous small independent firms in each sector, and then applied the era's high technologies—the Bessemer steel process, the Portland cement process, and so on—to the resulting larger-scale operations. Criticized for building monopolies, Aitken moved to England in 1910 to build a vast publishing empire.

How crucial Canada's first-generation business groups were to coordinating capital allocation so as to bring about successful development is unclear. Certainly, their resemblance to Japanese zaibatsu and Korean chaebol is obvious: before their rise Canada was an agrarian economy; after their rise Canada was an industrial economy. That they played analogous roles in early industrialization seems plausible.

If business groups promote rapid industrialization of an agrarian economy by coordinating investment through central (i.e. group headquarters) planning in an economy whose market institutions are not yet well developed, their success renders them superfluous (Morck, Wolfenzon, and Yeung, 2005). Once the whole spectrum of firms, industries, and institutions of a modern economy come into existence, the cost of market transactions plausibly falls, making intra-group central planning a relatively costly way of allocating capital. This fits with the decline of business groups by the 1940s evident in Figure 17.1, but leaves their 1970s resurgence somewhat of a mystery. Using pyramiding to magnify control and the political influence that goes with it is one possibility (Morck and Yeung, 2004; Morck, 2010).

17.4.2 Business Groups as Efficient Capital Allocators

The major Japanese business groups all contained banks as prominent affiliates (Morck and Nakamura, 2007), and Khanna and Yafeh (2007) posit that these served as private equity investors in funding projects throughout their business groups, and that groups therefore remain important in countries where arm's-length financing is costly or unavailable. In Canada, securities law is delegated to provincial governments, so the country subjects listed firms to a patchwork of regulations. This attracts much criticism for making compliance unnecessarily expensive (Puri, 2010) and for permitting numerous high-profile frauds because provincial governments lack resources to appropriately police listed firms (Armstrong, 2015).

The resurgence of business groups does correspond to unusually high-profile scandals in Canadian capital markets, though these were concentrated on the Vancouver Stock Exchange, which Forbes dubbed the "scam capital of the world" (Cruise and Griffiths, 1991).[8] However, the business groups' resurgence was mainly a phenomenon of the Toronto Stock Exchange, which retained a better reputation through this era. Still, the hypothesis that business groups returned because external capital grew less available is not prima facie unreasonable. Rajan and Zingales (2003) document a "reversal" in Canadian financial development in the mid-twentieth century: bank deposits fell from 22 percent of GDP in 1913 to only 13 percent in 1960 and then rose monotonically thereafter to 66 percent in 1999. Stock-market capitalization, 74 percent of GDP in 1913, rose to 175 percent of GDP by 1970, but then plummeted to only 46 percent of GDP in 1980 as the pyramidal groups resurged. As the groups fell away, stock-market capitalization rose again—to 111 percent of GDP by 2012. The timing is not quite tight though: Figure 17.1 shows the resurgence of business groups cresting around 1990, while Rajan and Zingales (2003) show Canada's financial development reaching its lowest ebb a decade or more earlier.

Canadian business groups did not contain banks after the early 1920s, when a recession precipitated government bailouts of several large banks via subsidized forced mergers with healthier banks (Morck and Nakamura, 1995). Among these was the Molson Bank, an affiliate of the Molson family's business group. Concerns about related-party lending destabilizing banks led to a proscription against banks having controlling shareholders. Canada's surviving large banks are all freestanding and widely held, with voting caps guaranteeing that status in perpetuity.[9] No major Canadian bank has failed since, though most came closer than is generally appreciated (Kryzanowski and Roberts, 1993), and inept industrial policy triggered the collapse of several smaller banks in the 1980s (Fossum, 1997). After the 1990s, the banks were

---

[8] See "Scam Capital of the World" by Joe Queenan, *Forbes Magazine*, May 29, 1989: 132–40.
[9] A voting cap is a takeover defense that limits the voting power of any shareholder, or group of shareholders acting in concert, to a fixed percentage regardless of their ownership stake. Thus, a 4-percent voting cap would limit a shareholder's voting power to 4 percent regardless of how many shares she actually owned. If more than 4 percent of the firm's stock is in "friendly" hands, the firm cannot be taken over.

allowed to control insurance and investment firms, but the barriers against banks controlling non-financial firms remain.

Over the next decades, the major banks took over many of the country's most important insurance, investment banking, and financial analysis firms. In every case, the targets were private, and became divisions of the banks. The financial sector is now dominated by a small number of large universal banks, each organized as a financial conglomerate. Thus, the commercial bank TD Canada Trust, the investment bank and brokerage firm TD Waterhouse, and the insurance provider TD Insurance are all part of the Toronto Dominion (TD) Bank Group, as are TD operations in foreign countries. The Royal Bank of Canada (RBC), Bank of Montreal (BMO), Canadian Imperial Bank of Commerce (CIBC), and Bank of Nova Scotia (Scotiabank) likewise developed into financial conglomerates, each operating across many parts of the finance sector, but none with any operations at all outside of finance. The term conglomerate is appropriate because each appears to investors as one unified corporate entity.

However, many major business groups contain important "non-bank" financial institutions. Two examples are Power Financial Corporation of Desmarais group and PC Financial Holdings of Weston group. Power Financial, a diversified management and holding company, controls several large non-bank financial firms (including insurance) in Canada, the United States, and other parts of the world. Today, the holdings of Power Financial are central to the Desmarais group. PC Financial is wholly owned by Loblaw Companies, a Weston group member firm. PC Financial lets customers of Loblaw's supermarkets access credit card and banking services provided by the back offices of CIBC, a widely held bank. The Bronfman and Reichmann groups also contained non-bank financial institutions.

Khanna and Palepu (2005) argue that India's Tata business groups served as a venture capital provider and was critical to developing that country's information-technology sector. None of the four groups discussed in detail above was active in such a capacity in Canada. The most prominent high-tech business group firm in Canada was Nortel, a member of the widely held BCE business group. The BCE group was centered around legacy landline telephone networks, and broke itself up into free-standing firms upon Nortel's collapse amid alleged (but never proven) mismanagement problems (Hunter, 2002; Bagnal, 2013). Other Canadian high-tech firms, such as Corel and BlackBerry, were not group affiliates. The Thomson group has expanded aggressively into information technology, but mostly outside of Canada.

Canada's remaining pyramidal business groups are not prominent in venture capital. A nascent 1980s venture capital industry was crowded out by government subsidies to labor union-run venture capital funds, whose dismal performance tarred the sector for over a decade (Cumming and MacIntosh, 2006, 2007). Government investment funds, often cast as venture capital providers, can morph into politically driven industrial policy tools. For example, the Caisse de Dépôt et Placements du Québec, a provincial government investment fund, acquired asbestos mines to protect Quebec workers from mine closures, as litigation fears began forcing the industry to downsize (Arbour, 1993). More generally, federal and provincial government-sponsored venture capital funds systematically underperform (Brander et al., 2010).

Leveraged buyout (LBO) funds, which buy listed firms, restructure them to improve productivity, and then sell them back to public shareholders at higher prices, have long been present. More recently, federal and provincial government social security programs and public sector pension plans, having boosted contributions to become "substantially funded," are joining private equity deals in a new wave of LBOs. Some of these public sector investment funds also show signs of becoming corporate governance activists in listed firms (Doidge et al., 2015). Conceivably, these funds might develop into state-run business groups along the lines of Italy's Istituto per la Ricostruzione Industriale (Aganin and Volpin, 2005).

17.4.3 Business Groups as Market Internalization

Khana and Yafeh (2007) argue that business groups' key advantage is that they "internalize" markets. If intermediate goods markets function poorly—for example, if firms routinely try to cheat each other—control by a common shareholder can force both firms to deal honestly with each other. Membership in the same group lets firms rely on its well-functioning "internal" market, rather than the dysfunctional external markets. If this motivates group formation, group member firms would be highly vertically integrated. As described in detail above in the explanation of Figure 17.3, we follow Fan and Lang (2000) in quantifying the degree of vertically integration of every possible pair of industries in the economy. In Figures 17.3, 17.4, 17.5, and 17.6 the number flagged with "VI" above the name of each firm is the degree of vertical integration of its primary industry with its immediate parent firm's primary industry.

The first step in our assessment of the vertical integration of an entire group used annual WIOD data on Canadian IO tables for 1995 through 2010. From these we compute VI coefficients each year for all possible pairs of the industry categories in Table 17.1.

The second step applies these average pairwise VI coefficients to business groups. If a group operates in N different industries, there are $\frac{1}{2}N(N-1)$ ways of organizing them into pairs. For each year in question, we list all the industries in which the group operates and produce an input-output submatrix for those sectors only. The elements of this submatrix, the VI coefficients of all the industry pairs in which group firms operates, record the pattern of vertical integration within that group. The distribution of these VI coefficients measures the scope for vertical integration in the group.[10] We

---

[10] The method is imperfect for several reasons. First, these calculations are based on all relevant pairs of industries in each group—we do not consider whether a group firm is publicly listed or unlisted, the size of each firm, or how many firms are in a same industry. While an advantage of using listed firms only is that we know these are important firms, the number of unlisted entities in each major group is far more than that of listed firms and, ideally, we would like to take both types of firms into consideration. Unfortunately, unlisted firms in Canada provide little information to the public, so we have no readily available and comparable information about their primary industries or their sizes. Second, as mentioned earlier, some firms are conglomerates and they do not belong to any industry as classified by the input-output tables. This is obviously problematic. Third, some firms are larger than others, and

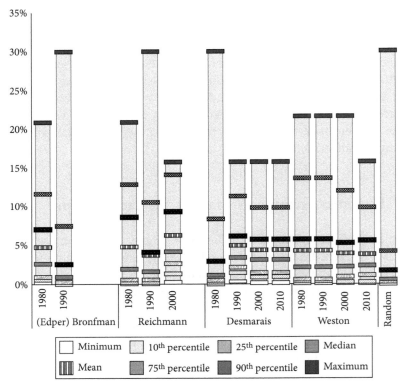

FIGURE 17.8. Vertical integration of major business groups.

Note: The vertical integration of each pair of firms is the average of share of the first firm's inputs that come from the second firm's industry and the share of the second firm's inputs that come from the first firm's industry. Vertical integration is measured for each possible pair of firms in each business group each year. The graph shows the distributional characteristics of these pairwise vertical integration measures within each group each year. The rightmost entry is the benchmark distribution of vertical integration between all industry pairs in the entire economy.

Source: Author's calculations based on figures from Statistics Canada's Inter-Corporate Ownership (ICO) and the Report on Business database.

characterize the distributions of each group's VI coefficients in terms of their means, medians, and other descriptive statistics.

If business groups were randomly selected collections of firms, the firms in them should be no more or less vertically integrated than are firms in the overall economy in general. As discussed previously, the mean and median VI coefficients for the entire economy over all years are 0.0179 and 0.0055, respectively. Neither figure varies much over time.

Figure 17.8 presents the distributional characteristics of each of the four most important family groups' vertical integration in 1980, 1990, 2000, and 2010. All four groups

some groups contain multiple firms in a given industry. A more precise approach would weight VI coefficients by the importance of each sector to each group. More technical econometric analysis capable of coping with these complications, at least to an extent, is beyond the scope of this chapter.

do operate in pairs of highly vertically integrated sectors, and the mean and median levels of vertical integration in all four groups are higher than would be expected if their member firms were drawn randomly from different industries. However, the groups appear to follow somewhat different diversification strategies. Immediately before the early 1990s recession and interest-rate spike, the average degrees of vertical integration were relatively low for Edper Bronfman and Reichmann compared with those for Desmarais and Weston. In more recent years, the two surviving groups—Desmarais and Weston—have both thrived on the back of focused-diversification strategy.

The Edper Bronfman and Reichmann groups were both relatively unintegrated vertically, and both collapsed in the early 1990s. Figure 17.3 shows the Edper Bronfman group spread out across unrelated industries in 1990. Through Hees International Bancorp, Edper controlled a large network of companies headed by Brascan (diversified) which formed Trilon Financial (financial), and acquired controlling interests in Noranda Inc. (mining) and John Labatt (liquor). Noranda, in turn, controlled Kerr Addison Mines (mining), Norcen Energy (petroleum), and MacMillan Bloedel (forestry). Through Carena Holdings, Edper Bronfman group also controlled several real estate companies, in particular Carena Properties, Trizec Corporation, and Bramalea Limited. Figure 17.4 shows a similarly broad diversification in the Reichmann group at the same time. Commercial real estate remained the core business, but the group also contained Abitibi-Price Inc. (pulp and paper), Gulf Canada Resources (petroleum), and Consumer's Gas (utilities). While the cement-making industry is highly vertically integrated with real estate development (VI = 0.1445), and pipeline transportation arguably supports the petroleum industry (VI = 0.0633), real estate and natural resources sectors are unrelated.

After gaining control of Power Corporation of Canada, Paul Desmarais extended his business group into ocean shipping, pulp and paper, and communications. The group's industrial configuration changed markedly after Paul's retirement in 1996. Figure 17.5 shows the group becoming more sharply focused on the financial sector between the early 1990s and 2010, most notably with the acquisitions of Canada Life Assurance in 2003 and Mackenzie Investments in 2001. Throughout, the core companies remain Power Corporation and Power Financial Corp and the number of industrial categories remains fairly stable, though their distribution in Figure 17.8 shifts towards less vertical integration in later decades.

Figure 17.6 shows the Weston group, after its 1970s divestitures and consolidations, comparatively focused on its core business: retailing. Successive generations preserved the group's key companies—George Weston Limited and Loblaw Companies Limited—and their focus. Like the Desmarais group, the Weston group kept to a roughly stable number of industries. The sole notable change is the group's expansion into commercial real estate (Super Center Development) and financial services (PC Financial Holdings), both of which are arguably relevant to retail. Also like the Desmarais group, the Weston group is shown to be have become less vertically integrated in more recent decades.

17.4.4 Business Groups as Financial Stabilizers

Hoshi, Kashyap, and Scharfstein (1991) posit that business group member firms co-insure each other against bankruptcy, letting group member firms carry higher debt loads than otherwise comparable independent firms could, while still comfortably surviving cyclical ups and downs.

The 1920s and 1930s were decades of exceptional economic volatility, in which stability might well have been a major advantage. Several major business groups that dominated 1920s Canada were indeed quite highly leveraged, e.g. BESCO, a large business group organized by Roy M. Wolvin with member firms in coal mining, steel, railways, and port operations. Another, Canadian General Investments, controlled by Prime Minister Arthur Meighan, was a multi-tiered pyramid assembled with transactions that Bliss (1987) describes, essentially correctly, as leveraged buyouts. The 1920s was a period of generally loose credit, so arguments about business group member firms co-insuring each other may not have been necessary to justify their high leverage.

In any case, both collapsed—BESCO just before the Crash of 1929 and CGI just after. Their member firms were bought up by other groups—for example, many of the former member firms of BESCO ended up as member firms of another business group, DOSCO, controlled by the industrialist C. B. McNaught. Their business group structures were apparently not up to the task of seeing them through such volatile times.

The Crash of 1929 and subsequent Great Depression were huge economy-wide shocks—the unemployment rate peaked at 27 percent in 1933. The epic of BESCO and DOSCO is not unique: other major business groups imploded, while yet other groups expanded by acquiring their debris. It seems likely that high leverage played a role in these implosions, though data needed to formally test this are unavailable. The Bronfman group grew rapidly during these decades with little need for debt financing: its sales of liquor to anonymous buyers at its distilleries near the US border during that country's Prohibition era provided ample earnings.

In the 1960s highly diversified pyramidal business groups—the Argus, BCE, and Canadian Pacific groups, for example—were commonly referred to as conglomerates. However, this is not strictly true because, unlike US conglomerates of the era, their individual member firms were usually quite focused. Massey Harris, though a member of the Argus pyramid, was a farm equipment manufacturer and nothing else. Public shareholders were offered the shares of undiversified Argus operating companies. Pyramidal groups with widely held apex firms, such as BCE and Canadian Pacific, also let public shareholders invest in their apex firms, whose assets were relatively undiversified physical assets plus relatively diversified intercorporate control chains. Neither Canadian organizational structure resembled a 1960s US public conglomerate—that is, with multiple operations in diverse industries organized as divisions or fully owned subsidiaries of a single listed entity.

The 1970s and 1980s were turbulent decades too, with oil price hikes bringing successive booms in the 1970s and an oil price collapse wreaking havoc in the late 1980s. However, in recent decades, when comparable financial data are readily available,

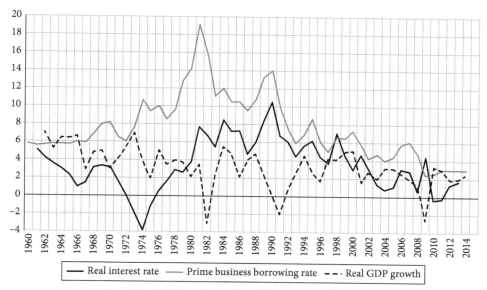

FIGURE 17.9. Interest rates and real GDP growth in Canada.
Source: Statistics Canada CANSIM database.

many of group member firms became remarkably more highly leveraged than comparable freestanding firms. For example, using 1980s data, Daniels et al. (1994) report a 32.6-
percent median debt-to-assets ratio for firms in the Edper Bronfman group, and contrast
this with an 18.5-percent debt-to-assets ratio for a size and industry matched set of
freestanding firms.

Canada's early 1990s recession featured high nominal interest rates and unprecedent-
edly high real interest rates, illustrated in Figure 17.9. Unable to sustain its debt load, the
Edpre Bronfman group collapsed in the 1990s. Another large business group, ultimately
controlled by the Reichmann family, also collapsed under an unsustainable debt load in
the 1990s, though the family later restored its standing by making good on its debts.

The Report on Business Corporate database (ROB), from which we source firm-level
financial leverage information, contains both text and numeric data on Canadian
companies (Tian, 2009). These data are reliable for Canadian companies included in
the TSX Composite Index from January 1985 onward. The most proximate ICO
directory to 1985 is for 1987, and the largest family-controlled groups identified in
the ICO 1987 were Edper Bronfman group, Desmarais group, Reichmann group, and
Weston group. For firms in each of these four groups that we are able to identify in
ROB, we retrieve their financial leverage data of roughly every four years over the
period 1987 to 2010. Financial leverage is defined as the ratio of total debt over total
asset. With regard to industries, similar to the analysis of corporate diversification
described previously, we use an input-output based industry classification system.

Figure 17.10 shows that business group affiliates were more levered than the median
firms for their industries. Panels A and B contrast the very high leverage levels for the

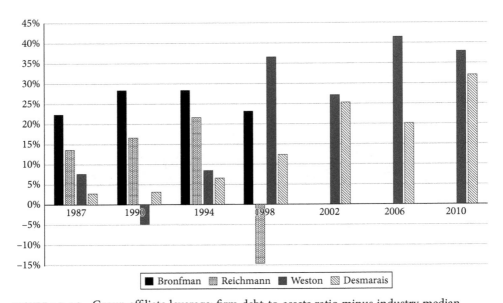

FIGURE 17.10. Group affiliate leverage: firm debt-to-assets ratio minus industry median.

Note: Debt-to-assets is total debt divided by total assets. Industry medians are based on listed firms, each assigned to one of 36 input-output industries.

Source: Author's calculations based on figures in Statistics Canada's Inter-corporate Ownership directories and the Report on Business database.

Edper Bronfman group affiliates (except for a pivotal listed holding company) with the far less levered firms of the Desmarais pyramid. Edper Bronfman group expanded very quickly in the 1970s and 1980s, diversifying into both real estate and natural resources. The economic downturn in the early 1990s hit both sectors pretty hard. Two unsustainably highly levered group firms in real estate failed—Bramalea in 1992 and its immediate parent company, Trizec, shortly thereafter. The once almighty Edper empire collapsed by the end of the twentieth century, and the Bronfman brothers and their heirs lost control of the group. Desmarais group was also extensively diversified during the 1980s, involved in transportation, pulp and paper, communications, and financial industries. However, prior to the early 1990s recession and its interest-rate spike, Paul Desmarais had sold Consolidated Bathurst and Montreal Trustco. Power Corporation of Canada was thus almost debt-free and sailed unscathed past the floundering Edper Branfman group.

Panel C plots the mean excess leverage—firm leverage minus median leverage for its industry—of listed group affiliates for the four major family-controlled groups. Those whose firms had more debt—Edper and Reichmann—perished, while those whose firms avoided over-leverage—Desmarais and Weston—survived.

The logic that healthy group member firms can help out their troubled sibling firms holds if bankruptcies are independent random events. Unfortunately, bankruptcies are highly correlated and countercyclical—they come in waves during recessions, especially recession with very high interest rates such as Canada's early 1990s downturn.

An economy-wide downturn hits many firms and sectors at once, and co-insurance offers no help when the whole group is afflicted. If group firms, deeming themselves immunized against bankruptcy, take on exceptionally high debt loads, the group's collapse is all the more spectacular when it comes. The Edper Bronfman and Reichmann groups were both highly diversified, and a belief that this allowed their higher leverage levels was obviously misplaced. Remarkably, Figure 17.10 shows both the Desmarais and Weston groups exhibiting markedly higher leverage in later years, even as Figure 17.8 shows their industrial conformations becoming less integrated, strategies reminiscent of the Edper Bronfman and Reichmann groups in the 1980s.

17.4.5 Political Economy and Business Groups

The Great Depression generated a remarkable popular backlash against business elites in the 1930s United States. That backlash let President Franklin Delano Roosevelt enact, as part of his New Deal, sweeping reforms that curtailed the power of business elites. Prominent among these reforms were measures explicitly designed to break up business groups: the taxation of dividends paid by one firm to another, restrictions on regulated utilities belonging to business groups, and the regulation of firms that owned shares in other firms as mutual funds (Morck, 2005). While the relative importance of these reforms is debated (Banks and Cheffins, 2010), pyramidal business groups in the United States rapidly faded away as the reforms took hold and became permanent fixtures of the institutional environment (Kandel et al., 2013).

Canada, by contrast, had no New Deal. Inter-corporate dividends remained untaxed, public utilities remained prominent in business groups, accounting and disclosure standards changed little until the 1960s, and firms whose assets were largely shares in other firms were not subject to significant additional regulation. Porter (1965) attributes these differences to Canadians' greater subservience to elites.

This may reflect Canada's unique status as a former colony of both France (1608–1759) and Britain (1759–1867). Canada is usually counted an Anglo-Saxon country. However, one in five Canadians speaks French as their first language; a French civil code is used in Quebec and in the Supreme Court of Canada; and senior government officials are influenced by French political and economic ideas.

French Canada was an inward-looking, devotedly Roman Catholic "solitude" until the 1960s, when the Quiet Revolution abruptly transformed the region into a skeptical, secular society with an elite intent on restoring ties with France and asserting its influence in Canada (Behiels, 1985).[11] Throughout the 1960s successive governments worked to bring French Canadians into ever more senior government positions. In 1968 Pierre Trudeau swept to power on a nationwide wave of support for bilingualism—the state-sanctioned restoration of the French language to national prominence. Until 1969 the language of government and business was English. After

---

[11] Hugh MacLennan's 1945 novel *Two Solitudes* coined the term.

1969 the Official Languages Act required the federal parliament, government departments, courts, and state-owned enterprises to provide services in both French and English everywhere. The Act further mandates that French and English have equal status as working languages in government offices in the national capital region and all regions with substantial French- and English-speaking populations, that French be their working language where the predominant language is French, and that English be their working language where the predominant language is English. English and French were also given equal status as languages of work within the federal public service in regions designated as bilingual, including the national capital region, Montreal, and New Brunswick, as well as in government offices abroad and in regions with sufficient demand for services in both official languages.

The need for fluent French speakers in government thus rose abruptly, but proficiency in French increased only gradually among anglophones. This necessitated the active recruitment of French Canadians, the great majority of whom were already bilingual, in the civil service. A new generation of civil servants read French newspapers, magazines, and books on political economy issues as students, and accepted French ideas about the role of the state in society (Nemni and Nemni, 2010).

The result was the transformation in the 1960s, 1970s, and early 1980s of an Anglo-Saxon liberal democracy into a European social democracy—with all the requisite taxes, business subsidy programs, state-owned enterprises, and industrial policy (Bliss, 1987; English, 2010; Cohen and Granatstein, 2011). Figure 17.11 plots the changing extent of state intervention in the economy, and shows a clear peak in these years, followed by a retreat of the state as the initial enthusiasm for French and European ideas gave way to a renewed confidence in free markets under Trudeau's successors. Figure 17.2 shows a similar pattern, with state-owned enterprises attaining maximal importance in the late 1970s.

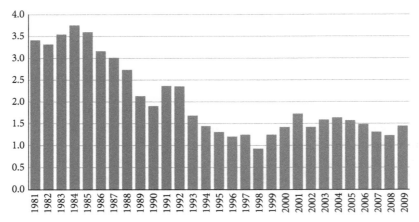

FIGURE 17.11. Government subsidies to private sector businesses, state-owned enterprises, and consumers as percentage of GDP in Canada.

Source: Statistics Canada as reported in Milke (2014).

European-influenced policies were ascendant for a substantial period. One industrial policy initiative, the National Energy Program (MacDonald, 2004), expropriated foreign-owned oilfields and provided substantial subsidies to oil companies that were certifiably Canadian owned. This forced remaining foreign controlling shareholders to sell their stakes in oil companies, and the largest of these that were not nationalized ended up as cash cows in abruptly swelling family business groups—notably those of the Reichmanns and Edper Bronfmans. These transactions are evident in Figure 17.2 as an abrupt drop in foreign-owned firms in the early to mid-1980s.

Morck and Yeung (2004) develop a series of arguments suggesting that the families controlling large business groups are uniquely advantaged in political rent-seeking, the term Krueger (1974) coins for legally investing in political connections. Overt favor trading, where a politician favors a firm that does her a favor in return, is illegal in Canada. However, business groups let the favor-receiving firm and the favor-returning firm be entirely different. Moreover, the long-standing wealth of the controlling families lets politicians wait for their return favor with a high degree of confidence that it will in fact be returned. Though she does not highlight business groups, Krueger (1974) argues that such favor-trading is legal in many contexts, and is part of normal business practice to varying degrees in every country. That the old-moneyed families in charge of the country's largest business groups might have been uniquely well positioned to profit from this abrupt intrusion of the state into the economy seems a reasonable explanation for the equally abrupt increase in the importance of business groups in precisely these years. That business groups did not regain prominence after the collapse of the Bronfman and Reichmann groups is also consistent with politicians downgrading their confidence in controlling families being able to return favors.

Prime Minister Pierre Trudeau, heir to a minor Quebec business group, also abolished the federal inheritance tax in 1972, replacing it with an estate tax (capital gains tax realization on death). After 1974 these became deferrable for a generation or more via expensive and complicated family trust arrangements. By contrast, US inheritance taxes remained high and largely unavoidable throughout these decades, though US President George W. Bush suspended them briefly. Accounts of Canadian business family successions suggest that inheritance tax played a major role in the downsizing of early twentieth-century business groups (Morck, Tian, and Yeung, 2005). Moreover, the abolition of inheritance tax roughly coincides with the beginning of the resurgence of business groups in Figures 17.1 and 17.2. In one case, a branch of the Bronfman family obtained an unprecedented, and never repeated, waiver of all capital gains taxes due on such a family trust.

The extent and distribution of subsidies to businesses are carefully guarded state secrets, so the reliance of business group firms, or any other firms, on political connections is difficult to assess. However, successive governments, especially those led by prime ministers Jean Chrétien and Stephen Harper, adopted much more liberal economic policies. That political connections decayed in value during this period is certainly plausible. If business groups relied on such connections, their ebbing in these years is also explained.

17.5. CONCLUSIONS

The business groups that dominated the economy at the beginning of the twentieth century may well have resembled those in successfully emerging economies, such as South Korea and Taiwan, at the century's end. Data sufficiently detailed to confirm this empirically are unavailable, but the structure and industrial portfolio composition of group firms is consistent with their allocating capital across mutually interdependent firms in related newly forming industries. These business groups faded away by the middle of the century, consistent with the completion of the country's industrialization having rendered them obsolete.

The second wave of business groups that arose in the 1970s and 1980s contained firms that were not especially vertically integrated, nor did they allocate capital to new high-technology firms to any great degree. Rather, these groups' industrial portfolio seems more consistent with broad industrial diversification to reduce risk. Risk reduction via diversification is more effective in more developed economies (Morck et al., 2000; 2013), but pyramiding, especially highly leveraged pyramiding, magnifies risk. The two largest such groups, the Edper Bronfman and Reichmann groups, became increasingly highly leveraged in these years, perhaps theorizing that such wide-ranging diversification reduces risk enough to make higher debt loads sustainable. In fact, both groups collapsed in a brief recession in the early 1990s that featured very high interest rates. The two groups that survived this episode, the Desmarais and Weston groups, were substantially less levered and their member firms were more integrated vertically. However, both groups subsequently grew less vertically integrated and took on higher debt after the 1990s.

The second wave of business groups corresponds to an abrupt change in political economy: Canada's transformation from a liberal democracy into a social democracy. The 1970s and early 1980s saw a rapid and far-reaching expansion of state intervention, the adoption of European-style industrial policies with high taxes and complicated systems of business subsidies, and the introduction of French notions about the role of the state into the country's political discourses by newly assertive French Canadian politicians. We posit that this made political connections more valuable for a time, and that business groups were uniquely well positioned to flourish in this political economy environment. From the 1990s on, Anglo-Saxon concepts of the role of the state regained standing, industrial policies were scrapped, and more liberal economic policies took their place. We posit that business groups' advantages faded in this environment.

ACKNOWLEDGMENTS

We are grateful for very helpful comments from Asli M. Colpan, Takashi Hikino, and participants in Kyoto University's conference on Business Groups in Developed Economies. We are grateful to the Bank of Canada for partial funding.

REFERENCES

Acharya, V. V., Gottschalg, O. F., Hahn, M., and Kehoe, C. 2013. "Corporate Governance and Value Creation: Evidence from Private Equity," *Review of Financial Studies*, 26 (2): 368–402.

Actualidad Económica. 2012. "Grupos," *Actualidad Económica*, December, 2012: 12–26.

Aganin, A., and Volpin, P. 2005. "The History of Corporate Ownership in Italy," in R. Morck (ed.), *The Global History of Corporate Governance*. Chicago: University of Chicago Press: 325–61.

Agnblad, J., Berglof, E., Högfeldt, P., and Svancar, H. 2001. "Ownership and Control in Sweden: Strong Owners, Weak Minorities, and Social Control," in F. Barca and M. Becht (eds.), *The Control of Corporate Europe*. Oxford: Oxford University Press: 228–58.

Ahlstrom, D., and Bruton, G. D. 2004. "Guest Editors' Introduction to Special Issue. Turnaround in Asia: Laying the Foundation for Understanding This Unique Domain," *Asia Pacific Journal of Management*, 21 (1–2): 5–24.

Ahmadjian, C., and Lincoln, J. 2001. "Keiretsu, Governance, and Learning: Case Studies in Change from the Japanese Automobile Industry," *Organization Science*, 12: 683–701.

Ahrens, R., Gehlen, B., and Reckendrees, A. 2013. "Die Deutschland AG als Historischer Forschungsgegenstand," in R. Ahrens, B. Gehlen, and A. Reckendrees (eds.), *Die "Deutschland AG." Historische Annäherungen an den Bundesdeutschen Kapitalismus*. Essen: Klartext: 7–30.

Alexander, M., Murray, G., and Houghton, J. 1994. "Business Power in Australia: the Concentration of Company Directorship Holding Among the Top 250 Corporates," *Australian Journal of Political Science*, 29: 40–61.

Almeida, H., and Wolfenzon, D. 2006a. "A Theory of Pyramidal Ownership and Family Business Groups," *Journal of Finance*, 61 (6): 2637–80.

Almeida, H., and Wolfenzon, D. 2006b. "Should Business Groups Be Dismantled? The Equilibrium Costs of Efficient Internal Capital Markets," *Journal of Financial Economics*, 79 (1): 99–144.

Almeida, H., Park, S., Subrahmanyam, M., and Wolfenzon, D. 2010. "The Structure and Formation of Business Groups: Evidence from Korean Chaebols," *Journal of Financial Economics*, 99: 447–75.

Amaral, L. 2010. *Economia Portuguesa: As Últimas Décadas*. Lisbon: Relógio d'Água/Fundação Francisco Manuel dos Santos.

Amaral, L. 2013. "Imperfect but True Competition: Innovation and Profitability in Portuguese Banking During the Golden Age (1950–1973)," *Financial History Review*, 20 (3): 305–33.

Amatori, F. 1997. "Growth via Politics: Business Groups Italian Style," in T. Shiba and M. Shimotani (eds.), *Beyond the Firm. Business Groups in International and Historical Perspective*. Oxford: Oxford University Press: 109–34.

Amatori, F., and Bezza, B. (eds.). 1990. *Montecatini. Capitoli di Storia di Una Grande Impresa.* Bologna: Il Mulino.

Amatori, F., and Colli, A. 1999. *Impresa e Industria in Italia dall'Unità ad Oggi.* Venice: Marsilio.

Amatori, F., and Colli, A. 2011. *Business History. Complexities and Comparisons.* London: Routledge.

Ammann, M., Hoechle, D., and Schmid, M. 2012. "Is there Really No Conglomerate Discount?" *Journal of Business Finance & Accounting,* 39 (1–2): 264–88.

Amsden, A. 1992. *Asia's Next Giant: South Korea and Late Industrialization.* Oxford: Oxford University Press.

Anand, B. N. 2005, 2016. Lecture on "Strategies of Multi-Business Firms."

Anand, B. N. 2012. "Corporate Strategy." *Harvard Business School Module Note,* 713–415.

Anand, B. N., and Byzalov, D. 2011. "Systematic Heterogeneity versus Average Effects in the Returns to Diversification," Working Paper.

Anand, B. N., Collis, D. J., and Hood, S. 2008, rev. 2015. "Danaher Corporation," Harvard Business School Case, no. 708–445.

Anand, B. N., and Jayanti, S. P. 2005. "Strategies of Unrelated Diversification." Harvard Business School Background Note, no. 705–480.

Ancona, D., Kochan, F., Scully, M., Van Maanen, J., and Westney, D. 1996. "Module 1: The New Organization," in Ancona, D.G. (ed.), *Managing for the Future: Organizational Behavior and Processes.* Cincinnati, OH: South-Western College Publishing: 1–30.

Andrieu, C., Le Van, L., and Prost, A. 1987. *Les Nationalisations de la Libération. De l'Utopie au Compromise.* Paris: Presses de Sciences-Po.

Arbour, P. 1993. *Québec Inc. and the Temptation of State Capitalism* (translated by M. Hébert). Montreal: Robert Davies Publishing.

Armstrong, C. 2015. *Moose Pastures and Mergers: The Ontario Securities Commission and the Regulation of Share Markets in Canada, 1940–1980.* Toronto: University of Toronto Press.

Asanuma, B. 1985. "Manufacturer–Supplier Relationships and the Concept of Relation-Specific Skill," *Journal of the Japanese and International Economies,* 3: 1–30.

Bagnal, J. 2013. *100 Days: The Rush to Judgement that Killed Nortel.* New York: HarperCollins.

Baker, G., and Montgomery, C. 1994. "Conglomerates and LBO Associations: A Comparison of Organizational Forms," Harvard Business School Working Paper, no. 10–024.

Banks, S. A., and Cheffins, B. R. 2010. "The Corporate Pyramid Fable." *Business History Review,* 84 (3): 435–58.

Barca, F., et al. (eds.). 1994. *Assetti Proprietari e Mercato delle Imprese.* 2 vols., Bologna: Il Mulino.

Barca, F., and Becht, M. (eds.). 2001. *The Control of Corporate Europe.* Oxford: Oxford University Press.

Barca F., and Böhmer, E. 2001. "Ownership and Voting Power in Germany," in F. Barca and M. Becht (eds.), *The Control of Corporate Europe.* Oxford: Oxford University Press: 128–52.

Barca, F., and Mayer, C. 2001. "Introduction," in F. Barca and M. Becht (eds.), *The Control of Corporate Europe.* Oxford: Oxford University Press: 1–45.

Barendregt, J., and Visser, H. 2009. "Towards a New Maturity, 1940-1990," in M. 't Hart, J. Jonker, and J. L. van Zanden (eds.), *A Financial History of The Netherlands.* Cambridge: Cambridge University Press: 152–95.

Barjot, D. 1992. "Francis Bouygues: L'Ascension d'un Entrepreneur (1952–1989)," *Vingtième Siècle, Revue d'Histoire*, no. 35.

Barnard, A. 1961. *Visions and Profits: Studies in the Business Career of Thomas Sutcliffe Mort*. Melbourne: Melbourne University Press.

Barney, J. B. 1991. "Firm Resources and Sustained Competitive Advantage," *Journal of Management*, 17 (1): 99–120.

Barry, P. 1990. *The Rise and Fall of Alan Bond*. Sydney: Bantam Books.

Bartlett, C. A., and Ghoshal, S. 1989. *Managing across Borders: The Transnational Solution*. Boston, MA: Harvard Business School Press.

Bartlett, C. A., and Ghoshal, S. 1993. "Beyond the M-form: Toward a Managerial Theory of the Firm," *Strategic Management Journal*, 14 (S2): 23–46.

Bartlett, C. A., and Wozny, M. 1999, rev. 2005. "GE's Two-Decade Transformation: Jack Welch's Leadership." Harvard Business School Case, no. 399-150.

Barucci, E., and Pierobon, F. 2007. *Le Privatizzazioni in Italia*. Rome: Carocci.

Battiau, M. 1976. *Les Industries Textiles de la Région du Nord Pas-de-Calais: Etude d'une Concentration Géographique d'Entreprises et de sa Remise en Cause*. Lille: Service de Reproduction des Thèses.

Battilani, P., and Schröter, H. G. (eds.). 2012. *The Cooperative Business Movement, 1950 to the Present*. Cambridge: Cambridge University Press.

Battilani, P., and Zamagni, V. 2010. "Co-operatives (1951–2001)," in A. Colli and M. Vasta (eds.), *Forms of Enterprises in 20th Century Italy. Boundaries, Structures and Strategies*. Cheltenham: Elgar: 273–93.

Battilani, P., and Zamagni, V. 2012. "The Managerial Transformation of Italian Co-operative Enterprises 1946–2010," *Business History*, 54 (6): 964–85.

Bauer, M., and Cohen, E. 1981. *Qui Gouverne les Groupes Industriels?* Paris: Le Seuil.

BBVA. (Various years). Annual reports, http://shareholdersandinvestors.bbva.com/TLBB/ tlbb/bbvair/ing/financials/reports/index.jsp, accessed September 13, 2013.

Beaud, M., Bellon, B., Lévy, A. M., Liénart, S. 1978. *Dictionnaire des Groupes Industriels et Financiers en France*. Paris: Editions du Seuil.

Becht, M., and DeLong, J. B. 2005. "Why Has There Been So Little Block Holding in America?" in Morck, R. (ed.), *A History of Corporate Governance Around the World: Family Business Groups to Professional Managers*. Chicago: University of Chicago Press.

Beckman, C., Haunschild, P., and Philips, D. 2004. "Friends or Strangers? Firm-Specific Uncertainty, Market Uncertainty, and Network Partner Selection," *Organization Science*, 15: 259–75.

Beckmann, P. 2006. *Der Diversifikations-Discount am Deutschen Kapitalmarkt*, Wiesbaden: Deutscher Universitäts-Verlag/GWV Fachverlage GmbH.

Behiels, M. 1985. *Prelude to Quebec's Quiet Revolution: Liberalism Vs Neo-Nationalism, 1945–60*. Montreal: McGill-Queen's University Press.

Belenzon, S., and Berkovitz, T. 2008. "Business Group Affiliation, Financial Development and Market Structure: Evidence from Europe," http://papers.ssrn.com/sol3/papers.cfm? abstract_id=1086882.

Belenzon, S., and Berkovitz, T. 2010. "Innovation in Business Groups." *Management Science*, 56 (3): 519–35.

Belenzon, S., Berkovitz, T., and Rios, L. 2013. "Capital Markets and Firm Organization: How Financial Development Shapes European Corporate Groups," *Management Science*, 59.6: 1326–43.

Belenzon, S., Patacconi, A., and Zelner, B. A. 2012. "Identifying Archetypes: an Empirical Study of Business Group Structure in 16 Developed Economies," https://faculty.fuqua. duke.edu/~sb135/bio/BPZ%20Final%2012_3_12.pdf.

Belenzon, S., and Tsolmon, U. 2016. "Market Frictions and the Competitive Advantage of Internal Labor Markets," *Strategic Management Journal*, 37 (7): 1280–1303.

Belmonte, A. 1999. "La Banca Toca Techo en su Estrategia Industrial (Banks Reach the Limits of Their Industrial Strategy)," *El Mundo, Su Dinero*, 181, July 18, 1999, http://www. elmundo.es/su-dinero/99/SD181/SD181-06.html, accessed November 7, 2014.

Beltran, A. 2002. *L'Électricité dans la Région Parisienne 1878–1946*. Paris: Rive Droite.

Beltrán Tapia, F. J. 2012. "Commons, Social Capital, and the Emergence of Agricultural Cooperatives in Early Twentieth Century Spain," *European Review of Economic History*, 16: 511–28.

Benedetti, E., and Toniolli, M. 1963. "Concentrazione Industriale e Potere di Disposizione," *Rivista Internazionale di Scienze Economiche e Commerciali*, 10: 633–52.

Berg, N. A. 1969. "What's Different about Conglomerate Management?" *Harvard Business Review*, 47 (6): 112–20.

Berger, P. G., and Ofek, E. 1995. "Diversification's Effect on Firm Value," in *Journal of Financial Economics*, 37 (1): 39–65.

Berglöf, E. 1990. "Capital Structure as a Mechanism of Control: A Comparison of Financial Systems," in M. Aoki, B. Gustavsson, and O. Williamson (eds.), *The Firm as a Nexus of Treaties*. Newbury Park, CA: Sage.

Bernard, A. B., Redding, S. J., and Schott, P. K. 2010. "Multiple-Product Firms and Product Switching," *American Economic Review*, 100 (1): 70–97.

Berneron-Couvenhes, M.-F. 2007. *Les Messageries Maritimes. L'Essor d'une Grande Compagnie de Navigation Française—1851–1894*. Paris: Presses de l'Université de Paris-Sorbonne.

Bernstein, S., Lerner, J., Sorensen, M., and Stromberg, P. 2015. "Private Equity and Industry Performance," *Management Science*, 63 (4): 1198–213.

Bertrand, M., Mehta, P., and Mullainathan, S. 2002. "Ferreting Out Tunneling: An Application to Indian Business Groups," *Quarterly Journal of Economics*, 117: 121–48.

Bianchi, M., Bianco, M., and Enriques, L. 2001. "Pyramidal Groups and the Separation Between Ownership and Control in Italy," in F. Barca, and M. Becht (eds.), *The Control of Corporate Europe*. Oxford: Oxford University Press.

Bianchi, M., Bianco, M., Giacomelli, S., Pacces, M., and Trento, S. 2005. *Proprietà e Controllo delle Imprese in Italia*. Bologna: Il Mulino.

Binda, V. 2013. *The Dynamics of Big Business: Structure, Strategy, and Impact in Italy and Spain*. New York: Routledge.

Bishel, W. 1996. "Fall from Grace: US Business Interests versus US Diplomatic Interests in Peru, 1885–1890," *Diplomatic History*, 20 (2): 163–84.

Blainey, G. 1966. *The Tyranny of Distance*. Melbourne: Sun Books.

Blázquez, S. 2014. "Las Cooperatives Toman el Mando (Cooperatives Take Charge)," *El Pais*, May 25, 2014: 14.

Bliss, M. 1987. *Northern Enterprise: Five Centuries of Canadian Business*. Toronto: McClelland and Stewart.

Bloemen, E. S. A., Fransen, A. W., Kok, J., and van Zanden, J. L. 1993. "De Vermogensontwikkeling van Nederlands Grootste Industriële Bedrijven. 1913–1950," *Jaarboek voor de Geschiedenis van Bedrijf en Techniek*, 10: 133–61.

Bloemen, E. S. A., Kok, J., and van Zanden, J. L. 1993. *De Top 100 van Industriële Bedrijven in Nederland 1913–1990*. The Hague: AWT.

Blomqvist, P. 2004. "The Choice Revolution: Privatization of Swedish Welfare Services in the 1990s," *Social Policy & Administration*, 38 (2): 139–55.

Boelaert, S., and Bonucci, N. 1988. "An Italian Raid on an Old Belgian Lady," *International Financial Law Review*, 7: 21.

Bolt, J., and van Zanden, J. L. 2014. "The Maddison Project: Collaborative Research on Historical National Accounts," *Economic History Review*, 67 (3): 627–51.

Bonacich, P. 1987. "Power and Centrality: A Family of Measures," *American Journal of Sociology*, 92: 1170–82.

Bonbright, J., and Means, G. 1932. *The Holding Company: Its Public Significance and its Regulation*. New York: McGraw-Hill.

Bonelli, F. 1975. *Lo Sviluppo di una Grande Impresa in Italia. La Terni dal 1884 al 1962*. Turin: Einaudi.

Bonelli, F. (ed.) 1982. *Acciaio per l'Industrializzazione. Contributi allo Studio del Problema Siderurgico Italiano*. Turin: Einaudi.

Bonin, H. 1987. *Suez, du Canal à la Finance, 1858–1987*. Paris: Economica.

Bonin, J. P., Jones, D. C., and Putterman, L. 1993. "Theoretical and Empirical Studies of Producer Cooperatives: Will Ever the Twain Meet?" *Journal of Economic Literature*, 31: 1290–320.

Borland, J. 2015. "Microeconomic Reform," in S. Ville and G. Withers (eds.), *The Cambridge Economic History of Australia*. Cambridge: Cambridge University Press.

Borsa, M. 1992. *Capitani di Sventura. Agnelli, De Benedetti, Romiti, Ferruzzi, Gardini, Pirelli: Perché Rischiano di Farci Perdere la Sfida degli Anni '90*. Milan: Mondadori.

Boussemart, B. and Rabier, J. C. 1983. *Le Dossier Agache-Willot: Un Capitalisme à Contre-courant*. Paris: Presses de Sciences-Po.

Bouvier, J. 1983. *Les Rothschild*, 2nd ed. Brussels: Editions Complexe.

Bouwens, B., and Dankers, J. 2010. "The Invisible Handshake: Cartelization in the Netherlands, 1950–2000," *Business History Review*, 84 (4): 751–71.

Bower, T. 2008. *Branson*. London: Harper Perennial.

Boyce, G., and Ville, S. 2002. *The Development of Modern Business*. Basingstoke: Palgrave.

Boyd, B. K., and Hoskisson, R. E. 2010. "Corporate Governance of Business Groups," in A. M. Colpan, T. Hikino, and J. R. Lincoln. (eds.), *Oxford Handbook of Business Groups*. Oxford: Oxford University Press: 670–95.

Brander, J. A., Egan, E. and Hellmann, T. F. 2010. "Government Sponsored versus Private Venture Capital: Canadian Evidence," in J. Lerner and A. Schoar (eds.), *International Differences in Entrepreneurship*. Calgary: University of Chicago Press.

Branstetter, L., and Sakakibara, M. 2002. "When Do Research Consortia Work Well and Why? Evidence from Japanese Panel Data," *American Economic Review*, 92: 143–59.

Brimson, S. 1987. *Ansett, the Story of an Airline*. Sydney: Dreamweaver Books.

Brinton, W. C. 1914. *Graphic Methods for Presenting Facts*. New York: Engineering Magazine Company: 13.

Brion, R., and J-L. Moreau, *La Société générale de Belgique 1822–1997*. 1999. Brussels: Fonds Mercator.

Brioschi, F., Buzzacchi, L., and Colombo, M. 1990. *Gruppi di Imprese e Mercato Finanziario*. Rome: NIS.

Brito, J. M. B. 1989. *A Industrialização Portuguesa no Pós-Guerra (1948–1965)*. Lisbon: Publicações D. Quixote.

Broadberry, S. N., and Crafts, N. F. R. 1992. "Britain's Productivity Gap in the 1930s: Some Neglected Factors," *Journal of Economic History*, 52 (3): 531–58.

Broberg, O. 2006. *Konsten att Skapa Pengar. Aktiebolagens Genombrott och Finansiella Modernisering Kring Sekelskiftet 1900*. Gothenburg: Göteborgs Universitet.

Brummer, A., and Cowe, R. 1994. *Hanson: The Rise and Rise of Britain's Most Buccaneering Businessman*. London: Fourth Estate.

Bruton, H. J. 1998. "A Reconsideration of Import Substitution," *Journal of Economic Literature*, 36 (2): 903–36.

Bucheli, M. 2003. "United Fruit Company in Latin America," in S. Striffler and M. Moberg (eds.), *Banana Wars: Power, Production, and History in the Americas*. Durham: Duke University Press.

Bucheli, M. 2005. *Bananas and Business: The United Fruit Company in Colombia, 1899–2000*. New York: New York University Press.

Bucheli, M., Mahoney, J., and Vaaler, P. 2010. "Chandler's Living History: The *Visible Hand* of Vertical Integration in Nineteenth Century America Viewed Under a Twenty-First Transaction Costs Economics Lens," *Journal of Management Studies*, 47 (5): 859–83.

Bud-Frierman, L., Godley, A., and Wale, J. 2010. "Weetman Pearson in Mexico and the Emergence of a British Oil Major, 1901–1919," *Business History Review*, 84: 275–300.

Bull, B., Castellacci, F., and Kasahara, Y. 2014. *Business Groups and Transnational Capitalism in Central America: Economic and Political Strategies*. Basingstoke: Palgrave Macmillan.

Bunkanwanicha, P., Gupta, J. P., and Wiwattanakantang, Y. 2014. "Family Business Groups and Organizational Structure: A Study of Bank Pyramidal Ownership in Thailand," European Corporate Governance Institute, Finance Working Paper No. 434.

Burgess, E. W., and Harbison, F. 1954. *Casa Grace in Peru*. Washington: National Planning Association.

Burns, T. and Stalker, G. 1961. *The Management of Innovation*. London: Tavistock.

Burt, R. 1992. *Structural Holes: the Social Structure of Competition*. Cambridge, MA: Harvard University Press.

Büschgen, H. E. 1983. *Die Großbanken*, Frankfurt am Main: Knapp.

Bussière, E. 1992. *Paribas. L'Europe et le Monde, 1872–1992*. Antwerp: Fonds Mercator.

Bussière, E. 2003. "The French 'Banques d'Affaires' in the Interwar Period: the Case of the Banque de Paris et des Pays-Bas (Paribas)," in M. Kasuya, *Coping with Crisis. International Financial Institutions in the Interwar Period*, Oxford: Oxford University Press.

Butler, C., and Keary, J. 2000. *Managers and Mantras. One Company's Struggle for Simplicity*. Singapore: John Wiley.

Butlin, N. G. 1959. "Colonial Socialism in Australia," in H. G. J. Aitken (ed.), *The State and Economic Growth: Papers of a Conference Held on October 11–13, 1956 under the Auspices of the Committee on Economic Growth*, Social Science Research Council.

Butlin, N. G., Barnard, A., and Pincus, J. J. 1982. *Government and Capitalism: Public and Private Choice in Twentieth Century Australia*. Sydney: George Allen & Unwin.

Buyst, E., Cassiers, I., Houtman-de Smedt, H., Kurgan-van Hentenryk, G., van Meerten, M., and Vanthemsche, G. 1998. *La Générale de Banque (1822–1997)*. Brussels: Editions Racine.

Byrne, J. 1993. "The Horizontal Corporation," *Business Week*, December 20, 1993: 80–1.

Caeiro, J. M. C. 2004. *Elites e Poder: os Grupos Económicos em Portugal do Estado Novo à Actualidade*. Lisbon: Universidade Lusíada.

Cahn, A., and Donald, D. C. 2010. *Comparative Company Law: Text and Cases on the Law Governing Corporations in Germany, the UK and the USA*. Cambridge: Cambridge University Press.

Campa, J. M., and Kedia, S. 2002. "Explaining the Diversification Discount," in *Journal of Finance*, 57 (4): 1731–62.

Campbell, E. W. 1963. *The 60 Rich Families Who Own Australia*. Sydney: Current Book Distributors.

Cancelo Alonso, A. 1999. "Mondragón Corporación Cooperativa. 'Historia de una Experiencia' (Mondragón Cooperative Corporation. The History of an Experience)," *Revista Internacional de Estudios Vascos*, 44: 323–57.

Canha, I., and Fernandes, F. S. 2011. *Champalimaud. Construtor de Impérios*. Lisbon: A Esfera dos Livros.

Cannadine, D. 2006. *Mellon: An American Life*. New York: A. A. Knopf.

Cannon, M. 1966. *The Land Boomers*. Melbourne: Melbourne University Press.

Cardoso, J. L. 2012. "The Great Depression in Portugal: diagnoses and remedies," in M. Psalidopoulos (ed.), *The Great Depression in Europe: Economic Thought and Policy in a National Context*. Athens: Alpha Bank: 361–93.

Carlsson, R. 2007. "Swedish Corporate Governance and Value Creation: Owners Still in the Driver's Seat," *Corporate Governance: An International Review*, 15 (6): 1038–55.

Carney, M. 2005. "Corporate Governance and Competitive Advantage in Family-controlled Firms," *Entrepreneurship Theory and Practice*, 29 (3): 249–65.

Carney, M., and Gedajlovic, E. 2002. "The Co-evolution of Institutional Environments and Organizational Strategies: The Rise of Family Business Groups in the ASEAN Region," *Organization Studies*, 23 (1): 1–29.

Caron, F. 1997–2005. *Histoire des Chemins de Fer en France*, 2 vols. Paris: Fayard.

Carosso, V. P. 1970. *Investment Banking in America: A History*. Cambridge, MA: Harvard University Press.

Carosso, V. P. 1987. *The Morgans: Private International Bankers, 1854–1913*. Cambridge, MA: Harvard University Press.

Carreras, A., Tafunel, X., and Torres, E. 2008. "The Rise and Decline of Spanish State-owned Firms," in P. M. Toninelli (ed.) *The Rise and Fall of State-owned Enterprise in the Western World*. New York: Cambridge University Press.

Cassis, Y. 1997. *Big Business. The European Experience in the Twentieth Century*. Oxford: Oxford University Press.

Cassis, Y. 2011. *Crises and Opportunities. The Shaping of Modern Finance*. Oxford: Oxford University Press.

Cassis, Y., Colli, A., and Schröter, H. G. (eds). 2016. *The Performance of European Enterprise during the 20th Century*. Oxford: Oxford University Press.

Cayez, P. 1989. *Rhône-Poulenc. 1895–1975*, Paris: Armand Colin.

Chalmin, P. 1987. "The Rise of International Commodity Trading Companies in Europe in the Nineteenth Century," in S. Yonekawa, *Business History of General Trading Companies*. Tokyo: Tokyo University Press.

Chandler, A. D., Jr. 1962. *Strategy and Structure: Chapters in the History of the American Industrial Enterprise*. Cambridge, MA: MIT Press.

Chandler, A. D., Jr. 1977. *The Visible Hand: the Managerial Revolution in American Business*. Cambridge, MA: Belknap Press.

Chandler, A. D., Jr. 1982a. "The M-form: Industrial Groups, American Style," *European Economic Review*, 19 (1): 3–23.

Chandler, A. D., Jr. 1982b. "Evolution of the Large Industrial Corporation: An Evolution of the Transaction Costs Approach," *Business and Economic History*, 11: 116–35.

Chandler, A. D., Jr. (with Hikino, T.) 1990. *Scale and Scope: the Dynamics of Industrial Capitalism*. Cambridge, MA: Belknap Press.

Chandler, A. D., Jr. 1991. "The Functions of the HQ Unit in the Multibusiness Firm," *Strategic Management Journal*, special issue: "Fundamental Research Issues in Strategy and Economics," 12: 31–50.

Chandler, A. D., Jr. 1992. "Organizational Capabilities and the Economic History of the Industrial Enterprise," *Journal of Economic Perspectives*, 6 (3): 79–100.

Chandler, A. D. Jr., and Hikino, T. 1997. "The Large Industrial Enterprise and the Dynamics of Modern Economic Growth," in A. D. Chandler, Jr., F. Amatori, and T. Hikino (eds.), *Big Business and the Wealth of Nations*. Cambridge: Cambridge University Press: 24–57.

Chang, S. J. 2003. *Financial Crisis and Transformation Korean Business Groups: The Rise and Fall of Chaebols*. New York: Cambridge University Press.

Chang, S. J., and Hong, J. 2000. "Economic Performance of Group-affiliated Companies in Korea: Intragroup Resource Sharing and Internal Business," *Academy of Management Journal*, 43: 429–48.

Channon, D. F. 1973. *The Strategy and Structure of British Enterprise*. London: Macmillan Press.

Chapman, S. D. 1985. "British-based Investment Groups before 1914," *Economic History Review* 38 (2): 230–47.

Chapman, S. D. 1992. *Merchant Enterprise in Britain*. Cambridge: Cambridge University Press.

Chaves, R., Soler, F., and Sajardo, A. 2008. "Co-operative Governance: The Case of Spanish Credit Co-operatives," *Journal of Co-operative Studies*, 41 (2): 30–7.

Cheffins, B. R. 2008. *Corporate Ownership and Control. British Business Transformed*. Oxford: Oxford University Press.

Cheffins, B. R., and Armour, J. 2007. "The Eclipse of Private Equity," *European Corporate Governance Institute*, Working Paper Series in Law no. 82.

Chernow, R. 1993. *The House of Morgan: An American Banking Dynasty and the Rise of Modern Finance*. New York: Simon & Schuster.

Chittoor, R., Kale, P., and Puranam, P. 2015. "Business Groups in Developing Capital Markets: Towards a Complementarity Perspective." *Strategic Management Journal*, 36: 1277–96.

Chittoor, R., Narain, A., Vyas, R., and Tolia, C. 2013. "Creating a Corporate Advantage: The Case of the Tata Group," Indian School of Business, case no. ISB005.

Chlepner, B. S. 1930. *Le Marché Financier Belge Depuis Cent Ans*. Brussels: Falk Fils.

Chung, J., Sensoy, B. A., Stern, L., and Weisbach, M. S. 2012. "Pay for Performance from Future Fund Flows: the Case of Private Equity," *Review of Financial Studies*, 25 (11): 3259–304.

Cinco Dias. 2003. "Rumasa Aún Colea Cuatro Lustros Después (Rumasa Still Alive Twenty Years Later)," *Cinco Dias*, February 22, 2003, http://cincodias.com/cincodias/2003/02/22/empresas/1045924787_850215.html, accessed November 6, 2014.

Clark, J. 2012. *Mondo Agnelli: Fiat, Crysler, and the Power of a Dynasty*. Hoboken, NJ: John Wiley & Sons, Inc.

Clarke, F., Dean, G., and Oliver, K. 2003. *Corporate Collapse. Accounting, Regulatory and Ethical Failure.* Cambridge: Cambridge University Press.

Clarke, T. (ed.). 2007. *Theories of Corporate Governance.* London/New York: Routledge.

Clayton, L. 1999. *Peru and the United States: The Condor and the Eagle.* Athens, GA: University of Georgia Press.

Coase, R. H. 1937. "The Nature of the Firm," *Economica,* 4 (16), 386–405.

Cohen, A., and Granatstein, J. L. 2011. *Trudeau's Shadow: The Life and Legacy of Pierre Elliott Trudeau.* Toronto: Random House.

Colli, A. 2013. "La Grande Stagione dell'IRI," in F. Amatori. (ed.), *Il Miracolo Economico e il Ruolo dell'IRI 1949–1972,* Bari: Laterza, PP.

Colli, A. 2016. "Forms of Corporate Hierarchical Control in Italy: Reflections between History and Theory," Working Paper.

Colli, A., and Merlo, E. 2006. *Fontana: un Storia di Vita.* Milan: Egea.

Colli, A., Rinaldi, A., and Vasta, M. 2016. "The Only Way to Grow? Italian Business Groups in Historical Perspective," *Business History,* 58 (1): 30–48.

Colli, A., and Vasta, M. 2010. "Introduction," in A. Colli and M. Vasta (eds.), *Forms of Enterprise in Twentieth Century Italy. Boundaries, Structures and Strategies.* Cheltenham: Elgar: 1–21.

Colli, A., and Vasta, M. 2015. "Large and Entangled: Italian Business Groups in the Long Run," *Business History,* 57 (1): 64–95.

Collin, S-O. 1998. "Why Are These Islands of Conscious Power Found in the Ocean of Ownership? Institutional and Governance Hypotheses Explaining the Existence of Business Groups in Sweden," *Journal of Management Studies,* 35 (6): 719–46.

Collins, M. 1991. *Banks and Industrial Finance in Britain 1800–1939.* London: Macmillan.

Collis, D. J. 1991, rev. 1997. "Beatrice Companies—1985," Harvard Business School Case, no: 391–191.

Collis, D. J., and Anand, B. N. 2014. "Dynamic Capabilities at the Danaher Corporation," Working Paper.

Collis, D. J., and Kind, E. A. 2010, rev. 2014. "Silver Lake," Harvard Business School Case, no: 711–420.

Collis, D. J., and Montgomery, C. A. 1998. "Creating Corporate Advantage," *Harvard Business Review,* May–June, 1998: 71–83.

Collis, D. J., and Montgomery, C. A. 2005. *Corporate Strategy.* Boston, MA: McGraw Hill Professional.

Colpan, A. M., and Hikino, T. 2010. "Foundations of Business Groups: Towards an Integrated Framework," in A. M. Colpan, T. Hikino, and J. R. Lincoln. (eds.), *The Oxford Handbook of Business Groups.* Oxford: Oxford University Press: 15–66.

Colpan, A. M., Hikino, T., and Lincoln, J. R. (eds.) 2010. *The Oxford Handbook of Business Groups.* Oxford: Oxford University Press.

Colpan, A. M., and Jones, G. 2011. "Vehbi Koç and the Making of Turkey's Largest Business Group," Harvard Business School Case, no. 811–081.

Coltorti, F. 1988. "Note sulla Modificazione della Struttura Finanziaria delle Imprese Italiane Negli Ultimi Venti Anni," in *Atti del Seminario: Ristrutturazione Economica e Finanziaria delle Imprese.* Rome: Banca d'Italia: 593–657.

Commerzbank. 1954–2000, *Wer Gehört zu Wem?* Frankfurt am Main and Hamburg: Commerzbank.

Comos Tovar, C. 2004. "La Economía Social y sus Organizaciones Representativas en España (The Social Economy and its Representative Organizations in Spain)," *Mediterraneo Economico*, 6: 55–86.

Confalonieri, A. 1974–76. *Banca e Industria in Italia, 1894–1906*. 3 vols. Milan: Banca Commerciale Italiana.

Confalonieri, A. 1982. *Banca ed Industria in Italia dalla Crisi del 1907 all'Agosto 1914*. 2 vols. Milan: Banca Commerciale Italiana.

Confalonieri, A. 1992. *Banche Miste e Grande Industria in Italia 1914–1933*. vol. 1. Milan: Banca Commerciale Italiana.

Confraria, J. 1992. *Condicionamento Industrial: Uma Análise Económica*. Lisbon: Direcção-Geral da Indústria.

Confraria, J. 2005. "Política Económica," in P. Lains and A. F. Silva. (eds.), *História Económica de Portugal, Vol. III—O Século XX*. Lisbon: Instituto de Ciências Sociais: 305–41.

Consob. 2011. *Dall'Unità ai Giorni Nostri: 150 Anni di Borsa in Italia*. Rome: Consob.

Cook, K., Emerson, R., and Gillmore, R. 1983. "The Distribution of Power in Exchange Networks: Theory and Experimental Results," *American Journal of Sociology*, S 89: 275–305.

Costa, J., Louçã, F., Rosas, F., Fazenda, L., and Honório, C. 2010. *Os Donos de Portugal. Cem Anos de Poder Económico em Portugal*. Lisbon: Afrontamento.

Cottenier, J., Boosere, P., Gounet, T. 1989. *La Société Générale: 1822–1992*. Brussels: Editions Aden.

Crespí-Cladera, R., and García-Cestona, M. A. 2001. "Ownership and Control: A Spanish Survey," in F. Barca and M. Becht (eds.), *The Control of Corporate Europe*. New York: Oxford University Press.

Cruise, D., and Griffiths, A. 1991. *Fleecing the Lamb: The Inside Story of the Vancouver Stock Exchange*. London: Penguin Books.

Cuervo, A. 1988. *La Crisis Bancaria en Espana 1977–1985 (The Banking Crisis is Spain 1977–1985)*. Barcelona: Editorial Ariel.

Cuervo-Cazurra, A. 1999. "Grandes Accionistas y Beneficios Privados: El Caso de Bancos Como Accionistas de Empresas No Financieras (Large Shareholders and Private Benefits: The Case of Banks as Shareholders of Non-financial Firms)," *Investigaciones Europeas de Dirección y Economía de la Empresa*, 5 (1): 21–44.

Cuervo-Cazurra, A. 2006. "Business Groups and Their Types," *Asia Pacific Journal of Management*, 23 (4): 419–37.

Culpepper, P. 2005. "Institutional Change in Contemporary Capitalism: Coordinated Financial Systems Since 1990," *World Politics*, 57: 173–99.

Culpepper, P. 2011. *Quiet Politics and Business Power: Corporate Control in Europe and Japan*. New York: Cambridge University Press.

Cumming, D. J., and MacIntosh, J. G. 2006. "Crowding Out Private Equity: Canadian Evidence," *Journal of Business Venturing*, 21 (5): 569–609.

Cumming, D. J., and MacIntosh, J. G. 2007. "Mutual Funds that Invest in Private Equity? An Analysis of Labour-Sponsored Investment Funds," *Cambridge Journal of Economics*, 31 (3): 445–87.

Daems, H. 1977. *The Holding Company and Corporate Control*. Boston, MA: Springer.

Dahmén, E., and Carlsson, B. 1985. "Den Industriella Utvecklingen efter andra Världskriget," in Svensk Industri, Stockholm: Industriförbundets Förlag.

Dalzell, R. F. 1987. *Enterprising Elite: The Boston Associated and the World They Made*. Boston: Harvard University Press.

Dammers, D., and Fischer, H. 2016. "The Performance of German Big Business in the Twentieth Century," in Y. Cassis, A. Colli, and H.G. Schröter (eds.) *The Performance of European Business in the Twentieth Century*. Oxford: Oxford University Press.

D'Angio, A. 2000. *Schneider et Cie et la Naissance de l'Ingénierie. Des Pratiques Internes à l'Aventure Internationale 1836–1949*. Paris: CNRS Editions.

Daniels, R., Morck, R., and Stangeland, D. 1995. "In High Gear? A Case Study of the Hees-Edper Corporate Group," in R. Daniels and R. Morck (eds.), *Corporate Decision-Making in Canada*. Calgary: University of Calgary Press: 223–37.

Dankers, J. J., and Verheul, J. 1993. *Hoogovens 1945–1993. Van Staalbedrijf tot Twee-metalenconcern*. Den Haag: SDU.

Daumas, J. C. 2010. *Dictionnaire Historique des Patrons Français*. Paris: Flammarion.

David, G. 2007. Comments from the Dean's Innovative Leader Series. MIT Sloan School of Management, February 22, 2007.

David, T., and Westerhuis, G. (eds.). 2014. *The Power of Corporate Networks: A Comparative and Historical Perspective*. New York, Abingdon: Routledge.

Daviet, J. P. 1989. *Une Multinationale à la Française. Saint-Gobain, 1665–1989*. Paris: Fayard.

Davis, G., Diekman, K., and Tinsley, C. 1994. "The Decline and Fall of the Conglomerate Firm in the 1980s: The Deinstitutionalization of an Organizational Form," *American Sociological Review*, 59: 547–70.

Davis, J. A., Bertoldi, B., and Quaglia, R. 2012. "The Agnellis and Fiat: Family Business Governance in a Crisis (A)," Harvard Business School Case, no. 9-812-128.

Daws, G. 1968. *Shoal of Time: A History of the Hawaiian Islands*. New York: Macmillan.

De Bree, L. 1918. *Nederlandsch Indië in de Twintigste Eeuw: Het Bankwezen*. Batavia: Ruygrok & Co.

De Cock, C., and Nyberg, D. 2014. "The Possibility of Critique under a Financialized Capitalism: The Case of Private Equity in the United Kingdom," *Organization*, published online December 22, 2014.

De Jong, A., and Röell, A. A. 2005. "Financing and Control in the Netherlands. A Historical Perspective," in: R.K. Morck (ed.), *A History of Corporate Governance around the World: Family Business Groups to Professional Managers*. Chicago: National Bureau of Economic Research, The University of Chicago Press: 467–515.

De Jong, A., Sluyterman, K., and Westerhuis, G. 2011. "Strategic and Structural Responses to International Dynamics in the Open Dutch Economy, 1963–2003," *Business History*, 53 (1): 63–84.

De Long, J. 1991. "Did J. P. Morgan's Men Add Value? An Economists Perspective on Financial Capitalism," in P. Temin (ed.), *Inside the Business Enterprise: Historical Perspectives on the Use of Information*. Chicago: University of Chicago Press: 205–49.

Delvaux, B., and Michielsen, S. 1999. *Le Bal des Empires: Les Dessous du Capitalisme Belge*. Brussels: Racine.

De Secada, C. A. 1985. "Arms, Guano, and Shipping: The W. R. Grace Interests in Peru, 1865–1885," *Business History Review*, 59 (4): 597–621.

Desjardins, B., Lescure, M., Nougaret, R., Plessis, A., and Straus, A. 2003. *Le Crédit Lyonnais 1863–1986*. Geneva : Droz.

De Vries, J. 1968. *Hoogovens Ijmuiden 1918–1968. Ontstaan en Groei van een Basisindustrie*. IJmuiden: Koninklijke Nederlandsche Hoogovens en Staalfabrieken.

Didrichsen, J. 1972. "The Development of Diversified and Conglomerate Firms in the United States, 1920–1970," *The Business History Review*, 46 (2): 202–19.

Dierickx, I., and Cool, K. 1989. "Asset Stock Accumulation and Sustainability of Competitive Advantage," *Management Science*, 35 (12): 1504–11.

Doidge, C., Dyck, A., Mahmudi, M., and Virani, A. 2015. "Can Institutional Investors Improve Corporate Governance Through Collective Action?" University of Toronto Rotman School of Management Working Paper No. 2635662, available at SSRN, http://ssrn.com/abstract=2635662.

Dore, R. 1983. "Goodwill and the Spirit of Market Capitalism," *British Journal of Sociology*, 34: 459–82.

Dreyfus, J. M. 2003. *Pillages sur Ordonnances. Aryanisation et Restitution des Banques en France 1940–1953*. Paris: Fayard.

Dunning, J. H., and Lundan, S. M. 2008. *Multinational Enterprises and the Global Economy*. Cheltenham: Elgar.

Dyas, G. P., and Thanheiser, H. 1976. *The Emerging European Enterprise*. London: Macmillan.

Dyer, J., and Hatch, N. 2004. "Using Supplier Networks to Learn Faster," *Sloan Management Review*, 45: 57–63.

Ebrahimi, H. 2013. "Britain's Private Equity Titans Have Tumbled," *Daily Telegraph*, March 30, 2013.

Economist. 2015. "Meet Shinzo Abe: Shareholder Activist." June 6, 2015, print edition: 21.

Edelstein, M. 1988. "Professional Engineers in Australia: Institutional Response in a Developing Economy, 1860–1980," *Australian Economic History Review*, 28 (2): 8–32.

Elbaum, B., and Lazonick, W. (eds.). 1987. *The Decline of the British Economy*. Oxford: Clarendon Press.

Elderkin, K. 1997. "The Takeover of the Norton Company," Harvard Business School Case, no. 9-291-002, rev. December 15, 1997.

Elio, E. 2004. "Mondragón Corporación Cooperativa, el Paradigma del Desarrollo del Primer Grupo Industrial en España a Través del Cooperativismo de Trabajo Asociado. (Mondragón Corporación Cooperativa, the Development Paradigm of The Largest Industrial Group in Spain through Associated Workers Cooperation)," *Mediterraneo Economico*, 6: 335–54.

El Mundo. 2005. "La Nueva Rumasa (The New Rumasa)," *El Mundo*, February 20, 2005, http://www.elmundo.es/nuevaeconomia/2005/262/1108854001.html, accessed November 6, 2014.

El País. 1990. "La Corporación Industrial de Banesto Alcanza un Valor de 320.000 Millones de Pesetas a Precios de Mercado (The Banesto Industrial Corporate Reaches a Value of 320,000 Million Pesetas at Market Prices)," *El País*, April 21, 1990, http://elpais.com/diario/1990/04/21/economia/640648807_850215.html, accessed March 1, 2014.

English, J. 2010. *Just Watch Me: The Life of Pierre Elliott Trudeau, 1968–2000*. Toronto: Vintage Canada.

Esteves, J. P., and Jesus, A. 2015. *Caso BES. A Realidade dos Números*. Lisbon: Clube de Autor.

Exor. 2016. Annual Report.

Faccio, M., and Lang, L. H. P. 2002. "The Ultimate Ownership of Western European Corporations," *Journal of Financial Economics*, 65: 365–95.

Fan, J., and Lang, L. 2000. "The Measure of Relatedness: An Application to Corporate Diversification," *Journal of Business*, 73(4): 629–60.

Federico, G., and Vasta, M. 2015. "What Do We Really Know about Protection Before the Great Depression: Evidence from Italy," *Journal of Economic History*, 75 (4): 993–1029.

Feldenkirchen, W. 1997. "Business Groups in the German Electrical Industry," in T. Shiba and M. Shimotani (eds.), *Beyond the Firm. Business Groups in International and Historical Perspective* (Fuji conference series II). Oxford: Oxford University Press: 135–66.

Feldman, G. 1995. "Die Deutsche Bank vom Ersten Weltkrieg bis zur Weltwirtschaftskrise," in L. Gall et al. (eds.), *The Deutsche Bank, 1870–1995*. London: Weidenfeld & Nicolson: 138–314.

Fellman, S., Iversen, M., Sjogren, H., and Thue, L. (eds.) 2008. *Creating Nordic Capitalism: The Business History of a Competitive Periphery*. Basingstoke: Palgrave Macmillan.

Ferguson, N. 1998. *The World's Banker. The History of the House of Rothschild*. London: Weidenfeld & Nicolson.

Ferguson, N. 2011. *High Financier*. London: Penguin Books.

Fernandes, F. 2008. *O Homem SONAE*. Lisbon: Academia do Livro.

Fernandes, F. 2014. *As Vítimas do Furacão Espírito Santo*. Lisbon: Oficina do Livro.

Ferreira, M. E. 2002. "Nacionalização e Confisco do Capital Português na Indústria Trans-formadora de Angola (1975–1990)," *Análise Social*, 37 (162): 47–90.

Ferris, S. P., Kim, K., and Kitsabunnarat, P. 2003. "The Costs (and Benefits?) of Diversified Business Groups: The Case of Korean Chaebols," *Journal of Banking and Finance*, 27 (2): 251–73.

Fiedler, M. 1999. "Die 100 Größten Unternehmen in Deutschland – Nach der Zahl Ihrer Beschäftigten – 1907, 1938, 1973 und 1995," in *Zeitschrift für Unternehmensgeschichte*. H. 1: 32–66

Fieldhouse, D. K. 1994. *Merchant Capital and Economic Decolonization*. Oxford: Clarendon Press.

Fields, L. P., Fraser, D. R., and Kolari, J. W. 2007. "Is Bancassurance a Viable Model for Financial Firms?," *Journal of Risk and Insurance*, 74 (4): 777–94.

Fischer, W. (ed.). 1986. *Handbuch der Europäischen Wirtschafts- und Sozialgeschichte*. Vol. 5. Stuttgart: Ernst Klett.

Fitzpatrick, B. 1944. *The Rich Get Richer: Facts of the Growth of Monopoly in the Economic Structure of Australia Before and During the War*. Melbourne: Rawson's Book Shop.

Fleming, G. A., Merrett, D., and Ville, S. P. 2004. *The Big End of Town: Big Business and Corporate Leadership in Twentieth-Century Australia*. New York: Cambridge University Press.

Fleming, L., and Waguespack, D. 2007. "Brokerage, Boundary Spanning, and Leadership," *Organization Science*, 18: 165–80.

Fligstein, F. 1985. "The Spread of the Multidivisional Form among Large Firms, 1919–1979," *American Sociological Review*, 50: 377–91.

Fligstein, N. 1990. *The Transformation of Corporate Control*. Cambridge, MA: Harvard University Press.

Fligstein, N. 1991. "The Structural Transformation of American Industry: An Institutional Account of the Causes of Diversification in the Largest Firms, 1919–1979," in W. Powell and P. DiMaggio (eds.), *The New Institutionalism in Organizational Analysis*, Chicago: University of Chicago Press: 311–36.

Focus magazine, 1999. no. 51, online, accessed April 28, 2013.

Fohlin, C. 2007. *Finance Capitalism and Germany's Rise to Industrial Power*. Cambridge: Cambridge University Press.

Fomento de la Producción. Various Years. *Las 2500 Mayores Empresas Españolas (The 2500 Largest Spanish Firms)*. Barcelona: Fomento de la Producción.

Forbes. 2014. "The World's Billionaires," *Forbes*, November 7, 2014, http://www.forbes.com/billionaires/list/#tab:overall_country:Spain, accessed November 7, 2014.

Forbes. 2015. "The World's Billionaires." *Forbes,* July 29, 2015, http://www.forbes.com/billionaires/#version:static_country:Spain, accessed July 29, 2015.

Foreman-Peck, J., and Hannah, L. 2012. "Extreme Divorce: the Managerial Revolution in UK companies before 1914," *Economic History Review,* 65 (4): 1217–38.

Fortune, 2014. Fortune Global 500.

Fossum, J. E. 1997. *Oil, the State, and Federalism: The Rise and Demise of Petro-Canada as a Statist Impulse.* Toronto: University of Toronto Press.

Fracchia, E., Mesquita, L., and Quiroga, J. 2010. "Business Groups in Argentina," in A. M. Colpan, T. Hikino, and J. R. Lincoln (eds.), *The Oxford Handbook of Business Groups.* Oxford: Oxford University Press: 325–53.

Francis, D. 1986. *Controlling Interests: Who Owns Canada?* Toronto: Macmillan Canada.

Francis, D. 2008. *Who Owns Canada Now? Old Money, New Money and the Future of Canadian Business.* New York: HarperCollins.

Frankfurter Allgemeine Zeitung, 2007. December 20, online, accessed April 28, 2013.

Franks, J., and Mayer, C. 2001. "Ownership and Control of German Corporations," in *Review of Financial Studies,* 14 (4): 943–77.

Franks, J., Mayer, C., and Rossi. 2005. "Spending Less Time with the Family: The Decline of Family Ownership in the United Kingdom," in R. Morck (ed.) *A History of Corporate Governance around the World: Family Business Groups to Professional Managers.* Chicago: University of Chicago Press: 581–607.

Franz Haniel and Cie. (eds.). 2006. *Haniel 1756–2006: eine Chronik in Daten und Fakten.* Duisburg: Haniel.

Freeland, R. F. 1996. "The Myth of the M-Form? Governance, Consent, and Organizational Change," *American Journal of Sociology,* 102 (2): 483–526.

Freeman, C., and Louçã, F. 2001. *As Time Goes by: From the Industrial Revolution to the Information Revolution.* Oxford: Oxford University Press.

Freeman, C., and Soete, L. 1997. *The Economics of Industrial Innovation.* Cambridge, MA: MIT Press.

Freundlich, F., Grellier, H., and Altuna, R. 2009. "Mondragon: Notes on History, Scope and Structure," *International Journal of Technology Management and Sustainable Development,* 8: 3–12.

Fridenson, P. 1972. *Histoire des Usines Renault,* i. *Naissance de la Grande Entreprise.* Paris: Le Seuil.

Fritz, M., and Karlsson, B. 2006. *SKF—Världsföretaget: 1907–2007.* Stockholm: Informationsförlaget.

Fruin, W. M. 2008. "Business Groups and Interfirm Network," in G. Jones and J. Zeitlin (eds.), *The Oxford Handbook of Business History.* Oxford: Oxford University Press.

Galambos, L. 1966. *Competition and Cooperation: The Emergence of a National Trade Association.* Baltimore: Johns Hopkins University Press.

Galasso, G. (ed.). 1993. *Storia dell'Industria Elettrica in Italia. Vol 3. Espansione e Oligopolio 1926–1945.* Bari: Laterza.

Gales, B. P. A., and Sluyterman, K. E. 1998. "Dutch Free-standing Companies, 1870–1940," in M. Wilkins and H. Schröter (eds.), *The Free-standing Company in the World Economy, 1830–1996.* Oxford: Oxford University Press: 293–322.

Gall, L. 1995. "Die Deutsche Bank von ihrer Gründung bis zum Ersten Weltkrieg, 1870–1914," in L. Gall, G. Feldman, H. James, C.-L. Holtfrerich, and H. Büschgen, *Die Deutsche Bank, 1870–1995.* Munich: C. H. Beck: 1–136.

Garner, P. 2011. *British Lions and Mexican Eagles. Business, Politics, and Empire in the Career of Weetman Pearson in Mexico, 1889–1919*. Stanford: Stanford University Press.

Garrido, Á. 2005. "Conjunturas Políticas e Economia," in P. Lains and A. F. Silva (eds.), *História Económica de Portugal, Vol. III—O Século XX*. Lisbon: Instituto de Ciências Sociais: 451–73.

General Electric. "GE Company Organization Chart (updated November 2014)," http://www.ge.com/pdf/company/ge_organization_chart.pdf.

Gerlach, M. 1992. *Alliance Capitalism: The Social Organization of Japanese Business*. Berkeley: University of California Press.

Gerschenkron, A. 1962. *Economic Backwardness in Historical Perspective*. Cambridge: Belknap.

Ghai, S., Kehoe, C., and Pinkus, G. 2014. *Private Equity: Changing perceptions and new realities*. London: McKinsey & Co.

Ghemawat, P., and Khanna, T. 1998. "The Nature of Diversified Business Groups: A Research Design and Two Case Studies," *Journal of Industrial Economics*, 46: 35–61.

Ghoshal, S., and Bartlett, C. 1990. "The Multinational Corporation as an Interorganizational Network," *Academy of Management Review*, 15: 603–25.

Giannetti, R., and Vasta, M. 2006. "The Concentration of the Industrial Structure," in R. Giannetti and M. Vasta (eds.), *Evolution of Italian Enterprises in the 20th Century*. Heidelberg: Physica-Verlag: 49–61.

Giannetti, R., and Vasta, M. 2010. "Big Business (1913–2001)," in A. Colli and M. Vasta. (eds.), *Forms of Enterprise in Twentieth Century Italy. Boundaries, Structures and Strategies*. Cheltenham: Elgar: 25–51.

Gille, B. 1965–7. *Histoire de la Maison Rothschild, Vol. 1, Des Origines à 1848; Vol. 2, 1848–1870*. Geneva: Droz.

Gillingham, J. 1974. "The Baron de Launoit: a Case Study in the 'Politics of Production' of Belgian Industry during Nazi Occupation," https://www.journalbelgianhistory.be/nl/journal/belgisch-tijdschrift-voor-nieuwste-geschiedenis-1974-1-2/baron-launoit-case-study-politics, accessed October 17, 2016.

Glete, J. 1987. *Ägande och Industriell Omvandling*. Stockholm: SNS Förlag.

Glete, J. 1993. "Swedish Managerial Capitalism: Did It Ever Become Ascendant?" *Business History*, 35 (2): 99–110.

Glete, J. 1994. *Nätverk i Näringslivet*. Stockholm: SNS Förlag.

Godelier, E. 2006. *Usinor—Arcelor: du Local au Global*. Paris: Lavoisier.

Goey, F. de. 2005. "The Cruise Industry in the Twentieth Century," *Revista de Historia Transportes, Servicios y Telecomunicaciones, (TST)* 9: 90–110.

Goey, F. de. 2013. "A Case of Business Failure: The Netherlands Trading Company (NHM) in Japan, 1859 to 1881," *Zeitschrift für Unternehmensgeschichte*, 58 (1): 105–26.

Goldstein, A. 2003. "Privatisation in Italy 1993–2002. Goals, Institutions, Outcomes and Outstanding Issues," *Cesifo WP 912*.

Gompers, P., and Lerner, J. 2001. "The Venture Capital Revolution," *Journal of Economic Perspectives*, 15 (2): 145–68.

Gonzalez, M. J., Anes, R., and Mendoza, I. 2007. *BBVA, 1857–2007. 150 Años, 150 Bancos. (BBVA, 1857–2007. 150 Years, 150 Banks)*, Madrid: BBVA.

Goold, M., and Campbell, A. 1987. *Strategies and Styles: The Role of the Centre in Managing Diversified Corporations*. Oxford: Blackwell.

Gordon, S. 2014 . "Brand it Like Branson," *Financial Times*, November 6, 2014.

Gordon, S. and Sanderson, R. 2017. "Agnelli Heir Makes Bet on Family Fortune," *Financial Times*, April 4, 2017.

Gossweiler, K. 1975. *Großbanken, Industriemonopole, Staat. Ökonomie und Politik des Staatsmonopolistischen Kapitalismus in Deutschland 1914–1932*. Berlin: deb-Verlag.

Goto, A. 1982. "Business Groups in a Market Economy," *European Economic Review*, 19: 53–70.

Gourevitch, P., and Shinn, J. 2005. *Political Power and Corporate Control: The New Global Politics of Corporate Governance*. Princeton, NJ: Princeton University Press.

Graaf, T. de. 2012. *Voor Handel en Maatschappij. Geschiedenis van de Nederlandsche Handel-Maatschappij 1824–1964*. Amsterdam: Boom.

Grace, J. P. 1953. *W. R. Grace (1832–1904) and the Enterprises He Created*. New York: Newcomen Society.

Graham, J. R., Lemmon, M. L., and Wolf, J. G. 2002. "Does Corporate Diversification Destroy Value?," *Journal of Finance* 57 (2): 695–720.

Granovetter, M. 1973. "The Strength of Weak Ties," *American Journal of Sociology*, 78: 1360–80.

Granovetter, M. 1995. "Coase Revisited: Business Groups in the Modern Economy," *Industrial and Corporate Change*, 4 (1): 93–130.

Granovetter, M. 2005. "Business Groups and Social Organization," in N. Smelser and R. Swedberg (eds.), *The Handbook of Economic Sociology*. Princeton, NJ: Princeton University Press, 429–50.

Grupo Villar Mir. Various Years. "Annual Report," http://www.grupovillarmir.es/Informes-Anuales/Descargas-PDF, accessed February 19, 2014.

Guillén, M. F. 2000. "Business Groups in Emerging Economies: A Resource-Based View," *Academy of Management Journal*, 43 (3): 362–80.

Guillén, M. F. 2001. *The Limits of Convergence. Globalization and Organizational Change in Argentina, South Korea, and Spain*. Princeton, NJ: Princeton University Press.

Guillén, M. F., and García-Canal, E. 2010. *The New Multinationals. Spanish Firms in a Global Context*. New York: Cambridge University Press.

Guillot, D. and Lincoln, J. 2005. "Dyad and Network: Models of Manufacturer-Supplier Cooperation in the Japanese TV Manufacturing Industry," in A. Bird and T. Roehl, (eds.), *Advances in International Management: Special Issue on Changing Japan*. Greenwich, CT: JAI Press.

Guinnane, T. W., and Martínez-Rodríguez, S. 2010. "Did the Cooperative Start Life as a Joint-Stock Company? Business Law and Cooperatives in Spain, 1869–1931," *Economic Growth Center, Yale University*, discussion paper no. 987. New Haven, CT: Yale University Press.

Gulati, R. 1998. "Alliances and Networks," *Strategic Management Journal*, 19: 293–317.

Hall, P., and Soskice, D., eds. 2001. *Varieties of Capitalism: The Institutional Foundations of Comparative Advantage*. New York: Oxford University Press.

HAL Trust. 2014. *Annual Report 2013*. Willemstad: Hal Holding NV.

Hamilton, G., and Biggart, N. 1988. "Market, Culture, and Authority: A Comparative Analysis of Management and Organization in the Far East," *American Journal of Sociology* 94: S52–S94.

Hancké, B., Rhodes, M., and Thatcher, M., (eds). 2007. *Beyond Varieties of Capitalism: Conflict, Contradiction and Complementarities in the European Economy*. Oxford: Oxford University Press.

Handbuch der Aktiengesellschaften, 1950–2012, Darmstadt: Hoppenstedt.

Handbuch der Großunternehmen, 1950–2012, Darmstadt: Hoppenstedt.

Handelsblatt, 2014. April 16, online, accessed April 28, 2013.

Haniel, 2015. Annual Report.

Hannah, L. 1976. *The Rise of the Corporate Economy.* London: Methuen.

Hannah, L. 1980. "Visible and Invisible Hands in Great Britain," in A. D. Chandler and H. Daems (eds.), *Managerial Hierarchies. Comparative Perspectives on the Rise of the Modern Industrial Enterprise.* Cambridge, MS: Harvard University Press.

Hannah, L. 2007a. "J. P. Morgan in London and New York before 1914," *Business History Review*, 85: 113–50.

Hannah, L. 2007b. "The 'Divorce' of Ownership from Control from 1900 Onwards: Re-calibrating Imagined Global Trends," *Business History*, 49 (4): 404–38.

Hannah, L. 2009. "Strategic Games, Scale and Efficiency, or Chandler goes to Hollywood," in R. Coopey and P. Lyth (eds.), *Business in Britain in the Twentieth Century.* Oxford: Oxford University Press.

Hannecart, R. 2010. Le Dernier Carré: les Charbonniers Belges, Libres Entrepreneurs Face à la CECA (1950–1959). Brussels; New York: P.I.E. Peter Lang.

Harris, R. S., Jenkinson, T., and Kaplan, S. N. 2014. "Private Equity Performance: What Do We Know?" *Journal of Finance,* 69 (5): 1851–82.

Heerding, A. 1980. *Geschiedenis van de NV Philips' Gloeilampenfabrieken.* Vol. 1: "Het Ontstaan van de Nederlandse Gloeilampen Industrie." The Hague: Nijhoff.

Heerding, A. 1986. *Geschiedenis van de NV Philips' Gloeilampenfabrieken.* Vol. 2: "Een Onderneming van Vele Markten Thuis, 1891–922." Leiden: Nijhoff.

Henrekson, M., and Jakobsson, U. 2003. "The Transformation of Ownership Policy and Structure in Sweden: Convergence Towards the Anglo-Saxon Model?" *New Political Economy*, 8 (1): 73–102.

Henrekson, M., and Jakobsson, U. 2011. "The Swedish Corporate Control Model: Convergence, Persistence or Decline?" IFN Working Paper No. 857, Stockholm: Research Institute of Industrial Economics.

Herrigel, G. 1994. *Industrial Constructions: The Sources of German Industrial Power.* New York: Cambridge University Press.

Hertner, P. 1986. "Financial Strategies and Adaptation to Foreign Markets: the German Electrotechnical Industry and its Multinational Activities: 1890s to 1939," in A. Teichova, M. Lévy-Leboyer, and H. Nußbaum (eds.), *Multinational Enterprise in Historical Perspective.* Cambridge: Cambridge University Press: 145–59.

Heugens, P. M. A. R., and Zyglidopoulos, S. C. 2008. "From Social Ties to Embedded Competencies: the Case of Business Groups," *Journal of Management and Governance,* 12 (4): 325–41.

Hidy, R., and Hidy, M. 1955. *History of Standard Oil Company of New Jersey: Pioneering in Big Business: 1882–1911.* New York: Harper.

Hikino, T., and Amsden, A. H. 1994. "Staying Behind, Stumbling Back, Sneaking Up, Soaring Ahead: Late-Industrialization in Historical Perspective," in W. J. Biumol, R. R. Nelson, and E. N. Wolff (eds), *Convergence in Productivity: Cross-country Studies and Historical Evidence.* New York and Oxford: Oxford University Press.

Hilferding, R. 1910. *Das Finanzkapital: eine Studie über die Jüngste Entwicklung des Kapitalismus.* Vienna: Verlag der Wiener Volksbuchhandlung.

Hill, A. 2011. "Tata Can Take a Long View on Succession," *Financial Times*, November 28, 2011.

Hill, C. W. L. 1985. "Diversified Growth and Competition: the Experience of Twelve Large UK Firms," *Applied Economics*, 17: 827–47.

Hitt, M., Ireland, D., and Hoskisson, R. 2007. *Strategic Management.* Ohio: Thompson South-Western.

Högfeldt, P. 2005. "The History and Politics of Corporate Ownership in Sweden," in R. Morck (ed.), *A History of Corporate Governance Around the World: Family Business Groups to Professional Managers.* Chicago: University of Chicago Press.

Holland, M. 1989. *When the Machine Stopped: A Cautionary Tale from Industrial America.* Boston, MA: Harvard Business School Press: 145–7.

Holmén, M., and Högfeldt, P. 2009. "Pyramidal Discounts: Tunneling or Overinvestment?" *International Review of Finance,* 9 (1–2): 133–75.

Holmén, M., and Knopf, J. D. 2004. "Minority Shareholder Protection and the Private Benefits of Control for Swedish Mergers," *Journal of Financial and Quantitative Analysis,* 39 (1): 167–91.

Homburg, E. 2004. *Groeien door Kunstmest. DSM Agro 1929–2004.* Hilversum: Verloren.

Hoshi, T., Kashyap, A., and Scharfstein, D. 1991. "Corporate Structure, Liquidity, and Investment: Evidence from Japanese Industrial Groups," *The Quarterly Journal of Economics,* 106 (1): 33–60.

Hoskisson, R. E., Hill, C. W. L., and Kim, H. 1993. "The Multidivisional Structure: Organizational Fossil or Source of Value?" *Journal of Management,* 19 (2): 269–98.

Hoskisson, R. E., Johnson, R. A., Tihanyi, L., and White, R. E. 2005. "Diversified Business Groups and Corporate Refocusing in Emerging Economies," *Journal of Management,* 31 (6): 941–65.

Houtman-De Smedt, H. 1994. "Le Système Bancaire en Belgique à Travers les Siècles," in Pohl, M. (ed.), *Handbook on the History of European Banks.* Uitgave, Aldershot: Elgar: 56–63.

Huber, E., and Stephens, J. 2001. *Development and Crisis of the Welfare State: Parties and Policies in Global Markets.* Chicago: University of Chicago Press.

Hund, J., Monk, D., and Tice, S. 2012. "Apples to Apples: the Economic Benefit of Corporate Diversification," SSRN Working Paper No. 2023786.

Hunter, D. 2002. *The Bubble and the Bear: How Nortel Burst the Canadian Dream.* New York: Doubleday.

IMTECH. 2010. *De Rijke Geschiedenis van de Europese Technische Dienstverlener 1860–2010. Imtech N.V. 150 jaar Technologie & Ondernemerschap.* Gouda: IMTECH.

Industrivärden. 2009. Annual Report.

INI. Various Years. *Informe Annual (Annual Report).* Madrid: Instituto Nacional de Industria.

Instituto de la Empresa Familiar. 2009. "El Instituto de la Empresa Familiar (The Family-Owned Firm Institute)," http://www.ehu.es/p200-content/eu/contenidos/informe_estudio/cef_estudios_situacion/eu_estudios/adjuntos/Estudio_Instituto.pdf, accessed November 7, 2014.

Investor. 2009. Annual report.

Investor. 2014. Annual Report.

Irwin, N. 2015. "Next Berkshire Head May Struggle to Match Founder's Record," *International New York Times,* March 4, 2015.

ITW (Illinois Tool Works). 2013. Annual Report.

Iversen, M. J., and Thue, L. 2008. "Creating Nordic Capitalism–the Business History of a Competitive Periphery," in S. Fellman et al. (eds.), *Creating Nordic Capitalism.* New York: Palgrave.

Iversen, T., and Soskice, D. 2009. "Distribution and Redistribution: The Shadow of the Nineteenth Century," *World Politics*, 61 (3): 438–86.

Jackson, G. 2003. "Corporate Governance in Germany and Japan: Liberalization Pressures and Responses during the 1990s," in K. Yamamura and W. Streeck (eds.), *The End of Diversity?*, Ithaca: Cornell University Press: 261–305.

James, H. 2005. *Familienunternehmen in Europa. Haniel, Wendel und Falck*. Munich: C. H. Beck.

James, H. 2006. Family Capitalism: Wendels, Haniels, Falcks, and the Continental European Model. Cambridge, MA: Belknap Press.

James, M. 1993. *Merchant Adventurer: The Story of W. R. Grace*. Wilmington: Scholarly Resources.

Jensen, M. C. 1986. "Agency Costs of Free Cash Flow, Corporate Finance, and Takeovers," *American Economic Review*, 76 (2): 323–9.

Jensen, M. C., and Ruback, R. S. 1983. "The Market for Corporate Control: The Scientific Evidence." *Journal of Financial Economics*, 11 (1–4): 5–50.

John, R. 1997. "Elaborations, Revisions, Dissents: Alfred D. Chandler, Jr's *The Visible Hand* after Twenty Years," *Business History Review*, 71: 151–206.

Johnson, M. 2013. "Spain's Ownership Web Set to Untangle," *Financial Times*, June 9, 2013.

Johnson, S., LaPorta, R., Lopez -de-Silanes, F., and Schleifer, A. 2000. "Tunneling," *American Economic Review*, 90 (2): 22–7.

Jones, G. (ed.). 1986. *British Multinationals: Origins, Management and Performance*. Aldershot: Gower.

Jones, G. 1994. "British Multinationals and British Business Since 1850," in M. W. Kirby and M. B. Rose (eds.), *Business Enterprise in Modern Britain*. London: Routledge.

Jones, G. 1997. "Great Britain: Big Business, Management and Competiveness in Twentieth-century Britain," in A. D. Chandler, F. Amatori, and T. Hikino (eds.), *Big Business and the Wealth of Nations*. Cambridge: Cambridge University Press.

Jones, G. 2000. *Merchants to Multinationals: British Trading Companies in the Nineteenth and Twentieth Centuries*. Oxford: Oxford University Press.

Jones, G. 2005a. *Multinationals and Global Capitalism: From the Nineteenth to the Twenty-First Century*. Oxford: Oxford University Press.

Jones, G. 2005b. *Renewing Unilever*. Oxford: Oxford University Press.

Jones, G. 2010. *Beauty Imagined. A History of the Global Beauty Industry*. Oxford: Oxford University Press.

Jones, G., and Colpan, A. M. 2010. "Business Groups in Historical Perspectives," in A. M. Colpan, T. Hikino, and J. R. Lincoln (eds.), *The Oxford Handbook of Business Groups*. Oxford: Oxford University Press.

Jones, G., and Khanna, T. 2006. "Bringing History (Back) into International Business," *Journal of International Business Studies*, 37 (4): 453–68.

Jones, G., and Wale, J. 1998. "Merchants as Business Groups: British Trading Companies in Asia Before 1945," *Business History Review*, 72: 367–408.

Jonker, J. 2009. "The Alternative Road to Modernity: Banking and Currency, 1814–1914," in M. 't Hart, J. Jonker, and J. L. van Zanden (eds.), *A Financial History of The Netherlands*. Cambridge: Cambridge University Press: 94–124.

Jonker, J., and Sluyterman, K. E. 2000. *Thuis op de Wereldmarkt. Nederlandse Handelshuizen door de Eeuwen Heen*. 's-Gravenhage: SDU (English Translation: *At Home on the World*

Markets: Dutch International Trading Companies from the 16th Century Until the Present. Montreal: McGill-Queen's University Press).

Jonker, J., and Zanden van, J. L. 2007. *From Challenger to Joint Industry Leader, a History of Royal Dutch Shell, vol. 1*. Oxford: Oxford University Press.

Kandel, E., Kosenko, K., Morck, R., and Yafeh, Y. 2013. "Business Groups in the United States: A Revised History of Corporate Ownership, Pyramids and Regulation, 1930–1950," Working Paper.

Kandel, E., Kosenko, K., Morck, R., and Yafeh, Y. 2015. "The Great Pyramids of America: A Revised History of US Business Groups, Corporate Ownership and Regulation, 1930–1950," *National Bureau of Economic Research (NBER)* Working Paper no. 19691. Washington: NBER.

Kanter, R. 1989. "The New Managerial Work," *Harvard Business Review*, November–December, 1989.

Kanter, R. 1994. "Collaborative Advantage: The Art of Alliances." *Harvard Business Review*, July–August, 1994.

Kaplan, S. N., and Schoar, A. 2005. "Private Equity Performance: Returns, Persistence, and Capital Flows," *Journal of Finance*, 60 (4): 1791–823.

Katz, R. 1998. *Japan, the System That Soured: The Rise and Fall of the Japanese Economic Miracle*. Armonk, NY: M. E. Sharpe.

Katzenstein, P. J. 1985. *Small States in World Markets: Industrial Policy in Europe*. Ithaca and London: Cambridge University Press.

Keister, L. 1998. "Engineering Growth: Business Group Structure and Firm Performance in China's Transition Economy," *American Journal of Sociology*, 104: 404–40.

Kelly, J. 2011. "TPG: The Operators," *Bloomberg Businessweek*, February 17, 2011.

Kenwood, A. 1995. *Australian Economic Institutions Since Federation: An Introduction*. Melbourne: Oxford University Press.

Khanna, T., and Palepu, K. 1997. "Why Focused Strategies May Be Wrong for Emerging Markets," *Harvard Business Review*, 75 (4): 41–51.

Khanna, T., and Palepu, K. 1999. "Policy Shocks, Market Intermediaries, and Corporate Strategy: The Evolution of Business Groups in Chile and India," *Journal of Economics and Management Strategy*, 8 (2): 271–310.

Khanna, T., and Palepu, K. 2000. "The Future of Business Groups in Emerging Markets: Long-Run Evidence from Chile," *Academy of Management Journal*, 43: 268–85.

Khanna, T., and Palepu, K. 2005. "The Evolution of Concentrated Ownership in India: Broad Patterns and a History of the Indian Software Industry," in R. Morck (ed.) *A History of Corporate Governance Around the World: Family Business Groups to Professional Managers*. Chicago: University of Chicago Press: 283–324.

Khanna, T., and Palepu, K. 2010. *Winning in Emerging Markets. A Roadmap for Strategy and Execution*. Cambridge, MA: Harvard Business Press.

Khanna, T., and Rivkin, J. W. 2001. "Estimating the Performance Effects of Business Groups in Emerging Markets," *Strategic Management Journal*, 22 (1): 45–74.

Khanna, T., and Rivkin, J. W. 2006. "Interorganizational Ties and Business Group Boundaries: Evidence from an Emerging Economy," *Organization Science*, 17 (3): 333–52.

Khanna, T., and Yafeh, Y. 2005. "Business Groups and Risk-sharing Around the World," *Journal of Business*, 78: 310–40.

Khanna, T., and Yafeh, Y. 2007. Business Groups in Emerging Markets: Paragons or Parasites?, *Journal of Economic Literature*, 45 (2): 331–72.

Khanna, T., and Yafeh, Y. 2010. "Business Groups in Emerging Markets: Paragons or Parasites?" in A. M. Colpan, T. Hikino, and J. R. Lincoln (eds.), *Oxford Handbook of Business Groups*. Oxford: Oxford University Press.

Kim, H., Hoskisson, R. E., Tihanyi, L., and Hong, J. 2004. "The Evolution and Restructuring of Diversified Business Groups in Emerging Markets: The Lessons from Chaebols in Korea," *Asia Pacific Journal of Management*, 21 (1–2): 25–48.

Klein, P. G. 2001. "Were the Acquisitive Conglomerates Inefficient?," *RAND Journal of Economics*, 32 (4): 745–61.

Knoke, D., and Kuklinski, J. 1982. *Network Analysis*. Thousand Oaks, CA: Sage.

Kock, C., and Guillén, M. F. 2001. "Strategy and Structure in Developing Countries: Business Groups as an Evolutionary Response to Opportunities for Unrelated Diversification," *Industrial & Corporate Change*, 10 (1): 1–37.

Korpi, W. 2006. "Power Resources and Employer-Centered Approaches in Explanations of Welfare States and Varieties of Capitalism: Protagonists, Consenters, and Antagonists," *World Politics*, 58 (2): 167–206.

Krueger, A. 1974. The Political Economy of the Rent-seeking Society. *American Economic Review*, 64 (6): 291–303.

Kryzanowski, L., and Roberts, G. S. 1993. "Canadian Banking Solvency, 1922–1940," *Journal of Money, Credit and Banking*, 25 (3): 361–76.

Kuisel, R. F. 1967. *Ernest Mercier, French Technocrat*. Berkeley and Los Angeles: University of California Press.

Kurgan-van Hentenryk, G. 1982. *Rail, Finance et Politique: les Entreprises Philippart, 1865–1890*. Brussels: Editions de l'Université de Bruxelles.

Kurgan-van Hentenryk, G. 1996. *Gouverner la Générale de Belgique. Essai de biographie collective*, Louvain-la-Neuve: De Boeck Université.

Kurgan-van Hentenryk, G. 1997. "Structure and Strategy of Belgian Business Groups," in T. Shiba and M. Shimotani (eds.), *Beyond the Firm. Business Groups in International and Historical Perspective*. Oxford: Oxford University Press: 88–107.

Lambrecht, P. 2002. "The 13th Directive on Takeover Bids—Formation and Principles," in Ferrarini G., Hopt K.J., and Wymeersch E., *Capital Markets in the Age of the Euro*. Norwell, MA: Kluwer Law International.

Lamoreaux, N., Raff, D. M. G., and Temin, P. 2002. "Beyond Markets and Hierarchies: Toward a New Synthesis of American Business History," Working Paper 9029 at http://www.nber.org/papers/w9029.

Lamoreaux, N., Raff, D. M. G., and P. Temin. 2003. "Beyond Markets and Hierarchies: Toward a New Synthesis of American Business History," *American Historical Review*, 108 (2): 404–33.

Lang, L. H., and Stulz, R. M. 1994. "Tobin's q, Corporate Diversification, and Firm Performance," *Journal of Political Economy*, 102 (6): 1248–80.

Langlois, R. 2010. "Economic Institutions and the Boundaries of Business Groups," in A. M. Colpan, T. Hikino, and J. R. Lincoln (eds.), *The Oxford Handbook of Business Groups*. Oxford: Oxford University Press: 629–49.

Langlois, R. N. 2013. "Business Groups and the Natural State," *Journal of Economic Behavior and Organization* 88: 14–26.

Lanthier, P. 1988. "Les Constructions Électriques en France: Financement et Stratégie de Six Groupes Industriels Internationaux, 1880–1949," Ph.D. thesis, Université de Paris-X Nanterre.

Lanthier, P. 1994. "Les Entreprises du Secteur Électrique: la Construction Électrique," in M. Lévy-Leboyer and H. Morsel, *Histoire Générale de l'Électricité en France*, t. 2. Paris: Fayard.

La Porta, R., López-de-Silanes, F., and Shleifer, A. 1999. "Corporate Ownership around the World," *Journal of Finance*, 54: 471–517.

La Porta, R., López-de-Silanes, F., Shleifer, A., and Vishny, R. 1997. "Legal Determinants of External Finance," *Journal of Finance* 52 (1, 3): 1131–50.

La Porta, R., López-de-Silanes, F., Shleifer, A., and Vishny, R. 2000. "Investor Protection and Corporate Governance," *Journal of Financial Economics* 58 (1): 3–27.

Larsson, M. 1991. *En Svensk Ekonomisk Historia 1850–1985*. Stockholm: SNS Förlag.

Larsson, M. 1998. *Staten och Kapitalet—det Svenska Finansiella Systemet under 1900-talet*. Stockholm: SNS Förlag.

Larsson, M. 2001. *Bonniers en Mediefamilj. Förlag, Konglomerat och Mediekoncern 1953–1990*. Stockholm: Albert Bonniers Förlag.

Larsson, M. 2002. "Storföretagande och Industrikoncentration," in M. Isacson and M. Morell (eds.), *Industrialismens tid. Ekonomisk-historiska Perspektiv på Svensk Industriell Omvandling under 200 år*. Stockholm: SNS Förlag.

Larsson, M., Lindgren, H., and Nyberg, D. 2008. "Entrepreneurship and Ownership: the Long-term Viability of the Swedish Bonnier and Wallenberg Family Business Groups," in S. Fellman et al. (eds.), *Creating Nordic Capitalism: The Business History of a Competitive Periphery*. Basingstoke: Palgrave Macmillan.

Lawriwsky, M. 1978. *Ownership and Control of Australian Corporations*. Sydney: University of Sydney.

Leff, N. H. 1978. "Industrial Organization and Entrepreneurship in the Developing Countries: The Economic Groups," *Economic Development and Cultural Change*, 26 (4): 661–75.

Leff, N. 1986. "Trust, Envy, and the Political Economy of Industrial Development: Economic Groups in Developing Countries." Graduate School of Business, Columbia University.

Leite, António N., Machado, J. A. F., and Cúrdia, V. 2001. *Portugal como Destino do Investimento Directo Estrangeiro/Estado da Competitividade da Economia Nacional*. Lisbon: Câmara de Comércio Americana em Portugal.

Leontief, W. 1986. *Input-Output Economics, 2nd edn*. Oxford: Oxford University Press.

Levy-Leboyer, M. 1980. "The Large Corporation in Modern France," in A. D. Chandler and H. Daems, *Managerial Hierarchies*. Cambridge, MA: Harvard University Press.

Levy-Leboyer, M., and Morsel, H. 1994. *Histoire Générale de l'Électricité en France*. t. 2. Paris: Fayard.

Liedke, R. 1993–2006. *Wem Gehört die Republik? Die Konzerne und ihre Verflechtungen. Namen, Zahlen, Fakten*, Frankfurt am Main: Büchergilde Gutenberg.

Liedke, R. 2007. *Wem Gehört die Republik? Die Konzerne und ihre Globalen Verflechtungen in der Globalisierten Wirtschaft*, Frankfurt am Main: Eichborn Verlag.

Liefmann, R. 1921. *Beteiligungs- und Finanzierungsgesellschaften: eine Studie über den Modernen Effektenkapitalismus in Deutschland, den Vereinigten Staaten, der Schweiz, England, Frankreich und Belgien*. Jena: G. Fischer.

Lincoln, J, and Choi, E. 2010. "Strategic Alliances in the Japanese Economy," in H. Miyoshi, and Y. Nakata. *Have Japanese Firms Changed?*. Basingstoke: Palgrave Macmillan.

Lincoln, J., and Gerlach, M. 2004. *Japan's Network Economy: Structure, Persistence, and Change*. New York: Cambridge University Press.

Lincoln, J., Gerlach, M., and Takahashi, P. 1992. "Keiretsu Networks in the Japanese Economy: A Dyad Analysis of Intercorporate Ties," *American Sociological Review*, 57: 561–85.

Lincoln, J., and Shimotani, M. 2010. "Business Networks in Postwar Japan: Whither the Keiretsu?" in A. Colpan, T. Hikino, and J. Lincoln, (eds.), *The Oxford Handbook of Business Groups*. Oxford: Oxford University Press: 127–56.

Lincoln, J., Guillot, D., and Sargent, M. 2017. "Business Groups, Networks, and Embeddedness: Innovation and Implementation Alliances in Japanese Electronics, 1985–1998." *Industrial and Corporate Change*, 26: 357–78.

Lindgren, H. 1987. *Banking Group Investments in Swedish Industry*. Uppsala Papers in Economic History 15, Department of Economic History, Uppsala University.

Lindgren, H. 1988. *Bank, Investmentbolag, Bankirfirma. Stockholms Enskilda Bank 1924–1945*. Stockholm: Skandinaviska Enskilda Banken.

Lindgren, H. 1994. *Aktivt ägande. Investor under Växlande Konjunkturer*. Stockholm: Stockholm School of Economics.

Lindgren, H. 2009. *Jacob Wallenberg 1892–1980: Swedish Banker and International Negotiator*. Stockholm: Atlantis.

Lindgren, H. 2011. Affärsbankerna och det Svenska Näringslivet," in M. Larsson (ed.), *Företagsfinansiering, Från Sparbankslån till Derivat*. Stockholm: SNS Förlag.

Lindgren, H. 2012. "The Long-term Viability of the Wallenberg Family Business Group: the Role of a Dynastic Drive," in A. Perlinge and H. Sjögern (eds.), *Biographies of the Financial World*. Hedemora: Gidlunds.

Lindgren, H., and Sjögren, H. 2003. "Banking Systems as 'Ideal Types' and as Political Economy," in D. Forsyth and D. Verdier (eds.). *The Origins of National Financial Systems*. London: Routledge.

Linge, G. 1979. *Industrial Awakening: A Geography of Australian Manufacturing, 1788 to 1890*. Canberra: ANU Press.

Ljungqvist, A., and Richardson, M. 2003. "The Cash Flow, Return and Risk Characteristics of Private Equity," National Bureau of Economic Research Working Paper No. w9454.

Lockwood, W. W. 1968. *Economic Development of Japan: Growth and Structural Change*. Princeton, NJ: Princeton University Press.

Lopes, J. S. 1999. *A Economia Portuguesa desde 1960*. Lisbon: Gradiva.

Loubet, J. L. 2009. *La Maison Peugeot*. Paris: Perin.

Louis Dreyfus. 1951. *A L'occasion de Son Centenaire*. Montrouge.

Lubinski, C., Fear, J., and Perez, P. F. 2013. *Family Multinationals: Entrepreneurship, Governance and Pathways to Internationalization*. New York: Routledge.

Lucena, M. 1976. *A Evolução do Sistema Corporativo Português*. Lisbon: Perspectivas e Realidades.

Lumpkin, G. T., and Brigham, K. H. 2011. "Long-term Orientation and Intertemporal Choice in Family Firms," *Entrepreneurship Theory and Practice*, 35 (6): 1149–69.

Lundström, R. 1999. *Bank, Industri, Utlandsaffärer. Stockholms Enskilda Bank 1910–1924*. Stockholm: Stockholm School of Economics.

Luo, X., and Chung, C. 2005. "Keeping It All in the Family: The Role of Particularistic Relationships in Business Group Performance during Institutional Transition," *Administrative Science Quarterly*, 50: 404–39.

Luyten, D. 2010. "The Belgian Economic Elite and the Punishment of Economic Collaboration after the Second World War: Power and Legitimacy (1944–1952)," *Jahrbuch für Wirtschaftsgeschichte*, 2: 95–10

Luzzatto Fegiz, P. 1928. "Il Consiglio di Amministrazione e l'Indipendenza delle Imprese," *Giornale Degli Economisti e Rivista di Statistica*, 43: 197–231.

MacCormack, A. 2001. "Virgin.com," Harvard Business School Case, no. 9-601-041, rev. August 29, 2001.

Macdonald, G. 2004. *The National Energy Program*. Oxford: Oxford University Press.

McKay, J. P. 1986. "The House of Rothschild (Paris) as a Multinational Industrial Enterprise: 1875–1914," in A. Teichova, M. Lévy-Leboyer, and H. Nussbaum, *Multinational Enterprise in Historical Perspective*. Cambridge: Cambridge University Press.

McKenna, C. D. 2006. *The World's Newest Profession: Management Consulting in the Twentieth Century*. Cambridge: Cambridge University Press.

McLean, I. W. 2013. *Why Australia Prospered: The Shifting Sources of Economic Growth*. Princeton, NJ: Princeton University Press.

MacLennan, H. 1945. *Two Solitudes*. Toronto: Macmillan.

Maddison, A. 1991. *Dynamic Forces in Economic Development*. Oxford: Oxford University Press.

Maddison, A. 2009. "Statistics on World Population, GDP and Per Capita GDP, 1–2006 AD." http://www.ggdc.net/maddison.

Maddison, A. 2013. "Historical Statistics for the World Economy: 1–2003 AD," *Maddison Project*, http://www.ggdc.net/maddison/maddison-project/home.htm.

Madureira, N. L. 2002. *A Economia dos Interesses. Portugal entre as Guerras*. Lisbon: Livros Horizonte.

Magnusson, L. 2010. *Sveriges Ekonomiska Historia*. Stockholm: Norstedts.

Mahmood, I., Chung, C., and Mitchell, W. 2013. "Business Group Innovativeness as a Market Evolves," *Management Science*, 59: 1142–61.

Maijoor, S. J. 1990. *The Economics of Accounting Regulation. Effects of Dutch Accounting Regulation for Public Accountants and Firms*. Ph.D. thesis, Maastricht University.

Maksimovic, V., and Philips, G. M. 2013. "Conglomerate Firms, Internal Capital Markets, and the Theory of the Firm," *Annual Review of Financial Economics*, 5: 225–44.

Maman, D. 2002. "The Emergence of Business Groups: Israel and South Korea Compared," *Organization Studies*, 23: 737–58.

Manager Magazine, 2002. March 15. online, accessed April 28, 2013.

Mani, D., and Moody, J. 2014. "Moving Beyond Stylized Economic Models: The Hybrid World of the Indian Firm Ownership Network," *American Journal of Sociology*, 119: 1629–69.

Markides, C. C., and Williamson, P. J. 1994. "Related Diversification, Core Competencies and Corporate Performance," *Strategic Management Journal*, 15: 149–65.

Marquis, J. 1993. *Merchant Adventurer: The Story of W. R. Grace*. Wilmington: Scholarly Resources.

Marrus, M. 2000. *Mr. Sam: The Life and Times of Samuel Bronfman*. Lebanon, NH: University Press of New England.

Marseille, J. 2004. *Les Wendel, 1704–2004*. Paris: Perrin.

Marseille, J., and Torres, F. 1992. *Alcatel Alsthom. Histoire de la Compagnie Générale d'Electricité*. Paris: Larousse.

Martin, R. 1980. *Patron de Droit Divin*. Gallimard, Paris.

Martin Aceña, P., and Comín, F. 1991. *INI. 50 Años de Industrialización en España (INI. 50 Years of Industrialization in Spain)*. Madrid: Espasa Calpe.

Martins, M. B. 1973. *Grupos e Sociedades em Portugal*. Lisbon: Estampa.

Masulis, R. W., Kien Pham, P., and Zein, J. 2011. "Family Business Groups around the World: Financing Advantages, Control Motivations, and Organizational Choices," *Review of Financial Studies*, 24 (11): 3556–601.

Maville, X., Tulkens, C. H., and Vincent, A. 1997. *La Société Générale de Belgique 1822–1997. Le Pouvoir d'un Groupe à Travers l'Histoire*. Brussels: CRISP.

Mayer, M., and Whittington, R. 1996. "The Survival of the European Holding Company," in R. Whitley and P. H. Kristensen (eds). *The Changing European Firm*. London: Routledge.

Mediobanca, 2014. *Le Principali Società Italiane*. Milan: Mediobanca.

Mees, A. C. 1939. *NV Internationale Crediet- en Handelsvereniging "Rotterdam." Gedenkboek Uitgegeven bij het Vijf-en-zeventig Bestaan op 28 Augustus 1838*. Rotterdam: NV Internationale Crediet- en Handelsvereniging "Rotterdam."

Mehrotra, V., Morck, R., Shim, J., and Wiwattanakantang, Y. 2013. Adoptive Expectations: Rising Sons in Japanese Family Firms," *Journal of Financial Economics*, 108: 840–54.

Merrett, D. T. 2002. "Australian Firms Abroad Before 1970: Why So Few, Why Those, and Why There?," *Business History*, 44 (2): 65–87.

Merrett, D. 2004. *William Lionel Buckland*. Melbourne: William Lionel Buckland Foundation.

Merrett, D. 2015. "Big Business and Foreign Firms," in S. Ville and G. Withers (eds.), *The Cambridge Economic History of Australia*. Cambridge: Cambridge University Press.

Merrett, D. T., and Ville, S. 2009. "Financing Growth: New Issues by Australian Firms, 1920–1939," *Business History Review*, 83 (3): 563–89.

Metrick, A. and Yasuda, A. 2010. "The Economics of Private Equity Funds," *Review of Financial Studies*, 23 (6): 2303–41.

Michie, R. 1999. *The London Stock Exchange: A History*. Oxford: Oxford University Press.

Milgrom, P., and Roberts, J. 1992. *Economics, Organization and Management*. Englewood Cliffs, NJ: Prentice-Hall.

Milgrom, P., and Roberts, J. 1994. "Complementarities and Systems: Understanding Japanese Economic Organization," *Estudios Económicos*, 9 (1): 3–42.

Milke, M. 2014. *Government Subsidies in Canada*. Vancouver: Fraser Institute.

Miller, R. 1976. "The Making of the Grace Contract: British Bondholders and the Peruvian Government, 1885–1890," *Journal of Latin American Studies*, 8 (1): 73–100.

Miller, R. 1983. "The Grace Contract, The Peruvian Corporation, and Peruvian History," *Ibero-amerikanisches Archiv*, Neue Folge, 9 (3/4): 319–48.

Mitchell, J., and Hohl, B., 2008. "Fiat's Strategic Alliance with Tata," IES 202 0-308-023. Barcelona: IESE Business School.

Moine, J. M. 1989. *Les Barons du Fer*. Nancy: Editions Serpenoise.

Mondragon Corporation. 2012. "Annual Report," http://www.mondragon-corporation.com/eng/about-us/economic-and-financial-indicators/annual-report/, accessed September 13, 2014.

Mondragón Corporation. 2014. "Companies and Cooperatives," http://www.mondragon-corporation.com/eng/our-businesses/our-companies/, accessed September 13, 2014.

Moody's Investors Service. 2015. *Investment Holding Companies: One Size Does Not Fit All*, October 8, 2005.

Morck, R. 2003. "Why Some Double Taxation Might Make Sense: The Special Case of Inter-Corporate Dividends," University of Alberta Center for Financial Research Working Paper, No. 03-01.

Morck, R. 2005. "How to Eliminate Pyramidal Business Groups: The Double Taxation of Intercorporate Dividends and Other Incisive Uses of Tax Policy," in J. M. Poterba (ed.), *Tax Policy and the Economy*. Cambridge, MA: MIT Press: 135–79.

Morck, R. 2010. "The Riddle of the Great Pyramids," in A. M. Colpan, T. Hikino, and J. R. Lincoln (eds.), *The Oxford Handbook of Business Groups*. Oxford: Oxford University Press: 602–28.

Morck, R., and Nakamura, M. 1995. "Banks and Corporate Governance in Canada," in R. Daniels and R. Morck (eds.), *Corporate Decision Making in Canada*. Calgary: University of Calgary Press: 481–501.

Morck, R., and Nakamura, M. 1999. "Banks and Corporate Control in Japan," *Journal of Finance*, 43: 319–39.

Morck, R., and Nakamura, M. 2005. "A Frog in a Well Knows Nothing of the Ocean: A History of Corporate Ownership in Japan," in R. Morck (ed.), *A Global History of Corporate Governance*. National Bureau of Economic Research and University of Chicago Press: 367–459.

Morck, R., and Nakamura, M. 2007. "Business Groups and the Big Push: Meiji Japan's Mass Privatization and Subsequent Growth," *Enterprise & Society*, 8 (3): 543–601.

Morck, R., Percy, M., Tian, G. Y., and Yeung, B. 2005. "The Rise and Fall of the Widely Held Firm: A History of Corporate Ownership in Canada," in R. Morck (ed.), *A History of Corporate Governance around the World*. National Bureau of Economic Research & University of Chicago Press: 65–140.

Morck, R., Stangeland, D., and Yeung, B., 2000. "Inherited Wealth, Corporate Control and Economic Growth: The Canadian Disease?," in R. Morck (ed.), *Concentrated Corporate Ownership*, National Bureau of Economic Research ND University of Chicago Press: 319–69.

Morck, R., Tian, G. Y., and Yeung, B. 2005. "Who Owns Whom? Economic Nationalism and Family Controlled Pyramidal Groups in Canada," in L. Eden and W. Dobson (eds.), *Governance, Multinationals & Growth: Essays in Honour of Ed Safarian*. Cheltenham: Elgar: 44–67.

Morck, R., Wolfenzon, D., and Yeung, B. 2005. "Corporate Governance, Economic Entrenchment, and Growth," *Journal of Economic Literature* 43 (3): 655–720.

Morck, R., and Yeung, B. 2004. Family Firms and the Rent-seeking Society. *Entrepreneurship: Theory and Practice*, 28 (4): 391–409.

Morck, R., Yeung, B., and Yu, W. 2013. "R-squared and the Economy," *Annual Review of Financial Economics*, 5 (1): 143–66.

Morsel, H. 1981. "Les Groupes dans les Industries Électriques en France avant les Nationalisations," *Cahiers d'Histoire*, 26 (4).

Muñoz, J. 1969. *El Poder de la Banca en España*. Madrid: ZYX.

Munro, J. F. 2003. *Maritime Enterprise and Empire*. Woodbridge: Boydell.

Musacchio, A., and Lazzarini, S. G. 2012. "Leviathan in Business: Varieties of State Capitalism and their Implications for Economic Performance," Working Paper at http://ssrn.com/abstract=2070942.

Nadal, J., Carreras, A., and Sudria, C. (eds.). 1991. *La Economía Española en el Siglo XX. Una Perspectiva Histórica. (The Spanish Economy in the 20th Century. A Historical Perspective)*. Barcelona: Ariel.

Nanda, A., and Bartlett, C. 1990. "Corning, Inc.: A Network of Alliances," Harvard Business School Case, no. 9-391-102.

Naylor, R. 1975. *The History of Canadian business 1867–1914*. Toronto: James Lorimer.

Nelson, R. R. 1991. "Why Do Firms Differ, and How Does It Matter?," *Strategic Management Journal*, 12 (2): 61–74.

Nelson, R. R., and Winter, S. G. 1977. *An Evolutionary Theory of Economic Change*. Cambridge: Belknap Press.

Nemni, M., and M. Nemni. 2010. *Young Trudeau: 1919–1944: Son of Quebec, Father of Canada*. Toronto: McClelland & Stewart.

Neuburger, H. 1977. "The Industrial Politics of the Kreditbanken 1880–1914," *Business History Review*, vol. 51: 190–207.

Nilsson, G. B. 2005. *The founder: André Oscar Wallenberg 1816–1886: Swedish Banker, Politician and Journalist*. Stockholm: Almqvist & Wiksell International.

Nishiguchi, T., and Beaudet, A. 1998. "The Toyota Group and the Aisin Fire," *Sloan Management Review*, Fall, 1998: 49–59.

Nygren, I. 1985. *Från Stockholm Banco till Citibank, Svenska Kreditmarknad under 325 år*. Stockholm: Liber.

Olcutt, G., and Oliver, N. 2014. "Social Capital, Sensemaking, and Recovery: Japanese Companies and the 2011 Earthquake," *California Management Review*, 56: 5–22.

Olsson, U. 1997. *At the Centre of Development: Skandinaviska Enskilda Banken and its Predecessors 1856–1996*. Stockholm: Skandinaviska Enskilda Banken.

Olsson, U. 2002. *Furthering a Fortune: Marcus Wallenberg: Swedish Banker and Industrialist 1899–1982*. Stockholm: Ekerlids.

Ormaechea, J. M. 1993. *The Mondragon Cooperative Experience*. Lezo, Guipúzcoa: Litografía Danona Sociedad Cooperativa.

Östlind, A. 1945. *Svensk Samhällsekonomi 1914–1922, med Särskild Hänsyn till Industri, Banker och Penningväsen*. Stockholm: Svenska Bankföreningen.

Owen, G. 2009. "Industrial Policy in Twentieth Century Britain," in R. Coopey and P. Lyth (eds.), *Business in Britain in the Twentieth Century*. Oxford: Oxford University Press.

Pagano, M., and Volpin, P. 2005a. "Managers, Workers, and Corporate Control," *Journal of Finance* 60 (2): 841–68.

Pagano, M., and Volpin, P. 2005b. "The Political Economy of Corporate Governance," *American Economic Review*, 95 (4): 1005–30.

Pagano, M., and Volpin, P. 2006. "Alfred Marshall Lecture Shareholder Protection, Stock Market Development, and Politics," *Journal of the European Economic Association*, 4 (2–3): 315–41.

Palmisano, S. 2006. "The Globally Integrated Enterprise." *Foreign Affairs*, May/June, 2006.

Pavan, R. J. 1976. *Strutture e Strategie delle Imprese Italiane*. Bologna: Il Mulino.

Pavan, R. J. 1978. "Making the Divisional Structure the Legal Structure in Italy. Why and How," unpublished manuscript, Chandler Papers, Baker Library Historical Collections, Harvard Business School.

Perrow, C. 1992. "Small Firm Networks," in N. Nohria and R. G. Eccles (eds.), *Networks and Organizations*. Boston: Harvard Business School Press: 445–70.

Peteraf, M. A. 1993. "The Cornerstones of Competitive Advantage: A Resource-based View. *Strategic Management Journal*," 14 (3): 179–91.

Pfeffer, J., and Salancik, G. 1978. *The External Control of Organizations*. New York: Harper & Row.

Phalippou, L., and Gottschalg, O. 2009. "The Performance of Private Equity Funds," *Review of Financial Studies*, 22 (4): 1747–76.

Pinkstone, B., and Meredith, D. 1992. *Global Connections: A History of Exports and the Australian Economy*. Canberra: AGPS Press.

Pintado, M. R., and Mendonça, A. 1989. *Os Novos Grupos Económicos*. Lisbon: Texto Editora.

Piore, M., and Sabel, C. 1984. *The Second Industrial Divide: Possibilities for Prosperity*. New York: Basic Books.

Pisano, G., and Corsi, E. 2012. "Virgin Group: Finding New Avenues for Growth," Harvard Business School Case, no. 9-661-070 (rev. May 9, 2012).

Plessis, A. 2000. "Une Maison de la Haute Banque Parisienne, les Mirabaud, et le Financement des Entreprises de la Fin du XIXe Siècle à la Seconde Guerre Mondiale," in P. Marguerat, L. Tissot, and Y. Froixdevaux, *Banques et Entreprises Industrielles en Europe de L'Ouest, XIXe et XXe Siècles: Aspects Internationaux, Nationaux et Régionaux*. Neuchâtel: Université de Neuchâtel.

Podolny, J., and Page, K. 1998. "Network Forms of Organization," *Annual Review of Sociology*, 24: 57–76.

Porter, J. 1965. *The Vertical Mosaic: An Analysis of Social Class and Power in Canada*. Toronto: University of Toronto Press.

Porter, M. E. 1987. "From Competitive Advantage to Corporate Strategy," *Harvard Business Review*, 65 (3): 43–59.

Porter, M. E. 1990. *The Competitive Advantage of Nations*. London: Macmillan.

Powell, W. 1990. "Neither Market nor Hierarchy: Network Forms of Organization," in B. M. Staw and L. L. Cummings (eds.), *Research in Organizational Behavior*, vol. 7: 295–336.

Poynter, J. R. 1967. *Russell Grimwade*. Carlton, Vic.: Melbourne University Press.

Poynter, J. R. 1979. "Baillieu, William Lawrence (Willie) (1859–1936)," in *Australian Dictionary of Biography*. National Centre of Biography, Australian National University.

Pratley, N. 2004. "Legacy of the Lord with the Midas Touch," *The Guardian*, November 2, 2004.

Prechel, H. 1997. "Corporate Transformation to the Multilayered Subsidiary Form: Changing Economic Conditions and State Business Policy," *Sociological Forum*, 12 (3): 405–39.

Prechel, H., Morris, T., Woods, T., and Walden, R. 2008. "Corporate Diversification Revisited: The Political-legal Environment, the Multilayer-Subsidiary Form, and Mergers and Acquisitions," *Sociological Quarterly*, 49: 849–78.

Prêcheur, C. 1959. *La Lorraine Sidérurgique*. Paris: S.A.B.R.I.

Priemel, K. C. 2007. *Flick. Eine Konzerngeschichte vom Kaiserreich bis zur Bundesrepublik*. Göttingen: Wallstein Verlag.

Private Equity International, 2016, https://www.privateequityinternational.com/PEI/PEI300.

Prizkoleit, K. several years 1953–1963. *Männer, Mächte, Monopole*, Frankfurt am Main: Büchergilde Gutenberg.

Puri, P. 2010. "The Capital Markets Perspective on a National Securities Regulator," *Supreme Court Law Review*, 51 (2d): 603–22.

Quote magazine, 2014. "Quote 500."

Radar (pseud. of Emanuele Rienzi). 1948. *Organizzazione del Capitale Finanziario Italiano*. Rome: Edizioni Italiane.

Rajan, R., and Zingales, L. 2003. "The Great Reversals: The Politics of Financial Development in the Twentieth Century," *Journal of Financial Economics*, 69: 5–50.

Ramsay, I. M., and Stapledon, G. P. 2001. "Corporate Groups in Australia," *Australian Business Law Review*, 29 (February 2001): 7–32.

Ravenscraft, D. J., and Scherer, F. M. 1987. *Mergers, Sell-offs, and Economic Efficiency*. Washington, DC: Brookings Institution Press.

Rawling, J. N. 1939. *Who Owns Australia?* Sydney: Modern Publishers.

Reckendrees, A. 2000. *Das "Stahltrust"-Projekt. Die Gründung der Vereinigten Stahlwerke A.G. und ihre Unternehmensentwicklung 1926–1933/34*. Munich: C. H. Beck.

Reingold, J. 2015. "Everybody Hates Pearson," *Fortune*, January 21, 2015.

Reiter, J. 2003. "Changing the Microfoundations of Corporatism: The Impact of Financial Globalisation on Swedish Corporate Ownership," *New Political Economy*, 8 (1): 103–25.

Rinaldi, A., and Vasta, M. 2005. "The Structure of Italian Capitalism, 1952–1972: New Evidence Using the Interlocking Directorates Technique," *Financial History Review*, 12 (2): 173–98.

Rinaldi, A., and Vasta, M. 2012. "The Italian Corporate Network after the 'Golden Age' (1972–1983): from Centrality to Marginalization of State-Owned Enterprises," *Enterprise & Society*, 13 (2): 378–413.

Rinaldi, A., and Vasta, M. 2014. "Persistent and Stubborn: the State in the Italian Capitalism, 1913–2001," in T. David and G. Westerhuis (eds.), *The Power of Corporate Networks. A Comparative and Historical Perspective*, New York, Abingdon: Routledge: 169–88.

Roberts, M. J., Sahlman, W. A., and Barley, L. 2007, rev. 2008. "Texas Pacific Group—J. Crew," Harvard Business School Case, no. 808–017.

Roe, M. 2003. *Political Determinants of Corporate Governance: Political Context, Corporate Impact*. Oxford: Oxford University Press.

Rolfe, H. 1967. *The Controllers: Interlocking Directorates in Large Australian Companies*. Melbourne: Cheshire.

Romano, R. 1992. *L'Industria Cotoniera in Italia dall'Unità al 1914*. Milan: Banca Commerciale Italiana.

Rosenkopf, L., and Padula, G. 2008. "Investigating the Microstructure of Network Evolution: Alliance Formation in the Mobile Communications Industry," *Organization Science*, 19: 669–87.

Rosenstein-Rodan, P. 1943. "Problems of Industrialization of Eastern and South Eastern Europe," *Economic Journal*, 53: 202–11.

Rossi, E. 1955. *I Padroni del Vapore*. Bari: Laterza.

Rothschild, G. de. 1983. *Contre Bonne Fortune*. Paris: Belfond.

Rueschemeyer, D., Huber Stephens, E., and Stephens, J. 1992. *Capitalist Development and Democracy*. Cambridge: Polity.

Rukstad, M. G., Collis, D. J., and Levine, T. 2001, rev. 2009. "The Walt Disney Company: The Entertainment King," Harvard Business School Case, no. 701–035.

Rumelt, R. P. 1974. *Strategy, Structure, and Economic Performance*. Boston: Division of Research, Graduate School of Business Administration, Harvard University.

Rust, M. J. 1973. "Business and Politics in the Third Republic: The Comité des Forges and the French Steel Industry, 1896–1914," Ph.D. thesis, Princeton University.

Salings Börsenjahrbuch. 1882–1932. Berlin: Saling.

Samphantharak, K. 2002. "Internal Capital Markets in Business Groups," at http://cier.uchicago.edu/papers/.

San Román, E., Fernández Pérez, P., and Gil López, A. 2014. "As Old as History: Family-controlled Business Groups in Transport Services: the Case of SEUR," *Business History*, 56 (8): 1–23.

Sanchez Montes de Oca, M., and Saavedra Acevedo, J. 2008. "Entrevista Juan Miguel Villar Mir (Interview Juan Miguel Villar Mir)" *Escuela de Organizacion Industrial*, http://www.eoi.es/portal/guest/alumni/entrevistas/entrevista-juan-miguel-villar-mir, accessed February 19, 2014.

Saxenian, A. 1996. *Regional Advantage: Culture and Competition in Silicon Valley and Route 128*. Boston, MA: Harvard University Press.

Schaafsma, J. R. 1946. "De Belastingheffing van de Groot-Industrie," in P. J. A. Adriani, *Fiscale Ervaringen in Bezettingstijd 1940–1945*, Amsterdam: L. J. Veen's Uitgeverijmaatschappij N. V.

Schedvin, C. 1987. *Shaping Science and Industry: A History of Australia's Council for Scientific and Industrial Research, 1926–49*. Sydney: Allen & Unwin.

Schneider, B. R. 2008. "Economic Liberalization and Corporate Governance: The Resilience of Business Groups in Latin America," *Comparative Politics*, 40: 379–98.

Schneider, B. R. 2009. "A Comparative Political Economy of Diversified Business Groups, or How States Organize Capitalism," *Review of International Political Economy*, 16: 178–201.

Schneider, B. R. 2010. "Business Groups and the State: the Politics of Expansion, Restructuring and Collapse," in A. M. Colpan, T. Hikino, and J. R. Lincoln (eds.), *The Oxford Handbook of Business Groups*. Oxford: Oxford University Press: 651–69.

Schneider, B. R. 2013. *Hierarchical Capitalism in Latin America; Business, Labor and the Challenges of Equitable Development*. New York: Cambridge University Press.

Schröter, H. G. 2005. *Americanization of the European Economy. A Compact Survey of American Economic Influence in Europe since the 1880s*. Dordrecht: Springer.

Schröter, H. G. 2011. "Germania," in G. Nardozzi (ed.), *Lo Stato da Gesture di Grandi Imprese a Referente nel Loro Governo. Privatizzazioni e Competitive delle Imprese*. Milan: Fondazione Ansaldo Editore, B 06–118.

Schwartz, P., and Gonzalez, M. J. 1978. *Una Historia del Instituto Nacional de Industria (A History of the National Institute of Industry)*. Madrid: Editorial Tecnos.

Schweitzer, S. 1982. *Des Engrenages à la Chaîne: Les Usines Citroën, 1915–1935*. Lyons: Presses Universitaires de Lyon.

Schwetzler, B., and Reimund, C. 2003. "Conglomerate Discount and Cash Distortion: New Evidence from Germany," in *Handelshochschule Leipzig Arbeitspapier* 60 (March 31, 2003).

Sensoy, B. A., Wang, Y., and Weisbach, M. S. 2014. "Limited Partner Performance and the Maturing of the Private Equity Industry," *Journal of Financial Economics*, 112 (3): 320–43.

SEPI. 2013. *Informe Annual (Annual Report)*, http://www.sepi.es/img/resources/publicaciones/Esp/InformeAnualSEPI2012.pdf, accessed February 14, 2014.

SEPI. 2014. "History: Grupo INI," http://www.sepi.es/img/default.aspx?cmd=0004&IdContent=345&idLanguage=_EN&idContraste, accessed February 14, 2014.

Servaes, H. 1996. "The Value of Diversification during the Conglomerate Merger Wave," *Journal of Finance*, 51 (4): 1201–25.

Shanley, M. 1996. "Straw Men and M-Form Myths: Comment on Freeland," *American Journal of Sociology*, 102 (2): 527–36.

Sheldon, P., and Thornwhaite, L. 1999. "Swedish Engineering Employers: The Search for Industrial Peace in the Absence of Centralized Collective Bargaining," *Industrial Relations Journal*, 30 (5): 514–32.

Sherman, S. P. 1988. "GE's Costly Lesson on Wall Street," *Fortune*, May 9, 1988.

Shleifer, A., and Vishny, R. W. 1991. "Takeovers in the '60s and the '80s: Evidence and Implications," *Strategic Management Journal*, 12 (S2): 51–9.

Siciliano, G. 2001. *Cento Anni di Borsa in Italia*. Bologna: Il Mulino.

Siegel, J. 2007. "Contingent Political Capital and International Alliances: Evidence from South Korea," *Administrative Science Quarterly*, 52: 621–66.

Siegel, J., and Choudhury, P. 2013. "A Reexamination of Tunneling and Business Groups: New Data and New Methods," *Review of Financial Studies*, 25: 1763–98.

Silva, A. F. 2011. "The Circulation of Management Knowledge: Management Consulting in Portugal in the Early 1970s." Paper Presented to the Business History Conference, St. Louis.

Silva, A. F., Amaral, L., and Neves, P. 2015. "Business Groups in Portugal in the Estado Novo Period (1930–1974): Family, Power and Structural Change," *Business History*, 58 (1): 49–68.

Silva, A. F., and Neves, P. 2014a. "Business Coalitions and Segmentation: Dynamics of the Portuguese Corporate Network," in G. Westerhuis, and T. David (eds.), *The Power of Corporate Networks: A Comparative and Historical Perspective*. New York and Abingdon: Routledge: 191–212.

Silva, A. F., and Neves, P. 2014b. "In the Making: Portuguese Business Groups and the Financial Crisis." Paper Presented to the Association of Business Historians Conference, Newcastle.

Silva, A. F., and Neves, P. 2018a. "Ties That Bind: Ownership and Control Configurations in Portuguese Business Groups," Nova SBE Working Paper.

Silva, A. F., and Neves, P. 2018b. "Big Business and Corporate Networks in Portugal: A New Approach," APHES Working Paper.

Silverman, B. S. 1999. "Technological Resources and the Direction of Corporate Diversification: Toward an Integration of the Resource-based View and Transaction Cost Economics," *Management Science*, 45 (8): 1109–24.

Sjögern, H. 2011. "Breaking the Industrial Logic – a Comparative Study of Swedish Family Dynasties," *Research Report no. 24*. Institute for Economic and Business History Research, Stockholm School of Economics.

Sjögern, H. 2012. *Den Uthålliga Kapitalismen: Bolagsstyrningen i Astra, Stora Kopparberg och Svenska Tändsticksaktiebolaget*. Stockholm: SNS.

Sköld, M. and Karlsson, C. 2012. "Technology Sharing in Manufacturing Business Groups," *Journal of Product Innovation Management*, 29 (1): 113–24.

Sluyterman, K. E. 1998. "Dutch Multinational Trading Companies in the Twentieth Century," in: G. Jones (ed.), *The Multinational Traders*. London and New York: Routledge: 86–101.

Sluyterman, K. E. 2005. *Dutch Enterprise in the Twentieth Century. Business Strategies in a Small Open Economy*. London and New York: Routledge.

Sluyterman, K. E. 2015. "Introduction," in K. Sluyterman (ed.) *Varieties of Capitalism and Business History. The Dutch Case*. London: Routledge.

Sluyterman, K. E., and Bouwens, B. 2014. *Brewery, Brand and Family. 150 Years of Heineken*. Amsterdam: Boom.

Smångs, M. 2006. "The Nature of the Business Group: A Social Network Perspective," *Organization*, 13 (6): 889–909.

Smångs, M. 2008. "Business Groups in 20th-Century Swedish Political Economy. A Sociological Perspective," *American Journal of Economics and Sociology*, 67 (5): 889–913.

Smith, M. S. 2006. *The Emergence of Modern Business Enterprise in France, 1800–1930*. Cambridge, MA: Harvard University Press.

Smith, R. G., and Barrie, A. 1976. *Aspro—How a Family Business Grew Up*. Melbourne: Nicholas International Limited.

Sobel, R. 1984. *The Rise and the Fall of the Conglomerate Kings*. NY: Stein and Day. Société Générale de Belgique, 1988. Annual Report.

Söderstrom, H. T., Berglöf, E., Holmström, B., Högfeldt, P., and Meyersson Milgrom, E. M. 2003. *Corporate Governance and Structural Change: European Challenges*. SNS Economic Policy Group Report, Studieförbundet Näringsliv och Samhälle.

Spender, J. A. 1930. *Weetman Pearson. First Viscount Cowdray 1856–1927*. London: Cassell.

Stavrou, E., Kassinis, G., and Filotheou, A. 2007. "Downsizing and Stakeholder Orientation among the Fortune 500: Does Family Ownership Matter?," *Journal of Business Ethics*, 72 (2): 149–62.

Streitwieser, M. L. 1991. "The Extent and Nature of Establishment-level Diversification in Sixteen US Manufacturing Industries," *Journal of Law and Economics*, 34 (2): 503–34.

Stretton, H. 1985. "The Quality of Leading Australians," in S. R. Graubard (ed.), *Australia, the Daedalus Symposium*. Sydney: Angus & Robertson.

Strouse, J. 1999. *Morgan: American Financier*. New York: Random House.

Süddeutsche Zeitung, 2011. August 13–15, accessed June 20, 2015.

Sundin, A., and S-I Sundqvist. 2009. *Ägarna och Makten i Sveriges Börsföretag*. Stockholm: DN.

Sundin, A., and S-I Sundqvist. 2016. *Ägarna och Makten i Sveriges Börsföretag 2015*. Stockholm: SNS.

Swedish Bankers' Association. 2017. *Bank and Finance Statistics*. Stockholm.

Swensen, D. F. 2009. *Pioneering Portfolio Management: An Unconventional Approach to Institutional Investment, Fully Revised and Updated*. New York, NY: The Free Press.

Sykes, T. 1994. *The Bold Riders: Behind Australia's Corporate Collapses*. St. Leonards, NSW: Allen & Unwin.

Szeless, G. 2001. *Diversifikation und Unternehmenserfolg*. Diss., St. Gallen: Universität St.Gallen.

Tamames, R. 1967. *Los Monopolios en España*. Madrid: Editorial Zix.

Tamames, R. 1977. *La Oligarquía Financiera en España*. Barcelona: Planeta.

Tamames, R. 1992. *Introducción a la Economía Española (Introduction to the Spanish Economy)*. Madrid: Alianza Editorial.

Taylor, G. 2006. "From Shirtsleeves to Shirtless: The Bronfman Dynasty and the Seagram Empire," *Business and Economic History Online*, 4 (1): 1–36.

Taylor, G., and Baskerville, P. 1994. *A Concise History of Canadian Business*. Oxford: Oxford University Press.

Tedlow, R. 1988. "Trade Association and Public Relations," in H. Yamazaki and M. Miyamoto (eds.), *Trade Associations in Business History*. Tokyo: University of Tokyo Press: 139–72.

Teece, D. J., Pisano, G., and Shuen, A. 1997. "Dynamic Capabilities and Strategic Management," *Strategic Management Journal*, 18 (7): 509–33.

Tell, F. 2008. "From ASEA to ABB; Managing Big Business the Swedish Way," in S. Fellman et al. (eds.), *Creating Nordic Capitalism: The Business History of a Competitive Periphery*. Basingstoke: Palgrave Macmillan.

TheCityUK. 2012. "Financial Markets Series: Private Equity," http://www.thecityuk.com/assets/Uploads/Private-Equity-2.pdf.

Thomsen, S., and Pedersen, T. 1994. "European Ownership Structures: The 100 Largest Companies in Six European Nations," in *Institute of International Economics and Management*, Working Paper 5–94, Copenhagen: Institute of International Economics and Management.

Thunholm, L-E. 2007. *Flydda Tider*. Stockholm: Fischer & Co.

Thurow, L. 1993. *Head to Head: The Coming Economic Battle among Japan, Europe, and America*. New York, NY: Warner Books.

Tian, G. Y. 2006. *Three Essays on Corporate Control in Canada*. Ph.D. thesis, University of Alberta.

Tian, G. Y. 2009. "Pyramid Groups and Firm Performance: Empirical Evidence from Canadian Corporations," *Corporate Ownership and Control*, 7 (3): 104–22.

Toninelli, P. A. (ed.). 2000. *The Rise and Fall of State-Owned Enterprise in the Western World*. Cambridge: Cambridge University Press.

Toninelli, P. 2008. "From Private to Public to Private Again: A Long-term Perspective on Nationalization," *Análise Social*, vol. XLIII (4): 675–92.

Toninelli, P. A. and Vasta, M. 2010. "State-owned enterprises (1936–83)," in A. Colli and M. Vasta (eds.), *Forms of Enterprise in Twentieth century Italy. Boundaries, Structures and Strategies*. Cheltenham: Elgar: 52–86.

Tortella, G. 1994. *El Desarrollo de la España Contemporánea. Historia Económica de los Siglos XIX y XX (The Development of Contemporary Spain. Economic History of the 19th and 20th Centuries)*. Madrid: Alianza Editorial.

Tortella, G., and García Ruiz, J. L. 2013. *Spanish Money and Banking: A History*. New York: Palgrave McMillan.

Useem, J. 2004. "Another Boss Another Revolution—Jeff Immelt is Following a Time-Honored GE Tradition: Abandoning the Most Treasured Ideas of His Predecessor," *Fortune*, April 5, 2004.

Uzzi, B. 1996. "The Sources and Consequences of Embeddedness for the Economic Performance of Organizations: The Network Effect," *American Sociological Review*, 61 (4): 674–98.

Van der Wee, H. 1996. *The Industrial Revolution in Belgium*, in M. Teich, and R. Porter (eds.), *The Industrial Revolution in National Context: Europe and the USA*. Cambridge: Cambridge University Press.

Van der Wee, H., and Verbreyt, M. 1997. *La Générale de Banque (1822–1997): Un Défi Permanent*. Brussels: Racine.

Van Gerwen, J., and Goey, F. de. 2008. *Ondernemers in Nederland. Variaties in Ondernemen*. Amsterdam: Boom.

Vanthemsche, G. 1991. "State, Banks and Industry in Belgium and The Netherlands, 1919–1939" in H. James, H. Lindgren, and A. Teichova. *The Role of Banks in the Interwar Economy*. Cambridge: Cambridge University Press.

Van Wolferen, K. 1990. *The Enigma of Japanese Power: People and Politics in a Stateless Nation*. New York: Vintage Books.

Varian, H. 2007. "An iPod Has Global Value. Ask the Many Countries that Make It," *New York Times*, June 28, 2007.

Vartiainen, J. 1998. "Understanding Swedish Social Democracy: Victims of Success?" *Oxford Review of Economic Policy*, 14 (1): 19–39.

Vasta, M. 2006a. "Appendix: the Source and the Imita.db Dataset," in R. Giannetti and M. Vasta (eds.), *Evolution of Italian Enterprises in the 20th Century*. Heidelberg, New York: Physica-Verlag: 269–73.

Vasta, M. 2006b. "The Largest 200 Manufacturing Firms (1913–2001)," in R. Giannetti and M. Vasta. (eds.), *Evolution of Italian Enterprises in the 20th Century*. Heidelberg, New York: Physica-Verlag: 87–110.

Vedres, B., and D. Stark. 2010. "Structural Folds: Generative Disruption in Overlapping Groups," *American Journal of Sociology*, 115: 1150–90.

Vernon, R. 1966. "International Investment and International Trade in the Product Cycle," *Quarterly Journal of Economics*, 80 (2): 190–207.

Vietor, D. 1994. *Contrived Competition: Regulation and Deregulation in America*. Cambridge, MA: Harvard University Press.

Villalonga, B. 2004. "Diversification Discount or Premium? New Evidence from the Business Information Tracking Series," *Journal of Finance*, 59 (2): 479–506.

Ville, S. 1998. "Business Development in Colonial Australia," *Australian Economic History Review*, 38 (1): 16–41.

Ville, S., and D. Merrett. 2016. "Big Business in Twentieth-Century Australia," Source Papers in Economic History, 12: 1–34, Australian National University.

Vincent, A., and Lentzen, E. 1983. "La Concentration Économique et les Groupes Société Générale de Belgique COBEPA, Bruxelles Lambert et Frère-Bourgeois en 1981–1982," *Courrier Hebdomadaire du CRISP*, 1: 993–994.

Vincent, A., and Tulkens, C. X. 1998. La Société Générale de Belgique et la Générale de Banque: Intégration dans Deux Groupes Distincts. *Courrier Hebdomadaire du CRISP*, 28 (1): 1613–1614.

Vuillermot, C. 2001. *Pierre-Marie Durand et l'Energie Industrielle. L'Histoire d'un Groupe Électrique 1906–1945*. Paris: CNRS Editions.

VV. AA. 1992–1994. *Storia dell'industria elettrica in Italia*. Bari: Laterza.

Wailerdsak, N., and Suehiro, A. 2010. "Business Groups in Thailand," in A. M. Colpan, T. Hikino, and J. R. Lincoln (eds.), *The Oxford Handbook of Business Groups*. Oxford: Oxford University Press.

Wasserman, S., and Faust, K. 1994. *Social Network Analysis. Methods and Applications*. Cambridge: Cambridge University Press.

Watts, D. 1999. *Small Worlds: The Dynamics of Networks between Order and Randomness*. Princeton, NJ: Princeton University Press.

Weder, D. 1968. *Die 200 Größten Deutschen Aktiengesellschaften. Beziehungen Zwischen Größe, Lebensdauer und Wettbewerbschancen von Unternehmen*. Frankfurt: Universität Frankfurt.

Weiner, C. 2005. "The Conglomerate Discount in Germany and the Relationship to Corporate Governance," in Discussion Paper 2005–063, December 12, 2005, Berlin: Humboldt-Universität, Sonderforschungsbereich 649.

Welch, K. 2014. "Private Equity's Diversification Illusion: Economic Comovement and Fair Value Reporting," SSRN Working Paper No. 2379170.

Wellhöner, V. 1989. *Großbanken und Großindustrie im Kaiserreich*. Göttingen: Vandenhoeck & Ruprecht.

Wengenroth, U. 1997. "Germany: Competition Abroad Cooperation at Home, 1870–1990," in Chandler, A. D. Jr., F. Amatori, and T. Hikino (eds.), *Big Business and the Wealth of Nations*. Cambridge: Cambridge University Press.

Wennekes, W. 1993. *De Aartsvaders. Grondleggers van het Nederlandse bedrijfsleven*. Amsterdam: Atlas.

Wernerfelt, B. 1984. "A Resource-based View of the Firm," *Strategic Management Journal*, 5 (2): 171–80.

Westerhuis, G., and De Jong, A. 2015. *Over Geld en Macht*. Amsterdam: Boom.

Wheelwright, E. L. 1957. *Ownership and Control of Australian Companies: A Study of 102 of the Largest Public Companies Incorporated in Australia*. Sydney: Law Book Co of Australasia.

Whittington, R., and Mayer, M. 1996. "The Survival of the European Holding Company: Institutional Change and Contingency," in R. Whitley and P. H. Kristensen. *The Changing European Firm: Limits to Convergence*, London: Routledge.

Whittington, R., and Mayer, M. 2000. *The European Corporation. Strategy, Structure, and Social Science*. Oxford: Oxford University Press.

Whittington, R., Mayer, M., and Curto, F. 1999. "Chandlerism in Post-War Europe: Strategic and Structural Change in France, Germany and the United Kingdom, 1950–1993," *Industrial and Corporate Change*, 8 (3): 519–551.

Wijnen, H. van. 2004. *Grootvorst aan de Maas. D.G. Van Beuningen*. Amsterdam: Balans.

Wilkins, M. 1970. *The Emergence of Multinational Enterprise*. Cambridge, MA: Harvard University Press.

Wilkins, M. 1988. "The Free-standing Company, 1870–1914: An Important Type of British Foreign Direct Investment," *Economic History Review*, XLI (2): 259–82.

Wilkinson, H. L. 1914. *The Trust Movement in Australia*. Sydney: Critchley Parker Pty Ltd.

Williamson, O. E. 1975. *Markets and Hierarchies: Analysis and Antitrust Implications*. New York: The Free Press.

Williamson, O. E. 1979. "Transaction-Cost Economics: The Governance of Contractual Relations," *Journal of Law and Economics*, 22 (2): 233–61.

Williamson, O. E. 1981. "The Economics of Organization: the Transaction Cost Approach," *American Journal of Sociology, 87* (3): 548–77.

Williamson, O. E. 1985. *The Economic Institutions of Capitalism*. New York: The Free Press.

Williamson, O. 1999. "Strategy Research: Governance and Competence Perspectives," *Strategic Management Journal*, 20: 1087–108.

Williot, J. P. 2010. *L'Industrie du Gaz à Paris au XIXe Siècle*, Paris: Rive droite.

Wilson, C. 1954. *The History of Unilever*, 2 vols. London: Cassell.

Wilson, C. 1968. *Unilever 1945–1965*. London: Cassell.

Womack, J. P., Jones, D. T., and Roos, D. 1990. *The Machine that Changed the World*. Glencoe, IL: Free Press.

Woodman, H. 1981. "The Business of Agriculture," "Business and Economic History," Papers Presented at the 27th Annual Meeting of the Business History Conference, May 5–7, 1981, 10 (1): 1–12.

Wrigley, L. 1970. "Diversification and Divisional Autonomy," DBA Thesis, Boston, MA: Harvard Business School.

Yacob, S., and Md Khalid, K. 2012. "Adapt or Divest? The New Economic Policy and Foreign Businesses in Malaysia (1970–2000)," *Journal of Imperial and Commonwealth History*, 40 (3): 459–82.

Yan, A. 2006. "Value of Conglomerates and Capital Market Conditions," *Financial Management*, 35 (4): 5–30.

Yiu, D. W., Lu, Y., Bruton, G. D., and Hoskisson, R. E. 2007. "Business Groups: An Integrated Model to Focus Future Research," *Journal of Management Studies*, 44 (8): 1551–79.

Yiu, D., Ng, F. W., and Ma, X. 2013. "Business Group Attributes and Internationalization Strategy in China," *Asian Business and Management*, 12: 14–36.

Yule, P. 2012. *William Lawrence Baillieu. Founder of Australia's Greatest Business Empire*. Melbourne: Hardie Grant Books.

Zahra, S. A., Hayton, J. C., and Salvato, C. 2004. "Entrepreneurship in Family vs. Non-family Firms: A Resource-based Analysis of the Effect of Organizational Culture," *Entrepreneurship: Theory and Practice*, 28 (4): 363–79.

Zalan, T. and Lewis, G. 2007. "The Administrative Heritage," in H. W. Dick and D. Merrett (eds.), *The Internationalisation Strategies of Small-Country Firms. The Australian Experience of Globalisation*, Cheltenham: Edward Elgar Publishing.

Zamagni, V. 2007. "The Rise and Fall of the Italian Chemical Industry 1950s–1990s," in L. Galambos, T. Hikino, and V. Zamagni (eds.), *The Global Chemical Industry in the Age of the Petrochemical Revolution*. Cambridge: Cambridge University Press: 347–67.

Zanden, J. L. van. 1998. *The Economic History of the Netherlands, 1914–1995. A Small Open Economy in the "Long" Twentieth Century*. London and New York: Routledge.

Zanden, J. L. van. 2009. "Old Rules, New Conditions, 1914–1940," in M. 't Hart, J. Jonker, and J. L. van Zanden, *A Financial History of the Netherlands*. Cambridge: Cambridge University Press: 124–52.

Zanden, J. L. van., and Riel, A. van. 2000. *The Strictures of Inheritance. The Dutch Economy in the Nineteenth Century*. Princeton, NJ: Princeton University Press.

Zerini, E. (pseud. of Emanuele Rienzi) 1947. "L'Economia Capitalistica ed i Vari Aspetti delle Egemonie Economiche in Italia," *Critica Economica*, 5, 6, 7: 67–102 and 108–42.

Zorn, D., Dobbin, F., Dierkes, J., and Kwok, M. 2004. "Managing Investors: How Financial Markets Reshaped the American Firm," in K. Cetina and A. Preda, *The Sociology of Financial Markets*. London: Oxford University Press.

Zorzini, M. 1925. "L'Organizzazione dell'Industria Idroelettrica in Italia," *Economia*, 7: 166–76.

Zwan, A. van der. 2006. *Hij Overwon Iedereen op een Vrouw na. F. H. Fentener van Vlissingen 1882–1962*. Amsterdam: Balans.

Zysman, J. 1990. *Governments Markets and Growth: Financial Systems and the Politics of Industrial Change*. Ithaca, NY: Cornell University Press.

Index

Note: Tables and figures are indicated by an italic *t* and *f*, respectively, following the page number.